Reenchantment without Supernaturalism

La Nouvelle Agence
7, rue Corneille
75006 Paris

A volume in the series

Cornell Studies in the Philosophy of Religion

EDITED BY WILLIAM P. ALSTON

A full list of titles in the series appears at the end of the book.

David Ray Griffin

Reenchantment without Supernaturalism

A Process Philosophy of Religion

Cornell University Press, Ithaca and London

First published 2001 by Cornell University Press
First printing, Cornell Paperbacks, 2001

Printed in the United States of America

Library of Congress Cataloging-in-Publication Data

Griffin, David Ray, 1939–
   Reenchantment without supernaturalism : a process philosophy of religion / David Ray Griffin.
     p.   cm. — (Cornell studies in the philosophy of religion)
   Includes bibliographical references and index.
   ISBN 0-8014-3778-4 (alk. paper) — ISBN 0-8014-8657-2 (pbk. : alk. paper)
   1. Natural theology. 2. Process theology. 3. Process philosophy.
I. Title. II. Series.
BL182 . G75 2000
210 — dc21

00-009506

Cloth printing   10 9 8 7 6 5 4 3 2 1
Paperback printing   10 9 8 7 6 5 4 3 2 1

Contents

To
John Buchanan and Eugene Long,
who both know why,
and to the memory of George Nordgulen (1933–2000),
who also may

Preface

By using the word *reenchantment* in the title of this book, I allude to Max Weber's well-known claim that modern thought has resulted in the "disenchantment" of the world, by which Weber meant that the world is no longer believed to contain any inherent meaning or normative values around which human beings should orient their lives. One implication is that at the same time that democracy has become almost universally accepted as the only legitimate form of political organization, many of the best-known cultural theorists, having thought through the implications of disenchantment, claim that democracy is not supported by any universally valid moral values. It is now widely held in intellectual circles that this disenchantment is irreversible—that it is not possible to overcome it, for example, by seeing that it was based on a set of intellectual mistakes.

Among those who do believe that disenchantment is reversible, the majority opinion has been that the major mistake was the rejection of a supernatural creator. According to these thinkers, the way to reenchant the world, thereby providing a cosmic basis for morality, is to return to supernaturalism. My title, *Reenchantment without Supernaturalism,* signals that this is not my view. Completely rejecting supernaturalism—understood as the belief in the possibility of occasional interruptions of the world's most fundamental causal order—I present a worldview that, although saturated with values, is fully natural. This worldview *does* involve a form of theism, but it is a fully naturalistic theism, according to which divine influence is a natural dimension of the world's most fundamental causal order, never an interruption thereof.

The term *process philosophy* in the book's subtitle points to the fact that the worldview presented here is based on the process philosophy developed primarily by Alfred North Whitehead. That this book is a philosophy of *religion* means, of course, that the focus is on those dimensions of process philosophy which bear directly on issues of religious concern. Considerable attention, however, is also given to other dimensions, especially the capacity of this worldview to provide a basis not only for morality—as the theme of reenchantment indicates—but also for science. The book can serve, therefore, as a general introduction to process philosophy.

Because this book involves extensive quotations of others, especially Whitehead, I must add a comment about language. Besides employing male pronouns for God, Whitehead often used the term *man* for human beings in general, a practice that is now generally associated with sexist views. At the time Whitehead wrote, of course, this practice was virtually universal, among women as well as men. Whitehead himself, furthermore, was very critical of sexism. In addition to being active in the movement for women's suffrage (Lowe 1985, 314), he considered the "rule of men over women" in modern societies, along with the resulting "inequality of men and women," to be "a hang-over from barbarism" with its "rule of individual masters over slaves" (AI 83). In any case, although avoiding the use of male terms for divinity or humanity in developing my own thoughts, I do not change or comment upon the use of such language by people I quote.

I have, of course, incurred many debts in the writing of this book. Most of them are indicated in my list of references at the end. More directly, I received helpful suggestions from Bill Alston, Richard Amesbury, John Cobb, Derek Malone-France, Gene Reeves, Robert Segal, Ted Vitali, John Woell, members of my 1999 class, "Whitehead's Philosophy and Its Religious Relevance," and some anonymous readers, to all of whom I hereby express my gratitude. I am also indebted to my wife, Ann, and our white-headed West Highland terrier, Evelyn ("Evey"), for their forbearance for many missed walks on the beach.

Just before receiving page proofs, I learned of the death of George Nordgulen, who had retired from a long career of teaching, most recently at Eastern Kentucky University. Besides being a good friend, George is the one who—in conjunction with Douglas Straton, whose class at the University of Oregon we were taking—introduced me to process philosophy. One of the reasons I especially regret his premature death concerns Chapter 5 of this book. George had always been unhappy that John Cobb and I, in our *Process Theology*, had suggested that arguments for the existence of God "are not an essential part of its work." George agreed with our main point—namely, that process philosophy makes its primary contribution to theistic belief by presenting a credible idea of God. But he argued that it is important to emphasize the various reasons for believing in such a divine reality and that process philosophy provides a novel slant on what these reasons are. I wish that the fruits of my belated realization that George was right had been published while he was still with us.

DAVID RAY GRIFFIN

Santa Barbara, California

Abbreviations

Although all other writings referred to in the text are cited by author and year, the writings of Alfred North Whitehead are cited by standard abbreviations (as employed in the journal *Process Studies*).

AE   *The Aims of Education and Other Essays.* New York: Macmillan, 1929.

AI   *Adventures of Ideas* (1933). New York: Free Press, 1967.

ESP   *Essays in Science and Philosophy.* New York: Philosophical Library, 1947.

FR   *The Function of Reason* (1929). Boston: Beacon Press, 1958.

MT   *Modes of Thought* (1938). New York: Free Press, 1968.

PR   *Process and Reality* (1929), corrected edition, edited by David Ray Griffin and Donald W. Sherburne. New York: Free Press, 1978.

R   *The Principle of Relativity.* Cambridge: Cambridge University Press, 1922.

RM   *Religion in the Making* (1926). Cleveland: World, 1960.

S   *Symbolism: Its Meaning and Effect* (1927). New York: Capricorn, 1959.

SMW   *Science and the Modern World* (1925). New York: Free Press, 1967.

Reenchantment without Supernaturalism

Introduction
A Process Philosophy of Religion

This book is an articulation, from the point of view of an advocate, of a process philosophy of religion. It is written, of course, from one particular understanding of the best way to develop a self-consistent process philosophy of religion. Other process philosophers of religion, with different perspectives, would have written quite different books, and I have made no attempt to try to represent these various perspectives (which would have been impossible without greatly increasing the size of this volume). Although these other books would largely agree with regard to the central tenets of process philosophy, they would have different emphases and would differ more or less greatly with regard to other matters. In this introductory chapter, I will first lay out the understanding of *process philosophy* that informs this book. I will then explain my understanding of the nature and tasks of a *process philosophy of religion* in particular.

1. Process Philosophy

Toward a Definition of Process Philosophy

Although the label "process philosophy" can legitimately be used quite broadly to refer to a wide range of positions emphasizing the ultimate reality of becoming, process, and change, it is now widely used in a much more limited sense to refer to the movement initiated by Alfred North Whitehead

(1861–1947) and Charles Hartshorne (b. 1897). It is used here in this more limited sense.

This formal definition, however, does not tell us what process philosophy is because Whiteheadian-Hartshornean process philosophy cannot be simply equated with everything that Whitehead and Hartshorne happened to believe. For one thing, the writings of these two philosophers differ on several issues (L. Ford 1973). Although that point might suggest that process philosophy could simply be equated with everything on which Whitehead and Hartshorne agree, even that solution would be unsatisfactory because they may have just happened to agree on a number of beliefs that are not entailed by what can arguably be considered their core doctrines. If, for example, they both believed our universe to be 15 (rather than 10 or 20) billion years old, that belief would not ipso facto belong to process philosophy. If we are to talk intelligibly about (Whiteheadian-Hartshornean) process philosophy, accordingly, we must be able to point to *a set of core doctrines shared by Whitehead and Hartshorne*. I will suggest a list of ten such doctrines. Although this set of core doctrines would permit an indefinite number of fully worked out process philosophies of religion (as well as process philosophies of science, process political philosophies, and so on), it does exclude various doctrines held by other schools of thought. A process philosophy of religion, for example, could not affirm a doctrine of divine omniscience according to which God knows the details of what will happen in the future. Although the core doctrines allow considerable flexibility, therefore, they also serve to distinguish Whiteheadian-Hartshornean process philosophy from other schools of thought.

The failure to distinguish core doctrines from other matters of opinion has been responsible for much confusion about what "process philosophy says," especially with regard to religious issues. For example, Whitehead probably did not believe in life after death, and Hartshorne and some other process philosophers and theologians have explicitly rejected this belief. On the basis of statements by Hartshorne and some of these other process thinkers, it is often said, by both advocates and critics, that process philosophy *as such* rules out belief in life after death. The truth, however, is that process philosophy's position on the mind-body relation makes life after death possible. What is important about Whitehead and Hartshorne in this regard is not the fact that they did not personally believe in life after death— Whitehead probably, Hartshorne definitely—but that they are two of only a handful of twentieth-century philosophers included in the prestigious "Library of Living Philosophers" whose ontologies *allow for its possibility*. It is the ontology that allows for the possibility of life after death—not the personal opinion of Whitehead or Hartshorne (or any other self-identified process thinker) about whether this possibility is realized—that belongs to the core doctrines of process philosophy and theology.

Although critics of process philosophy have, to use the old language of "essence" and "accidents," often been guilty of confusing one or more of its accidents with its essence, this confusion is largely excusable because the advocates of process philosophy have heretofore failed to set out clearly what does and does not belong to its core doctrines. Although some process thinkers may consider the attempt to formulate these core doctrines distasteful, there are three good reasons for attempting it. First, if we do not spell out somewhat clearly what we take process philosophy as such to be, we can hardly say what its implications are for religion (or anything else). Second, if we do not state process philosophy's core doctrines explicitly, we will nevertheless operate with an *implicit* list of such doctrines. The refusal to discuss them explicitly will not lessen their controlling power; it will only shield them from scrutiny. Third, as the example about life after death illustrates, if we do not provide a list of core doctrines, we have no basis for distinguishing "process philosophy as such" from any opinion on any topic uttered by anyone self-identified as a process philosopher in the Whiteheadian-Hartshornean tradition.

In limiting my list of core doctrines to ten, I do not mean that no other doctrines could be added. Because this book is a process philosophy of *religion,* my focus is on doctrines that are especially germane to topics of religious concern. If I had written a process philosophy of science or of politics, a somewhat different list would probably have been provided. I do maintain, however, that none of the substantive doctrines[1] listed here could be eliminated without serious damage to the coherence of the position as a whole. Insofar as this is true, one can claim with some objectivity, not just as a matter of arbitrary personal opinion, that this set of doctrines belongs to the very core of process philosophy.

Three qualifications of this claim, however, are necessary. First, this is one place where my statement in the opening paragraph about different perspectives is especially important. Some process philosophers—holding perhaps that Whiteheadian process philosophy is a dynamic movement, not a set of ideas—may consider the very idea of trying to state a set of core doctrines inappropriate. This is a fully legitimate matter for debate. The present

---

[1] Two of the doctrines, as pointed out later, are formal rather than substantive.

book constitutes, among other things, an argument by example that the effort to provide a list of core doctrines is appropriate and that the advantages of doing so outweigh any possible dangers.

Second, although various other process philosophers may agree with the effort to achieve clarity by providing a list of core doctrines, they might give lists that differ more or less greatly from mine. Besides including doctrines that I did not, they might even argue that one or more of those that I have included should be regarded as unessential, perhaps even as inconsistent with the truly core doctrines. This kind of debate within the camp of process philosophers, far from being inconsistent with the spirit of my attempt to give a list of core doctrines, is a result that I would welcome. It would be good for us to attain more clarity about the extent to which various ideas generally associated with process philosophy are mutually implicated.

Third, although I believe that none of the substantive doctrines on my list could be rejected without creating problems of incoherence, it does not follow that anyone who rejects one of these doctrines is ipso facto not a process philosopher in the Whiteheadian tradition. For one thing, being a member of any tradition, even a tradition in which ideas are central, is more a matter of self-identification than it is of holding various beliefs. Also, even to the extent that being a member of a philosophical tradition does imply holding some common ideas, being a member in this sense is a matter of degree, not an all-or-nothing matter. Some members of this tradition, for example, refer to themselves as neo-Whiteheadians. In any case, the purpose of the effort to list a set of core doctrines is simply to state clearly what I take the central ideas to be and why I take them to be essential to Whiteheadian-Hartshornean process philosophy. Although there is, to be sure, always the danger that a list of core doctrines could be used by ideologues to read others out of the camp, I came to regard such a list as necessary, as I indicated above, for the opposite reason: to try to prevent others from reading *into* process philosophy as such opinions of some of its advocates that are not entailed by its central ideas.[2] With this apologia for doing so, I will now lay out ten doctrines that arguably belong to the core of process philosophy.

---

[2] My list provides no complete protection even from this danger because this list is not exhaustive. However, simply by distinguishing between core doctrines, on the one hand, and doctrines that are optional or even in tension with core doctrines, on the other hand, we underline the fallacy involved in the following syllogism, which is rather commonplace in critiques of process thought: (1) so-and-so denies X; (2) so-and-so is a process philosopher; (3) therefore process philosophy denies X.

Core Doctrines of Process Philosophy

For those not already familiar with process philosophy, this initial discussion of core doctrines, which must be brief, will probably be rather opaque. Each of these doctrines, however, will be central to one or more of the following chapters. In this initial discussion of each doctrine, accordingly, I will indicate the chapter(s) in which it will be further developed.

1. *The integration of moral, aesthetic, and religious intuitions with the most general doctrines of the sciences into a self-consistent worldview as one of the central tasks of philosophy in our time.* By understanding "religious intuitions" broadly to include intuitions of moral and aesthetic values, this purpose can be stated more succinctly as *the integration of science and religion into a single worldview.* This (formal) doctrine will be developed in Chapter 1.

2. *Hard-core commonsense notions as the ultimate test of the adequacy of a philosophical position.* Although this doctrine is in part, like the first one, formal, it is also partly substantive, in that it says that there *are* some hard-core commonsense notions, meaning *notions that are inevitably presupposed in practice by all human beings.* Insofar as they are *inevitably* presupposed, any philosophy that denies one or more of them violates the law of noncontradiction because it is guilty of explicitly denying what it implicitly affirms. This doctrine provides the primary means by which process philosophy avoids the complete relativism that is affirmed, whether explicitly or only implicitly, by much modern and postmodern philosophy. This doctrine is laid out in the first chapter, then developed further in the final chapter.

3. *Whitehead's nonsensationist doctrine of perception, according to which sensory perception is a secondary mode of perception, being derivative from a more fundamental, nonsensory "prehension."* This epistemological doctrine, which involves the development of a central feature of William James's "radical empiricism," allows for genuine religious experience in the sense of a direct perception of a Holy Reality, as shown in Chapter 2. It also allows for the perception of moral norms, as discussed in Chapter 8. Finally, because this doctrine also allows for the direct perception of some other things (such as causality, the past, and the external world) that could not be perceived if the sensationist[3] theory of perception were true, it will be central to the critique of Reformed epistemology in the final chapter.

---

[3] Although Whitehead, in line with convention, referred to the doctrine that all our perception is by means of our physical sensory organs as the *sensationalist* doctrine of perception, or simply as *sensationalism,* I prefer the shorter terms *sensationist* and *sensationism,* partly because sensationalism has a much different meaning in ordinary parlance.

4. *Panexperientialism with organizational duality, according to which all true individuals — as distinct from aggregational societies — have at least some iota of experience and spontaneity (self-determination).* The affirmation of panexperientialism involves the rejection of the early modern dualism between two kinds of actual entities: physical actualities *devoid* of experience and mental actualities (minds) *with* experience. The addition of "organizational duality" provides the basis for avoiding the counterintuitive suggestion, which some versions of panexperientialism make, that self-determination and a unified experience are enjoyed by literally everything in the actual world, including sticks and stones. This doctrine is central to discussion of the mind-body relation and freedom in Chapter 3.

5. *The doctrine that all enduring individuals are serially ordered societies of momentary "occasions of experience."* This doctrine, according to which enduring individuals, such as molecules and minds, are analyzable into momentary *events,* is fundamental to process philosophy's reconciliation of final and efficient causation and, therefore, of freedom and determinism. The salient point is that each enduring individual, such as a living cell or a human mind, oscillates between two modes of existence: the *subjective* mode, in which it exerts final causation or self-determination, and the *objective* mode, in which it exerts efficient causation upon subsequent events. This unique doctrine will be central to the discussion of the mind-body relation, especially the issue of human freedom, in the third chapter.

6. *The doctrine that all actual entities have internal as well as external relations.* This doctrine, according to which all actual entities are fundamentally *relational* — in the sense of first being internally (constitutively) related to prior actual entities, then externally related to (constitutive of) subsequent actual entities — has led some advocates of this position to call it "process-relational philosophy." This relational doctrine of actuality, besides being explicated in the third chapter, is central to the doctrine of God's activity and immanence in the world in the following chapters and to the discussion of the relation between the individual and society in Chapter 8.

7. *The Whiteheadian version of naturalistic theism, according to which a Divine Actuality acts variably but never supernaturally in the world.* This doctrine — the centrality of which is signaled by the phrase *without supernaturalism* in the book's title — says that although there is a divine actuality that influences human experience and, in fact, all finite beings, this divine influence never involves an interruption of the normal pattern of causal relations, being instead a *natural dimension* of this normal pattern. The reason for this absence of divine interruptions, furthermore, is metaphysical, not merely moral, being based on the fact that the fundamental God-World relation is fully natural, grounded in the very nature of things, not in a contingent divine decision. This naturalistic theism, although developed in Chapter 4, is already presupposed in the reconciliation of science and religion provided in the first chapter.

8. *Doubly Dipolar Theism.* Better known than process philosophy's naturalistic theism is its dipolar theism, according to which the divine reality has two aspects, or "poles." There has been considerable confusion, however, about exactly how to understand the divine dipolarity, mainly because process theism actually involves *two* dipolarities, one of which has been emphasized more by Whitehead, the other more by Hartshorne. In the fourth chapter, I draw on John Cobb's integration of these two views to develop a doctrine of God that, by overcoming inconsistencies in Whitehead's doctrine of God and an inadequacy in Hartshorne's, is intended to do justice to both dipolarities.[4]

9. *The provision of cosmological support for the ideals needed by contemporary civilization as one of the chief purposes of philosophy in our time.* Like the first core doctrine, which refers to the task of integrating science and religion, this one is purely formal. It complements the first one, however, by bringing out the fact that the overall purposes of process philosophy are practical as well as theoretical. This point, the centrality of which is signaled by the use of the word *reenchantment* in the title, is developed primarily in Chapter 8, although it is introduced in Chapter 1 and is implicit throughout the book.

10. *A distinction between verbal statements (sentences) and propositions and between both of these and propositional feelings.* This doctrine is central to the discussion of language and truth in Chapter 9 and thereby to the discussion of knowledge in Chapter 10.

2. The Nature of a Process Philosophy of Religion

Having discussed what process philosophy as such is, I turn now specifically to a process philosophy of religion. Although the "nature" and the "tasks" of philosophy of religion are closely intertwined, I first discuss the former, then the latter.

In order to understand the distinctive nature of a process philosophy of religion, it will be helpful to look at various recent enterprises that have been called *philosophy of religion.* Sometimes this term is used for the enterprise more commonly called *philosophical theology,* which deals primarily with the existence and nature of deity. Under this general rubric, there are many types. One distinguishing issue involves the author's *methodological stance.* Some philosophical theology understands itself to be *natural theology,* which (in contrast with so-called *revealed theology*) seeks to rest its argument entirely

---

[4] As I suggested in the first paragraph, this book represents my own understanding of "the best way to develop a self-consistent process philosophy of religion." With regard to most issues, this goal leads me primarily to explain the position of Whitehead and/or Hartshorne. With regard to some issues, however, this goal leads me to develop alternative doctrines, which I take to be more self-consistent and/or adequate to the relevant evidence.

on the basis of evidence (sometimes called "general revelation") that is in principle available to everyone (not simply to those privy to the "special revelation" of a particular tradition). Traditional Thomistic theology involves natural theology thus understood. By contrast, some philosophical theologians, believing that natural theology in this sense is impossible—because one's interpretation and even perception of the evidence is always colored by one's religious tradition—have argued that an identifying adjective must always be used, so that Christian philosophers engaged in this enterprise would call it "*Christian* natural theology" or simply "*Christian* philosophy" (Cobb 1962, 1965). Although I accept this second view, the enterprise is still *natural* or *philosophical* theology insofar as the position is justified in terms of the philosophical criteria of adequacy and self-consistency rather than in terms of the alleged origin of the ideas in a truth-guaranteeing revelation.

Besides methodological stance, another distinguishing issue among philosophical theologies concerns what *concept of God* is defended. *Traditional* philosophical theologies defend some version of traditional Western theism, such as an Augustinian, Thomist, or Calvinist doctrine of God. There are, however, also *revisionist* philosophical theologies in which traditional theism is rejected in favor of a revised concept of deity. Included among these revisionist positions are *feminist* philosophical theologies, which argue that Western and, in fact, all the major religions for the past several thousand years have had a one-sided male bias (Keller 1986, 1988, 1990; Christ 1997).

Still another division among those who understand philosophy of religion to involve philosophical theology concerns the *data* on which the idea of God is based. Quite often the "arguments for the existence of God" are understood to be based on data other than religious experience, such as the order, beauty, and/or bare existence of the world. Overagainst this enterprise, some have argued that the philosophy of religion, as distinct from philosophical theology, should be understood as the *philosophy of religious experience,* in the sense that it would take actual religious experiences as they have occurred in history—especially in the lives of the saints in the various religious traditions—as its primary data (Widgery 1954). A mediating position is provided by those philosophical theologians who include an "argument from religious experience" among the various arguments for the existence of God (Swinburne 1979, 1996).

All the above types of philosophy of religion are positive, arguing that religion is justified, at least insofar as it involves belief in a divine reality. Philosophy of religion, however, can also be negative, in the sense of anti-theistic, carried out by those who consider belief in a divine reality philosophically indefensible. Most anti-theistic philosophies of religion are directed against traditional theism. Although their exponents often give the impression that they have shown *all* "belief in God" to be irrational, they seldom devote serious attention to any of the revisionary forms of theism. Much that passes for "philosophy of religion" in the contemporary scene, therefore, consists simply of arguments for or against the truth of traditional Christian theism.

Still other types of philosophy of religion try to avoid the need for even this limited kind of argumentation. One of these, while defending traditional Christian theism, does not believe that this defense requires an appeal to evidence that could in principle be accepted by those outside the Christian community of faith. The purpose of philosophy of religion, from this perspective, is to defend traditional Christian beliefs by merely showing that critics cannot convict Christians of being irrational for holding these beliefs (Plantinga 1979, 1981, 1983a; Wolterstorff 1983a). This type of philosophy of religion, which is really "the philosophy of Christian beliefs," is discussed in the final chapter.

Another way to "do" philosophy of religion in a positive way without having to argue for the truth of any philosophically debatable beliefs is simply to deny that religion involves any such beliefs. The task of philosophy of religion, accordingly, largely consists in arguing for a "nonrealist" understanding of religious language, especially language about God (Phillips 1976, 1986). It is argued, for example, that praising God for creating the world does not involve any cognitive beliefs that would put one at odds with the neo-Darwinian theory of evolution, according to which our world came about without any cosmic directivity. Those engaged in negative philosophy of religion often devote considerable attention to this position (as well as to traditional theism), arguing that it distorts beyond recognition the meaning of the language of belief, which does intend to describe objective realities (Nielsen 1982, 1985, 1989a).

Whereas the three-way discussion involving traditional theists, nonrealists, and critics of both is generally carried on in terms of Christian beliefs, some philosophers of religion regard this whole discussion as extremely provincial. To be legitimately called philosophy of religion, they argue, an enterprise should not simply be concerned with the Christian religion but must deal with religion as such and hence with all (or at least many) religions. They advocate, therefore, *cross-cultural* or *comparative* philosophy of religion (Dean 1995; N. Smart 1983, 1995b). This approach may be simply *descriptive,* but it can also be *normative,* seeking to develop a global religious philosophy based on insights from various religious traditions.

Not all these approaches, of course, are mutually exclusive. A philosophy of religion might involve a combination of two or more of them. One could, for example, combine a revisionary theism with a defense of the rationality (rather than the truth) of religious faith as such (rather than of, say, Christian faith in particular), thereby providing a non-apologetic, revisionary, cross-cultural philosophy of religion (Hick 1989).

Although there are still other types of enterprises that are, or at least could be, called philosophy of religion, the purpose of this survey is not to be exhaustive but to provide a basis for an initial characterization of process philosophy of religion. In terms of the issues just discussed, a process philosophy of religion involves a *realist, truth-seeking* approach. Its discussion of God is based primarily on *religious experience,* but this primacy does not exclude the more traditional types of arguments for a divine reality. Process philosophy, however, thinks that these arguments support not traditional theism but a version of *revisionary* theism, one that has much in common with many feminist approaches. Process philosophy also supports the contention that a philosophy of religion should in principle, and in practice as much as possible, be *cross-cultural,* taking account of religious experience and reflection thereon from many traditions.

3. The Tasks of a Process Philosophy of Religion

Traditionally, the tasks of philosophy of religion have included the following: (1) providing an account of the nature of religion and (2) assessing the validity of religion (thus understood), which includes assessing the genuineness of religious experience and evaluating the truth of religious beliefs. The acceptance of these two tasks has often been understood to imply a third task, namely, *ranking* the various historic religions in terms of how well they exemplify the very nature of religion and/or how close their beliefs come to the philosophical truth about the universe. Not surprisingly, Christian philosophers of religion have judged Christianity to be the highest religion while Hindu philosophers of religion have found Hinduism superior. The reaction against this third task has sometimes led, owing to guilt by association, to suspicion about the first two tasks as well. Process philosophers of religion agree with the widespread rejection of the effort to rank various religions, but they do accept the first two tasks.

Defining Religion

The task of coming up with a definition of religion has been greatly resisted in recent times. Commentators with historical knowledge of the great diversity that exists have concluded that there is no one thing that all religions have in common, such as belief in life after death or belief in a god or gods. This lack of a common essence is especially clear, some add, when we include movements such as Nazism, Communism, and other ideologies, which must at least be considered "quasi-religions." This very discussion illustrates, however, that *some* notion of what makes something a religion is presupposed. Philosophy of religion should not duck the task, no matter how problematic, of trying to provide a generally acceptable formulation of what that is. Although this issue will be discussed in more detail in Chapter 7, it is necessary here to provide an initial statement of my working definition of religion.

The denials of any common essence connecting all the religions almost always illustrate the point in terms of substantive matters (such as "belief in spirits"). It is less obvious, however, that there is no *formal* characteristic shared by all those traditions that we intuitively regard as religions. Whitehead's own sense of such a formal characteristic is suggested by his observation that "whatever suggests a cosmology, suggests a religion" (RM 136). The presupposition behind this statement was brought out by the observation of historian Carl Becker that "[t]he desire to correspond with the general harmony springs perennial in the human breast" (1932, 63). All religious activity, in other words, is based on the desire to be in harmony with ultimate reality. The Christian, for example, wants to be in harmony with the nature and purpose of God; the Muslim with the will of Allah; the Confucian with the Mandate of Heaven; the Taoist with the supreme Tao; the Buddhist with Nirvana, Emptiness, or the Dharma; the ideological Marxist with the dialectical process of history; the ideological (social Darwinian) capitalist with the law of the survival of the fittest; and so on. The fact that this is what Whitehead had in mind is shown in his comment about the practical importance of different ideas of "law" in different cosmologies.

> The directions of human activities in various epochs, and the clashings of such directions in the same epoch, are the outcome of rough and ready solutions of the problem of cosmology, popularized throughout the masses of mankind. Millions of men have marched to battle fiercely nerved by intense faith in Law imposed by the will of inflexible Allah. . . . Millions of Buddhists have . . . rel[ied] on the impersonal immanence of Law, made clear to them by the doctrines of the Buddha. Millions of humans have shaped their lives according to the compromise between these two doctrines due to the Platonism of Christianity. (AI 135)

The recognition that all religions involve the desire to be in harmony with ultimate reality—which in some cases may mean realizing one's *identity* with that reality—provides one step toward a definition of religion.[5]

Those movements that we regard as *full-fledged* (as distinct from *quasi-*) religions, which would include all in the above list except Marxism and capitalism, involve another element, however. In full-fledged religions, the ultimate reality with which harmony is desired is explicitly conceived to be *holy* or *sacred*. Although these terms, which are here used interchangeably, are largely indefinable, they include the notion of that which is of ultimate intrinsic value. A second step toward a definition of full-fledged religions is the recognition of the essential role played by this idea of the holy.

By virtue of having ultimate, nonderivative value, the holy reality is understood to provide derivative value, and thereby meaning, to the universe. A third step toward a definition of full-fledged religions is this recognition that they portray the world as meaningful. As Michael J. Perry says: "If a worldview is not grounded or embedded in a vision of the finally or ultimately meaningful nature of the world and of our place in it, it is a confusion . . . to think of that worldview as 'religious'—even if the worldview, like Marxism, is all-encompassing" (1998, 14–15).

A fourth step is the recognition that any concrete religion involves a great variety of factors: beliefs, including myths and stories as well as doctrines; history and traditions; emotions, attitudes, and dispositions; rituals and other cultic practices; ethical activities, both individual and sociopolitical; institutions; and artistic creations, such as icons, statues, and buildings.[6]

In light of this discussion, we can now provide a preliminary definition of a full-fledged religion: *a complex set of beliefs, stories, traditions, emotions, attitudes, dispositions, institutions, artistic creations, and practices—both cultic and ethical, both communal and individual—oriented around the desire to be in harmony with an ultimate reality that is understood to be holy and thereby to provide life with meaning.*

Although this definition will be refined and more fully explored in Chap-

---

[5] To claim that religion "involves" and is even "oriented around" the desire to be in harmony with ultimate reality is not to deny that the actual religious practices of people are often, perhaps usually, focused on much more concrete concerns, such as being healed, getting a better job, passing an exam, getting along better with one's spouse, or having a better birth in one's next life. That this recognition does not contradict the proffered definition can be seen by the twofold fact that these utilitarian goals are to be achieved by coming into proper relationship with ultimate reality (perhaps as embodied in a particular deity or saint) and that the recognized saints of the religious tradition in question are individuals who sought harmony with ultimate reality for its own sake.

[6] These elements correspond closely to Ninian Smart's nine "dimensions of the sacred" (1996).

ter 7, it is important to note now the irrelevance, from the perspective of this definition, of all nonrealist philosophies of religion. If the very motive force behind religion in all its forms involves the desire to be in harmony with that which is truly ultimate in the nature of things,[7] then nonrealist interpretations of language referring to God (or Brahman, or the Tao, or the Buddha-nature) cannot do justice to the intentions of religious devotees.[8] It has often been observed that nonrealist interpretations of religious language are not descriptive but purely prescriptive—that is, rather than describe how religious believers use language, they prescribe how believers *should* use it. In light of the present definition of religion, we can add that this is a prescription that could not possibly be adopted by any religious community—at least not without undermining the very basis of its being a *religious* community.

My position on both these controversial points—on the possibility of a general characterization of religion and on the nature of religion as involving beliefs about ultimate reality—is supported by the highly respected anthropologist Clifford Geertz. On the first point, although Geertz is an emphatic particularist, rejecting all attempts, such as that of Mircea Eliade, to describe the "universal forms" of religion, he does believe that we can characterize what he calls "the religious perspective." After dismissing various ways of characterizing this perspective—such as belief in "the supernatural" or in the existence of an "invisible world" or in "a divine presence [that] broods over the world"—as not universally applicable, Geertz says that the religious perspective is "the conviction that the values one holds are grounded in the inherent structure of reality, that between the way one ought to live and the way things really are there is an unbreakable inner connection" (1968, 97). Put more simply, a religion always consists of a "world view" and an "ethos," with the latter understood as values, attitudes, emotions, motivations, and conduct—both moral and ritualistic conduct (1973, 89–125). In a religion, more precisely, these two elements combine to reinforce each other: "The world view is believable because the ethos, which grows out of it, is felt to be authoritative; the ethos is justifiable because the

[7] My contention here, that any conception of religion that regards it as separable from all metaphysical commitments is ipso facto inadequate, is supported by Franklin Baumer's statement, in his study of religion and scepticism, that "all genuine religion would seem to be bound up [with] the metaphysical sense" (1960, 57).

[8] It might be thought that this criticism would not apply to those nonrealist interpretations that mean not to deny the reality of Something Holy but only to question the adequacy of any language for describing it. If, however, there is no description of it that is better than others—so that, for example, describing it as compassionate is no more adequate than referring to it as indifferent—then we have no hint as to what kind of life would constitute being in harmony with it.

world view, upon which it rests, is held to be true" (1968, 97). Geertz would reject, accordingly, any attempt to characterize as *religious* a way of life that is not thought to be supported by the way things really are.

Assessing the Validity of Religion

If the attempt to provide a generic definition of religion has been out of vogue, equally controversial, at least in academic-study-of-religion circles, would be any positive assessment of the validity of religion (especially theistic religion), including both the genuineness of religious experience and the truth of religious beliefs, especially about a divine or holy reality. In these circles, it is widely assumed that an account of religion, to be properly "academic," must either avoid any assessment of the validity of religion or else give a negative assessment.

The idea that judgments about the validity of religion are to be avoided is especially prevalent in departments of religious studies. The question of truth, it is widely held, is to be bracketed. For example, although Arvind Sharma has made contributions to the philosophy of religion, he states: "Religious studies does not typically concern itself with the validity of religious claims, understood as truth claims rather than as meaning claims" (1997, 51). However, recognizing that what is typically the case is not universally so, Sharma adds: "The philosophy of religion, no doubt, addresses the question of truth claims but it only constitutes a subset of religious studies." Many commentators would add the adjective "peripheral" before "subset."

Given this widespread attitude, it is philosophy of religion's task not only to assess the validity of religious experience and of related religious beliefs but also to make a case for the propriety and even centrality of doing so.[9] Philosophers of religion should not accept the growing sense that their discipline is peripheral to the academic study of religion, perhaps eventually to be excluded altogether. Given a broad view of the history of modernity, there is surely no question more central to the cultural realm than that of the validity of religion. If that question cannot be addressed in departments of religious studies, where *can* it be addressed in an intellectually responsible—that is, in an empirically informed and philosophically sophisticated—way? There are surely many legitimate reasons for engaging in the empirical study of religion. Why should we say that answering the question of religious truth is not one of them, or at least that the attempt to answer this question should not occur in departments of religious studies? The

---

[9] One contemporary philosopher of religion who has done so is H. G. Hubbeling: "The question of the truth of religious statements is in my opinion the central problem of the philosophy of religion" (1987, 3).

question *will* be answered, both in other departments and outside the academy. Departments of religious studies should not exclude themselves from being central participants in this discussion, which means that they need to have people prepared to engage in normative cross-cultural philosophy of religion.

This issue, of the propriety and centrality of focusing on the truth-question, has been confused by the fact that it has usually been discussed in terms of *theology.* This loaded, highly ambiguous term is customarily understood to mean not only *Christian* theology but also a particular type of Christian theology, namely, *confessional* theology—in the sense of a stance that simply assumes the truth of various doctrines, usually on the basis of their alleged origin in a supernatural, perhaps infallible, revelation. The desire to avoid or marginalize the question of truth in departments of religious studies is largely due to the fact that these departments have developed out of, and in reaction to, "departments of religion" that were de facto largely departments of theology in that sense.

The term *theology,* however, need not be thus understood. For example, Delwin Brown, in "Academic Theology and Religious Studies," points out that two very different kinds of theology now exist. One kind, which I have called confessional theology, is "a mode of study that begins with the assumption of some divine revelation, an assumption immune to rational critique, and seeks to understand and interpret this self-disclosure so as to nourish and assure the faithful continuation of it" (1997, 65). Insofar as that kind of theology engages in the evaluation of religious beliefs, this evaluation "will be governed by the norms of the religious community under study." Such theology, Brown argues, should not even have a peripheral place in the academy, understood as "the community of scholarly inquiry where the effort to find out what is the case in each area of knowledge is governed by defensible and revisable canons of investigation and validation, and where no claims to truth are privileged." There is, however, another kind of theology, which can be called academic theology precisely because it rejects the idea that some truth-claims are immune to criticism, seeking instead "to be responsible to the same kinds of criteria, and to the same criteriological debates, that fallibly and somewhat unstably guide other analyses within the academy" (65). Theology in this sense, Brown continues, should be included in the academic study of religion.[10]

---

[10] A similar analysis is provided in Robert Neville's presidential address to the American Academy of Religion, "Religious Studies and Theological Studies," in which he says that "like the value-neutral approaches the theological disciplines ought to be publicly objective in the sense . . . that their normative judgments need to make themselves vulnerable to criticism from all sides" (1993, 191).

Although Brown is entirely right, it may be less problematic to use the term *philosophy of religion* to name the enterprise he advocates (which corresponds to the task of philosophy of religion that I have called "assessment of the validity of religious beliefs"), given the deep-seated equation of "theology" with confessional theology. The deep-seatedness of this equation is illustrated in an essay, "Religious Studies and Theology," by Ninian Smart, who virtually equates "theology" with the expression of a particular faith, such as the Christian faith, and thereby as the activity of a denominational community (1997, 66). Theology, which is "trying, in an intellectual manner, to preach," Smart says, is in no way a social science (67, 68). By contrast, Smart adds, religious studies *is* a social science, having "at its core informed empathy" and thereby a purely phenomenological approach (67). As such, contends Smart, religious studies is "methodologically agnostic" and "on the whole empirical," that is, descriptive rather than evaluative (68).

After setting out this extreme contrast in most of the article, however, Smart adds a qualification:

> There is, however, one approach to religion which is not so much like the others: namely, the philosophy of religion. For it goes more directly into matters not so much of the power of religion as of the truth and coherence of worldviews. This means that it can engage with Christian, Islamic and other theologies or religious philosophies. . . . This is characterized in the academy as "cross-cultural philosophy of religion." . . . The cross-cultural philosophy of religion is the only sort commensurate with a Religious Studies program. It would go beyond the thin agenda of Kant to consider issues about rebirth, nirvana, types of religious experience, and so on. But there is another range of reflections which concern the criteria of what is a good (and true) faith. . . . This is what might be called "extended cross-cultural philosophy of religion." (67)

Smart also points out that although theology is typically understood as a denominational activity, "there are those who defend a more general 'theology,' involving thoughts about gods and the ultimate, [which] is a kind of denser version of the philosophy of religion" (66). Smart, in other words, recognizes that the term can refer to something like Delwin Brown's academic theology. Throughout most of the article, however, Smart simply speaks of theology (without a qualifying adjective) as if it were necessarily a denominational, confessional, homiletical enterprise. If someone as sophisticated as Ninian Smart almost automatically thinks of theology in this way, the effort to get an enterprise called theology, even prefaced by the adjective academic, accepted as a legitimate dimension of religious studies will probably be futile.

Smart's article also illustrates the extent to which the need of the burgeoning field of religious studies to distinguish itself from confessional theology has produced an overreaction in the self-understanding of the field. Although Smart is himself a philosopher of religion who enters into the question of the truth and coherence of religious worldviews, he accedes to the consensus that this task is peripheral, saying that "Religious Studies' main thrust is descriptive and explanatory" (67). Although the statement that religious studies is explanatory might be taken to mean that a practitioner could explain the existence of religion as a response to a divine reality, Smart excludes this interpretation, adding that religious studies "does not deny belief in God nor does it affirm it" (67–68). In light of this widespread understanding of the "main thrust" of religious studies, illustrated by Smart as well as Sharma, one of the tasks of a process philosophy of religion is to argue that the assessment of the validity of religion—including the assessment of both the genuineness of religious experience and the truth of religious beliefs—should be regarded as a proper and even central dimension of the academic study of religion.

Members of the academy, however, do not universally hold that the question of truth should be bracketed. Among those engaged in the "social scientific study of religion," it is often assumed that evaluations of the validity of religion are permissible, *if* those evaluations are negative. Robert A. Segal, in *Explaining and Interpreting Religion,* says that every social science explanation of religion involves "a naturalistic rather than divine origin" (1992, 19). J. Samuel Preus, in *Explaining Religion,* similarly says that the study of religion should operate in terms of a "naturalistic paradigm," meaning "an altogether nonreligious point of view," thereby explaining the existence of religion on the assumption that "God is not given" (1987, xiii, xiv, xv). On the basis of this assumption—that religions do not originate in genuine religious experience, meaning the experience of a divine or holy reality distinct from the totality of finite things—Segal and Preus both conclude, logically enough, that beliefs about such a divine reality are most likely entirely false. If the Segal-Preus proposal for the academic study of religion were to be fully implemented, only explanations of religion that deny the essential truth of religious beliefs could count as academic. This is a dogmatism as inhibitive of free inquiry as the theological dogmatism against which it is reacting.

This position is partly fueled by another confusion about the nature of "theology," closely related to the one already discussed. Segal and Preus assume that theology is inherently supernaturalistic, thereby being necessarily antithetical to the naturalistic perspective of the sciences, including the social sciences. Any theistic, and in that sense "theological," explanation of religion would, they conclude, necessarily be anti-scientific. This argument, however, involves two quite distinct meanings of *naturalism*. Naturalism is usually taken to entail the claim that "nature is all there is," with *nature* understood as the totality of finite entities, processes, and events.[11] But naturalism in this sense is not necessarily entailed by the naturalism properly presupposed by science, which, at least arguably, merely involves the rejection of supernatural interruptions of the normal causal processes of the world. It is part of a process philosophy of religion to make this argument, thereby showing that (nonsupernaturalistic) theistic explanations are not necessarily excluded from the academic study of religion.[12]

Although its nature and tasks have now been discussed, the distinctive character of a process philosophy of religion has not yet been fully brought out. This character was pointed to in the first core doctrine of process philosophy, according to which its overall task includes "the integration of moral, aesthetic, and religious intuitions with the most general doctrines of the sciences into a self-consistent worldview." Process philosophy is thereby meant to be equally a moral, aesthetic, religious, and scientific philosophy. It is, in other words, meant to provide a new framework for the academy as a whole, equally adequate as a presuppositional matrix for thought in the natural sciences, social sciences, arts, and humanities.

If this sounds audacious, it may be because Whitehead is correct in saying that "the ideal of the attainment of a harmony of the understanding" is "an excellency of which we have nearly forgotten the existence" (SMW 76). The fact that such a harmony is now not even widely thought to be an ideal, at least one toward which we should strive, is illustrated by the Humean contrast between theory and practice, the Kantian contrast between theoretical and practical reason, the existentialist contrast between objective and existential thinking, the neo-Darwinian contrast between biological and cultural evolution, and the academy's contrast between the natural sciences (*Naturwissenschaften*) and the humanities or human sciences (*Geisteswissenschaften*) with its methodological contrast between (scientific) "explanation" and (hermeneutical) "interpretation."

Since the latter part of the nineteenth century, to be sure, there has been increasing pressure in the academy to base all thought on the materialistic, atheistic form of naturalism that has come to be considered the "modern sci-

---

[11] It is surely in large part owing to this fact that Whiteheadian-Hartshornean process philosophy has thus far not been widely recognized as a form of naturalism.

[12] I have developed my critique of the Segal-Preus position at much greater length elsewhere (Griffin 2000b).

entific worldview." The proposals by Preus and Segal both reflect and express that pressure. The endurance of the dualisms just mentioned, however, expresses a widespread conviction that this experiment in reductionism has failed. Whiteheadian-Hartshornean process philosophy agrees entirely with Preus and Segal on the need for what can be called "domain uniformitarianism," according to which explanation and understanding should be sought in all domains of the academy in terms of a single set of categories. But it is based on the conviction that if we are to gain such a harmony of understanding it will need a more adequate basis. Process philosophy consists of a proposal for such a basis.

This philosophy as a whole, we have seen, can be considered equally a philosophy of religion, of morality, of aesthetics, and of science. This does not mean, however, that a presentation of it as a philosophy of religion requires laying out the whole philosophy in all its details. Rather, although each dimension does in a sense presuppose the whole, a presentation of one dimension can prescind from the details of the other dimensions. What makes this book a process philosophy of *religion,* accordingly, is its focus on matters that are especially important from a religious perspective. It is distinctive in relation to most other contemporary philosophies of religion, however, by being part and parcel of a proposal to move beyond the two mind-sets presently dominant in the academy—the contentment with, or at least resignation to, the present absence of any harmony of understanding, and the pressure to understand all phenomena in terms of the reductionistic version of naturalism.[13] Process philosophy makes this proposal by providing a nonreductionistic version of naturalism, which in principle allows all phenomena to be interpreted in terms of one scheme of ideas. Chapter 1 addresses this issue in terms of what has been the chief impediment to a harmony of understanding: the apparent conflict between religion and scientific naturalism.

[13] This orientation of the book—the fact that the position of process philosophy on various issues is offered as an alternative to the presently dominant positions in the academy—accounts for one of its lacunae. Except in a few cases, I have not referred to the interpretations of, and debates among, other process philosophers, such as those that have appeared in *Process Studies* since its founding in 1971. Although I had originally planned to incorporate much more of this internal discussion, the scope of the project, combined with my decision that it should be directed primarily outward, meant that to keep the manuscript down to a publishable length most of that internal discussion had to be eliminated.

[1]

Religion, Science, and Naturalism

Overcoming the apparent conflict between science and religion is at the very heart of process philosophy's purpose. Referring to "its close relations with religion and with science, natural and sociological," Whitehead says that philosophy "attains its chief importance by fusing the two, namely, religion and science, into one rational scheme of thought" (PR 15). This estimation of importance is based on the fact that Whitehead considers the terms *religion* and *science* to point not merely to two types of ideas but to two *forces*—"the force of our religious intuitions, and the force of our impulse to accurate observation and logical deduction"—which he considers, apart from bodily impulses, "the two strongest general forces" influencing human thought and behavior (SMW 181). In light of this view of what religion and science are, Whitehead says, "it is no exaggeration to say that the future course of history depends [upon our decision] as to the relations between them" (SMW 181). This reference to "the future course of history" brings out the connection between the science-religion issue and the even more inclusive purpose of process philosophy, which is to be of service to civilization (as will be discussed in Chapter 8). One of the main ways in which philosophy in our time could serve the future of civilization, Whitehead believed, is by overcoming the conflict of religious ideas and scientific ideas that has existed especially since the latter part of the nineteenth century.[1]

The attempt to integrate science and religion into a single scheme of

---

[1] Although here, for the most part, I simply presuppose that there is still a widespread conviction that religion, insofar as it presupposes ideas about the nature of reality, is in conflict with science, I have supported the idea elsewhere (Griffin 2000a).

thought,[2] he believed, is important for two basic reasons. One is simply that we should not give up "all hope of a vision of a harmony of truth" (SMW 185). He was deeply committed, in other words, to what I called "domain uniformitarianism" at the close of the introductory chapter. An even more important reason is that the future of civilization is endangered by this lack of integration, for at least three reasons. First, as long as the scientific and religious communities regard each other with suspicion and hostility, it will be difficult for them to cooperate wholeheartedly to overcome the problems threatening civilization today, such as the global ecological crisis. Second, religion that has not taken account of the truths revealed by science can be very dangerous. Third, the development of a "scientific worldview" that does not incorporate the truths revealed by religious experience has led, as highlighted by this book's title, to the view that the universe provides no normative values to guide the future course of civilization. The reasons for these judgments can be provided only later (mainly in Chapters 4 and 8). For now, the point is simply that moral as well as intellectual passion lay behind Whitehead's desire to integrate scientific and religious ideas.

1. Two Meanings of "Naturalism" Implicit in Whitehead's Solution

The key to understanding Whitehead's solution to the apparent conflict between scientific and religious ideas is to see that he provided a new form of naturalism,[3] one that is equally religious *and* scientific. To say that it is a form of *naturalism* is to say, and *only* to say, that it *rejects supernaturalism,* meaning the idea of *a divine being who could (and perhaps does) occasionally interrupt the world's most fundamental causal processes.* Being naturalistic in this limited sense does not, however, prevent Whitehead's process philosophy from being religious and even theistic. After having been agnostic or even atheistic most of his adult life, Whitehead came, soon after beginning to develop his

---

[2] This view of how to overcome apparent conflicts between science and religion sets process philosophy apart from those views that try to show that science and religion, properly understood, are so different that they cannot possibly conflict, and those that hold that science and religion can, through dialogue, be seen to be "consonant" with each other while remaining distinct bodies of thought that cannot be integrated into an inclusive worldview usable by both communities. Helpful discussions of these four positions—conflict, independence, dialogue, and integration—have been provided by Ian Barbour (1990, 3–30; 1995, 21–45).

[3] Although Whitehead himself, besides not making the distinction between the two meanings of naturalism that I bring out here, did not even employ the term, he did, as shown in James Bissett Pratt's *Naturalism* (1939), develop such a position.

metaphysical position, to believe that an intelligible cosmology requires a form of theism. But it is a *naturalistic* theism, allowing for no supernatural incursions. Having long been involved in the world of scientific thought himself—he had, for example, written a book (R) in which he developed an alternative to Einstein's theory of relativity—he saw nothing inherent to the nature of science that would prevent it from accepting a theism of this type.

What he *did* take to be essential to "the full scientific mentality" is the assumption "that all things great and small are conceivable as exemplifications of general principles which reign throughout the natural order" (SMW 5), so that "every detailed occurrence can be correlated with its antecedents in a perfectly definite manner, exemplifying general principles" (SMW 12). The conviction that the most fundamental of these "general principles" can never be overridden, which the scientific community adopted in the latter part of the nineteenth century, is what I am calling the basic conviction of scientific naturalism, which can be called *naturalism$_{ns}$* (with "ns" standing for "nonsupernaturalist").

As this naturalistic worldview developed concretely, however, it contained other elements that went far beyond this mere denial of supernatural interventions. It retained the sensationist doctrine of perception,[4] which had been adopted in the seventeenth century. It also retained that century's mechanistic doctrine of physical nature while rejecting its doctrine of a nonphysical mind or soul, with the result that everything in the world, including human behavior, was to be understood in terms of a mechanistic materialism. Finally, in rejecting the *interventionist* supernaturalism of the early modern scientific worldview, it did so, after a brief interlude of *deistic* supernaturalism (which Darwin still held), in favor of a completely atheistic worldview.

The resulting form of naturalism can be called *naturalism$_{sam}$* (with "sam" symbolizing "sensationist-atheistic-materialistic"). Once this metaphysical position replaced the previous one as the scientific worldview, any attempt to explain some phenomenon in other than sensationist, mechanist, materialist, reductionist terms would risk being rejected as unscientific, regardless of the rigor of the methodology and the logic. It is this naturalism$_{sam}$, called "scientific materialism" by Whitehead, to which he provided an alternative.[5]

---

[4] On the term *sensationist,* see note 3 of the Introduction.

[5] Although most philosophers today write as if "naturalism" self-evidently means some variant of reductionistic materialism, some make a distinction. For example, Hilary Putnam, having rejected his earlier materialism, now sometimes uses an adjective, such as *scientistic, reductionist,* or *disenchanted,* to characterize the type of naturalism he rejects, in distinction from the type he affirms (1994, xxii, lxxiv n. 58, 312).

2. The Two Sources of Conflict

Whitehead's solution to the conflict between the presently dominant world-views of the scientific and religious communities—and thereby the *apparent* conflict between science and religion themselves—implies that this conflict has two fundamental sources. In light of the scientific community's acceptance of naturalism$_{ns}$, which Whitehead believed to be philosophically justified, one source of conflict between these communities is the *continued association of religion with supernaturalism*. Given that association, the religious worldview would necessarily conflict with the worldview of the scientific community, even if the latter were to adopt a less restrictive form of naturalism$_{ns}$ in place of naturalism$_{sam}$. The other source of conflict is precisely this *present association of science with naturalism$_{sam}$*,[6] which rules out *any* significant religious beliefs, not simply supernaturalist ones. As long as either of these two associations is maintained, an integration of scientific and religious beliefs into a cosmology suitable for both scientific and religious communities will be impossible.

Naturalism$_{sam}$ as a Source of Conflict

To illustrate the way in which this currently dominant form of naturalism necessarily creates conflict, we can use a recent statement by William Provine, a historian of science, especially Darwinism:

> [M]odern evolutionary biology tells us . . . that nature has no detectable purposive forces of any kind. . . . Modern science directly implies that the world is organized strictly in accordance with deterministic principles or chance. . . . There are no purposive principles whatsoever in nature. There are no gods and no designing forces that are rationally detectable. . . .
>
> Second, modern science directly implies that there are no inherent moral or ethical laws. . . .[7]

[6] To speak of this present association is not to say that all present-day scientists accept naturalism$_{sam}$. Many of them, insofar as they have philosophical convictions at all, presuppose a dualistic and perhaps even a supernaturalistic worldview, and some hold ideas something like those of process philosophy. To say that science is now "associated" with naturalism$_{sam}$ is to say that this worldview is the one presupposed, and sometimes even aggressively advocated, by the ideological leaders of the present-day scientific community. This association is still so close, in fact, that the kind of argument I make in the present chapter—that naturalism$_{sam}$ provides an inadequate framework for science—is commonly perceived as an attack on science itself.

[7] This point and the previous one—which together say that the universe embodies no divine purpose, no inherent meaning, and no moral principles—spell out what Max Weber meant by speaking of "the disenchantment of the world" brought about by modern thought.

Third, human beings are marvelously complex machines. The individual human becomes an ethical person by means of only two mechanisms: deterministic heredity interacting with deterministic environmental influences. That is all there is.

Fourth, we must conclude that when we die, we die and that is the end of us. . . . There is no hope of life everlasting. . . .

[F]ree will, as traditionally conceived, the freedom to make uncoerced and unpredictable choices among alternative possible courses of action, simply does not exist. . . . [T]he evolutionary process cannot produce a being that is truly free to make choices. . . .

The universe cares nothing for us. . . . Humans are as nothing even in the evolutionary process on earth. . . . There is no ultimate meaning for humans. (Provine 1988, 64–70)

In making all these claims, Provine is simply spelling out the implications of naturalism$_{sam}$.[8] As long as science is associated with this form of naturalism, science will be regarded as antithetical to any significantly religious outlook. The dominance of this view in the academic community is illustrated by the efforts of Samuel Preus and Robert Segal, discussed in the introductory chapter, to bring even the field of religious studies into line with it.

Supernaturalism as a Source of Conflict

Many religious thinkers, of course, resist this effort. Aside from the futile effort to claim that religion is only to be interpreted, not explained, the most prominent forms of resistance have been mustered on behalf of some form of supernaturalism, thereby illustrating the continued prevalence of the other source of conflict. The most extreme version is "scientific creationism," which seeks to argue on scientific grounds that, as suggested by a rather literal reading of the biblical account, the Earth is only a few thousand years old.

Less obviously at variance with known facts is "progressive creationism." While accepting the view that the universe has been billions of years in the making, this view still rejects the idea that later species have evolved out of

---

Although much modern philosophy has been devoted to the effort to provide some basis for human meaning and morality in the light of this disenchantment, Whitehead, believing not only that these efforts are futile but also that the disenchantment has been based on philosophical errors, devoted his efforts to providing what could be called a reenchanted worldview.

[8] Some advocates of this worldview do not emphasize, and may even try to disguise, its hostility to any significantly religious viewpoint—as pointed out by Michael Ruse, an advocate who "deplore[s] this strategy" (quoted in Johnson 1993a, 165).

earlier ones, maintaining instead that the various species have been brought about by a series of special creations. For example, Alvin Plantinga considers "the claim that God created mankind as well as many kinds of plants and animals separately and specially" to be more probable, given a theistic perspective, than the claim that all living things have a common ancestry (1991a, 22). Explicit about the fact that this view involves supernatural exceptions to the normal causal processes, Plantinga holds that "God has often treated what he has made in a way different from the way in which he ordinarily treats it," illustrating this point by reference to miracles.

Plantinga argues that there is no reason why scientists qua scientists could not refer to this kind of supernatural causation:

> If after considerable study, we can't see how [some event] could possibly have happened by way of the ordinary workings of matter, the natural thing to think, from [a theistic perspective], is that God did something different and special here. . . . And why couldn't one conclude this precisely as a scientist? Where is it written that such a conclusion can't be part of science? (1991b, 98)

Plantinga is right that the idea that science cannot refer to divine causation is a recently adopted convention and that, like other conventions, it could be changed. But he evidently underestimates how deeply convinced the current scientific community is of the idea that there are never, because there *could not* be, any exceptions to the most general principles involved in the way in which events are normally related to antecedent and subsequent events. Given that deep-seated conviction, no proposal for the reform of science involving the suggestion that the universal causal nexus can be interrupted will be taken seriously. William Hasker reflects this point by saying that the "theistic science" proposed by Plantinga "might better be termed 'quixotic science'" (1995, 483).

Hasker's criticism is made from the perspective of yet a third way to resist scientific naturalism$_{sam}$, a way that involves accepting the convention that science is "methodologically atheistic." Advocates of this view agree that, in Hasker's words, "scientific explanation cannot appeal to supernatural intervention" (1995, 483). They argue, however, that scientific naturalism with its atheism is, in the words Ernan McMullin, "a way of characterizing a particular *methodology,* no more" (1991, 57). Science's naturalism is said to be purely methodological, not ontological. Given this view, coupled with the claim that the natural sciences by definition deal with only a limited domain (the "natural" or "creaturely" domain), they then argue that science with its (methodological) naturalism can be *placed within a supernaturalistic framework.*

Howard Van Till, saying that science necessarily gives "an incomplete picture of reality," maintains that it "needs to be placed within the framework
of an all-encompassing, biblically-informed, theistic worldview" (1991, 45).
Advocating this position against progressive creationism, Hasker says that
"divine purpose enters into the process at another level—not in the origins
of specific creatures, but in establishing the process as a whole" (1995, 485).
In a replay of Leibniz's argument against Newton (through Newton's proxy
Samuel Clarke), McMullin argues against Plantinga that such a view is really
more in keeping with the implications of the wisdom and power of God:

> The Creator whose powers are gradually revealed in [the Hebrew Bible] is
> omnipotent and all-wise. . . . His Providence extends to all His creatures; they
> are all part of His single plan. . . . Would such a Being be likely to "intervene"
> in His creation in the way that Plantinga describes? . . . He must be thought
> of as creating in that very first moment the potencies for all the kinds of liv-
> ing things that would come later, including the human body itself. (1991, 75)

Besides regarding this view as more consistent with divine omnipotence, its
proponents believe that it eliminates, or at least greatly mitigates, the possibility of conflict between science and religion.

From the perspective of the analysis of the sources of conflict given earlier, however, this proposal does not address the fundamental problem. By
saying that divine interventions *could* occur, it is still supernaturalistic. For
example, McMullin says that although God has chosen to work through natural or secondary causes, "God *could* also, if He so chose, relate to His creation in a different way, in the dramatic mode of a grace that overcomes nature" (1991, 76–77). Some exponents of this position, furthermore, say that
God actually does intervene now and again. Hasker, after his statement that
"scientific explanation cannot appeal to supernatural intervention," adds
that the Christian should "refuse to make the assumption that every actual
event has a scientific explanation" (1995, 483). His point is that it may be
that "there just *is* no scientific (i.e., naturalistic) explanation of the origin of
life." This proposal would be no more palatable from the point of view of
the scientific community, even if its naturalism were restricted to natural-
ism$_{ns}$, than Plantinga's proposal for a supernaturalistic science. That is, more
fundamental than whether the scientist qua scientist can affirm supernatural
interventions is whether such interventions are thought actually to occur.
The most basic issue, in other words, is worldview, not the nature of science.

It could be argued, however, that the problem lies not in this third stance
as such, but only in the fact that theologically conservative proponents of it,

such as Hasker, McMullin, and Van Till, do not hold to it consistently. Perhaps more liberal proponents could, by maintaining that God works *exclusively* through natural causes, avoid any conflict with scientific naturalism$_{ns}$. Such a position was fully developed at the outset of the twentieth century in Rudolf Otto's *Naturalism and Religion* (1907) and his later "Darwinism and Religion" (1931). Advocating full acceptance of the (naturalistic$_{ns}$) view that "a similar mode of causal connection binds all things together," Otto strongly rejected the reductionistic, materialistic, deterministic, atheistic version of naturalism that had become the dominant worldview of the scientific community (1907, 19).

Believing that "there can be no religion without the supernatural," Otto proposed replacing the "lower supernaturalism" with the "higher supernaturalism" (1931, 129). Against the lower supernaturalism, which accepts "the notion that by individual special acts, the supernatural intrudes upon the normal course of things," Otto insisted that no exceptions should be allowed, even for the origin of life and of human beings (129, 134–37). All this is consistent, he said, with the higher supernaturalism, according to which the whole world, with its uninterrupted causal nexus, is the product of purposive design. Given "the belief that eternal wisdom has purposely determined the existence of life and human intelligence in this world," said Otto, "the processes of evolution working themselves out strictly in accordance with natural law . . . are then nothing but so many different means for making certain of this end" (137–38).

Although this position overcomes the most obvious problems of the stance represented by Hasker, McMullin, and Van Till, it still does not fully embody naturalism$_{ns}$. There are no interventions *within* the world, but the original creation of the world is still a fully supernatural event, involving a type of causality absolutely different in kind from anything since then. It thereby violates at the outset the naturalistic conviction that, in Otto's own words, "a similar mode of causal connection binds all things together." Furthermore, although Otto consistently maintained that God in fact never does intervene supernaturally, his acceptance of the view that God created the universe ex nihilo implies that God *could* do so, and even the allowance of this possibility violates naturalism$_{ns}$.[9]

The supernaturalistic idea of the origin of our universe also results in a number of other problems that undermine Otto's contention that his "higher supernaturalism" is far more rational than the reductionistic naturalism he opposed. One problem, which Otto's position has in common

[9] See note 8 of Chapter 4.

with all the previously mentioned versions of supernaturalism (except scientific creationism with its young Earth), is the tension between the slow-
ness of the creative process and the alleged omnipotence of the Creator. If
the whole purpose of the creation was, as Otto claims, to bring forth human
beings (1931, 137–38), it is an enormous mystery as to why an all-wise, omnipotent being would take ten to twenty billion years to do so.

At least equally serious is the problem of evil created by Otto's position.
Although his God never intervenes, the reason for this nonintervention is a
divine decision, not a metaphysical necessity. Accordingly, people can still
justifiably ask why God does not intervene to prevent particularly horrible
events. Otto's answer would be that God in the beginning planned all the
details to work out for the best. For example, rejecting the view that divine
providence extends only to a few exceptional events, Otto's higher supernaturalism holds that "everything has come about in such a way that it reveals intention, wisdom, providence, and eternal meaning" (1907, 37). The
old question, however, is whether, given the enormous evils of the evolutionary process and human history, this view of the universe is even re-
motely credible. Otto frankly admitted the problem, saying that his position
leaves "many gaps and a thousand riddles," so that faith means "going against
appearances" and requires "a courageous will to believe" (1907, 15). A
position that can be advocated only on this basis has little chance of being
regarded by the scientific community as more rational than its present
worldview.[10]

Overcoming the Two Sources of Conflict

The foregoing summary of recent discussions illustrates the analysis implicit in Whitehead's position as to the two fundamental sources of the present conflict between science and religion. As long as religion seems to require supernaturalism while science seems to support naturalism$_{sam}$, science
and religion will seem to be completely opposed to each other. Furthermore, even if one of these associations is overcome, conflict will remain
if the other is not. This conflict is removed, to be sure, in those forms of
liberal theology that fully accept the presuppositions and implications of nat-
uralism$_{sam}$. Insofar as they accept those implications, however, these theologies lose their religious character. Although they can perhaps claim a recon-

---

[10] Otto, who affirmed a Cartesian dualism between mind and body in order to defend human freedom, also admitted that this position made the mind-body relation inexplicable
(1907, 153, 300, 311, 349).

ciliation of science and *theology,* the conflict between science and *religion* remains.

If there is to be a real reconciliation, it will require the kind of basis proposed by Whitehead: *a scientific-religious naturalism, supportive of the necessary presuppositions of the scientific and religious communities.* Of course, the scientific and religious communities will adopt such a position not simply because doing so is a precondition for achieving harmony between the two communities, but only if doing so will help them express their own proper concerns more adequately.

With regard to the religious communities, I have already suggested two reasons why supernaturalism, with its idea of God as possessing coercive omnipotence, creates difficulties for theistic religion: it allows the evil of the world to create doubt as to the goodness and even the existence of a divine creator, and it is in extreme tension with the evolutionary account of the world. Later chapters will elaborate on these reasons and provide some more. Many theists, to be sure, readily admit that the idea of divine omnipotence creates many problems but maintain that they are overridden by the fact that the positive affirmations of theistic religion require supernaturalism. One argument of this book is that theistic religions can express their fundamental convictions better within the framework of process philosophy's naturalistic theism than within that of a supernaturalistic theism.

Even assuming that this argument can be made, however, the fact remains that the intellectual leaders of the scientific community certainly will not reject naturalism$_{sam}$ in favor of a more open form of naturalism simply because doing so might overcome the apparent conflict of science and religion. They will do so only if they become convinced that *naturalism$_{sam}$ has become a problem and that a new form of naturalism will provide a better basis for science itself* (see Section 4).

3. The Criterion of Hard-Core Common Sense

As stated in the introductory chapter, one of the core doctrines of process philosophy involves the primary criterion for evaluating the adequacy of any theory, be it a philosophical, theological, or scientific theory. This criterion is that the theory do justice to what I call our hard-core commonsense notions, which Whitehead referred to as the inevitable presuppositions of practice. In his words, "we must bow to those presumptions, which, in despite of criticism, we still employ for the regulation of our lives. Such presumptions are imperative in experience" (PR 151). The reason why such presumptions are imperative, so that our theories to be rational must include them, is that we *inevitably* presuppose them in practice. And if our theories involve "negations of what in practice is presupposed" (PR 13), then we contradict ourselves, explicitly denying what we are implicitly affirming. This criterion can, therefore, be regarded as an implication of the law of noncontradiction, usually considered the first rule of reason.[11] *Any scientific, philosophical, or theological theory is irrational, accordingly, to the extent that it contradicts whatever notions we inevitably presuppose in practice.*[12]

In referring to these notions as (hard-core) commonsense notions, I am drawing attention to the fact that Whitehead stands in the tradition of "commonsense philosophy," with which the name of Thomas Reid is especially associated. As I will point out in the final chapter, Whitehead's version of this philosophy differs from that of Reid himself and thereby the advocates of Reformed epistemology, who appeal to it. For now, however, the point is that Whitehead affirms the *basic* approach of Reid, who said that because the very act of denying such notions verbally would involve an implicit affirmation of them, such a denial would be "metaphysical lunacy" (1997 [1764], 268–69). Because this set of notions cannot be consistently denied, it should provide the basic criterion for deciding the adequacy of any theory.

Whitehead articulates this criterion, as had Reid, overagainst David Hume's position. Hume had also recognized the existence of various "natural beliefs," such as the beliefs in an external world and in causal influence, which we inevitably presuppose in practice. He saw, however, that some natural beliefs, including these two, could not be justified by his own brand of empiricism. Affirming *conceptual* empiricism (as does Whitehead), Hume held that, in Whitehead's words, "nothing is to be received into the philosophical scheme which is not discoverable as an element in subjective experience" (PR 166). But because Hume affirmed the *sensationist* version of this

---

[11] Putnam had earlier denied, in agreement with the position Willard Van Quine articulated in "Two Dogmas of Empiricism" (1953), that there are any a priori truths different in kind from empirical truths, thereby suggesting that even the most fundamental laws of logic are in principle revisable. In "There Is at Least One A Priori Truth," however, Putnam argues that the principle of noncontradiction is an absolutely unrevisable a priori truth (1983, 98–114).

[12] Jürgen Habermas and other members of the school of thought known as "critical theory," especially Karl-Otto Apel, employ a version of this criterion in their criticism of modes of discourse that force their proponents into "performative self-contradictions." Such self-contradictions arise, explains Martin Jay, "when whatever is being claimed is at odds with the presuppositions or implications of the act of claiming it" (1993, 29). For my own most complete critique of the attempt to deny hard-core commonsense notions, see my chapter on Mark C. Taylor in Griffin, Beardslee, and Holland 1989.

conceptual empiricism, he was led to deny that we directly experience a real world beyond ourselves or any causal influence. Rather than use this conclusion as a reductio ad absurdum of the sensationist theory of perception (as Whitehead believes he should have), Hume justified such natural beliefs by appealing to "practice," saying that in *practice* he necessarily presupposed various beliefs that could have no place in his metaphysical *theory*. Regarding this move as wholly irrational, Whitehead says:

> Whatever is found in "practice" must lie within the scope of the metaphysical description. When the description fails to include the "practice," the metaphysics is inadequate and requires revision. There can be no appeal to practice to supplement metaphysics. . . . Metaphysics is nothing but the description of the generalities which apply to all the details of practice. (PR 13) [13]

Instead of using the inevitable presuppositions of practice to *supplement* his theory, Hume should have employed them to *revise* it (PR 156). Had he done so, Whitehead suggests, we would rightly revere him "as one of the greatest of philosophers" (S 52). As it is, however, Hume is to be regarded as "the high watermark of anti-rationalism in philosophy" (PR 153). This is because rationalism is the attempt to show how all our beliefs can be coordinated with one another. Hume, by contrast, rested content with two sets of uncoordinated beliefs (PR 153).

Rationalism is, more particularly, the attempt to show how all our hard-core commonsense beliefs can be rendered consistent with one another. After stating his basic rule of evidence—"that we must bow to those presumptions, which, in despite of criticism, we still employ for the regulation of our lives"—Whitehead adds: "Rationalism is the search for the coherence of such presumptions" (PR 151). With this statement, Whitehead is taking issue with most forms of modern thought, which he considers anti-rational insofar as they are not devoted to showing how to coordinate such presumptions with one another and with all the other beliefs we take to be well founded. Modern thought, in other words, has by and large followed Hume in *not* taking hard-core common sense as the basic criterion for evaluating the adequacy of theories. [14]

[13] As Putnam points out, the classical pragmatists—Peirce, James, and Dewey—rejected the idea "that there is a 'first philosophy' higher than the practice that we take most seriously when the chips are down. There is no Archimedean point from which we can argue that what is indispensable in life *gilt nicht in der Philosophie*" (1994, 154). Many have recently rejected metaphysics in the name of pragmatism. Given Whitehead's definition of metaphysics in terms of practice, however, we could say that he has developed a "pragmatic metaphysics."

[14] Criticizing his Harvard colleague's scientistic physicalism on this basis, Putnam says: "The task of philosophy is not the examination of our intuitive notions, in Quine's view, but

Whitehead's suggestion that rational thought *should* do so may be rejected by many as anti-scientific. Our common sense, it is often said, consists simply of all the beliefs we have inherited from the society in which we were brought up, most of which are false. Indeed, science has come to be regarded as a systematic assault upon common sense. Whereas common sense once said that the Earth is flat, stationary, and at the center of the universe, that matter is solid and inert, and that human beings could not fly to the moon, science has shown all these beliefs to be false. Intellectual progress, in short, is perceived as the continual modification of common sense in the light of scientific discoveries. With something like this idea of common sense in mind, Kant rejected the appeal to it by Reid (whose writing he evidently knew only through a hostile secondary source), charging that Reid took as his criterion the uncritical prejudices of people rather than the well-considered reflections of trained thinkers (Woozley 1941, xiv, xxxiii).

It is precisely because the term *common sense* is often understood in this way that I add the adjective *hard-core* when referring to the kind of common sense that *should* be used as the primary test of adequacy for all theories. The kind of common sense discussed in the previous paragraph can, by contrast, be called "soft-core common sense," thereby indicating that it is different in kind from hard-core common sense. Commonsense beliefs of the soft-core variety, unlike those of the hard-core variety, are *not* inevitably presupposed in practice; they are *not* common to all human beings at the presuppositional level; and they *can* be denied verbally without self-contradiction. Soft-core common sense, therefore, certainly does not provide a criterion to which theories should conform. Science has rightly modified this kind of common sense in the past and will surely continue to do so in the future. Whitehead himself sometimes uses the term with this meaning, saying that it is "part of the special sciences to modify common sense," that "an excess of common sense has its disadvantages," and that his own philosophy is an attempt to modify "the general common-sense notion of the universe" (PR 17; MT 16, 129).

The fact that the term *common sense* is often used in this way, accordingly, does not count against the proposal that our *hard-core* common sense should

rather the construction of a substitute for those notions based on first-class science [i.e., physics]" (1994: 334). Ironically, Putnam had earlier praised Quine for stressing, in relation to the argument for the indispensability of mathematical entities (see notes 24 and 25), "the intellectual dishonesty of denying the existence of what one daily presupposes" (1979, 347). The difference is that Quine takes seriously only those notions that are presupposed in physics, whereas Putnam has recently come, with the pragmatists, to take seriously the notions that are presupposed in human life in general.

be the primary criterion for evaluating the adequacy of all theories, including scientific theories. The two kinds of common sense have little in common except the name. They are different in kind, not merely in degree. What makes hard-core commonsense beliefs different is, again, the fact that we *inevitably* presuppose them, even in the act of verbally denying them. To illustrate this point, we can use the two beliefs already mentioned—the beliefs in an external world and in causality. If I announce to an audience, or write on my computer, that I am a solipsist, doubting the existence of an actual world beyond myself, I show by my act (of speaking *to the audience* or writing *on my computer*) that I do not doubt this at all. Likewise, if I try to convince some colleagues that there is no such thing as causal influence, I prove by my very attempt to cause them to change their minds that I know otherwise.[15] The same kind of self-refutation would be involved in denials of any of the other hard-core commonsense beliefs to be mentioned later, such as our beliefs in the past, in purposive causation, and in freedom.

In making the inevitable presuppositions of practice fundamental, Whitehead was, as he knew (PR 13; MT 106), accepting one of the meanings of the "pragmatism" advocated by Charles Peirce and William James. Hartshorne makes the connection even more explicitly. Besides endorsing Peirce's "critical common-sensism," Hartshorne says that he accepts the "pragmatic principle" that "what we have to be guided by in our decision-making, we should not pretend to reject theoretically" (1991b, 676, 624). Although the idea that *any* notions should not be subject to doubt is sometimes said to contradict the principle of "fallibilism," which we should all affirm, it is to be noted that the same Peirce who made fallibilism famous also affirmed commonsensism (1931–53, 5:376n, 416).[16] The attempt to give a *precise formulation* of any hard-core commonsense notion should, of course, be regarded as a fallible enterprise.

It should not be assumed, however, that the burden of proof is on the one

[15] As Habermas and Apel would say (see note 12), such statements involve "performative self-contradictions." In "Cogito, Ergo Sum," Jaakko Hintikka showed that Descartes's famous argument involved such a contradiction: If I say, "I doubt herewith, now, that I exist," then, explains Hintikka, "the propositional component contradicts the performative component of the speech act expressed by that self-referential sentence" (1962, 32). The commonsense tradition, to which both Whitehead and Apel belong, points out that this kind of self-contradiction is not limited to the instance focused on by Descartes.

[16] As Apel says (1987, 266), Peirce himself did not satisfactorily show how his fallibilism and commonsensism were consistent. What Peirce should have said, Apel points out, is that fallibilism must not be absolutized: "The principle of fallibilism and the principle of criticism derived from it are meaningful and valid only if they are restricted in their validity from the outset, so that at least some philosophical evidence is excluded from possible criticism— namely the evidence on which these principles are themselves based" (274).

making the claim about any particular notion, such as causal influence or
(partial) freedom. No universal claim can be proved by any number of instances, however great. But as William James said, it takes only one white
crow to prove that not all crows are black (1986, 131). A universal claim can,
in other words, be *disproved* by a single negative instance. The proper approach for those who resist the anti-relativism involved in this criterion, accordingly, would not be simply to express scepticism about it or to condemn
it by association with some now disreputable position, such as foundationalism. The proper approach would be to find someone who can live consistently without presupposing the notion in question. Insofar as no such person can be located, there is good reason to suppose the notion to be indeed
universally presupposed. In carrying out this test, of course, it is important
to keep in mind the distinction between hard-core and soft-core common
sense. The non-universality of the former cannot be shown by using an
example of the latter—a point that should be too obvious to mention but,
alas, is not.[17]

The most common way of resisting the anti-relativism of this position is
not, of course, to deny that some beliefs are universally presupposed in practice. Even Hume, after all, did not do this. The most common approach is
simply, with Hume, to deny that such beliefs should, by virtue of their de
facto universality at the presuppositional level, be given *normative* status. One
might speculate, for example, that because acting as if they were true helped
our ancestors survive, they have been programmed into us by evolutionary
mechanisms. One could even recognize that this explanation itself presupposes the very notions in question, such as the external world, the past, and
causation. One could argue, nevertheless, that we can recognize that we, as
products of the evolutionary process, inevitably presuppose various notions
while remaining sceptical of the ontological (as distinct from the merely instrumental) truth of these notions.

[17] Even after I had made this point, a reader wrote in response to my argument: "It seems
to me very complicated to determine 'what we inevitably presuppose in practice.' For instance, in practice when we do all kinds of measurement we presuppose that we are at rest.
However, we have nonetheless come to the conclusion that the situation is better described as
the Earth rotating, circling the Sun, and the Solar system moving in the Galaxy." However (I
reply), the "presupposition" that we are at absolute rest is clearly *not* an example of what I call
hard-core common sense, as is shown by the very fact that it is a belief that we *can* give up
without falling into self-contradiction. This critic, in fact, implicitly admitted this. After quoting my stipulation that hard-core commonsense beliefs are *inevitably* presupposed, this critic
(correctly) did *not* put this adverb before "presuppose" in the second sentence. This apparent
recognition that my claim about hard-core common sense was being refuted in terms of an
example of merely soft-core common sense, however, did not lead the critic to withdraw the
refutation.

Such an argument, however, would be self-contradictory. If we verbally express doubt about the truth of some proposition while presupposing its truth in the very act of expressing the doubt, we are affirming and doubting it at the same time. And once we have allowed ourselves to hold a self-contradictory position on one matter, we have renounced the right to appeal to the first rule of reason, the principle of noncontradiction,[18] in criticizing alternative positions. In arguing against the creationist account of fundamentalist Christians, for example, one would not be able to use any self-contradictions or contradictions with fact inherent in that view as reasons to reject it. One would, therefore, have no reason to affirm the truth of an evolutionary account of our origins. Accordingly, the very reason for assuming the ideas to be true in merely an instrumentalist sense—the argument that we accept them because they facilitated survival in the evolutionary struggle—would be undermined. Although it may go against the fashionable relativism of our time, there really is no alternative, if we want to engage in rational discussion, to accepting our hard-core common sense as the basic criterion of adequacy.

In any case, having discussed the most fundamental of the criteria to be used to evaluate the adequacy of theories, I turn now to the question of the adequacy of naturalism$_{sam}$ for expressing scientific beliefs. Whitehead recognizes that the enormous successes of science will make it especially difficult to transcend the set of ideas with which science has been associated (SMW 18). What is important to see, however, is that these successes have been limited to certain areas. In the eighteenth and nineteenth centuries, for example, the "triumph of materialism was chiefly in the sciences of rational dynamics, physics, and chemistry" (SMW 60). Besides recognizing these triumphs, it is important to recognize, against materialistic triumphalism,[19] all the areas in which the present scheme of concepts has, far from leading to progress, actually prevented it.

4. Science and Naturalism$_{sam}$

Whitehead carried out his critique of scientific materialism, or what I am calling naturalism$_{sam}$, in the interests of *science itself* (SMW 66, 83–84; PR xiv).

---

[18] "[T]he rules of a minimal logic," says Apel, belong to the "conditions of the possibility of criticism itself" (1987, 274).

[19] A recent example of such triumphalism is provided by E. O. Wilson's *Consilience* (1998).

His goal was "to widen the scientific scheme in a way which is useful for science itself" (SMW 68). The philosophical worldview with which science is presently associated is problematic, he argued, because it prevents the scientific community from providing rational explanations for a wide range of phenomena. Problems created by the sensationism, materialism, and atheism of naturalism$_{sam}$ will be discussed in order.

Problems Created for Science by Sensationism

Science, Whitehead points out, is urged forward by an "ultimate rationalism," which is "the belief that clarity can only be reached by pushing explanation to its utmost limits" (FR 61; PR 153). The fact that modern science has accepted the sensationist doctrine of perception, however, has meant that this urge for ever more complete explanation has been stifled with regard to many issues.

The most well-known of such issues are probably the interrelated problems of causation and induction. Hume famously showed that sense perception as such provides no basis for the belief that there is any necessary connection between what in any particular instance we call the "cause" and the "effect." All that we actually see is a "constant conjunction" between two *kinds* of events. Having observed this constant conjunction, we call the event that comes first "the cause" and the one that follows "the effect." This means that the causal connection, as far as we know, is entirely arbitrary. We have no good reason, therefore, to expect the same kinds of "causal relations" that we observe today to obtain tomorrow. The implication is that the belief in the "uniformity of nature" is rationally groundless.

Science, however, presupposes this uniformity. The basic method of science is generally held to involve induction, in which general laws are drawn from a few cases. If two hydrogen atoms combined with one oxygen atom form a water molecule today, we expect the same to have been true billions of years ago. If a vaccination of penicillin prevents pneumonia in Boston this year, we assume that the same thing will be true in Edinburgh next year (barring, of course, the development of a penicillin-resistant form of pneumonia). In general, more or less universal laws of nature are commonly based upon a single experiment and a few replications. What Hume's demonstration showed is that there is no rational basis for this whole enterprise, insofar as the sensationist theory of perception is presupposed. The result has been, Whitehead points out, that "since the time of Hume, the fashionable scientific philosophy has been such as to deny the rationality of science" (SMW 4). The dominant reaction has been simply to ignore the problem of justifying induction, being content, Whitehead says sardonically, "to base it upon our vague instinct that of course it is all right" (SMW 43).[20]

The attitude criticized by Whitehead is illustrated by one of the most famous of the logical positivists. As Jeffrey Stout points out, "A. J. Ayer accepts the Humean principles that lead toward the problem of induction, but he cannot bring himself to take the problem at all seriously" (Stout 1981, 91). In fact, Ayer simply said that it is time "to abandon the superstition that natural science cannot be regarded as logically respectable until philosophers have solved the problem of induction" (1952, 49). Whitehead, by contrast, does not think that the scientific community, especially the philosophy-of-science community, should rest content with this anti-rationalism.[21]

The problems, furthermore, do not stop with causation and induction. Hume's argument also showed that sensory perception gives no knowledge of an external world, that is, of actual things beyond our own minds.[22] George Santayana extended this Humean argument for solipsism by pointing out that sensory perception also gives no knowledge of the past, so that the sensationist form of empiricism leads to "solipsism of the present moment" (1955, 14–15). If we have no knowledge that there has been a past and that there will be a future, furthermore, we have no knowledge of time. If scientific theories could not speak of a real world, causation, the past, and time, we could have no scientific theories, such as a theory of evolution. As Whitehead says, "pure sense perception does not provide the data for its own interpretation" (MT 133).

It might be argued, of course, that because no one really doubts the reality of causation, the past, time, and an external world, no problem is created by the fact that sense perception does not provide the empirical data for discussing these matters. We can rest content with sensationism as a general philosophy, while recognizing that we have to presuppose a few ideas that are not, strictly speaking, justified by sensory perception. These few exceptions create no problem because all these ideas are noncontroversial, being presupposed by everybody.

[20] Defining the "naturalism" he advocates as the view that natural science requires no external justification, Quine says that one of the sources of this naturalism is "unregenerate realism, the robust state of mind of the natural scientist who has never felt any qualms beyond the negotiable uncertainties internal to science" (1981, 72). Quine thereby perfectly illustrates the state of mind Whitehead was criticizing.

[21] Whitehead's view was shared by one of the most prominent logical positivists, Hans Reichenbach, who says of Hume: "He is not alarmed by his discovery; he does not realize that if there is no escape from the dilemma pointed out by him, science might as well not be continued . . . if it is nothing but a ridiculous self-delusion" (1938, 346).

[22] "The belief in an external world independent of the perceiving subject," said Einstein in opposition to phenomenalist-positivistic views, "is the basis of all natural science" (1931, 66).

This contention, however, is precisely Hume's argument from "practice," which not only builds irrationalism into the very foundation of scientific thought but leads to irrational arguments. It has been common, for example, for scientists and science-based philosophers to ignore claims of empirical evidence for extrasensory perception, such as telepathy, on the grounds that no such evidence could exist because extrasensory perception is impossible. Also, the exclusion of aesthetic, ethical, and religious notions from the cognitive domain, and therefore from cosmology, has been based on the claim that these notions are unempirical, not being rooted in perception. The basis for these arguments is the assumed truth of the sensationist theory of perception, which says that we can perceive things beyond our own bodies only by means of our physical sensory organs. The scientific and the larger intellectual community is acting wholly irrationally, insofar as it so argues, because it is using the sensationist theory or perception to exclude ideas that it does not want to include in its official worldview while allowing in other ideas—such as causality, time, and a real world—that equally fail to meet the critical standard.[23] We should surely want a "scientific rationality" that is more truly rational.

The problems created by the sensationist theory of perception run even deeper: there are still other notions presupposed in the practice of science that are not grounded in sensory perception, such as the mathematical objects involved in physics and the logical principles involved in all scientific

[23] For example, Quine endorses the (sensationist) empiricist principle that "whatever evidence there *is* for science *is* sensory evidence" (1969, 75), which means that "our statements about the external world face the tribunal of sense experience" (1953, 41). He agrees with Hume, furthermore, that sense experience gives no knowledge of an external world, so that physical objects are merely convenient posits, "comparable, epistemologically, to the gods of Homer." And yet he "believe[s] in physical objects and not in Homer's gods" (1953, 44), accepting, in fact, a physicalist or materialist ontology (1995, 14, 40). Although he accords "epistemological priority" to the "phenomenalistic conceptual scheme," in terms of which the ontology of physical objects is a "myth" (1953, 19), he has no doubt as to the truth of this mythical ontology, confessing his "unswerving belief in external things—people, nerve endings, sticks, stones" (1981, 21). (Quine's position, says Putnam, sounds "like Hume saying that when he is in his study he sees that total skepticism is correct, but whenever he leaves his study he is a 'robust realist'" [1994, 347].) Besides letting in the external world, furthermore, Quine's tribunal of sense experience lets temporality sneak past. Saying that sensory experience gives us merely the "specious present," Quine asks how we make the "momentous" step involved in "the transcending of the specious present" (1995, 36). But then he assumes that we begin with "a state of language that is limited to the specious present *and to short-term memories and expectations*" (1995, 36; emphasis added), thereby presupposing the very temporality that was to be explained. He seems simply to ignore the point, driven home by Santayana, that sense data give no clue whatsoever of a past or a future, whether remote or contiguous. When it comes to moral objects, however, Quine enforces his tribunal of sensory experience, excluding moral judgments from the realm of cognitive assertions (Hahn and Schilpp 1986, 663–65).

reasoning. One of the central issues in the philosophy of mathematics and of logic in the past century has been how to make sense of the objectivity of mathematical and logical truths, which everyone presupposes. Because, as Hilary Putnam points out, "the nature of mathematical truth" and "the nature of logical truth" are one and the same problem (1994, 500), we can discuss the problem in terms of only one of them; I will use mathematics.

The traditional view, usually called "Platonic realism" or simply "realism" or "Platonism," is that "mathematical entities exist outside space and time, outside thought and matter, in an abstract realm" (Hersh 1997, 9). Since the rise of the sensationist doctrine of perception, this traditional affirmation of the existence of "abstract entities" raises the question how we could apprehend them. This sensationist doctrine was rejected by one famous mathematician and logician, Kurt Gödel, who said:

> [D]espite their remoteness from sense experience, we do have something like
> a perception also of the objects of set theory, as is seen from the fact that the
> axioms force themselves upon us as being true. I don't see any reason why we
> should have less confidence in this kind of perception, i.e., in mathematical
> intuition, than in sense perception. (1990, 268)

However, many philosophers of mathematics, affirming the sensationist doctrine of perception, have strongly rejected Gödel's thesis. For example, in "A Gödelian Thesis Regarding Mathematical Objects: Do They Exist? And Can We Perceive Them?" C. Chihara asks rhetorically: "What empirical scientist would be impressed by an explanation this flabby?" (1982, 217). Also in reaction to Gödel's view, Putnam at one time declared:

> The trouble with this sort of Platonism is that it seems flatly incompatible
> with the simple fact that we think with our brains, and not with immaterial
> souls. . . . One does not have to be an "identity theorist" in the philosophy
> of mind (that is, one who holds that sensations, intuitions, and perceptions are
> identical with brain events) to recognize the difficulties with the kind of du-
> alism that Gödel believes in. We cannot envisage *any* kind of neural process
> that could even correspond to the "perception of a mathematical object."
> (1994, 503)[24]

[24] Although this essay was included in Putnam's 1994 collection, it was originally published in 1979, when Putnam still held a materialist worldview, with a functionalist, cybernetic view of the mind. Putnam now endorses the attitude of Quine, who, in Putnam's words, "ignores the problem . . . as to how we can know that abstract entities exist unless we can interact with them in some way," simply affirming their existence on the basis of the "indispensability argument," namely, that the abstract entities of mathematics are indispensable for physics (1994, 153). Although Putnam now rejects arguments of the type he formerly gave, saying that we should not "confuse the 'intuitions' of metaphysicians with genuine argument" (156), it is clear

Reuben Hersh, in the same vein, charges mathematicians who accept the Platonic view with being "unscientific" (1997, 11). Asking rhetorically, "How does this [alleged] immaterial realm . . . make contact with flesh and blood mathematicians?" Hersh adds: "Ideal entities independent of human consciousness violate the empiricism of modern science" (12). In all these statements, we see the assumption that empiricism, the doctrine that we can know of the existence of things only through perceptual experience, is equated with *sensate* empiricism, according to which all perception is by means of our sensory organs.

Because this attitude is so widespread, there has been strong pressure to reject the Platonic, realistic conception of mathematical truth. One result has been that mathematicians have tended to hold one view in public—usually "formalism," according to which mathematics is just a game with meaningless symbols—and another in practice. That is, most mathematicians in practice, virtually everyone evidently agrees, presuppose the Platonic view (Hersh 1997, 7; Maddy 1990, 2–3). As Y. N. Moschovakis says: "The main point in favor of the realistic approach to mathematics is the instinctive certainty of most everybody who has ever tried to solve a problem that he is thinking about 'real objects,' whether they are sets, numbers, or whatever" (1980, 605). But the clash of this worldview with naturalism$_{sam}$ makes it difficult to confess this belief, so that, Moschovakis adds, "most mathematicians claim to be formalists (when pressed) while they spend their working hours behaving as if they were unabashed realists" (605–6).[25] This is clearly unsatisfactory.

---

that his earlier intuitions are alive and widespread in the philosophical, mathematical, and scientific communities. A philosophical position aspiring to adequacy cannot avoid this issue simply by appeal to the indispensability argument, as true as it is.

[25] Another result has been the attempt by philosophers of mathematics to develop, in opposition to the assumptions of working mathematicians, anti-Platonic doctrines, as witnessed by the appearance of books with titles such as *Science without Numbers* (Field 1980) and *Mathematics without Numbers* (Hellman 1989). The depth of the conflict between naturalism$_{sam}$ and the presuppositions of mathematicians is strikingly manifest in the position of Penelope Maddy (1990). Insisting (rightly) that philosophers must take the presuppositions of working mathematicians seriously (vii), Maddy tries to develop a materialistic version of the Platonic or realistic view. We can overcome the problem of "unobservable Platonic entities" (44), she suggests, by "bringing [mathematical] sets into the physical world" so that they are no longer "abstract" but have "spatio-temporal location" (59). As a result, Gödel's "perception-like connection is just [sensory] perception itself" (178). Being fully explicit about what she is doing, Maddy states: "Of course, my motivation for bringing sets into the physical world and for tying mathematical intuition so closely to ordinary perception is naturalism" (by which she means Quine's materialism). Her new approach seems to her "the most promising approach for bringing mathematical ontology and epistemology into line with our overall scientific world-view" (78). Process philosophy suggests, by contrast, that we should instead try to bring "our overall scientific world-view" into line with the inevitable presuppositions of mathematics (as well as of logic, science, and life more generally).

Besides presupposing the existence of mathematical and logical truths, science presupposes many other notions not rooted in sensory perception. By engaging in the quest for truth, science presupposes the twofold notion that there is such a thing as truth and that truth is important. But sensory perception is not the source of either part of this twofold notion. Science also presupposes beauty, as in the sense that certain proofs are especially "elegant." Moral ideals are also presupposed, such as when medical research is motivated by a desire to alleviate suffering. As long as the scientific community continues to endorse the sensationist theory of perception, it implies that its own practice—insofar as it presupposes cognitive, aesthetic, and moral ideals as well as mathematical and logical truths—is based upon wholly fictional notions.

It might be said, of course, that the job of science is not to deal with such matters but simply to discover facts about the world, leaving the presuppositions of scientists as a topic for philosophers. However, although this kind of division of labor makes sense, it can be carried out *only if the scientific community does not lend its prestige to theories that make it impossible.*

The proposed division of labor also breaks down for another reason, which is that there is now no part of the world that is beyond the domain of science. There was a time when science was equated with *natural* (or *physical*) science, so that it dealt with only a limited portion of the world, leaving the human mind (along with God and any other "spiritual beings") to philosophy and theology. Now, however, partly because the dualism of mind and matter upon which that division of domains was based is generally rejected, "science" is understood to include the social (or human) sciences as well as the natural sciences. Accordingly, there can no longer be a division between study of the *world* and study of *scientists* because scientists are themselves part of the world given to science to understand. It belongs to the task of science, then, to explain the knowledge about mathematical, logical, cognitive, moral, and aesthetic principles presupposed by scientists.

Problems Created for Science by Materialism

The term *materialism* is ambiguous. It can, in the first place, refer merely to the idea that the ultimate units of nature are bits of matter, with "matter" understood to mean things that are *vacuous actualities,* in the sense of being entirely devoid of experience. Such bits of matter can have only *external relations* with one another, meaning that relations to other things cannot be internal to (constitutive of) them. The only kind of motion that can be attributed to them, furthermore, is *locomotion,* meaning motion from one place to another, as opposed to any sort of *internal* becoming. This view, which is also called the "mechanistic" view of nature, was in early modern thought part and parcel of a dualistic ontology, according to which the human mind was an actuality of another kind. The term *dualism* is usually used to refer to this early modern view, with the fact that it embodies a mechanistic or materialistic view of the ultimate units of nature being simply presupposed.

The second meaning of materialism, which is the more common one, refers to the rejection of this dualistic ontology in favor of the view that there are no actual things other than material ones.[26] Whitehead uses the term *scientific materialism* in both senses: for the idea that the ultimate units of nature are bits of matter and for the later expansion of this idea of physical nature into a complete worldview, in which all complex things, including human experience and behavior, are to be understood in terms of the locomotions and external relations of vacuous actualities. In my discussion of naturalism$_{sam}$, materialism refers to this later view. It is important to keep in mind, however, that ontological dualism likewise presupposes the materialistic (or mechanistic) view of the ultimate units of nature. This section deals first with problems created for science by this view of the ultimate units of nature as vacuous actualities and then moves to some further problems created by full-fledged materialism.

Although materialism is usually equated, or at least closely aligned, with *physicalism,* which says that the world is to be understood entirely in terms of the entities of physics, Whitehead argues that the materialistic view of matter is not even adequate for physics. For one thing, although modern cosmology is based on the idea of gravitation, the materialistic view of the ultimate units of nature gives no hint as to why there should be any stresses between them (MT 134).[27] A second problem results from the fact that the material of which nature is comprised, according to this view, is indifferent to the division of time, so that "the lapse of time is an accident, rather than

[26] Materialism is, in fact, usually defined not merely as the doctrine that there are no non-physical *actual* things but as the doctrine that *nothing whatsoever* exists except material entities. Although materialism thus defined is often used interchangeably with "physicalism," some advocates of physicalism—understood as the doctrine that physics is the final arbiter of ontology—diverge from strict materialism. For example, Quine, whose "indispensability argument" for the existence of mathematical entities has already been mentioned, says that his physicalism "is materialism, bluntly monistic except for the abstract objects of mathematics" (1995, 14) and that he assumes "abstract objects over and above the physical objects" (1981, 14–15). But he does not explain how or where such abstract objects exist or how physical objects—included among which, for Quine, is the human mind—could involve these abstract objects and thereby how the mathematician can know of the existence of mathematical objects.

[27] Whitehead did not believe that the Einsteinian notion of the curvature of space provided a real answer to, or a way to avoid, that problem, as he explained in *The Principle of Relativity* (1922).

of the essence, of the material" (SMW 50). Matter, accordingly, should be able to exist at an "instant," meaning a durationless slice through time. Physics, however, now implies that it takes time to exist, so that there can be no "nature at an instant" (SMW 35, 124; MT 146). A third problem is that quantum physics, insofar as it is taken to imply *anything* about the real nature of the ultimate units of nature, suggests that they have no undifferentiated existence through time but instead involve a series of discrete events—as when an electron suddenly jumps from one state to another (SMW 34–35, 129–31). All these developments, Whitehead points out, are incompatible with the inherited idea of matter.

A problem shared by physics and all the other physical sciences is that of the justification of induction. Although this problem is partly rooted in the sensationist theory of perception, as pointed out earlier, it is also rooted in the materialistic idea that the units of nature have only external relations to one another. That is, if events called "causes" are in no way internal to and thereby constitutive of their "effects," then no study of these effects, regardless of how penetrating, can reveal why they should result from their "causes." Likewise, "[i]f the cause in itself discloses no information as to the effect," then "science is impossible, except in the sense of establishing *entirely arbitrary* connections which are not warranted by anything intrinsic to the natures of either causes or effects" (SMW 4). Many philosophers of science are contented with such a view of science, but Whitehead believed that science should and could become rational.

Closely related to this is the problem of having any meaningful concept of physical causation whatsoever. We saw earlier how this problem is created by the sensationist theory of perception. However, even if a nonsensationist theory of perception could show how we do indeed have a direct experience of causation as real influence, which would give us an empirical basis for using the term *causation* meaningfully, a materialistic view of the ultimate units of nature would imply that their causal interactions are different in kind from the causal interactions involved in human perception. Our empirically rooted notion of causation could not, therefore, intelligibly be applied to the interactions studied by physics and chemistry.

Yet another problem created by this view of matter, according to which past events are in no sense internal to later events, is that it provides no way to make sense of the reality of time, in the sense of an asymmetrical, irreversible process. Accordingly, as I have discussed elsewhere (Griffin 1986b, 1998d), many thinkers who have thought about this problem have held that time is not really real. But this idea violates our hard-core common sense because we cannot help presupposing that some things are settled, hence in the past, and that other things are still unsettled, hence still in the future. The other option, given the modern view of matter, is that time is an emergent product of some evolutionary development. But this doctrine results in the self-contradictory view that there were millions or even billions of years of evolution before time emerged, so that *time emerged at some point in time*.[28]

If the materialistic view of nature is inadequate for physics, it is even more inadequate, Whitehead argued, for the biological sciences (SMW 41, 66). In the first place, this view, according to which all the ultimate units are related to one another only externally, does not "provide any elementary trace of the organic unity of a whole" (SMW 73). This is even a problem for physics and chemistry, insofar as electrons, protons, and molecules behave as organic unities (SMW 73). But it is biology that has the most obvious unsolved problem: to account for living organisms "[g]iven configurations of matter with locomotion in space as assigned by physical laws" (SMW 41). One solution, of course, is vitalism, according to which living matter is different in kind from nonliving matter because it acts in accord with purposive, teleological principles, not mechanical ones. Whitehead agrees with the scientific community's rejection of this view because vitalism "involves an essential dualism somewhere" (SMW 79). He does not believe, however, that a satisfactory view of living organisms is possible on the basis of the wholly reductionistic position in terms of which vitalism is usually rejected. What is needed is a view of the ultimate units of nature that allows for the emergence of organic unities of various degrees of complexity.

More generally, the problem can be stated in terms of a clash between materialism and evolution. Although it has been customary to think of evolution as giving support to materialism, it really gives support only to a *nondualistic* position. Most thinkers have assumed that this means a materialistic position, but that would be true only if the ultimate units of nature are to be understood in materialistic terms. It is precisely this view, however, that is inconsistent with the fact of evolution.

[A] thoroughgoing evolutionary philosophy is inconsistent with materialism. The aboriginal stuff, or material, from which a materialistic philosophy starts is incapable of evolution. . . . Evolution, on the materialistic theory, is reduced to the role of being another word for the description of the changes of the external relations between portions of matter. There is nothing to evolve, because one set of external relations is as good as any other set of external relations. There can merely be change, purposeless and unprogressive. (SMW 107)

[28] As with most arguments that I summarize briefly, while referring to my development of them elsewhere, I do not expect this very brief summary to be fully convincing. The purpose of the reference to my treatment elsewhere is to allow readers seriously interested in the issue to evaluate the argument in terms of its fuller statement.

If we believe that evolution of more complex organisms *has* occurred, we should be sceptical of a metaphysical view of the ultimate units of nature that would make such evolution inconceivable.

An especially crucial stage of evolution in which this is true is the emergence of the minds of humans and other animals. Since the time of Descartes, scientists and philosophers have been struggling, unsuccessfully, with the problem of how mind and matter, being entirely different in kind, could interact. Since the rise of the evolutionary picture of the world, there is the additional problem of explaining how mind, with its experience, could have *emerged out of* bits of matter wholly devoid of experience. Although, as mentioned earlier, evolution has generally been taken to count against dualism, the problem is equally great for materialism. It makes no difference, in other words, whether what we call the "mind" is thought to be a distinct actuality, as dualism holds, or merely a property of the brain, as materialism holds. In either case, the problem of how conscious experience could have emerged out of wholly insentient matter is *insoluble in principle,* as an increasing number of both dualists and materialists have acknowledged (see Griffin 1998, intro., chap. 6). Accordingly, as long as science presupposes the materialistic view of the ultimate units of nature, it will make itself incapable of making sense of the feature of the world of which we are most certain, our own experience. This inherited view of nature, in other words, *makes science incapable of making rational sense of the existence of scientists.*

The problems, furthermore, do not stop there. Minds, besides having experiences, intentionally produce effects. And they do so with a degree of freedom. Our hard-core common sense contains the twofold presupposition that we *intentionally* and *freely* bring about movements in our bodies and, through them, the world beyond. We would presuppose this twofold reality of mental causation and freedom in ourselves and our audience in the very act of trying to deny it. This fact is recognized by dualists, who argue against materialists that we can do justice to the dual reality of mental causation and freedom only if we affirm the existence of a mind, distinct from the brain, that can freely formulate intentions and then cause the brain to enact them. The perennial problem, however, is how such a mind, being different in kind from the (supposedly) insentient neurons of which the brain is composed, could produce any effects in the brain.

(Full-fledged) materialism, in seeking to avoid the problem of dualistic interaction by denying the existence of a nonphysical mind, is even less well equipped to deal with our hard-core commonsense beliefs about mental causation and freedom. Having rejected a distinct mind that could serve as a causal agent, materialism denies that intentions or purposes exert causal efficacy, saying instead that the behavior of human beings and other animals must be explained, ultimately, in terms of the same principles that are said to explain the behavior of sticks and stones—namely, the laws of physics and chemistry. Whitehead especially emphasizes the contradiction between current scientific opinion and our inevitable presuppositions: "The conduct of human affairs is entirely dominated by our recognition of foresight determining purpose, and purpose issuing in conduct. Almost every sentence we utter and every judgment we form, presuppose our unfailing experience of this element in life" (FR 13). As Whitehead points out, however, the "prevalent scientific doctrine" says that everything is determined by efficient causes, so that final causes and, therefore, purposes play no real role. To illustrate the implications of this doctrine, he refers to the building of a ship.

> We are asked to believe that the concourse of atoms, of iron, and of nitrogen, and of other sorts of chemical elements, into the form of the ship . . . was purely the outcome of the same physical laws by which the ocean waves aimlessly beat on the coasts of Maine. There could be no more *aim* in the one episode than in the other. The activity of the shipbuilders was merely analogous to the rolling of the shingle on the beach.

"The very idea," Whitehead concludes, "is ridiculous" (FR 14). And surely he is right, because we cannot help presupposing that human behavior is guided by aims or purposes. In denying that it is, scientists and philosophers would be contradicting themselves. Whitehead draws attention to this self-refuting behavior, remarking that "[s]cientists animated by the purpose of proving that they are purposeless constitute an interesting subject for study" (FR 16). The conclusion that materialism cannot do justice to our presuppositions about mental causation is, it should be noted, not simply that of outside critics. After many years of working on the problem, Jaegwon Kim (1993, 367) has recently concluded the same thing from the inside (Griffin 1998, chap. 10).

Materialist philosophers are even more unanimous, furthermore, about the conflict of their position with our presupposition about freedom. John Searle, for example, agrees that nothing can shake this presupposition, saying that it is "impossible for us to abandon the belief in the freedom of the will" because that belief "is built into every normal, conscious intentional action" (1984, 92, 97). Searle, however, believes that "[s]cience allows no place for the freedom of the will" (92). In referring to "science" in this statement, Searle really means *science as interpreted in materialist terms,* according to which "the world consists entirely of physical particles in fields of force"

(1992, xii), everything is determined by "bottom-up causation" so that all the features of the world "are determined at the basic microlevels of physics" (1984, 93), "consciousness is just an ordinary biological, that is, physical, feature of the brain" (1992, 13), and "like the rest of nature, [the mind's] features are determined at the basic microlevels of physics" (1984, 94). Given this materialistic reading of science, Searle concludes: "Now, ideally, I would like to be able to keep both my commonsense conceptions and my scientific beliefs. . . . But when it comes to the question of freedom and determinism, I am . . . unable to reconcile the two" (1984, 86). And rather than use the fact that he cannot help presupposing freedom to revise the premises of his philosophical theory, he concludes that his sense of freedom must be illusory (1984, 94, 98).[29] In so doing, Searle is representative of materialist philosophers in general—except for those who redefine freedom to make it compatible with complete determination by antecedent conditions, which, as Searle points out, is *not* freedom as we presuppose it in practice, so that this solution is a sham (1984, 87, 92, 95).

The impossibility of freedom also implies the impossibility of rational activity. If we, as we constantly assume, have the capacity to engage in the rational activity of deciding what is true and what is false, we must have the capacity to be guided by norms, such as coherence and adequacy to the facts. This means that these norms must function as final causes in terms of which we decide what is rational to believe. The materialistic view of human experience, however, implies that our seemingly rational activity is illusory because our "rational conclusions" are in reality as determined by efficient causation as is the behavior of billiard balls. The paradoxical conclusion is that we have no reason to believe the arguments of mechanistic philosophers. As Putnam now says, most science-based schools of thought have produced "*philosophies which leave no room for a rational activity of philosophy.* This is why these views are self-refuting" (1983, 191).

In sum, the inadequacy of materialism as a worldview for science is especially obvious with regard to the human sciences, which, if they are to be adequate to the inevitable presuppositions of the scientists themselves, must recognize not only the reality of conscious experience but also the reality of freedom and purposive causation. Although this realization by itself could lead to the conclusion that we should exclude human experience and behavior from the domain of the real sciences, materialism is also inadequate

---

[29] Searle's position in this respect, accordingly, is similar to that of those deconstructionists who consider many of our inevitable presuppositions to be "transcendental illusions" in the Kantian sense (McCarthy 1993, 102–3).

for the other domains as well, including that of physics. The materialism of naturalism$_{sam}$, like its sensationism, is detrimental to the explanatory adequacy of science.

Problems Created for Science by Atheism

It has become commonplace to say that "science cannot speak of God" and to assume that science is, almost by definition, atheistic. Whitehead himself held, as we have seen, that science should be naturalistic in the sense of excluding any idea of supernatural interruptions of the normal pattern of causal relations. Insofar as *that* is what is intended by saying that science is not to speak of God, he agreed. After having been agnostic or even atheistic for most of his professional life, however, Whitehead came to believe that the effort to explain *all* features of the world requires that we, with Plato, posit "a basic Psyche whose active grasp of ideas conditions impartially the whole process of the Universe" (AI 147). His discussion points to several features of the world for which science, if it continues its prohibition against the recognition of any such agency, will be unable to give a satisfactory explanation. These features—which include the basic order of the world, the upward trend of the evolutionary process, the novelty that has appeared in this process, the world's "excessive" beauty, and the objectivity of normative ideals and other ideal (nonactual) entities, such as those of mathematics and logic—will be discussed in Chapter 5.

5. Science, Religion, and Philosophy

In Whitehead's view, the two problems created by naturalism$_{sam}$—the apparent conflict between science and religion and the obstacle to adequate scientific treatments of a wide range of phenomena—have the same root cause: the fact that this philosophical worldview has been grounded in only *part* of the evidence about reality available to human experience. Traditionally, Whitehead points out, cosmologies have been suggested by aesthetics, ethics, and religion as well as by science (SMW vii). Since the seventeenth century, however, "the cosmology derived from science has been asserting itself at the expense of older points of view with their origins elsewhere." The meaning of this statement can be seen more fully by looking at a passage in which Whitehead contrasts religious and scientific doctrines:

> The dogmas of religion are the attempts to formulate in precise terms the truths disclosed in the religious experience of mankind. In exactly the same

way the dogmas of physical science are the attempts to formulate in precise
terms the truths disclosed in the sense-perception of mankind. (RM 57)

As this passage indicates, the crucial difference is that science focuses on
truths disclosed in *sensory* perception whereas religious teaching focuses on
truths disclosed in *nonsensory* experience. This difference of focus does not,
of course, point to a complete separation. On the one hand, many scientific
categories, such as causality and time, involve ideas learned from nonsensory
perception, as we have seen, and the science of parapsychology focuses explicitly on nonsensory perception. On the other hand, many religious doctrines, such as that of creation, involve truths of sensory perception. It remains true, nevertheless, that science and religion focus primarily on the
truths of sensory and nonsensory perception, respectively. Whitehead's point,
in any case, is that the cosmology now dominant in the scientific community, and thereby in the intellectual world in general, has been designed on
the assumption that only the data of sensory perception provide information
about the nature of reality. That assumption leads to the widespread acceptance of, in the words of J. J. C. Smart, "the omnicompetence of science as a
cognitive activity" (1996, 222)—meaning that science is the only means
through which truth about the nature of reality can be discovered.[30]

Because this assumption is so deeply ingrained that many thinkers do not
even realize it is merely an assumption, much that passes for rational criticism is circular. The position regarded as the "rational viewpoint" is derived
from only a limited portion of human experience. Religious, aesthetic, and
ethical experiences are excluded from making any contribution to this rational viewpoint. Thinkers then employ this rational viewpoint to examine
the status of aesthetic, ethical, and religious ideas and conclude, predictably
enough, that these ideas contribute nothing to our rational knowledge of
reality.[31]

What we need to insist on, Whitehead urges, is "the retention of the

[30] J. J. C. ("Jack") Smart should not be confused with Ninian Smart (his brother), discussed
in the Introduction.

[31] For Habermas, the modern disenchantment of the world (see note 7), which he assumes
to be irreversible, means that religion has been "deprived of its worldview functions" (1992,
51). This means that philosophers seeking to provide a grounding for ethics must do so in
terms of purely formal, procedural reason, "without recourse to the substantial reason of religious or metaphysical world-views, and thus on the level of learning attained by our modern
understanding of the world" (1982, 248). The crucial figure for determining this "modern understanding" for Habermas is Kant, who stipulated that only those concepts that are rooted in
sensory perception can contribute to our theoretical-scientific-cognitive (*wissenschaftliche*) understanding of the universe.

whole of the evidence in shaping our cosmological scheme" (SMW vii). What is needed for the pursuit of truth, he emphasizes, is an "unflinching determination to take the whole evidence into account" (SMW 187). This is what he has tried to do in his attempt to devise a scheme of ideas applicable to all the dimensions and data of human experience. The attempt to include the parts of this evidence that have been left out in the late modern period involves, primarily, the effort to include our hard-core commonsense ideas, especially those rooted in our aesthetic, ethical, and religious intuitions.

The basic idea behind Whitehead's approach to achieving an integrated worldview is that human beings tend to exaggerate the truths they see: "[T]he chief error in philosophy is overstatement" (PR 7); religious dogmas "are only bits of the truth, expressed in terms that are in some ways over-assertive" (RM 139). The main form of this overstatement or over-assertiveness is "the fallacy of misplaced concreteness," in which a set of abstractions about something, based on some limited interest, is mistaken for the concrete reality in its entirety (PR 7; SMW 51). Because this truth as overstated implies "an exclusion of complementary truths" (RM 144), it may be used to deny the truths that have been seen by others, which is the original sin of intellectuals: "Thought is abstract; and the intolerant use of abstractions is the major vice of the intellect" (SMW 18). Religious thinkers may use their exaggerations to deny truths seen by science, whereas scientific thinkers may use their exaggerations to deny truths derived from religious experience.

The task for philosophic thought is to overcome the exaggerations involved in different schemes of abstractions, especially those of science and theology (with "theology" understood as the attempt to systematize the truths discovered in religious experience). Believing that both theology and science have truths to contribute to philosophy and that philosophy's task is to modify the partial truths of each in terms of those of the other, Whitehead says: "You cannot shelter theology from science, or science from theology; nor can you shelter either of them from metaphysics, or metaphysics from either of them. There is no short cut to truth" (RM 76–77). The goal is the discovery of "wider truths and finer perspectives within which a reconciliation of a deeper religion and a more subtle science will be found" (SMW 185). Although the expected benefits to religion and science stand out in this statement, the phrase "wider truths and finer perspectives" points to the expected benefits to metaphysics, understood as "the science which seeks to discover the general ideas which are indispensably relevant to the analysis of everything that happens" (RM 82n). Its task, in other words, is to discover a scheme of generic notions in terms of which *all* our experiences,

including our religious and scientific experiences, can be equally well interpreted (PR 3).

This approach means that philosophy exists in a relation of *mutual modifi-
ation* with both science and religion. With regard to science, Whitehead's
approach is distinctive in relation to most modern philosophy in saying that,
besides learning from science, philosophy should modify it—that is, the
currently dominant scientific scheme of thought. In its role as the "critic of
abstractions" (SMW 59), philosophy is to "challenge the half-truths constituting the [presently dominant] scientific first principles" in the light of "yet
wider generalities" (PR 10). With regard to religion, Whitehead's position
differs from most recent thought by saying that, besides the fact that religious
doctrines should be modified in the light of metaphysics (PR 10), religion
"contributes its own independent evidence, which metaphysics must take
account of in framing its description" (RM 76). In *Religion in the Making,*
Whitehead emphasizes this point by including a section on "The Contribution of Religion to Metaphysics" (84).[32] This approach involves the assumption that truths about reality are revealed not only by scientific experience
but also by religious experience—which brings us to the next chapter.

[32] Given that, as Charles Larmore points out, the term *metaphysics* "today functions mostly
as a term of abuse" (1996, 116), I should probably say something more about the fact that process philosophy *is* a type of metaphysical philosophy. The most salient point is that those who
reject "metaphysics" as impossible or undesirable usually mean by the term something very
different from what Whitehead meant. I have already pointed out, in relation to the assumption that metaphysics involves an anti-pragmatic "first philosophy" that belittles the ideas we
necessarily presuppose in practice, that process philosophy can be called a *pragmatic metaphysics*.
Another common understanding of metaphysics is the Kantian conception of it as the attempt
to talk about things beyond the limits of possible experience, but Whitehead understands it as
the endeavour to construct a coherent scheme of ideas "in terms of which every element of
our experience can be interpreted," adding that the "elucidation of immediate experience is
the sole justification for any thought" (PR 3, 4). Some philosophers reject metaphysical systems on the grounds that they arrogantly claim to attain certainty, but Whitehead regards a
metaphysical system as a tentative hypothesis, an "experimental adventure," adding that "the
merest hint of dogmatic certainty as to finality of statement is an exhibition of folly" (PR 8, 9,
xiv). With regard to the necessity of metaphysics, Whitehead would have endorsed Peter
Dews's observation that "the idea that metaphysics can no longer function foundationally, as
'first philosophy,'" does not imply "that metaphysics should also be suppressed in its role as
'last philosophy'" (1995, 13).

[2]

Perception and
Religious Experience

One of the most important goals of process philosophy, as we have seen, is to integrate the truths of science with the truths of religion. This view makes sense, of course, only if religion is at least partly based upon a distinctive kind of experience that provides some distinctive truths about the nature of reality. This issue is at the heart of process philosophy qua philosophy of religion.

It is now widely held in intellectual circles that religion is not a truth-providing enterprise. Religious beliefs are held to be either "noncognitive"—meaning that they are neither true nor false because they do not really intend to make any factual assertions about reality—or simply false. In either case, religious beliefs would not provide any truths to be integrated with the truths provided by science. The main reason for assuming that religious experience provides no distinctive truths about the nature of reality is, as we have seen, the acceptance of naturalism$_{sam}$. The atheism and materialism of this view assure its adherents that there is no holy reality, or even a realm of ideal realities, to be experienced,[1] and its sensationism assures them that even if such things existed, our experience could involve no perceptual access to them. Naturalism$_{sam}$, in other words, implies that any belief in a nonsensory mode of perception would be a violation of naturalism. For example, J. J. C. Smart, whose acceptance of "the omnicompetence of science

---

[1] As we have seen, an exception is often (inconsistently) made for the ideal objects studied by mathematics and logic. The negative implications of sensationism and materialism for the ideal objects of morality and aesthetics, however, are rigorously enforced.

as a cognitive activity" was quoted in Chapter 1, says that genuine religious experience could not occur naturally:

> It would seem that if mystical experiences are not mere aberrations of feelings, that are explicable in naturalistic terms, then they must be in some way miraculous. . . . Physics and physiology enable us to explain, in outline at least, how we can get in touch with rabbits or even with electrons. "Getting in touch" involves responses to physical stimuli, and it is clear that no naturalistic account could be given of mystical cognition of the supernatural. (1996, 222–23)

Given the widespread equation of naturalism$_{sam}$ with the "scientific" or "rational" view of reality, which Smart illustrates, the acceptance of genuine religious experience is assumed to be anti-scientific.

In Chapter 1, however, we saw that there are many reasons to doubt the truth of naturalism$_{sam}$, including the fact that this form of naturalism is not adequate for science itself. Indeed, insofar as the scientific community endorses this metaphysical viewpoint, scientific activity itself is rendered irrational because this viewpoint denies the rationality of many presuppositions necessarily involved in the scientific enterprise. The basis that has increasingly been used since the eighteenth century to declare religion irrational turns out, Whitehead shows, to render science equally irrational. Although Hume had already seen this fact, his followers, like Hume himself, have generally spelled out the negative implications only for religion, ethics, and aesthetics, not also for science. Recently, however, the more sweeping implications have been recognized by thinkers other than Whiteheadians. One result has been a relativistic—or, as some advocates prefer to call it, "historicist"—form of postmodernism, in which science is put on the same level as other cultural activities, such as religion, ethics, and aesthetics, by denying cognitive status to science as well (Rorty 1979, 176–79; 1982, xvi–xxvi; Stout 1981, 91–96).

Whitehead also provides the basis for a postmodernism in which the modernist view of science as uniquely cognitive is rejected, but he does this by providing a new basis for the traditional view that truths are supplied by religious, ethical, and aesthetic experience as well as by scientific experience. Part and parcel of this new basis is his nonsensationist doctrine of perception, which is the third core doctrine of process philosophy. This doctrine, worked out in critical dialogue with Hume's discussion of perception, overcomes the basis for the Humean conclusion that science, when judged in the light of a critical empiricism, has no theoretical justification. This same Whiteheadian doctrine of perception simultaneously overcomes the basis for the Humean charge, echoed repeatedly in the intervening centuries, that religion, when judged in the light of a critical empiricism, has no theoretical justification.

This chapter proceeds in the following way. Section 1 lays out Whitehead's nonsensationist doctrine of perception, showing how it provides a naturalistic explanation of our knowledge of several things that we inevitably presuppose in practice, even though we could not know them if the sensationist form of empiricist naturalism were true. Section 2 then explains how this nonsensationist doctrine of perception allows for genuine religious experience without any violation of what I have called *domain uniformitarianism*—without, in other words, explaining religion in terms of principles different from those needed in other intellectual domains. The third section, finally, discusses the truths Whitehead believed to be derivable from religious experience.

1. Nonsensory Perception as More Fundamental than Sensory

Although the sensationist form of empiricism cannot explain our knowledge of mathematical and logical principles, our cognitive, moral, and aesthetic ideals, or even our ideas of an external world, the past, time, and causal influence, scientific activity presupposes all these ideas. Whitehead summarizes this situation by saying that "science conceived as resting on mere sense perception, with no other source of observation, is bankrupt" (MT 154). It is not science as such that he here calls bankrupt but only science insofar as it is based on the sensationist theory of perception, according to which sense perception provides our only way of observing the world beyond our own minds.

Two Versions of Empiricism

To understand Whitehead's criticism of this view of perception, it is essential to understand that his whole epistemological enterprise is based on the acceptance of empiricism. This sets him apart from many contemporary philosophers who, having realized that "empiricism" as normally conceived—namely, *sensationist* empiricism—is wholly inadequate, have rejected empiricism altogether. Whitehead, by contrast, affirmed empiricism more broadly conceived. For example, citing the principle that "all knowledge is derived from, and verified by, direct intuitive observation," he adds: "I accept this axiom of empiricism as stated in this general form" (AI 177).

He accepts, furthermore, the normal empiricist idea that this "direct intuitive observation" involves *perception*. In maintaining that "all knowledge
is grounded on perception," he says, "philosophy started on a sound principle" (PR 158).

Where philosophy went wrong epistemologically, however, was in holding that all such perception had to be *sensory* perception—"that all perception is by the mediation of our bodily sense-organs, such as eyes, palates,
noses, ears, and the diffused bodily organization furnishing touches, aches,
and other bodily sensations" (AI 177–78). "The unfortunate effect has
been," Whitehead says, "that all direct observation has been identified with
sense-perception" (AI 217).

The "critical" aspect of modern philosophy resulted from the combination of this sensationism with a new epistemological question: "[T]he an-
cients asked what have we experienced, and the moderns asked what can we
experience" (AI 224). In other words, far from promoting a genuinely empirical approach, which would sincerely inquire into what people *do* experience, the sensationist doctrine of perception became an a priori weapon,
employed to tell people that they cannot really experience several things that
they think they do. Although we do have "impressions of reflection," they
are all derivative from "impressions of sensation," said Hume (1739, Bk. I,
Sect. II), which are "impressions through the organs of sensation" (Bk. III,
Sect. II). If someone claims to have had some other kind of experience, such
as a telepathic experience of another person's mind or religious experience
of a divine spirit, the Humean replies: "No you did not, because such experiences are impossible." Hume's critical weapon, however, does not exclude only such "esoteric" experiences. This same principle is the basis for
Hume's claim that we have no direct experience of causation or an external
world of other actual things.

This critical weapon, furthermore, is used to tell people what ideas they
really can and cannot have in their minds. This employment follows simply
from the general empirical principle that all meaningful ideas are rooted in
immediate experience. In Hume's words:

[A]ll our ideas are nothing but copies of our impressions, or, in other
words, . . . it is impossible for us to think of any thing, which we have not an-
tecedently felt, either by our external or internal senses. (1902, Sect. VII, Pt. I)

Whitehead, as we have seen, accepts the general principle of empiricism
involved here. He, in fact, explicitly "accepts Hume's doctrine that nothing
is to be received into the philosophical scheme which is not discoverable as

an element in subjective experience" (PR 166). He considers "entirely justifiable," therefore, "Hume's demand that causation be describable as an element in experience" (PR 166–67). The problem arises only from Hume's
additional requirement that causation must be describable as an element in
sensory experience. Because it is not, Hume concludes that we really have no
idea of causation as real influence. Rather than have the idea of "necessary
connection"—according to which the "cause" is necessary for the "effect"
and in some sense necessitates it—we have only the idea, Hume assures us,
of a "constant conjunction" between two kinds of events: we notice that
when an event of Type A occurs, it is always followed by an event of Type
B, and that, conversely, when a Type B event occurs, it is always preceded
by an event of Type A. Because of the constant conjunction that we notice
between these two types of events, we come to call instances of Type A
events "causes" and instances of Type B events "effects" (at least, Hume
added, if the two events are contiguous). Despite what we may think, we really have no idea that some events *actually influence* other events, because
there is no "impression of sensation" from which such an idea could be
derived.

The way in which Hume wielded this critical weapon can be illustrated
by his criticism of the belief that we have any genuine idea of a "substance."
Although Whitehead agrees with Hume's rejection of the idea of substance
as a nonexperienced something that underlies an enduring thing, Hume's attack is also directed against any idea of things that are *actual* in the sense of
being something more than simply a collection of abstract qualities. Against
philosophers who employ such a notion of substance, Hume says:

> I would fain ask . . . whether the idea of *substance* be derived from the im-
> pressions of sensation or reflection? If it be conveyed to us by our senses, I ask,
> which of them, and after what manner? If it be perceived by the eyes, it must
> be a colour; if by the ears, a sound; if by the palate, a taste; and so of the other
> senses. But I believe none will assert that substance is either a color, or a
> sound, or a taste. The idea of substance must, therefore, be derived from an
> impression of reflection, if it really exist. But the impressions of reflection re-
> solve themselves into our passions and emotions; none of which can possibly
> represent a substance. We have, therefore, no idea of substance, distinct from
> that of a collection of particular qualities. (1739, Bk. I, Sect. VI; quoted by
> Whitehead in S 33–34)

This argument is the basis for Hume's denial that we have any genuine idea
of an actual external world (as distinct from various collections of qualities,

such as sounds and colored shapes). The same argument supports his denial that we have any idea of causation as real influence.

These are, of course, paradoxical assertions. If Hume really did not have the ideas of actual things and of causation as real influence, he would not know what he was denying. This fact illustrates the wholly unempirical, a priori nature of Hume's critical epistemology: although he clearly has these ideas, knowing what they mean, he has to deny that he has them because if his sensationist empiricism were true, he could not have them. Rather than use this point (with Kant) to reject his empiricism or (with Whitehead) to reject his sensationism, Hume simply denies that he has the ideas in question. Actually, however, he does not even quite do this. Rather, he says that he must continue "in practice" to operate in terms of a world of actual things exerting causal influence. By admitting that he does employ ideas about the world that have not come through impressions of sensation, he thereby implicitly rejects either his empiricism or his sensationism while verbally maintaining both of them. He can then use his critical weapon against ideas that he does not like, such as the ideas of religious experience and of a divine creator, while sneaking in other ideas under the cloak of "practice." His whole procedure, as Whitehead says, involves the height of irrationality. This irrationality results not from the acceptance of conceptual empiricism, according to which meaningful concepts must be rooted in perception, but from wedding this doctrine to the sensationist theory of perception.

This sensationist theory has been almost unanimously accepted in modern science and philosophy. Contemporary philosophers sometimes state their acceptance explicitly. For example, Quine says that the "stimulation of his sensory receptors is all the evidence anybody has to go on, ultimately, in arriving at his picture of the world" (1969, 76–76).[2] Usually, however, the equation of perception with sense perception is simply assumed. For example, in his introduction to the anthology *Perceptual Knowledge,* Jonathan Dancy asserts blandly, as if it were not controversial, that perceptual knowledge is the sort of knowledge we get by "using our senses" (1988, 1).

This contemporary consensus in part reflects the rootage of most contemporary philosophy in Hume or Kant. Recognizing that neither science

---

[2] This statement, far from being made casually, expresses a central feature of Quine's position. "I do emphasize," he points out, "that our data regarding the world reach us only through sensory stimulation" (Hahn and Schilpp 1986, 364). Also, having said that "the triggering of our sensory receptors . . . is all we have to go on," he adds explicitly that "there is no extrasensory perception" (1981, 1–2). See, however, note 8.

nor ordinary life would be possible on the basis of Hume's sensationist empiricism and not being willing to accept Hume's wholly arbitrary appeal to practice, Kant rejected his empiricism by saying that sense data are appropriated in terms of the mind's a priori concepts. But he fiercely insisted on the twofold idea that (1) all genuine concepts are rooted in perceptions or intuitions (saying, famously, that "concepts without intuitions are empty")[3] and (2) all perceptions or intuitions of the world arise from the physical senses.[4] Both the Anglo-American and the Continental scientific and philosophical traditions, thereby, have largely presupposed the equation of perception with sensory perception.

In opposition to this virtual unanimity, Whitehead does not consider sense perception to be our only mode of perception. We need not, therefore, call upon it to provide the basis for all that we seem to know (or, when we realize that it does not, supplement it, as do Hume and Kant, with notions thought not to be rooted in direct perception). Instead, a significant portion of our knowledge can be explained in terms of *another mode of perception*.

Besides not thinking of sensory perception as our *only* mode of perception, Whitehead does not even consider it to be our *primary* mode, portraying it instead as a secondary, derivative mode. This differentiates his position from that of thinkers who reject sensationism in the name of some higher, more advanced mode of perception. The "extrasensory perception" studied by parapsychology, for example, is sometimes thought of as a uniquely human capacity, being perhaps a harbinger of the future, in which this mode of communication will be commonplace. For Whitehead, however, the nonsensory mode of perception is not a more advanced mode, perhaps

[3] Kant's employment of this idea has been extremely fateful. Besides being the root of his own "Copernican revolution" and thereby his version of idealism, which led then to Hegelianism and, by inversion, Marxism, this doctrine (in conjunction with sensationism) lies behind Kant's denial of the possibility of metaphysics, including natural theology. Whitehead's nonsensationist epistemology, which shows that (nonsensory) intuitions *do* lie behind our concepts of actuality, causation, time, and so on, is the primary basis for his return to "pre-Kantian modes of thought" (PR xi). In developing an explicitly *metaphysical* form of philosophy, in other words, Whitehead is *not* advocating that we try to do "metaphysics" in the sense rejected by Kant, which meant speculating about objects beyond the limits of possible experience. Whitehead's account of perception assigns an experiential basis for precisely those concepts that Kant, because of his sensationism, assumed had to be a priori concepts provided by the mind.

[4] With regard to the latter idea: Kant became so aroused by reports that Sweden's greatest scientist, Emanuel Swedenborg, had had veridical clairvoyant visions and other nonsensory experiences that he went to great lengths to investigate their truth. For a long time, the best report of Kant's relationship to Swedenborg, at least in English, was that of the philosopher C. D. Broad (1969, 116–55). Recently, however, much more complete accounts have been provided by Gottlieb Florschütz (1993–96) and Gregory Johnson (1999a, 1999b).

shared only with angelic and divine beings, but a more fundamental mode, shared with all other individuals whatsoever.

His argument for this position is based partly on the need for a purely naturalistic account of the evolutionary rise of human experience. As mentioned in the first chapter, a naturalistic account is impossible if it involves the idea of the emergence of experience out of wholly nonexperiencing things. Such a transition would be possible only through the action of a supernatural, omnipotent being. The only kind of experiential emergence that is conceivable in a naturalistic universe is the emergence of higher forms of experience out of lower forms. Some mode of experience, accordingly, must go all the way down. Because not all beings have sensory organs, there must be a mode of experience more fundamental than sensory experience. This argument in terms of ontology, however, anticipates the discussion of panexperientialism in the next chapter. Whitehead held, in any case, that the argument can be made in purely epistemological terms—by analyzing, in fact, Hume's own epistemological discussion.

Perception in the Mode of Presentational Immediacy

In Whitehead's analysis, *actual sensory perception* is distinguished from *sensory perception as understood by Hume*. Sensory perception in the Humean sense—which is the sense in which it has been considered in our discussion thus far—is called "perception in the mode of presentational immediacy." The point of this name is that the data of perception in this mode, namely, the *sense* data, are immediately present to conscious experience and, as such, tell us nothing about anything beyond this present experience. For example, I see a small, bright, white light in the night sky and call it a "star." In actual fact, however, there may at the moment be no real star in the region in question. The star from which the light was emitted may, indeed, no longer exist anywhere, having exploded long ago. Furthermore, the colored shapes I am seeing may not even have any causal connection to any stars in the past, having resulted instead from drugs or a blow to my head. To carry the analysis even further, the colored shapes in themselves do not say anything whatsoever about their origin. Hume makes this point in saying that these data arise in our experience from "unknown causes" (1739, Bk. I, Pt. I, Sect. II). From this mode of perception alone, in fact, we could not even speak meaningfully of "causes" because, as Whitehead points out (PR 123), Hume showed that perception in this mode provides no notion of causal efficacy. Indeed, the implication of Hume's analysis is that if this were our only mode of perception, solipsism would be the result. In Hume's own words, "the mind [cannot] go beyond what is immediately present to the senses, either to discover the real existence or the [causal] relations of objects" (1739, Bk. III, Sect. II). Also, as Whitehead's term *presentational immediacy* indicates, perception in this mode "gives no information as to the past or the future" (PR 168). It was this realization that led Santayana, assuming this perceptive mode to be our sole source of information, to speak of "solipsism of the present moment" (1955, 14–15).

The fundamental problem, which leads to this self-refuting dead end, is that "empiricism" is tied to the doctrine that our experience originates with sense data. Pointing out how far this doctrine is from our actual experience, Whitehead says: "A young man does not initiate his experience by dancing with impressions of sensation, and then proceed to conjecture a partner. . . . The unempirical character of the philosophical school derived from Hume cannot be too often insisted upon" (PR 315–16). A truly empirical doctrine must be based upon the recognition of a more fundamental mode of perception. One of the keys to Whitehead's version of empiricism is his dictum, to be explained later, that "consciousness presupposes experience, and not experience consciousness" (PR 53). This doctrine means that the *primary* elements in experience are generally not the elements of which we are most clearly conscious.

Perception in the Mode of Causal Efficacy

Whitehead usually distinguishes actual sensory perception (which I will sometimes call "full-fledged" sensory perception) from perception in the mode of presentation immediacy, with which Hume equates sensory perception. In some passages, however, Whitehead speaks as if sensory perception *could* be identified with perception in the mode of presentational immediacy. The reconciliation of these two ways of speaking is provided by the fact that in some of the latter passages Whitehead speaks of "pure sense perception" (thereby referring to what I have called sensory perception *as such*). The reason for the qualifying adjective "pure" is that *full-fledged* sense perception involves a synthesis of this pure mode of perception with another pure mode, which is more fundamental. Having in mind Hume's denial that we directly perceive causal influence, Whitehead calls this more fundamental mode "perception in the mode of causal efficacy." In this mode, we perceive other things as *actual* and as *exercising causal efficacy on us*. It is because actual sensory perception involves this mode as well as presentational immediacy that we are all realists, automatically taking colored shapes and other sense data to refer to actual things. This full-fledged sensory perception, understood as a mixed mode of perception, is called "perception in the mode of symbolic reference," the point being that the data from one mode (usually presentational immediacy) are employed to refer to, and thereby interpret, data from the other mode (usually causal efficacy). Given this analysis of sensory perception, Whitehead agrees with the insistence of some realist philosophers that it *does* directly tell us about actual things, not simply about sense data that we have ourselves produced. Whitehead agrees with these realists while also agreeing with Hume's conclusion that sense data as such do not provide the ground for realism. What is needed, he argues, is a recognition that full-fledged sensory perception involves data other than sense data. It involves, more precisely, the derivation of presentational immediacy's sense data from data provided by perception of one's body in the mode of causal efficacy.

The Nonsensory Perception of One's Own Body

Our awareness of this fact, Whitehead points out, is shown by Hume's own analysis. Referring back to Hume's argument, quoted above, that if we had a direct perception of actual substances, it would have to be perceived by the eyes or some other sensory organ, Whitehead comments:

> Thus in asserting the lack of perception of causality, he implicitly presupposes it. For what is the meaning of "*by*" in "*by* the eyes," "*by* the ears," "*by* the palate"? His argument presupposes that sense-data, functioning in presentational immediacy, are "given" by reason of "eyes," "ears," "palates" functioning in causal efficacy. . . . Hume with the clarity of genius states the fundamental point, that sense-data functioning in an act of experience demonstrate that they are given *by* the causal efficacy of actual bodily organs. He refers to this causal efficacy as a component in direct perception. Hume's argument first tacitly presupposes the two modes of perception, and then tacitly assumes that presentational immediacy is the only mode. (S 51)

The complete datum provided by visual perception, then, does not consist simply of the sights that we see, namely, the colored shapes. "The ultimate momentary 'ego' has as its datum," instead, "the 'eye as experiencing such-and-such sights'" (PR 118). The datum, in other words, includes *the eye as exerting causal efficacy* on the percipient (the "momentary ego") by causing it to see those sights.

One reason that philosophers have overlooked this obvious point is that they tend to ignore the body, tacitly treating it as part of the self, forgetting that it is simply that part of nature that is most intimately related to the self.

When they ask about our direct experience of *nature,* accordingly, they ask what our sensory organs tell us about the world outside our bodies. The question of solipsism, however, is not simply whether I know whether anything beyond my body exists but whether I know that anything exists beyond my conscious experience. (More precisely, as Santayana reminds us, it is whether I know about anything beyond my *present* conscious experience, to which Whitehead refers by speaking of the "momentary ego.") Hume in his argument completely ignores this point, simply taking it for granted that he has an actual physical body, the sensory organs of which cause him to see sights, hear sounds, taste flavors, and so on.

Hume does, however, sometimes remember that his principles require scepticism about this fact, as when he writes that impressions of sensation arise in the soul "from unknown causes." But, Whitehead points out, this statement simply illustrates "the 'make-believe' character of [Hume's] empiricism" because, as revealed in the other passage, "the heat of the argument elicits his real conviction—everybody's real conviction—that visual sensations arise '*by* the eyes.'" Having some fun at Hume's expense, Whitehead continues:

> The causes are not a bit "unknown," and among them there is usually to be found the efficacy of the eyes. If Hume had stopped to investigate the alternative causes for the occurrence of visual sensations—for example, eye-sight, or excessive consumption of alcohol—he might have hesitated in his profession of ignorance. If the causes be indeed unknown, it is absurd to bother about eye-sight and intoxication. The reason for the existence of oculists and prohibitionists is that the various causes *are* known. (PR 171)

We have here an example of Whitehead's argument from hard-core common sense.

Our awareness of our body's causal efficacy for our experience is due to our nonsensory perception of this efficacy. This perception is obviously not itself a form of sensory perception. I do not see my eyes or hear my ears. My capacity to enjoy sights and sounds through my eyes and ears depends upon my more basic perception of my body through which I receive the information these sensory organs have brought in from the world beyond my body. My most *direct* perception of my body, furthermore, is not my perception of these organs but my perception of my brain. In Whitehead's words:

> Common sense, physical theory, and physiological theory, combine to point out a historic route of inheritance . . . first physically in the external environ-

ment, then physiologically—through the eyes in the case of visual data—up
the nerves, into the brain. (PR 171)

I indirectly perceive my eyes and ears, then, by directly perceiving my brain.

We are not, to be sure, consciously aware of this perception of the brain.
We are consciously aware of the causal efficacy only of those bodily organs,
such as the eyes and the skin, in which physiological processes of transmission originate (PR 120, 171), not of that central organ in which they culminate. We know from physiology, however, that our sensory perceptions depend directly upon the brain. Sensory percepts can be induced, for example,
by direct stimulation of certain parts of the brain. Accordingly, by combining what we know from immediate experience with what we know from
science, we must conclude that it is primarily by means of a nonsensory perception of the brain that we perceive the causal efficacy of various parts of
the body, and through them of external things, for our experience. (The
term *primarily* is inserted because process philosophy allows for a direct prehension of things beyond the body, to be discussed later.)

The idea that "I perceive my brain" depends, of course, upon a distinction between the brain, understood as a society composed of billions of neurons, and "myself" in the strictest sense, meaning my mind, psyche, or soul,
which unifies data received from the brain. Assuming this distinction, we
can see that the mind's sensory perceptions presuppose its nonsensory perception of its body, most directly its brain.

The Nonsensory Perception of One's Own Past

This perception of the reality and causal efficacy of one's own body is not
our only example of nonsensory perception. Whitehead even suggests that
it is not the clearest one, saying that "the most compelling example of non-
sensuous perception is our knowledge of our own immediate past" (AI 181).
He is referring to memory, which involves one's perception in the present
of one's own experiences in the past.

Most philosophers, of course, have not thought of memory as an example,
compelling or otherwise, of nonsensory perception, for a number of reasons.
One of these has been the assumption that the mind or soul is a "substance"
in the sense of a single actual entity enduring through time. Insofar as philosophers hold that assumption, it would not occur to them to think of the
present memory of a past experience as an example of the perception by one
actual entity of *another* actual entity. The fifth core doctrine of Whiteheadian process philosophy, however, is that all enduring individuals are serially

ordered societies of momentary "occasions of experience," with *occasion of experience* being a technical term for *actual entity.* The explanation of and justification for this view of enduring individuals, including minds or souls, will be provided in the following chapter. For now the point is that, given this view, one's present memory of a past experience *is* an instance of the perception by one actual entity of another one.

A second reason for not thinking of memory as an example of perception is simply the fact that we call it "memory," thereby assuming that we have an explanation for it. But, as Whitehead says, "The mere word 'memory' explains nothing" (AI 183). And if, as Whitehead suggests (along with Buddhism [see Hartshorne 1960]), the enduring mind or soul is to be understood as a serially ordered society of actual entities, and if the reception by a moment of experience of data from actualities beyond itself is by definition a "perception," then each act of remembrance is an instance of perception. If this thought had been pervasive when our language was being formed, the words for memory in the various languages might have been words connoting "past-self-perception." The mere fact that the word "memory" does not immediately suggest a form of perception should not, accordingly, prevent us from considering memory to be an example of nonsensory perception.

A third reason why memory has not been regarded in the way suggested by Whitehead is the widespread view, generally thought to be *the* scientific view, that memories are to be explained in terms of "traces" in the brain. Even with this view, however, memory would involve a nonsensory perception of the brain by the mind—given the assumption that mind and brain are numerically distinct. The dominance of materialism in scientific circles, of course, means that such a distinction between brain and mind is usually *not* assumed. But some of the problems with mind-brain identism, such as its inability to do justice to our hard-core assumptions about freedom and mental causation, were discussed in the previous chapter, and the difficulties in this view will be discussed more fully in the next chapter. For now, the point is that, assuming the truth of Whitehead's view that the mind is a serially ordered society of occasions of experience distinct from that society of billions of cells that we call the brain, memory does involve a nonsensory perception of a past actual entity by a present one.

A fourth obstacle to this way of thinking, especially to regarding memory as an especially clear example of the nonsensory perception of causal efficacy, is the tendency to think of memory in relatively long-range terms. In speaking of "our knowledge of our own immediate past" as "the most compelling example of non-sensuous perception," Whitehead says: "I am not referring to our memories of a day past, or of an hour past, or of a minute past" but, instead, to "that portion of our past lying between a tenth of a second and half a second ago" (AI 181). Whitehead provides an illustration that, because of the importance of this point to his rebuttal of Hume's "associationist" position on perception and causation, is worth quoting at length:

> Consider a reasonably rapid speaker enunciating the proper name "United States." There are four syllables here. When the third syllable is reached, probably the first is in the immediate past; and certainly during the word "States" the first syllable of the phrase lies beyond the immediacy of the present. Consider the speaker's own occasions of existence. Each occasion achieves for him the immediate sense-presentation of sounds, the earlier syllables in the earlier occasions, the word "States" in the final occasion. As mere sensuous perception, Hume is right in saying that the sound "United" as a mere sensum has nothing in its nature referent to the sound "States," yet the speaker is carried from "United" to "States" . . . by the energizing of the past occasion . . . in the present. The immediate past as surviving . . . in the present is the palmary instance of non-sensuous perception. (AI 181–82)

Hume's explanation, to be sure, would be that the speaker has learned to associate the word *United* with the word *States,* so that it is this habitual *association* that leads from the one word to the other, not a nonsensory perception of causal influence by the past upon the present. Whitehead gives another example to respond to this possible objection:

> The speaker, a citizen of the United States and therefore dominated by an immense familiarity with that phrase, may in fact have been enunciating the phrase "United Fruit Company"—a corporation which . . . he may have not heard of till half a minute earlier. . . . In this latter example it is to be noted that while association would have led him to "States," the fact of the energizing of the immediate past compelled him to conjoin "Fruit" in the immediacy of the present. He uttered the word "United" with the non-sensuous anticipation of an immediate future with the sensum "Fruit," and he then uttered the word "Fruit" with the non-sensuous perception of the immediate past with the sensum "United." But, unfamiliar as he was with the United Fruit Company, he had no association connecting the various words in the phrase "United Fruit Company." . . . Perhaps, indeed, he was the founder of the Company, and also invented the name. He then uttered the mere sounds "United Fruit Company" for the first time in the history of the English language. There could not have been the vestige of an association to help

him along. . . . [T]here was direct observation of the past with its intention
finding its completion in the present fact. This is an instance of direct intuitive observation which is incapable of reduction to the sensationalist formula.
(AI 182–83)

As this example shows, our whole lives depend upon the continuity afforded
from moment to moment by the direct perception of the immediately past
moment of experience.

This type of nonsensory perception is especially important to our sense of
time. As we have seen, perception in the mode of presentational immediacy
provides, by definition, no knowledge of the past or the future and therefore no knowledge of time. As Whitehead says, the separation of the world
"into past and future lies with the mode of causal efficacy and not with that
of presentational immediacy" (PR 170). It is from the causal efficacy of our
past experiences, in particular, that this sense arises, which we then generalize to the world at large: "Time is known to us as the succession of our acts
of experience, and thence derivatively as the succession of events objectively
perceived in those acts" (S 35). It is the fact that memory involves the direct
perception of past occasions of experience *as past,* in other words, that answers Santayana's query as to why we are not afflicted by "solipsism of the
present moment."

To point to the causal efficacy of the actual world—"the fact that whatever is settled and actual must in due measure be conformed to" (S 36–
37)—Whitehead liked William James's term *stubborn fact.* For example,
Whitehead summarized his criticism of Hume's philosophy by saying: "According to Hume there are no stubborn facts" (S 37). This was true for
Hume, as we have seen, because of his equation of perception and sensory
perception, combined with his equation of sensory perception and the perception of sense data immediately present to consciousness. Whitehead,
summarizing the twofold way in which the recognition of a nonsensory
mode of perception allows us to recognize the reality of stubborn fact, says:

[W]e essentially arise out of our bodies which are the stubborn facts of the
immediate relevant past. We are also carried on by our immediate past of personal experience; . . . it remains remorselessly true, that we finish a sentence
because we have begun it. We are governed by stubborn fact. (PR 129)

The Reformed Subjectivist Principle

To emphasize the point that we directly perceive other actualities, Whitehead speaks of "the reformed subjectivist principle" (which is the central

concept of this chapter). Although Whitehead's somewhat confusing discussion of this concept requires some sorting out (Griffin 1977), his position is that there is a *general* subjectivist principle, which is to be accepted, but that it exists in two versions, unreformed and reformed, only the latter of which is to be accepted. The general subjectivist principle is that "the whole universe consists of elements disclosed in the analysis of experience" (PR 166).[5] This principle is closely related to what he calls the "subjectivist bias," introduced by Descartes, according to which "those substances which are the subjects enjoying conscious experiences provide the primary data for philosophy, namely, themselves as in the enjoyment of such experience" (PR 159). Whitehead also endorses this principle. What he rejects is the subjectivist interpretation of the *datum* of experience (which he, confusingly, also simply calls "the subjectivist principle"), according to which "the datum in the act of experience can be adequately analysed purely in terms of universals" (PR 157). In other words, the datum is said—by Descartes and Locke in some passages, by Hume more consistently—*not* to include any actualities, or stubborn facts, which can be called the *unreformed* version of the subjectivist principle. In discussing the *reformed* version of it, Whitehead says that "Descartes' discovery on the side of subjectivism requires balancing by an 'objectivist' principle as to the datum for experience" (PR 160). Therefore, while agreeing with Descartes's subjectivist bias, according to which philosophy's primary data consist of the conscious experiences of subjects, he adds that these experiences include perceptions of other actualities, which is why none of us are solipsists in practice.[6]

The Importance of Recognizing Nonsensory Perception

Whitehead is able to avoid modern philosophy's subjectivist, solipsistic interpretation of the datum of experience because his analysis of ordinary human experience uncovered two types of nonsensory perception. Pointing to the philosophical importance of this analysis, he says: "If we discover such instances of non-sensuous perception, then the tacit identification of perception with sense-perception must be a fatal error barring the advance of

---

[5] Whitehead's way of working out the implications of this principle, which I call his pan-experientialism, is discussed in the next chapter.

[6] Descartes's subjectivist starting point, "I think, therefore I am," cannot explain why we all assume the "external world" to be as unproblematic as our own existence. Whitehead's reformed subjectivist starting point, which could be summarized as "I prehend other actual things, therefore we are," does explain this fact.

systematic metaphysics" (AI 180). Given the intimate relation between science and metaphysics, this error has also, as we saw in Chapter 1, been fatal for the rationality of science. Illustrating his general point that most errors are simply exaggerations of truths, Whitehead says that the idea that all data are provided by the activity of the sensory organs, especially the eyes, "has a vague, general truth, very important for practical affairs. In particular all exact scientific observation is derived from such data." However, he adds: "The scientific categories of thought are obtained elsewhere" (AI 225). By "the scientific categories of thought," he means the categories of the type we have been discussing: actuality, causality, pastness, and time.[7] Kant argued that the "elsewhere" from which these categories are obtained is the mind itself, equipped with a priori categories—an explanation that presupposed the implantation of the categories into the mind by a supernatural deity. Kant thus originated an idealist movement that degraded the natural and social sciences to the study of mere appearance. Whitehead, by contrast, provides a naturalistic account, showing how these categories arise out of a nonsensory perception of the actual world. Whitehead thereby gave support to a realistic view of science.

The fact that metaphysics and scientific thought are also intimately related to religious thought means that the exaggeration in question—the expansion of the truth that all *exact* perception is derived from the senses to the view that *all perception whatsoever* is thus derived—must be fatal for an adequate treatment of religion. By explicitly rejecting this sensationist exaggeration, Whitehead's metaphysics provides a basis for taking religious experience as cognitive, as really pointing to truths about the nature of reality.

2. Nonsensory Perception and Religious Experience

As we saw in the introductory chapter, it has widely come to be considered "unscientific" and even "unacademic" to explain the origin and persistence of religion in terms of the idea that people have genuine religious experiences that evoke religious beliefs and activities. The primary reason for this

[7] Quine, maintaining that "our information about the world is limited to irritations of our surfaces," describes the epistemological question as "the question how we human animals can have managed to arrive at science from such limited information" (1981, 72). Whitehead's answer would be: "In no way." Quine, as we have seen in prior notes, gives the impression of providing an answer only by presupposing the existence of all sorts of things, such as the external world, time, the past, and mathematical truths, of which his principles, if consistently enforced, would make him confess ignorance.

widespread attitude is simply the assumption that genuine religious experiences, defined as experiences in which a Holy Reality is experienced *as* holy, simply do not occur. In *Explaining Religion,* as we saw, Preus says that the existence of religion is to be explained on the assumption that "God is not given" (1987, xv). The naturalistic[sam] analyst rejects the religious participants' own account of their religious experience, says Preus approvingly, "because the analyst does not believe their explanation that mysterious transcendent powers beyond the realm of natural [read "finite"] causation . . . really create this experience" (174). Likewise, Segal, in *Explaining and Interpreting Religion,* expresses his conviction that social scientists are correct to assume that "believers never encounter God" (1992, 71).

The same sort of explanatory reductionism is supported in Wayne Proudfoot's *Religious Experience* (1995, 197, 215). Arguing in particular for "a historical or cultural explanation" of religious experience, Proudfoot says that what William James described as a religious *sense* is really a *thought* (223, 161). What constitutes an experience as a *religious* experience, in other words, is not something inherent to the experience but the interpretive categories brought to it from the person's culture. Rather than religion's being a product, at least partly, of religious experience, so-called religious *experience* is entirely a product of religious *beliefs*—which are themselves to be explained in nonreligious terms.

This assumption shared by Preus, Segal, and Proudfoot has been based in large part on the equation, insisted on so forcibly by Hume, of perception with sensory perception. Indeed, Hume's philosophical position itself has played a large role in the social scientific tradition to which these contemporary thinkers belong. Although the idea that *philosophical* ideas have played a determinative role in the *scientific* study of religion might be questioned by some, Segal is clear on this point. He sometimes, to be sure, speaks as if the reductionistic, nonreligious approach to religion that he favors were somehow uniquely scientific. For example, besides describing naturalistic (meaning atheistic) explanations of religion as "social scientific explanations" (1989, 78; 1992, 19), Segal says that the question of the ultimate nature of religion "must be settled by *research*" (1992, 7), thereby suggesting that the issue is primarily empirical. As Segal shows elsewhere (1989, 80 n. 15, 83; 1992, 16, 31, 123), however, he knows better, as he repeatedly points out that for the classical social scientists, such as Karl Marx, E. B. Tylor, James Frazer, Auguste Comte, Emile Durkheim, and Sigmund Freud, "religion is false on philosophical, not social scientific, grounds" (1992, 16). These social scientists, in other words, "do not argue [the falsity of religion]

on the basis of their social scientific findings" but instead "argue for the secular origin and function [of religion] on the grounds of the falsity of religion," which they believed to have been established philosophically (1992,
16). The idea that this philosophical point goes back to Hume is supported
by Tylor's statement, quoted by Preus (1987, 142), that Hume's *Natural History of Religion* "is perhaps more than any other work the source of modern opinions as to the development of religion." This estimation fits with
Preus's own characterization of Hume as the one in which the "naturalistic
paradigm" for explaining religion first became fully operative (1987, xiv–xv,
84). Preus, in fact, thinks of Hume as the founder of the *scientific* study of
religion (84n).

Whatever the actual historical influence of Hume, there can be no doubt
that the sensationist theory of perception, with which he is closely identified, has been fundamental for the tradition to which Preus and Segal belong. It is noteworthy that in spite of the impact of his *Varieties of Religious
Experience,* William James, whose "radical empiricism" involved an explicit
rejection of sensationism, is not even mentioned in Preus's historical survey
of major modern thinkers engaged in the task of "explaining religion" scientifically. Evidently because James, on the basis of his nonsensationist view
of perception, explained the existence of religion in terms of genuine religious experience, his explanation could not be considered "scientific."

As Whitehead has shown, however, science itself presupposes various
ideas that, if they are to be explained naturalistically, can be explained only
in terms of nonsensory perception. The use of the sensationist theory of perception to exclude the possibility of genuine religious experience involves,
therefore, a selective application. Referring to the appeal to "practice" made
by "Hume and his followers" to supplement their epistemological theory,
Whitehead says that "the general procedure of modern philosophical 'criticism' is to tie down opponents strictly to the front door of presentational
immediacy as the sole source of information, while one's own philosophy
makes its escape by a back door veiled under the ordinary usages of language" (PR 174). That is, whether one speaks of this "back door" in terms
of "ordinary language" or simply "practice," the sensationist thinkers allow
their own theories to be supplemented with notions that would not pass the
entrance requirements laid down by the sensationist version of empiricism—notions such as the real world, causal influence, the past, and time—
while not allowing this right to religious thinkers. The ideas of God and religious experience are excluded as "unempirical."

The way to overcome this radical inconsistency at the heart of modern critical thought, Whitehead argues, is to develop an epistemology that is truly adequate for the inevitable presuppositions of human practice, including scientific practice. Such an epistemology, it turns out, also allows for genuine religious experience. Criticism of truth-claims based on religious experience, accordingly, cannot be carried out wholesale by the application of an a priori dogma. Rather, criticism of such claims must, like the criticism of claims based on sensory experience, be carried out on a retail basis, asking whether particular claims make sense in the light of everything else we think we know.

The widespread acceptance of the sensationist view of perception is not, however, the only reason for the a priori rejection of religious experience as cognitively significant. I turn now to the response of Whiteheadian process philosophy to other reasons for this rejection.

Religious Experience and Arguments for the Existence of God

Besides the acceptance of sensationism, the other most obvious reason for doubting the reality of genuine religious experience, understood as direct perception of a Holy Power, is simply the doubt that any such power exists, so that there is no "object" for religious experience to be a genuine experience *of*. This topic is to be addressed in Chapter 5, in which arguments for the existence of God will be discussed. The topic is somewhat more complex, however, in light of the fact that some religious experience seems to be nontheistic, meaning that the "object" seems not to be a personal being—indeed, not *a* being at all. This apparent disagreement as to the object of religious experience is, in fact, often used as an argument against the genuineness of all such experience. This topic will be addressed in Chapter 7, which develops John Cobb's suggestion that theistic and nontheistic religious experience are different because they are oriented to different ultimate realities.

Religious Experience and Secular Explanations of Religion

Another reason for doubting the reality of genuine religious experience is the assumption that the origin and persistence of religion has been explained in terms of purely secular causes by theorists such as Marx, Durkheim, and Freud. The modern study of religion has, in fact, largely consisted in showing how religion as it actually exists is shaped by social, political, economic, and psychodynamic factors. To return to talking about genuine religious experience would, it is widely assumed, be redundant at best, regressive at worst.

This assumption, however, often conflates two distinct issues. One issue is whether these secular factors go far toward explaining the shape taken by religions in their various contexts, and there can be no doubt about this. A very different issue is whether these factors, even in combination, completely explain the very phenomenon of religion. As Segal recognizes (1989, 82), for secular social scientific explanations to show theistic explanations of religious experience to be redundant, the former would have to provide *sufficient* explanations. An examination of the accounts given thus far reveals that they have not come close. Indeed, although Preus hails the "success of Durkheim and Freud" as marking the "completion of a naturalistic paradigm for the study of religion," even making the grandiose claim that they described secular processes *sufficient* to generate and sustain religious responses to reality (1987, 161, 197), an examination of Preus's own review of their work shows otherwise. In a more circumspect statement, which points out (in a considerable understatement) that the theories of Freud and Durkheim are "not wholly compatible as they stand," Preus says that they pose "the challenge of producing a unified theory of religion" (158). Posing such a "challenge" is not quite the completion of the Humean project by describing secular factors sufficient to account for the existence of religion! Furthermore, commentators not convinced of the truth of naturalism$_{sam}$, and therefore of the possibility of a fully nonreligious explanation of religious experience, are even less impressed with the adequacy of what has been produced along these lines. For example, at the end of his *Theories of Primitive Religion,* E. E. Evans-Pritchard says: "I have to conclude that I do not feel that on the whole the different theories we have reviewed, either singly or taken together, give us more than common-sense guesses, which for the most part miss the mark" (1965, 120).

Process philosophers of religion, in any case, take the view that an adequate explanation of religion would require a combination of religious and secular factors. In such an explanation, genuine religious experience would account both for the very fact that people always and everywhere have been religious, believing in something Holy, and for some of their particular beliefs and attitudes, while the secular factors would account for the rest. Segal recognizes the possibility of this kind of both-and explanation, saying that "surely religion can have an origin that is partly sociological and partly religious," but he dismisses this possibility as "unlikely" (1992, 9). The reason for this dismissal, however, seems to be simply Segal's conviction as to the truth of naturalism~sam~. Insofar as we have good reason to reject naturalism~sam~, however, the partly-partly explanation would *not* seem unlikely.

Telepathy and Religious Experience

Another objection to the acceptance of theistic religious experience as involving the perception of a Cosmic Mind is based on the assumption that such a perceptual experience would be absolutely singular, being devoid of any analogy to render it plausible. Although, it might be argued, Whitehead has undermined the sensationist theory of perception somewhat by pointing to nonsensory perceptions of our own bodies and our own past occasions of experience, these exceptions still involve relations to what would ordinarily be considered simply different aspects of the person in question. They do not, therefore, show the possibility of direct, nonsensory perceptions of *another mind*. Only evidence of such perceptions would provide an analogical basis for thinking of a direct perception of a Cosmic Mind.

Most directly relevant to this objection is process philosophy's endorsement of, along with the empirical evidence for, the reality of telepathic experience, meaning the direct feeling of one mind by another. Although Whitehead did not base much upon it, he did endorse the reality of telepathy in his writings (SMW 150; PR 308; AI 248) and also in private conversation (A. Johnson 1969, 364). His acceptance of it was probably influenced by the fact that he spent his adult life in the three leading centers for the study of such phenomena: Cambridge, England, where Henry Sidgwick, the first president of the Society for Psychical Research (SPR), was a highly respected professor of moral philosophy, whose *Memoirs* Whitehead evidently read (SMW 142); London, where the SPR had its headquarters since its founding in 1882; and Cambridge, Massachusetts, where William James had been the leading light of the American branch of the SPR.

The beginning of process philosophy's endorsement of telepathy could, in fact, be traced back to James, many of whose ideas were absorbed by Whitehead. Whitehead's doctrine of perception in particular is an expansion of James's "radical empiricism." The most well-known feature of this type of empiricism, with which Whitehead agreed, is the insistence that relations, including causal relations, are directly perceived. But James said the "thicker and more radical empiricism" he advocated would also include an examination of "the phenomena of psychic research so-called" (1971, 271). Although the centrality of these phenomena to James's thought has been largely ignored in secondary works on James, as Marcus Ford has shown

(1998), one of James's most famous statements was made in a context in which James confessed his belief in telepathy. Discussing "the orthodox belief that there can be nothing in any one's intellect that has not come in through ordinary experiences of sense," James uttered his oft-quoted logical point that it takes only one white crow to prove that not all crows are black.[8] He continued:

> My own white crow is Mrs. Piper. In the trances of this medium, I cannot resist the conviction that knowledge appears which she has never gained by the ordinary waking use of her eyes and ears and wits. What the source of this knowledge may be I know not . . . ; but from admitting the fact of such knowledge I can see no escape. (1986, 131)

In a recent study (Griffin 1997a), I have argued that the evidence for telepathy, which is even stronger now than in the days of James and Whitehead, puts its reality beyond reasonable doubt. Given the central role played by the sensationist theory of perception in the widespread rejection of the reality of genuine religious experience in intellectual circles, it is surprising that philosophers of religion seldom appeal to the evidence for nonsensory perception provided by parapsychology, which some of its advocates have referred to as "religion's science" (Rhine 1953, 220; Setzer 1970).

One reason that parapsychology's evidence is especially important is that

---

[8] Although Quine quotes both what he calls the "empiricist manifesto," *nihil in mente quod non prius in sensu,* and the aviary dictum that "all ravens are black" (1995, 4, 27), he does not mention that a Harvard philosopher from an earlier period had used these same two dicta in a discussion aimed at showing the need for a broader version of empiricism. Quine does say, however, that the (sensationist) empiricist manifesto should not be considered an a priori dogma, because his "naturalistic epistemology" means the rejection of any "first philosophy," in the sense of any "supra-scientific tribunal" to which science is answerable (1981, 72). He is, to be sure, firmly convinced that "it is a finding of science itself . . . that our information about the world comes only through impacts on our sensory receptors," which "warn[s] us against telepaths" (1990, 19). His naturalistic epistemology, however, makes science itself the final arbiter, "and science is fallible and corrigible," so that "[e]ven telepathy and clairvoyance are scientific options" (1990, 20–21). If "some extraordinary evidence" were to support them, says Quine, "then empiricism itself—the crowning norm . . . of naturalistic epistemology— would go by the board" (21). From the perspective of James and Whitehead, of course, Quine should have said that the *sensationist version* of empiricism would go by the board. But the main point is that Quine's formal position, that science is the final arbiter, implies that he must remain open to the possibility that his substantive conviction that there is no extrasensory perception will be falsified by the science of parapsychology. Quine himself is relaxed about the absence of any a priori, definitional bulwarks against this contingency because he considers it "implausible" (1990, 21). It is significant, nonetheless, that Quine's naturalistic epistemology, to which many philosophers now profess allegiance, implies the need to examine the best available evidence *against* the sensationist theory of perception.

it is *scientific* evidence, in the sense that it can be empirically tested.[9] This is not true, by contrast, of the other types of nonsensory perception discussed here: there is no way to test empirically whether our perceptions of our own bodies or our own past experiences are really nonsensory perceptions, and there is certainly no way to set up an empirical test to see if religious experience sometimes involves a direct perception of a Cosmic Mind. Empirical tests *have* been set up, however, to rule out alternative interpretations of experiences apparently involving extrasensory perception of other human minds (for a summary, see Griffin 1997a, chap. 2). Insofar as such tests have shown the reality of telepathic influence beyond a reasonable doubt, they cast an aura of credibility on the nonsensory interpretation of the other types of experience. Once we have one indubitable white crow, the acceptance of a second and a third is not so difficult.

Whitehead's acceptance of telepathy, furthermore, illustrates a feature of perception in the mode of causal efficacy not yet discussed. This is the fact that it involves an appropriation of influences from every actuality in the perceiver's environment. This means that a moment of human experience does not arise solely out of the causal influences provided by the brain. Rather, whatever has become actual is available to be perceived. Whitehead makes this point in discussing the possibility of telepathy. Having said that we must "allow for the possibility that we can detect in ourselves direct aspects of the mentalities of higher organisms," he adds: "The fundamental principle is that whatever merges into actuality, implants its aspects in every individual event" (SMW 150). This principle implies that we are directly perceiving the minds of others all the time, so that those moments in which people have what are normally termed "telepathic experiences" would be special only in the sense that the ongoing prehensions of the other minds in question had, for some reason, momentarily risen to the level of *conscious* awareness. This same principle would imply that if there is a divine actuality, it would implant aspects of itself in all human experiences, which would mean that we would actually be perceiving God all the time. From this perspective, those moments in which people have what are normally termed (theistic) "religious experiences" would be special only in the sense that the perception of God, which is an aspect of every experience, had momentarily risen to the level of consciousness. This is another respect in

---

[9] Probably the main reason for the neglect (if not outright dismissal) of this evidence is the widespread feeling that parapsychology is *not* a science but merely a pseudo-science. I have dealt with this objection at considerable length in a chapter titled "Parapsychology, Science, and Religion" in Griffin 2000a.

which the analogical use of telepathy serves to naturalize religious experience, showing it not to be an exception to the principles involved in other forms of perception.

Givenness and Religious Experience

Yet another reason for assuming religious experience not to involve perceptual experience of a Holy Power is the assumption that our conscious experience is entirely *constructed,* with no element in it that is simply *given* to the experience. This is, of course, precisely the position that most of Whitehead's epistemology, with its reformed subjectivist principle, is directed against. It is because most modern philosophers have ignored perception in the mode of causal efficacy, focusing only on presentational immediacy, that they have ended up with a purely subjectivist account of experience, according to which every element in our experience is thought to be created or constructed by the experiencing subject. This wholly subjectivist account leads, of course, to solipsism. Whitehead's alternative analysis is aimed at showing how it is that other actualities *are* given to experience, which explains the fact that we are all realists in practice, presupposing that we are in the midst of other actualities. Whitehead does not, by any means, deny that conscious experience is *largely* constructed by the percipient. He in fact praises Kant as "the great philosopher who first, fully and explicitly, introduced into philosophy the conception of an act of experience as a constructive functioning" (PR 156). Kant's own way of conceptualizing this constructive act was problematic, however, because he had accepted Hume's purely subjectivist account of perceptual experience, according to which no stubborn facts are given.

In Whitehead's account, by contrast, each moment of experience is an act "of self-production arising out of some primary given phase" (S 8). Being able to speak of a "primary" phase that is "given" depends upon the recognition of a presensory perceptual mode of causal efficacy, in which the causal efficacy of other actualities is directly apprehended. The data of presentational immediacy arise only in a later phase: these data are "data"—that is, *given* elements—not in the sense of being given *to the occasion of experience from beyond itself* but only in the sense of being given *to perception in the mode of presentational immediacy by the prior functioning of that occasion of experience itself* (PR 172, 180). And "symbolic reference," which involves the integration of the data from the two pure modes of perception, occurs in a still later phase of an occasion of experience (PR 121, 168). Whitehead fully agrees, accordingly, that the prominent data of *sensory* perception are constructed by, not given to, a moment of experience. But data of sensory perception are constructed out of data that *are* given from beyond an occasion of experience to its primary phase, the phase of perception in the mode of causal efficacy.

Of course, the extreme position that experience in general is *wholly* constructed is not taken seriously by many thinkers. The *wholly* constructivist analysis is usually applied only selectively, to forms of experience in which the content, if given to the experience rather than constructed by it, would have to be given in a nonsensory way. For example, theologian Gordon Kaufman, agreeing with Kant not only that concepts without percepts are empty but also that percepts are exclusively sensory, asks to what the word *God* might refer. "Certainly not to anything we directly experience," Kaufman answers, suggesting instead that the idea of God is an "imaginative construction" (1993, 415).[10] In a statement with which, under one interpretation, Whitehead would agree, Kaufman says that all our ideas—our ideas of trees as well as our ideas of God—are products of the imagination (1993, 39). Kaufman, however, makes an addition with which Whitehead would not agree, showing that he regards the sense in which the idea of God is "imaginative" to be different in kind from the sense in which the idea of a physical object is imaginative: "God is simply not the sort of reality that is available to direct observation or experience. . . . The idea of God, thus, should not be regarded as epistemically similar to the idea of a perceptual object (for example, a table or a person or a mountain); it is not based on direct human perceptions of God. Rather it is constructed imaginatively in the mind" (1993, 323). By contrast, given Whitehead's (non-Kantian) epistemology, including his recognition of the telepathic perception of other minds, the idea of a Cosmic Mind *could* be regarded as "epistemically similar" to some ideas of some (other) "perceptual objects."

Conformal Feelings and Experience of the Holy

I will conclude this discussion by treating one final reason why philosophers, presupposing the traditional view of perception, have found the notion of genuine religious experience problematic. The issue involved is the idea of religious experience as involving a perception of a Holy Reality— that is, a perception of the reality *as* "holy" or "sacred." The problem is simply, What basis do we have in our ordinary experience for assuming that this

[10] In saying this, Kaufman is simply following the lead of Kant himself, who said that to affirm a "feeling of the immediate presence of the Supreme Being" would be a "fanatical religious illusion" because it would be to affirm "a receptivity for an intuition for which there is no sensory provision in man's nature" (1960, 163). Kant, of course, assumed that there could be no cognitive intuitions that are not sensory.

kind of extraordinary experience could be a genuine experience—that is, that the experience of the reality *as holy* would involve a *perceptual response* to a quality, which we can call "holiness," inherent in the reality itself?

Insofar as the sensationist theory of perception is presupposed, it would seem that there is no such basis because sensory perception does not, at least obviously, involve affective responses to its data. For example, Durkheim said that the primary problem for the scientific understanding of religion is "explaining the sacred"—that is, explaining why religious people think in terms of a distinction between the "sacred" and the "profane," even though "nothing in sensible experience seems able to suggest the idea of so radical a duality to them" (1963, 57).[11] Otto, famous for his book *The Idea of the Holy,* solved this problem, while holding a basically Kantian view, by adding another a priori category to the Kantian mind, namely, the category of the holy (1958, 175). Mircea Eliade likewise says that "the 'sacred' is an element in the structure of consciousness" (1978, 1:xiii). Such a solution, however, raises a question that cannot be answered naturalistically. "[I]n an academic setting where other scholars are struggling with the evolutionary emergence of our species," Preus rightly says, "one legitimately wants to know how Eliade's remarkable 'element in the structure of consciousness' might have gotten there" (1987, xix). An answer, as Otto explicitly recognized, would require reference to a supernatural implantation. Much of the hostility to Eliade's approach has been due to its apparent violation of domain uniformitarianism, combined with the implicit supernaturalism upon which this violation seems to be based. Is it possible to consider religious experience inherently distinctive without implying supernaturalism?

Whitehead's epistemology is directly relevant to this question. Although perception in the mode of presentational immediacy is devoid of affective response, at least virtually, the opposite is true of perception in the mode of causal efficacy. In this mode, the perception of a datum, which is something actual, always involves a conformal response to affective tones inherent in

---

[11] Another example of this view is found in Bryan Rennie's critique of Ninian Smart's treatment of religious experience. Asking how we should understand the relation between experience and emotion in what Smart calls the "experiential and emotional dimension" of religion, Rennie suggests that a clearer distinction "would be that of stimulus and response. The stimulus is an object or event. The response is an internally generated reaction *to* the stimulus." On this basis—in which Smart's examples of religious experience, such as "awe," would be responses that are (entirely) *internally generated*—Rennie concludes that the experiential and emotional dimension of religion should be understood "as primarily involving response rather than stimuli" (1999, 65). Having thus interpreted "Smart's treatment of the experiential dimension as involving reaction rather than reception," Rennie claims his support for his own conclusion that "there is nothing identifiable as 'religious' experience" per se (68). Whitehead's epistemology, I will show, provides a basis in terms of which Smart could more clearly articulate his conviction that religious emotions can involve a receptive response.

that actuality itself. To explain this point, it is necessary to introduce some more technical terms: *prehension, feeling,* and *subjective form.*

Whitehead's more general word for perception is *prehension,* which is derived from the Latin *prehensio,* from *prehendere,* meaning "to seize." More common, of course, is the adjective *prehensile,* as in "a prehensile tail." Also common, of course, is the term *apprehension,* which suggests a *conscious* grasp of something. In using *prehension* without the *ap,* Whitehead meant to indicate a grasp that could be either conscious or unconscious (SMW 69). He recognized that for most people the term *perception* suggests both *sensory* perception and *conscious* perception (SMW 69; AI 178). Although he continued to use that term in the phrase "perception in the mode of causal efficacy" to point to a kind of perception that is not sensory and is also usually not conscious, the term *prehension* emphasizes the fact that something more fundamental than conscious sensory perception is intended. The meaning of this term—a seizing or a grasping—also serves to make clear Whitehead's rejection of the theory of *representative* perception, according to which the perception of an actuality involves nothing other than the perceiving mind's having ideas, understood as its private qualities, which for some reason "represent" exterior things (PR 54, 144). The term *prehension,* by contrast, indicates that the perceiver actually incorporates aspects of the perceived thing into its own constitution.

Prehensions are of two fundamental types: physical and mental (or conceptual). A *physical* prehension is the type we have been discussing: the prehension of a prior *actuality.* "Physical prehension" is, in fact, a synonym for "perception in the mode of causal efficacy." The data of *mental* (or *conceptual*) prehensions, by contrast, are mere possibilities or universals (which Whitehead calls "eternal objects"), such as the color *white* and the shape *round.* Perception in the mode of presentational immediacy consists entirely of mental (or conceptual) prehensions. Hume's epistemology, then, involves the doctrine that perception begins with mental or conceptual prehensions. Although the term *impressions of sensation* seems to suggest that a moment of experience begins with the reception of data impressed upon it by outer things, Hume, as we saw, denies this, saying instead that the data consist entirely of sense data understood to be mere universals or eternal objects, such as colored shapes. Whitehead's alternative doctrine is that every occasion of experience begins with *physical* prehensions, the data of which are prior *actualities.*

It is important not to let this point be distorted by the meaning that the word *physical* has in dualistic philosophy, in which physical things, being different in kind from mental things, are wholly devoid of experience. Given that connotation, one might think that physical prehensions are those that grasp purely physical things, such as sticks, stones, and bodily organs, whereas the prehension of a mind—whether one's own past mind (in memory), or another person's mind (in telepathy), or a Cosmic Mind (in theistic religious experience)—would be a mental prehension. That emphatically is *not* Whitehead's meaning. If a prehension's datum is an *actuality,* as distinct from a mere possibility, then it is a *physical* prehension, whether that actuality be the brain, a past occasion of one's own experience, another mind, or a Cosmic Mind. Given *this* meaning of "physical prehension," Whitehead insists that each occasion of experience begins with physical prehensions.

One reason why this insistence is important, beyond avoiding solipsism, is that it provides the basis for saying that each moment of experience begins with an *affective* or *emotional* response to things prehended. This point, which illustrates the way in which Whitehead's ontology and epistemology presuppose each other, is correlated with the ontological doctrine that all actualities are, or are composed of, occasions of experience, thereby having emotional feelings to be prehended. But this ontological doctrine is based largely upon Whitehead's epistemological point that when we see that our most fundamental form of perception is physical prehension, or perception in the mode of causal efficacy, then we will recognize that *things as directly perceived are perceived as themselves embodying emotional feelings.* They are perceived this way because they are perceived as evoking conformal emotional responses in us when we perceive them.

This doctrine, which is fundamental for Whitehead's ontology as well as his epistemology, he calls "the Doctrine of the Conformation of Feeling" (AI 183). It could also be called the doctrine of the initial conformation of subjective form (AI 253). I have here introduced the two other new technical terms of this subsection, *feeling* and *subjective form.* A *subjective form* is the way in which a subject prehends a datum. Every prehension, in other words, involves a datum, which is *what* is prehended, and a subjective form, which is *how* that datum is prehended. If a man kicks me, I will probably prehend him with the subjective form of anger because I consider him responsible for the fact that I am prehending my leg with the subjective form of pain. The term *feeling* is employed, as a virtual synonym for prehension, in order to bring out "this double significance of subjective form and of the apprehension of an object" (AI 233). That is, the term *feeling* suggests both that *something* is felt and that it is felt *with emotion.* The centrality of this notion for Whitehead is shown by his suggestion that his whole philosophy aspires to be "a critique of pure feeling" (PR 113). At the root of this critique is the idea of the *initial conformation of subjective form,* according to which the subjective form of the feeling of a prior feeling initially conforms to, or reenacts, the subjective form of that prior feeling. For example, when I feel my leg's pain (the datum), I feel it painfully (the subjective form). Likewise, moments later, when I remember the moment in which I became angry at the man for kicking me, I will remember my past anger at him angrily. I am not, to be sure, forever destined to prehend this past event with the same subjective form. Other factors can enter which may lead me to forgive the man, perhaps by realizing that he did not intend to do it. I may even, by prehending this event through the mediation of intervening events, come to recall my past anger primarily with humor. The doctrine speaks only of the *initial* conformity of subjective form. It says that the physical feelings constituting the initial phase of an occasion of experience conform to the subjective forms of the past feelings that are felt. "The first phase in the immediacy of the new occasion is that of the conformation of feelings. The feeling as enjoyed by the past occasion is present in the new occasion as datum felt, with a subjective form conformal to that of the datum" (AI 183). To emphasize this point, Whitehead also calls physical feelings "conformal feelings" (PR 164, 237–38). They could also be called *sympathetic* feelings: if the present occasion be called B and the prior occasion A, the "continuity of subjective form is the initial sympathy of B for A" (AI 183).

At the root of Whitehead's nonsensationist doctrine of perception, therefore, is the idea that our most fundamental perception of the world is not a conscious, sensory perception of it, in which it is represented by barren, unemotional sense data, but a preconscious feeling of it, in which other things are felt sympathetically:

> The primitive form of physical experience is emotional—blind emotion— received as felt elsewhere in another occasion and conformally appropriated as a subjective passion. In the language appropriate to the higher stages of experience, the primitive element is *sympathy,* that is, feeling the feeling *in* another and feeling conformally *with* another. (PR 162)

This doctrine, based on the priority of feeling, involves a complete inversion of the Humean brand of empiricism.

> Hume and Locke, with the overintellectualist bias prevalent among philosophers, assume that emotional feelings are necessarily derivative from sensations. . . . The converse doctrine is nearer the truth: the more primitive mode of objectification is via emotional tone, and only in exceptional organisms does objectification, via sensation, supervene with any effectiveness. (PR 141)

The traditional doctrine of perception, in other words, has regarded the derivative elements as primary and the truly primary elements as derivative.

The mistake behind this traditional doctrine involved a confusion between two kinds of priority: "The order of dawning, clearly and distinctly, in consciousness," Whitehead points out, was assumed to be the same as "the order of metaphysical priority" (PR 162), meaning the order in which the elements arose in an act of experience. "[T]he opposite doctrine," Whitehead contends, "is more nearly true" (PR 173).

The basis for this opposite doctrine, beyond what has already been said, is a new view of the nature of consciousness. Rather than being the stuff of which a mind is composed, as most modern philosophy has followed Descartes in assuming, consciousness is a subjective form, which requires a very complex datum to provoke it into existence. This complex datum, called an "intellectual feeling," involves an integration of feelings that had arisen in earlier phases of the becoming, or "concrescence," of an occasion of experience. Consciousness, therefore, cannot exist in the early phases of an act of experience but arises, if at all, only in a late phase. If, by contrast, it were simply the stuff of which human experience were composed, we could assume that it would be, as it were, *lying in wait at the outset of an occasion of experience, ready to illuminate the first elements to arise.* In that case, priority in consciousness *would* signal priority in experience. Given Whitehead's alternative doctrine, however, the opposite conclusion follows. As he has famously said, "consciousness presupposes experience, and not experience consciousness" (PR 53).

Because of the centrality of this point for Whitehead's philosophy in general, as well as for the issue of religious experience in particular, it is worth quoting his most important statement on it at some length:

[C]onsciousness only arises in a late derivative phase of complex integrations. . . . Consciousness only illuminates the more primitive types of prehension so far as these prehensions are still elements in the products of integration. Thus those elements of our experience which stand out clearly and distinctly in our consciousness are not its basic facts; they are the derivative modifications which arise in the process. For example, consciousness only dimly illuminates the prehensions in the mode of causal efficacy, because these prehensions are primitive elements in our experience. But prehensions in the mode of presentational immediacy are among those prehensions which we enjoy with the most vivid consciousness. These prehensions are late derivatives in the concrescence of an experient subject. The consequences of the neglect of this law, that the late derivative elements are more clearly illuminated by consciousness than the primitive elements, have been fatal to the proper analysis of an experient occasion. In fact, most of the difficulties of philosophy are produced by it. (PR 162)

For our present purposes, the implication of this point is that although each occasion of experience begins with perceptions in the mode of causal efficacy and thereby with feelings that conform to the subjective forms of the actualities felt, consciousness tends to hide this fact. As stated earlier, each occasion of experience is an act of self-construction arising out of a primary given phase. Consciousness primarily illuminates the products of our self-constructive activity, leaving the given elements largely in the dark—that is, in what we call the unconscious portion of experience, which is most of it. These *given* elements are contained in *conformal feelings,* which, in feeling other things as actual and as causally efficacious for our experience, conform to emotional feelings in those other things, sympathetically reenacting those emotional feelings. The fact that this element of our experience is not primary in our conscious awareness is no sign that it is not primary in the depths of our experience.

We can, in fact, become consciously aware of this sympathetic, conformal prehension of other things if we will turn our attention away from sensory perception of the world external to our bodies, turning it instead to our prehensions of our bodies themselves and our own past experiences. We naturally sympathize with the feelings of our bodies, feeling their pains as our pains, their enjoyments as our enjoyments. We also tend to sympathize with our immediately antecedent occasions of experience, feeling their joy as our (present) joy, their disappointment as our (present) disappointment, their anger as our (present) anger. These facts are consistent, furthermore, with the nature of telepathic experiences: it is common for the perceiver not simply to receive bare information from the mind of the other person but to feel the other's feelings, sometimes taking on the other's emotional state. Indeed, the very word *telepathy,* which means "feeling at a distance," reflects this feature of such experiences.

The relevance of all this to religious experience should now be clear. If, as the discussion of "panentheism" in Chapters 4 and 5 will suggest, we are encompassed by a loving, holy actuality, we would feel this actuality in every moment, and we would do so with conformal subjective form. If this feeling were to rise to the level of consciousness, we would, therefore, naturally describe it as an awareness of a *holy* reality, power, or presence.

Genuine religious experience thus understood requires no special religious sense, a priori or otherwise, no supernatural intervention into the normal causal processes involved in human experience, and no special pleading in terms of the beliefs and practices of a particular religious community. It follows instead from the general principles of process philosophy's epistemology, which are defended primarily in terms of their ability to do justice to the inevitable presuppositions of our ordinary experience (rather than having been constructed primarily to do justice to religious experience in particular). The employment of this interpretation of religious experiences, whether in departments of religion, philosophy, sociology, anthropology, or psychology, would in principle involve no violation of domain uniformity because this interpretation would be employing epistemological categories proposed for all disciplines of study, including the natural sciences. Of course, insofar as sensationist assumptions about perception continue to be used in most other fields, the interpretation of putative religious experience in these terms would de facto mean the use of categories not generally accepted in the academic community. But besides the fact that this would not add significantly to the chaos of interpretive schemes presently extant in the intellectual world, the resulting problem would be the practical one of achieving consensus, not the theoretical one of proposing a unique epistemology for religious studies. Indeed, the proposal that at least some religious experiences could be thus interpreted is part and parcel of a proposal to overcome the present chaos of interpretive schemes. Whether it succeeds, of course, depends upon whether the leading thinkers of the coming generations in the various fields find it convincing and helpful.

3. Truths Provided by Religious Experience

Whitehead's complaint about the philosophical tradition generally called "empiricist," as we have seen, is that it is wholly unempirical. While excluding Locke himself from this charge, Whitehead says that "Locke's successors, who arrogated to themselves the title of 'empiricists,' have been chiefly employed in explaining away the obvious facts of experience in obedience to the a priori doctrine of sensationalism" (PR 145). The fact they have been most devoted to explaining away is religious experience. That religious experience is a response to Something Holy in the nature of things is not, to be sure, as obvious as the reality of causation, time, the past, and the external world. But it is obvious that human beings always and everywhere have been religious and that, furthermore, religion is not disappearing in the light of modern criticisms and substitutes. "The religious spirit," observes Whitehead, "is always in process of being explained away, distorted, buried. Yet, since the travel of mankind towards civilization, it is always there" (AI 172).

Whitehead's explanation for this fact is that rather than being based simply on intellectual mistakes or contingent social conditions, "religion is the expression of one type of fundamental experiences of mankind" (SMW 190). In light of the discussion in the previous sections, combined with the discussion of God to be provided in later chapters, we can expand this statement by saying that the existence of religion is rooted in the twofold fact that (1) all people at all times feel, albeit usually only at an unconscious level, the existence of a Holy Actuality, which accounts for what is sometimes called "the religious dimension of experience," and (2) in some people this direct prehension sometimes rises to the level of conscious awareness, producing what is called an "experience of the Holy" or a "mystical experience." Because all people (by hypothesis) have religious experience in the first sense, a responsive chord may be evoked in them by verbal reports of religious experiences in the second sense. Psychological, sociological, economic, political, moral, and aesthetic factors play significant roles in the actual shape of, and even the very existence of, particular religious communities. But the distinctively religious dimension of a religion—that which makes it identifiable as "a religion"—is explainable in terms of these two fundamental forms of religious experience. Nothing would be lost by the qualification that these two fundamental forms are probably best thought of as two ends of a continuum.

Besides considering religious experiences to constitute a fundamental type of experience, Whitehead considers them potentially cognitive, meaning that they can give rise to truths. This belief is expressed in a statement quoted earlier: "The dogmas of religion are the attempts to formulate in precise terms the truths disclosed in the religious experience of mankind" (RM 57). The purpose of the present section is to point to the truths Whitehead believed to be disclosed by religious experience. *Whitehead's ideas about such truths were,* more than has usually been recognized, *essential to the whole shape of his cosmology,* the exploration of which will begin in the next chapter. It is important to see, therefore, just what truths he believed to come uniquely from religious experience.

First, acknowledgment must be made of an ambiguity in Whitehead's discussion of religious experience and truth to which I have earlier only alluded. Sometimes, as when he says that the "peculiar character of religious truth is that it explicitly deals with values" (RM 120), he thinks of religious truths in a broad sense, as inclusive of all truths derivable from nonsensory value experiences. When used in this broad sense, the truths derivable from religious experience are inclusive of the truths derivable from ethical and aesthetic experience. In other passages, however, he is thinking of religious experience in a narrower sense, so that its truths are distinct from those of ethical and aesthetic experience. This usage is reflected, for example, in his statement that it is cosmology's task to bring scientific concepts into relation with "the aesthetic, moral, and religious interests" (PR xii). Although this double usage can be confusing, it is understandable for two reasons. On the one hand, being based on nonsensory prehensions, aesthetic and ethical ideas, as well as religious ideas in the narrow sense, have been widely thought not to reveal any truths about the nature of reality. They are all, therefore, in the same cognitive boat, so that to defend the possibility that religious experience (in the narrow sense) can be truth-providing, by showing that nonsensory perception can be cognitive, also serves to vindicate the possibility that aesthetic and ethical notions express truths about the nature of reality. On the other hand, as we will see in later chapters, Whitehead explains the impact of aesthetic and ethical ideals on our experience in the same way in which he explains distinctively religious experiences, namely, in terms of our prehension of divine influence. For these two reasons, it was appropriate for Whitehead, while recognizing a sense in which religious truths are distinctive in relation to aesthetic and ethical truths, also to think of the latter as aspects of religious truths. In the ensuing discussion, I will also refer to religious experiences and truths in this twofold way, trying in each case to make clear whether the broad or the narrow meaning is intended.

Cosmological Truths about Values

In holding that the "peculiar character of religious truth is that it explicitly deals with values" (RM 120), Whitehead was probably influenced by the Ritschlean school of thought (begun by the neo-Kantian German theologian Albrecht Ritschl [1822–1899]). Whitehead rejected, however, the view of some members of this school who, having distinguished between value-judgments (*Werturteile*) on the one hand and judgments about the nature of reality (*Seinsurteile*) on the other, declared religion to be interested only in the former. As we saw earlier, Whitehead considered religion to be inseparable from cosmological beliefs. "The theme of Cosmology," he even says, "is the basis of all religions" (PR 349). The truths about values disclosed by religious experience, he held, provide clues as to the nature of the cosmos: value-judgments can point to truths about the nature of reality. The task of philosophy is to develop a self-consistent, adequate cosmology by combining the truths derived from sensory experience, which science has sought to systematize, with the truths about values derived from religious experience, which have been systematized in various ways by the various systems of religious thought.

A Character of Permanent Rightness in the Nature of Things

Whitehead's most fundamental religious conviction was that the universe contains a "character of permanent rightness" (RM 60). The main evidence for this truth is "the intuition of immediate occasions as failing or succeeding in reference to the ideal relevant to them. There is a rightness attained or missed" (RM 59). This intuition involves "a revelation of character, apprehended as we apprehend the characters of our friends. But in this case it is an apprehension of character permanently inherent in the nature of things" (RM 60). In early forms of religious experience, Whitehead suggests, this notion of "rightness is mixed up with the notion of preservation. Conduct is right which will lead some god to protect you" (RM 39–40). A purified religion, however, "rises to the conception of an essential rightness of things," which involves a "new, and almost profane, concept of the goodness of God," with the result that you no longer "study the will of God in order that He may preserve you"; rather, "you study his goodness in order to be like him" (RM 40).

To understand what Whitehead is claiming, it is important to see what he is *not* claiming. He is emphatically not saying that we have an intuition that all things fully conform to this character of rightness:

> It is not true that every individual item of the universe conforms to this character in every detail. There will be some measure of conformity and some measure of diversity. The whole intuition of conformity and diversity forms the contrast which that item yields for the religious experience. So far as the conformity is incomplete, there is evil in the world. (RM 60)

The idea that we experience a principle or character of rightness, "equally compelling recognition and permissive of disregard" (RM 59), so that we experience ourselves as either failing or succeeding in relation to ideals—or as partly succeeding and partly failing—is one that Whitehead repeats often. And he explicitly refers to this experience as an experience of a divine reality. After having said, "There are experiences of ideals—of ideals entertained, of ideals aimed at, of ideals achieved, of ideals defaced," he adds: "This is the experience of the deity of the universe" (MT 103). The idea that this deity is an all-determining power, however, is the main exaggeration of religious experience that his philosophy of religion seeks to overcome.

Whitehead is also not claiming that universal religious experience supports the idea that the character of permanent rightness is the character of a personal deity. There is, indeed, "a large concurrence in the negative doctrine that this religious experience does not include any direct intuition of a definite person, or individual" (RM 60). Sometimes this denial, made in *Religion in the Making,* has been overinterpreted to mean that Whitehead, at least while writing this book (which was only the second of his American, metaphysical period), did not himself think of God as a personal being, meaning one who responds to the world as well as influencing it. Whitehead's concern here, however, is only with the nature of the evidence directly provided to philosophy by universal religious experience as such (RM 84). His point is that "if you make religious experience to be the direct intuition of a personal being substrate to the universe," your evidence is weakened "because there is no widespread basis of agreement to appeal to" (RM 62–63; cf. 84). "[T]here is a large consensus," he argues, only for "the concept of a rightness in things, partially conformed to and partially disregarded" (RM 65). The consensus, in other words, is only for that which he would later call "the primordial nature of God," God as influencing the world in terms of ideals.

A Divine Reality Responsive to the World

Whitehead does not say, however, that an inference from the religious experience of a character of rightness to a personal deity would be unjustified. Indeed, after saying that "the notion of a direct vision of a personal God" has been rejected by the majority of the advanced religions, he adds: "As soon, however, as it comes to a question of rational interpretation, numbers rapidly sink in importance. Reason mocks at majorities" (RM 64–65). Why Whitehead himself was led by "reason" to affirm a personal deity will be discussed in Chapter 5.

For now it is important to note that, besides not denying that God should be understood as a personal being, Whitehead evidently even came to believe that people can and do have experiences of God as personal, as responsive to the world—which would mean, in his later language, of God's "consequent nature."[12] For example, in *Process and Reality,* after discussing this

---

[12] By contrast, early-nineteenth-century German theologian Friedrich Schleiermacher—who, in spite of being called "the father of modern liberal Protestant theology," accepted the traditional doctrine of God's omnipotence and impassibility—defined religious experience as a feeling of *absolute* dependence, which is said to be the awareness of being dependent on something upon which one exerts no counterinfluence whatsoever (1928 [1830], 14–18). Whitehead's alternative view, that religious experience can include an awareness of the divine responsiveness, was independently supported by the Jewish theologian Abraham Joshua Heschel. In his great work *The Prophets* (1962), Heschel, who rejected the idea of divine impassibility (224), said that the prophets, being "open to the presence and emotion of the transcendent Subject" (309), spoke out of a "state of suffering in sympathy with the divine pathos" (118).

consequent nature, which he also calls "the love in heaven," he says that this love "floods back again into the world," which makes God "the great companion—the fellow-sufferer who understands" (PR 351). We can, in other words, experience God as one who loves the world, suffering with it. Later, in *Adventures of Ideas,* in which Whitehead refers to the primordial and consequent natures together as forming "the Great Fact," he says that the "sense of Peace" involves the "immediate experience of this Final Fact" (AI 295–96). In a still later discussion, in *Modes of Thought,* he describes an experience in which "our sense of the value of the details for the totality dawns upon our consciousness. This is the intuition of holiness, the intuition of the sacred, which is at the foundation of all religion" (MT 120). Whitehead is here speaking of "our sense of the value, for its own sake, of the totality of historic fact in respect to its essential unity." Leaving no doubt about his meaning, he adds: "There is a unity in the universe, enjoying value and (by its immanence) sharing value" (MT 119–20). It is our intuition of this value-enjoying unity that he calls our intuition of holiness. These passages do not mean that Whitehead modified his historical judgment that the majority of the religious traditions have denied that an intuition of a personal divine reality, responsive to the world, is given in religious experience itself. They suggest only that Whitehead himself evidently came to believe that certain religious experiences involve this intuition, even if it is not as widespread and indubitable as the intuition of a character of rightness in the nature of things.

The World as Oriented toward the Production of Value

These intuitions about what Whitehead came to call the primordial and consequent natures of God are abstractions from what he regarded as the overall import of religious experience, which involves the interaction of the divine reality with the world. With regard to the world, the first contribution of religious experience is "the recognition that our existence is more than a succession of bare facts" (RM 77). Spelling this out, Whitehead says: "Religion is founded on the concurrence of three allied concepts in one moment of self-consciousness" (RM 58). These three concepts, contained in this basal religious experience, are:

1. That of the value of an individual for itself.
2. That of the value of the diverse individuals of the world for each other.
3. That of the value of the objective world which is a community derivative from the interrelations of its component individuals, and also necessary for the existence of each of these individuals.

Although this threefold value-experience does not exhaust the content of religious experience, it provides the basic presuppositions: that the world is a place in which values are realized, that individuals have value for themselves and for one another, and that the world as a whole is necessary if these value-realizing individuals are to exist. Although "religious consciousness starts from self-valuation," Whitehead suggests, it "broadens into the conception of the world as a realm of adjusted values, mutually intensifying or mutually destructive" (RM 58–59). In a statement bringing out the fact that religious experience, by providing this insight, makes a contribution to cosmology not provided by science's systematization of the data of sensory perception, Whitehead says: "Religion insists that the world is a mutually adjusted disposition of things, issuing in value for its own sake. This is the very point that science is always forgetting" (RM 138).

This conviction, that a cosmology constructed without regard to our value-experiences will be inadequate, is reflected in many of Whitehead's comments about "scientific materialism," meaning the "scientific cosmology which presupposes the ultimate fact of an irreducible brute matter [that is] senseless, valueless, purposeless" (SMW 17). According to this cosmology, he says critically: "Nature is a dull affair, . . . merely the hurrying of material, endlessly, meaninglessly" (SMW 54). This cosmology implies the "complete futility" of the ultimate entities of nature, regarding them as having "no intrinsic reality" but instead as being "wholly occupied in moving each other about" (SMW 155). Stressing the irrationality of this Cartesian cosmology, Whitehead writes:

> The bodily substances have, on this theory, a vacuous existence. They are sheer facts, devoid of all intrinsic values. It is intrinsically impossible to give any reason why they should come into existence, or should endure, or should cease to exist. Descartes tells us that they are sustained by God, but fails to give any reason why God should care to do so. (FR 30)

A rational cosmology, this statement implies, must be based through and through on the insight that all individuals have intrinsic value, that the order of the world always issues in "value for its own sake."

The intuition of the existence of a divine power is integrally connected with the intuition that "[t]he order of the world is no accident" but exists for the sake of value:

> The religious insight is the grasp of this truth: That the order of the world, the depth of reality of the world, the value of the world in its whole, and in

its parts . . . are all bound together—not accidentally, but by . . . the completed ideal harmony, which is God. (RM 115)

"The purpose of God," Whitehead says explicitly, "is the attainment of
value in the temporal world" (RM 97). Presupposed in this statement is the
idea not only that all individuals have intrinsic value—"Value is inherent in
actuality itself" (RM 97)—but also that there are degrees of intrinsic value:
"Occasions differ in importance of actuality" (RM 100). This twofold idea
leads Whitehead, in spite of his reluctance to describe God as "creator" (because of this term's association with creation ex nihilo), to assert: "Thus the
purpose of God in the attainment of value is in a sense a creative purpose"
(RM 100). The order of the world, in other words, reflects the divine purpose of evoking individuals with increasingly greater degrees of intrinsic
value. *The world is a locus of value-realization.* Although less poetic than Keats's
description of the world as a "vale of soul-making," this phrase provides an
estimation of the divine purpose that is far less anthropocentric.

The religious response to the universe involves harmony with this purpose. In a statement in which Whitehead corrects the one-sided view of his
concept of religion that results from an exclusive focus on his most famous
but preliminary definition—"Religion is what the individual does with his
own solitariness" (RM 16)—he says: "In its solitariness the spirit asks, What,
in the way of value, is the attainment of life? And it can find no such value
till it has merged its individual claim with that of the objective universe. Religion is world-loyalty" (RM 59). It is value in this sense, in fact, that Whitehead had in mind in saying that the "peculiar character of religious truth is
that it explicitly deals with values." Directly after that statement, he adds this
clarification: "[Religious truth] brings into our consciousness that permanent side of the universe which we can care for. It thereby provides a meaning, in terms of value, for our own existence, a meaning which flows from
the nature of things" (RM 120). As this statement emphasizes, religious value
cannot be disconnected from cosmology because this value involves a sense
of ultimate meaning that "flows from the nature of things,"[13] from an aspect
of the "permanent side of the universe." This permanent aspect, of course,
is the character of rightness inherent in the nature of things. Our lives attain
meaning insofar as their claims are brought into harmony with *its* claim.

---

[13] In affirming such a meaning, Whitehead is challenging the idea that the modern disenchantment of the world is irreversible. The connection of Weberian disenchantment with the
issue of meaning has been emphasized by Peter Dews in *The Limits of Disenchantment* (1995,
1–2, 209–10).

The fact that the resulting religion involves "world-loyalty" indicates that it is no individualistic relation between the soul and God. Rather, the universe disclosed in religious experience is "through and through interdependent" (RM 85). In a statement that nicely brings out the implications of his doctrine of internal relatedness to this issue, Whitehead writes:

> The individual is formative of the society, the society is formative of the individual. Particular evils infect the whole world, particular goods point the way of escape. . . . The actual world . . . is a community of many diverse entities; and these entities contribute to, or derogate from, the common value of the total community. . . . The topic of religion is individuality in community. (RM 85–86)

Religious meaning, therefore, involves not only the sense of being in harmony with the character of the deity of the universe but also the sense of making a positive contribution to the world. "Religion is the direct apprehension that, beyond [obvious] happiness and [obvious] pleasure, there remains the function of what is actual and passing, that it contributes its quality as an immortal fact to the order which informs the world" (RM 77–78).

The Immortality of Achieved Value

When writing *Religion in the Making,* as we have seen, Whitehead only hinted at the possibility that religious experience involves the idea that the value evoked becomes, in turn, value *for* God. Insofar as religious experience implied actualized value to be immortal, it was primarily in the sense of making an immortal contribution "to the order which informs the world." In Whitehead's later works, the early hint becomes a major theme. In his last book, the threefold value-experience is said to involve a dim division into "'The Whole,' 'That Other,' and 'This-My-Self,'" with the first of these indicating "the totality of value experience" (MT 110). "Everything has some value," accordingly, "for itself, for others, and for the whole" (MT 111). A cosmology, to be adequate to religious experience, would now have to provide a basis for this conviction—that the values we realize are immortal because they are contributions to the everlasting, divine reality of the universe. And indeed, the "consequent nature of God" already loomed large in Part V of *Process and Reality,* which was presented as "an interpretation of the religious experience of mankind" (PR 167).

In this chapter, we first saw how Whitehead's epistemology allows for re-

ligious experience within a naturalistic framework, then examined his estimation of the truths, relevant for cosmology, that come from this experience. In the following chapters, we will see how Whitehead's cosmology includes these notions, thereby providing a version of naturalism that is neither
materialistic nor atheistic.

Panexperientialism, Freedom, and the Mind–Body Relation

The primary method for overcoming the apparent conflict between science and religion, Whitehead has suggested, is to overcome the exaggerations on both sides. From the side of religion, the primary exaggeration has been supernaturalistic theism. The proposed correction of this exaggeration, a panentheistic version of naturalistic theism, will be developed in Chapters 4 through 8. From the side of the scientific community, the primary exaggeration since the latter part of the nineteenth century has been the sensationist, atheistic, materialistic form of naturalism, which, besides precluding a harmony between science and religion, is not adequate for science itself. Beginning with the issue of sensationism, Chapter 2 provided a naturalistic doctrine of perception that shows sensationism to involve an exaggeration of the truth that our physical sensory organs provide all our *clear and distinct, reliably accurate* perceptions of the world beyond ourselves.

The task of the present chapter is to provide a naturalistic alternative to the materialistic ontology of naturalism$_{sam}$. *Materialism* as used here, it should be recalled, involves a combination of two doctrines: (1) the mechanistic doctrine of nature, according to which the ultimate units of nature are entirely devoid of experience and self-determination; (2) the doctrine of non-dualism, according to which there are no other actualities, different in kind from the ultimate units of nature, to explain the activities of human beings and other living things.[1] Process philosophy also affirms a nondualistic on-

---

[1] To anticipate the discussion below: the truth involved in this materialistic position, from the perspective of process philosophy, is its replacement of dualism with a (pluralistic) monism, so that we need think of only one kind of efficient causation. The exaggerations in it follow

tology, but on the basis of a panexperientialist rather than a mechanistic account of the ultimate units of nature. To claim that panexperientialism is superior to materialism (as well as dualism) requires, of course, some criteria. I employ three.

First, an ontology should be *adequate to "the whole of the evidence."* This criterion means, above all, that the ontology should do justice to our *hard-core commonsense presuppositions* about the reality of human consciousness, mental causation, freedom, and normative ideals—which means, in effect, overcoming modernity's mind-body problem. An ontology should also be adequate to well-established *scientific facts* (insofar as these go beyond hard-core commonsense notions), such as the fact that there is no "nature at an instant," that the ultimate units of nature are discrete events, and that the present state of the world has come about through a long evolutionary process. It should also be able to explain such things as how time could have existed at the earliest stages of the evolution of our universe, how an intelligible notion of causation can be applied at the level of nature studied by physics and chemistry, and how scientific induction is rationally justifiable.

Second, an ontology should be *fully self-consistent* and *fully consistent with the epistemology* with which it is connected. This means, most elementarily, that the ontology should have *no logical inconsistencies* within itself. The ontology also should, as William Wainwright says (1998, 337), avoid *self-stultification.* That is, assuming the truth of the epistemology with which the ontology is connected, the ontology should contain no ideas that the epistemology declares unknowable, so that they must be slipped in through some back door.[2] The ontology should, furthermore, provide *an explanation for the epistemology with which it is connected.* It must, for example, account for the existence of scientists and philosophers with their conscious sensory percepts, their mathematical abilities, their concern for truth, and their logical, moral, and aesthetic norms.

Third, an ontology should be *fully naturalistic,* which most obviously means rejecting the possibility that the world's causal nexus could be interrupted. Being *fully* naturalistic, however, means that the ontology does not even contain an *implicit* supernaturalism, such as evolutionary transitions that, to be explained, would require supernatural interventions.

It would be hard, it seems, for any advocates of naturalism$_{sam}$ to take issue

---

from the fact that it retained the mechanistic doctrine of nature, which led it to two false conclusions: that all efficient causation is mechanistic and that all causation whatsoever is efficient (as distinct from final) causation.

[2] Self-stultification is similar, therefore, to the "performative self-contradiction" emphasized by Habermas and other critical theorists (see note 12 of Chapter 1).

with these criteria. Given this agreement, the argument that process philosophy, with its panexperientialism, can fulfill these criteria far better than can naturalism$_{sam}$ is of potentially momentous importance for the future of human culture. This chapter makes this argument. The development of the ontology in this chapter is oriented around the fourth, fifth, and sixth of the core doctrines of process philosophy, namely, (4) the doctrine of panexperientialism with organizational duality, (5) the doctrine that enduring individuals are serially ordered societies of actual entities, and (6) the doctrine that all actual entities have internal as well as external relations. The three-fold thesis of this chapter is that this ontology is more fully naturalistic than naturalism$_{sam}$, that it is otherwise more adequate for science than naturalism$_{sam}$, as illustrated especially by its capacity to solve the mind–body problem in a way that does justice to our hard-core commonsense assumptions, and that it provides a basis upon which ontological naturalism can express the belief, based on evidence from our religious intuitions, that the world is a locus of value-realization.

This chapter unfolds in the following way. The first section provides several reasons for being suspicious of the idea that the ultimate units of nature are "vacuous actualities," meaning individuals that are fully actual and yet devoid of experience. The second section provides some positive arguments in favor of panexperientialism, according to which all fully actual individuals do have experience. The third section explains a distinctive feature of the Whiteheadian form of panexperientialism, the doctrine that all *enduring* individuals are serially ordered *societies* of momentary actual entities (actual occasions), then shows how this doctrine allows us to conceptualize the relation between efficient and final causation, thereby the relation between freedom and determinism. The fourth section applies this doctrine to the problem of the compatibility of internal relations with pluralistic realism. The fifth section, pointing out that panexperientialism by itself would not necessarily allow for human freedom, mental causation, or even the unity of a moment of experience, explains another crucial feature of the Whiteheadian form of panexperientialism: the organizational duality between compound individuals and mere aggregational societies, which provides the final element needed to overcome modern philosophy's mind–body problem and thereby to affirm our hard-core commonsense assumptions about the reality, freedom, and efficacy of our conscious experience. The sixth section explains how persons can in a sense be different in kind, without being ontologically different, from elementary particles.

1. Reasons to Be Suspicious of Vacuous Actualities

At the root of modern ontology, in both its dualistic and materialistic forms, is the mechanistic view of nature. Although the term *mechanistic* refers primarily to doctrines about causation—that all causation is *efficient* (vs. final) causation, that all efficient causation occurs between contiguous events, and that all such causal relations are *external* relations—these causal doctrines presuppose a particular notion about what the ultimate units of nature are in themselves, namely, that they are wholly devoid of experience. It is because they have no experience and therefore no "inside" that they have no power to exercise final causation (self-determination in terms of a finis, or goal), no capacity to influence and be influenced by noncontiguous things, and no capacity to receive influence from other things into themselves. Whitehead uses the term *vacuous actuality* (PR 29, 167) to refer to this idea of things that are (1) fully actual and yet (2) wholly devoid of experience.

Although the assumption that the ultimate units of nature are vacuous actualities has been so widespread in modern thought as to seem to many thinkers to be a self-evident, commonsense truth if there ever was one, it is really only an example of soft-core common sense. It is *not* a hard-core commonsense notion because one can explicitly reject it without inconsistency. And, Whitehead argues, we have many reasons to reject it in favor of some version of panexperientialism.

The term *panexperientialism,* I should add, is my own,[3] not Whitehead's or Hartshorne's. The traditional term for the position that the ultimate units of the world contain experience (and perhaps spontaneity) is *panpsychism.* Although Whitehead did not use this term either, Hartshorne has. But this term, which is based on the word *psyche,* is less suitable for two reasons. It suggests, in the first place, that the ultimate units of the world are enduring things, as are psyches, whereas for Whitehead the ultimate units are momentary experiences ("occasions of experience"). In the second place, the term *panpsychism* suggests that these ultimate units contain rather high-level mentality, with consciousness. This second problem was, in fact, evidently Whitehead's own reason for not using the term (A. Johnson 1969, 354). Although Hartshorne later gave up this term, he replaced it with *psychicalism,* which still has the same two problems. Upon seeing the term *panexperientialism* used to expound his position, Hartshorne wrote: "I do not object to

---

[3] I first used the term *panexperientialism* in print, to my knowledge, in Cobb and Griffin 1977, 98.

'panexperientialism' instead of 'psychicalism,' and see advantages in that terminology" (Kane and Phillips 1989, 181).

In the next section, I will provide several positive reasons for affirming
panexperientialism. To prepare the way for that discussion, the present section provides several reasons for at least being suspicious of the modern assumption that the ultimate units of nature are vacuous actualities.

Suspect Motives behind the Early Modern Affirmation of Vacuous Actualities

One reason for being suspicious of this conception of the ultimate units
of nature—a reason that I have discussed at length elsewhere (Griffin 2000a,
chap. 5)—is that this idea was adopted by its seventeenth-century advocates,
such as Mersenne, Descartes, Boyle, and Newton, for sociological and theological rather than empirical reasons. The idea that the ultimate units of nature are bits of insentient matter, wholly devoid of experience and spontaneity, was useful in arguing for an omnipotent deity, supernatural miracles,
and the immortality of the human soul (which could, as such, fear hell and
hope for heaven after death). Such arguments supported the authority of the
hierarchical church and thereby the monarchy. The idea was adopted primarily for such reasons, not on the basis of any experimental facts.

Vacuous Actuality as a Doubly Speculative Idea

A second reason for suspicion is that the only idea we have of what something is *in itself* that is based on direct knowledge, rather than speculation, is
our idea of our own conscious experience. Any other ideas about the nature
of things *in themselves* are necessarily speculative. Some speculations, however, are more warranted by the relevant evidence than others.

The question at hand is which of the two speculative ideas about the ultimate units of nature—that they *do* or *do not* have experience—has more
evidential support. Many thinkers reject panexperientialism on the grounds
that it is too "metaphysical," meaning too speculative. What they fail to realize, however, is that the contrary idea, that the ultimate units of nature do
not have experience, is equally speculative.

It is, in fact, even *more* speculative. That is, we have direct knowledge that
"experiencing actualities" can exist because we are examples of such. In supposing that the ultimate units of nature are experiencing actualities, therefore, process philosophers are merely speculating that these entities are further exemplifications of this mode of existence. The position of materialists
and dualists, by contrast, involves not only a speculation about what these

entities are in themselves but *the additional speculation that a "vacuous actuality" is a metaphysically possible mode of existence.* That is, we have no direct experience of any actualities *as devoid of experience.* Many dualists and materialists, to be sure, seem to think they can tell, just by looking at things, that they are devoid of experience. The assumption implicit in this conclusion is that sensory perception, especially visual perception, involves a direct observation of nature. As Whitehead has emphasized, however, it is a very indirect way of perceiving nature. The fact that visual perception reveals no experience in nature, accordingly, may tell us more about the nature of sensory perception than it does about the nature of nature. In any case, because we have no direct knowledge that the phrase "vacuous actuality" even names a possible type of thing, the idea that the ultimate units of nature are vacuous actualities is far more speculative than the panexperientialist idea that they are experiencing actualities.

Berkeley's Question

A closely related reason to be suspicious of the very idea of "vacuous actuality" is the question famously raised by Bishop Berkeley. In response to the idea, endorsed by Cartesians and Newtonians alike, of "nature" as composed of insentient matter, Berkeley asked, What does it *mean* to say that things such as sticks and stones exist? Advocating, like Hume after him, conceptual empiricism, according to which concepts are meaningful only insofar as they are rooted in immediate experience, Berkeley asked what the phrase "to be" means. His answer was that it has only two experiential meanings: "to perceive" (*percipere*) and "to be perceived" (*percipi*). We know what it means to be a mind, defined as a perceiver, by being one. We thereby have an idea of what it means *to be actual.* Accordingly, we can meaningfully attribute minds to other people, and we can even meaningfully speak of God as an omniscient mind. If sticks and stones are *not* perceivers, however, then they must exemplify the only other intelligible sense we can give to the idea that they exist, which is that for them to exist is *to be perceived.* But something whose whole essence is to be perceived is simply an idea in a mind because it by definition cannot exist apart from being perceived by some mind. So although we can meaningfully attribute *actual* existence to God and other minds, Berkeley argued, we cannot do the same for sticks and stones: we do not know what it *means* to say that something is actual and yet devoid of experience. Such things, said Berkeley, should be attributed only ideal, not actual, existence.

Berkeley used this analysis to argue for the existence of God: because we cannot believe that sticks and stones go out of existence when no finite mind is perceiving them, there must be an omniscient mind who is perceiving them all the time. Like most other philosophers, Whitehead rejects this argument, holding instead that we know sticks and stones to have actual, not merely ideal, existence. However, Whitehead adds, Berkeley "made all the right criticisms" and asked the right question, namely, "What do we mean by things being realised in the world of nature?" (SMW 66, 67). The fact that we rightly reject Berkeley's idealist answer—that their existence is constituted by "being perceived within the unity of mind" (SMW 69)—does not mean that we can justifiably ignore either his question or his contention that "vacuous actuality" is a meaningless combination of words.

Spontaneity and Some Objects of Sensory Perception

Perhaps the main reason for assuming that the ultimate units of nature must be devoid of experience is that the inorganic world seems to be devoid of the primary basis for *inferring* that something has experience, namely, the capacity for spontaneity, self-determination, self-motion. We unhesitatingly attribute experience to squirrels and dogs because of their obviously spontaneous movements, but our paradigmatic examples of "physical things," such as rocks and tables, seem to be completely inert.

Science itself, however, has undermined this argument, showing that sensory perception of things such as rocks does not reveal their ultimate constituents. Of course, it has long been assumed that the ultimate units of visible things were to be understood by analogy with them: atoms were assumed to be essentially like billiard balls, only smaller. However, the chief philosophical implication of quantum physics, as stressed by both White-head (SMW 35–36) and Milič Čapek (1991, 135, 205–11), is that this assumption is false. The fact that sticks and stones as such are devoid of spontaneity, accordingly, is not a valid basis for assuming their ultimate constituents to be devoid of this usual concomitant of experience. (In distinguishing between the sticks or stones as such and their "ultimate constituents," suggesting that the latter could have experience and spontaneity while the former do not, I am anticipating the discussion of "aggregational societies" in the fifth section.)

The Abstract Character of Physics

One reason why many people, including many philosophers, suppose the ultimate units of nature to be devoid of experience is that physics, the branch of science that studies such entities, ascribes no experience to them. That position, however, assumes that by *not ascribing* experience to them, physics *positively denies* that they have experience. The truth is that physics as such, at least physics as it has existed thus far, takes no position on this issue. In Whitehead's words, "physics ignores what anything is in itself. Its entities are merely considered in respect to their extrinsic reality" (SMW 153).[4] To assume that electrons have no experience because the descriptions of (present-day) physics say nothing about experience, therefore, is to commit the "fallacy of misplaced concreteness," which involves taking an abstract description of something, produced in terms of certain limited interests, for a complete description of the thing in its concreteness (SMW 51; PR 7).

Inadequacy for Science

Besides not being justified by physics, the materialistic idea of the ultimate units of nature has even proved to be *inadequate for* physics and the other natural sciences, as was discussed in the fifth section of Chapter 1. Being inconsistent with the durational character of the ultimate units of nature, the rationality of induction, the intelligible attribution of causation to the entities studied by physics and chemistry, the intelligible attribution of time to the billions of years of evolution prior to the rise of life, the evolutionary emergence of living organisms, and the emergence of organisms with consciousness and freedom, the idea that the ultimate units of nature are vacuous actualities is an inadequate basis for a scientific realism.

The Mind-Body Problem

Although the mind-body problem—understood as the twofold problem of how the mind emerged and how it interacts with the body—is now recognized as a problem for science, it has for much longer been recognized as a problem, perhaps the *chief* problem, for philosophy. Given the notion that the ultimate units of nature are vacuous actualities, the only two options for thinking of the relation between one's body, including the brain, and one's experience, usually referred to as "the mind," are dualism and materialism. Dualists, who point out the insuperable problems in materialism, and mate-

---

[4] That statement, true of physics in Whitehead's time, is still largely true today. But a few physicists, believing that physics now must ask what things such as electrons are in themselves, have argued that they must involve experience (see the mention of Bohm and Hiley [1993] in Section 2). One philosopher who supports this development is Galen Strawson, who has (rightly) suggested that the mind-body problem can be solved from a physicalist viewpoint only with the development of a "qualitative-character-of-experience physics" (1994, 88–89).

rialists, who point out the insuperable problems in dualism, have been de-
bating each other since the time of Descartes and Hobbes. After more than
three centuries, neither side is close to providing an adequate position.

Indeed, leading advocates on both sides are now admitting that a solution
to the mind-body problem seems to be impossible in principle. From the
side of dualism, this admission has been made by Karl Popper (Popper and
Eccles 1977, 105) and, more forthrightly, Geoffrey Madell (1988), who admits that "the appearance of consciousness in the course of evolution must
appear for the dualist to be an utterly inexplicable emergence" (140). From
the materialist side, the difficulty of understanding how human experience
could have arisen out of purely physical brain cells has been underscored by
Thomas Nagel (1986, 176), William Seager (1991, 4), William S. Robinson
(1988, 29), Galen Strawson (1994, 50), and Colin McGinn (1991), who, besides saying that the "difficulty here is one of principle: we have no understanding of how consciousness could emerge from an aggregation of non-
conscious elements" (213), states that the time has come "to admit candidly
that we cannot resolve the mystery" (viii). When we bring in the problem
of understanding how this human experience could make free decisions that
would then guide bodily behavior, we can add the names of many others
who admit defeat, such as John Searle (1984, 85–97) and Jaegwon Kim
(1993, 367).[5] This dead end reached by both dualists and materialists should
be taken—as I have argued at length elsewhere (Griffin 1998a)—as a reductio ad absurdum of the assumption they hold in common: the idea that
the ultimate units of nature are vacuous actualities.

Understanding the World's Order

The conception of the ultimate units of the world as vacuous actualities
also makes it impossible to understand how the world's most fundamental
order could have arisen. The early modern worldview understood it in
terms of an external imposition by a supernatural deity. The late modern rejection of this explanation does not change the fact it is the only possible
one, given the assumption that the ultimate units of nature are nonexperiencing actualities, which are incapable of being influenced inwardly. Insofar

---

[5] Habermas apparently holds, in spite of his disavowal of any "metaphysical" beliefs about
what nature is "in itself," that it contains no iota of subjectivity and self-determination. In criticism, Peter Dews rightly asks: "[W]here does the subjective freedom of human beings emerge
from, if pre-human nature reveals no self-related structures and no capacity—even an
unreflective one—for self-determination in accordance with an immanent norm?" (1995,
158).

as we reject supernaturalism and yet believe that the world's order requires an explanation, we should be sceptical of a conception of nature's ultimate units that makes a naturalistic explanation impossible.

Understanding the World as a Locus of Value-Realization

Religious experience, as we have seen, suggests that the world is ordered for the sake of the realization of intrinsic values. If the ultimate units of nature are thought of as vacuous actualities, which by definition means devoid of intrinsic value, it is impossible to understand how things with intrinsic value could have arisen—unless a supernatural insertion is assumed.[6] Although this problem can be regarded as simply a rephrasing of the mind-body problem, it is helpful to bring out the distinctively religious aspect of this problem. The issue of value as well as order, therefore, should especially lead religious thinkers to be sceptical of the idea of vacuous actualities at the base of nature.

2. Positive Reasons to Affirm Panexperientialism

To have several reasons for being dubious of the hitherto dominant view of nature's ultimate units is, of course, already to have a basis for moving toward the alternative form of realism, according to which they are *not* vacuous. The hitherto dominant view has been so pervasive, nevertheless, that it would be helpful also to have some positive evidence for panexperientialism, understood here as the doctrine that the ultimate units of nature have both experience and spontaneity. Whitehead's philosophy provides several such reasons.

Human Experience as a Fact of Nature

The most obvious reason, once dualism has been rejected, is that our own conscious experience must be regarded as part of "nature." Although a moment of human experience is a particularly high-grade event, it should not be regarded as different in kind from other natural events. Whitehead thereby accepts the central demand of materialistic mechanism, "that no arbitrary breaks be introduced into nature" (SMW 73), while providing the basis for

---

[6] This point has been emphasized both by Richard Swinburne (1979, chap. 9; 1986, 198–99), who accepts the idea of such an insertion, and by Colin McGinn (1991, 17n, 45), who rejects it.

overcoming its inadequacies. What makes my own experience different from any other occurrence in the world is that it is the only one I know from the inside. We each should take our own self-knowledge, accordingly, as a privileged peek into the nature of nature (in spite of the criticisms that have been raised against the idea of "privileged access"). Although we have tended to think of our experience itself as an event different in kind from the things that we experience, we should realize instead that the uniqueness here is epistemic, not ontological: "The private psychological field is merely the event considered from its own standpoint" (SMW 150). Given this inside view into the nature of nature, we can then generalize what we have learned about natural units to other such units (SMW 73). In so doing, of course, we have to decide which elements in our high-level experience are plausibly generalizable to all experiences whatsoever. But the very rejection of dualism between experience and nature, in favor of the view that experience is fully natural, implies that experience of some sort does go all the way down, characterizing even the most primitive units of nature.[7]

Knowledge of Nature Acquired from Direct Prehension of Our Bodies

The truth of panexperientialism is suggested not only by our direct knowledge of our own conscious experience but also by our direct knowledge of our bodily parts. Although the lingering effects of dualism may leave many philosophers reluctant to accept their own experience as a full-fledged instance of a natural thing or event, it is widely accepted that our own bodies, at least, are part of the natural world. And they are the part that, aside from our conscious experience itself, we observe most directly: our sensory perception of the world beyond our bodies is a far less direct mode of observation, being dependent upon our direct prehension of data transmitted to our brains from our sensory organs. If we are truly empirical, therefore, we should base our ideas of the nature of nature more on our prehensions of our bodies than we do on our sensory perceptions of the world beyond our bodies. "The human body," emphasizes Whitehead, "provides our closest experience of the interplay of actualities in nature" (MT 115). The question, then, is what we learn from this experience.

As we saw in Chapter 2, physical feelings are *conformal* feelings, in which we feel the feelings of other things with sympathetic subjective forms. This

---

[7] As Hans Jonas declared: "Since finality—striving towards a goal—appears in a subjectively manifest form in certain natural beings, namely living beings, and can hence become effective in an objectively causal way, it cannot be entirely alien to nature, which brought it forth; it must itself be 'natural'" (1988, 23; translated in Dews 1995, 163).

description, Whitehead emphasizes, is true of our prehensions of our bodies. "[A]mong our fundamental experiences," he emphasizes, is the "direct feeling of the derivation of emotion from the body" (MT 159–60). Whitehead's point, in other words, is that *we directly experience the fact that our bodily parts have their own experiences.* He says, in fact, that "the predominant basis of perception is the perception of the various bodily organs, as passing on their experiences" (PR 119).

Whitehead is providing here, it should be noted, a phenomenological account of what is directly given to experience. It is very different, however, from phenomenologist Edmund Husserl's account of the given in terms of "essences" (which for Whitehead are abstracted products of construction and simplification). Commenting on the fact that both he and Whitehead had independently been influenced by Wordsworth, Hartshorne writes:

> [Wordsworth] was describing nature so far as given to our direct intuitions. . . . The "ocean of feelings" that Whitehead ascribes to physical reality is not only thought; so far as our bodies are made of this reality, it is intuited. What is not intuited but only thought is nature as consisting of absolutely insentient stuff or process. No such nature is directly given to us. . . . Wordsworth was doing a phenomenology of direct experience far better than Husserl ever did. . . . Wordsworth seems to have influenced Whitehead much as he did me. He saved us from materialism and even dualism. Both result from an inadequate phenomenology. (1991a, 13)

Whitehead himself pointed to this phenomenological basis for his position. Remarking that his philosophy "attributes 'feeling' throughout the actual world," he adds: "It bases this doctrine upon the directly observed fact that 'feeling' survives as a known element constitutive of the 'formal' existence of such actual entities as we can best observe" (PR 177). From his phenomenology of bodily experience, it follows that "the body is composed of various centres of experience imposing the expression of themselves on each other" (MT 23).

Given this insight into that part of nature that—aside from our own minds—we are in position to observe most directly, Whitehead concluded, we should generalize this knowledge to the rest of nature. After the remark that "the predominant basis of perception is the perception of the various bodily organs, as passing on their experiences," he adds:

> It is the accepted doctrine in physical science that a living body is to be interpreted according to what is known of other sections of the physical universe. This is a sound axiom; but it is double-edged. For it carries with it the con-

verse deduction that other sections of the universe are to be interpreted in accordance with what we know of the human body. (PR 119)

We have here, it should be emphasized, Whitehead's answer to the question as to how we can think of *causality* in nature: we can do so by thinking of actualities as passing on their experiences to other actualities. Whitehead denies the reality of causation "in the old sense of separate and distinct substances having accidental interaction" (A. Johnson 1969, 359). Efficient causation is to be understood instead wholly in terms of experiences receiving content from prior experiences.

This panexperientialist conclusion is supported, furthermore, by our sensory perception itself. The idea that the ultimate actualities of nature are vacuous is mutually implicated with the assumption that they are "simply located," which means that they contain no essential reference either to the past or to the future (SMW 49; S 38). As such, they would be different in kind from our own experience, with its incorporation of past events and its anticipation of future events. Our sensory perception, however, implies that this is not true of the bodily cells constituting our sensory system. This implication follows from a twofold fact about sensory perception: on the one hand, sensory perception directly depends entirely upon functionings that occur within our bodies; on the other hand, it usually tells us about things beyond our bodies. In Whitehead's words: "Your perception takes place where you are, and is entirely dependent on how your body is functioning. But this functioning of the body in one place, exhibits for your cognisance an aspect of the distant environment. . . . If this cognisance conveys knowledge of a transcendent world, it must be because the event which is the bodily life unifies in itself aspects of the universe" (SMW 91–92). The general reliability of sensory perception, in other words, implies that the bodily cells comprising the sensory system are *prehenders,* grasping aspects of prior events and passing them on to subsequent events. If I see the sun, for example, I can do so only because the cells in the retina of my eye grasped photons that had been emitted from the sun eight minutes earlier. The cells in the retina then had to transmit this information to the brain by means of a chain of neuronal events in the optic nerve. Each of these events, rather than being simply located, involved an essential reference to past events and to future events in this temporal chain of transmission. So even though the *data* of sensory perception give us a purely spatial world, the *process* of sensory perception itself suggests that the cells in our bodies are not purely spatial but are *prehensive unifications of data from prior events,* being in this respect analogous to moments of our own experience. Whitehead's double-edged axiom then leads to the conclusion that this must be true of all the events comprising nature.

The Unessential Nature of Consciousness and Sensory Perception

Whitehead's doctrine of perception, by showing consciousness and sensory perception to be secondary, unessential features of experience, provides support for panexperientialism. By saying that "consciousness presupposes experience, and not experience consciousness" (PR 53), Whitehead could intelligibly attribute *experience* to things surely not capable of *consciousness* (understood to involve clear discrimination among data of experience, including a contrast between what *is* given and what *might* have been given but is not). And by regarding sensory perception as *derivative* from perception in the mode of causal efficacy, he not only could intelligibly attribute perceptual experience (in the mode of causal efficacy) to entities devoid of sensory organs but also could appeal to the behavior of lower forms of existence to confirm the derivative nature of sensory perception. "It does not seem to be the sense of causal awareness that the lower beings lack," Whitehead observes, "so much as variety of sense-presentation, and then vivid distinctness of presentational immediacy" (PR 176). He could, furthermore, give more content to the idea of low-grade experience by his rejection of the Humean view that emotional and purposeful experience are derivative from sensory perception because he could say that "the emotional appetitive elements in our conscious experience are those which most closely resemble the basic elements of all physical experience" (PR 163). In these ways, Whitehead's epistemology provides support for his description of the world, cited by Hartshorne, as an "ocean of feeling" (PR 166).

Indirect Evidence from Physics

Indirect evidence for the experiential nature of the ultimate units of nature is also supplied, Whitehead argued, by twentieth-century physics. This physics, as we have seen, says nothing about experience as such. It does, however, suggest that the ultimate units of nature involve *duration,* apart from which experience would be inconceivable. This suggestion is made by the idea that there is no "nature at an instant," which implies that the ultimate units of nature are not purely spatial entities but *spatiotemporal events.* The same thing is implied by relativity physics, with its dictum that space and time are inseparable. The relevant background idea here is the rejection of the "absolute" view of both space and time, according to which space would exist even if there were no objects and time would exist even if there

were no events. Almost all physicists and philosophers now hold the "relational" view, according to which space depends on the relations among spatial objects and time on the relations among temporal events. When this idea
is combined with the idea that space and time are inseparable, the implication is that *space-time exists only because spatiotemporal events occur.* The ultimate
units of nature, accordingly, must be events, with temporal duration as well
as spatial extension. This point is important because if they have *duration,*
they have a necessary condition for experience. It is, in fact, hard to understand of what the duration could consist *except* experience.

The idea that the ultimate units of existence are spatiotemporal events
is expressed by Whitehead's doctrine that the fully actual entities of the
world are "actual occasions," the term he used to emphasize precisely this
combination of temporal and spatial extensiveness (PR 77). The idea that
such occasions, with their duration, are best thinkable as momentary *experiences* is expressed in his doctrine that all actual occasions are "occasions of
experience."

More Direct Evidence from Science

In addition to the indirect scientific evidence for panexperientialism provided by the reasons just discussed for thinking of the ultimate units of nature as durational events, more direct evidence has been forthcoming. For
example, whereas it was common until rather recently to assume that experience is limited to the higher animals, some leading ethologists, including
Donald Griffin (1992), now give reasons to attribute experience at least as
far down as bees. Going much further down, Stuart Hameroff has recently
summarized a wide range of evidence suggesting that single-cell organisms,
such as amoebae and paramecia, have a primitive type of experience (1994,
97–99). Going even further down, from eukaryotic to prokaryotic cells,
some biologists have provided evidence for a rudimentary form of decision
making, based on a rudimentary form of memory, in bacteria (Adler and Tse
1974; Goldbeter and Koshland 1982). Going still further down, macromolecules, such as DNA molecules, are now understood more as organisms than
as machines (E. Keller 1983). Finally, going all the way down, quantum
physics implies, according to some philosophers (Seager 1995, 282–83) and
some physicists (Bohm and Hiley 1993, 384–87), that the behavior of the
elementary units of nature can best be explained by attributing to them
something analogous to our own mentality.

There is, in sum, a strong cumulative case for the Whiteheadian idea that
the ultimate units of nature are best understood as "occasions of experience." Because dualism has equated *experience* with *mentality,* the doctrine

that all actual entities are occasions of experience might sound like simply a new version of idealism, according to which everything is mental. That, however, is emphatically not Whitehead's doctrine. Every occasion of experience is said to be *dipolar,* having both a physical pole and a mental pole (PR 108, 239). The physical pole is the occasion's prehension of influences from past actual occasions; the mental pole, which originates with conceptual prehensions (prehensions of pure possibilities, or eternal objects), is the occasion's self-determination. The physical pole, in other words, is constituted by *efficient causation* from the past, while the mental pole is the occasion's *final causation* in the sense of self-determination in terms of an ideal.

With this set of ideas, we move toward Whitehead's solution to the problem of freedom and determinism. Panexperientialism by itself does not necessarily solve this problem, as shown by the fact that some forms of it, under the name *panpsychism,* have been deterministic (e.g., Rensch 1977). Essential to Whitehead's solution is his view that the most individual actual entities are momentary, dipolar occasions of experience, which means that *enduring* individuals, such as human psyches, are serially ordered societies of such occasions. I turn now to this fifth core doctrine of Whiteheadian-Hartshornean process philosophy.

3. Enduring Individuals as Serially Ordered Societies

"The real actual things that endure," stipulates Whitehead, "are all societies" (AI 204). The negative point here is that the fully actual entities, the things that are actual individuals in the strictest sense of the term, are not *enduring* individuals, such as electrons, but *momentary events.* An electron is already a *society* of individual actual entities, which are, as we have seen, momentary "actual occasions." An electron is, to be sure, different from what we normally think of as a society, in which there are social relations among a number of coexisting individuals. In an electron, there is only one member—namely, one electronic occasion—at a time, so the relations between the members are purely temporal: each member is socially related to the earlier and the later members of that society. Such a society, therefore, has purely temporal or serial order. It is a society insofar as (1) each member shares a common form and (2) that form is derived from prior members and passed on to later members of that society. Protons, atoms, molecules, living cells, and animal psyches are other examples of serially ordered societies. Whitehead also sometimes speaks of these enduring individuals as *personally* ordered societies, but he recognizes that this term, by virtue of suggesting that consciousness is necessarily involved, can be misleading (PR 34–35).

He also refers to such things as "enduring objects" (PR 34–35), thereby bringing out the fact that what endures is not a subject (or substance) but merely an "object," meaning the common element of form that is transmitted from occasion to occasion. Another term, which I often use, is *enduring individuals*.

Although some philosophers have assumed this doctrine to be an unessential feature of this form of process philosophy, so that it could be rejected without seriously affecting the coherence of the position, nothing could be further from the truth. This doctrine is essential both to Whitehead's defense of freedom and to his reconciliation of internal relatedness with pluralistic realism. I will deal with the issue of freedom—that is, reconciling final with efficient causation—in the present section, saving internal relations for the next.

Reconciling Efficient and Final Causation

Having commented that Aristotle's philosophy "led to a wild overstressing of the notion of 'final causes' during the Christian middle ages; and then, by a reaction, to the correlative overstressing of the notion of 'efficient causes' during the modern scientific period," Whitehead adds: "One task of a sound metaphysics is to exhibit final and efficient causes in their proper relation to each other" (PR 84). As his statement suggests, modern thought has had difficulty doing justice to our inevitable presuppositions about these two kinds of causation. For example, I know that my conscious experience is heavily influenced by the efficient causation of my body on it. But I also presuppose that this influence is not total determination because I presuppose that I have a degree of freedom to decide just how to respond to it. I presuppose, in other words, that I make this decision on the basis of influences from the world but also in the light of some goal I want to achieve, some possibility I want to realize—which is final causation. I also anticipate, furthermore, that this free decision will in turn become an efficient cause, directing my bodily activity in the next moment. "A satisfactory cosmology," Whitehead points out, "must explain the interweaving of efficient and final causation" (FR 28).

The Failure of Modern Thought

Modern philosophical and scientific thought has been unable to explain this interweaving of final and efficient causation. Descartes's dualism, for example, attributed the capacity for final causation only to mental substances, saying that physical substances could exercise only efficient causation. He did endorse the interaction of our bodies and our conscious experience described in the previous paragraph. But he could not explain how this inter-action is conceivable—how a mental substance capable of final causation could also exert efficient causation upon purely physical substances, and how these physical substances could exert causal influence back upon a mental substance. He could not explain this interaction, that is, without appealing to divine omnipotence.

Some of Descartes's successors, most notably Nicolas Malebranche, took this solution further, or at least made it more explicit, by saying that there is really no interaction between mind and body. When I see my dinner before me, it is not because my sensory organs are really conveying information to my mind but only because, on the occasion of there being food in front of me, God causes me to see food; when I decide to use a fork to get some food, my hand moves not because my decision causes it to do so but only because God, on the occasion of my decision, causes my hand to move. In this doctrine of "occasionalism," there is really no interaction of final and efficient causation. Carrying this denial a step further, Leibniz articulated a doctrine of "pre-established harmony," according to which God created the mind and the body as autonomous systems running along parallel with each other: I see the food because it was ordained at the moment of creation that it would be there and that I would see it, and my hand moves following my decision to lift it because God had likewise ordained that it would do so. Leibniz was not a dualist, but he might as well have been. Although he ar-ticulated a form of panpsychism, saying that all things in the world are, or are composed of, "monads," all of which enjoy perception, he declared all the monads to be "windowless," meaning that they had no openings to the outside world, so that they could not *really* perceive one another. Even more ridiculously, if that is possible, some more recent thinkers have affirmed this "parallelism" between mind and body without a God to establish it: some-how mind and body just happen to run along "in sync" with each other. In all these post-Cartesian views, the mind makes decisions, thereby exercising final causation, but this causation makes no difference in the physical world, in which efficient causation is alone operative.

The doctrine of *epiphenomenalism,* according to which the mind is a "non-efficacious byproduct of the brain," also does violence to the relation we presuppose between efficient and final causation. Epiphenomenalism allows the body to exert causation upon conscious experience (although without any explanation as to how this is possible); and one version of epiphenome-nalism allows this conscious experience to exercise a degree of final causa-tion, in the sense of determining some of its own experiences. But epiphe-nomenalism, by definition, does not allow any such final causation to become "mental causation" in the sense of efficient causation upon the body (sometimes called "downward causation"): my decision still cannot cause my hand to move.[8]

The interweaving of final and efficient causation that we all presuppose in practice also cannot be explained by materialism. Some versions of materialism portray themselves as more adequate to our experience than epiphenomenalism, by allowing our decisions to exert downward causation upon our bodies. However, besides the fact that these "decisions" turn out, upon examination, to involve no final causation, being instead completely determined by the (upward) efficient causation from the body, they are not given any truly causal role but are said to be mere concomitants, as epiphenomenalism more explicitly says, of bodily causation, which is understood to be devoid of any final causation (see Griffin 1998a, 37–38 and 218–42). Materialism, accordingly, is even less capable than dualism and epiphenomenalism of conceptualizing the interweaving of final and efficient causation that we all presuppose in practice.

Whitehead's Solution

Whitehead's solution to this problem depends upon his doctrine that the fully actual entities are not enduring individuals but momentary events understood as "occasions of experience."[9] This core doctrine is crucial because it lies behind the distinctive nature of the Whiteheadian type of process philosophy, according to which there are *two fundamental types of process:* concrescence and transition (PR 210). The term *concrescence* is used for the process of becoming that occurs *within* an occasion of experience because this is the process through which it becomes fully concrete. The term *transition* refers to the process that occurs *between* one occasion and succeeding occasions. These two kinds of process involve our two kinds of causation: "Concrescence moves towards its final cause," whereas "transition is the vehicle of the efficient cause" (PR 210). This distinction between two types of process is crucial for conceptualizing how final and efficient causation are related because it allows them to occur successively rather than simultaneously.

To explain: Whitehead accepts the Aristotelian principle, which he calls

---

[8] The term *epiphenomenalism* was suggested by Thomas Huxley, who said that consciousness appears to be "completely without any power of modifying [the] working of the body, just as the steam whistle . . . of a locomotive engine is without influence on its machinery" (1893, 239–40). For a recent explication and defense of epiphenomenalism, see Campbell 1984; for a critique, see Griffin 1997a, 24–25.

[9] In many recent discussions of causation and agency, *personal agency* has been strongly contrasted with *event causation*. Whitehead's philosophy, by understanding the most fundamental events of the world as "occasions of experience," shows how these two models can be reconciled.

the "ontological principle," that only fully *actual* entities can *act*—that is, exert causation of any type, whether final causation (in the sense of self-determination) [10] or efficient causation (PR 24, 40). The question, then, is what the fully actual entities are. To answer that they are enduring individuals, such as the enduring human mind or soul, creates a problem: if we remain true to human experience, saying that the mind not only exercises self-causation but also both *receives* efficient causation from the body and *exerts* efficient causation back upon the body, we face a conceptual difficulty. Final causation (as understood here) is self-causation or self-determination, a process through which something becomes fully determinate, and it is only as fully determinate that something could conceivably exert efficient causation, that is, causal influence upon something else. In every fraction of a second, however, billions of causal influences are being exerted upon the mind from the neurons in the brain. The question is how the mind's process of self-determination could ever culminate in a definite decision. This decision, of course, is to be made largely on the basis of information being received from the body. But, we would have to imagine, just as a decision was about to be made, more information would be received. Then, just as a decision was about to be made on the basis of this new information, still more information would need to be taken account of, and so on. This process would go on endlessly, with the result that the mind would never be able to make a definite decision with which to influence the body.

In Whitehead's view, by contrast, we need not think of final causation as occurring simultaneously with either the reception or the exercise of efficient causation. These three processes happen successively. An actual occasion begins by receiving efficient causation from the past; this is the occasion's physical pole or phase. It then, *without letting in any more influences from without,* [11] exercises its self-determining final causation; this is the occasion's mental pole or phase. Then, after this process of final causation is complete, it exerts efficient causation upon subsequent occasions. It is part and parcel of this doctrine that each actual entity exists in two modes. It exists first *subjectively,* as a subject of experience, with its physical and mental poles. It then exists *objectively,* as an object for later subjects, thereby exerting efficient causation upon them.

To emphasize the idea that an enduring individual, such as a psyche or a proton, involves a rapid succession of occasions of experience, each of which

[10] Although Whitehead primarily uses the term *final causation* in this sense, to refer to an actual occasion's act of aiming toward an ideal end, he sometimes uses it for the ideal aimed at, as in the quotation from PR 151 a few paragraphs later.

[11] During the occasion's mental phase, one could say, it is a "windowless monad," as no influences can either enter or leave.

exists first as a subject of experience exercising final causation and then as an object exerting efficient causation, Whitehead uses Locke's phrase "perpetual perishing." Whitehead's point is simply that the occasion's *subjectivity,* or *subjective immediacy,* must perish before the occasion can exist as an object for later occasions, because until an occasion's final causation or self-determination is complete, it *is* nothing determinate and therefore could not exert causal influence upon anything else.

Whitehead's choice of terms, however, has led to great confusion. Some interpreters have taken the term *perishing* too literally, to mean that the occasion loses its very actuality. For example, according to Ivor Leclerc, "only concrescing, i.e., 'acting' entities are *actual* in the full, proper sense. The acting of antecedent actualities is completed; as such, they are, in the strict sense, no longer 'actual'" (1958, 101). In the same vein, William Christian says of a completed occasion that it "has now perished and is no longer actual" (1959, 322). Then, pointing out that "the only 'reasons' according to the ontological principle are *actual* entities" (Christian 1959, 322), Leclerc and Christian conclude that past occasions, being no longer actual, could not exert efficient causation upon the present. Christian even says that because they have perished, past occasions "cannot serve as the reason for the fact that they are now given." Having created this artificial problem, Christian suggests a solution—reminiscent of Malebranche's occasionalism (as Christian is aware [329])—based on Whitehead's doctrine, to be discussed in later chapters, that all actual occasions are taken up into God. Although present occasions, says Christian, could not *directly* prehend past occasions, they can *indirectly* prehend them by prehending them in God. To influence my body, then, I must first influence God, who influences my body. A greater distortion of Whitehead's position can hardly be imagined.

That this is not at all what Whitehead meant by *perishing* can be seen simply by looking at the passages in which he explains what he does mean. In his first definition of the term, he says:

> [A]ctual entities "perpetually perish" subjectively, but are immortal objectively. Actuality in perishing acquires objectivity, while it loses subjective immediacy. It loses the final causation which is its internal principle of unrest, and it acquires efficient causation. (PR 29)

What perishes, in other words, is not actuality but merely subjective immediacy, with its final causation or self-determination. Indeed, this perishing of subjective immediacy is *the very means by which the actual occasion acquires objectivity and thereby the capacity to exert efficient causation.* In a later statement, discussing Plato's suggestion that "not-being is itself a form of being," Whitehead says: "When they perish, occasions pass from the immediacy of being into the not-being of immediacy. But that does not mean that they are nothing. They remain 'stubborn fact.'" He adds: "Thus 'perishing' is the assumption of a role in a transcendent future. A pure physical prehension is how an occasion in its immediacy of being absorbs another occasion which has passed into the objective immortality of its not-being. It is how the past lives in the present. It is causation" (AI 237). As these passages show, Whitehead's doctrine of the perishing of actual entities, far from being in tension with his doctrine that all actual entities exert efficient causation, is the *basis* for this doctrine.

Because the term has proved to be so misleading, however, it would be better to replace the language of *perpetual perishing* with that of the *perpetual oscillation* between the two kinds of process, concrescence and transition. The creative advance of the world, therefore, involves a perpetual oscillation between efficient and final causation. Employing the idea that concrescence is a private process, internal to an occasion, whereas transition is a public process, Whitehead expresses this idea of a rhythmic process:

> The creative process is rhythmic: it swings from the publicity of many things to the individual privacy; and it swings back from the private individual to the publicity of the objectified individual. The former swing is dominated by the final cause, which is the ideal; and the latter swing is dominated by the efficient cause, which is actual. (PR 151)

Using this notion that all enduring individuals, such as minds and brain cells, involve a perpetual oscillation between efficient and final causation, we can give conceptual expression to our hard-core commonsense assumptions about our free mental causation. In any particular moment, my conscious experience arises out of the efficient causation of past actualities, most impressively the immediately antecedent occasions of my own experience and the immediately antecedent occasions of experience constituting my body at that moment. (This is the physical pole of the occasion of experience.) Then, being initially constituted by these influences from the past (including an "initial aim" from God, to be discussed in later chapters), I freely decide exactly how to respond to them, which involves deciding upon my "subjective aim," meaning the complex aim to be realized in that occasion of experience. This aim is twofold, being directed both at my immediate "satisfaction" and at my intended influence upon subsequent events, including most directly my immediately following occasions of experience and the state of my body in the next moment. Deciding upon and realizing this

twofold aim constitutes the final causation, or self-determination, of that occasion of experience (which is its mental or conceptual pole). When satisfaction is reached, the occasion of experience then exerts efficient causation
upon subsequent occasions, most immediately my next occasion of experience and the living occasions of experience in my brain cells, which prehend
that previous occasion of experience in terms of its aims for them.

In this way, Whitehead's doctrine that all enduring individuals are serially
ordered societies of occasions of experience provides one of the essential ingredients in his explanation of our threefold presupposition that our conscious experience is heavily influenced by our bodies, that our conscious
experience nevertheless makes somewhat free decisions, and that these decisions then influence our bodily behavior.

The fact that Whitehead's social doctrine of enduring individuals is central to his explanation of the interweaving of final and efficient causation
seems to be widely unappreciated among Whitehead scholars. For example,
several philosophers have argued that Whitehead's conception of the human
being should be rejected in favor of some version of the traditional view that
the human being as a whole, or at least the human soul, is a single actual entity (Bertocci 1972; Edwards 1975; Fetz 1991; Kirkpatrick 1973; Moreland
1988; Pailin 1989, 54). Not one of them, however, mentions the fact that this
modification would entail the loss of Whitehead's distinctive way of doing
justice to our hard-core commonsense presuppositions as to the interweaving of final and efficient causation in the relation between the body and the
mind,[12] which was one of the chief purposes of his philosophy and arguably
one of his greatest achievements.

A more complete understanding of Whitehead's solution to the mind-
body problem will require an examination of his doctrine of compound in-

[12] These critiques of Whitehead's position typically claim to be upholding common sense
against Whitehead's violation of it, on the grounds that a person *seems* to be a single actual entity enduring through time rather than a temporally ordered society of distinct occasions of
experience. But these critiques really amount to an appeal to merely *soft-core* common sense
as a basis for rejecting Whitehead's way of doing justice to our *hard-core* common sense. Although there is no space here for an extensive response to these critiques, it can be pointed
out that they generally share a number of misinterpretations of Whitehead's position: the idea
that if the human being enduring through time is not simply a single actual entity, we cannot
say that the same "self," "person," or "I" exists at different times (see especially Moreland
1988, 196, which suggests that Whitehead regards the enduring person as "a mere heap of successive temporal moments"); the idea, spread by Ivor Leclerc (1958, 1972, 1977) and Edward
Pols (1967, 1975, 1982), that Whitehead considered only subatomic occasions to be truly actual entities (see especially Fetz 1991, 1–4); and that, therefore, Whitehead's description of the
human being as a society means that it is a mere multiplicity of extremely minute events, with
no higher unity (see especially Fetz 1991, 4–6).

dividuals. First, however, we need to look at another of the benefits of the doctrine of enduring individuals as serially ordered societies: how it allows us to affirm pluralistic realism as well as internal relations, both of which also belong to our hard-core common sense.

4. Internal Relations, External Relations, and Pluralistic Realism

"[O]ur general sense of existence," Whitehead observes, involves being "one item among others, in an efficacious actual world" (PR 178). To be adequate, accordingly, a philosophy needs to affirm *pluralistic realism,* the doctrine that reality consists of a plurality of actual entities. And as our discussions of perception, causation, induction, and time have shown, adequacy also requires the affirmation that actual entities are internally related to— that is, partially constituted by their prehensions of—other actual entities. Philosophers have generally found it impossible, however, to affirm both these doctrines. Most who have affirmed pluralistic realism have done so by insisting that the actualities are only externally related to one another, as exemplified both by modern materialism, which is generally endorsed by the present scientific community, and by Leibniz's system of windowless monads. Most who have affirmed internal relations have been led to a monistic universe.

At the root of this problem, according to Whitehead's analysis, is the assumption that the ultimate units of the world are enduring individuals. Given this assumption, philosophical analysis was led to the conclusion that actual entities are "substances with undifferentiated endurance of essential attributes" (PR 77). The activity of such substances was described as "the occasional modification of their accidental qualities and relations" (PR 78). A fully actual entity was described in terms of "continuous stuff with permanent attributes, enduring without differentiation, and retaining its self-identity through [some] stretch of time" (PR 78). Driving home what he finds problematic in that traditional view, Whitehead adds: "The stuff undergoes change in respect to accidental qualities and relations; but it is numerically self-identical in its character of one actual entity throughout its accidental adventures." Then, emphasizing one of his reasons for rejecting this view, he declares: "The admission of this fundamental metaphysical concept has wrecked the various systems of pluralistic realism" (PR 78).

One of the reasons why pluralistic realism was wrecked by the notion of enduring substances followed from the fact that according to that traditional view "an individual substance with its [private] predicates constitutes the ultimate type of actuality" (PR 137). I have inserted the word *private* to bring out the point that according to this traditional view *the predicates are not derivative from relations to other substances*.[13] Although this view *could* in principle lead either to monism, according to which there really is only one such individual substance, or to pluralism, according to which there are many (PR 137), this view in fact tends to promote monism because it makes pluralism problematic: "With this metaphysical presupposition, the relations between individual substances constitute metaphysical nuisances: there is no place for them" (PR 137). Accordingly, thinkers such as Spinoza and F. H. Bradley, who value self-consistency over adequacy to our hard-core commonsense presuppositions—Whitehead refers here to their "defiance of the most obvious deliverance of our intuitive 'prejudices'" (PR 137)—are led to (quantitative) monism, according to which the idea that there is a plurality of actual things is an illusion.[14]

What allows Whitehead to combine self-consistency with real relations and thereby pluralism is his doctrine that enduring individuals are really serially ordered societies of actual entities. Each actual entity, understood as a momentary actual occasion, arises out of its prehensions of, hence its relations to, prior actual occasions. The most influential of these prior actual occasions is usually the immediately preceding occasion in the enduring individual to which the present occasion belongs. For example, although each electronic occasion is influenced by all prior events, it for the most part repeats the form of the prior occasion of the enduring electron to which it belongs. The present occasion's qualities or properties, accordingly, are derivative from its relations to prior occasions. In this view, we can still say that the enduring electron has an "essential form," consisting of qualities or properties. But this form, with its qualities, is derived by each electronic occasion from its relations to prior members of its serially ordered society. Whereas Descartes had retained the traditional "dominance of the category of 'quality' over that of 'relatedness,'" in Whitehead's position "'relatedness' is dominant over 'quality'" (PR xiii). Given that reversal, relations, far from

[13] Whitehead himself uses the term *private* in a parallel passage, saying that if we understand the universe as comprised of "substantial things, each thing in its own way exemplifying its private bundle of abstract characterers," we render the interconnectedness of the world unintelligible (AI 133).

[14] Bradley's metaphysical position developed in *Appearance and Reality* (1893), with its denial of relations and thereby of pluralistic realism, was instrumental to the revulsion against metaphysics in the early part of the twentieth century—hence the importance of Whitehead's demonstration that "metaphysics" need not reach Bradley's conclusion. On the relation of the two positions, see Leemon McHenry's comparative analysis (1992).

being nuisances, are essential to each actual entity: "In Cartesian language, the essence of an actual entity consists solely in the fact that it is a prehending thing (i.e., a substance whose whole essence or nature is to prehend)" (PR 41). And pluralism, rather than being in tension with internal relations, is demanded by them, as each actual entity by definition arises out of its prehensions of a multiplicity of prior actual entities and contributes itself to future actual entities: "The many become one, and are increased by one" (PR 21).

The idea that a person is really a personally ordered *society* of actual entities, each of which is constituted out of its relations to prior actual entities, is one of the reasons why many feminist philosophers of religion have found Whitehead's philosophy helpful. For example, according to Catherine Keller's analysis in a book subtitled *Separation, Sexism, and Self*, one of the main bases for sexism has been the ideal of the self as separate from the world, including other selves, which men—who formulated the ideal—have been better able to approximate. The fact that women are more obviously internally related to nature and other people has been used to regard them as not as fully human. This ideal of the self as separate, argues Keller, has been supported by the notion of the self as an enduring substance that remains essentially the same through its changes: "The consequence is that all changes are merely external or accidental. Moreover, the influences of the world, of other actual entities, are then external as well." Enduring individuals, concludes Keller, "cannot flow in and out of each other if they consist of abiding, presiding subjects" (1986, 182). The result is that that view of the self "blocks awareness of the influent effects of the world, the others" (31). Suggesting that we "replace substantial with connective selves," Keller endorses Whitehead's notion that the person is a society, a "nexus in which the members feel each other in an especially intimate way" (183, 196).

This social view of actual entities as internally related to their environments is also at the root of Whitehead's solution to the problem of induction—which he took to be not the derivation of general, eternal laws applying to all events whatsoever but simply the "divination of some characteristics of a particular future from the known characteristics of a particular past." This divination is justifiable, he points out, on the assumption that all events within a particular community of events "are in some respects mutually qualified by reason of their inclusion within that same community" (SMW 44). Given this framework, we have a reason "why we should put some limited trust in induction. For if we assume an environment largely composed of a sort of existences whose natures we partly understand, then we have some knowledge of the laws of nature dominating that environment" (AI 112).

5. Panexperientialism with Organizational Duality

After the first two sections of this chapter provided reasons to affirm some form of panexperientialism, the third and fourth sections developed one of the distinctive features of the Whiteheadian version of panexperientialism, namely, the idea that enduring individuals are temporally ordered *societies* of momentary events. We are now in position to look at the other distinctive feature of Whiteheadian panexperientialism, its organizational duality. This doctrine, also one of the core doctrines of process philosophy, is crucial for providing a naturalistic account of the mind-body relation that can do justice to the unity of our experience and our presuppositions about human freedom and mental causation.

Compound Individuals

Organizational duality refers to two basic ways in which large numbers of purely temporal societies of occasions of experience can come together to form spatiotemporal societies. Either the organization is such as to give rise to a "regnant," "presiding," or "dominant" member, or it is not. If there *is* a dominant member, the total society is, to use the term coined by Hartshorne (1972), a *compound individual*. The most obvious example is a human being or any other animal with a central nervous system, in which the bodily cells are organized so as to give rise to a temporally ordered society of higher-level occasions of experience, which we call the "mind" or "soul." Although these dominant occasions of experience are not different in kind from the living occasions of experience in the bodily cells, they are enormously different in degree (a fact that reflects the billion years of evolution it took to get from eukaryotic cells to human souls).

Although the human being is composed of trillions of cells, it is an *individual* by virtue of its soul, which is a personally ordered society of dominant occasions of experience. The bodily organization is such that in each moment experiences from every part of the body are poured into the dominant occasion, which, by integrating these experiences into a higher-level experience, gives the society as a whole an experiential unity.[15] Then, thanks

[15] In Whitehead's words, "the animal body is composed of entities, which are mutually expressing and feeling. . . . By reason of [the body's] organization, an adjusted variety of feelings is produced in that supreme entity which is the one animal considered as one experiencing subject" (MT 23).

again to the bodily organization, this higher-level occasion of experience can exert a dominant influence on the behavior of the society as a whole, thereby causing the whole body to act as a unity. This explanation presupposes, of course, the distinction between the two forms of process discussed in the previous sections. The experienced unity of the psychophysical society is enjoyed by a dominant occasion in its process of concrescence, during which it exercises self-determination, deciding, among other things, how to exert its influence upon its body in the next moment. Then, after its concrescence has reached satisfaction, its decisions exert influences upon various parts of the brain, thereby giving instructions to various parts of the body. This is the "mental" or "downward" causation that materialism is unable to affirm. Insofar as the efficient causation of the dominant occasion upon its brain cells was based upon the self-determination of an individual occasion of experience, we have an explanation, also impossible for materialism, as to why we assume the person's bodily behavior to be free action, for which the person is responsible.

One of the respects in which other process philosophers have improved upon Whitehead's own formulation of his core ideas involves the spatial relation between the regnant or dominant member of a compound individual and the subordinate members. Evidently thinking of all actual occasions as spatially minute, Whitehead spoke of the regnant, living occasions of the cell as occurring in the "empty space" of the cell, meaning the space not filled with enduring objects, and of the dominant occasions in a human being as occurring in empty spaces of the brain: "Life lurks in the interstices of each living cell, and in the interstices of the brain" (PR 105–6). This view led him to assume that the dominant occasion "wanders" from one part of the brain to another, depending upon which part is receiving the greatest variety of experience from the body (PR 106). In further developing the notion of the compound individual, Hartshorne suggested that each higher member would fill the whole spatial region of the lower members from which it emerged, so that molecular occasions would fill the entire region of the molecule, living occasions would fill the entire region of the cell, and dominant occasions would fill the entire region of the brain. This idea has been further developed by Cobb, who points out that it makes better sense of the fact that we seem to receive data from many parts of the brain simultaneously (1965, 82–91; 1984). This understanding of compound individuals also provides the basis for the doctrine of panentheism, which will be discussed in the next chapter.

Aggregational Societies

Not all spatiotemporal societies are compound individuals. There are also aggregational societies, in which there is no dominant member. In referring to an inorganic example, such as a rock, Whitehead used the term *corpuscular society* (PR 35); in referring to a living example, such as a tree, he spoke of a "democracy" (MT 24), thereby indicating that there is no "regnant" member to make the society a "monarchy." There are, of course, enormous differences between rocks and trees, but they have a structural similarity: there are billions of the highest-level type of enduring individual constituting the society—molecules in the case of rocks, cells in the case of plants. Because of the absence of a still-higher-level, more powerful member to coordinate the spontaneities occurring in its various cells, a plant's response to its environment is not analogous to that of an animal. Even more is there no analogy between the rock and a human being. Whereas the bodily behavior of a human being is directed by the purposes of a series of dominant occasions of experience, the behavior of a rock is simply a statistical result of the average effect of its billions of members. These two kinds of societies— compound and aggregational—are, therefore, different in kind, not simply in degree.[16]

Duality without Dualism

Dualists, of course, have always made this point, saying that the fact that the behavior of a rock is totally determined by environmental forces does not mean that human behavior is equally determined, because the human being's behavior is directed by a self-determining mind or soul. For dualists, however, this *organizational duality* involved an *ontological dualism:* the soul or mind was said to be not only numerically distinct but also different in kind from the cells of which the brain is made. Accordingly, dualists could not explain the mind-brain interaction apart from an appeal to supernatural causation.

In rejecting supernaturalism and thereby ontological dualism, materialists also lost the strength of dualism, which was its recognition of the organiza-

---

[16] Some of Whitehead's most influential interpreters, unfortunately, have not understood this point. For example, Leclerc has said that for Whitehead "all composites are alike in philosophical status; that is, there are no fundamentally different kinds among them . . . which means that the diversity among composites is to be understood entirely in terms of degrees of complexity of relationships among the constituents . . . [so that] composites cannot be any more than pure aggregates" (1977, 104).

tional duality between things that are self-moving and things that are not. Materialists could not affirm this duality because of their retention of the mechanistic view of nature, according to which its ultimate units are vacuous actualities: there is simply no conceivable way in which such things could be organized so as to produce compound individuals. Materialists have assumed that all visible things exemplify the same part–whole relationship, in which the whole is simply the sum of the parts, never a partially self-determining individual that, while arising out of its parts, can act back upon them. Materialists have thereby assumed all visible things to be behaviorally analogous, so that the behavior of dogs and human beings is to be understood in terms of the same principles required to explain the behavior of rocks and ocean waves. In neither, in other words, is the category of "aim" or "purpose" to be used. As we saw in Chapter 1, Whitehead rejects as "ridiculous" the idea that the activity of shipbuilders is "analogous to the rolling of the shingle on the beach" (FR 14).

Thanks to his version of panexperientialism, Whitehead is able to affirm organizational duality without ontological dualism. The key idea is that "diverse modes of organization" can produce "diverse modes of functioning" (MT 157). In inorganic aggregational societies, on the one hand, the mutual influence between the various enduring individuals "is predominantly of a formal character expressible in formal sciences, such as mathematics. The inorganic is dominated by the average. It lacks individual expression in its parts. Their flashes of selection (if any) are sporadic and ineffective. Its parts merely transmit average expressions" (MT 27). Because there is no ontological dualism, the individual actual occasions making up a rock have mentality, which means that they have spontaneous functionings. But "for lifeless matter these functionings thwart each other, and average out so as to produce a negligible total effect" (AI 207). The scientific study of such aggregational societies can, therefore, ignore these individual spontaneities; a science of average effects is adequate. In compound individuals, on the other hand, these individual spontaneities are no longer negligible because they give birth to a dominant member, which can coordinate these spontaneities into a unified effect. A science of the average, based on impartial effects, is no longer adequate.

> An angry man . . . does not usually shake his fist at the universe in general. He makes a selection and knocks his neighbour down. Whereas a piece of rock impartially attracts the universe according to the law of gravitation. The impartiality of physical science is the reason for its failure as the sole interpreter of animal behavior. . . . The fist of the man is directed by emotion seeking a novel feature in the universe, namely, the collapse of his opponent. In

the case of the rock, the formalities predominate. In the case of the man, explanation must seek the individual satisfactions. These enjoyments are constrained by formalities, but in proportion to their intensities they pass beyond them, and introduce individual expression. (MT 28–29)

In other words, even though rocks and human beings are both physical bodies, subject to the law of gravitation, their movements are not equally explained by this law or the efficient causation whose average effects it and other laws summarize. To explain human movements, we must also refer to final causation, the aim toward various types of satisfaction. The idea that such explanations are "unscientific" is simply a prejudice created by the recent association of science with the materialistic ontology, which has no place for the self-determining freedom we all presuppose in practice.

Habits and Downward Causation

Besides having no place for dominant occasions of experience, distinct from the brain, which could make free decisions, this materialistic ontology has no place for the idea that such decisions could exert "downward causation" on the brain cells and thereby the rest of the central nervous system so as to direct the body's movements. For materialists, such causation would involve the (impossible) influence of a purely mental entity upon purely physical brain cells. Moreover, downward causation would violate the materialists' assumption that all causation is what Searle calls "bottom-up causation." This assumption, as Searle points out with approval, implies that all the features of the world, including the world of human experience, "are determined at the basic microlevels of physics" (1984, 93). For Searle, this view is simply regarded as a scientific axiom. Many other materialists, however, base it on another assumption, which is that all events are determined by laws of nature, with the laws of physics being the most fundamental of these, from which all others are supposedly derived. Because the molecules in our bodies follow the same laws of nature that determine the behavior of molecules in rocks, they argue, our bodily behavior is as determined by bottom-up causation as is the behavior of rocks. Using a line by Tennyson alluding to the problem of mechanism—"The stars," she whispers, "blindly run"—Whitehead formulates the deterministic argument thus: "Each molecule blindly runs. The human body is a collection of molecules. Therefore, the human body blindly runs, and therefore there can be no individual responsibility for the action of the body" (SMW 78).

Whitehead's response to this argument involves a rejection of the idea that the actions of molecules, atoms, and electrons are fully determined by "laws of nature," which is a holdover from the early modern view that such laws were imposed on matter by an omnipotent creator. One of the irrationalities of materialism is that it has kept the imposed laws while rejecting the Imposer. In Whitehead's view, which he held in common with Peirce and James, the regularities discovered by physics are simply the most widespread, long-standing "habits of nature," its "communal customs" (MT 154; AI 41). As such, they describe *the average behavior of the entities in inorganic environments*. In a living cell, however, electrons and molecules are subject to different influences, so they behave differently. If this cell is in a living human body, it will be subject to influences from the human soul, and these influences will be mediated by the cell to its molecular and electronic components. The behavior of the molecules and their electrons will still be "blind," in the sense that they will not themselves have any *conscious* experiences, but they will blindly run in accord with the plan of the whole body, which is significantly guided by purposive influences from the dominant occasions of experience. In Whitehead's words:

> The concrete enduring entities are organisms, so that the plan of the *whole* influences the very characters of the various subordinate organisms which enter into it. In the case of an animal, the mental states enter into the plan of the total organism and modify the plans of the successive subordinate organisms until the ultimate smallest organisms, such as electrons, are reached. Thus an electron within a living body is different from an electron outside it, by reason of the plan of the body. The electron blindly runs either within or without the body; but it runs within the body in accordance with . . . the general plan of the body, and this plan includes the mental state [of the dominant occasions]. (SMW 79)

We see here one of the most important implications of Whitehead's view that enduring individuals such as electrons and molecules are serially ordered societies of occasions of experience. The fact that they are *experiential* in nature, hence not different in kind from our own experiences, provides part of the explanation as to why our experiences can influence them. The other part is provided by the fact that they consist of *momentary* occasions, so that they are open many times per second to influences from higher-level occasions of experience. These ideas are essential aspects of Whitehead's organizational duality, which allows us to explain downward causation from the mind to the body, which we presuppose all the time.

The Importance of Organizational Duality

It would be hard to overestimate the importance of this organizational duality for the Whiteheadian type of panexperientialism. This type, with its distinction between aggregational societies and those with a dominant member, goes back to Leibniz, who referred to the mind of the human being (or any other animal) as the "dominant monad." Leibniz's own version of this doctrine was problematic, of course, insofar as his monads, being windowless, could not really influence one another. But in distinguishing genuine individuals, which act and feel, from aggregational collections of low-grade forms of these individuals, which neither act nor feel, he made a crucial conceptual breakthrough. In making this distinction, Hartshorne says, "Leibniz took the greatest single step in the second millennium of philosophy (in East and West) toward a rational analysis of the concept of physical reality" (1977a, 95).

One reason this distinction is so important is that it overcomes various prevalent criticisms of panexperientialism, usually discussed as "panpsychism." The charge that panexperientialism is absurd because it implies that things such as rocks and telephones have feelings, or even consciousness, has been the most common of these criticisms (McGinn 1982, 32; Popper and Eccles 1977, 55, 517). There is, to be sure, a version of panpsychism, affirmed by Spinoza and some later thinkers (Rensch 1977), to which this criticism is applicable. It does not apply, however, to the type affirmed by Leibniz, Whitehead, and Hartshorne. Another criticism, offered by some dualists (Popper and Eccles 1977, 53–55, 516), is that panpsychism is a form of parallelism, according to which the mind's experiences and the brain's activities simply run along in parallel with each other, not really interacting, so that human behavior is not really free. This criticism is, again, applicable to the Spinozistic version of panpsychism, which regards the "mind" as simply the brain as known from within (Rensch 1977), but it is not applicable to the Whiteheadian-Hartshornean version, in which the mind is a series of much higher-level occasions of experience numerically distinct from all the occasions of experience constituting the brain. This form of panexperientialism, accordingly, can do justice to human freedom without ontological dualism and thereby without supernaturalism.

6. Living Persons

Although panexperientialism can solve many problems, including the long-standing mind-body problem, it probably still seems counterintuitive to many readers. One may wonder, in particular, whether we can really conceive of the human psyche as merely different in degree from a proton. The concept of a "living person," which has not previously been introduced, is directly relevant to this issue. This concept entails that although a proton and a human psyche are in one sense analogous, in that each is a serially ordered society of occasions of experience, there is another sense in which they are different in kind.

A large part of the difference can be explained simply in terms of the huge difference in degree between an individual protonic occasion and an individual human occasion. In a protonic occasion there is a mental pole, but it is vanishingly small, whereas in a typical human occasion of experience the mental pole, with its novel elements, plays an enormous role. This capacity for considerable novelty of response, which human occasions of experience share with canine occasions and even cellular occasions, is fundamental to what Whitehead means by "living" (PR 102). Human mentality, however, far surpasses that of cells and even dogs. In this respect, human and protonic occasions of experience probably approach being as different in degree as any creaturely enduring objects could be.

The full difference between a proton and a human psyche, however, involves not just the degree of mentality in each occasion but also a difference in the *role played by this mentality,* a difference that involves a distinction between two kinds of physical prehensions. A physical prehension, meaning the prehension of a prior actual occasion, can be either pure or hybrid. In a *pure* physical prehension, the prior occasion is prehended in terms of its *physical* pole, which consists of data that this prior occasion had inherited from still earlier occasions. In a *hybrid* physical prehension, by contrast, the prior occasion is prehended in terms of its *mental* pole, which contains any novelty that had appeared in that occasion.

Given this distinction, we can see that, besides the enormous difference of degree between a proton and a psyche, there is a difference in kind between these two kinds of societies (without, however, an *ontological* dualism between two kinds of actual entities). In a proton, each protonic occasion inherits from its predecessor almost entirely in terms of *pure* physical prehensions. So, besides the fact that very little novelty shows up in the successive occasions, the tiny bit that does occasionally appear gets ignored. This is why the abstract essence of the enduring proton remains virtually the same for billions of years. In a human psyche, by contrast, each occasion can inherit from its predecessor by means of *hybrid* physical prehensions. So, besides the fact that significant novelty crops up in many human occasions, this novelty can get absorbed into the abstract essence of the enduring individual, so that this essence can be continually enlarged. It is this twofold characteristic to which Whitehead points by referring to a psyche as a "living person." A proton is, technically, a person, being a personally (serially) ordered society of occasions of experience. But it is not a *living* person because its individual occasions have very little mentality and because its identity over time is sustained by means of pure physical prehensions. A proton seems "purely physical" compared with a human soul because it *is*.

Still another question to ask about this naturalistic panexperientialism is whether there is any way to conceptualize how an evolutionary process, without benefit of supernatural intervention, could have led from subatomic particles, such as protons and electrons, to human beings. This question will be addressed in Chapter 6, which will also develop the point, introduced at the end of the previous chapter, that the purpose of the evolutionary process is to promote the realization of value-experiences. Before dealing with the question of divine influence in the evolutionary process, however, it is necessary to lay out process philosophy's naturalistic theism.

[4]

Naturalistic, Dipolar Theism

The form of naturalism with which science has been associated for the past century and a half, as we have seen, involves sensationism, atheism, and materialism. The fact that science has been so closely identified with this naturalism$_{sam}$ has created the widespread presumption that this version of naturalism is uniquely "scientific." This presumption has created, in turn, the widespread belief that science is incompatible with any significantly religious worldview and, more generally, that taking science seriously entails the adoption of a wholly disenchanted worldview. In the first chapter, I provided reasons to question the adequacy of naturalism$_{sam}$ for science itself. In the second chapter, I showed how Whiteheadian process philosophy provides a naturalistic but *nonsensationist* account of perception that, besides being more adequate for science, allows for genuine religious experience. In the third chapter, I explained how this philosophy provides a naturalistic but *nonmaterialistic* ontology that allows for the freedom, purposive causation, and nonsensory perception presupposed by both science and religion. In the present chapter and the next, I lay out process philosophy's naturalistic but *nonatheistic* view of the universe—in other words, its naturalistic theism—which provides the third modification of scientific naturalism required to overcome the late modern conflict between science and religion and, more generally, to overcome the late modern disenchantment of the universe.

The claim that this aspect of the conflict can and should be overcome by the adoption of naturalistic theism, especially as formulated by process philosophy, is based on a twofold argument. In the first place, this naturalistic theism fulfills the criteria of rational consistency and adequacy to the facts of experience better than does atheism, thereby providing a better framework for the scientific community. In the second place, it is more adequate for religious purposes than the supernaturalistic theism with which religious faith in the West has traditionally been associated.[1] The argument for this second point will be continued in subsequent chapters. Insofar as this twofold argument is successful, process philosophy provides a version of theism upon which the scientific and religious communities could in principle agree.

The first part of this twofold argument—that the naturalistic theism proffered by process philosophy is more rational than atheism—involves a plunge into "natural theology" in the sense of arguments for the existence of a divine reality. Although the term *natural theology* can properly be used more broadly to include the discussion of various issues of religious interest from a philosophical point of view, in this chapter and the following one I am referring to natural theology in the narrower sense of arguments for the existence of God. Some forms of confessional theology and even some forms of philosophy of religion have, of late, avoided this enterprise, regarding it as harmful or at least unnecessary. Those approaches, however, are essentially defensive in nature, concerned merely to show that adherents of those theologies cannot be convicted of irrationality. The goal of process philosophy of religion, by contrast, is to provide a new worldview that can be seen by the scientific community, the philosophical community, and the various religious communities to be *more adequate* than previous worldviews. It cannot be content, therefore, with a defensive stance but must argue that its position is *more probable* than atheistic and supernaturalistic positions. This argument involves engaging in natural theology in the sense of positive arguments for the truth of naturalistic theism.

Although naturalistic theism and natural theology are very different things—the former being a position, the latter an enterprise—they are closely related features of process philosophy of religion. Process philosophers hold, in fact, that natural theology, in the sense of arguments for the existence of *theos,* can be successful if and only if the *theos* of which it speaks is that of naturalistic theism. What was wrong with traditional natural theology, in other words, was not so much the general types of arguments it offered but the particular conception of *theos* to which it tried to make those arguments point. In Hartshorne's words, "the fallacies in the older proofs

---

[1] My argument also presupposes, of course, that the position presented here is superior to other forms of naturalistic theism. For some critiques from a process perspective of other positions that could be considered forms of naturalistic theism, see Hartshorne 1937, chap. 3; Cobb 1962, chap. 4, and 1969, chap. 2; and Griffin 1973a, chaps. 1–4; 1973b; 1989c, chap. 4; 1996; and 2000a, chap. 3.

were largely due to the attempt to justify an erroneous conception of God" (1953, 191). In agreement with most atheistic philosophers, process philosophers hold that that conception was, if not internally incoherent, at least morally problematic and in strong tension with several features of the world as known through modern science.

To discuss traditional theism fairly, a distinction must be made between the two major versions it has taken: the all-determining version and the free-will version. According to the all-determining version of traditional theism—which, being the version articulated by its classical exponents, such as Augustine, Thomas Aquinas, Luther, and Calvin, could also be called the "classical" version of traditional theism[2]—God not only has the *power* to determine all events in the world but actually *does* so. For example, although in some passages Augustine seems to attribute free will to human beings, in more precise statements he says that even those wills "which follow the world are so entirely at the disposal of God, that He turns them whithersoever He wills, and whensoever He wills," which means that God "does in the hearts of even wicked men whatsoever He wills" (1948b, XLI, XLII). Luther, explicitly denying the idea that God simply foreknows, without determining, future events, says that God "does all things according to His own immutable, eternal and infallible will" (1957, 80). Calvin, rejecting the suggestion that the divine omnipotence is a mere *ability* to do all things, which sometimes remains "idle," insists that God is called omnipotent because "he regulates all things according to his secret plan, which depends solely upon itself" (1960, I, xvi, 3; III, xxiii, 7). This classical version of traditional theism also holds that God is *impassible,* being incapable of being affected by the world, and, indeed, *immutable* in all respects, being incapable of being changed from within as well as from without. This latter insistence follows from the idea that God is *eternal* in all respects, meaning completely outside time. The idea that God must determine all things is implied in fact by the idea that the divine will must be immutable, as clearly stated by Luther. Having said of God that "His will is eternal and changeless, because His nature is so," Luther says that "it follows, by resistless logic, that all we do, however it may appear to us to be done mutably and contingently, is in reality done necessarily and immutably in respect of God's will" (1957, 80).

---

[2] Although in prior writings I have distinguished between the all-determining and free-will versions of traditional theism, I had not previously referred to the former as the "classical" version. Most process philosophers and theologians use *classical theism* and *traditional theism* interchangeably—largely through the influence of Charles Hartshorne, who contrasted his "neo-classical theism" with the classical theism of (primarily) Augustine, Anselm, and Aquinas.

This all-determining version of traditional theism, process philosophers agree with many other philosophers and theologians, is incoherent. For example, although Augustine, Luther, and Calvin said that God fully determined the sinful actions of sinners, they also said that God *justly* punished them for their sins. The dominant way of maintaining that this twofold doctrine is not self-contradictory has been to argue that the idea that human beings act freely, so as to be responsible for their actions, is compatible with the idea that their actions, including their decisions, are fully determined by God. Although this "compatibilism" was defended by Augustine, Aquinas, and (sometimes) Calvin, it is—process philosophers agree not only with many other philosophers but also with Luther—self-contradictory.[3] Some other self-contradictions in the classical version of traditional theism will be mentioned in Section 2.

Among those philosophers and theologians who find the all-determining version of traditional theism incoherent are some who have developed a free-will version of traditional theism, such as Alvin Plantinga, who was discussed in Chapter 1, and evangelical thinkers who advocate what they call the "open" view of God (Pinnock et al. 1994).[4] According to this position, the creatures—at least the human ones—have freedom vis-à-vis God, being able to act contrary to the divine will, and time is real for God, so that there can be genuine *interaction* between God and the world, with God responding to the free decisions of the creatures (as well as vice versa). Thanks to these revisions, the self-contradictions in the classical version of traditional theism are overcome. From the perspective of process philosophers of religion, however, this free-will version of traditional theism still exemplifies the other two problems of the classical version—namely, being morally problematic and being in tension with many features of the world as known through modern science.

This latter problem can be illustrated by two such tensions. First, the idea that God can override human self-determination, and thereby human fallibility, led to the expectation that God would have provided infallibly inspired religious scriptures. This assumption, in its Christian form, lay behind the enormous cultural importance of the modern study of the Bible, as this

---

[3] For an argument against a (Thomistic) theological version of compatibilism, see Griffin 1991, chap. 4. For an argument against a materialistic version of compatibilism, according to which human freedom is compatible with complete determination by physical causes, see Griffin 1998a, 212–17. Other philosophers who reject this latter form of compatibilism include Jaegwon Kim (1993, 239, 281, 291), Thomas Nagel (1986, 110–17), and John Searle (1984, 87, 92, 95).

[4] For a dialogue between process theologians and advocates of this "openness" version of traditional theism, see Pinnock and Cobb 2000.

study demonstrated that the biblical writings show no signs of any supernatural overriding of normal human sinfulness, ignorance, and cultural conditionedness. Second, the idea that God's creative power is the power to create ex nihilo, in the sense of "from absolutely nothing," led many traditional
theists to the expectation that scientific study would reveal the world in its
present form to have been created virtually all at once—in, say, six days—
only a few thousand years ago. Scientific evidence, however, revealed that
our world, with its plants and animals, has instead been created through an
evolutionary process over many billions of years. Many supernaturalists were
still led by their view of how God *could* have created the world to the expectation that each species would have been created ex nihilo rather than
from earlier species. The rejection of this view, however, is the central and
arguably the best-confirmed feature of Darwin's theory. Although neither of
these "expectations" was strictly entailed by traditional theism, so that theories reconciling it with contemporary views of the Bible and evolution are
possible, these expectations followed so naturally from traditional theism
that they constituted the dominant opinion for many centuries. Even though
there is no outright contradiction between traditional theism and this modern knowledge, there *is* tension.[5]

With regard to the widespread view that the God of traditional theism is
morally problematic, the chief difficulties arise in relation to the problem of
evil, which will be discussed in Chapter 6. Although, as we will see, the free-
will version softens this problem, it does not entirely remove it. But there
are other morally problematic implications of traditional theism, which the
free-will version also does not completely remove. For example, to many
persons and groups interested in overcoming oppressive social, economic,
and political structures, the chief ideological enemy has seemed to be the
traditional idea of God because the idea of divine omnipotence has been
used to suggest that God sanctions the status quo. Although this idea follows
most clearly from the doctrine that God in fact determines all events, it is
also suggested by the assumption that God *could* simply overcome the social
evils in question.

[5] Another tension, which was discussed in Chapter 1, is that between supernaturalism's basic assumption, that God can interrupt the world's normal web of causes and effects, and the
scientific community's naturalism$_{ns}$, according to which this web is inviolable. This naturalistic conviction, being merely an assumption, cannot strictly be called modern *knowledge,* but it
is now the scientific community's most fundamental ontological assumption. Although I am
arguing that some of this community's present assumptions—namely, those involved in its
naturalism$_{sam}$—could and should be modified, there are two major differences. First, natural-
ism$_{ns}$, unlike naturalism$_{sam}$, involves no violation of our hard-core commonsense assumptions.
Second, naturalism$_{ns}$ is a much more fundamental assumption, as evidenced by the many scientists who continue to accept it while rejecting naturalism$_{sam}$.

A closely related problem with traditional theism, say many feminist philosophers of religion, is that its image of God as male and wholly transcendent has had negative consequences for women. Catherine Keller, for example, says that this image of God has been supportive of "the oppression of women" (1986, 38), and Carol Christ regards it as "morally and spiritually reprehensible" (1997, 104).

From the view of process philosophy, then, the reason that natural theology has fallen on hard times—aside from the widespread acceptance of naturalism$_{sam}$—is not that there is a lack of evidence for the existence of a divine power but that most of those engaged in the enterprise have been committed to using this evidence to support a doctrine that was morally objectionable (and it is notoriously difficult to convince people of the truth of ideas that they do not *want* to be true),[6] in strong tension with our knowledge of the world, and, in its classical version, incoherent (and just as no amount of evidence can prove the existence of a round square, no amount evidence can prove the existence of a deity incoherently conceived).

Given this analysis of the chief reason for the failure of traditional natural theology, the most important ingredient needed to produce a viable natural theology would be not a new argument but a *new conception of deity*.[7] This statement presupposes, of course, that this new conception of deity would be in sufficient continuity with more traditional conceptions to be worthy of the name *God*. It also presupposes that one or more of the traditional types of arguments for the existence of God did provide good reason to affirm the existence of a divine reality of some sort. It also presupposes, finally, that this new conception of deity can be seen to be adequate to the types of experience that lie behind the very idea of a Holy Power. The most important contribution a philosophy of religion can make to belief in the existence of a divine reality, accordingly, is a conception of a divine reality that is in harmony with, rather than in opposition to, our best logical, moral, and religious intuitions and our best thinking about the nature of the universe.

Such a conception of the divine reality is the primary contribution that

---

[6] One of our leading and most reflective biologists, Richard Lewontin, has provided a particularly clear statement of the way in which the equation of theism with supernaturalism has prevented many modern thinkers from entertaining theistic explanations for any phenomena, even if such explanations could overcome what he calls "the patent absurdity" of some of the explanations offered from a purely materialistic standpoint. "[W]e cannot allow a Divine Foot in the door," says Lewontin, because "[t]o appeal to an omnipotent deity is to allow that at any moment the regularities of nature may be ruptured, that miracles may happen" (1997, 31).

[7] In light of the previous note, what is needed, more precisely, is a new conception of deity as *an integral part of a naturalistic worldview* more convincing than naturalism$_{sam}$.

process philosophy of religion seeks to make to the enterprise of natural or philosophical theology. The distinctive features of process philosophy's conception of deity are summarized by the seventh and eighth of the core doctrines listed in the introductory chapter, namely, the Whiteheadian version of naturalistic theism and doubly dipolar theism. The first two sections of the present chapter lay out these two doctrines, which deal with the nature of deity and of deity's relation to the world. The third section responds to the charge, often made by atheists as well as supernaturalists, that this conception is not really a conception of *God*. Only after this discussion of the nature of God do I, in the next chapter, turn to the question of the evidence for the existence of such a divine reality, showing how *naturalistic theism* requires a reevaluation of the validity of *natural theology*.

1. The Whiteheadian Version of Naturalistic Theism

Although there are many versions of naturalistic theism (see note 1), they all have in common the acceptance of naturalism$_{ns}$, which denies the existence of a supernatural being that does—or even could—occasionally interrupt the world's normal causal processes. For process theism, at least, this means that God could not totally determine some events in the world, thereby interrupting the creatures' twofold power to exert self-determination and to exert causal influence on subsequent creatures. Hartshorne says, for example, that divine influence "could not possibly suppress all freedom in the recipient" (Hartshorne and Reese 1953, 275). This definition of naturalistic theism excludes one doctrine that is sometimes considered a form of it, namely, that version of deism according to which God *could* supernaturally intervene but has decided never to do so. Given my definition, this doctrine, by virtue of making the lack of interventions volitional rather than metaphysical, is a species of supernaturalism. A truly naturalistic theism understands naturalism$_{ns}$ to mean that the universe is such that any supernatural interruption of its basic causal nexus is metaphysically impossible.[8]

---

[8] Although the title of a book by Peter Forrest, *God without the Supernatural* (1996), suggests that he endorses a naturalistic theism, his position is quite different from what I mean by that term. Forrest calls himself an "antisupernaturalist" by virtue of not affirming any divine violations of the laws of nature (2–4), but his intention is only to "avoid the assumption that God has actually exercised any power to break the laws of nature" (4). The fact that he believes that God (metaphysically) *could* act otherwise is shown by his rejection of "those accounts in which the laws of nature are beyond even God's control," his statement that his "reluctance to admit violations of the natural order [is] based on aesthetic considerations" (59), and his speculation that "if there was not another way of ensuring an afterlife, divine providence might result in a violation of the divinely instituted natural order" (58). Forrest even hints, in fact, that if he turned to explicating Christianity, he might have to affirm "the super-

Beyond agreement on this point, however, the various forms of naturalistic theism differ on some important points. One issue is, granted the agreement that there are no supernatural interventions into the world's normal causal processes, whether these normal processes include variable divine influence. Deistic versions of naturalistic theism say no, whereas process philosophy's version says yes. Another issue is whether the divine reality is thought to be a personal being, in the sense of responding consciously to the world. Most versions of naturalistic theism, such as that of Henry Nelson Wieman (1946), say no, whereas process theism says yes. A still more basic issue is whether the divine reality is thought to be an actuality distinct from the universe, when "the universe" is understood as the totality of finite things, processes, and relationships, including the energy embodied in them. Pantheistic (Gustafson 1981), Tillichean (Tillich 1951), Deweyan (Dewey 1934; Cupitt 1981), and Kaufmanian (Kaufman 1993) versions of naturalistic theism say no, whereas process theism says yes.

In the case of this last issue, there is a sense in which process theism could intelligibly be considered a type of supernaturalism. As mentioned earlier, "naturalism" is sometimes defined as the doctrine that "nature is all there is," with "nature" understood to be the totality of finite agents, processes, and relationships, including the energy embodied in them. In terms of *that* definition of naturalism, process philosophy would *not* be a version of naturalism. In terms of *that* definition of naturalism, process theism could intelligibly be called a version of supernaturalism$_{da}$ (with "da" standing for "distinct actuality" or "distinct agency") because process theism affirms that God is an actuality distinct from the totality of all finite things—an actuality with its own experience, its own power of self-determination, and its own power to exert influence on other things. This point is important for showing that process theism really is a form of theism, not a disguised form of atheism or pantheism. Nevertheless, it would be misleading to refer to process theism as a version of supernaturalism because that term almost inevitably—no matter which definition of naturalism has been given—suggests the power to interrupt the world's normal causal processes. This problem is avoided by clearly defining naturalism as naturalism$_{ns}$.

---

natural" (5). Forrest's position does contain one element in common with what I mean by naturalistic theism in affirming that God created the world not out of absolute nothingness but out of "a maximally indeterminate something" (83) that involves metaphysical as well as logical laws (70, 84, 85). He does not, however, suggest that the metaphysical laws involve causal principles that even God could not violate. Given my definitions, then, Forrest's position is a version of supernaturalistic theism.

In any case, this set of differences between process theism and other versions of naturalistic theism is the reason for listing the Whiteheadian version of naturalistic theism,[9] not simply naturalistic theism, as one of the core doctrines of process philosophy. In the remainder of this section, I first discuss the basis for Whitehead's acceptance of naturalism$_{ns}$. I then explain how this version of naturalistic theism nevertheless allows for variable divine influence in the world.

Creation Out of Chaos and the Impossibility of Supernatural Interventions

Given process philosophy's analysis of causal relations, the acceptance of naturalism$_{ns}$ would mean that a divine being could not prevent an actual occasion from being influenced by the efficient causation of prior occasions, from exercising self-determination on itself, or from exerting efficient causation upon subsequent events. There can be no "miracles" as traditionally defined, namely, events that are produced by God's interruption of the normal causal relations among finite entities.

This denial is rooted in the rejection of the traditional, albeit nonbiblical (Levenson 1988; May 1994; Griffin forthcoming b), doctrine of creation ex nihilo, which said that our world was created by God out of absolute nothingness rather than out of a previously existing realm, perhaps in a state of chaos, of finite entities or processes. The main implication of this (postbiblical) doctrine of creation ex nihilo is that the world has no inherent power, no power of its own, with which it could resist the divine will. This implication is brought out explicitly by contemporary evangelical theologian Millard Erickson, who says: "God did not work with something which was in existence. He brought into existence the very raw material which he employed. If this were not the case, God would . . . have been limited by having to work with the intrinsic characteristics of the raw material which he employed" (1985, 374). Given the doctrine of creation ex nihilo, then, God *can* unilaterally determine states of affairs in the world. And insofar as the world usually runs according to "laws of nature," God can suspend these laws from time to time. Affirming the name as well as the substance of what I have called supernaturalism, Erickson says that his theology is based on "a definite supernaturalism—God resides outside the world and intervenes

---

[9] In using this term, I mean to refer only to that aspect of Whitehead's doctrine of God that I am calling his naturalistic theism, not his doctrine of God in its entirety, as shown by my criticism of his version of divine dipolarity in the next section. The resulting position is appropriately called "Whiteheadian," nevertheless, because it is more coherent with Whitehead's own metaphysical principles than is his own doctrine.

periodically within the natural processes through miracles" (304). The so-called laws of nature can be interrupted because they are not really "natural" laws, in the sense of being inherent in the very nature of things. Nature, having been created by God out of nothing, "is under God's control; and while it ordinarily functions in uniform and predictable ways in obedience to the laws he has structured into it, he can and does also act within it in ways which contravene these normal patterns (miracles)" (1985, 54).

Whitehead formulated his naturalistic theism in opposition to this supernaturalistic position, which he calls the Augustinian-Newtonian "theology of a wholly transcendent God creating out of nothing an accidental universe" (PR 95). In rejecting a "wholly transcendent God," Whitehead means one that exists independently not simply of our *present* universe (which Whitehead affirms) but of any universe of finite existents whatsoever. By "an accidental universe," Whitehead means one that is *wholly* contingent, in the sense that there is no necessity for *any* universe of finite existents. This twofold point, along with the implication that such a God could wholly determine the states of affairs in such a world, is expressed in Whitehead's rejection of the idea of "one supreme reality, omnipotently disposing a wholly derivative world" (AI 166).

Whitehead, by contrast, regards the world as, in one sense, existing naturally, in the sense of necessarily. Besides portraying "the World as requiring its union with God," Whitehead's philosophy portrays "God as requiring his union with the World" (AI 168). The fact that "World" is here capitalized is significant. Whitehead does not mean that our particular world, with its particular forms of order—such as its electrons, protons, and neutrons and its inverse square law of gravitation—is necessary to the divine existence. Referring to this particular world as "our cosmic epoch" (PR 35–36, 84, 288), Whitehead holds that it exists only contingently. In speaking of "the World" as necessary to God, he means that beneath the contingent order of our cosmic epoch there is a more fundamental order, a *metaphysical* order, which is necessarily embodied in some world or other, and that "the World" in this sense is internally related to God, so that it belongs to the very nature of God to be related to *some* world embodying this metaphysical order.[10]

The contrasting position of traditional theism, with its supernaturalism, is illustrated by William Wainwright's statement, made in an explication of Eric Mascall's position, that "because [God] *freely* creates the world, its or-

[10] "What really interests me," Einstein has been quoted as saying, "is whether God had any choice in the creation of the world." Whitehead's answer would have been "yes and no."

der will be contingent" (1997, 58). In Whiteheadian process philosophy, God did indeed freely create our cosmic epoch. In fact, the point made by Mascall (1949, 9), as Wainwright mentions (1997, 58), was based in part on Whitehead's endorsing observation that modern science, with its combination of rationalism and empiricism, presupposed the vision of the world as the product of a free decision of a rational creator (SMW 12, 178). In Whitehead's view, however, our world embodies metaphysical principles, which were not freely created, so the order of our world is partly necessary as well as partly contingent.

With this point, we are approaching the full difference between the naturalistic and the supernaturalistic forms of theism. The essence of supernaturalism, as exemplified by Erickson and Mascall, is *extreme voluntarism,* according to which the very existence of a world of finite existents is due to the divine will. Whether God is related to any world at all is said to be an entirely voluntary matter on God's part. Given the fact that there is a world, it follows that the *nature* of God's relation to the world is entirely voluntary, being wholly determined by a divine decision. Not being even partly based on necessity, therefore, the normal God–world relationship can be changed at will. For example, in the first chapter I quoted Plantinga's statement that "God has often treated what he has made in a way different from the way in which he ordinarily treats it" (1991a, 22). Lying behind that statement is Plantinga's belief that no causal laws are outside God's control because "God is the author of the causal laws that do in fact obtain" (1984, 31).

Whitehead, by contrast, holds that "the World's nature is a primordial datum for God; and God's nature is a primordial datum for the World" (PR 348). This mutual internal relatedness implies that "the relationships of God to the World . . . lie beyond the accidents of will," being instead "founded upon the necessities of the nature of God and the nature of the World" (AI 168). Because God's way of influencing the world is founded on the necessities of the (metaphysical) nature of world as well as upon the necessities of the (metaphysical) nature of God, it cannot occasionally reflect a different modus operandi. The term *naturalistic theism,* accordingly, means that the basic God–world relationship lies in the very nature of things. Because the most fundamental of the *contingent* features of our cosmic epoch are said to have been freely chosen, this position does involve a *moderate* voluntarism. But the basic principles of process philosophy rule out *extreme* voluntarism, according to which the very existence of a world of finite entities and thereby the most fundamental causal principles exemplified in our world are contingent upon a divine decision.

The difference between that supernaturalistic, extremely voluntaristic

form of theism and Whitehead's naturalistic theism is expressed in his famous dictum that "God is not to be treated as an exception to all metaphysical principles" but instead as "their chief exemplification" (PR 343).
Within the framework of supernaturalistic theism, by contrast, the most
fundamental causal principles of our universe are not really metaphysical in
the sense of necessarily being exemplified in any possible universe. They
were freely chosen. It is this speculative hypothesis that lies behind the assumption that God can interrupt the most fundamental causal principles of
our universe. Whiteheadian-Hartshornean process theism, by contrast, involves the hypothesis that these principles are really metaphysical, so that
God, rather than existing over and above these principles, is their "chief exemplification." According to Hartshorne's interpretation of this idea, it
means that God's eternal essence is "no mere case under the categories, nor
yet a mere exception to them," but is instead "the categories in their pure
or unqualified meaning, as fixed characteristics of an individual life" (1961b,
171). If the metaphysical principles belong to the very essence of God, then
it makes no sense to speak of God as interrupting them. As eternal metaphysical principles, they describe not only the way in which finite actual entities necessarily interact with one another but also the way in which they
necessarily interact with God.

In this version of naturalistic theism, in other words, what exists necessarily is not simply God, as traditional theism holds, or simply the world of
finite existents, as atheism holds, but God-and-a-world. This position can be
expressed by saying, as does Hartshorne, that God is essentially "the soul of
the universe," being related to the universe somewhat in the way in which
the human soul, as the dominant member of the human being, is related to
its body (1941, 174–87; 1984, 52–62; 1991b, 649). As the word *somewhat*
indicates, the God-world relationship is merely analogous to the soul-body
relationship. For example, human souls are contingent emergents of the
evolutionary process, with this emergence being dependent upon the organization of the human body, whereas God, by contrast, exists necessarily
and thereby primordially. God, Whitehead says, "is not there as derivative
from the world" (RM 150). Referring to God as the soul of the universe, accordingly, does not imply that God's existence is dependent upon our particular world or even that God's existence is in any sense contingent. One
thing it does imply, however, is that being related to a realm of finite actualities is part and parcel of the very nature of God.[11]

One of the central terms used by Hartshorne for this type of theism is *pan-*

---

[11] In this respect, the Whiteheadian-Hartshornean position is similar to that of the great
philosophical theologian Frederick Tennant, who portrayed God as "essentially world-
ground" and thereby *not* as "a being who might or might not have created" (1930, 18).

entheism, which means "all (finite) things are in God." This idea follows from the combination of two ideas—the interpretation of compound individuals given in Chapter 3, according to which the dominant member includes the regions of the subordinate members, and the idea that God is the soul of the universe. Just as the brain is in the soul, the universe is in God. It might be thought, incidentally, that although *panentheism* is for this reason a good term for Hartshorne's position, it would not fit Whitehead's, because he did not hold this view of the mind–brain relation, so that, by analogy, he would not have thought of God as omnipresent. That is, it is sometimes suggested that whereas Hartshorne answers the question "Where is God?" by saying "everywhere," Whitehead would have said "nowhere." However, in response to the question "Is it possible to indicate God's locus?" Whitehead replied, that "in respect to the world, God is everywhere. Yet he is a distinct entity. The world (events in it) has a (specific) locus with reference to him, but he has no locus with reference to the world. This is the basis of the distinction between finite and infinite. God and the world have the same locus" (A. Johnson 1969, 372).

It would seem, then, that Whitehead would have agreed with Hartshorne and others who have argued in favor of regional inclusion (Cobb 1971, 1972b), saying that the divine experience includes the regions of all the world's experiences.

Even apart from this notion of regional inclusion, furthermore, the term *panentheism* is appropriate for Whitehead's position because all worldly occasions are said to be prehended by, and thereby included in, the divine experience (which Whitehead calls the "consequent nature" of God, to be discussed later). Besides the fact that God is internal to the world (as traditional theism said), the world is internal to God: "It is as true to say that the World is immanent in God, as that God is immanent in the World" (PR 348).

Being arguably the most illuminating term for the naturalistic theism of process philosophy, *panentheism* brings out the fact that it combines features of both pantheism, which regards God "as essentially immanent and in no way transcendent," and traditional theism, which regards God "as essentially transcendent and only accidentally immanent" (AI 121). Like pantheism, panentheism says that the universe is not a wholly contingent, external creation of God. Rather, being related to a universe belongs to the very nature of God (as *essentially* soul of the universe). With traditional theism, however, panentheism affirms the transcendence of God over *this particular* universe. Although God can be said to be "the universe as a whole," the "whole" in this phrase is not an aggregational whole but *the universe as an experiencing individual.* In the words of Hartshorne: "The world as an integrated individual is not a 'world' as this term is normally and properly used, but 'God.'

God, the World Soul, is the *individual integrity* of 'the world,' which otherwise is just the myriad creatures" (1984, 59). The universe, in other words,
is a compound individual with God as its dominant member.[12]

Panentheism is crucially different from pantheism because God transcends the universe in the sense that God has God's own creative power, distinct from that of the universe of finite actualities. Hence, each finite actual
entity has its own creativity with which to exercise some degree of self-
determination, so that it transcends the divine influence upon it. "Every actual entity, in virtue of its novelty, transcends its universe, God included"
(PR 94). This position, by thereby providing the basis for a distinction between what *is* and what *ought* to be, avoids the worst implication of pantheism, which is that whatever happens is divine, and therefore right, no matter how horrible. Because the world's actual occasions have their own
creativity, the evil in the world does not impugn the goodness of the influences from God (a point to be discussed at greater length in Chapter 6).

This notion of creativity provides the basis for the distinctively Whiteheadian-Hartshornean way of denying creation ex nihilo. Whitehead's naturalistic theism is based on the denial that God creates this creativity. Traditional theism also, of course, thought of creativity as uncreated, in the sense
that God's own creative power, belonging to the essence of God, was said to
exist necessarily. Insofar as the universe of finite actualities also embodied
creativity, however, it did so only contingently, because God freely gave creative power to worldly creatures. Whitehead, by contrast, rejects the "suggestion that the ultimate creativity of the universe is to be ascribed to God's
volition" (PR 225). This rejection is expressed in Whitehead's famous dictum about the "unfortunate habit" of paying "metaphysical compliments"
to God. Although this statement, taken out of context, has often been used
to suggest that Whitehead denies that God is in any respects metaphysically

---

[12] Many feminist theologians have found this panentheistic vision appealing. For example,
Carol Christ, while expressing appreciation for the pantheistic notions of some feminist theologians insofar as they express a sense of divine immanence, says that her religious experience
suggests that "the Goddess is also a personal presence, a power . . . who cares about my life
and the fate of the world," which leads her to say: "Process theology's notion of 'pan-*en*-
theism' (all is *in* God) provides a way of understanding God that moves beyond the polarities
of immanence and transcendence, pan-theism (all is God) and theism (God is above or beyond
all)." In contrast to traditional theism, she affirms process theology's view that "God is internally related to everything in the world," meaning that "God is affected in the depth of God's
being by everything that exists and everything that happens in the world. God suffers with our
suffering and rejoices in our joy." In contrast to pantheism, she affirms process theology's view
that "God is transcendent as well as immanent because God is 'more' than the sum total of all
the discrete beings in the world," being "the 'mind' or 'soul' of the world body" (1997, 104–
5). See also Keller 1986, 37–44.

unique, Whitehead had in mind only one particular "compliment": the conception of God "as the foundation of the metaphysical situation with its ultimate activity" (SMW 179). Whitehead does emphatically reject that view, holding instead that this ultimate activity is necessarily embodied in a world as well as in God. Although "God is the aboriginal instance of this creativity" (PR 225), this creativity is also eternally embodied in some realm or other of finite actual entities. (The relationship between God and creativity, as "the two ultimates," will be further discussed in Chapter 7.)

The creation of our particular universe or cosmic epoch, therefore, was "not the beginning of [finite] matter of fact, but the incoming of a certain type of order" (PR 96). Whitehead's panentheism involves, in other words, a return to the ancient position, expressed in the Bible (Levenson 1988; May 1994), that the creation of our world involved bringing order out of chaos. In Whitehead's view, this would not have been pure or absolute chaos: "The immanence of God gives reason for the belief that pure chaos is intrinsically impossible" (PR 111). There would always, at the least, be the order expressive of the metaphysical principles. We can suppose, however, that between the decay of the previous cosmic epoch and the beginning of the present one, there would have been "a state of chaotic disorder," meaning "disorder approaching an absolute sense of that term" (PR 92). In such a state, there would have been no social order, no societies—no electrons, protons, photons, or even quarks, which are already temporally ordered societies. All finite actual occasions would have happened randomly, so there would have been no "congruent unity of effect" out of which higher-level actual entities could have emerged (PR 92). All finite occasions, accordingly, would have been extremely trivial. The first stage of the creation of our cosmic epoch would have involved the formation of very low-grade serially ordered societies (perhaps quarks) out of such a chaotic state (FR 24). Later stages would have involved the creation of more complex societies out of these simpler ones.

If the creation of our particular world occurred in this manner, there was no stage at which God could unilaterally determine the state of affairs. At each stage, God was working with actual occasions, each of which had the twofold power of creativity: the power to exercise self-determination, then the power to exert efficient causation on subsequent occasions. Although God embodies creativity to the maximal degree possible, the divine creativity can never obliterate or override the creativity of the creatures. This means, in Whitehead's language, that divine power is always persuasive, never coercive. Plato's final conviction, "that the divine element in the world is to be conceived as a persuasive agency and not as a coercive agency,"

Whitehead suggests, is "one of the greatest intellectual discoveries in the history of religion" (AI 166).

Variable Divine Influence in the World

Now, having seen how God does *not* act, according to this naturalistic panentheism, we need to see how God *does* act. The difference between "liberal" philosophies of religion and theologies, on the one hand, and "conservative" ones, on the other, has largely revolved around the issue of variable divine influence in the world. Liberal positions, beginning with the eighteenth-century deists, have usually denied variable divine influence whereas conservative positions have usually affirmed it. Because virtually all parties to the discussion have assumed that variable divine causation in the world would mean supernatural interruption of the normal web of cause-effect relations, the issue of variable divine influence has been nearly identical with the question of the compatibility of religious thought with scientific naturalism$_{ns}$.

The historical reason for this assumption was the primary-secondary scheme for understanding the relation between divine and worldly causation, which the early modern thinkers inherited from the medieval period. According to this scheme, God is the primary cause of all events. Being omnipotent, God as the primary cause is the *sufficient* cause of all events, so that no supplementation by other causes is needed. God usually does not bring events about directly, however, but uses secondary causes, also called natural causes. These secondary causes are *also* sufficient causes, as long as attention is focused on the *nature* of the events that are brought about, on their *whatness*. If, by contrast, the question of the *thatness* of the events is raised—that is, why a world, with its chains of causal events, exists at all—one must refer to God, as the being who created the whole universe and sustains it in existence. This answer, however, requires no reference to *variable* divine influence: God's influence with regard to most events consists simply in the undifferentiated activity of sustaining them in existence. But a few events, such as the creation of life, the inspiration of the prophets, and the incarnation in Jesus, were said to be "special" acts of God in which God acted in an extraordinary way.

With regard to these extraordinary events, the primary-secondary scheme had disastrous implications. Given the assumption that most events were in principle fully explicable without reference to variable divine influence, to speak of *extraordinary* divine influence in any event was necessarily to speak of a *supernatural interruption* of the chain of natural causes and effects. For example, if one maintained that the creation of life must have involved divine causation beyond the undifferentiated divine influence that sustains all beings in existence, one thereby necessarily implied that the creation of life involved an interruption of the causal principles involved in most events.

This background explains why, when scientific naturalism emerged in the nineteenth century, it involved atheism. Scientific naturalism as such, involving only the denial of supernatural interruptions of the world's basic causal processes, would have been compatible with the idea of variable divine influence in the world, as long as this influence had been held to be part of, rather than an interruption of, the normal causal processes. The primary-secondary scheme, however, ruled out this possibility: by excluding variable divine influence from the normal causal processes, this scheme entailed that any such influence had to constitute a supernatural intervention into these processes. Given that assumption, accepted by virtually all parties, naturalism implied atheism—at least "methodological atheism," the doctrine that although the world may have been created by God, all the concrete features of events are to be explained without appeal to any divine influence.

This issue is often discussed in terms of a "God of the gaps," a derogatory phrase that is used both epistemically and ontologically. In the *epistemic* sense, it refers to the appeal to God to explain some gap in our present scientific knowledge of the world. This practice has become disreputable because of cases in which the advance of science closed the gap. The classic example is Newton's appeal to God to provide an adjustment of the planetary orbits required by his faulty calculations, a blunder immortalized by the (probably apocryphal) quip of the astronomer Pierre Laplace to Napoleon that he had "no need for that hypothesis." In the *ontological* sense, "God of the gaps" refers to the idea of a supposed gap in the chain (or web) of finite causes that is allegedly filled by a supernatural cause, the idea that naturalism$_{ns}$ explicitly rejects. Given the primary-secondary schema for thinking of the relation between divine and worldly causation, however, divine influence could contribute to the content of any event only by displacing some finite causation, so *any* variable divine causation in the world implied this kind of supernatural gap-filling.

This development has confronted philosophers of religion and theologians with a dilemma: on the one hand, if they reject a God of the gaps, thereby rejecting all variable divine causation, they deny one of the basic presuppositions of all theistic religions. On the other hand, if they do justice to this presupposition by affirming variable divine causation, they affirm a God of the gaps, thereby putting religious belief at odds with the most fundamental ontological belief of the scientific community. This is the basic reason why both liberal and conservative theologies have been problematic in the late modern period.

Whiteheadian process philosophy, by having a God-shaped hole that is not filled by a God of the gaps, provides a solution to this dilemma. The key to this solution is a fundamentally different way of understanding the relation between divine and worldly causation. Every actual entity prehends all the actual entities in its environment, which includes God (as the term *panentheism* emphasizes). An actual occasion is, therefore, partially constituted by its (physical) prehension of God. Because physical prehension and efficient causation are simply two ends of the same relationship, there is divine causation on, thereby divine influence in, every event. In Whitehead's words: "Every event on its finer side introduces God into the world. . . . He adds himself to the actual ground from which every creative act takes its rise. The world lives by its incarnation of God in itself" (RM 149). In saying that the world "lives by its incarnation of God," Whitehead is reaffirming the traditional view that the world's continued existence in each moment depends upon the sustaining influence of God. He goes beyond the traditional view, however, insofar as it thought of this divine sustaining activity as invariable. Although Whitehead regards this activity as the same for all events in one sense, he regards it as variable in another sense. Hence, reference to the divine influence is necessary for explaining the *whatness* (or content) of all events, not simply their *thatness*.

Whitehead's term for this divine influence in every event is the *initial subjective aim*. As we saw, every actual occasion has a "subjective aim," which is its overall aim or purpose during its moment of subjective immediacy. This subjective aim is its final causation. More precisely, its final causation, in the sense of its self-determination, is its decision as to exactly what its subjective aim is to be. Although this decision as to its own aim is the occasion's act of self-creation, the occasion does not create this aim out of nothing or entirely out of influences from the past world of finite occasions of experience. Rather, an occasion of experience's subjective aim is partially created out of an *initial* subjective aim derivative from the occasion's prehension of God.

It is important, in stating this point, *not* to say—as some critics of process theism have taken it to say—that a finite occasion simply derives its subjective aim from God. If that were the doctrine, we would have a new version of divine determinism. Whitehead is usually careful to specify that what is derived from God is the *initial* (or *basic*) stage of the subjective aim (PR 108, 224, 225, 244), which is sometimes simply called the "initial aim" (PR 244). Although preferences are built into this initial aim, there are alternatives to be decided among. Each finite occasion, Whitehead writes, "derives from God its basic conceptual aim, relevant to its actual world, yet with indeterminations awaiting its own decisions" (PR 224). Again, "the initial stage of the aim is rooted in the nature of God, and its completion depends on the self-causation of the subject–superject" (PR 244).

According to this conception, divine influence in the world is always formally the same but variable in content. It is *formally the same* because God acts in relation to all finite actual occasions by providing them with initial aims. But it is *variable in content* because different initial aims are appropriate for different actual entities.[13] The initial aim for any occasion of experience is toward that ideal possibility that would be best for that occasion, given its location and complexity (PR 84, 244). What is best for one occasion, however, will differ more or less greatly from what is best for another occasion. The best possibility for an electronic occasion will differ radically from the best possibility for a human occasion. The best possibility for a young child in a particular moment will differ greatly from the best possibility for an adult. And the best possibilities for adult human beings in one cultural tradition may differ significantly from the best possibilities for adult human beings in another tradition.

Besides being variable in content, the divine influence in the world is *variable in effectiveness*. This kind of variability occurs primarily in high-grade occasions of experience, such as those of human beings, which have a great degree of complexity and freedom. Because of their complexity, vast numbers of possibilities are open to them in each moment. Because of their great freedom, they have the power to go radically against the initial aim received from God. The possibility that they choose to make their subjective aim may be greatly different from the initial aim received from God.

Thanks to this idea that God acts in the world by means of initial aims, the above-described dilemma, with the resulting polarization between liberal and conservative approaches, can be avoided. On the one hand, this doctrine does not involve a God of the gaps, either epistemically or ontologically. The role played by God in the formation of each finite actual occasion is *in principle* not a role that could be played by some finite agency, so it is not a "gap" in our present empirical knowledge that might be closed by some future scientific discovery. And the divine influence is not an interruption of the world's normal causal process but a regular, even necessary, factor *in* this process. Therefore, as I have suggested elsewhere (Griffin 1988,

---

[13] Those process theists who insist that God acts in "one and the same way always and everywhere" are correct, therefore, insofar as they are emphasizing the fact that, from a Whiteheadian perspective, God always acts by giving initial aims, so that there is only one *mode* of divine agency. But they are misleading insofar as they fail also to say that the *content* of the divine aims can differ drastically in different times and places. My first publication (Griffin 1967) was a critique of Schubert Ogden's position on this point.

73–77), process philosophy has a God-shaped hole that is *not* filled by a God of the gaps.

Process philosophy's idea that the divine aims for occasions differ in both content and effectiveness allows theologians of the theistic religions to accept and conceptualize the assumption, central to these religions, that some events, such as certain crucial events reported in the scriptures of these traditions, are far more important than others for revealing the divine nature and purpose (Griffin 1983). Christian theologians, for example, can develop a Christology that supports the conviction that Jesus' life especially incarnated God in a way that makes it appropriate to receive Jesus as especially revelatory of God (Griffin 1973a, chap. 9; Cobb 1975, chaps. 8–10). Accordingly, the religious idea that has created the most severe problem for modern theology, the idea of variable divine influence in the world, has been reconciled with naturalism$_{ns}$.

2. Doubly Dipolar Theism

Although the most important dimension of Whiteheadian-Hartshornean process theism is arguably its complete rejection of supernaturalism combined with its affirmation of variable divine agency, its best-known feature is probably its dipolarity. However, because of several factors—that process theism actually involves *two* dipolarities, that Whitehead's doctrine is designed primarily for one of them and Hartshorne's primarily for the other, and that Whitehead's doctrine involves violations of his own metaphysical principles—the dipolar theism of process philosophy has been one of its greatest sources of confusion and justified criticism. Since this dipolar theism involves a rejection of what Hartshorne calls the "monopolarity" of classical theism (Hartshorne and Reese 1953, 3–6),[14] we can begin by looking at that older doctrine.

The Monopolarity of Classical Theism

Classical monopolar theism resulted in two distinguishable denials: that God could be *affected by the world* (impassibility) and that God could *change in any respect* (immutability). Accordingly, the monopolarity involved two dimensions. First, God exerts causal efficacy upon the world but receives no

---

[14] Speaking, as Hartshorne does, of classical theism is appropriate here because this description applies not to the temporalistic, free-will version of traditional theism but only to what I have called the classical version (see note 2).

causal influence back from the world, which means that God is *entirely active,* not at all responsive. Second, whereas in a finite substance there is a distinction between its essence and its actual states (which involves many unessential or "accidental" features), in God *essence and actuality are identical,* which means that, assuming God's *essence* to be unchanging, God must be unchanging *in all respects.* Both these dimensions follow from classical theism's assumption that the world with its temporal process is a wholly derivative creation, so that the existence of the temporal process is not metaphysically necessary. Because God is therefore not "subject" to the temporal process, according to this view, the idea of an unchanging essence that is instantiated in a succession of actual states cannot be applied to God, and the changing world can produce no effects in God.

These implications produced grave problems for classical theism, resulting in some of the incoherencies referred to in the introduction to this chapter. For example, the idea that there is no distinction between the divine essence and the divine actuality, so that there are no contingent ("accidental") relations in God, seemed to imply that God's relation to our world, in all its details, was essential to God, a logical deduction that led to Spinoza's monistic pantheism (Hartshorne and Reese 1953, 189–91; Griffin 1976, 96–99). So whereas classical theism said that God is wholly independent of the world and the world's existence wholly contingent, it also implied that the world, in all its details, exists necessarily.

Another contradiction involved the (Greek) idea that God does not respond to the world, which conflicted with the (biblical) idea that God loves the world. St. Anselm, facing this problem directly in the twelfth century, wrote in a prayer:

> Although it is better for thee to be . . . compassionate, passionless, than not to be these things; how art thou . . . compassionate, and, at the same time, passionless? For, if thou art passionless, thou dost not feel sympathy; and if thou dost not feel sympathy, thy heart is not wretched from sympathy for the wretched; but this it is to be compassionate. (1903, 11, 13)

The best that Anselm could do to resolve this paradox was to say: "Thou art compassionate in terms of our experience, and not compassionate in terms of thy being" (13). In other words, God is not really compassionate but only seems so to us. In the next century, Thomas Aquinas (1952, I, Q. 20, art. 1) felt called upon to respond to the argument that "in God there are no passions. Now love is a passion. Therefore love is not in God." Rather than deny the first premise, Thomas solved the problem by simply saying that God "loves without passion." Insofar as passion, compassion, or sympathy is part and parcel of the very nature of love, however, these solutions are self-contradictory.

The Double Dipolarity of Process Theism

Process philosophy's dipolar theism reflects its naturalistic theism, with its different assessment of the relation between God and the world. The temporal process belongs to the metaphysical nature of things. It is, accordingly, real for God, a point that is reinforced by the statement that God is the chief exemplification of the metaphysical principles, not the exception thereto (PR 343). God changes, therefore, and these divine changes involve responses to the world. But God does not change in all respects; there is an aspect of God that is strictly unchanging. Hartshorne emphasized this dipolarity—God as *unchanging* and God as *changing*—by speaking, respectively, of God's "abstract essence" and God's "concrete states." However, there is another way of speaking of two divine aspects or poles—namely, God as *influencing* the world and God as *being influenced* by the world in return. Whitehead emphasized this dipolarity by speaking, respectively, of God's "primordial nature" and God's "consequent nature."

Considerable confusion has resulted from the fact that most expositions of process theology refer simply to its "dipolar theism" without pointing out that there are really two dipolarities. Although one of them is more emphasized by Whitehead, the other more by Hartshorne, both thinkers affirmed both dipolarities. Although Whitehead's distinction between the "primordial nature" and the "consequent nature" of God most readily points to the distinction between God as influencing and as being influenced, he also means this distinction to refer to God as unchanging and as changing. The primordial nature, in other words, is God *both* as unchanging *and* as influencing the world, whereas the consequent nature is God *both* as changing *and* as influenced by the world. Whitehead's dipolar theism is deeply problematic partly because of this attempt to make the same distinction account for both dipolarities.

Problems in Whitehead's Doctrine

Two of the problems in Whitehead's doctrine are due to the fact that the initial aims, through which God influences the world, are usually said to come from the primordial nature (alone). This idea is problematic, in part, because of Whitehead's dictum that God is not to be made an exception to metaphysical principles. One of these principles is the "ontological prin-

ciple," according to which only full-fledged actualities can supply explanatory reasons (PR 19, 24). God's primordial nature, as Whitehead himself
points out, is an abstraction, "a mere factor in God, deficient in actuality"
(PR 34; cf. 344–45). It therefore cannot be said to be the source of initial
aims. When Whitehead was asked by A. H. Johnson about this fact—that
he had in effect treated a mere abstraction in God as if it were an actuality
in its own right—Whitehead conceded, reports Johnson, that this had been
a "great carelessness" on his part (1969, 370). A second problem created by
the idea that initial aims come from the primordial nature of God alone is
related to the idea, discussed earlier, that initial aims are said to be for the
best possibility open to each actual occasion, *given its concrete situation*. If the
aims come from the unchanging primordial nature, we have the "perplexing problem," as Cobb puts it (1965, 180–81), of how these aims can be
relevant to the concrete situations of the various actual occasions in the
world.

Both these problems point to the necessity of saying that the act of providing initial aims is an act of *God as a whole* at that moment, not simply of
God's primordial nature. These problems could be handled in the following
way: God is, analogously to a human soul, a serially ordered society of occasions of experience. On this view, the "consequent nature" of God is, in
Hartshorne's language, "simply the abstract principle that there must always
be for each new state of the world process a new Consequent State of deity" (1964b, 323). It is, in other words, an abstraction from the fact that in
each moment God prehends all the actual occasions that have just occurred,
then unifies all these prehensions into a divine satisfaction, which includes
initial aims for the next moment of the universe. These initial aims are based
on God's primordial aims *combined with God's sympathetic knowledge of the present situation*. The next actual occasions of the world, which receive their initial aims from this divine satisfaction, are then prehended by the following
divine occasion, which can thereby provide relevant aims for the subsequent
state of the universe, and so on. This conceptuality, according to which initial aims are provided in each moment by God as a full-fledged actual entity,
honors the ontological principle and explains the relevance of the divine
aims for the present state of the universe. Whitehead himself moved in this
direction: in speaking of God as exerting "particular providence for particular occasions" (PR 351), he was referring to the influence of God's *consequent* nature and thereby of God as a whole.

This solution involves a modification of Whitehead's position, however,
because Whitehead had conceived of God as a single actual entity, *not* as a

serially ordered society of divine occasions of experience.[15] Whitehead's view would mean that whereas all other enduring entities would embody both kinds of process, God would embody only concrescence: there would be no transition from divine occasion to divine occasion, as there would be no such occasions. As pointed out in Chapter 3, Whitehead associated time and temporality with transition. For this reason, he often referred to God as the "non-temporal actual entity," thereby contrasting God with "the temporal world" and "temporal actual entities." But he never meant to deny the reality of process *in* God and even, in a late passage, said that God's nature, though "non-temporal" in one sense, "in another sense is temporal" (AI 208). Whitehead's decision to regard God as a single actual entity, however, meant that he had no conceptuality, consistent with his principles, for ascribing temporality to God. Einstein called his adjustment of his calculations to make them fit his preconceived idea of a nonexpanding universe his "greatest blunder"—although some physicists now think otherwise (Cole 1988). Whitehead's decision to conceive of God as a single, everlasting actual entity was arguably *his* greatest blunder—although some Whiteheadians think otherwise.[16]

This decision lay behind the two problems already discussed, one of which involves a violation of a metaphysical principle. Given the idea of God as a single actual entity, it followed that the divine dipolarity would be understood by analogy with the dipolarity of a finite actual entity ("analogously to all actual entities, the nature of God is dipolar" [PR 345]). This meant that the two poles, which Whitehead called the "primordial" and the "consequent" natures of God, had to be understood by analogy with an actual entity's mental and the physical poles, respectively. That is, given the notion of the primordial nature as the appetitive prehension of the eternal objects, it was thought of as the mental or conceptual pole of God, whereas the consequent nature, which is said to originate with God's prehension of the actual world, was thought of as God's physical pole. Although, given the idea that God is a single actual entity, these equations seem inevitable, they create problems.

[15] Although Whitehead otherwise used the terms *actual entity* and *actual occasion* interchangeably, he specified that *actual occasion* would "always exclude God from its scope" (PR 88).

[16] Although the coherence of Whitehead's view of God as a single actual entity has been defended by several interpreters, including William Christian (1959, 294–301), Marjorie Suchocki (1975, 1988, 1989), and Jorge Nobo (1989), the most extensive defense has been offered by Palmyre Oomen (1998). Problems with this defense will be mentioned in subsequent notes.

For one thing, these equations mean that the same distinction, that between the two poles of a single actual entity, must account for both divine dipolarities. At first glance, Whitehead's distinction between the "primordial" and "consequent" natures of God seems up to this twofold task. The term *primordial,* which is similar to *eternal,* suggests that which is unchanging, whereas the term *consequent* suggests that which changes (in response to something else). Likewise, just as the term *consequent* suggests God as influenced by the world, the term *primordial* can be understood to refer to God as prior to, and thereby influential upon, a particular state of the world. Upon closer examination, however, the problems created by Whitehead's equations become apparent. The fact that the primordial nature is not only God as *influencing the world* but also God as *unchanging* lies behind the problem, noted earlier, of how a wholly unchanging aspect of God can by itself supply initial aims that are relevant to the concrete situation of finite actual occasions, thereby accounting for "particular providence for particular occasions." Likewise, the understanding of this primordial nature as God's mental pole lies behind the other problem discussed earlier, namely, the idea that initial aims are derived from a mere abstraction, which violates the ontological principle.

Still another problem created by Whitehead's equation of the divine dipolarity with the two poles of an actual entity, which follows from his categorization of God as a single actual entity, involves a reversal of the usual relation between the physical and mental poles of an actual entity: "The origination of God is from the mental pole, the origination of an actual occasion is from the physical pole" (PR 36). The idea that God, unlike finite occasions, cannot originate from a physical pole follows, of course, from the identification of God as consequent with the divine physical pole. Likewise, the equation of God as primordial with God's mental pole implies that God originates from the mental pole. In any case, this reversal of the poles seems to make God an exception to a second metaphysical principle. Although the idea that actual entities, understood as occasions of experience, originate with physical feelings is never explicitly called a metaphysical principle, it is clearly one of the fundamental principles of Whitehead's system, as illustrated by his prolonged debate with Hume's doctrine of perception, which had experience beginning with purely conceptual data rather than with physical prehensions of other actualities.[17]

---

[17] Far from regarding the reversal of the poles as a problem, Oomen makes it central to her position (1998, 114, 115, 116, 119). She argues that it is not a problem by saying that God can be regarded as "qualitatively different" in some respects without thereby necessarily being "an

In these ways, Whitehead's decision to regard God as a single actual entity led him to treat God, against his own dictum, as an exception to metaphysical principles. Furthermore, this decision led to violations of some additional metaphysical principles.

One of these principles is that all *enduring* things are temporally ordered *societies* of actual entities. "The real actual things that endure are all societies" (AI 204). As we saw in Chapter 3, Whitehead's whole ontology is based on the rejection of the idea that an enduring individual is a single actual entity, which remains numerically one while undergoing changes of relationships and qualities (PR 78). But that is exactly the description of his God. We have here a clear case of his making God an exception to a metaphysical principle, because Whitehead explicitly refers to the principle involved as *metaphysical*. Having said that the traditional notion of an enduring substance "expresses a useful abstract for many purposes of life," he adds:

> But in metaphysics the conception is sheer error. This error does not consist in the employment of the word "substance"; but in the notion of an actual entity which is characterized by essential qualities, and remains numerically one amidst the changes of accidental relations and of accidental qualities. (PR 79; emphasis added)

In defining God as a single actual entity that endures everlastingly, Whitehead has affirmed what he himself calls a metaphysical error.[18]

Besides being a serious problem in itself, this violation of a third metaphysical principle, in conjunction with Whitehead's affirmation that God

---

exception to the metaphysical scheme" (111). Although she is right about that, the question, with regard to any particular difference that is affirmed, is whether it involves an exception to a metaphysical principle. Although she does not address the objection that the reversal of the poles involves such an exception (at least in her article, which is a translation of a portion of her dissertation, written in Dutch), her approach, as shown in relation to other issues, is to argue that a principle is not metaphysical unless Whitehead explicitly labels it as such (117). Whitehead simply was not that fastidious, however. Some principles are so central to his position and so interlocked with other central principles that they must be considered metaphysical, even if we have no passage in which he calls them such.

[18] In responding to my argument on this point in an earlier publication (Griffin 1989b), Oomen argues that "there is no relapse into substantivism in Whitehead's conception of God." Her basis for this conclusion is the assumption that Whitehead was merely rejecting the idea of "substances" according to which relations are purely accidental for them. Whitehead's view of God would hence not violate his own dictum because although God's particular relations to the world are accidental, "the relatedness as such is not" (Oomen 1998, 117). As Whitehead's statement shows, however, his objection was aimed not only at the Cartesian view of substances, according to which relatedness as such is accidental to them, but at the notion of an actual entity that "remains numerically one amidst the changes of accidental relations," precisely the view that Oomen reaffirms of God, saying that "physical prehensions are constantly added" (115).

and the world are internally related to each other, created two additional violations. If God is a single, everlasting actual entity, as Whitehead suggests, then God is *contemporaneous* with every finite actual occasion—"in unison of becoming with every other creative act" (PR 345). Contemporary actual occasions, however, are *mutually independent,* with neither exerting influence on the other. That indeed is the very definition of two contemporary actual occasions. In particular, if two actual occasions, A and B, are in "unison of becoming," A cannot influence B, because when B prehends its actual world, A has not yet reached satisfaction and therefore, not being anything determinate, cannot be prehended; and B cannot influence A for the same reason. This would seem to be a metaphysical principle if anything is. And yet Whitehead's discussion of the interaction between God and the world *doubly* violates this principle.

On the one hand, in affirming that God has a consequent nature, Whitehead says that *God prehends the world.* But because God is said to be everlastingly in concrescence, this would mean that God, unlike all finite occasions, *can receive efficient causation while exercising final causation,* which seems to give us a fourth violation of a metaphysical principle. The seriousness of this violation is highlighted by a passage in which Whitehead implies that his position is not subject to the Humean critique that talk of theistic causation between God and the world is meaningless because such causation has to be different in kind from causation within the world. In discussing the way in which worldly actual occasions are taken into the divine experience, Whitehead says that this occurs "according to the same principle as in the temporal world the future inherits from the past" (PR 350). However, given the idea that the divine experience is said to be in unison of becoming with the finite occasions it prehends, rather than in their future, inheritance "according to the same principle" is precisely what *cannot* occur.

On the other hand, in affirming that God influences the world, Whitehead says that all finite actual occasions *prehend God.* This affirmation makes God an exception to a fifth metaphysical principle, that an actual entity cannot be prehended until it reaches satisfaction. Whitehead does speak of a divine "satisfaction" (PR 32, 88), which may refer to a satisfaction of the primordial nature alone or of God as a whole, but neither concept makes sense: the primordial nature, being a mere abstraction, cannot have a satisfaction; and God as a whole could never, as an everlasting actual entity, reach satisfaction.[19] Whitehead himself, in fact, evidently admitted the self-contradiction. After getting Whitehead's confirmation that according to his view God

[19] Considering this the central problem to be solved in order to defend the consistency of the conception of God as a single actual entity, Oomen argues that God, although everlast-

never reaches completion in the sense of "perishing," Johnson put the following question to him: "If God never 'perishes,' how can he provide data for other actual entities? Data are only available after the 'internal existence' of the actual entity 'has evaporated.'" Whitehead replied: "This is a genuine problem. I have not attempted to solve it" (Johnson 1969, 373).[20]

And a serious problem it is, especially given Whitehead's early criticism of the "easy assumption that there is an ultimate reality which, *in some unexplained way,* is to be appealed to for the removal of perplexity" (SMW 92; emphasis added). Whitehead does appeal to God to remove many perplexities, such as why the world has an order that supports the emergence of high-level value-experiences, how novel forms can be realized in the world, why we experience moral ideals, and how our lives can have ultimate importance. There is nothing objectionable in principle about appealing to God to explain such things *if* the explanation, besides not involving an appeal to a God of the gaps, does not simply say that God does these things "in some unexplained way." But Whitehead's own doctrine, by portraying God as in unison of becoming with the worldly occasions that both prehend and are prehended by God, finally amounts to saying just that.

Reconceiving God as a Living Person

Given these five ways in which Whitehead's doctrine makes God, contrary to his own dictum, an exception to metaphysical principles, it seems

---

ingly incomplete, is always fully determinate, so that "God is 'satisfied' and [therefore] prehensible at every moment" (1998, 112). Her basis for this claim is the idea that because of the priority and completeness of the primordial nature, God's physical prehensions of the world do not "have to be brought to unity" but can be "instantaneously absorbed into [God's conceptual] unity" (114–15). But her position makes God an exception to several principles, beyond those discussed earlier, that are arguably metaphysical. First, maintaining that God is "always fully determinate" (112), she says that when Whitehead uses the term "concrescence" in regard to God, "this is not concrescence in the usual sense of the word; in other words, not concrescence as the transition from indeterminateness to determinateness" (113). Second, because the other kind of process, that which occurs *between* occasions, also does not occur in God, "the two forms of process mentioned by Whitehead do not apply to God" (119). A third exception is that God is said to have *two* concrescences, one for the consequent nature and one for the primordial nature (120). Finally, her view, which involves saying that God is "always subject, never merely object," entails that the perishing of subjectivity is not needed in the divine case to make prehensibility possible (117). Her attempt to defend Whitehead against the charge of violating one of his metaphysical principles, therefore, results in a position in which several such principles are violated.

[20] Although Oomen (1998, 109) acknowledges that Whitehead evidently gave this reply, she fails to point out that if he had really held the position she attributes to him, he could simply have said: "This is not a problem. God, being an exception in this respect, need not perish to be prehended."

clear to many process philosophers and theologians that to make the concept of God coherent with the basic principles of the system, we must reconceive God as a living person—that is, as an everlasting personally ordered society of divine occasions of experience. Those who have, to the contrary, decided that Whitehead's doctrine of God as a single actual entity is to be retained evidently assume that Whitehead had some very good basis for this doctrine, one important enough to override the fact that it created multiple violations of his own principles. There are two reasons, however, for doubting this assumption. First, Whitehead himself said that he had not worked out a clear doctrine of God. Second, the reason Whitehead himself gives for defining God as a single actual entity, rather than as a living person, is not a strong one.

Given the fact that Whitehead was a pioneer in working out a doctrine of divine dipolarity and that he came to this task rather late in life, it would not be surprising if his doctrine of God is less clear and less well integrated into his total position than other aspects of his philosophy. And this was, furthermore, Whitehead's own judgment, according to Hartshorne, who was Whitehead's assistant at Harvard. Whitehead, reports Hartshorne (1961a, 26), characterized his own ideas about God as "very vague." This report is confirmed by Johnson, who says that "Whitehead remarked that in the last part of *Process [and Reality]*, he was not clear on what he wanted to say" (1969, 371). Whitehead also said, Johnson reports, that he was less interested in working out his idea of God as such than in showing that God "belonged"—that an affirmation of God is necessary to make sense of things (1969, 365). Given all these considerations, there is no a priori reason to assume that Whitehead had some well-considered reason for his decision to conceptualize God as an everlasting actual entity rather than as an everlasting personally ordered society of divine occasions of experience.

The main reason given for this decision, furthermore, does not justify it. This reason consisted of Whitehead's twofold conviction that there could be no loss in God and that in personally ordered societies there is always loss. Regarding the latter point, Whitehead said:

> The ultimate evil in the temporal world is deeper than any specific evil. It lies in the fact that the past fades, that time is a "perpetual perishing." Objectification [prehension of past actual entities] involves elimination. The present fact has not the past fact with it in any full immediacy. . . . In the temporal world, it is the empirical fact that process entails loss: the past is present under an abstraction. But there is no reason, of any ultimate metaphysical generality, why this should be the whole story. (PR 340)

His assumption seemed to be that any transition in God from occasion to occasion would involve loss because "[o]bjectification involves elimination." This assumption is reflected in his answer to Johnson as to whether he could think of God (as consequent) as a society. Whitehead replied that he had considered this possibility because a society is what endures, whereas an actual entity passes away. Nevertheless, Whitehead said, he had rejected this possibility because (in Johnson's paraphrase [1969, 372] of Whitehead's answer): "In a society the past is lost (i.e., one ordinary AE [actual entity] fades away and only some of its data are passed on to another AE). But, in God, his past is not lost."

But this is not a good reason, certainly not good enough to justify multiple violations of Whitehead's own principles. As Whitehead himself indicated, the fact that objectification entails loss is an *empirical* fact about *finite* actual entities, not a *metaphysical* truth. There is no reason, therefore, why perfect preservation of the past would be incompatible with the idea of God as a living person. Hartshorne, who holds this view, says that "there is no lapse of memory, no loss of immediacy, as to occasions already achieved" (Hartshorne and Reese 1953, 274). And Cobb, in defending the idea of God as a personally ordered society of divine occasions of experience, has said: "[L]oss in the temporal world is the result of the very fragmentary way in which past occasions are reenacted in the present. . . . In God we may suppose that no such loss occurs. . . . His experience grows by addition to the past, but loses nothing" (1965, 190–91).

Given this Hartshornean-Cobbian conception of God as a living person, the dipolarity between the unchanging and changing aspects of God need not be equated either with the distinction between the mental and the physical poles of a single actual entity or with the distinction between God as exercising influence and as receiving influence. Rather, this dipolarity can be described as the distinction between, in Hartshorne's terms, the "abstract essence" and the "concrete states" of God (1991b, 571, 644, 700). The abstract essence of God is analogous to what we call the "character" of a human being, meaning that set of characteristics that remains virtually the same day after day, month after month, while the person lives through millions of experiences, these occasions of experience being the "concrete states" in which the abstract essence is exemplified now in this way, now in that. The difference, which is why we have here only an analogy, is that a human being's personality can change whereas the abstract essence of God is strictly immutable (Hartshorne 1951, 531). One attribute of God's abstract essence, for example, is omniscience, the characteristic of knowing everything knowable at any given time. God's concrete *knowledge* grows, insofar as new events happen which add new knowable things to the universe. But the abstract attribute of *omniscience*—the attribute of always knowing everything that is (then) knowable—is exemplified in every concrete state of the divine existence (Hartshorne 1964a, 120–21; 1970, 234). In Hartshorne's writings, "dipolar theism" always refers to this distinction between the abstract essence and the concrete states of God, which provides a coherent way of distinguishing that aspect of God that does not change from that which does.

In light of this Hartshornean idea of God, the dipolarity that was most important to Whitehead, that between God as influencing the world and God as being influenced by the world, can be understood simply in terms of the distinction between concrescence and transition, or subjectivity and objectivity. A divine occasion begins its moment of subjectivity, its process of concrescence, by being influenced by all actual occasions that have reached satisfaction. When this divine occasion's concrescence is completed, so that it has reached satisfaction, it becomes a superject and thereby an object for, meaning an efficient cause on, subsequent actual occasions. The dipolarity of God as influencing and being influenced involves, accordingly, not different aspects or natures of God but simply the distinction between the two modes in which a divine occasion exists. The divine individual, therefore, involves the same perpetual oscillation between efficient and final causation that occurs in worldly individuals.

Although Hartshorne's revision, according to which God is to be conceived as a living person, provides a necessary condition for this solution, Hartshorne himself did not adequately develop it, partly because he did not retain the idea of a realm of eternal objects primordially envisaged by God,[21] which was fundamental for Whitehead's understanding of God's influence by means of initial aims. The fact that Hartshorne's discussion of God does not include this element, however, does not mean that it is incompatible with Hartshorne's idea of God as a living person. In fact, Cobb, in developing this Hartshornean idea, includes within it the idea that God "envisages all possibility eternally" (1965, 187). This eternal envisagement, which is what Whitehead meant by the "primordial nature of God," is common, Cobb suggests (191–92), to every divine occasion of experience, which would mean that it belongs to the abstract essence of God.[22] As suggested

[21] More precisely, although what Whitehead calls "eternal objects of the objective species," meaning the "mathematical Platonic forms" (PR 291), are retained by Hartshorne (1991b, 645), he rejects the existence of Whitehead's "eternal objects of the subjective species," in terms of which Whitehead's God lures the world to actualize moral, aesthetic, and religious values. Hartshorne thinks of this dimension of abstract possibility as a continuum.

[22] The same is true of the "consequent nature" of God. That is, insofar as this name refers to an abstract nature, as distinct from God's concrete states, it also, like the "primordial na-

earlier, the initial aims provided by each divine satisfaction would be based upon this eternal envisagement of possibilities combined with God's prehension of the immediately past state of the world. Adopting the Hartshornean idea of God as a living person does *not,* therefore, necessitate giving up the distinction between the primordial and consequent natures of God. By combining elements of Whitehead's position with elements of Hartshorne's position, we can develop a coherent doctrine of God that does equal justice to the two kinds of divine dipolarity essential to process theism.

This discussion provides a good illustration of the importance of the distinction between the core doctrines of process philosophy on the one hand and the personal ideas of various process philosophers, including Whitehead and Hartshorne, on the other. Some critics, seeing the incoherencies in Whitehead's doctrine of God, have rejected process philosophy itself, at least as a basis for philosophy of religion or theology. The problems in Whitehead's theism would betoken a problem in Whiteheadian process philosophy as such, however, only if these problems followed from its basic principles. But these problems, as we have seen, result from the fact that Whitehead's own doctrine of God is *inconsistent* with some of these principles. Therefore, overcoming the problems requires only, in Cobb's words, "achieving greater coherence of first principles" (1965, 179).

The Importance of the Distinction between God's Abstract Essence and Concrete States

The twofold argument concerning process philosophy's theism is that it is more adequate, rationally as well as religiously, than both atheism and traditional theism. This argument is made throughout this book as a whole. In the present subsection, I look specifically at how the divine dipolarity emphasized by Hartshorne, that between the abstract essence and the concrete states of God, is important for a doctrine of God that is both rationally intelligible and religiously adequate.

To be religiously adequate, a doctrine of God must be able to affirm that God is absolute and therefore unchanging in one sense and yet really related to the (changing) world and therefore changing in another sense. It is pri-

---

ture," belongs to what Hartshorne calls the "abstract essence" of God, which refers to those features of God that are instantiated in every concrete state. In other words, each concrete state of God—each divine occasion of experience—not only appetitively envisages the eternal objects but also responds sympathetically to the world.

marily because of this twofold emphasis that Hartshorne refers to his theism as "neo-classical." Classical theists, in speaking of God as the necessary, timeless absolute, completely independent of and thereby unaffected by the temporal world, were enunciating a vitally important aspect of the idea of God. Their mistake, however, was to equate this aspect with God as a whole, thereby committing the fallacy of misplaced concreteness. What makes Hartshorne's view *neo*-classical is the idea that the attributes of timelessness, necessity, absoluteness, independence, immutability, and impassibility apply not to God as a whole but merely to the abstract essence of God. God as concrete, meaning God as a whole, is temporal, contingent, relative, dependent, changeable, and passible.

This affirmation, Hartshorne emphasizes, is essential to the religious adequacy of a doctrine of God. Unless time is real for the divine perspective, which is the final truth, then time is ultimately unreal, so that the histories of individuals, nations, religions, and civilizations are ultimately meaningless. If God is not affected by the world, then in attributing "love" to God, says Hartshorne, we empty the notion of love "of its most essential kernel, the element of sympathy, of the feeling of others' feelings" (1984, 29). If God is in no sense dependent upon and therefore contingent upon and relativized by the world, then no real meaning can be given to the religious idea that we are to "serve God" (1941, 48, 114). This point is of utmost importance to Hartshorne, for whom the highest religious aspiration, and the very meaning of life, is to be able consciously to make a permanent contribution to the divine life (1991b, 662; 1987, 94). In expounding his "religion of contributionism," Hartshorne says: "We contribute our feelings to others, and above all to the Universal Recipient of feeling, the One 'to Whom all hearts are open'" (1990, 379). "My sharpest objection to classical theism," he adds,

> is its making God the giver of everything and recipient of nothing. I feel a need for a divine recipient of our contributions as definitely as I feel the need for a divine contributor to or enabler of our existence. We need a God to serve, not just a God who serves us. But a timeless God does not fit these requirements. A "first" cause is not enough. . . . There is equal need of a last effect, or rather an everlasting effect. (1991b, 672)

Religious adequacy, however, also requires the attributes insisted on by classical theists. The idea of God, Anselm insightfully said, is the idea of "that greater than which none can be conceived," which is the idea of perfection. Although God must be contingent in some respects, Hartshorne says, God must certainly *exist* necessarily. And although God cannot be independent, unchanging, and impassible in *all* respects, the divine *character* must exemplify these attributes. For example, although to be loving God must be affected by the world, the *fact* that God is loving must be an unchanging characteristic of God, independent of anything that may happen.

To have a religiously adequate idea of God, therefore, we must think of God as both necessary and contingent, both absolute and relative, both unchanging and changing, both independent and dependent, both nontemporal and temporal. It might seem as if Hartshorne is affirming a self-contradictory view of God, which would mean that religious adequacy is being purchased, as some critics have charged, at the expense of rational intelligibility. However, as Hartshorne points out: "No rule of logic forbids saying that a thing has a property and also its negative, provided the positive and the negative properties are referred to the thing in diverse aspects" (1970, 233). Lying behind this statement is Hartshorne's dipolar theism with its distinction between the abstract essence and the concrete states of God. It is the abstract essence that is necessary, absolute, unchanging, independent, and nontemporal, whereas God as concrete is contingent, relative, changing, dependent, and temporal.

To illustrate by means of the distinction between necessity and contingency: every concrete state of the divine existence is contingent because it involves prehensions of the world, so that if the world's creatures had made different decisions, the divine experience would have been different. For example, if Al Gore's parents had not had any children, God's love for the world would not include love for Al Gore. This contingency of the concrete states or experiences of God, however, is compatible with the necessary existence of God. Although each concrete state of God is far more than the abstract essence of God, each such state does include that abstract essence, which exists necessarily. Therefore, although the content of each concrete state of God is partly contingent, it is necessary that some such state will occur. In this way, the dipolarity of Hartshorne's theism supports its rational intelligibility as well as its religious adequacy.

Although some of the critics of this form of theism complain that it does not make God "transcendent enough," it actually, Hartshorne likes to emphasize, involves a doctrine of "dual transcendence," which means that there are two ways, not just one, in which God is perfect and thereby categorically unique. Classical theism attributed to God only the uniquely excellent way of being independent and necessary, but there is also, Hartshorne argues, a uniquely excellent way of being dependent and contingent (1991b, 643). Besides the divine absoluteness, meaning that respect in which God excludes all others, there is, to use the title of one of Hartshorne's books, "the divine relativity," which refers to God's perfect inclusion of all others.

These two kinds of transcendence are distinguishable in terms of two kinds of perfections: absolute perfections, in which a maximum is possible, and relative perfections, in which it is not. For example, it is possible for God to have *omniscience,* understood as the abstract capacity to know everything knowable, but maximal knowledge is impossible because there will always be new events to know.[23] Whereas God's omniscience exemplifies *absolute* perfection because it is unsurpassable (even by God in a subsequent state), God's concrete knowledge exemplifies *relative* perfection because it can be surpassed (although only by God in a subsequent state).[24] Hartshorne's doctrine of dual transcendence, accordingly, does not put transcendence at odds with either rational intelligibility or religious values.

Some critics have alleged, however, that process theism is not really a doctrine of *God.* I will look at this issue before moving, in the next chapter, to the reasons for thinking the God of process theism to exist.

3. Process Theism and the Generic Idea of God

As I pointed out earlier, process theism's main contribution to the question of the existence of God is to provide a concept of God that is free from the problems that undermined the arguments provided by traditional theists. Whitehead and Hartshorne both refer to this issue. Whitehead, for example, introduces his idea of God with the statement that it is "an attempt to add another speaker to that masterpiece, Hume's *Dialogues Concerning Natural Religion*" (PR 343). Having already agreed that "Hume's *Dialogues* criticize unanswerably" more traditional ways of explaining the world theistically, he

[23] The fact that God at any moment does not know "future events," incidentally, does not detract from the divine omniscience because nothing more can be demanded of omniscience than the capacity to know everything knowable, and such events are, given process philosophy's ontology, simply not knowable. In Hartshorne's words, "[F]uture events, events that have not yet happened, are not there to be known. . . . *God does not already or eternally know what we do tomorrow, for, until we decide, there are no such entities as our tomorrow's decisions*" (1984, 39).

[24] The same distinction can be made with regard to the divine beauty. As a feature of the abstract essence of God, the divine beauty is absolutely perfect, unsurpassable in principle, whereas the beauty of the divine experience in any moment is only relatively perfect, which means that it can always be further enriched by our contributions (Hartshorne 1991b, 594).

thereby indicates that he is presenting an idea of deity not considered by Hume. Hartshorne, with reference to Kant's claim "to have defined the one and only philosophically legitimate 'ideal of reason' or idea of God," says that Kant's *ens realissimum* ("most real being") is not simply indemonstrable and only barely possible, as Kant argued, but "demonstrably impossible." Also, Hartshorne notes, this concept is "not what 'God' as a religious term ought to mean" (1970, 277). It is, therefore, simply sloppy (or perhaps wishful) thinking to accept the widespread idea, repeated in countless books and essays, that Hume and Kant demolished every possible argument for the existence of God, thereby settling the question for all time.[25]

This is a logical point. There are numerous ideas as to what the word *God* means. Arguments against two of those ideas—Hume's *Dialogues,* for example, considers only supernaturalistic Christian theism, represented by Demea, and supernaturalistic deism, represented by Cleanthes—can at best refute those two ideas. Some critics, to be sure, recognize this point. For example, in *The Miracle of Theism: Arguments for and against the Existence of God,* John Mackie directed his arguments against traditional theism, according to which the definition of God includes the attribute "able to do everything (i.e. omnipotent)" (1982, 1). Mackie concludes that the existence of such a being is highly improbable, especially in light of the problem of evil. He points out, however, that those who believe in a deity that is "though powerful, not quite omnipotent,[26] will not be embarrassed by this

[25] For example, Kai Nielsen reports with approval the "very considerable consensus among contemporary philosophers and theologians that arguments like those developed by Hume and Kant show that no proof (*a priori* or empirical) of God's existence is possible" (1985, 18). One problem with this consensus is that Kant offered what he considered a proof, namely, his moral argument for the existence of God. More germane to the point at hand is that when Kant claims all the traditional arguments fail, his point is that they do not prove the existence of a supreme being who, being self-sufficient in all respects, created the world ex nihilo. With regard to the argument from design (which Kant called the "physico-theological proof"), for example, he said that it shows "the contingency of the form merely, but not of the matter . . . of the world," so that it can at most "demonstrate the existence of an *architect of the world,* whose efforts are limited by the capabilities of the material with which he works, but not of a *creator of the world,* to whom all things are subject" (1952, 188, 189). In light of the fact that the God of which Whitehead and Hartshorne speak, like the God of the Bible (see note 28), created our world out of chaos, not out of absolute nothingness, their view that the world's order provides evidence for such a being is supported, not undermined, by Kant. Finally, because Kant's view of causation, like Hume's, serves to undermine *all* arguments for a being that transcends the world known in sensory perception, it is dependent on the Humean-Kantian assumption that our perception is limited to *sense* perception, which James, Whitehead, and much empirical evidence have shown to be false.

[26] Hartshorne would not make the point in this way, which seems to imply that although a being possessing omnipotence in the traditional sense would be possible, the divine being who happens to exist has less power. Hartshorne insists that God's power is the greatest pos-

difficulty" (151). Many critics of theistic arguments are, unfortunately, not as circumspect. They say, or at least imply, that in refuting the arguments for the existence of the God of traditional theism, they have established the probable truth of complete atheism. The fallaciousness of this conclusion is illustrated by the fact that most proponents of nontraditional forms of theism also agree that the case for traditional theism has been refuted. For example, Hartshorne, referring to the classical version of traditional theism, says that the arguments against it are "as conclusive as philosophical arguments could well be" (1941, 58). Because of its many problems, especially its problem of evil, the traditional idea of God is an easy target. Most critics of theism have ignored less easily refutable ideas of divinity.

One way to avoid the necessity of examining such ideas is to claim that they are not really ideas of God (sometimes, in such statements, pronounced *Gawd*). For example, Antony Flew, having equated Christian theism with the all-determining version of traditional theism, argues that Christian theism is incoherent because it holds that nothing happens without God's consent while maintaining that human beings sin by violating the will of God (1966, 47). In making this argument, Flew is simply repeating the charge made by many theists, including Whitehead and Hartshorne, who have offered an alternative form of theism in which this inconsistency no longer exists. But Flew then claims that any doctrine that would suggest that God cannot control all events would not be "true theism," so that it could be dismissed with the rebuke, "Your God is too small" (51–52). In the same vein, Roland Puccetti argues that "reflective theists" understand that God, to be an "adequate object of religious attitudes," must have unlimited power, knowledge, and goodness (1964, 244–45). Then, while rejecting this "reflective" concept of God as *incoherent,* he dismisses all coherent doctrines as *not really reflective.* This strategy is also employed by Kai Nielsen. Rejecting traditional, nonanthropomorphic doctrines as incoherent, Nielsen then dismisses all other concepts as anthropomorphic, "Zeus-like conceptions" that speak of God "as if he were some kind of great green bird" (1989a, 2, 244) or "a sort of cosmic Mickey Mouse" (1982, ix). The positions thus dismissed as "not really theistic" by Flew, Puccetti, and Nielsen would include, by implication, those of such respected philosophers and theologians as Otto Pfleiderer, C. Lloyd-Morgan, Frederick Tennant, Hastings Rashdall, James Ward, William Temple, Charles Raven, William James, E. S. Brightman, and

---

sible. This different formulation, however, does not subvert Mackie's point that if the traditional doctrine of omnipotence is rejected, the existence of God is not refuted by the world's evil.

Reinhold Niebuhr, as well as Whitehead, Hartshorne, Cobb, Schubert Ogden, Marjorie Suchocki, Daniel Day Williams, and other process theists.

The credibility of such dismissals in relation to process theism, in any case,
can be examined in terms of what I call the "generic idea of God," meaning an idea of deity that is widely shared by Christians, Jews, and Muslims
as well as theists in many other traditions. According to this generic idea, the
term *God* (or its equivalent) refers to a being that is:

1. A personal, purposive being.
2. Perfect in love, goodness, and beauty.
3. Perfect in wisdom and knowledge.
4. Supreme, perhaps even perfect, in power.
5. Creator and sustainer of our universe.
6. Holy.
7. Omnipresent.
8. Necessarily and everlastingly existent.
9. Providentially active in nature and history.
10. Experienced by human beings.
11. The ultimate source of moral norms.
12. The ultimate guarantee of the meaning of life.
13. The ground of hope for the victory of good over evil.

Whether all these features are *necessary* for a concept of God could be argued,
but that these features are *sufficient* is beyond reasonable debate. No one believing in a being thus characterized could plausibly be said not to believe in
God. All these features are affirmed by traditional theism.[27] They are also all
affirmed by process theism.

Process theism, of course, gives a different interpretation to some of these
features. The crucial ones, for the debate about whether process theism is
really a doctrine of *God,* are the fourth, fifth, and ninth features. With regard to the fourth, process theism denies that being "supreme in power"
means being "omnipotent" in the sense of *essentially* having *all* the power (so
that any power possessed by creatures would be merely on loan). With re-

---

[27] At least most of these features are included in the definition proffered by Swinburne of
God as "a person without a body (i.e., a spirit), present everywhere, the creator and sustainer
of the universe, a free agent, able to do anything (i.e., omnipotent), knowing all things, perfectly good, a source of moral obligation, immutable, eternal, a necessary being, holy, and
worthy of worship" (1977, 2). I did not, incidentally, include Swinburne's last attribute, "worthy of worship," in my list because unlike the other characteristics, it is an evaluation, not a
description, and including it would have rendered tautological my conclusion that the being
described is worthy of the name *God.*

gard to the fifth feature, process theism, while affirming that God created our universe, denies that this creation was ex nihilo in the sense of "out of absolute nothingness." [28] With regard to the ninth feature, process theism, while affirming God's providential activity in the world—with, as we have seen, variable divine influence—denies that this activity ever involves interruptions of the normal causal processes. But—returning to the fourth feature—process theism does affirm that God is the supreme power of the universe, and Hartshorne in particular emphasizes the *perfection* of God's power, saying that God's power is "absolutely maximal, the greatest possible, but even the greatest power is still one power among others, is not the only power" (1964a, 138).

Because all the remaining features of the generic idea of God are affirmed by process philosophy's naturalistic, doubly dipolar theism—as has already been shown or will be shown in the following chapters—it cannot credibly be said not really to be a doctrine of *God*. Process theists, in fact, claim that their doctrine explicates the *religious* idea of deity, as that which is alone worthy of worship, far better than does traditional theism (Hartshorne 1964a, vii, ix–x, 1; 1991b, 721). Process theism is said, furthermore, to explicate the kind of divine actuality that the "evidence for God" really suggests: "Fully developed," says Hartshorne, "each of the arguments points not simply to the theistic conclusion, but to the neo-classical form of this conclusion" (1970, 296).

If there is to be harmony between the scientific and the religious communities in terms of basic worldview, it is necessary not only for the scientific

---

[28] It has widely been assumed by Christian philosophers and theologians that any acceptable idea of God must affirm the doctrine of creation ex nihilo, with the further assumption being that this is the biblical doctrine. These assumptions have been so deeply ingrained (as illustrated by Kant in note 25) that although I have already mentioned that studies by Jon Levenson and Gerhard May have shown the doctrine of creation out of absolute nothingness *not* to be biblical, I should expand on this point. The book by Levenson (1988) shows that the doctrine of creation out of chaos is reflected not only in Genesis 1 but also throughout the Hebrew Bible, having been central to the cultic life of the Hebrew people. Although Christian scholars have long accepted the fact that creation ex nihilo is not in the Old Testament, they have held that it does emerge in the inter-testamental literature, especially 2 Maccabees, and therefore could be assumed to lie behind the handful of passages in the New Testament traditionally taken to reflect this doctrine. The book by May (1994) shows that the doctrine of creation ex nihilo was articulated by Christian theologians only in the latter half of the second century C.E. in response to Marcion's form of gnosticism. Until that time, Christian thinkers, like prior and contemporary Jewish thinkers, had considered the biblical view to be quite compatible with the idea of creation out of chaos as articulated in Plato's *Timaeus*. I discuss the books of Levenson and May at some length in Griffin forthcoming b.

community to replace naturalism$_{sam}$ with a less restrictive form of naturalism$_{ns}$ but also for theistic religious communities to replace, both substantively and rhetorically, supernaturalism with a naturalistic form of theism. Whitehead has provided most of the ingredients for such a theism. By employing Hartshorne's reconception of God as a living person, thereby modifying Whitehead's doctrine of God to bring it into harmony with his own metaphysical principles, we can have a form of naturalistic theism that is both fully coherent and religiously adequate, clearly affirming all the features of our generic idea of God. With this conclusion, we now turn to the question of the evidence for the existence of God thus conceived.

[5]

Natural Theology Based
on Naturalistic Theism

In the previous chapter, I explicated Whitehead's version of naturalistic theism and argued that in spite of some problems in Whitehead's own position a coherent version of naturalistic theism, consistent with the basic principles of process philosophy, can be developed. I also showed why this version of theism cannot be dismissed as too far removed from the ordinary meaning of the word *God*. In the present chapter, I discuss the major reasons to believe that such a divine reality actually exists, showing how natural theology is transformed when carried out on the basis of this naturalistic theism. Before doing so, however, I look at the *nature* of process philosophy's multifaceted argument for the existence of God.

1. The Nature of Process Philosophy's Argument
for the Existence of God

Although process philosophy employs various kinds of evidence to construct a number of arguments, not one is to be thought of as a wholly independent argument, to be evaluated in complete separation from the others. The various arguments are instead to be regarded as part of what is sometimes called a "cumulative argument." As Hartshorne puts it, "[A]ll the arguments are phases of one 'global' argument, that *the properly formulated theistically religious view of life and reality is the most intelligible, self-consistent, and satisfactory one that can be conceived*" (1970, 276). In such a cumulative or global argument, each of the constitutive arguments has some independence from the others and, therefore, can lend support to the others. Because of the relative independence of each of its constitutive arguments, the global argument is not like a "chain" that is "no stronger than its weakest link" but like a cable, each strand of which strengthens the others (Hartshorne 1991b, 595). Hence, the background considerations for evaluating the probability of each argument include the considerations lifted up by the other arguments. This point is often ignored, as critics will typically examine each argument independently of the others, asking *ad seriatim* whether each argument, all by itself, is sufficient to demonstrate the strong probability of the existence of a being worthy of the name *God*.

Also, the global argument, with each of its strands, is not to be taken in isolation from Whiteheadian process philosophy as a whole. The relationship is, again, one of only partial independence. The global argument is partially independent of the whole system insofar as the same general kinds of evidence can be used to argue, from the standpoint of different metaphysical assumptions, for more or less different versions of theism. Because of this partial independence, the global argument, considered in abstraction from any particular philosophical system, provides various considerations against atheism. But this independence is *only* partial because the soundness of process philosophy's cumulative argument for God cannot finally be evaluated apart from process philosophy as a whole.

The negative point implicit here is directed against the tendency of critics to evaluate the cogency of the various arguments not only in isolation from one another but also in terms of various background assumptions involved in naturalism$_{sam}$. The employment of this procedure against the arguments to be given here would be question-begging because process philosophy's reasons for affirming a naturalistic, dipolar theism presuppose its panexperientialism and its nonsensationist doctrine of perception. Insofar as the philosophical position is coherent, furthermore, this ontology and epistemology finally make sense only in the context of this form of theism. "If, without psychicalism, theism is incoherent," says Hartshorne, "so, without theism, is psychicalism" (1991b, 692). This mutual dependence is implicit in the inclusion of Whiteheadian naturalistic theism with its double dipolarity among the core doctrines of process philosophy. The various theistic arguments as formulated by process philosophy, therefore, involve pointing out respects in which there is a "God-shaped hole" in process philosophy's way of construing the world in general and human experience in particular. The formal structure of the global argument is that *insofar as process philosophy's construal of the world is otherwise convincing, seeming more adequate and self-consistent than other known options, the reality of a divine being, as portrayed by process philosophy, is implied.*

The question, accordingly, is not whether process philosophy's panentheism is convincing when examined through materialistic, sensationistic lenses. The question is *which overall worldview is most adequate.* Process philosophy has provided a new naturalistic worldview, a way of embodying naturalism$_{ns}$ that is radically different from naturalism$_{sam}$. If we use the term *prehensive* to point to its naturalistic but nonsensationist doctrine of perception, we can call it naturalism$_{ppp}$ (for prehensive-panentheistic-panexperientialist). The question of the probable truth of its panentheism, therefore, involves the question whether naturalism$_{ppp}$ is superior to both naturalism$_{sam}$ and supernaturalistic theism. A complete judgment, of course, would have to bring in all the other living options, but it is here necessary to limit explicit comparisons to its two chief rivals in the contemporary Western world (although a beginning move toward a more cross-cultural philosophy of religion is made in Chapter 7).

Now that this point about the holistic nature of this argument for theism has been made, it is necessary to caution against exaggerations. It is only the *precise shape* of process philosophy's concept of God and thereby of its global theistic argument that is mutually implicated with its other core doctrines. The various arguments in more general form carry some weight independently of any particular system with which they may be associated. It is for this reason that one can recognize the inadequacy of complete atheism even before having a better worldview to put in its place. The ensuing global argument, therefore, should be taken as the completion of the discussion, begun in Chapter 1, of the inadequacies of atheism.

Most of the arguments, says Hartshorne, "may be interpreted as showing that the idea of God, taken as true, is required for the interpretation of some fundamental aspect of life or existence" (1970, 280). The one exception in his list, he points out, is the ontological argument. Although Hartshorne has devoted considerable attention to this argument (1962, chap. 1; 1964a, chap. 9; 1965), I will not discuss it partly because I, evidently like Whitehead (RM 68), do not find it convincing[1] and partly because—which is perhaps the same thing—this argument is *not* "required for the interpretation of some fundamental aspect of life or existence." In any case, the other arguments for God can be divided into two fundamental types: those that are

---

[1] Even Hartshorne says that, some of his interpreters notwithstanding, he has "not used this argument as *the* way, or even as, by itself, a very good way, to justify belief in God" (1984, 126; cf. 1991b, 668).

based on some "fundamental aspect of life or existence" in the world in general and those that are based on some fundamental aspect of human experience in particular. I will give five of the first type, then four (or eight, depending upon how one counts) of the second type, for a total of nine (or thirteen).[2]

2. Arguments from Fundamental Aspects of the World in General

The fundamental aspects of the world in general, on which the five arguments of first type are based, are the metaphysical order of existence as such, the basic contingent order of our cosmic epoch, the teleological order of our cosmic epoch, the emergence of novelty, and the world's excessive beauty.

The Metaphysical Argument

The argument from existence as such has traditionally been called the "cosmological argument." Beginning with the assessment of the world as contingent—that is, as not bearing the necessity for its existence within itself—this argument concluded that the world's existence can be explained only by reference to a being that does exist necessarily. Traditional theists took the argument to point to the existence of a God *in all respects* necessary and a world *in all respects* contingent.

Process theists, of course, do not accept this conclusion. On the one hand, as Hartshorne points out, the idea that God exists necessarily does not mean that God is in all respects necessary. On the other hand, the fact that our particular universe is contingent does not imply that the very existence of a universe of finite beings is contingent. In spite of rejecting the cosmological argument in its traditional form, however, process philosophers do believe that it is based on a sound intuition. From the perspective of process philosophy, in fact, what has been called the cosmological argument contains *two* distin-

---

[2] One of my major surprises in writing this book involved this chapter. I had assumed that it would rely heavily on Hartshorne, who discussed the arguments for the existence of God much more extensively and systematically than Whitehead, whose arguments are found in brief passages—often appearing (misleadingly) to be casual asides—scattered throughout his writings. When I focused on the question of which arguments were really convincing to me, however, I found the formulations provided by Whitehead more powerful (although I found that some of them required revision). My conclusion that Whitehead's arguments for God's existence are actually stronger than his formulation of the nature of God is consistent with his statement, cited in the previous chapter, that he was less interested in working out his position on the latter than in simply showing that God "belonged."

guishable arguments: besides a properly cosmological argument, which I will discuss later, there is a metaphysical argument, to be explained here.

A point made earlier, that the precise form of every argument employed by process philosophy will reflect its particular construal of the nature of reality, is especially true with regard to this metaphysical argument. For process philosophy, as we have seen, a finite actual entity is an actual occasion. As in the Aristotelian view that forms and prime matter are ingredients of every finite substance, in process philosophy the "formative elements" of every actual occasion include the realm of ideal forms (eternal objects) and creativity (RM 88). Also, just as "Aristotle found it necessary to complete his metaphysics by the introduction of a Prime Mover—God," so Whitehead was led by his own "metaphysical train of thought [as to] the general character of things" to affirm "an entity at the base of all actual things" (SMW 173–74), thereby coming to affirm God as a third formative element in all actual occasions (RM 88). Although Whitehead recognized that the exact form of Aristotle's argument was based upon an erroneous physics, he also said that, given his (Whitehead's) own metaphysical analysis, "an analogous metaphysical problem arises which can be solved only in an analogous fashion" (SMW 174). While agreeing with Whitehead on this, I think his version of the argument needs to be revised.

According to Whitehead's analysis, "the universe exhibits a creativity with infinite freedom, and a realm of forms with infinite possibilities." By themselves, however, "this creativity and these forms are together impotent to achieve actuality" (RM 115). Whitehead's explanation for the joint impotence of creativity and the eternal forms is that for an actual occasion to come into existence, a task must be performed that cannot be assigned to either of them because of the ontological principle, according to which only *actual* entities can act: creativity is not an actual entity (RM 90), and the ideal forms are, by definition, ideal rather than actual. The task to be performed follows from the twofold fact that although the realm of eternal forms is infinite, our world involves a set of particular limitations that must reflect a primordial selection from this infinite realm of possibility. Whitehead's argument is formulated thus:

> [T]he spatio-temporal relationship, in terms of which the actual course of events is to be expressed, is nothing else than a selective limitation within the general systematic relationships among eternal objects. By "limitation," as applied to the spatio-temporal continuum, I mean those matter-of-fact determinations—such as the three dimensions of space, and the four dimensions of the spatio-temporal continuum—which are inherent in the actual course

of events, but which present themselves as *arbitrary* in respect to a more abstract possibility. (SMW 161; emphasis added)

Whitehead later says that these arbitrary elements include, besides the causal relations mentioned in the above quotation, logical relations and standards of value. These arbitrary elements point to the existence of an actuality that performed this antecedent selection (SMW 174–78).[3] This antecedent selection is what Whitehead later comes to call the "primordial nature of God," understood as a primordial "decision" (PR 46, 47, 164). If we combine the discussion in *Science in the Modern World* with most of the relevant passages in *Process and Reality,* Whitehead's position would seem to be that a divine primordial decision is responsible for both (1) the basic contingent laws of our cosmic epoch (meaning what are normally called the laws of physics) and (2) the ultimate principles of metaphysics.

Several interlocking reasons exist for rejecting both aspects of this view as inconsistent with Whitehead's own core principles. In the first place, Whitehead in *Process and Reality* comes to distinguish more clearly than he previously had between the contingent (arbitrary) laws of our cosmic epoch, on the one hand, and the metaphysical principles applying to all possible worlds, on the other. Regarding the former, he says: "The arbitrary, as it were 'given,' elements in the laws of nature warn us that we are in a special cosmic epoch" (PR 91). He includes among these arbitrary elements "the four dimensions of the spatio-temporal continuum," which had been mentioned in the statement quoted from *Science and the Modern World.* Because these factors are peculiar to our cosmic epoch, they cannot be ascribed to a primordial decision: the primordial is *eternal* (PR 13, 345), whereas our cosmic epoch, by definition, has existed only for a limited period.

The metaphysical principles, by contrast, are "necessary" (PR 3, 4). The reason to suppose certain features of the world to be metaphysical is that they are "characteristics so general that we cannot conceive any alternatives" (PR 288). In light of this distinction between metaphysical principles and the arbitrary elements in the laws of our cosmic epoch, Whitehead should *not* have said that the metaphysical principles result from a decision. Elsewhere using the word *decision* in terms of "its root sense of a 'cutting off,'" Whitehead points out that a decision cuts off alternative possibilities, resulting in

[3] In *Science and the Modern World,* in which Whitehead first developed this argument, he described God not as an actuality but as merely a principle (called alternatively the "principle of limitation" and the "principle of concretion"), saying that "God is not concrete, but He is the ground for concrete actuality" (SMW 178). I have phrased the argument, however, in terms of Whitehead's later acceptance of the implications of the ontological principle, according to which only that which is itself a concrete actuality can be the "ground" of anything else.

that which is "given" as distinct from that which is "not given" (PR 42–43). It is this "element of 'givenness' in things," he adds, that "implies some activity procuring limitation" (PR 43). The metaphysical principles, however, are precisely those principles that are necessary, having no alternatives, so they are *not* "given" in the sense of "arbitrary." They cannot, accordingly, intelligibly be attributed to a decision, even a primordial one. Whitehead should not, therefore, have said that God's primordial nature, *understood as a decision,* "at once exemplifies *and establishes* the categoreal conditions" (PR 344; emphasis added) or that a primordial decision "constitutes the metaphysical stability whereby the actual process exemplifies general principles of metaphysics" (PR 40). He should instead have regarded these principles as obtaining independently of any decision.

This alternative idea is, in fact, sometimes reflected in Whitehead's statements. He says, for example, that the primordial nature of God "presupposes the *general* metaphysical character of creative advance, of which it is the primordial exemplification" (PR 344). The metaphysical principles are simply the principles descriptive of this general character of creative advance. If they are presupposed by God's primordial nature, that primordial nature cannot be a decision that *establishes* these principles.

Another reason to reject the idea of a "primordial decision" is that, as Hartshorne has said, the very notion is incoherent. A decision, as we have seen, is that which cuts off alternative possibilities. But the primordial is the eternal and, as Hartshorne emphasizes (1965, 141) in agreement with Aristotle, the eternal is equatable with the necessary: if something is eternal, it could not have been otherwise; and if something exists necessarily, it could never have failed to exist. "Primordial decision," therefore, makes no more sense than "round square."

Whitehead was probably misled here by the same feature of his thought that created so many other incoherencies—his idea of God as a single actual entity, which resulted in his equation of the primordial nature of God with God's "mental pole." The mental pole, to recall, is that aspect of an actual entity in which it is *causa sui,* making a free decision as to what it is to be. Whitehead's equation of God's primordial nature with the divine mental pole implied, therefore, that this primordial nature must consist of a free decision. "A temporal occasion in respect to the second element of its character, and God in respect to the first element of his character," says Whitehead, "satisfy Spinoza's definition of substance, that it is *causa sui*" (PR 88).

As we have seen, however, the double dipolarity implied by Whitehead's position can be made intelligible only by thinking, with Hartshorne, of God as an everlasting society of divine occasions of experience exemplifying an eternal, abstract essence. From this perspective, the metaphysical principles are *neither* independent of God *nor* dependent upon a divine decision. Rather, Whitehead's statement that God is the "chief exemplification" of the metaphysical categories would mean that these categories belong to the eternal essence of God, as Hartshorne suggests (1941, 41; Hartshorne and Reese 1953, 277). So, rather than being either independent of God or dependent upon a divine decision, they are dependent on God without being in any way contingent. Being part of the eternal essence of God, they share its necessity.

This position is more in harmony, in fact, with Whitehead's later position in *Adventures of Ideas,* which was fundamental for the discussion of Whiteheadian naturalistic theism in the previous chapter. According to this position, as we saw, "metaphysics requires that the relationships of God to the World should lie beyond the accidents of will" (AI 168). Whitehead's earlier suggestion that the metaphysical principles are due to a divine decision, by contrast, seems dangerously close to the idea that the causal relationships between God and the world *are* due to the divine will, which would significantly undermine process philosophy's answer to the problem of evil.[4]

This position, however, still implies a metaphysical argument for the divine existence. According to one formulation of Whitehead's ontological principle: "Everything must be somewhere; and here 'somewhere' means 'some actual entity'" (PR 46). The implication is that because the eternal metaphysical principles must be in some actuality, there must be some necessarily existent individual actuality in which they reside. Their home could not be simply the world of finite occasions: although some such world exists necessarily and therefore always, there is no finite enduring individual that has always existed. Being localized, furthermore, a finite being could not explain the universality of the metaphysical principles. This point seems to be implied in one of Whitehead's explications of the ontological prin-

---

[4] For example, much of Stephen Ely's criticism of Whitehead's theism follows from Ely's judgment that Whitehead's God, while not metaphysically ultimate, is nevertheless "responsible for the choice of all types of order that actually prevail, and this makes him responsible, one would suppose, for whatever happens" (Ely 1983 [1942], 178). Given the self-determination vis-à-vis God attributed to all actual occasions, Ely's charge that Whitehead's God is responsible "for whatever happens" is an exaggeration. However, if Whitehead's God freely chose even the most fundamental order of our world, which we call its metaphysical order, then it would be correct to say that this God is responsible for whatever *can* happen, and it would be reasonable to wonder whether God could not have chosen a fundamental order that would, while still allowing for the positive values of our world, not allow for so much evil. This problem is not raised by the Hartshornean position that the metaphysical principles belong to the eternal, abstract essence of God, so that they could not have been otherwise.

ciple. Having said that "the reasons for things are always to be found in the composite nature of definite actual entities," he adds: "in the nature of definite temporal actual entities for reasons which refer to a particular environment" and "in the nature of God for reasons of the highest absoluteness" (PR 19).

If we take "the nature of God" in that statement to mean the abstract essence of God, the universality of the metaphysical principles is explainable by the fact that they are inherent in this abstract essence. Because it is exemplified by every divine occasion of experience, this abstract essence, with its metaphysical principles, is prehended by every finite occasion of experience. "[T]he primordial Being," Whitehead says, "shares his nature with the world," thereby being "a component in the natures of all [actual occasions]" (AI 130). It is in this sense, I suggest, that we should understand Whitehead's statement that "a primordial actual entity constitutes the metaphysical stability whereby the actual process exemplifies general principles of metaphysics" (PR 40).

What I am calling the metaphysical argument, then, contends that *the fact that the "actual process exemplifies general principles of metaphysics" can be understood only by positing the existence of an omnipresent, everlasting individual to whose abstract essence the metaphysical principles belong, and who shares these principles by being prehended by all finite actual entities.* What makes it an argument from the very existence of finite actual entities is its contention that apart from the metaphysical order thus provided, finite actual occasions could not even occur. In Whitehead's words:

> Apart from God, the remaining formative elements would fail in their functions. There would be no creatures, since, apart from harmonious order, the perceptive fusion would be a confusion neutralizing achieved feeling. . . . It is not the case that there is an actual world which accidentally happens to exhibit an order of nature. There is an actual world because there is an order in nature. If there were no order, there would be no world. Also since there is a world, we know that there is an order. The ordering entity is a necessary element in the metaphysical situation presented by the actual world. (RM 100–101)

I have interpreted Whitehead's argument here as referring to the *metaphysical* order of the world. He did not, however, clearly distinguish the metaphysical order from the most basic contingent order of our cosmic epoch, particularly at the time he articulated this argument in *Religion in the Making*. Accordingly, his statement can equally be used for the distinctively cosmological argument, to which I now turn.

The Cosmological Argument

The nature of the second argument, built on the *basic contingent* order of our cosmic epoch, has already been adumbrated. Once this contingent order is clearly distinguished from the necessary, metaphysical dimension of the order of the universe, it becomes evident that this contingent order requires a different explanation. This explanation must be, as Whitehead suggested, the decision of a primordial being, but this decision cannot be primordial in the sense of eternal partly because the very notion is incoherent and partly because the eternal cannot by itself explain a contingent temporal development. This decision could be primordial only in the sense of being *prior to our cosmic epoch.*

Accordingly, process philosophy's cosmological argument can be stated thus: *Universal throughout our cosmic epoch are, besides the metaphysical principles, some basic contingent laws, which we call the laws of physics. Without the order provided by these laws, which is more particular than the order provided by the metaphysical principles, actual occasions of the types at the root of our universe—such as electronic, protonic, and photonic occasions—could not come into existence. The universality of actual occasions embodying these contingent laws implies the existence of a primordial actuality that, besides having unfathomable wisdom, can make temporal, contingent decisions, then make the content of these decisions effective throughout the universe, so as to bring our type of universe into existence. The existence of our particular cosmos, therefore, suggests the existence of a being with at least many of the attributes of "God" as generically conceived.* This argument is stronger than the metaphysical argument, not only because the contingent order it explains implies a being with more of the attributes belonging to our generic idea of God but also because this order would be more difficult to explain away. That is, even if advocates of "Whitehead without God" (Sherburne 1967, 1971, 1986) could plausibly claim that the metaphysical order somehow *just is* without needing to be instantiated in a primordial actuality, they would still be faced with the more difficult problem of explaining the universality of the contingent laws of our cosmic epoch.

Although that is the essence of the argument, it belongs to the self-understanding of process philosophy not simply to *affirm* divine agency but to *explain,* consistently with the metaphysical principles, *how such agency can be efficacious.* The question here is how such agency can result in what are usually called the laws of nature. Whitehead's explanation is in terms of a combination of two traditional understandings of law: law as imposed, based on external relations, and law as immanent, based on internal relations. Descartes, Newton, and Leibniz, given their substances with purely external relations to other substances, thought of law as wholly imposed by a "transcendent imposing Deity" (AI 113). An atom behaves as it does because an omnipotent God imposed certain laws of behavior on it (AI 113–14, 131–34). By contrast, Whitehead, given his actual entities with internal relations, thinks of law as immanent, which means that an atom behaves as it does because of its inner nature, which is due to its internal relations to other things (AI 111–12). This concept is central to Whitehead's justification of induction. Because the doctrine of imposition implies that the laws of nature will be exactly obeyed whereas the doctrine of immanence implies that they will not, the discovery that the laws of physics are statistical rather than absolute supports the doctrine of immanence (AI 112).

However, Whitehead adds, a doctrine lacking *any* element of imposition, so that law would be based purely on the internal relations of finite enduring individuals with one another, would not be adequate. Such a doctrine would never have inspired science because it would not have provided the faith in definite laws underlying the apparent capriciousness of nature (AI 114–15). Also, "apart from some notion of imposed Law, the doctrine of immanence provides absolutely no reason why the universe should not be steadily relapsing into lawless chaos" (AI 115). What is needed, Whitehead suggests, is a doctrine of *quasi-imposition,* resulting from the immanence of a supreme being in all other beings. In a statement partially quoted earlier, he says:

> [T]he primordial Being, who is the source of the inevitable recurrence of the world towards order, shares his nature with the world. In some sense he is a component in the natures of all [actual occasions]. Thus, an understanding of the nature of temporal things involves a comprehension of the immanence of the Eternal Being. This doctrine effects an important reconciliation between the doctrines of Imposed Law and Immanent Law. For, with this doctrine, the necessity of the trend towards order does not arise from the imposed will of a transcendent God. It arises from the fact, that the existents in nature are sharing in the nature of the immanent God. (AI 130)

Whitehead not only *says* that "'God' is that actuality in the world, in virtue of which there is physical 'law'" (PR 283). He also explains, in line with his metaphysical principles, *how it can be* that the laws of nature are dependent upon God: worldly occasions all prehend God, thereby receiving initial aims.[5] We should say, I suggest, that *these initial aims embody*—among other things—*both the metaphysical principles, reflecting God's eternal essence, and the*

5 Reporting that a physicist had said to him, "It is as if an electron knew the mathematics of its behavior," Hartshorne comments: "It does not know this, but it feels in a way that gets

basic contingent laws of this cosmic epoch, reflecting a divine decision at the outset of this epoch. These divinely derived initial aims are essential to the very existence of the kinds of actualities studied by physics.

This position overcomes one of the main problems in the cosmological argument in its early modern, Newtonian form, which was criticized by Hume. That form of the cosmological argument, which involved a "supernatural origin" of the world, is, Whitehead says, "now generally abandoned as invalid; because our notion of causation concerns the relations of states of things within the actual world, and can only be illegitimately extended to a transcendent derivation" (PR 93). That, of course, was the essence of Hume's criticism—that the "causation" attributed to God in creating the world is different in kind from causation as known in human experience, so that the term *causation* is used equivocally, making the cosmological argument invalid. Whitehead's point in this passage is that this criticism does not apply to his reformulated version of this argument, in which the idea of creation ex nihilo is rejected and God's causal influence on worldly actual occasions is not different in kind from the causal influence of one worldly occasion on another. The importance of this point in Whitehead's thinking is shown by the fact that his famous statement that "God is not to be treated as an exception to all metaphysical principles" follows directly upon his statement that his discussion is "an attempt to add another speaker" to Hume's *Dialogues* (PR 343). To revise Whitehead's own doctrine of God as suggested in the previous chapter so that the account of the causal relations between God and the world really do not violate his metaphysical principles, therefore, is to carry out Whitehead's own deepest intentions.

Solving that philosophical problem, however, does not show that a divine actuality without coercive omnipotence could account for the origin of our cosmic epoch, with its "finely tuned" laws of physics, which provided the precondition for the emergence of a universe capable of bringing forth life. This aspect of the cosmological argument will be saved for Chapter 6.

The Teleological Argument

Beyond the evidence for a creator provided by the metaphysical principles and the basic contingent laws of our universe, there is evidence from the

---

the statistical result; and this is because it feels God so far as there is in God what is relevant to it" (1991b, 646). Whitehead and Hartshorne are, of course, providing here an answer to what many physicists consider, in the words of Roger Penrose, "a very great mystery," namely that "somehow the structure of the physical world is rooted in mathematics" (1994, 23). Neither Whitehead nor Hartshorne believes, to be sure, that the behavior of subatomic individuals is derived entirely from God; they both speak of the "laws" followed by these individuals as long-standing "habits."

"upward trend" of the evolutionary process (FR 24). The question "Why has the trend of evolution been upwards?" Whitehead points out, "is not in the least explained by the doctrine of the survival of the fittest" (FR 7). That doctrine explains only why some kinds of organisms, having emerged, manage to survive. If survival were the only goal, however, then the very emergence of living things would be inexplicable: "life itself is comparatively deficient in survival value. The art of persistence is to be dead" (FR 4). What we unhesitatingly call the higher organisms, furthermore, are even less capable of survival than lower ones: otters, whales, and humans are transient species compared with viruses, bacteria, and even beetles. "The problem set by the doctrine of evolution is," Whitehead concludes, "to explain how complex organisms with such deficient survival power ever evolved" (FR 5). His answer involves the rejection of the "evolutionist fallacy," which assumes "that fitness for survival is identical with the best exemplification of the Art of Life" (FR 4). The point is that the evolutionary process is driven by some criterion of success other than mere survival, this criterion being "increase in satisfaction" (FR 8), meaning increase in the realization of intrinsic value. This criterion provides another reason to regard our world as created by a divine power.

In modern times, the teleological argument, which argues that the order of nature reflects a divine purpose, has been called the "argument from design." This language suggests exactly the kind of deistic, external imposition that process philosophy rejects. Such an argument, which was the target of Darwin's attack, has recently been revived under the title of the "anthropic principle," one version of which says that the most basic laws of the universe were designed to bring forth human beings. Whitehead does not entirely reject this idea. Indeed, in discussing the "order of nature," Whitehead cites as "fundamental for any discussion of this subject" (PR 89 n. 2) three books by L. J. Henderson, who is sometimes regarded as having given an early version of the anthropic principle. Henderson, however, does not endorse the anthropocentrism suggested by the term *anthropic,* instead describing our universe as "biocentric" (1913, 312). Insofar as Whitehead endorses Henderson's picture, therefore, he endorses only the idea that the basic laws seemed to be oriented toward the creation of life. And Whitehead emphatically rejects the notion, presupposed by many advocates of the theistic version of the anthropic argument, of an omnipotent, external deity imposing life-producing laws upon a world created out of nothing. "The Platonic 'persuasion' is required," he says, to explain the "inevitable trend towards order" (AI 115). Whitehead's position differs greatly, then, from the most well-known form of the teleological argument, which has been widely (and rightly) rejected.

Although what I am calling Whitehead's teleological argument is distinct from his cosmological argument, it is not completely separable from it because even the laws of physics, as he understands them, reflect an aim toward value. Saying that his philosophy, in contrast with Kant's, "finds the foundations of the world in the aesthetic experience," Whitehead adds: "All order is therefore aesthetic order" (RM 101). The laws of physics reflect the fact that the endurance of individuals such as electrons, atoms, and molecules involves the repetition and intensification of a certain kind of value ("the most general principles of harmony and intensity," says Hartshorne, "are more ultimate than the laws of physics and are the reasons for there being natural laws" [1991b, 590]). Just after the passage in which Whitehead uses *value* for the intrinsic reality of an event, he says: "The endurance of things has its significance in the self-retention of that which imposes itself as a definite attainment for its own sake" (SMW 94). In other words, the simplest kinds of temporally ordered societies already reflect a cosmic aim at value.

Unlike deistic positions, however, Whitehead's position is not committed to the idea that all the later evolutionary developments, such as the emergence of mammalian life or even life as such, were implicit in the elementary enduring individuals of our cosmic epoch, including their typical ways of interacting, the description of which we call the laws of physics. Rather, his view allows for considerable contingency at each stage of the evolutionary process. Given his view of compound individuals, in which higher kinds of occasions of experience emerge, he can portray God as continuing to be active throughout the whole evolutionary process, directly influencing the higher-level actualities, not simply influencing them indirectly by means of having created the entities studied by physics.

Whitehead does, nevertheless, affirm a fundamental, unchanging divine purpose that is reflected at every level of the evolutionary process: "What is inexorable in God, is valuation as an aim towards 'order'; and 'order' means 'society permissive of actualities with patterned intensity of feeling arising from adjusted contrasts'" (PR 244). God's aim, in other words, is at the creation of societies that give birth to higher-level actualities capable of greater intrinsic value, with "intrinsic value" understood to involve feeling that combines harmony with intensity. Although all occasions of experience have *some* intrinsic value, "[o]ccasions differ in importance of actuality." Therefore, Whitehead adds, "the purpose of God in the attainment of value is in a sense a creative purpose" (RM 100). It is this aim that lies behind the upward trend of the evolutionary process: "The problem of evolution is the development of enduring harmonies of enduring shapes of value, which merge into higher attainments of things beyond themselves" (SMW 94).

God, accordingly, is creator of our universe in two senses. In the first sense, as explained in the two previous arguments, God is responsible for the very existence of the finite occasions of experience of our universe. In the second sense, God is also responsible for evolutionary progress, meaning the emergence of creatures with greater intrinsic value. Although some neo-Darwinists, having no way to account for evolutionary progress, have tried to deny its reality (see Nitecki 1988; Griffin 2000a, chap. 8), the fact that the evolutionary process has reflected an upward trend over billions of years is too evident for such denials to be persuasive. This fact provides the basis for the distinctively teleological argument for the existence of God.

The Argument from Novelty

Closely related to this teleological argument—indeed, presupposed by it—is an argument based on the emergence of novelty, a feature of our universe that has been made especially evident by the discovery of its evolutionary nature. Within Whiteheadian process philosophy in particular, this emergence means the actualization of certain abstract forms that had not previously been actualized in our world. In light of the fact that the previous three arguments are all different phases of an argument from order, it is not surprising that Whitehead often refers to God as the "ground of order." The fact that he often adds "and novelty" (PR 88, 108, 247) suggests that this factor came to be of comparable importance for his affirmation of a divine actuality.

This supposition is supported by a later remark attributed to Whitehead. In *Process and Reality,* God is not included in Whitehead's discussion of his "categoreal scheme" (PR 20–30), in which all his basic notions are supposed to be introduced. God is formally introduced only in a chapter entitled "Some Derivative Notions," a fact that has been the source of no end of criticism from traditional theists. According to A. H. Johnson (1969, 367), however, Whitehead himself later realized that this treatment was inappropriate, saying that the primordial nature of God should have been included in the categoreal scheme to answer the question, "[W]here does novelty come from?" Given Whitehead's insistence on the necessity of God for the order of the world, of course, one can only wonder why he had not included God in the categoreal scheme for that reason. As Whitehead himself later reportedly said to William Hocking about his concept of God, primordial and consequent: "I should never have included it, if it had not been strictly required for descriptive completeness. You must set all your essentials into the foundation. It's no use putting up a set of terms, and then remarking, 'Oh, by the way, I believe there is a God'" (Hocking 1963, 16). In any case,

Whitehead did recognize, if belatedly, that the emergence of novelty in the world constitutes a God-shaped hole in process philosophy's categoreal scheme.

The argument from novelty is based on the fact that novel eternal objects, meaning possibilities previously unrealized in our cosmic epoch, do get realized. This fact implies that these possibilities, before they got realized, were somehow *relevant* to the actual entities that realized them. This implication raises the twofold question how such possibilities could exist and how any such existence could be relevant to the actual world. Combined with the ontological principle, this question provides a distinct argument for the existence of God, which is contained in a passage about the ontological principle, partially quoted earlier:

> Everything must be somewhere; and here "somewhere" means "some actual entity." Accordingly the general potentiality of the universe must be somewhere; since it retains its proximate relevance to actual entities for which it is unrealized. . . . This "somewhere" is the non-temporal actual entity. Thus "proximate relevance" means "relevance as in the primordial mind of God." (PR 46)

In a parallel passage, Whitehead makes the point in a way that more clearly brings out the argument from novelty:

> In what sense can unrealized abstract form be relevant? What is its basis of relevance? "Relevance" must express some real fact of togetherness among forms. The ontological principle can be expressed as: All real togetherness is togetherness in the formal constitution of an actuality. So if there be a relevance of what in the temporal world is unrealized, the relevance must express a fact of togetherness in the formal constitution of a non-temporal actuality.[6] (PR 32)

This argument from novelty is presupposed in the notion of God as the ground of the upward trend of the evolutionary process because every stage of this upward trend involves the realization of novel forms. The argument, in brief, is that *the upward trend of the evolutionary process, in which novel forms are continually incorporated into a richer order, is best explained on the assumption of a divine reality in which these forms are envisaged with appetition for them to be realized in the world for the sake of increasing the world's realization of value.* In

---

[6] Although Whitehead's treatment of God as a single actual entity led him to refer to the world and God as "temporal" and "non-temporal," respectively, the argument would not be affected by inserting other contrasting terms, such as "worldly" and "divine" or "finite" and "infinite." (For the relevant sense in which God is infinite, see p. 141.)

Whitehead's words: "'Order' and 'novelty' are but the instruments of [God's] subjective aim which is the intensification of 'formal immediacy'" (PR 88). Summarizing the arguments from basic order, teleological progress, and novelty, Whitehead writes: "Apart from the intervention of God, there could be nothing new in the world, and no order in the world. . . . The novel hybrid feelings derived from God, with the derivative sympathetic conceptual valuations, are the foundations of progress" (PR 247). The term *intervention* is dangerous, of course, because it suggests *occasional* interventions that interrupt the normal causal pattern of the world. Whitehead's meaning, however, is that God "intervenes" all the time, in every actual entity in the universe, so that this "divine intervention" is a regular, necessary part of the normal causal pattern of the universe, not an interruption thereof. Naturalism$_{ns}$ is not violated.

This passage, besides summarizing Whitehead's arguments from order and novelty, reminds us that he portrays God as providing the ground for order and novelty in terms of the general causal principles applicable to the interactions between all actual entities: God envisages various aims for the world. The worldly actual occasions prehend God by means of hybrid physical feelings, thereby feeling the relevant divine aims. Because God entertains those aims with the subjective form of appetition that they be actualized, the worldly occasions, by the principle of the initial conformity of subjective form, feel those aims sympathetically, thereby with an initial urge to actualize them. When this point is combined with the understanding of God as a living person, which allows the God-world interactions truly to exemplify the same metaphysical principles involved in all other interactions, process philosophy has an account of divine causation that is not vulnerable to the Humean critique that the notion of causation is being used equivocally. Whitehead has truly added "another speaker" to Hume's *Dialogues,* one not refuted therein.

The Argument from Excessive Beauty

The beauty of the world has often been regarded as the basis for a distinct argument for the divine existence, especially by traditions (such as Eastern Orthodoxy) and individual theologians (such as Jonathan Edwards) that have emphasized the divine beauty. The argument is that the world's beauty is explainable only as an embodiment of, or at least reflection of, the divine beauty. In our time, given the prominence of the neo-Darwinian account of the way our world came about, this argument takes its start from the appearance of *excessive* beauty, meaning *beauty beyond that which seems explainable in neo-Darwinian terms.*

Neo-Darwinism is a utilitarian, functional theory, explaining the various features of the evolutionary process in terms of their contribution to the adaptability, and thereby survivability, of organisms. The beauty of various plants and animals is among the features to be thus explained. Much of the world's beauty is indeed explainable, at least partly, in such terms. The bright colors of flowers, for example, are explained in terms of the selection of bees: insofar as bees are attracted to the brightest flowers, those flowers will be pollinated and hence will survive. In the "struggle for survival" in the coming generations, the flowers that have a slight edge in brightness will again have a greater tendency to survive, and so on. Another famous example is the otherwise dysfunctional tail of the male peacock, which evidently, because of its attractiveness to female peacocks, achieved its color and length through sexual selection (Cronin 1991).

After all such explanations have been given, however, there is still much beauty left over, which seems to demand another kind of explanation. For example, physicist Steven Weinberg says:

> I have to admit that sometimes nature seems more beautiful than strictly necessary. Outside the window of my home office there is a hackberry tree, visited frequently by a convocation of politic birds: blue jays, yellow-throated vireos, and, loveliest of all, an occasional red cardinal. Although I understand pretty well how brightly colored feathers evolved out of a competition for mates, it is almost irresistible to imagine that all this beauty was somehow laid on for our benefit. (1994, 250)

Although Weinberg's final sentence states the point in a more anthropocentric way than would process philosophers, it does express the sense that the beauty of the world appears, from a purely utilitarian point of view, excessive.

Weinberg draws back, however, from the idea that this beauty really *is* excessive, or at least from the implicit theistic conclusion, because "the God of birds and trees would have to be also the God of birth defects and cancer"— and, he adds in the next paragraph, the Holocaust. This is a particularly poignant example of the way the omnipotent God of supernaturalistic theism renders the world ambiguous, so that all the evidence *for* God is neutralized by the enormous amount of evidence *against* (such a) God. Weinberg's assumption, obviously, is that if there were a God, this God could intervene to prevent evils such as birth defects, cancer, and holocausts. Given process theism's different understanding of divine "intervention," by contrast, it can add the world's excessive beauty to its order and novelty as grounds for affirming the reality of a divine being. The argument, in brief, is that *our world's beauty, especially the beauty that cannot be explained in purely utilitarian, functionalist terms, is best explained in terms of influence from a divine creator, characterized by beauty, that has evoked beauty in its creatures.*

This argument is especially appropriate for process theism because it has emphasized the divine beauty. For Whitehead, the fundamental order of the world is *aesthetic* order, which results from the fact that all worldly occasions prehend God: "The actual world is the outcome of the aesthetic order, and the aesthetic order is derived from the immanence of God" (RM 101). In the next chapter, we will see how this understanding of divine influence in the world leads to an alternative to the neo-Darwinian understanding of evolution.

3. Natural Theology and a God-Shaped Hole

The preceding discussion of the way in which God does and does not intervene is related to the discussion in Chapter 4 of the fact that process philosophy has a God-shaped hole that is not filled by a God of the gaps. Because this issue is central to arguments for the existence of God, it will be helpful to pause to discuss it before moving on to further arguments.

In the previous chapter, we saw how the primary-secondary scheme for thinking of divine and worldly causation forced theists either to affirm a God of the gaps or to deny that ongoing divine influence plays any constitutive role in the world. The fact that most liberal and even some conservative theologians have grasped the second horn of this dilemma has been significantly responsible for the widespread neglect of arguments for the divine existence.

The background to the problem is provided by the fact that most of the traditional arguments started with some feature of the world that seemed to require a divine being for its explanation. The reaction against the God of the gaps led to the conclusion that *any* such argument would constitute an appeal to a "gap" in the disreputable sense. And given the primary-secondary scheme for thinking of divine and worldly causation, that would indeed be the case because a complete rejection of supernatural interventions would entail that purely *natural* (in the sense of *finite*) causes must, in principle, provide a *sufficient* explanation for every dimension of all events (apart from their mere thatness). This conclusion applies not only to the movements of physical bodies, such as the planetary orbits, but also to the emergence of every kind of order in our world, from the formation of electrons and atoms to the evolutionary development of life in general and human life in particular. There could be, therefore, no argument from the basic order of our world or the teleological direction apparently manifested in the evolutionary process.

The conclusion that finite causation is sufficient for all effects must also be applied to the deepest recesses of human experience. Even the beliefs by Jeremiah and Jesus that they were called by God must be assumed to be explainable, at least in principle, in terms of purely mundane causal factors, with no appeal to any direct influence by God. The theologian, of course, may believe that God, as the primary cause of all events, *used* certain psychodynamic processes, perhaps of a type postulated by Freud, Jung, or Maslow, to call such individuals to their prophetic tasks. But the fact that Jesus, Jeremiah, and many others have evidently felt called by God could not be used as counterevidence to the assumption that the entire content of every human experience is, in principle, fully explainable without appeal to divine influence. There could, in other words, be no arguments from aesthetic, moral, and religious experience, as well as no arguments from order and novelty.

Given this way of seeing things, there are only two alternatives. One can reject the idea that there are any objective reasons for believing in God (thereby either rejecting belief in God altogether or else taking it purely on faith). Or one can rest the entire case for the existence of God on those arguments that are compatible with the assumption that the content (the *whatness*) of all events is in principle explainable in terms of purely finite causes. This would mean reducing the arguments to two: the ontological argument, which most philosophers and theologians reject, and the traditional cosmological argument in its pure form, according to which the world's finitude or contingency is its only feature said to point to the existence of a divine being, so that the appeal to God explains nothing about the whatness of the world. In this way, some religious philosophers mean to conform to naturalism$_{ns}$ while still having an objective basis for affirming the existence of God.

The primary-secondary scheme combined with the acceptance of naturalism$_{ns}$ has thereby led, if not to a complete rejection of arguments for the divine existence, at least to the elimination of the kinds of argument that most people would be most likely to find convincing. For example, Ernan McMullin, who accepts this elimination, admits that "since there are no real 'gaps' to fill, we may be left without an argument for God's existence of the kind that would convince a science-minded generation" (1995, 74).

This situation provides an ideal dilemma for critics who wish to reject all arguments for the existence of God out of hand. If the arguments point to some aspect of the world that is said to require the existence of a divine being, they can be dismissed as appeals to a God of the gaps. But if the arguments avoid this charge by *not* explaining any feature of the world, the idea of God to which they point can be dismissed as superfluous.

Process philosophy, with its radically different conception of the relation between divine and worldly causation, avoids this dilemma. Although it rejects a God of the gaps, it does portray divine influence as playing a constitutive role in all events, so that a description of any event, to be adequate, would have to refer to this influence. It is especially here that process philosophy's arguments for panentheism must be evaluated in terms of the rest of its system of thought. Looked at from the outside, in terms of the assumption that any constitutive divine influence in the world would necessarily involve supernatural interruptions, process philosophy's God-shaped hole might be dismissed as simply one more God of the gaps. To see that it is not,[7] one must examine it from the inside, in terms of its panexperientialist ontology and its prehensive doctrine of perception. With this clarification of the relation between process philosophy's God-shaped hole and its arguments for the divine existence, I return to the latter, now dealing with those that are based on fundamental aspects of human experience.

4. Arguments from Fundamental Aspects of Human Experience

The arguments discussed in Section 2 are, of course, based on human experience in one sense, because it is human experience that has discerned the world's order, upward trend, novelty, and excessive beauty. Human experience has discerned those aspects, however, by looking at the world as objective to itself. The present arguments commence with aspects of human experience as such, these aspects being our experiences of ideals, truth, importance, and the holy.

The Argument(s) from Ideals

As we saw in Chapter 2, Whitehead believes that the immediate experience of people gives evidence of a character of rightness in things. The experience is "the intuition of immediate occasions as failing or succeeding in

---

[7] As I pointed out in Chapter 4, a position has a God of the gaps in the strongest sense if it has divine causation not only interrupting the normal web of causation but also doing so by accounting for some effect that in principle could be explained by finite causes.

reference to the ideal relevant to them" (RM 65). That this experience was one of Whitehead's major reasons for coming to affirm the existence of God is suggested by the fact that he mentions it in a summary statement of evidence for God in the same breath with order: the world, he says, "exhibits an order in matter of fact, and a self-contrast with ideals, which show that its creative passage is subject to the immanence of an unchanging actual entity" (RM 96). Whitehead returns time and time again to this self-contrast with ideals, in which we have a sense of "an excellence, partly attained and partly missed" (AI 148). In his most complete formulation of an argument for God on this basis, he says:

> There are experiences of ideals—of ideals entertained, of ideals aimed at, of ideals achieved, of ideals defaced. This is the experience of the deity of the universe. The intertwining of success and failure in respect to this final experience is essential. . . . Human experience explicitly relates itself to an external standard. The universe is thus understood as including a source of ideals. The effective aspect of this source is deity as immanent in the present experience. (MT 103)

This argument presupposes the form of the ontological principle according to which ideal, nonactual entities can exist only in actual entities. Because we experience these ideals as *objective* to ourselves—not as created by ourselves and projected onto the universe, as John Dewey (1934) and Donald Cupitt (1981) would have it—there must be an actual being in which they reside.[8] This argument also presupposes Whitehead's doctrine of perception, according to which all *conceptual* prehensions, the data of which are mere possibilities, arise out of *physical* prehensions, the data of which are other actualities. Our conceptual prehensions of ideal possibilities, Whitehead concludes, must arise out of physical prehensions of an actuality in which those ideal possibilities subsist. Our experiences of ideals arise, then, from hybrid physical prehensions of God's appetitive envisagement of these ideals (PR 32–33, 247, 250)—of God as the "Eros of the Universe," as the "poet of the world," leading it by a "vision of truth, beauty, and goodness" (AI 11; PR 346). The fact that we feel these ideals with an initial urge to realize them, or at least a sense that we *ought* to realize them, is in accord with the general category of the initial conformity of subjective form: because God prehends

---

[8] The central notion, which Whitehead attributes to Plato, is that "the agency where ideas obtain efficiency in the creative advance" is "a basic Psyche whose active grasp of ideas conditions impartially the whole process of the Universe" (AI 147). Whitehead's formulation of this notion is an attempt, he says, at "understanding how the Ideals in God's nature, by reason of their status in his nature, are thereby persuasive elements in the creative advance" (AI 168).

those ideal possibilities with purpose that they be actualized (AI 277), this subjective form is attached to our own prehension of them. Thus arises our initial aim.

This argument is important not only in itself but also because the experience on which it is built provides the basis for Whitehead's more general discussion of God's way of influencing the world. This human experience of ideals, partly conformed to and partly disregarded, is generalized to all occasions of experience, all of which are assumed to receive an analogous initial (or ideal) aim. Whitehead's discussion of divine agency thus conforms to his acceptance of conceptual empiricism, according to which all concepts, to be meaningful, must be rooted in immediate experience.

Although thus far the argument from ideals has been discussed as if it were a single argument, the ideals include truth, beauty, and goodness. It is inclusive, therefore, of what could be treated as three distinct arguments: a *cognitive* argument, based on the experience of the normative status of truth; a *moral* argument, based on the experience of the inescapable feeling of moral obligation attached to the awareness of moral ideals; and an *aesthetic* argument, based on the apparent objectivity of ideals of beauty. Furthermore, two more arguments, based on the objectivity of both *logical* and *mathematical* principles, can be added. That is, although I have interpreted the reality of "ideals" in the most common way, to mean the ideals of truth, beauty, and goodness, it is also the case, as discussed in Chapter 1, that the objects treated by logic and mathematics are ideal, not actual, entities. Before turning to metaphysics, Whitehead had primarily dealt with such entities, which he later came to call "eternal objects of the objective species" (PR 291). Given the ontological principle, the relevance of *these* types of entities to the actual world also implies the existence of a primordial actual individual in which they eternally reside and through which they can have causal efficacy.[9] Whitehead, in fact, mentioned that "logical notions must themselves find their places in the scheme of philosophic notions" (PR 3). We can say,

---

[9] The problem of how mathematical (as well as logical) entities could be perceived, mentioned in Chapter 1, was made even more pressing by Paul Benacerraf's "Mathematical Truth" (1983), in which he argued that true beliefs can be considered knowledge only if that which makes the belief true is *causally* responsible for the belief in an appropriate way. Summarizing the resulting problem for the Platonic view of mathematical entities, Penelope Maddy says: "But how can entities that don't even inhabit the physical universe take part in any causal interaction whatsoever? Surely to be abstract is also to be causally inert. Thus if Platonism is true, we can have no mathematical knowledge" (1990, 37). Reuben Hersh poses the problem in terms of the demise of theism: "For Leibniz and Berkeley, abstractions like numbers are thoughts in the mind of God. . . . [But] Heaven and the Mind of God are no longer heard of in academic discourse. Yet most mathematicians and philosophers of mathematics continue to believe in an independent, immaterial abstract world—a remnant of Plato's Heaven . . . , with all entities but the mathematical expelled. Platonism without God is like the grin on Lewis

accordingly, that "the argument from ideals" is really a set of five distinguishable arguments—the cognitive, moral, aesthetic, logical, and mathematical arguments.

The Argument from Truth

Although the "cognitive argument" in the previous subsection is an argument from truth, it is an argument from truth *as a normative ideal*. As such, it is an argument, like the others considered thus far, pointing to God as influencing the world. The present argument from truth begins the discussion of some dimensions of experience that point to *the world's reception into God*.

One of the relevant types of evidence is our presupposition that there is such a thing as "the truth," in the sense of a perspective (1) on the general nature of reality that corresponds to that general nature and (2) on concrete occurrences that corresponds to what has actually occurred. Our own asymptotic search for truth is an attempt to reach ever-greater approximations of that complete truth. The ongoing debates about the neo-Darwinian theory of evolution, for example, involve an attempt to arrive at the real truth about the general nature of the evolutionary process and about the actual developments that occurred—exactly *what* occurred, exactly *when* it occurred, and exactly *how* it occurred. Apart from the assumption that there are true answers to those questions to be found, all the debates would be nonsense.

Some modern and self-styled postmodern philosophers, however, have denied the existence of truth in this sense. Insofar as their point is epistemological, merely denying that any of our finite, human perspectives is to be equated with *the* truth, their point is a truth of which we cannot be reminded too often. But some philosophers make the quite different assertion, the *ontological* assertion, that there is no such thing as "the truth."

The ontological denial of the existence of truth is sometimes based on the acceptance of atheism. As such, the denial is not without merit: if the universe contains only a plurality of finite perspectives, no all-inclusive perspective, there *would be* no perspective that corresponds with the general nature of reality, let alone one that correctly reflects the concrete events that have occurred. With no impartial perspective in which all the partial perspectives are coordinated, there would simply be no place for "the whole

---

Carroll's Cheshire cat. . . . The grin remained without the cat" (1997, 12). In Whitehead's position, which almost seems tailor-made to respond to Benacerraf and Hersh, there is again a cat behind the grin.

truth" to exist. This conclusion follows from the ontological principle, according to which everything non-actual must be somewhere, with "somewhere" understood as an actuality. The (Nietzschean) denial of truth, therefore, is a reasonable deduction from atheistic premises.

The denial, nevertheless, is problematic because, insofar as it presupposes the truth of atheism, it involves the self-contradictory assertion that it is true that there is no truth. The denial of the existence of truth, in other words, is self-refuting, which means that the existence of truth is one of our hardcore commonsense notions. If, therefore, the only way to make sense of the reality of truth is to assume the existence of an all-including perspective in which this truth resides, we have an argument for the existence of a being with at least some of the attributes historically associated with the idea of God. Although traditional theism, with its all-determining, immutable, impassible deity, undermined the validity of this argument by making this truth timeless in all respects, the argument can be formulated in terms of a form of theism that allows truth to have a growing as well as a changeless aspect.

Whitehead formulated this argument very briefly, again employing the ontological principle, saying that "there can be no determinate truth, correlating impartially the partial experiences of many actual entities, apart from one actual entity to which it can be referred" (PR 13). Presupposing that the denial of "determinate truth" would be self-refuting, he affirms its reality by affirming the existence of a divine being who prehends the world in its entirety as it evolves: "The truth itself is nothing else than how the composite natures of the organic actualities of the world obtain adequate representation in the divine nature. Such representations compose the 'consequent nature' of God, which evolves in its relationship to the evolving world" (PR 12). Given our revision of Whitehead's doctrine, of course, "divine nature" in this passage would be replaced with "divine occasions of experience," and "consequent nature" would be replaced with "concrete states."

The Argument from Importance

Truth, as we have seen, plays a role not only in the argument here named for it but also in the argument from ideals. The two dimensions of our presuppositions about truth thus employed—that achieving truth is a normative ideal and that there is a total truth (at any given time)—thereby point to the two dimensions of God emphasized by Whitehead's distinction between the primordial and consequent natures of God, namely, God as *influencing* the world by means of ideals and God as fully and impartially *prehending* the world into the divine experience.

These two dimensions of God are also pointed to by our presuppositions about importance. Importance, Whitehead emphasizes, is one of the "ultimate notions" presupposed in our directed activities (MT 1). In spite of the positivistic effort to reduce everything to matter-of-fact, "the notion of importance is like nature itself: Expel it with a pitchfork, and it ever returns" (MT 8). When we reflect on this notion, furthermore, we see that it implies the two dimensions of God. In seeking to point to the meaning of this fundamental notion, Whitehead connects it to "the unity of the Universe" (MT 8). Saying that the "whole notion of importance is referent to this ultimate unity," he adds that this unity includes both "unity of purpose" and "unity of enjoyment" (MT 51).

The "unity of purpose" involves God's primordial nature, which is "the unity of ideal inherent in the universe" (MT 28). The argument to be made with regard to this dimension of importance is closely related to the argument from ideals. Whitehead, in fact, concludes his chapter titled "Importance" by referring to "the impact of aesthetic, religious and moral notions" (MT 19). He argues, however, that importance is a generic notion that "stretches beyond any finite group of species" (MT 11). In assuming morality, religion, art, and logic to be important, in other words, we are presupposing importance as "a fundamental notion not to be fully explained by any reference to a finite number of other factors" (MT 8). Accordingly, although the argument from importance is closely related to the arguments from truth, beauty, and goodness, it is distinguishable from them.

The sense of importance arises, Whitehead contends, from the immanence of the universe as one, with its unity of ideal and purpose, in the universe as many—that is, from the "immanence of infinitude in the finite" (MT 20). Speaking of "the derivation of importance from the one into the many" and of "that ultimate unity of direction in the universe, upon which all order depends, and which gives its meaning to importance" (MT 49, 51), Whitehead's point is that our sense of importance—the very fact that we have this notion, which cannot be exorcised[10]—exists because the same unity of purpose that is immanent in all other finite occasions, accounting for the direction of the universe in general, is also immanent in our experience.

The immanence of God as a unified envisagement of ideals does not, however, fully account for our presuppositions about importance. The reference earlier to the "unity of enjoyment" indicates another dimension: "Does not 'importance for the finite,'" Whitehead asks, "involve the notion

---

[10] For example, one who tried to refute this claim would be presupposing that it was important to do so.

of 'importance for the infinite'?" (MT 86–87).[11] With this transition, he moves to the way in which our presuppositions about importance point to the *consequent* nature of God. Whitehead's original reason for affirming God's responsiveness to the world was the consideration that if God is actual, God must prehend as well as being prehended. But once it was affirmed for *metaphysical* reasons, the consequent nature of God soon became closely related to the *religious* issue of ultimate meaning.

Although it would probably be going too far to say that this issue of ultimate meaning became, as it did for Hartshorne, the most important religious issue, it certainly became central. In *Process and Reality*, in which Whitehead first explicitly introduces the idea of God as having a consequent nature, he describes the "ultimate evil in the temporal world," which is "deeper than any specific evil," as "the fact that the past fades." His point is not that this fading is an evil in general but that it is the ultimate evil for the "higher actualities," by which he means distinctively human experiences, which are "haunted by terror at the loss of the past" and thereby seek "escape from time in its character of 'perpetually perishing'" (PR 340). His crucial statement is that "the culminating fact of conscious, rational life refuses to conceive itself as a transient enjoyment, transiently useful" (PR 340). Human life, in other words, needs to regard itself as *permanently* useful, as making some permanent contribution to the universe. The character of the world as perpetually perishing *would* be the "ultimate evil" for human beings *if* the fact that "process entails loss," which is empirically true within finite existence, "should be the whole story" (PR 340). Whitehead's doctrine of the consequent nature of God says that this is *not* the whole story, that "the fluent world become[s] 'everlasting' by its objective immortality in God" (PR 347). Whitehead then concludes, speaking explicitly to our topic: "In

[11] Bernard Williams, who seems simply to presuppose the truth of atheism, has a discussion of importance quite similar to Whitehead's, in which he firmly rejects the assumption that one type of importance, *moral* importance, is always more important than other kinds (1985, 182–87). His attempt to discuss the notion of "importance as such" within his nontheistic framework, however, is rather tortured. Besides having the merely *relative* idea of importance, according to which something is found important by someone, says Williams, "we have another notion, of something's being, simply, important (important *überhaupt*, as others might put it, or important *period*). It is not at all clear what it is for something to be, simply, important. *It does not mean that it is important for the universe: in that sense, nothing is important*. . . . I doubt that there can be an incontestable account of this idea. . . . It does not matter for the present discussion that this notion is poorly understood. I need only [the fact] that there is such a notion" (182; final emphasis added). Whitehead would fully agree that if the answer "important for the universe" is ruled out, no satisfactory notion of importance can be given. But he would reject the idea that we can complacently rule out an answer if we cannot, without it, make sense of one of our inevitable presuppositions.

this way, the insistent craving is justified—the insistent craving that zest for existence be refreshed by the ever-present, *unfading importance* of our immediate actions, which perish and yet live for evermore" (PR 351; emphasis added).

As summarized thus far, Whitehead's position would seem to be that the idea that God is responsive to the world, which is to be affirmed for metaphysical reasons, turns out to be of great religious significance. As such, we would have a happy coincidence, not a distinct argument for the existence of the God of process theism. There is, however, an argument contained in Whitehead's discussion. After saying that "conscious, rational life refuses to conceive itself as a transient enjoyment, transiently useful," he adds:

> But, just as physical feelings are haunted by the vague insistence of causality, so the higher intellectual feelings are haunted by the vague insistence of another order, where there is no unrest, no travel, no shipwreck: "There shall be no more sea." (PR 340)

Superficially read, this argument might be dismissed as simply a species of wishful reasoning: we want our lives to have permanent meaning so we posit a divine being who cherishes them for evermore. Whitehead's statement, however, is built around a parallel between the way physical and intellectual feelings are "haunted." The latter are haunted by the "vague insistence" of a nontransient order "just as" physical feelings are haunted by the "vague insistence" of causal efficacy. Having examined Whitehead's epistemology, with its rebuttal of Hume's brand of empiricism, we know that Whitehead takes this latter hauntedness to be revelatory of a deep truth: physical feelings involve this vague insistence of causal derivation because they *really*, if only dimly, *prehend* the causal efficacy that is actually exerted by other things. The point of the parallelism, therefore, is that intellectual feelings, in being similarly haunted by a vague insistence of a nontransient world, are likewise revelatory of a deep truth.

The importance of this argument to Whitehead is suggested by the fact that he recurs to it in his last significant writing, "Immortality." Distinguishing between the intuition of the truth of immortality, which he again describes in terms of a "haunting" feeling, and the possibility of adequately conceptualizing it, he says:

> This immortality of the World of Action, derived from its transformation in God's nature, is beyond our imagination to conceive. The various attempts at description are often shocking and profane. What does haunt our imagination

is that the immediate facts of present action pass into permanent significance for the Universe. (ESP 94)

What haunts the human imagination, he says, is *not* the idea that our actions *should* pass into permanent significance but the idea that they *do*. His wording in both passages suggests an argument, not merely a wish. When the two passages are put together, the argument seems to be that *the reason why we are not satisfied with the conception of ourselves as purely transient phenomena of the universe, even if our lives be otherwise immensely enjoyable, is that we have a direct prehension of the consequent nature of God*—Whitehead's description of which, he hopes, is less "shocking and profane" than more traditional accounts of heaven. And as we saw at the end of Chapter 2, Whitehead came to affirm that *we directly prehend this dimension of God*. Against the widespread modern view that religious belief is simply a product of the longing for immortality, then, Whitehead seems to argue that *the religious longing for immortality is itself a product of a veridical perception*.

To provide support for this reading of Whitehead's statements, I turn to James, by whom, I suggest, Whitehead was influenced on this issue. The relevant side of James's thought, concerning the "will to believe," has been insightfully explored by Wainwright in *Reason and the Heart: A Prolegomenon to a Critique of Passional Reason* (1995). James, of course, has been repeatedly criticized for his endorsement of this notion, which seems to sanction wishful thinking under certain conditions. Wainwright argues, however, that James's discussion of the "will to believe" actually involves two different positions. One of them is that under certain conditions we have a *right* to believe the view that we find most satisfactory. This argument *is* guilty, as critics have charged, of providing an alternative to epistemic justification. But the other position, rather than defending the right to believe in the face of insufficient evidence, is referring to *a kind of evidence* provided by our passional nature. "The dumb region of the heart in which we dwell alone with our willingness and unwillingness, our faiths and fears," says James, is "our deepest organ of communication with the nature of things" (1956, 62). In a similar passage, James says that "our power of moral and rational response to the nature of things [is] the deepest organ of communication therewith" (1956, 141). In related passages, James suggests that the tendencies in our emotional life can be "prophetic" and that our passional nature includes "concrete perceptions" (1975, 5, 140). In these discussions, then, James is speaking not of the will but of a mode of perception deeper than sensory perception.

James's argument depends as well on his idea that the human mind involves a threefold structure: it receives influences, reflects on them, and then discharges itself in action. Insofar as we trust our perceptual experience and our thought, contends James, we are assuming that the structure of our mind is "in accordance with the nature of reality." That assumption would be justified, however, only if the third dimension of the mind, its impulse to action, is also to be trusted. We cannot regard a view as fully rational, therefore, if it leaves "some one or more of our fundamental active and emotional powers with no object outside of themselves to react on or live for" (1956, 125).

Whitehead's argument seems similar—perhaps, I am suggesting, because of actual influence from the side of James's argument lifted up by Wainwright. Whitehead clearly believed that our passional natures—our emotions and purposes, our subjective forms and subjective aims—are most fundamentally rooted in a mode of receiving influences from the universe that is far deeper than our conscious sensory perception. He believed that this deeper mode—this perception in the mode of causal efficacy, this physical *feeling*—puts us in touch with reality, whereas sensory data give us mere appearance. He believed that the reality to which it connects us includes the divine reality, with its consequent nature (as well as its primordial envisagement of possibilities). And he believed, like James, that the mind—each occasion of experience, Whitehead would say—always includes a future orientation, so that its *anticipation* of its impact upon future events is as essential to it as its reception of influences from the past and its present enjoyment. Putting all these ideas together, we could formulate the argument thus: *Included among our deepest desires is the desire for our actions to make a permanent contribution to the universe. Given the fact that our most fundamental emotional-purposive responses to reality generally reflect the actual nature of reality, we can reasonably take this desire to be prophetic—to point to the reality of a permanent but growing dimension of the universe, to which our actions do make a contribution.*

Even if this argument was not in Whitehead's mind, it is fully in accord with Whiteheadian-Hartshornean philosophy. Hartshorne, in fact, regards a version of this argument to be, along with the argument from order, one of the two most important arguments for the existence of God (1991b, 665). Hartshorne's statement of this argument—that the ideal of contributing to the divine life, by promoting the good life among creatures, provides the only inclusive moral ideal for human existence that is fully satisfactory (1970, 287–89)—may seem like an argument only for why we should *wish* that a receptive God exists, not for believing that such a divine experiencer really does exist. His argument, however, is based on the conviction that we all, down deep, presuppose that life has meaning (1967, 47) and therefore that there is a supreme aim around which our lives could be rationally oriented (1970, 287; 1991b, 665). These presuppositions reflect our implicit awareness of "some highest level of feeling" through which all the other forms of feeling "can add up to a significant totality" (1990, 375).

The Argument from Religious Experience

I turn now to religious experience, which should be, from the point of view of any philosophy of religion, the most important basis for speaking of God—because without such experience, religion would not exist. Taking this position means, as explained in Chapter 2, rejecting typically modern explanations of religion, which try to explain its existence in purely psychosocial, functional terms.

In using the fact of religious experience as a basis for an argument for the existence of *God,* we are focusing on one of the two major types of religious experience, often called "theistic religious experiences," which can be, as Gary Gutting suggests, characterized as "perceptual but nonsensory experiences, purporting to be of a good and powerful being concerned with us" (1982, 145). In Chapter 7, we will look at the relation between theistic and nontheistic religious experiences. It may turn out that even nontheistic religious experiences are best interpreted as involving, as at least one element, an experience of God. But it is clearly theistic experience that provides prima facie evidence for the reality of a Divine Reality understood in terms of what I have called the "generic idea of God," hence as a purposive, responsive actuality.

Already narrowed to *theistic* religious experience, the scope of this discussion is furthered narrowed to what I, in Chapter 2, called religious experience in the narrow sense. In the broad sense, all the previous arguments in this section can be understood as arguments from religious experience because they are said to involve direct experiences of God. Those experiences are "religious" only by inference, however, insofar as we judge that they are best explained as involving direct prehensions of God. Religious experience in the narrow sense, by contrast, involves a direct apprehension of God *as Holy,* a sense of *being in the presence of a Holy Reality.*

This distinction can be clarified in terms of the conceptuality of process philosophy. Any experience of initial aims from God can be a religious experience in the broad sense, insofar as those aims are retrospectively judged to have come from a divine source. In such experiences, however, the focus is on the aims themselves (which includes both their content and the subjective form of an urge to realize them). In religious experience in the narrow sense, one *may* be aware of an aim (such as the experience of a religious "call"), but if so one is simultaneously aware of the aim as coming from a Holy Actuality. One is aware not simply of aims from the primordial nature of God, accordingly, but also of the concrete states—and thereby the consequent nature—of God. In some experiences, furthermore, the sense of receiving aims may be overwhelmed by this sense of simply being in the presence of God as a Holy Actuality.

The distinction between religious experience in the narrow and broad senses is not wholly identical, however, with experiences that do or do not involve awareness of the consequent nature of God, meaning God as responsive to the world. As we saw in the arguments from truth and importance, each of these presuppositions involves an inchoate awareness of God as prehending the world. In these experiences, however, there is no direct awareness of God as a personal, responsive being. Such experiences are "religious experiences" only insofar as they are interpreted as such, through the conclusion that our presuppositions about ultimate truth and importance are best explained as an inchoate awareness of the divine experience of the world. In religious experience in the narrow sense, by contrast, there is direct awareness of this divine experience—sometimes expressed as an awareness of being in the presence of Unconditional Love. This distinction, as explained in Chapter 2, involves a rejection of Wayne Proudfoot's view that every religious experience is such entirely because of beliefs, as distinct from any preconceptual aspect of the experience itself.

The question here is, Does (theistic) religious experience in the narrow sense provide the basis for a partially independent argument for the existence of God? Most philosophers of religion agree that it provides prima facie evidence. Apart from any other considerations, the simplest explanation of such experiences would be that they really result from, in Gutting's phrase, "perceptual but nonsensory experiences" of a Divine Actuality. The controverted question is whether this prima facie evidence is overridden by other considerations.

The most important of these other considerations are simply the two mutually reinforcing convictions (1) that there is no Divine Actuality to be experienced and (2) that even if there were, such an actuality would not be a possible object of human experience. In our time, as we saw in Chapter 2, this twofold conviction is supported by naturalism$_{sam}$, with its atheism denying the existence of a Divine Actuality, its materialism saying that such a being, understood as a cosmic experiencer without a brain, is impossible, and its sensationism ruling out any perceptual but nonsensory experiences. But this doctrine of perception, we saw, makes it impossible for an epistemology to explain how we know various things that we in fact show by our practice, including our scientific practice, that we do know. Chapter 3 demonstrated that a materialist ontology is far less adequate to a wide range of issues than a panexperientialist ontology. And the present chapter has shown that an atheistic view of the universe can do far less justice to a wide range of features than can a naturalistic theism. Because all these issues are interrelated, the more accurate way to state the point is that naturalism$_{ppp}$ has been shown to be far more adequate than naturalism$_{sam}$. Naturalism$_{sam}$, accordingly, does not provide a good reason for overriding the prima facie evidence for a Divine Actuality provided by (theistic) religious experience. Our best "background information" about the world, in other words, provides no reason to be dubious either of the reality of a Divine Actuality or of the human capacity to experience such a being.

Still other reasons, to be sure, have been given for challenging the view that theistic religious experiences should be given a theistic interpretation. One of these is the claim that a theistic interpretation is superfluous because such experiences can be explained in entirely secular terms, perhaps as filling a combination of psychological and sociological functions. As we saw in Chapter 2, however, this challenge is not really separate from the challenge provided by naturalism$_{sam}$ because the attempts to give psychosocial explanations of the origin and persistence of religion have been motivated, and given what plausibility they have, by the prior assumption, based on naturalism$_{sam}$, that the theistic explanation *must* be false.

Nothing close to an adequate explanation of this type, furthermore, has ever been provided, and there is good reason to suppose that none will be provided in the future. The relevant fact to be explained is not merely that some people in some times and places have reported such experiences but that insofar as we can tell, human beings at all times and all places have had such experiences. Besides explaining this universality, a theory must account for the tremendous diversity of religion. Those who are aware of this diversity find theories created with Judaism and Christianity primarily in mind, such as the theories of Marx and Freud, far from adequate. The task of coming up with a single functional theory, or even a finite set of theories, to explain such disparate religions as Christianity, Theravada Buddhism, Taoism, Korean Shamanism, and various African and Native American religions would be daunting indeed. By far the simplest explanation of the universality-with-diversity manifested by religion is that there is a (non-omnipotent) Divine Actuality, which peoples in all these traditions have experienced as Holy.

The way in which process theism can deal with the most commonly cited diversity—the fact that some religious experience seems to point to a personal ultimate, some to an impersonal ultimate reality—will be discussed in Chapter 7. Once that argument is made, we can conclude that, given the intellectual framework provided by process philosophy, there is no good reason to reject the view that religious experience involves, at least sometimes, a direct experience of a Divine Actuality.

5. The Cumulative Case for Naturalistic Theism

The thesis of this chapter, suggested by its title, is that the shift from supernaturalistic to naturalistic theism requires a reconsideration of the modern verdict against the possibility of a persuasive natural theology. Although natural theology in the service of supernaturalistic theism is indeed a failure, there can be a strong cumulative case for God as portrayed by the naturalistic theism of process philosophy.

The main reason for the failure of traditional natural theology was not the weakness of its arguments against atheism but the fact that traditional theism's concept of God was inconsistent with the world as we know it and, in its classical form, incoherent. These problems provide the basis, as Caroline Franks Davis points out, for a cumulative case *against* (traditional) theism (1989, 113, 140–42). Whether this negative cumulative case is stronger than the positive cumulative case *for* traditional theism is a matter of judgment. Atheists, of course, believe that it is. Some traditional theists argue that it only weakens, without destroying, this positive case. Richard Swinburne, for example, suggests that the various relevant considerations, apart from the argument from religious experience, show (traditional) theism to be *somewhat* "more probable than not," which is enough to allow us to take the argument from religious experience seriously. The addition of that argument, he then suggests, tips the balance in favor of theism so that it becomes "significantly more probable than not" (Swinburne 1996, 138–39). Atheists, of course, do not accept even this modest conclusion, which suggests that other factors, such as the will to believe or disbelieve, play a crucial role in the respective judgments. John Hick, accordingly, suggests that the world is religiously "ambiguous," so that atheism and theism are equally rational positions. That is, although theists have "the right to believe" (1989, 227), they should realize that theism cannot be "shown to be in any objective sense more probable than not" (211).

From the perspective of process philosophy, Hick's conclusion is partly right: insofar as the choice is between atheism and traditional theism, the considerations that count in favor of the latter are canceled out by those that count against it. The fuller truth, however, is that the standard theistic arguments provide arguments not *for* traditional theism but merely *against* atheism. They appear to be arguments also in favor of traditional theism only insofar as it is the sole form of theism considered. The reason why the arguments between atheists and traditional theists are interminable, with the deciding factor being extra-rational considerations, is not that the world is thoroughly ambiguous but that people have been forced to choose between two untenable positions, each of which has about equally strong considerations against it.

When the arguments against atheism are placed in service of process philosophy's naturalistic theism, however, the result is no longer a situation in which theism is objectively no more probable, or only "significantly" more probable, than atheism. Rather, it can now be seen that whereas there are many considerations that count against atheism, there are none that count against process theism.[12] The truth of something like process philosophy's naturalistic theism is *overwhelmingly* more probable than the truth of atheism.

This conclusion presupposes that process theism is not, unlike traditional theism, disconfirmed by an insoluble problem of evil. It also presupposes that it can provide a more convincing account of the creation of our world than not only traditional theism but also atheism, especially as now embodied in the neo-Darwinian theory of evolution. The next chapter turns to these two issues of evil and evolution, along with a third issue closely related to both of them, eschatology.

[12] No arguments, that is, that are not question-begging. Richard Dawkins, for example, rejects any idea of a theistic or deistic creator on the grounds that such a being would involve "organized complexity," whereas the scientific task is to explain all types of such complexity out of "primeval simplicity" (1987, 141, 316). The assumption that atheism is true, therefore, is simply built into Dawkins's description of the explanatory task.

[6]

Evolution, Evil, and Eschatology

The argument of Chapter 1 was that naturalism$_{sam}$, the form in which the scientific community's naturalism$_{ns}$ has been embodied for the past century and a half, not only prevents an integration of our scientific observations with our religious intuitions and our hard-core commonsense presuppositions into a single worldview but also provides an inadequate framework for scientific activity as such. Chapters 2 through 5 have shown how process philosophy's naturalism$_{ppp}$ provides a far more adequate way to embody naturalism$_{ns}$. After the second and third chapters presented process philosophy's naturalistic alternative to sensationism and materialism, the fourth and fifth chapters introduced its naturalistic alternative to both atheism and supernaturalism. The current chapter continues this presentation of process philosophy's version of naturalistic theism, showing how it portrays God as the creator of this evolutionary cosmos—but not in such a way as to be indictable for its evils.

By treating evolution and evil together, we bring out the potential tension between the second feature of the generic idea of God, according to which God is perfectly good and loving, and the fourth and fifth features, according to which God is the supremely powerful creator of our world, which is obviously filled with evil. The basis for process philosophy's defense of the goodness of our creator is its replacement of the supernaturalistic version of theism with a naturalistic version. In making this replacement, however, process philosophy raises the question whether it can really portray its divine actuality as creator of our universe. If the neo-Darwinian account of evolution is inadequate, as will be argued, can this inadequacy really be overcome apart from a supernaturalistic version of theism? That is the question of the first two sections of this chapter.

If this question can be answered positively, process theism faces a second question: Given the manifold and often horrendous evils of our world, can we attribute the direction of the evolutionary process through which this world came about to a divine being while maintaining the goodness of that being? If this deity's persuasion is sufficiently powerful to be responsible for the creation of our world, then this deity might seem indictable for the world's evils, even if not as fully indictable as the God of traditional theism. The third section deals with this issue.

Even if process theism successfully portrays the goodness of the world's creator, however, a third question arises. Most religions have been based partly on the belief that there are distinctively human problems that can be resolved, if at all, only through some sort of immortality. The fourth section, on eschatology, provides a version, from an evolutionary perspective, of this position.

1. The Inadequacy of Neo-Darwinian Evolutionism

The claim to be made is that process philosophy can provide a viable version of theistic evolutionism. That claim, however, presupposes that the nontheistic account of evolution given by neo-Darwinism, which is now generally accepted in scientific and philosophical circles, is inadequate.[1]

In giving nine (or thirteen) arguments for the existence of God in the previous chapter, I have thereby given that many reasons for doubting the adequacy of any nontheistic account of our universe. Many of these reasons explicitly refer to dimensions of the evolutionary process not explainable from a nontheistic perspective: its presupposed basic order, its upward trend, its perpetual realization of novel forms, and its production of human beings with an ineradicable sense of normative ideals along with a more general sense of importance and holiness. Besides problems that would apply to *any* nontheistic theory of evolution, there are some that are distinctive to the neo-Darwinian version in particular. The argument from excessive beauty already dealt with one of these. Far more serious, however, is the twofold

[1] In speaking of the neo-Darwinian theory of evolution as inadequate, I in no way mean to cast doubt on the idea of evolution itself. In a more complete discussion of this issue elsewhere (2000a, chap. 8), I sort out fourteen dimensions of "(neo-)Darwinian evolutionism," four of which I affirm—including the idea that all later species have arisen, without supernatural interventions, through "descent with modification" from earlier species.

clash of neo-Darwinian gradualism with both empirical facts and conceptual considerations.

The Conflict with the Fossil Record

Gradualism is the view that evolution always occurs by means of tiny steps, never by big jumps, known as "saltations" (from the Latin *saltare,* to leap). Darwin, who was committed to the dictum *natura non facit saltum* (nature makes no jumps), famously said: "Natural selection acts only by the preservation and accumulation of small inherited modifications. . . . [N]atural selection [will] banish the belief of the continued creation of new organic beings, or of any great and sudden modification of their structure" (1958, 100).

Darwin's commitment to this view was based on his rejection of supernatural interventions. Howard Gruber summarizes Darwin's position thus: "[N]ature makes no jumps, but God does. . . . [T]herefore if something is found in the world that appears suddenly, its origins must be supernatural" (1981, 125–26). Darwin's position is spelled out even more explicitly by Richard Dawkins in a reply to the question how living things, which *seem* "too beautifully 'designed' to have come into existence by chance," nevertheless did so: "The answer, Darwin's answer, is by gradual, step-by-step transformations from simple beginnings," says Dawkins with approval. "Each successive change in the gradual evolutionary process was simple enough, *relative to its predecessor,* to have come into existence by chance" (1987, 43). In other words, the thesis that each new development occurs entirely by chance, meaning with no purposive guidance, is plausible, Dawkins argues, if each development is very small. Dawkins then drives home the connection between this gradualism and Darwin's effort to provide a nonsupernaturalistic theory. Commenting on Darwin's rejection of the suggestion that the human mind can be explained only in terms of a divine intervention, Dawkins says:

> This is no petty matter. In Darwin's view, the whole *point* of the theory of evolution by natural selection was that it provided a *non*-miraculous account of the existence of complex adaptations. For Darwin, any evolution that had to be helped over the jumps by God was not evolution at all. . . . In the light of this, it is easy to see why Darwin constantly reiterated the *gradualness* of evolution. (1987, 249)

The negative point here is that Darwin's commitment to gradualism followed from his commitment to naturalism, *not* from his examination of the fossil record of the evolutionary process.

In fact, that fossil record, far from being the basis for Darwinian theory, has been against it from the beginning. One apparent problem was formulated by Darwin himself: "[W]hy, if species have descended from other species by insensibly fine gradations, do we not everywhere see innumerable transitional forms? Why is not all nature in confusion instead of species being, as we see them, well defined?" (1958, 287). This problem, Darwin pointed out, could be easily handled with the assumption that the transitional forms, being less well adapted for survival, had become extinct.

The fossil record, however, does not contain these "innumerable transitional forms." For this reason, the fossil record, Darwin said, provides "the most obvious and gravest objection" to his theory (1958, 287). He attempted to answer this objection by pointing out that the fossil record, as known then, was terribly incomplete. Further research, Darwin assumed, would discover many of these transitional forms, popularly known as "missing links."

One of the major problems for contemporary Darwinists is that this prediction has not been borne out. We now have the remains of some 250,000 extinct species, most of which were unknown in Darwin's time (Denton 1991, 162). Nevertheless, "the fossil record is about as discontinuous as it was when Darwin was writing the *Origin*" (Wesson 1991, 39–40). Indeed, says a former curator of the American Museum of Natural History, "Many of the discontinuities tend to be more and more emphasized with increased collecting" (Newell 1959, 267). In illustrating this absence of transitional forms, Michael Denton writes:

> [T]he sudden appearance of the angiosperms [flowering plants] is a persistent anomaly which has resisted all attempts at explanation since Darwin's times. . . . The first representatives of [the various] fish groups were already so highly differentiated and isolated at their first appearance that none of them can be considered even in the remotest as intermediate with regard to other groups. (1991, 162, 164)

Besides *not confirming* Darwinian theory, the fossil record even *contradicts* it. According to the theory, as we go higher up the taxonomical hierarchy from species to genera, to orders, to classes, and to phyla, we should find increasingly more transitional forms. But, says Denton, "there are fewer transitional species between the major divisions than between the minor," which "is the *exact reverse* of what is required by [Darwinian] evolution" (1991, 192).

Once species do appear, furthermore, they tend to remain about the same: "Species usually stand still" (Wesson 1991, 207). This fact is problematic for gradualism because if evolution was, through a series a tiny steps, to bring about elephants, whales, and humans from bacteria in only a few billion years, then directional change must have been occurring most of the time. If it was not, then neo-Darwinian gradualism seems refuted. As Steven Stanley says:

> The rapid adaptive radiation that is apparent today confronts gradualism with a seemingly insoluble problem. We now know that for many groups of marine invertebrates an average species lasts for five or ten million years without evolving enough to be given a new name. How, then, are we to explain the origin of advanced groups, like arthropods and mollusks, from primitive ancestors in a few tens of millions of years? (1981, 90)

In discussing the rapid radiation of mammals, Stanley drives home the problem:

> Today, our more detailed knowledge of fossil mammals lays another knotty problem at the feet of gradualism. Given a simple little rodentlike animal as a starting point, what does it mean to form a bat in less than ten million years, or a whale in little more time? [In that period, gradual evolution] might move us from one small rodentlike form to a slightly different one, perhaps representing a new genus, but not to a bat or a whale! (1981, 93–94)

The main effort to deal with this problem within a fundamentally neo-Darwinian framework is the theory of "punctuated equilibria" developed by Niles Eldredge and Stephen Jay Gould (1972).[2] Although this theory has sometimes been likened to (heretical) saltational theories, it is still Darwinian in saying that major changes occur through a series of small changes. As Dawkins points out, the theory of punctuated equilibria is still gradualistic: "The jumps that it postulates are not real, single-generation jumps. They are spread out over large numbers of generations" (1987, 244). This judgment is confirmed by Eldredge, who declares on behalf of Gould and himself that "Whatever we are, we are not saltationists!" (1995, 100). The very fact that the theory of punctuated equilibria is orthodox neo-Darwinism, however, means that it fails to reconcile evolutionary theory with the empirical facts. In a statement that both summarizes the essence of the theory and shows its inadequacy, Denton says:

> While Eldredge and Gould's model is a perfectly reasonable explanation of the gaps between species . . . , [t]he gaps which separate species . . . are utterly

---

[2] Steven Stanley, whom I have been quoting, also suggests a version of this theory.

trivial compared with, say, that between a primitive terrestrial mammal and a whale . . . and even these relatively major discontinuities are trivial alongside those which divide major phyla such as molluscs and arthropods. Such major discontinuities simply could not, unless we are to believe in miracles, have been crossed in geologically short periods of time through one or two transitional species occupying restricted geological areas. . . . To suggest that the hundreds, thousands, or possibly even millions of transitional species which must have existed in the interval between vastly dissimilar types were all unsuccessful species occupying isolated areas and having very small population numbers is verging on the incredible! (1991, 193–94)

Darwinian gradualism seems, therefore, to be disconfirmed by the fossil record.

The Conceptual Problem

Correlative to the empirical problem of the gaps in the fossil record, furthermore, is a conceptual problem, namely, the difficulty of conceiving "of functional intermediates through which the gap[s] might have been closed" (Denton 1991, 213). The term *functional* stresses the point that each of the intermediate species would have had to be viable. The problem is that in many cases several changes would have had to occur *simultaneously* for the new organism to be viable, and the possibility that all these coordinated changes could have occurred *by chance* is remote. For example, regarding the development of the amniotic egg, which would have been involved in the transition from amphibia to reptiles, Denton writes:

> Every textbook of evolution asserts that reptiles evolved from amphibia but none explains how the major distinguishing adaptation of the reptiles, the amniotic egg, came about gradually as a result of successive accumulations of small changes. . . . There are hardly two eggs in the whole animal kingdom which differ more fundamentally. . . . Altogether at least eight quite different innovations were combined to make the amniotic revolution possible. (1991, 218–19)

Saying that the amniotic egg was "a stunning advance on the simple blob of jelly that constituted the egg of frogs and fishes," Gordon Rattray Taylor adds that it was "a saltation if ever there was one" (1983, 64).

Critics of neo-Darwinism have pointed to hundreds of other examples in which a gradual evolution seems inconceivable, including and especially the very origin of life itself (Behe 1996; Denton 1991, 249–50). Michael Behe poses the problem in terms of the fact that every living system, including the most primitive bacterium, is "irreducibly complex," by which he means that the functioning of each of the parts presupposes that of the other parts. There is no way to imagine how such a system could have evolved through natural selection operating on small, random mutations, Behe argues: "Since natural selection can only choose systems that are already working, then if a biological system cannot be produced gradually it would have to arise as an integrated unit, in one fell swoop, for natural selection to have anything to act on" (1996, 39). The significance of such problems was pointed out by Darwin himself, who said: "If it could be demonstrated that any complex organ existed which could not possibly have been formed by numerous, successive, slight modifications, my theory would absolutely break down" (1958, 171).

The implication of these conceptual problems, combined with the fossil record, is that the Darwinian approach *has* broken down, at least as a complete explanation. Expressing a growing view, Taylor says that natural selection "accounts brilliantly for the minor adaptations but it is by no means clear that it explains the major changes in evolution" (1983, 13). Making this point even more emphatically, one paleontologist has said: "What Darwin described in the *Origin of the Species* was the steady background kind of evolution. But there also seems to be a non-Darwinian kind of evolution that functions over extremely short time periods—and that's where all the action is" (quoted in Nash 1995, 74).

Whiteheadian process philosophy provides a way to conceptualize "a non-Darwinian kind of evolution" that, while naturalistic, allows for saltations, which would overcome both the empirical and conceptual problems in Darwinian gradualism. Before turning to this alternative view, however, we need to see how nominalism provides the crucial connection between the gradualism of Darwinism and its atheism.

Gradualism, Nominalism, and Atheism

Most modern thinkers, as Whitehead points out (AI 129), have accepted nominalism, which comes from the Latin *nomen,* meaning "name." In reaction against the idea that there are (Platonic) forms in the nature of things, nominalism insists that the names for such forms are *merely* names, referring only to abstractions from particular things. Whitehead's doctrine of eternal objects involves, of course, a rejection of this nominalism. Darwinism, by contrast, is an example of modern nominalism. In a statement contrasting his view with the traditional view that the various taxa reflect forms in the mind of the creator, Darwin expresses his own nominalism:

> [T]he characters which naturalists consider as showing true affinity between any two or more species, are those which have been inherited from a common parent, all true classification being genealogical. . . . [C]ommunity of descent is the hidden bond which naturalists have been unconsciously seeking, and not some unknown plan of creation. (1958, 391)

All likenesses, in other words, are to be explained entirely in terms of *efficient* causation, not at all in terms of "formal" causes acting as final causes.

The Darwinian acceptance of nominalism is central to its commitment to gradualism. If nominalism were rejected, so that archetypal forms were thought to be real prior to the individual organisms that embody them, they could perhaps be thought to be efficacious as final causes, now sometimes called "attractors." The idea of jumps from one coherent type of organism to another would, therefore, be less inconceivable. Insofar as nominalism is presupposed, however, the idea that evolutionary developments could have occurred through such jumps is virtually inconceivable because such jumps would have to be entirely "random" or "chance" events. Each jump or saltation would involve *several changes* being made *simultaneously*. If such a jump were made on a purely random basis, not being based on the attractive power of some new type, the chance that it would result in a *viable* organism is infinitesimal. In sexually reproducing species, furthermore, a male and a female organism would have to make the same kind of jump simultaneously, and the chances that this would occur are virtually nil. Because of the nominalism of Darwinism, it must affirm gradualism, in spite of all the empirical and conceptual considerations against it.

The nominalism of Darwinism follows, furthermore, from its atheism. Although, as illustrated by the theological voluntarists of the fourteenth century, nominalism does not imply atheism, atheism does virtually imply nominalism: if there is no cosmic mind in which previously unactualized forms could subsist, we cannot conceive how they could exist, let alone how they could be efficacious in the actual world. Whitehead's "ontological principle," that everything nonactual must be in some *actual* entity, is simply a rephrasing of Aristotle's doctrine that forms can exist only in substances. Darwinian nominalism, accordingly, reflects the widespread agreement that if there is no divine being, there can be no efficacious forms in the nature of things.

Moreover, besides the evidence, both empirical and conceptual, against

gradualism, which indirectly suggests the falsity of nominalism, the empirical record supplies some direct evidence against Darwinian nominalism.
Although Darwinian theory predicts a *sequential* pattern, with multiple deri-
vations from a common ancestor, the record, says Denton, suggests a *hierarchical* pattern:

> The only sequence implied is a theoretical or abstract logical programme
> whereby a very general concept is successively subdivided into the more
> specific subcategories. The nodes and branches of the tree signify concepts in
> the mind of the logician. (1991, 122)

Although he is not himself a theist,[3] Denton points out that this hierarchical, typological view fits well with "the creative derivation of all the members of a class from the hypothetical archetype which existed in the mind of
God" (1991, 132).

2. Panentheism and Evolution

Having seen problems in the neo-Darwinian account of evolution that are
due to its atheism, we turn to how process philosophy, with its version of
naturalistic theism, can provide a better account. In this summary account
of a more extensive discussion provided elsewhere (Griffin 2000a, chap. 8),
I briefly indicate how process philosophy's theory of evolution answers the
following questions: Why should there be an evolutionary process? How
can divine influence bring about evolutionary changes? How can the evidently saltational nature of the evolutionary process be explained? How can
the very origin of our cosmic epoch be explained?

Why an Evolutionary Process?

One question to be answered by *any* position is, Why should there be an
evolutionary process at all? This question is difficult for traditional theism,
given its doctrine of omnipotence based on creation ex nihilo, according to

---

[3] In spite of this fact, some defenders of neo-Darwinism have suggested that Denton's arguments against it are discredited by the fact that these arguments have been *used* by creation-
ists! Besides avoiding this obviously fallacious argument, critics should note that, even if it were
valid to reject the arguments of thinkers because they *are* supernaturalists (which it is not), the
only arguments I have cited in this chapter that could thus be dismissed are those of Michael
Behe. There would still be the problems raised by the others, such as Denton, Eldredge,
Gould, Newell, and Stanley.

which there was no necessity for our world to have come about through a
long, slow evolutionary process. The question is also difficult for atheism,
given its view that there is no purpose behind the evolutionary process,
which makes the upward trend wholly mysterious. Process philosophy,
thanks to its naturalistic theism, can provide answers to both these questions.
There is an upward trend because the divine soul of the whole is seeking to
bring about more complex societies in which higher values can be realized.
The process has taken so long to reach its present state because the divine
power, being persuasive rather than coercive, needed continually to coax
creatures to overcome long-entrenched habits in order to embody novel
forms of experience.

How Can Divine Activity Induce Evolutionary Changes?

One of the reasons for the rejection of theistic evolutionism has been the
absence of any idea of *how* a divine actuality could influence the evolutionary process. Much of this problem has been due to materialism, which portrays nature as composed of vacuous bits of matter that can be causally affected only by other bits of matter. Process philosophy overcomes this
problem with its panexperientialism, according to which nature is composed of prehensive occasions of experience. This doctrine, by explaining
how cells, molecules, and even electrons in the human body can be influenced by the human mind, thereby explains how all the components of
the world could be influenced by a Cosmic Mind. However, this general explanation, while extremely important, needs to be supplemented by a more
particular explanation as to how divine influence could lead to progressive
change.

Whitehead's answer to this question revolves around the idea that mentality, in the sense of a mental or conceptual feeling, is to be understood as
appetition, and that such appetition can, by means of "hybrid physical feelings," play a causal role in the world. As explained in Chapter 3, a *hybrid*
physical feeling (or prehension) occurs when a present occasion prehends a
prior occasion in terms of that prior occasion's mental pole. In an occasion's
mental or conceptual pole, forms are embodied not in the full, unrestricted
way in which they are in the physical pole but only in a restricted way
(PR 291). To say that a form or possibility is felt conceptually, rather than
physically, is to say that this possible form of existence is felt *appetitively,* with
appetition for it to be realized physically, but that it is not yet thus realized.
The possibility is, in Whitehead's words, "an end realized in imagination but

not in fact" (FR 8). To desire a drink of water, for example, is not yet to enjoy it; to want to be loving is not yet to be loving. Thanks to hybrid physical feelings, however, this transition can occur, because in such a feeling the present occasion physically feels the form that was only conceptually felt in the prior occasion. In this way, that which is realized only conceptually or appetitively in one occasion can be fully realized, physically embodied, in the next.

Once a form is realized in the physical pole of an occasion, furthermore, it can then, without the need for any more hybrid physical feelings, become a regular part of the world's order. That is, once one occasion in a serially ordered society—such as a macromolecule, a living cell, or an animal mind—has prehended the new form physically, the subsequent occasions in that enduring individual can simply embody it by means of *pure* physical feelings. In this way, Whitehead says, novel forms become "canalized" (PR 107–8). Once this canalization occurs, so that the new form is a regular part of the world's order, the way is prepared for the appetitive entertainment of even more complex forms of order.

What still needs to be explained, however, is how these novel forms, or possible values, become appetitively entertained in the first place. Whitehead's explanation is that God acts in the world by, as it were, whetting the creatures' appetites for new forms. The concept of hybrid physical feeling is also central to the explanation of how this can occur. As mentioned earlier, the primordial nature of God, by virtue of consisting of God's conceptual prehension of the eternal objects, consists of God's *appetitive envisagement* of these possible forms of being (PR 32–34). It is for this reason that Whitehead can refer to this dimension of God as "the Eros of the Universe" (AI 11). As such, it is the "principle of unrest" in the universe (PR 32). That is, by means of their hybrid physical feelings of God, creatures feel the divine appetitions, in which novel forms are felt with appetition for them to be realized in the world. By the principle of the initial conformity of subjective form, the creatures feel the divine appetitions conformally and thereby with appetition to realize them.

If that were all there is to it, God would be able to bring about novel forms very rapidly. The fact that a creature feels God's appetitions with an *initial* conformity of subjective form, however, is not yet to have its appetite whetted, which occurs only when the creature, in its mental pole, itself feels the new possible form of existence with appetite for it to be realized in the future. Even this development, furthermore, is not sufficient to get the new form really embodied in the world. When the creature's appetite for this form becomes sufficiently strong and conditions are otherwise ripe, the full embodiment of the new form can occur by means of the process just described, in which the new form gets physically realized by means of a hybrid physical feeling, after which it can become canalized.

Assuming that this kind of threefold process—the hybrid physical feelings of a divine appetition for a new form to be realized, the creaturely appetition for this form, and the canalization of this form on the basis of a hybrid physical feeling—has occurred countless times over the past 15 billion years, we can understand how the varied and complex forms of order of our present world could have evolved out of extremely simple beginnings. Of course, once new creatures, which are more or less different from their ancestors, have emerged, they will reproduce and flourish only if environmental conditions permit. In most cases, probably, the environmental conditions do not permit, so that "natural selection" nips these embodiments of new forms of existence in the bud. In a few cases, however, the new organisms are viable in their environment, so that evolutionary developments occur.

Continuous Divine Activity and Discontinuous Evolution

The Darwinian assumption, as we have seen, is that discontinuous or saltational evolution would imply multiple supernatural interventions. This same assumption has been used by some supernaturalists to argue for "progressive creationism," which accepts the idea that the world has been billions of years in the making but argues that each species came about through a special creation rather than through evolution from a prior species.[4] Whitehead's explanation of the way in which divine activity becomes effective in the visible world, however, shows that this is not necessarily the case. Continuous, gradualistic divine activity can have discontinuous, saltational effects.

Divine activity is *continuous* because it exerts influence always and everywhere in terms of initial aims. Divine activity is *gradualistic* because the divine aims cannot induce creatures to actualize possibilities that are radically discontinuous with what they have already realized. There is an order among possibilities. We cannot run before we can walk, we cannot write poetry before we know a language. Likewise, God could not create mammals directly out of single-celled organisms, or human beings directly out of rodents. The divine aims can bring about novelty in the world only in terms of possibilities that are closely related to possibilities that have already been actualized.

---

[4] I have elsewhere discussed problems in this view as articulated by Phillip Johnson (Griffin 1998b) and by Johnson and Plantinga (Griffin 2000a, chap. 3).

Naturalistic theism, therefore, entails continuous, gradualistic divine action in the world.

This activity can, nevertheless, produce observable effects that are discontinuous. Although the divine activity works continually to whet the appetites of creatures for new possibilities, it may take a long time—perhaps years, centuries, millennia, or even much longer—for these appetites to get whetted—that is, for the occasions of experience of the types of enduring individual in question to begin feeling a new possibility conceptually, with appetition. Once this occurs, it may take an equally long period, or still longer, for this new form, entertained appetitively or imaginatively, to be embodied physically by means of a hybrid physical feeling and thereby canalized. Only when this happens would there be a change of shape that would be detectable by other organisms. When that process does finally occur, the organism might suddenly incorporate many more or less radical changes. A saltation will have occurred in the visible world. The divine activity lying behind it, however, had been entirely gradualistic.

This point illustrates the interrelatedness of the panexperientialism of process philosophy with its naturalistic theism. According to the panexperientialism, every individual has an inside, which is hidden to others, as well as an outside, which is observable. This philosophy thereby differs from the mechanistic, materialistic view of nature, according to which there is no inner, experiential reality behind the observable facade. Given the materialistic view, divine influence, if there were any, would have to act directly upon the observable world. Extraordinary *results* of divine activity would, therefore, imply that the divine activity itself had been extraordinary. Given the panexperientialist view, by contrast, there is an inner, hidden side to every actual entity, its concrescing subjectivity, which occurs before the occasion becomes an object for others. It is this inner, hidden side that the divine activity directly influences. Every enduring individual has an inner, hidden reality in which the effect of the divine activity can be building up behind the scenes, as it were, prior to its public manifestation. Because of its panexperientialism, therefore, process philosophy can account for the apparently saltational nature of the evolutionary process within a naturalistic$_{ns}$ context. Its solution, therefore, is one that the scientific community could in principle embrace.

The Origin of Our Cosmic Epoch

At this point, supernaturalistic theists may reply that although divine persuasion might be able to account for the evolution and even the origin of

life, it could not account for the origin of our universe itself. To explain this
origin, it is often argued, we need to appeal to divine coercion, especially
given the growing evidence that the universe has been able to exist so long
and to produce life only because it was "fine tuned" at the outset. If any one
of numerous variables, such as Planck's constant or the gravitational constant, were just slightly different, the universe would not have developed in
such a way that life could have evolved (Montefiore 1985, 169–71). Such
fine tuning, it is widely assumed, could be accounted for only by a creator
with coercive power.

This conclusion does not necessarily follow, however. The reason the
God of process theism usually cannot simply, by willing, have particular
forms instantiated is that the divine influence always faces competition from
the past world, with its well-entrenched habits, which are involved in long-
lasting enduring individuals such as protons, electrons, neutrons, atoms, and
molecules. Prior to the beginning of our particular cosmic epoch, however,
the realm of finite actualities was (by hypothesis) in a state of chaos, in the
sense that there were no societies, not even extremely simple serially ordered societies such as photons and quarks. So although our universe was not
created out of absolutely nothing, in the sense of a complete absence of finite
actualities, it *was* created out of a state of no-thing, in the sense of a state of
affairs in which there were no "things" in the ordinary sense of the term,
namely, *enduring* things. There *was,* by hypothesis, a multiplicity of finite actual occasions, but they were extremely brief events (enduring on the order
of a billionth of a second) happening at random. *Because there was no social order, these events embodied virtually no principles other than the purely metaphysical
principles.*

As explained in earlier chapters, an enduring individual, such as a quark
or an electron, involves a serially ordered society of actual occasions, in
which each occasion embodies not only the metaphysical principles but also
the more-or-less complex *contingent* form embodied in its predecessors in
that society. Each such enduring individual, in other words, embodies a habitual way of being, which through its long-standing repetition of a contingent form gives this form considerable power to implant itself in future
events. Prior to the emergence of any such habits, however, the divine
influence, in seeking to implant a set of contingent principles in the universe, would have had no competition from any other contingent principles.

*In the first instant of the creation of a particular universe, accordingly, divine per-
suasion could produce quasi-coercive effects.* A divine spirit, brooding over the
chaos, would only have had to think "Let there be X!" (with X standing for
the complex, interconnected set of contingent principles embodied in our

world at the outset, constituting its fine tuning). *From then on, however, the divine persuasive activity would always face competition from the power embodied in the habits reflecting these contingent principles,* so that divine persuasion would never again, as long as this world exists, be able to guarantee quasi-coercive results. In this way, process theism, while maintaining that God's agency *in* our universe is always persuasive, can nevertheless account for the remarkable contingent order *on* which our particular universe is based. This explanation completes the discussion of the cosmological argument given in Chapter 5.

3. God and Evil

Having seen how process philosophy can give a theistic explanation of the processes of cosmic, chemical, and biological evolution, as well as the very origin of our cosmic epoch—thereby portraying God as creator of our universe (the fifth feature of our generic idea of God)—we turn now to the question of theodicy: whether God's perfect goodness (the second feature) can be maintained in the face of the enormous evils of our world.

"All simplifications of religious dogma," Whitehead has famously said, "are shipwrecked upon the rock of the problem of evil" (RM 74). He was there referring primarily to the simple doctrine provided by traditional theism, according to which God is the sole formative element of our world, having created it ex nihilo. Because of this doctrine, the goodness of God is threatened by the existence of *any* evil in the world. The classical antitheistic argument from evil ran,

1. God is, by definition, all-powerful and all-good.
2. If God is all-powerful, God could unilaterally prevent all evil.
3. If God is all-good, God would want to prevent all evil.
4. Evil does occur.
5. Therefore God does not exist.

Using this formulation, I will, in preparation for explicating the theodicy of process philosophy, discuss that of traditional theism, which, as we saw in Chapter 4, exists in two versions: traditional *all-determining* theism, according to which God fully determines all occurrences in the world, and traditional *free-will* theism, according to which God has granted real freedom to some creatures so that some events are brought about by the free decisions of creatures.

Traditional All-Determining Theism

One way in which traditional all-determining theists can avoid the conclusion of the classical anti-theistic argument from evil is to reject the third premise, thanks to an ambiguity in it. The "evil" of which it speaks can be understood either as "prima facie evil," meaning *that which appears to be evil at first glance,* or as "genuine evil," meaning *that which actually makes the world less good than it might have been.* Apologists for traditional theism often take the term *evil* to refer merely to prima facie evil. They then point out that an event that is prima facie evil often provides the condition for a more-than-compensating good. For example, suffering through the momentary pain caused by a dentist is necessary for pain-free teeth in one's later years, and adversity provides an opportunity for spiritual growth. Then, generalizing from such examples, they suggest that all prima facie evils may be *only apparently* evil, so that none of them would be *genuinely* evil. On this basis, they deny the third premise, saying instead that God would surely have good reason for not preventing all (prima facie) evil.

This way out can be foreclosed from the outset, however, by specifying that "evil" in premises 3 and 4 refers to *genuine* evil. When this is done, traditional theism in its all-determining form has usually defended the existence of its God by rejecting the fourth premise—namely, that "evil does occur"—arguing that somehow everything will work out for the best. It thereby affirms that this is, in Leibniz's phrase, "the best of all possible worlds," down to its last detail.

It belongs to our hard-core common sense, however, that genuine evil does occur. As William James pointed out, no one can actually live in terms of "absolute optimism," meaning the belief that everything happens for the best. We all inevitably presuppose in practice that some things that happen are genuinely evil, meaning that something else could have happened that, if it had, would have made the world, all things considered, a better place. We show that we presuppose this by, for example, various emotions, such as anger, resentment, regret, and guilt feelings. If we truly believed that everything we and other people did worked out for the best, such emotions would never be appropriate. Illustrating the pervasiveness of the belief in genuine evil, Whitehead points out that "the imperfection of the world is the theme of every religion which offers a way of escape, and of every sceptic who deplores the prevailing superstition" (PR 47).[5] "The Leibnizian theory of the 'best of all possible worlds,'" Whitehead adds, "is an audacious

---

[5] The point of the latter clause is that although sceptics may verbally claim that they reject all standards of good and evil, their campaign against the evil of superstition proves otherwise.

fudge produced in order to save the face of a Creator constructed by contemporary, and antecedent, theologians."

If the denial of genuine evil is not a viable solution, the only way out for all-determining traditional theists is the desperate step of denying the validity of logic in theology. Karl Barth, Emil Brunner, and Emil Fackenheim, for example, all accept the four premises of the classical argument but reject the conclusion on the grounds that human logic does not apply to divine behavior (Griffin 1976, chaps. 12, 15). This solution, however, involves the rejection of a hard-core commonsense notion, this time the principle of noncontradiction. For theologians to deny that this principle applies to their reasoning is to deny their own enterprise, which as "theo-logy" is the application of logical reasoning to the idea of *theos*. Once this principle is rejected, furthermore, there can be no rational argumentation. Theologians who reject it have no logical basis, for example, to reject atheism on the grounds that it leads to inconsistencies.

The implausibility of the claim that none of the world's prima facie evils are *really* evil—because they are all canceled out by compensating goods—can be driven home by reflection upon the evolutionary process. This process, especially since the rise of animals with central nervous systems, has involved an enormous amount of pain and suffering. According to traditional theism, this entire process, with all its pain and suffering, was not necessary because a world such as ours, with the present types of creatures, could have been brought about suddenly (as, indeed, traditional theists historically assumed it had been). The suggestion that every instance of animal pain over the past 500 million years was somehow necessary for a compensating good is absurd.

Traditional Free-Will Theism

Less obviously problematic is the free-will version of traditional theism, according to which God, although *essentially* omnipotent, has *voluntarily* given freedom to the creatures, at least some of them, from which arises genuine evil. Because advocates of this position still affirm the traditional doctrine of divine power, they hold that God can do anything except that which is logically contradictory. They differ from traditional all-determining theologians, however, in maintaining that it is logically impossible for God fully to determine the actions of free creatures. In other words, they (rightly) deny that creaturely freedom is compatible with complete divine determinism. Therefore, they say, God, having granted real freedom to these creatures, cannot guarantee that they will not sin.

Having made this point, advocates of this position then reject the third premise of the above syllogism by saying that although God would ideally like to prevent genuine evil, God allows it to occur by virtue of granting its precondition, genuine freedom, to some of the creatures, at least human beings. This allowance for genuine evil is justified, these theists argue, because the existence of genuine freedom is the precondition for the highest possible values, such as the human virtues of faith, patience, generosity, compassion, and courage. A world containing freedom, even with all the evils it makes possible, is better, they contend, than an evil-free world without real freedom. The conclusion is that God's permission of evil is justified.

By recognizing that freedom and the higher values are necessarily associated, this solution moves, from the viewpoint of process philosophy, in the right direction. But it still has four serious problems. The first problem arises from the fact that it generally restricts real freedom to a few species on the Earth, typically to human beings alone. Its appeal to freedom thereby provides no answer to the question of what is usually called "natural evil," meaning the forms of evil that are not due to human volition. Besides all the pain and suffering in the prehuman evolutionary process mentioned above, the world's natural evils would include the fact that the face of the Earth is susceptible to earthquakes, tornadoes, and hurricanes, the fact that human beings and other animals are susceptible to cancer and other diseases, and the fact that the Earth contains the elements to produce nuclear weapons and other weapons of mass destruction. Because the nonhuman world is said to have been created ex nihilo and not to have any freedom vis-à-vis God, the implication is that God could have created a world that would be like ours in all respects except for not having these destructive elements. Some philosophers and theologians argue that a world with these elements is better because these evils provide the opportunity for human growth (Hick 1966; C. S. Lewis 1965). Others simply suggest that we can believe God has good reasons for allowing all these evils without our being able to discern what these reasons are (Plantinga 1981, 28; 2000, 466–67). Process philosophers share with atheists the conviction that these answers are unsatisfactory.[6]

This first problem with the traditional free-will theodicy could be overcome simply by positing that God has granted some degree of freedom to all creatures. A traditional free-will theist could, for example, adopt the Whiteheadian ontology—its panexperientialism with organizational duality—while stipulating that the creativity of the creatures, rather than being

---

[6] Saving my examination of Plantinga's position on faith and reason for Chapter 10, I here pass over the fact that he, offering not a theodicy but merely a "defense," claims that his answers need not be plausible.

inherent in the nature of reality, is derived from a free act of God. Even with this improvement, however, the second, third, and fourth problems confront the free-will version of traditional theism.

The second problem arises from the fact that according to this position, God could intervene to prevent any specific instance of evil. God could have diverted every bullet headed toward a human being "too young to die." God could have prevented any of the massacres that have occurred, including the Nazi Holocaust and the massacres carried out in the name of God during the Crusades. God could, in fact, prevent any sinful human intention from producing its intended effects. God could prevent any disease or any natural disaster from producing injury or death. God could, for example, prevent the millions of deaths that occur every year from starvation and polluted water. This position, therefore, retains the assumption of traditional theism that has led millions to question the existence or at least the goodness of a divine being. If there were a Superman who could prevent all these kinds of events but refused to do so—perhaps on the grounds that doing so would "prevent opportunities for human growth"—we would certainly question his moral goodness. A Superman, of course, could not prevent all genuine evils because, being finite, he could not be everywhere at once. But the God of traditional theism, understood as a Superman writ large, does not have this excuse.

A third problem for the traditional free-will theodicy is based on its position that even the freedom of human beings is an entirely gratuitous gift of God, not necessitated by anything in the nature of things—beyond the purely logical point that only genuinely free creatures can develop virtues that presuppose freedom. According to this position, God could have created beings identical with ourselves except that they would not have really been free to sin. They could have enjoyed all the kinds of values that we enjoy, from friendship and family to music and philosophy, except those that involve or presuppose genuine evil, such as murder and mayhem. They could even have believed that they were really acting freely while they were always doing good. Given the assumption that the omnipotent being who created our world could have chosen to create such a world instead, it is at least debatable whether this being made the best choice.

A fourth problem arises from the fact that even if we were to grant that our world, with its genuine freedom and correlative genuine evils, was the best choice, it would still be the case that, given the idea that human freedom was freely granted, this freedom could always be temporarily interrupted. Defenders of this position rightly point out that if God were to interrupt human freedom, the human being in that moment would not be fully human (given the definition of human beings as genuinely free): to have violated Hitler's freedom would have violated his full humanity. In response, however, the critic can ask: Would not this violation have been a small price to pay to have prevented Hitler from violating the freedom and humanity of millions of other people? Analogous questions arise, furthermore, every time human beings use their freedom to rob, injure, rape, murder, and otherwise violate the freedom and humanity of other human beings. The question remains: Can we consider perfectly good and loving an omnipotent being who, having the power to prevent such acts, does not do so?

In sum, although the free-will version of traditional theism can produce a somewhat better answer to the problem of evil than can the all-determining version, it still does not provide a satisfactory solution. In fact, this free-will version of traditional theism probably articulates, better than the all-determining version, the idea of the God-world relation that has actually been held by most people in the West. Insofar as traditional theism is thought to be refuted by the problem of evil, therefore, the refuted concept of God is that of traditional theism in general, not simply the all-determining version of it.

Process Philosophy's Answer to Why Evil Occurs

With regard to the reasons for the decline of belief in God in intellectual circles over the past centuries, the fact that the traditional idea of God creates a problem of evil without a satisfactory solution is equaled in importance only by the fact that this same idea has led to a perceived conflict between science and religion. Therefore, if process philosophy not only provides a worldview in terms of which science and religion can be integrated but does so in a way that overcomes the problem of evil, this twofold accomplishment could be of utmost importance for the prospects for belief in God in the coming centuries. Its solution to the problem of evil has, in any case, generally been recognized as one of its greatest advantages, even by some of its opponents (Hasker 1994, 139).

Most of the elements in this solution have already been provided. In contrast to traditional theism's simple doctrine, which posits God as the sole formative factor in our world, Whitehead's position has "additional formative elements" (RM 96), namely, creativity (as embodied in creatures as well as in God), the eternal forms or possibilities, and the metaphysical principles. It is the addition of these other, equally eternal elements that makes this a naturalistic, as distinct from a supernaturalistic, theism. Because our universe was created out of a chaos rather than out of absolute nothingness, so that creative power is inherent in the world (as well as in God), the creatures' twofold creative power of self-determination and efficient causation cannot be canceled, overridden, or completely controlled by God. On this basis, process philosophy denies the second premise in the argument given at the outset of this section, saying instead that although God *is* all-powerful—not only in the sense of being the supreme power of the universe but also in the sense of being perfect in power, having all the power one being could possibly have—God *cannot* unilaterally prevent all evil. If being "all-powerful" is taken to mean being omnipotent in the sense of essentially having all the power, however, then process philosophy simply denies the first premise's assertion that a being worthy of the name *God* is all-powerful by definition. In either case, the fact that genuine evil occurs is not in conflict with the existence of God. That is the first part of process theism's solution to the problem of evil.

Some critics, to be sure, argue that this type of approach, which depends on a reconception of divine power, cannot really be considered a solution. For example, Wainwright, discussing the reconception of divine sovereignty given by the Indian religious philosopher Ramanuja, says: "Ramanuja thus resolves the tension between human freedom and God's causal sovereignty by restricting the latter's range. This is to dissolve the problem, not solve it" (Wainwright 1997, 59). But why should this not count as a real solution? Imagine, for example, the following interchange at a neighborhood meeting:

A: How are we going to keep Jones from beating his wife?
B: Jones doesn't beat his wife.
A: But that is to dissolve the problem, not to solve it.

In other words, if the "problem" results solely from a peccant premise, to point out the erroneous assumption in the premise is to solve the problem precisely by dissolving it—that is, by showing that there is no real problem to be solved. This point was already made in Chapter 3 with regard to the mind-body problem. The essence of that problem, as formulated by both dualists and materialists, is how mind could evolve out of, and interact with, insentient matter. If we start with the alternative premise—that what we normally call matter is not really comprised of insentient, vacuous actualities—we have solved the essence of the mind-body problem precisely by dissolving it. In the same way, process theism solves the essence of the problem of evil—How is the occurrence of any genuine evil compatible with a perfectly good creator *who could have unilaterally prevented all genuine evil while still making possible all the good?*—by rejecting the italicized part of the premise, thereby dissolving the apparent problem.

Process Philosophy's Answer to Why So Much Evil Occurs

In most people's minds, the problem of evil is raised not simply or even primarily by the existence of *some* genuine evil (because most people, as distinct from philosophers and theologians, do not think through the fine point that God as traditionally defined is inconsistent with the existence of even one occurrence of genuine evil). Rather, what raises the problem of evil for most people is the *enormity* of the evil in world. For example, in *Candide,* which lampoons the sophism that "this is the best of all possible worlds," Voltaire builds his case on a long series of incidents, not simply on one unambiguous example of genuine evil.

Process philosophy's answer to why so much evil can occur in our world, in spite of its having been created by a good and loving divine power, involves what can be called the "law of the variables of power and value," which is implicit in Whitehead's philosophy. The variables in question are:

1. The capacity to experience intrinsic good.
2. The capacity to experience intrinsic evil.
3. The power to be extrinsically good—that is, to contribute positively to the experience of others.
4. The power to be extrinsically evil—that is, to contribute negatively to, or even be destructive of, the experience of others.
5. The power of self-determination—which in its higher forms we call "freedom."

The "law" in question is that *if any one of these variables rises, all the rest necessarily rise proportionately.* This law refers primarily to advances made in the evolutionary process.

The divine aim behind the evolutionary process, as we have seen, is to bring about increases in the first variable, the capacity to experience intrinsic good. The successive emergence of atoms, molecules, macromolecules, prokaryotic cells, eukaryotic cells, multicelled animals, animals with central nervous systems, mammals, and human beings can be understood as resulting from the divine aim at enduring individuals that can enjoy increasingly higher levels of positive intrinsic value. The point of the law of the variables is that *an increase in the capacity for intrinsic good is always accompanied by a correlative increase in the other four variables.*

To illustrate with the first and fifth variables: those creatures with greater intensity of feeling, and thereby greater capacity for experiencing intrinsic good, also have greater power to exercise self-determination. For example, human beings, who have far more power for self-determination than do their pet dogs, can also enjoy values, such as those involved in poetry, philosophy, and religious worship, that are far beyond any canine imagination. Dogs in turn have both far more freedom and far more capacity for enjoying positive values than do the fleas in their hair. These fleas in turn have both more freedom and more capacity for value-realization than any of their DNA molecules. And so on. Incidentally, although Whitehead does not explicitly formulate what I am calling the law of the variables of value and power, he alludes to the present correlation, between freedom and enjoyment, in his statement that "[e]ach occasion exhibits its measure of creative emphasis in proportion to its measure of subjective intensity" (PR 47).

This correlation between intrinsic value and freedom is obviously an *empirical* fact of our world: those beings with greater capacity for intrinsic value do, in fact, have more freedom. The law of the variables involves the supposition that this *empirical* fact reflects a *metaphysical* principle, so that this correlation would hold in any world that God could create. Given this correlation, God could not have created beings capable of experiencing great intrinsic good who would not also be capable of a corresponding degree of the power of self-determination. This power of self-determination includes, furthermore, power vis-à-vis God, power to act contrary to the initial aims received from God.

This point is directly relevant to one of the questions commonly asked by critics of theism, namely: Why didn't God create "rational saints," meaning *beings who are like us in all respects except guaranteed always to be good?* This is a difficult question for traditional all-determining theists because they either deny human freedom or, which comes to the same thing, declare it to be compatible with divine determinism. Because they cannot claim that human freedom requires the ability to act contrary to the divine will, they can give no good answer as to why God allows (that is, *causes*) human beings to sin.

Traditional free-will theists answer this question by first (rightly) denying that human freedom is compatible with divine determination, then stipulating that God does not want forced sainthood, that the only saints who are valuable in the eyes of God are those who have developed their virtues freely (Hick 1966, 308–10). Traditional free-will theists can, thereby, provide an initially plausible answer as to why God did not create human-like creatures who would be guaranteed to be good. This answer is problematic, however, because God would be the only one who would know that all these good people—leading healthy, happy, fulfilling lives, unmarred by theft, murder, rape, and warfare—were really not free to sin. We could think that we were really free, so that we could admire our own virtue and that of others. Such a situation would, it is true, involve an element of divine deception, to which advocates of this traditional free-will defense claim that God would not stoop. Some advocates of this view, however, speculate that God deliberately made the world more ambiguous than it needed to be by creating "epistemic distance" between God and humans, thereby making the divine existence less obvious than it might have been (Hick 1966, 317, 351–52).[7] It is unclear why this kind of deception, which results in much evil, is all right, whereas the other kind, which would prevent all evil, would be unacceptable. The question, therefore, remains: Can we completely admire the wisdom and goodness of a deity who would create our kind of world, instead of that other kind, simply for the satisfaction of knowing that those souls who do become good do so freely?

From the point of view of process theism, we need not debate that question because, by hypothesis, God could *not* have created beings like us in every way except guaranteed by God always to be and do good. *Any beings in any possible world capable of the kinds of values we can enjoy would also necessarily have the kind of freedom we have,* including the freedom to act contrary to the will of God.

This is another issue for which the difference between creation out of chaos and creation ex nihilo is crucial. Given its acceptance of creation ex nihilo, traditional theism implies that there are no metaphysical principles that would necessarily be embodied in any actual world that God could create. All the principles involved in our world are, by this hypothesis, purely contingent principles, which could have been otherwise. Although it is an empirical fact of our world that freedom and the capacity for intrinsic value rise proportionately, traditional theists must assume this correlation to be arbitrary, freely chosen by God. Part of their answer to the problem of evil, accordingly, must be an explanation as to why God chose to give us such dangerous freedom. Process philosophy supposes, by contrast, that there has always been a world of finite existents with both power and intrinsic value.

---

[7] Although John Hick was indeed an advocate of this traditional free-will theodicy when he wrote the book referred to here, he later, after developing the position to be discussed in Chapter 7, had to regard his earlier theodicy, with its language of "a personal being carrying out intentions through time," as "mythological" because, he has come to believe, such language "cannot apply to the ultimate transcendent Reality in itself" (Hick 1989, 359). This change, however, has not prevented Hick from republishing his earlier views (Hick forthcoming).

In harmony with this supposition, process philosophy affirms the existence of metaphysical principles, descriptive of how power and intrinsic value are related, which would necessarily hold true in any world that God could create. The previous question, therefore, does not arise. The only question is whether it was good for God to have brought forth a world with beings capable of the kinds of value-realization of which we human beings are capable—even though such beings would necessarily have a high degree of power to resist the divine aims for us.

The reason why this freedom makes us capable of experiencing and causing so much evil becomes clearer when we bring in the second variable, *the capacity to experience intrinsic evil*. It is sometimes wondered why we human beings are capable of such suffering, both physical and psychological. The capacity to experience physical pain can, of course, be partly explained in evolutionary terms, insofar as pain serves as a warning that some part of the body needs care. A mild amount of pain, however, could serve this function; there is no functional need for the intense, sometimes incapacitating pain to which we are susceptible. Process philosophy's explanation is that this capacity for pain is simply the reverse side of our capacity for physical enjoyment. As Whitehead suggests, the same "delicacy of perception" that allows an organism to "develop a finer and more subtle relationship among its bodily parts" also results in a corresponding capacity for pain (RM 93). Explicitly bringing out this correlation, as well as its metaphysical (which he calls "a priori") status, Hartshorne says: "[C]hances of evil overlap with chances of good. A dead man has no chance of suffering, also none of enjoyment. The principle is universal and a priori. Tone down sensitiveness and spontaneity, and one reduces the risk of suffering but also the opportunities for depth of enjoyment" (1953, 107). This principle applies even more to *psychological* suffering. Just as we human beings can experience forms and depths of joy of which our pets have no inkling, we are also susceptible to forms and depths of distress to which they are immune. Few pets commit suicide.

The full import of the positive correlation between the first two variables is brought out, however, only when we connect them with the fifth variable, *the freedom for self-determination*. Because this freedom is in some sense qualitatively different in human beings, compared with the rest of the animals, we are the uniquely *historical* species: we are able to shape, and be shaped by, a distinct historical tradition, so that human beings in one tradition can be radically different, psychologically, from human beings in other traditions. This same degree of freedom includes the power to shape ourselves—our historical traditions and our individual selves—in very unhealthy ways, so that being human can be far less intrinsically rewarding than it might be. It can, in fact, be a primarily miserable experience.

The reason why the metaphysical correlations make this such a dangerous world, in which horrible evils can occur, becomes even clearer when we bring in the third and fourth variables: *the capacity to be extrinsically good* and *the capacity to be extrinsically evil*. In reality, these two capacities are one— the power to exert causal efficacy on other experiences, for good or for ill. The principle that this power is correlative with the capacities for self-determination and intrinsic value means that *humanlike beings could not have been created so as to be less dangerous than we are.* In bringing about beings with the capacity for the accomplishments of a Jesus, a Gautama, a Hildegaard, a Michelangelo, a Shakespeare, a Newton, a Mozart, a Madame Curie, or a Sojourner Truth, God necessarily brought about beings with the capacity for creating the evils of slavery, genocide, pollution, and the extermination of entire species for sport and profit.

Given all these correlations of value and power inherent in the nature of things, the standard problem-of-evil question—Why didn't God bring about a world with all the good things of our world but guaranteed to have much less evil?—does not arise because God could not have done so. The only meaningful question is, Given the enormous amount of evil in our world, should God have stopped encouraging the evolutionary process forward before the world became so dangerous? If God had not brought forth human life, instead remaining content with a world in which the most sophisticated creatures were at the level of dolphins and chimpanzees, then the world would be free of the kinds of evil mentioned above. In *this* sense, God is partly responsible for all the evils caused and experienced by human beings, because if God had not encouraged the evolution of human beings, or other creatures with similar capacities, such evils would not have occurred.

The question is, however, whether God is *indictable*—that is, responsible in a blameworthy sense—for the evils of human history. One could give an affirmative answer to this question only if one could honestly can say that, in light of the evils made possible by human life, it would have been better if God had forever remained content with a simpler world, not encouraging the evolution of humanlike beings. When the choice is put in these terms— either a world with the risk of the kinds of evils our world has or a world with no humanlike beings at all—there are probably few who could indict God for making the wrong choice. As great as the evils caused and experienced by humans have been, a world without human (or at least humanlike) beings would be a far poorer world.

It is with this point that we see the full advantage of Whitehead's naturalistic theism, with its doctrine that God's relation to a world belongs to the very essence of God. This doctrine means not only that God cannot occasionally interrupt the world's causal nexus. It also means that the divine purpose to bring about a world rich in value cannot—*metaphysically* cannot—be carried out without the risk of great evils. In this way, process philosophy is able to reconcile the facts of our world, as horrible as they often are, with belief in the wisdom and perfect goodness of this world's creator. It thereby supports the second and third dimensions of the generic idea of God.

At this point, however, many critics will ask about the twelfth and thirteenth dimensions, which say that a being worthy of the name *God* must be portrayed as "the ultimate guarantee of the meaning of life" and "the ground of hope for the victory of good over evil." These issues bring us to eschatology, the doctrine of last or ultimate things. In Judaism, Christianity, and some other religions, this doctrine usually involves two parts, which correspond to two possible meanings of the "victory of good over evil"—namely, a victory on this planet, which in Judaism and Christianity has been called the arrival of the Reign of God, and a victory beyond death.

Process theism can provide a basis for both types of eschatological hope. With regard to the hope for a victory of good over evil on this planet, I have developed the case for such hope in two works in progress. Although I had originally planned to summarize this work in the present volume, the issue is really too complex to summarize briefly, and the present volume, in any case, was already sufficiently long. On this issue, therefore, I can only refer the reader to these other works (Griffin forthcoming a and c). I will, however, discuss the issue of hope for a victory of good over evil beyond this life. This issue is crucial because critics who deny the "religious adequacy" of process theology usually mean that its eschatology, by ruling out life after death, does not provide a sufficient response to the distinctively human problem, which is that we know we will die.

4. The Need for Life after Death

In the world's various religions, the doctrine of human destiny has usually involved some mode of existence beyond bodily death. On the one hand, it has widely been held that if some of the uniquely human problems are to be resolved, such a resolution could occur only in a life after death. On the other hand, some of the distinctively human capacities have suggested that human beings might uniquely be capable of such a mode of existence, at least with divine assistance. In theistic religions, this expectation has been central to the belief in God as the ground of hope for the ultimate victory of good over evil.

The Anticipation of Death

The distinctive nature of human consciousness, with its element of *self-consciousness*, makes death a special problem for human beings. Besides the fact that we, like all other animals, will die sooner or later, we can consciously anticipate this fact. The usual assumption that this anticipation is unique to us is probably correct, at least largely. Even if some of the other higher animals have an inchoate anticipation of their own deaths, we appear to be the only ones with elaborate rituals and meaning-systems connected with death. In any case, because we do anticipate our own death and that of others, death is a problem, which seems to have four distinguishable dimensions.

First, our awareness that we will die raises the question whether our lives have any ultimate meaning. We do seem to be meaning-demanding creatures. As Whitehead says, "[T]he culminating fact of conscious, rational life refuses to conceive of itself as a transient enjoyment, transiently useful" (PR 340). We feel a need instead to make some permanent contribution. The problem raised by this need is that if we believe that it is unfulfilled—that our lives *are* merely "transiently useful" at best—the resulting disappointment can empty our "transient enjoyment" of most of its enjoyment, a result that would mean that the evolutionary process had brought about a self-defeating result. That is, the purpose behind the evolutionary process is, by hypothesis, the development of creatures with increasingly greater capacity for intrinsic value. Human beings appear to be the apex of this development on our planet. And yet human existence, by virtue of its capacity to ask the question of ultimate meaning, can end up being less, rather than more, enjoyable than the other forms of animal existence.

We are aware that we will have a more or less extensive "social immortality," living on, in a sense, through the memory of others, through our descendants, and through other contributions we may have made to human society. But we also know that memory fades and that, for most of us anyway, our contributions will become less and less significant as time passes. If we really reflect on this issue, furthermore, we are aware that the human race itself will eventually perish, so that so-called *social* immortality provides no *real* immortality. The resulting suggestion that our lives make no permanent contribution to anything, so that the universe will eventually be as if we had never been, raises the question of the meaning of our lives in the strongest possible terms. We may have struggled mightily to realize certain aims, but reflection upon the impermanence of all finite structures raises the question whether our struggles really made any ultimate difference. As Hartshorne says: "Be the aim Nirvana, the Classless Society, the Welfare State, Self-realization, the query is never silenced, what good is it, from the cosmic and everlasting perspective, that one or the other or all of these aims be attained for a time on this ball of rock?" (1962, 132). If we give a nihilistic answer, that it makes no ultimate difference, this answer raises, in turn, the question of the reality of God, insofar as it belongs to the very idea of God to be the ultimate ground of the meaning of life. The nihilistic idea that life is meaningless, therefore, is closely connected to the idea that there is no Holy Reality. And that conclusion undermines the premise from which we started, that the evolutionary process is the expression of a cosmic purpose to realize value. Nihilism becomes total.

The second dimension of the problem created by our awareness that we all die is that of ultimate justice. We are aware that human life is terribly unfair, that some people, through no merit of their own, are extremely fortunate whereas others, through no fault of their own, are extremely unfortunate. Many are, for example, born into situations of abject poverty, from which there is no escape, or with terrible physical or mental deformities. Many others are born with great potential but die young, before having had much chance to develop this potential. Beyond these obvious facts, there is the problem, emphasized by Kant, that a gap between virtue and happiness often exists, with immoral people often having happier lives than truly good people. The resulting intellectual problem, as Kant pointed out, is that these discrepancies throw into doubt the validity of our sense that there *is* a moral order to the universe. That is, the universe seems to call us to be moral (most of the religions of the world agree, Whitehead points out, on the existence of a character of rightness inherent in the nature of things). But if the universe itself is not just, then our confidence that it really contains objective moral principles is undermined, with the result that we are led toward moral nihilism. Kant believed that we could prevent this undermining only by postulating a life after death in which the gap between virtue and happiness would be progressively overcome.

The third dimension of the problem raised by our anticipation of death is the fact that most people evidently have a longing for more life. Even apart from questions of ultimate meaning and justice, they are simply not ready to have their personal stream of experience extinguished. Much modern thought has, to be sure, assumed this longing to be a sign of immaturity or simply a lingering aftereffect of the traditional religions, which had created unrealistic expectations. The hope for continued life after death, in either case, has been seen as a problem that we will "get over." This assumption, however, has not been borne out. Most people still believe in a life after death, and at least most of the rest evidently find their lack of belief a problem. Some philosophers who completely reject this belief candidly admit that they wish they could accept it. In any case, if this longing is a permanent feature of human existence as such, as it seems, then it raises a problem about the goodness of the universe: if there is no continued life beyond bodily death, as most modern thought assumes, then the universe has created an ineradicable desire in us that it will not fulfill—a conclusion that implies a form of Manicheanism.

The fourth dimension of the problem created by our conscious anticipation of death involves the human religious desire for "salvation" in the sense of integrity or wholeness. Religious beliefs and practices are largely oriented around the sense that there is an ideal mode of existence and that through proper relation to the Holy Reality we can realize, or have realized in us, this mode of existence.[8] Most people, however, also have the sense of now being far from the goal, much too far for the gap to be traversed within the present life. The sense of this gap, between what we now *are* and what we *ought* to be, has been closely connected to ideas of a life beyond the present one, in which this gap may be overcome. For strongly religious people, in other words, the desire for *more* life, discussed earlier, has been intimately related to a desire for a *sanctified* life.

If we believe that there is no life after death, however, then we seem forced to the conclusion that it is impossible for the ideal to be realized, at least for most people, because of insufficient time, which produces a dilemma. On the one hand, if we hold to the religious ideal, we in effect accept a form of the view of Jean-Paul Sartre (1956) that the human being is a "futile passion," called to an ideal that cannot possibly be realized. On the other hand, in light of the widespread intuition that *ought* implies *can*, we may simply give up the religious ideal of wholeness, concluding that the old idea that human beings are called to realize such an ideal mode of existence was a colossal mistake. Part of Kant's reason for postulating life after death was that unless there would be time for us to develop the kind of virtuous character to which the moral law seems to call us, our confidence of the objectivity of this moral law itself would be undermined.

---

[8] This argument is unaffected if we, as I do, accept Cobb's view (1967) that there can be more than one ideal mode of existence.

Objective Immortality

The question before us, then, is what process philosophy says, or at least allows us to say, in the face of the distinctively human dimensions of the problem of death. A solution to the first dimension, that of *ultimate meaning,* is part and parcel of process philosophy's dipolar theism. Thanks to the doctrine of God's "consequent nature," according to which God is internally related to the world, all finite experiences are said to have "objective immortality" in God. This doctrine is presented by Whitehead and Hartshorne as an answer to the longing for ultimate meaning. Having affirmed, in his discussion of the "final application of the doctrine of objective immortality," that we have a sense of becoming "everlasting in the Being of God," Whitehead says: "In this way, the insistent craving is justified—the insistent craving that zest for existence be refreshed by the ever-present, unfading importance of our immediate actions, which perish and yet live for evermore" (PR 351). Discussing this same doctrine in terms of the idea that God is the supreme exemplification of the principle of internal relatedness, Hartshorne says:

> Deity is the highest possible form of the inclusion of others in the self. . . . Infallibly and with unrivaled adequacy aware of all others, God includes others—not, as we do, in a mostly indistinct or largely unconscious manner, but with full clarity. . . . Since God forgets nothing, loses no value once acquired, our entire worth is imperishable in the divine life. (1984, 110)

Due to the fact that Whitehead, while affirming this doctrine of objective immortality in the divine experience, does not affirm life after death, combined with the fact that Hartshorne, in affirming the former, explicitly denies the latter, it has widely been assumed that the promise of objective immortality is the only answer allowed by process philosophy of religion to the problem created by our anticipation of death. Because of this assumption, process philosophy of religion has been widely considered to provide an inadequate basis for theological reflection. And given the preceding analysis of the fourfold problem created by our anticipation of death, there is considerable justification for this response because the doctrine of objective immortality answers, at most, only the first dimension of this problem. It provides no answer to the problems created by the injustice of this life,[9]

---

[9] Marjorie Suchocki has suggested that by seeing objective immortality as involving an element of subjectivity, we could address the problem of justice (Suchocki 1988; 1989). I have argued that her interpretation is neither allowable without violating Whiteheadian principles nor sufficient to the problem (Griffin 1989b).

the human desire for more life, and the desire for wholeness. These problems could be overcome, if at all, only in a life beyond bodily death.

Furthermore, it can be argued that even the answer to the first problem, that of ultimate meaning, is unsatisfactory apart from belief in a continued existence beyond bodily death. Hartshorne argues that our awareness that we make a permanent contribution to the divine life should be sufficient. This argument, however, seems to reflect the bias of a privileged life, especially one in which there have been great opportunities to make contributions to other creatures, and thereby to God, with which one could be pleased. The subtitle of Hartshorne's autobiography (1990), in fact, indicates that it involves reflections "upon his fortunate career." For example, besides attending and then teaching in some of the finest educational institutions in the world, Hartshorne has had a long and productive life during which he has published more than twenty books and five hundred essays. In a commentary on the scriptural idea that one's life should be a "reasonable, holy, and living sacrifice" to God, Hartshorne says: "[I]f I can inspire multitudes who will never see me in the flesh, then the incense I send up to God will continue to rise anew for many generations" (1962, 257–58). Not all people, however, can look back upon their lives, and the lives of their loved ones, with such satisfaction. Many individuals die young, before they have had an opportunity to make any significant contributions. Many other individuals have opportunities but waste them, either making no worthwhile contribution to others or, worse yet, being positively destructive of the lives of others, perhaps through theft, rape, murder, or selling drugs. These individuals often look back upon their lives with disgust. For such people, the message that our lives will be permanently retained in God will probably seem more like a threat than a promise. Better to be completely obliterated, such people may say, than to be a permanent blot on the divine memory! Although they may agree that the doctrine of the consequent nature of God provides life with a meaning, they may find it to be a *horrible* meaning.

Although the doctrine of objective immortality is necessary for a satisfactory solution to the distinctively human dimensions of the problem of death, it is not sufficient. It is necessary because, as Whitehead and Hartshorne say, the ultimate religious question is whether our lives are ultimately meaningful, and we can finally think of them as such only if we think of them as making a contribution to an everlasting Holy Reality. Apart from this assumption, life after death, even one that lasted forever, would ultimately be meaningless. But the doctrine of objective immortality is not sufficient by itself because of the inadequacies discussed earlier.

These inadequacies could in principle be overcome, however, if the doctrine of objective immortality were combined with a doctrine of life after death. Such a doctrine would answer the simple desire that the present life be followed not by extinction but by more life in which new experiences are enjoyed. It would also allow for the possibility that the injustices of the present life could be overcome, in the sense that all souls would have the opportunity to actualize their potentialities and to make amends for injustices to which they have contributed. It would also allow time for the religious ideal of ultimate wholeness to be realized. And in allowing us to realize our various potentialities and to reach perfection, a continuing life beyond bodily death would allow each of us to make a contribution to the Divine Reality of the universe with which we could be content, so that the doctrine of objective immortality would finally be the great source of joy that Hartshorne says it should be.

5. The Possibility of Life after Death

The next question, accordingly, is whether process philosophy allows for the possibility of life after death. It has widely been assumed that it does not, primarily for four reasons: (1) the fact that Whitehead did not affirm life after death; (2) the Whiteheadian doctrine that every actual entity has a physical pole as well as a mental pole; (3) the Whiteheadian doctrine that the human mind or soul could not have emerged apart from the human brain; and (4) the fact that Hartshorne has denied the reality of life after death.

Whitehead's Nonaffirmation of Life after Death

The fact that Whitehead does not affirm the reality of life after death might be used to infer that he thought life after death metaphysically impossible. In his most explicit treatment of this question, however, he says that his philosophy "is entirely neutral on the question of immortality, or on the existence of purely spiritual beings other than God. There is no reason why such a question should not be decided on more special evidence, religious or otherwise, provided that it is trustworthy" (RM 107). In saying that his position is "entirely neutral" on this question, Whitehead meant that his doctrine of the human soul did not, like those of Plato and Descartes, entail that the soul would necessarily survive the death of the body, and also did not, like materialistic philosophies, rule out this possibility. In saying that a positive answer could be given on the basis of "more special evidence, religious or otherwise," he probably had in mind, besides reported events associated with religions (such as the resurrection of Jesus), the evidence from psychical research. In any case, in declaring the question of the reality of life after death to be an empirical question, he clearly indicated that his philosophy did not make it metaphysically impossible.

In reply, it might be said that this discussion, which occurs in *Religion in the Making,* reflects an early stage in Whitehead's metaphysical development, before he had arrived at his doctrine that every actuality has a physical as well as a mental pole. In this earlier stage, Whitehead at times suggested a virtual dualism, distinguishing between the "physical world" and the "spiritual world," with the former consisting of "physical occasions" and the latter of "mental occasions" (RM 99). Later in the book, he overcame this dualism, saying that "[t]he most complete concrete fact is dipolar, physical and mental," so that so-called mental occasions would be occasions in which the mental pole is merely "negligible," not entirely absent (RM 114). In the passage referring to the possibility of life after death, however, the more dualistic position is still presupposed, insofar as it refers to "purely spiritual beings," which had been defined as "routes of mentality in respect to which associate material routes are negligible, or entirely absent" (RM 106). Therefore we cannot, one could argue, take that passage as evidence that Whitehead, after reaching his final position—according to which every actual occasion has a physical pole as well as a mental pole—still considered life after death metaphysically possible.

The Necessity for a Physical Pole

Indeed, some have suggested, that final position makes the survival of the soul apart from the physical body metaphysically impossible. This argument, however, which depends on the equation of the "physical pole" with the "physical body," is based on confusing the distinctively Whiteheadian meaning of the term *physical* and the ordinary meaning of the term, which has been derived from dualistic philosophies. In that ordinary, dualistic meaning, the body is purely physical, in the sense of devoid of experience, whereas the mind or soul, with its conscious experience, is purely mental or spiritual. Within that context, to say that the mental cannot exist without the physical is to say that the mind or soul cannot exist apart from the body. Within Whitehead's (later) philosophy, by contrast, every actual entity is an "occasion of experience" with both a physical pole and a mental pole. In its Whiteheadian technical sense, accordingly, the term *physical* does *not* refer uniquely to the body and its constituents in distinction from the mind or soul. To say that every actual entity has a physical pole merely means that every occasion of experience begins by prehending *other actualities* (whereas the mental pole begins with the prehension of possibilities). The fact that every actuality must have a physical pole, therefore, does not necessarily imply that the personally ordered society of occasions of experience that is the human mind or soul could not exist apart from the body with which it has been associated.

No Souls without Brains?

The best argument for this conclusion—namely, that the soul could not exist in a disembodied state—would be based on the idea that from the perspective of Whiteheadian process philosophy the human soul could not have arisen apart from the human brain, or, more generally, a high-level enduring individual like the human soul could not have arisen apart from some structured society with the complexity of the human brain. By analogy, the living occasions like those in the eukaryotic cell could not have arisen apart from a structured society something like the eukaryotic cell as a whole, with its macromolecules and organelles. The nexus constituted by the living occasions of the cell cannot continue to exist apart from the environment provided by the cellular body, with its organisms that support and protect this nexus. For this reason, Whitehead refers to the temporal nexus of living occasions in the cell as a *nexus* rather than a *society* (PR 103). In the same way, one could argue, the nexus of dominant occasions constituting the human soul could not exist apart from the environment provided by the brain.

Whitehead himself, however, evidently did not draw this conclusion. In the first place, he refers to the soul as a society, not simply a nexus. In the second place, in *Adventures of Ideas,* one of his latest writings, he again leaves open the possibility, as he had in *Religion in the Making,* that the human soul might exist apart from the body. Having defined the human soul as "a personal living society of high-grade occasions," he adds:

> How far this soul finds a support for its existence beyond the body is:—another question. The everlasting nature of God, which in a sense is nontemporal and in another sense is temporal, may establish with the soul a peculiarly intense relationship of mutual immanence. Thus in some important sense the existence of the soul may be freed from its complete dependence upon the bodily organization. (AI 208)

It should be noted that Whitehead's openness to this possibility does not contradict his doctrine that every occasion of experience must have a physical pole. He is suggesting here only that the physical prehensions required by each occasion of the soul's existence might not necessarily need to include prehensions of a brain. Although Whitehead's alternative suggestion seemed to be that the soul's (physical) prehensions of God might suffice, there are, as will be discussed later, other possibilities. One cannot, in any case, appeal to Whitehead's authority to support the contention that process philosophy makes life after death impossible.

Hartshorne's Rejection of Subjective Immortality

It might seem, however, that one *could* appeal to Hartshorne for such support. For example, in one of his later books, Hartshorne rejects "immortality as a career after death . . . in which our individual consciousnesses will have *new* experiences not enjoyed or suffered while on earth" (1984, 4). He even refers to that idea derisively, speaking of "tall tales about human careers after death" (117). As shown by these and many other passages, there is no doubt that Hartshorne explicitly rejects every form of belief that the human soul continues to have new experiences after bodily death.

Insofar as Hartshorne presents *arguments* for this rejection, however, they are arguments not against the idea of life after death as such but only against the idea of subjective *immortality*—the idea that our existence would literally continue *forever*. His rhetoric, accordingly, is usually directed against the idea that we would have "infinite careers" after death (47, 48, 117), careers with "temporally infinite futures" (36), careers that go on "forever" (40). His objections to this view are theological and metaphysical.

Hartshorne's *theological* argument is that belief in our subjective immortality tends "to make God a mere means for our everlasting happiness" (1984, 117), "to make God the means to our ultimate fulfillment, as Kant did" (1970, 289). Opposing this tendency is of extreme importance to Hartshorne, because for him the very meaning of life is to realize that it is our privilege to contribute to the life of God, who is "the only immortal being" (1984, 117). We will be unlikely to realize that only this idea provides an adequate answer to the human need for ultimate meaning, Hartshorne believes, unless we accept our own temporal finitude.

Hartshorne's *metaphysical* argument against subjective immortality is based on the idea that "[i]mmortality is a divine trait" (1970, 289). The argument is that only the perfect being could have the "ability to preserve personal individuality through an infinity of experiences without monotony or loss of integrity" (1984, 117–18). In another formulation of this idea, Hartshorne says: "Each of us is a theme with variations. No theme other than that of the divine nature can admit an infinity of variations" (1962, 261). Because God is spatially ubiquitous, whereas we "are mere fragments of the spatial whole," it would be unreasonable to think of ourselves as like God temporally, that is, as having "temporally infinite futures" (1984, 36).

Hartshorne's arguments do *not* say that the mind-body relation is such that life after death is impossible. He would have no philosophical argument, therefore, against the idea that the human soul might exist for a very long time. Hartshorne has, in fact, conceded in personal correspondence (1994) that his view of the mind-body relation makes survival possible. Accordingly, as Donald Viney has pointed out (1985, 116), Hartshorne's personal rejection of life after death does not mean that his philosophical position makes it impossible, if that extended life is not thought to be literally endless.

It might be objected, to be sure, that such a view would not be satisfactory, that what we want assurance of is precisely that we will live forever. To make such a claim, however, would be to go far beyond our present knowledge. What we know, at most, is only that people, at least most people, want more life. We do not know that after having more life for a considerable period—perhaps ten thousand, a hundred thousand, a million, or a billion years—we would want to continue having new experiences. Perhaps there is truth in the Hindu and Buddhist notion of "karmic" existence, according to which we continue as finite centers of experience only insofar as we participate in this existence with intensity. That notion, in fact, is similar to Whitehead's view that enduring individuals in general continue to endure insofar as each member experiences that form of existence with intensity, passing it along to future members with appetition for its continuation. It might be, then, that we will continue to exist as long as we, at a deep level, *want* to continue. Besides allowing us the continued life that we now want, life after death thus conceived would allow time for souls to actualize all their potentialities, to reach a state of wholeness, and thereby to have their lives finally make a contribution to the divine life with which they can be content.

There is nothing in process philosophy, accordingly, to prevent the affirmation of a kind of life after death in which the distinctively human problem of death would find its resolution. Such an affirmation would fill in the missing piece in process philosophy's theodicy as presented in the third section. To say that life after death is not metaphysically ruled out, however, does not by itself provide sufficient reason to affirm its plausibility. I turn now to this question.

6. The Plausibility of Life after Death

By virtue of its doctrine of the human being as a compound individual, process philosophy provides the basic necessary condition for the possibility of life after death within a naturalistic framework, namely, the numerical distinction between mind and brain, because that distinction means that the death of the brain does not logically entail the death of the mind. Cartesian dualism had, of course, provided for this possibility, but its inability to explain the interaction of mind and brain, at least without appeal to supernatural assistance, led to the collapse of dualism into various versions of materialistic identism. Thanks to its panexperientialism, process philosophy has a nondualistic version of interactionism, allowing the numerical distinction between mind and brain to be intelligibly affirmed.

Even if they would allow for this numerical distinction, however, many philosophers would claim that the mind is too dependent on the brain to be capable of extrabodily existence. In *The Illusion of Immortality,* for example, Corliss Lamont says that the possibility of life after death is disproved by modern psychology, which is said to show the mind to be wholly dependent on the brain (1965, 86, 123). "All the evidence," claims Bertrand Russell, "goes to show that what we regard as our mental life is bound up with brain structure and organized bodily energy" (1957, 51). "[T]he empirical evidence in favor of an invariable correlation between mental states and brain states is extremely strong," says J. J. C. Smart, so that "it is hard to believe that after the dissolution of the brain there could be any thought or conscious experience whatever" (1996, 221).

When Lamont, Russell, and Smart talk about "all the evidence," however, they really mean a materialist reading of the evidence. From the perspective of process philosophy, our experience is not wholly dependent upon the brain with its sensory system. Some of the mind's experiences are due to its own self-determination. Insofar as it derives experiences from elsewhere, furthermore, these experiences are derived from *nonsensory* prehensions of other actualities, and these other actualities are not limited to our brain cells. We directly prehend the past actual world beyond our bodies, including the minds of other people. And we directly prehend God, from whom we receive alternative possibilities, including normative values. Of course, the materialistic psychology presupposed by Lamont, Smart, and Russell rules out all such experiences. For example, Smart rejects any authentic religious perception on the grounds that all perception "involves response to physical stimuli" (1996, 223). All telepathic and clairvoyant perception would, of course, be ruled out on the same grounds. But as pointed out in Chapter 2, process philosophy's position on the reality of nonsensory perception is supported by a massive amount of scientifically verified empirical evidence. On the basis of a more open-minded reading of "all the evidence," therefore, the mind's dependence on the brain for its perceptions is not as complete as materialists assume. It is not so clear that "after the dissolution of the brain," in Smart's words, "there could be [no] thought or conscious experience whatever."

It might be objected, however, that even if we could *perceive* in a disembodied state, we would not be able to *act,* because we are able to act on the world only through our bodies, most immediately our brains. In process philosophy, however, causation and physical prehension are simply two sides of the same transaction. For B to prehend A is for A to exert causal efficacy upon B. Accordingly, if person B telepathically prehends the mind of person A, then person A has acted directly, without the mediation of his or her body, upon the mind of person B. If that kind of mind-to-mind influence is possible now, it might be even more possible in a disembodied state, when the mind is not swamped with data coming from a brain. It might be thought, to be sure, that telepathy provides a basis for only a very passive type of "action," dependent wholly upon the selectivity of the prehender. Several telepathic experiments have shown, however, the capacity of one person deliberately to send messages to another person. The capacity of the embodied mind to act upon the world beyond its body without the mediation of the body has been demonstrated, furthermore, by evidence for psychokinesis, understood as the direct influence of the mind on things beyond one's own body (Griffin 1997a, 85–89).

In spite of these reasons to believe that a mind, *if* it found itself in a disembodied state, might still be able to perceive and act, many people would find implausible the idea that it *might find itself in such a state.* When it is said that *all* the evidence shows the brain-dependent nature of the mind, the evidence in question is usually the variety of evidence showing that damage to the brain results in derangement, loss of various cognitive abilities, or even complete loss of consciousness. A response to this argument was provided by J. M. E. McTaggart, who was, Whitehead mentioned, one of his closest philosophical friends (ESP 116). The facts, McTaggart pointed out, support only the proposition "that, *while a self has a body,* that body is essentially connected with the self's mental life." For example, "the fact that an abnormal state of the brain may affect our thoughts does not prove that the normal states of the brain are necessary for thought" (1906, 105). Although Whitehead did not explicitly endorse his friend's position on this issue, at least in print, this position is consistent with Whitehead's philosophy, as suggested by his own speculation, quoted earlier, that "the existence of the soul may be freed from its complete dependence upon the bodily organization" (AI 208).

This philosophical position is empirically supported, furthermore, by evidence for out-of-body experiences. A great number of people who have experienced themselves to be out of their bodies have reported their perceptions and thoughts to have been just as clear as, or even clearer than, normal. Of course, the mere fact of *seeming* to be out of one's body is not by itself sufficient to prove that one's mind or soul really *is* perceiving the world from a different location. But as I have argued in a chapter devoted to out-of-body experiences (Griffin 1997a, chap. 8), considerable empirical evidence supports the view that such extrasomatic experiences do occur, whereas the intrasomatic interpretation of all such cases has nothing supporting it except materialistic prejudice.

A final type of evidence supporting the plausibility of life after death is evidence that it actually occurs. As is often pointed out, the best evidence that X is possible is that X is actual. Of course, if all the other relevant evidence suggests that X is *impossible,* we will be strongly inclined to give an alternative interpretation of evidence purporting to show the actuality of X. It is largely for this reason that the evidence for life after death has been either explained away or simply ignored by most intellectuals in the late modern world. For example, Kai Nielsen, from a materialistic perspective, has said that no amount of empirical evidence could lead him to believe in life after death. If "we think that the concept of disembodied existence makes no sense," says Nielsen, "then we will interpret the data differently." [10] That is, "we will say, and reasonably so, even if we do not have a good alternative explanation for it, that [disembodied existence] cannot be the correct description of what went on" (1989b, 61). Given his assumption that all the background evidence makes the idea of disembodied existence unintelligible, Nielsen's position is fully rational. From the perspective of process philosophy, however, the background evidence makes such existence possible. Evidence that such existence actually occurs, therefore, provides additional support for its possibility.

[10] The idea that life after death is impossible, or makes no sense, has become widespread among philosophers in religion. For example, although one of the main targets of Nielsen's criticisms is D. Z. Phillips's nonrealist interpretation of religious language, both evidently agree on the issue at hand. "One can see, intellectually," Phillips has said, "that it makes no sense to speak of surviving death" (1970, 265–66).

For example, in my book on parapsychology, I examined evidence for survival provided by apparitions, messages from mediums, cases of the possession type, and cases of the reincarnation type. It is possible, I showed, to give an alternative explanation for much of this evidence by supposing some individuals to have enormous extrasensory and psychokinetic powers, which is the so-called *superpsi* explanation. This kind of nonsurvivalist interpretation can be even more adequate than is usually supposed, I pointed out, if one employs Whitehead's philosophy to increase the usual superpsi arsenal. Nevertheless, this approach to the evidence creates a problem for the determined antisurvivalist. The reason for not taking the evidence at face value in the first place is the assumption that the human soul is not the kind of entity that is capable of surviving apart from the body. To attribute to the soul enormous extrasensory and psychokinetic powers, however, is to suppose it to be precisely the kind of entity that *could* be supposed to survive apart from the body. But if one does not attribute these enormous powers to the soul, one is faced with an enormous amount of evidence that, if it cannot be explained in terms of superpsi, rather directly implies that at least some souls do survive bodily death. Even if the superpsi approach is used, furthermore, there is some evidence that resists such explanations.

My own conclusion, as a process philosopher who has examined much of the available evidence supporting both the possibility and the actuality of life after death, is that its reality is considerably more probable than not. It cannot be said, of course, that "process philosophy supports the reality of life after death" because this is not one of its core doctrines. What can be said, however, is that process philosophy supports the *possibility* of life after death, mainly because of three of its core doctrines: its nonsensationist doctrine of perception, its panexperientialism with organizational duality, and its naturalistic theism (the relevance of which is pointed out later). Process philosophy makes it possible, therefore, to provide a plausible image of human destiny according to which the distinctively human problems occasioned by the anticipation of death will find resolution.

Before this discussion is concluded, however, one more objection to the idea of life after death for human souls needs to be addressed. Lamont suggests a reductio ad absurdum—that if we posit life after death for human beings, we must do the same for Neanderthals, chimpanzees, rats, and even fleas (1965, 116–17). That attempted reductio would work, however, only if we said that the soul or dominant member of all compound individuals, purely by virtue of being a soul, has the inherent capacity to exist apart from the body that was originally necessary to bring it forth. As we have seen, however, Whitehead explicitly rejected this all-or-none view, thereby implying a third possibility, which is that the capacity to survive apart from the body is a historical emergent.

Within a panexperientialist evolutionary perspective, the idea of historical emergents is not an unusual idea, as the argument from novelty in Chapter 5 emphasized. Although all actual occasions are occasions of experience, so that experience as such does not emerge, there are many capacities that do. *Conscious* experience, for example, emerged at some stage of the evolutionary process, and *self*-consciousness at a still later stage. The capacity to use symbolic language also emerged at a rather late stage of the evolutionary process, bringing about a mode of existence that is virtually different in kind from that which went before. This emergence, in fact, was probably part and parcel of the emergence of self-consciousness. The capacity to survive apart from the body, if it now exists, could have also been an emergent capacity. If it was, it might well have been simply one of the effects of that great increase in power involved in the human soul's development of symbolic language and self-consciousness. In other words, the capacity to *ask* whether we survive bodily death might have been one of the expressions of the capacity to do just that.

The idea of the capacity to survive separation from the body as an evolutionary emergent was evidently suggested by Whitehead himself. In the context of his earlier-quoted speculation about survival, he said: "[T]he personality of an animal organism may be more or less. It is not a mere question of having a soul or of not having a soul. The question is, How much, if any?" (AI 208). Cobb has developed this idea of "degrees of soul" in an account of the rise of human existence according to which it was fueled by a great increase in surplus psychic energy (1967, 37–39). Although all animals have soul, Cobb suggests, human beings have enormously more: more creative energy, more power to engage in symbolizing activities, and more social order through time, so that one's concern for one's past and future experiences may be much stronger than one's concerns for one's bodily welfare. Perhaps these distinctive features of the human soul give it the capacity to survive separation from the body without supernatural support.

To say that life after death would not require supernatural support, however, is not to imply the unimportance of divine influence. In the first place, if the human soul now has the capacity to survive bodily death, it has this capacity only because of billions of years of divine activity. In the second place, even if the soul now has the capacity to survive the death of its bodily organism, it would actually do so only because it is continually receiving fresh divine aims from God. To express the position of process philosophy of religion on this point, Cobb has spoken of the "resurrection of the soul"

(1987b), which combines the points made by the two traditional competing expressions. That is, like *immortality of the soul,* the expression *resurrection of the soul* points to the idea that the power to survive death is now inherent in the soul, so that no supernatural intervention is needed. Like *resurrection of the body,* however, *resurrection of the soul* points to the idea that the transition to a post-carnate mode of existence depends on present divine influence. It should be of some importance to Christian philosophers and theologians, furthermore, that a good case has been made for the twofold proposition that the earliest Christians spoke of the "resurrection of the soul" and that talk of the "resurrection of the body" did not emerge until the end of the first century (Riley 1995).

Process philosophy of religion can suggest an account of human destiny according to which, even if human sin and folly bring about a premature death of the human species on this planet, the divine aims in bringing about human existence will not have been completely defeated. On the one hand, the values already realized by human existence will permanently enrich the divine experience, so the universe will never be as if we had not been. On the other hand, all the human souls already created may, through an emergent capacity to survive bodily death, continue to exist indefinitely in new modes of existence, growing in wisdom, compassion, and sanctity, thereby overcoming the problems of injustice in the present life and enriching creaturely and divine life immensely.

This account of human destiny beyond this planet, however, even if accepted as a probable account, should in no way be used as a basis for complacency about the present state of our planet, with its current trajectory toward self-destruction. It should not be assumed, furthermore, that eschatology as presented here, with its objective immortality combined with life after death, is the only type that can be supported by process philosophy. In works referred to earlier (Griffin forthcoming a and c), I argue that process theism can also ground hope for a "reign of God on earth," in which the problems of war, human rights violations, ecological destruction, and economic injustice would be overcome. With that addition, process theism's portrayal of God as the ground of hope for the victory of good over evil is even more complete.

The Two Ultimates
and the Religions

One of the central tasks of a philosophy of religion in our time is to suggest a framework for understanding the relations of the various religions to one another. This task is central for three reasons. First, the problem of the intellectual conflicts among the various religions has provided one of the major objections to the truth of religious beliefs, especially because the claim that religious beliefs reflect genuine religious experience is arguably undermined by the existence of radically different ideas of ultimate reality. Second, religion has been put into disrepute by the mutual hostility of religious traditions, which has often led to war. The modern frustration with this feature of religion is expressed in Whitehead's exclamation: "Must 'religion' always remain as a synonym for 'hatred'?" (AI 172). The fact that Whitehead shared this modern criticism of religion did not blind him either to its achievements in the past—"Religion can be, and has been, the main instrument for progress" (RM 36)—or its promise for the future, that it might "make common life the City of God it should be" (RM 38). For many modern thinkers, however, revulsion at the negative side of religion has led to a perception of it as wholly devoid of value, both intellectual and moral. In any case, a third reason for dealing with the relation among the religions is that it is one of the burning issues of our time, with perhaps the very survival of civilization depending upon the development of relations of mutual respect and even cooperation among the historic religious traditions.[1] By

---

[1] Although this latter point is not discussed in the present book, it will be central to two works in progress (Griffin forthcoming a and c).

suggesting an intellectual framework that would facilitate this development, philosophers of religion could provide one of their greatest contributions to civilization.

Process philosophy provides a distinctive framework for thinking about the relations of the various religions to one another. Working out the relations between any two religious traditions is, of course, a task for the theologians of those two traditions, and in carrying out this task a general philosophical framework, even if fully accepted, will leave many questions unanswered. For example, Christianity's relation to Judaism involves issues that are not involved in its relation to Islam; its relation to Islam involves issues not involved in its relation to Judaism; and its relations to Hinduism and Buddhism involve very different issues from those involved in its relations to Judaism and Islam. The fact that a general framework cannot by itself answer all questions does not, however, mean that all such frameworks are wholly devoid of value. The discussion of the relations among the religions has always been carried on in terms of some such framework, whether explicitly or only implicitly. The distinctive framework provided by process philosophy will be valuable insofar as it is more helpful than those hitherto employed.

The distinctiveness of this framework follows from two features of process philosophy's naturalistic theism: its doctrine of divine power as persuasive, not coercive, and its doctrine that God is not the only ultimate reality. The significance for the relations among the religions of this second doctrine, that process philosophy has *two* ultimates, is the central concern of this chapter. The distinction between these two ultimates is relevant to the oft-noted fact that religious experience seems to consist of two major types: theistic and nontheistic. It is thereby relevant to the issue of the relation between two major types of religions: religions that are oriented around devotion to a personal God, and religions that are oriented around the realization of identity with an impersonal (or "transpersonal") ultimate reality. Process philosophy thereby provides the basis for a version of "religious pluralism" that differs significantly from the version associated primarily with John Hick.[2]

---

[2] There are several types of religious pluralism. For example, five types of pluralism—phenomenal (which Hick exemplifies), confessional, universal, ontological, and dialectical—have been identified by Anselm Min (1997). But because it was impossible, owing to limitations of space, to discuss all these types, I have focused on Hick's version as the one that would best help, by contrast, to bring out the distinctive nature of the Whiteheadian position. I should add that whether or not Min's categorization of Cobb as a "confessional pluralist" does full justice to his position, the Cobbian-Whiteheadian approach, as summarized here, could be used to develop what Min calls "universal pluralism," as I intimate in Chapter 10.

The discussion develops in the following way. The first section looks at the nature of religion, building on the discussion in the introductory chapter. The second section explores the implications for the relations among the religions of the doctrine that divine power is persuasive rather than coercive. The third section discusses the relation between process philosophy's two ultimates, God and creative experience. The fourth section shows the relevance of this position for the relation between two kinds of religious experience and thereby two kinds of religion.

1. The Nature of Religion

In the introductory chapter, I argued that a philosophy of religion cannot responsibly dodge the difficult question of defining religion. Some authors contend that no such definition is needed, saying that what they mean by *religion* will become tolerably clear in the course of their discussion. If some such definition is being implicitly employed, however, it is the author's responsibility to render it explicit so that it can be subjected to criticism. The author should at least provide a working definition to indicate how the term *religion* is being understood "for the purposes of this work." A definition is also needed to delimit the scope of the discussion.

A delimiting definition is especially necessary when discussing the interrelations among the religions. The treatment of this topic will be much different depending upon whether "the religions" in question include only those ways of life customarily thought of as religions, such as Christianity, Islam, and Buddhism, or whether those ideological movements sometimes called "quasi-religions," such as Nationalism, Nazism, Marxist Communism, and Social Darwinian Capitalism, are also included. While not denying that the discussion of these quasi-religious ideologies is important, I am here limiting "the religions" to those ways of life customarily thought of as religions, which in the introduction I called "full-fledged religions." The characterization of the nature of religion, accordingly, needs to apply only to them (although some of the dimensions of this characterization will, of course, apply also to quasi-religions).

The introductory chapter proffered a preliminary definition of a religion as *a complex set of beliefs, stories, traditions, emotions, attitudes, dispositions, institutions, artistic creations, and practices—both cultic and ethical, both communal and individual—oriented around the desire to be in harmony with an ultimate reality that is understood to be holy and thereby to provide life with meaning.* I will now enrich this preliminary definition by discussing its central terms and adding some elements that are at best only implicit in this preliminary definition.[3]

Ultimate Reality

The desire to be in harmony with that which is *ultimate in the nature of things* is the basic religious motive, which lies at the root of quasi-religions as well as full-fledged religions.[4] Recognition of this feature is of utmost importance because it reveals from the outset the irrelevance to real religion of various types of enterprises that have presented themselves as "theologies" or "philosophies of religion." One example is provided by those nonrealist positions according to which statements about "God" do not refer to anything. Equally irrelevant is any theology or philosophy of religion that, while giving the word *God* a real referent, makes the referent something less than ultimate in the nature of things, such as the suggestions that *God* refers to the "language-situation of human beings" (Ebeling 1967), to our "co-humanity" (Braun 1965), or to "creative interchange" understood as a solely human process (Wieman 1946).

Furthermore, if we say merely that the putative ultimate reality around which religion is oriented must be taken to be not only really real but also really ultimate in the nature of things, there would be no basis for a distinction between religious (including quasi-religious) worldviews, on the one hand, and purely ethical systems, on the other, because the "ultimate realities" to which one is oriented could be ethical ideals, thought to be inherent in the nature of things. The definition would, to be sure, rule out the position articulated by John Dewey (1934) and Donald Cupitt (1981), according to which the word *God* refers to a cluster of ideals that we have formulated and imaginatively projected onto the universe, because those ideals are not thought really to exist in the nature of things, independently of our formulation of them. Some thinkers, however, believe that ethical ideals (perhaps along with aesthetic ideals and mathematical patterns) do somehow really exist, so that we intuit (rather than invent) them, even though there is no divine being in which they subsist. The incoherence of this position—judged in light of the ontological principle—is irrelevant to the point at hand, which is that the ethical ideals are believed really to exist, complete with their normative status, as ultimate factors in the nature of things. Some

---

[3] It might be helpful to recall my discussion in the Introduction of Geertz's characterization of the "religious perspective" as always combining a worldview and an ethos in a mutually supportive way.

[4] See the explanation and qualification in note 5 of the Introduction.

people who orient their lives in terms of these ultimate ideals, furthermore, refer to themselves as thereby religious.

Given what is understood here by "ultimate reality," however, this ethical way of life would not be religious, even though its adherents might be more admirable than most adherents of most religions, unless the ethical ideals were held—incoherently from the perspective of process philosophy—to have power, entirely on their own, to exert causal efficacy in the world. Religion involves the desire to be in harmony with ultimate reality in the sense of ultimate *agency,* ultimate *power*—that which is ultimately determinative of the nature of existence, at least of human existence. In some religions, the ultimate power is understood to be creator as well as savior; in others, it is a saving but not a creating power. In any case, insofar as ethical ideals or forms have merely ideal as distinct from actual existence and thereby no power to bring about anything, they are not ultimate realities in the requisite sense. They acquire religious meaning only insofar as they are associated with ultimate actuality and thereby power to bring about transforming change.

Even if it is specified that ultimate reality means ultimate agency or power, however, another ambiguity remains. On the one hand, the ultimate reality around which a religion is oriented may be understood to be the ultimate *agent,* which is the case in theistic religions, in which the divine reality is the supreme *being.* On the other hand, the ultimate reality around which a religion's beliefs, affections, and practices are oriented may be understood to be ultimate *agency as such,* ultimate *power as such,* rather than *an* agent or *a* power. Tillich was right, accordingly, in thinking that ultimate concern could be oriented toward "being itself," understood as the "power of being." He was wrong to think that the term *God*—given its history and thereby what I call the generic idea of God—could be intelligibly used to refer to being itself rather than to a supreme being. He was also wrong to think that Christianity could be reoriented around this alternative understanding of the divine reality and still survive in recognizable form. But he was right to hold that real religion—of another sort—could be based upon this alternative understanding of the ultimate reality.

Ultimate Reality as Holy

I have suggested that the desire to be harmony with the ultimate reality understood as ultimate power—whether a supremely powerful being or power as such—lies at the root of religion but that this description applies to quasi-religions as well as to full-fledged religions. I now add that in full-fledged religions, as distinct from quasi-religions, the *ultimate* with which harmony is desired is explicitly conceived to be *holy* or *sacred*.[5] The notion of the "holy" can refer to a perception and/or a conception. The *perceptual* meaning of the holy, as discussed in Chapter 2, is the subjective form of a prehension. The holy in this sense, which is sometimes referred to as the "numinous," is indefinable. Like the color yellow, its unique quality can be grasped only by being experienced. As a *conception,* however, the term *holy* can be said to refer to *that which is of ultimate intrinsic worth, in relation to which everything else finally has its worth.* Each religion, in referring to the ultimate reality around which it is oriented as God, Allah, Nirvana, Emptiness, Brahman, the Tao, or the Mandate of Heaven, is referring to that which it *conceives* to be holy, which some of its adherents believe they have *perceived* to be holy. Although quasi-religions are based upon an implicit conception of some dimension or principle of reality as holy, only full-fledged religions typically involve an explicit affirmation of a holy reality.

This explicitness leads to another difference between full-fledged and quasi-religions. Theoreticians of a full-fledged religion typically devote attention to the question of the appropriateness of advocating that human life be oriented around its putative ultimate reality: Jews, Christians, and Muslims reflect on the perfection of God; Buddhists on the ultimacy of Nirvana, Emptiness, the Dharma, or the Buddha-nature; Taoists on the ultimacy of the Tao. In a quasi-religion, by contrast, the putative ultimate around which it is oriented is implicitly taken to be holy, in the sense of worthy of ultimate commitment, but the idea that this putative ultimate is truly worthy of ultimate commitment is usually assumed rather than argued. Because quasi-religions are thereby more likely to involve, in Tillich's terms, ultimate concern for that which is not really ultimate, they are even more likely than full-fledged religions to become demonic.

Ultimate Reality as Spiritual

Full-fledged religions typically differ from quasi-religions in yet another respect, which is brought out by the famous definition of religion given by

---

[5] Although these two terms can be used synonymously, as here, I usually prefer the term *holy* because the term *sacred* seems more to carry the connotation of *that which cannot be questioned,* which I do not want to suggest. In any case, the importance of emphasizing this dimension of full-fledged religions is illustrated by the fact that Ninian Smart's distinction between religious and secular worldviews, which is in most respects similar to mine, has been criticized as untenable (Rennie 1999, 66). This criticism is valid to the extent that Smart, at least in some passages, has emphasized the similarities between religious and secular worldviews without equally emphasizing the differences. (For other respects in which Smart's position could be better protected from Rennie's criticism, see note 11 of Chapter 2.)

E. B. Tylor as "belief in spiritual beings" or simply "spirits" (1871, I:424–26), with "spirits" understood to refer both to local, finite spirits, especially of human beings, and to a divine spirit (or spirits). Full-fledged religions, in other words, reject materialism (which in Tylor's view [1871, II:183, 445] made them irredeemably superstitious relics of bygone ages). In particular, the ultimate reality around which they are oriented is understood to be a *spiritual* being or principle, and insofar as this ultimate reality is understood to be the ultimate *power* within or behind the universe, this power is understood to be primarily *spiritual* power. This understanding of religion is reflected in a summary of three basic beliefs involved in the religious life suggested by William James:

1. That the visible world is part of a more spiritual universe from which it draws its chief significance;
2. That union or harmonious relation with that higher universe is our true end;
3. That prayer or inner communion with the spirit thereof—be that spirit "God" or "law"—is a process wherein work is really done, and spiritual energy flows in and produces effects . . . within the phenomenal world. (1902, 485)

By contrast, quasi-religions, such as nationalism, humanism, Marxism, Nazism, and capitalism (sometimes called *economism*), typically make no explicit appeal to a "spiritual" or "invisible" world.[6]

This distinction between spiritual and non-spiritual worldviews is closely related to yet another difference, which is that full-fledged religions are usually based explicitly on nonsensory experience. Given the orientation around an ultimate reality understood to be "spiritual" rather than "physical," in the sense of that which can in principle be perceived through the physical senses, it follows by definition that this ultimate reality can be experienced only in a nonsensory way.[7] Although this point was discussed in Chapter 2 only in relation to *theistic* religious experiences, it is also true, for example, of Buddhist experiences of Emptiness and Hindu experiences of Nirguna Brahman. This feature of full-fledged religions is closely related to their explicit conception of the ultimate reality to which they are oriented as *holy*. The experience of something as holy, as we have seen, involves a

---

[6] As Rennie points out (1999, 63–64), Ninian Smart has generally held that whether an invisible world is affirmed is central to the distinction between religious and secular worldviews (even if Rennie himself reinterprets the idea of the invisible world so that it would no longer play this role [67]).

[7] To say this is not to deny, of course, that religious experience often involves, in conjunction with nonsensory experience, also quasi-sensory elements, such as apparitions and voices, and even sensory elements, such as incense, sculpture, and the starry sky.

nonsensory perception. Although quasi-religious ideologies are in fact based upon an association of holiness with a particular principle (such as "blood and soil" or "the dialectical process of history leading to the classless society" or "the survival of the fittest in the competitive struggle leading to never-ending progress and prosperity"), these ideologies are not *explicitly* based on nonsensory perception of something holy.

Individual Transformation

One more feature of full-fledged religions is their explicit purpose to be transformative of individuals by bringing them into proper relationship with ultimate reality understood to be holy.[8] As James said, every religion involves two parts:

1. An uneasiness; and
2. Its solution.
1. The uneasiness . . . is a sense that there is *something wrong about us* as we naturally stand.
2. The solution is a sense that *we are saved from the wrongness* by making proper connection with the higher powers. (1902, 393)

Whitehead emphasized this purpose of religions to transform individuals in his definition of a religion, on its doctrinal side, "as a system of general truths which have the effect of transforming character when they are sincerely held and vividly apprehended," along with his conclusion that "what should emerge from religion is individual worth of character" (RM 15, 17). As John Hick has emphasized, this transformative purpose, at least in what are usually called the higher religions, can be described in most general terms as the "transformation of human existence from self-centredness to Reality-centredness," with "Reality" here referring to the ultimate reality as understood by the religion in question (1989, 300). Quasi-religious ideologies, by contrast, are oriented primarily to the condition of the social world. Indeed, insofar as their goal is to transform the social world, they may be critical of the emphasis of full-fledged religions on the condition of individuals. Ideologies can instead be conservative, however, seeking to preserve the status quo rather than to transform it. In either case, although an ideology may have the *effect* of drawing individuals out of their ego-centeredness, this result is a by-product of the ideology, not a primary goal.

[8] This dimension is emphasized in the working definition of religion proposed by James Livingston (1998, 11): "Religion is that system of activities and beliefs directed toward that which is perceived to be of sacred value and transforming power."

To make this contrast is *not* to say, I should emphasize, that full-fledged religions necessarily think of the transformation of society as unimportant or even as less important than the transformation of individuals. Indeed, insofar as religious thought assumes that individuals are internally related to the societies in which they exist, they will tend to see individual and social transformation as closely interdependent. This idea is reflected in Whitehead's statement, quoted at the outset of this chapter, about religion's potential for making "the common life the City of God" and in his statement—which corrects his better-known but one-sided assertion that "[r]eligion is what the individual does with his own solitariness" (RM 16)—that "the topic of religion is individuality in community" (RM 86). The point is only that full-fledged religions do give explicit attention to the transformation of individuals.

Given this clarification of the meaning of "the (full-fledged) religions" as employed here,[9] we turn now to the framework provided by process philosophy for thinking of the relations of these religions to one another, focusing on the question of beliefs.

2. Divine Persuasion and the Religions

The most extensive discussion of the relations of the religions to one another has been carried on by Christian philosophers and theologians, who have naturally discussed the question primarily in terms of the relation of Christianity to other religions, sometimes dealing with "non-Christian" religions in general, sometimes focusing on a particular religion, such as Judaism, Islam, Hinduism, or Buddhism. Great advances have been made since the eighteenth century, when this discussion, which had previously been sporadic at best, began to gain momentum. From the point of view of process philosophy, however, this discussion has been distorted from the outset by the fact that it has been carried out primarily by thinkers who have assumed the traditional doctrine of divine omnipotence, according to which God can unilaterally bring about states of affairs in the world. The relevant implication of this doctrine is that God could have given an infallible and complete revelation of the divine nature and plan of salvation for the human race. This revelation could have also been recorded in inerrant scriptures.

---

[9] Although I regard this characterization of religion as more adequate than any other I have encountered, I assume that it will prove to be less than fully adequate. It is offered here in the spirit of a suggestion, which I hope others will help improve.

An infallible interpreter of these infallible scriptures could have also been provided.

The traditional Christian position was that this was exactly what God had done, with the Christian Gospel, of course, being the definitive revelation (although Eastern Orthodoxy and Protestantism have rejected the Roman Catholic position that the papacy was provided as an infallible interpreter). Given that assumption, there were various positions that could be taken on the question of the truth and salvific value of other religions. Some Christian theologians have taken a completely exclusivistic position, according to which the other religions contain no truth (except insofar as they agree with Christianity) and provide no salvation: this position interprets in the harshest possible way the traditional statement that there is "no salvation outside the [Christian] church." Other theologians have taken an inclusivist position with regard to salvation, saying that God's saving act in Jesus Christ is efficacious for all people who live by whatever light is provided by their own traditions. A few Christian theologians have even taken a universalist stance, saying that the Christian salvation is efficacious for all people. While it allowed for these varying positions on salvation, however, the traditional position maintained that religious *truth* is uniquely possessed by Christians.[10] It thereby implied that there is nothing to be learned from other religions. Christianity already contained everything of importance there is to be known about the divine reality and the proper way to be in harmony with it.

Supernaturalism and Exclusivism

For an illustration of the exclusivist version of this view, we can turn to Alvin Plantinga's recent essay "Pluralism: A Defense of Religious Exclusivism," which Plantinga begins by saying that he holds the following two beliefs:

(1) The world was created by God, an almighty, all-knowing, and perfectly good personal being . . . and

(2) . . . God has provided a unique way of salvation through the incarnation, life, sacrificial death, and resurrection of his divine son. (1995, 192)

For his position to be an example of *exclusivism,* Plantinga adds, two other factors are necessary. First, besides holding these Christian tenets, he holds

---

[10] There can, of course, be positions called "inclusivist" and "universalist" that do not hold this view, especially because some such positions would not hold the traditional view of divine omnipotence.

"that any propositions, including other religious beliefs, that are incompatible with those tenets are false" (194). Second, he is aware of other faiths and has reflected on the problem of pluralism, having answered affirmatively the question whether it "could be really true that the Lord has revealed himself and his programs to us Christians, say, in a way in which he hasn't revealed himself to those of other faiths" (195).

Plantinga's position clearly illustrates the connection between exclusivism and supernaturalistic theism: besides the fact that his first proposition refers to God as an "almighty" being, we saw in Chapter 1 Plantinga's affirmation of occasional supernatural interventions. Indeed, his statement that God has been revealed to Christians "in a way in which he hasn't revealed himself to those of other faiths" is a special application of his statement, quoted in Chapter 1, that "God has often treated what he has made in a way different from the way in which he ordinarily treats it" (1991a, 22).

Naturalistic Theism vs. Exclusivism

Process philosophy, with its naturalistic theism, rules out religious exclusivism. God acts in one and the same way in relation to all human experience. Although process philosophy allows for variable divine influence, this variability, from the divine side, involves the content, never the mode of agency, which is always the mode of persuasion. This normal way of relating to human experience is not subject to interruptions in which God would cancel out or override our normal human belief-forming processes, with their sinfulness, cultural conditionedness, and invincible ignorance. Infallible revelations and inerrant scriptures are metaphysical impossibilities. The rejection of the traditional doctrine of divine power, accordingly, implies the rejection of religious exclusivism.

Supernaturalism and the Essential Identity of All Religions

Although Plantinga's exclusivism depends upon his doctrine that God is "almighty," his first proposition also affirms that God is "perfectly good." This twofold position could lead to a radically different position. To some more liberal philosophers of religion and theologians, for whom the divine goodness is as important as the divine omnipotence, the idea that God would arbitrarily give saving knowledge through only one religious tradition has been intolerable. In opposition to that exclusivist view, some theologians have deduced from the power and goodness of God that all religions must contain the *same* basic saving truths. A classic statement of this position was provided by the eighteenth-century deist Matthew Tindal in *Christianity as Old as Creation* (1730). The meaning of his title was that the essential message of Christianity is identical with the essential message of all the religions, including the primitive religions of the first human beings. This deistic position involved reducing Christian doctrines to a few general ideas that could more or less plausibly be regarded as central teachings of all the other religions.

More recently, a quite different version of this same basic position—that all the religions essentially teach the same thing—has been spread under the rubric of the "perennial philosophy," with Aldous Huxley (1945), Frithjof Schuon (1975), and Huston Smith (1977) being three of its best-known exponents. Although these thinkers recognize that the various traditions are very different, they regard these differences as belonging to the external, "exoteric" side of the religions. At the deeper, "esoteric" level, they hold, the religions all teach the same perennial (or primordial) truths, so that they have, as the title of Schuon's (1975) book says, a "transcendent unity."

This position is reached deductively, as illustrated by Smith's argument that from the divine benevolence "it follows" that God's "revelations must be impartial, which is to say equal: the deity cannot play favorites" (Griffin and Smith 1989, 41). The conclusion that all the religions are identical follows not from the doctrine of divine benevolence alone, however, but only from its conjunction with the doctrine of divine omnipotence, which Smith also affirms. Defending the idea that God, besides being all good, essentially has all the power and is therefore the first cause of all that is, Smith draws the logical conclusion that the world is perfect (Griffin and Smith 1989, 69–71, 82, 162). This perfection is taken to require the essential identity of all the religions.

Naturalistic Theism and Difference

From the point of view of process philosophy, the rejection of the idea that God has played favorites, arbitrarily giving saving truth to some and withholding it from others, is certainly admirable. Because of its rejection of divine omnipotence, however, process philosophy has no a priori basis for deducing the essential identity of all the religions. It has, in fact, grounds for suspecting the opposite. Although every moment of human experience begins with an initial aim that reflects the eternal character and purpose of God, this aim is never the sole determinant of any moment of experience. On the one hand, every moment of experience is partly self-determining, and human experiences, as we have seen, have a much greater capacity for self-determination vis-à-vis their initial aims than do other types of occasions of experience. On the other hand, every occasion of experience is also influenced by the past world out of which it arises. The self-determination is, therefore, always based upon the influences from that particular past world. It is also, to be sure, based partly upon the initial aim from God, but that initial aim is context-dependent, being, as Whitehead says, toward the best *abstract* possibility that is *really* possible, given the concrete context (PR 244). The extent to which the initial aim is shaped by the context is reflected in Whitehead's further acknowledgment that in some situations the "best [can] be bad" (PR 244).

From these two features of human experiences—their extraordinary capacities for both self-determination and being shaped by their contexts— follows the radical *historicity* of human beings, meaning their capacity to be shaped by, and shape themselves in terms of, a particular historical tradition. Even the highest nonhuman animals, by contrast, are largely nonhistorical,[11] in the sense that all the members of a given species are largely the same, regardless of their location. Birds of a certain type are all largely the same whether they were raised in Asia, Africa, or South America. The same is true, albeit surely to a lesser extent, even of monkeys. Human beings raised as Buddhists in Thailand, however, are significantly different from human beings raised as Muslims in Morocco, and both these are significantly different from human beings raised as Jews in New York City or as Christians in California. These modern-day Jews and Christians, furthermore, are significantly different from Jews and Christians in the Middle Ages, whereas birds and monkeys have remained virtually the same for thousands of years.

Given this radical historicity of human beings, we would expect their religious traditions to share in this historicity. Indeed, insofar as religion is, in Whitehead's phrase, "the art and the theory of the internal life" of human beings (RM 16), we would expect religion to be the part of culture in which the historicity of human subjectivity is most reflected, rather than the part that is, at least in its inner core, immune to this historical conditioning. In any case, given the noncoercive nature of divine influence plus the radical freedom and thereby historicity of human beings, we have no basis for assuming that all the religious traditions would teach essentially the same thing about ultimate reality and the way to be in harmony therewith, which would imply that members of one tradition have nothing of real importance to learn from other traditions. The implication is, rather, that each tradition would have much to contribute to, and to learn from, the other traditions.

---

[11] Although it has been common to claim that all (nonhuman) animals are *wholly* nonhistorical, this is probably an exaggeration.

3. The Two Ultimates: God and Creative Experience

The assumption that all religions teach the same thing has been deduced not only from the twofold doctrine of divine goodness and omnipotence but also from the assumption that all the religions are oriented around the *same* ultimate reality. For example, Huston Smith says that all the great religions are "equal revelations from, and of, the one true God" (1988, 288). Hick says that "the different encounters with the transcendent" are all "encounters with the one infinite reality" (1973, 139). "When the different traditions speak of the God of Abraham, Isaac and Jacob, or of the Holy Trinity, or Allah, or Vishnu, or Brahman, or the Dharmakaya/Nirvana/Sunyata, and so on," says Hick, they are affirming the same "putative transcendent reality" (1989, 10). Although he suggests that "the Real" is the best generic name "for that which is affirmed in the varying forms of transcendent religious belief," Hick sometimes uses "ultimate Reality" or simply "the Ultimate" as synonyms (1989, 11). Smith and Hick thereby clearly illustrate the assumption that there is only one ultimate, or ultimate reality, an assumption that has been extremely widespread in the West, thanks in large part to the doctrine that our world was created by the biblical God ex nihilo, which implies that this God is the only ultimate reality, from which all other realities are derivative.

Creativity as Ultimate Reality

As we have seen, however, Whitehead rejects this doctrine, holding instead with Plato and the Hebrew Bible that our world was created out of a chaotic situation. Whitehead's way of developing this ancient view is to hold that creativity—which is the twofold power to create oneself out of influences from a past multiplicity of actual entities and then to exert efficient causation upon future occasions—is itself uncreated. As explained in the first section of Chapter 4, this idea means not merely that creative power belongs to the very essence of God—who exists eternally and necessarily, as traditional theists hold—but also that creative power also belongs essentially to a world of finite actualities. This idea coheres with Whitehead's description of creativity as the process whereby "the many become one, and are increased by one" (PR 21). Creativity, thus understood, could never be instantiated in only a single actual entity. Indeed, in Whitehead's most careful description of the "category of the ultimate," he does not equate it simply with creativity but describes it in terms of *three* ultimate notions: "creativity," "many," and "one," saying that all three of these are involved in the notion of "being" (PR 21).

Given this understanding of what it means to be an actual being, not even a *supreme* being could exist all alone by itself because *to be* an actual being is *to be* a unification of a many. In Whitehead's words, "There is no entity, not even God, 'which requires nothing but itself in order to exist'" (RM 104). The motto of the United States engraved on U.S. currency, *e pluribus unum,* is the ultimate metaphysical truth: it is the very nature of a "one" to be a "unification of a many." And God, as we have seen, is to be understood not as the exception to metaphysical principles but as the chief exemplification thereof. This is the meaning behind Hartshorne's statement that God is *essentially,* not just contingently, the soul of the universe. It is the very nature of God to be the experiential unification of the multiplicity constituting the parts of the universe. Creativity, therefore, is *necessarily* instantiated in a multiplicity of finite actualities as well as in the supreme actuality. Although God is the "aboriginal instance" of creativity (PR 225), creativity is also aboriginally instantiated in some multiplicity or other of finite actual entities.

Once that point has been established, the exact relation between God and creativity can be further clarified by reflecting on their respective roles in the creative process. God can be called the *in-formed ultimate* because in God creativity is instantiated in an actual entity—or rather, I have argued, an everlasting personally ordered society of actual occasions—in which creativity is in-formed by the chief or perfect exemplification of the metaphysical principles that in-form all actual entities. As the in-formed ultimate, God is the source from which forms enter the world.

Creativity, by contrast, can be called the *formless ultimate,* the "ultimate behind all forms" (PR 20). As such, Whitehead says, it replaces the Aristotelian category that is sometimes translated as "prime matter," sometimes as "primary substance," by which Aristotle meant the stuff that is instantiated in all substances or actualities (PR 21). Thus understood, it was part of his analysis of all things in terms of four factors or elements, usually translated as the four "causes." According to this analysis, everything has an *efficient* cause, which brings it about; a *final* cause, which is the purpose for which it is brought about; a *formal* cause, consisting of the various forms embodied in it; and a *material* cause, which is the "matter" of which it is formed. The material cause of a table is wood, the material cause of a cannonball is iron, and so on. Underlying all these specific kinds of matter, Aristotle assumed, is a *primary* matter, of which wood, iron, and so on are instantiations. Wood, in other words, is a combination of primary matter and certain forms, iron is a combination of primary matter and other forms, and so on. Being devoid of form, prime matter cannot exist by itself. It exists only in its instantiations, as in-formed by particular forms. As such, it is not a concrete thing but an abstraction from all concrete things. It is not, however, an abstraction in the same sense in which forms are abstractions. Although any particular forms may or may not be instantiated in a given concrete thing, prime matter is necessarily instantiated in every concrete thing. It is, in fact, that which makes it a concrete thing, a substance, as distinct from a merely possible thing, which is what a mere combination of forms would be.

Making clear that his creativity is the ultimate reality in his philosophy in the same sense in which Aristotle's primary matter was in his, Whitehead says:

> In all philosophic theory there is an ultimate which is actual in virtue of its accidents. It is only then capable of characterization through its accidental embodiments, and apart from these accidents is devoid of actuality. In the philosophy of organism this ultimate is termed "creativity." (PR 7)

Calling creativity "another rendering of the Aristotelian 'matter,'" Whitehead explains the parallelism even further:

> Creativity is without a character of its own in exactly the same sense in which the Aristotelian "matter" is without a character of its own. It is that ultimate notion of the highest generality at the base of actuality. (PR 31)

In calling it "the ultimate behind all forms" (PR 20), Whitehead indicates that it is different from the forms, or eternal objects. Although he refers to it as a *universal,* which is a term traditionally used for forms, his statement is that it is "the universal of universals" (PR 21), which implies that insofar as it *is* a universal, it is different from all the others in being the one that is instantiated in *all* actual entities. Creativity is different from the rest in being, to use Hegel's term, the "concrete universal"—that which makes something a concrete thing rather than a mere possibility (Cobb 1982a, 87). This point was brought out especially well by Whitehead's earlier term for creativity, *substantial activity,* which indicates that it is the activity by virtue of which actual entities, traditionally called *substances,* have their substantiality, their actuality, their concreteness.

Besides being analogous to Aristotle's material cause of all substances, however, Whitehead's creativity is significantly different. Having said, "'Creativity' is another rendering of the Aristotelian 'matter,' and of the modern 'neutral stuff,'" Whitehead adds: "But it is divested of the notion of passive receptivity" (PR 31). Aristotle's primary matter, like the neutral stuff of some realistic philosophers, passively received forms, but Whitehead's creativity actively unifies them and then actively passes them on. This point, that the ultimate stuff of which all actualities is composed is not a passive stuff but a dynamic activity, is brought out by Whitehead's earlier term *substantial activity*. If the notions of creativity, many, and one are all involved in the category of "being," then "being itself" is nothing other than this dynamic process of the many's becoming one and being increased by one, which leads to still more unifications. In a passage that gives his most precise description of this ultimate process, Whitehead says:

> The ultimate metaphysical principle is the advance from disjunction to conjunction, creating a novel entity other than the entities given in disjunction. The novel entity is at once the togetherness of the "many" which it finds, and also it is one among the disjunctive "many" which it leaves. . . . The many become one, and are increased by one. (PR 21)

In being activity rather than passivity, therefore, Whitehead's creativity differs significantly from Aristotle's prime matter.

Creativity as Creative Experience

The two notions also differ in another, equally important respect. The Aristotelian term, both in the Greek and in its translations as "matter" and "substance," suggests that the ultimate stuff of which all actualities is composed is devoid not only of activity but also of experience. For Whitehead, by contrast, the process of creativity, in which the many become one, is always an *experiential* process, in which the feelings from past occasions of experience are brought together into an experiential togetherness, completed with a "satisfaction." At the heart of his philosophy, he says, is the principle that there is no meaning of "togetherness" other than "experiential togetherness" (PR 189). I have emphasized this feature of process philosophy, that all actual entities are occasions of *experience,* by using the term *panexperientialism*.

Although this dimension is not brought out by Whitehead's term *creativity,* it is brought out by the term *creative experience,* which is used by Hartshorne, who says that he "agree[s] with Whitehead that *creative experience,* as emergent synthesis of previous experience, is the form of forms" (1991b, 690). Creativity does not experience, of course, just as it does not act. By the ontological principle, only actual entities act and experience. The point is that the creative process, in which the many become one and are increased by one, is an *experiential* process. According to process philosophy, in other words, being itself is creative experience as such.

The Relation between God and Creative Experience

Now that the nature of creativity, including the fact that it is more completely described as creative experience, has been clarified, the next issue is its relation to God. There are four possibilities: (1) God and creative experience could be identical; (2) creative experience could be subordinate to, in the sense of derivative from, God; (3) God could be subordinate to, in the sense of derivative from, creative experience; or (4) God and creative experience could be equally primordial, equally ultimate, with neither subordinate to the other. Whitehead's position is the fourth. The idea that there are *two* ultimates, however, runs contrary to most philosophical and religious thought, not only in the West but also in the East (although, as we will see, it has there been more fully anticipated). It has been difficult, accordingly, for the true nature of Whitehead's position to be recognized, with many thinkers interpreting it in terms of one of the first three possibilities. Although a few interpreters have wrongly assumed that Whitehead simply equated God and creativity (the first possibility), the most common misinterpretations have involved the second and third possibilities.

The fact that Whitehead rejects the second possibility, that the creative experience embodied in finite occasions of experience was created by God, is part and parcel, as we have seen, of his naturalistic theism. I have emphasized the centrality of this point for process philosophy by including Whitehead's naturalistic theism among its core doctrines. Not all philosophers who think of themselves as following Whitehead's theism, however, have understood his position on this point. David Pailin, for example, endorses the traditional view that God (alone) is "ontologically ultimate" (1989, 41). Then, recognizing that Whitehead refers to creativity as the ultimate, Pailin says: "The 'ultimate' may be called 'creativity' because God, as the ultimate, is necessarily creative" (127). Although Pailin regards himself as denying the traditional doctrine of creation ex nihilo, he does not think of the finite actualities of the world as embodying a creative power that cannot be overridden by divine power (129–33). Hence, in discussing the existence of evil in the world brought about by human beings, he says that "God deliberately chooses to respect our personal freedom" (168), implying that God could do otherwise. Pailin's conclusion that the theodicy provided by process philosophy offers no improvement over "the standard free-will defence" (145) is no surprise because process theodicy as interpreted by Pailin is *no different from* "the standard free-will defence." Indeed, the same kind of criticism that I and many others have leveled against traditional free-will theism is leveled by Pailin against process theism as he understands it: "[T]he notion that God deliberately chooses to respect our personal freedom by having limited influence over what happens," says Pailin, seems "like careless irresponsibility when [human beings] are being demonically destructive" (168). The position Pailin criticizes is not the position of Whiteheadian process philosophy, as I have made clear not only in Chapter 6 but also in several earlier writings (Griffin 1976, 1981, 1991).

Some other Christian theists, while recognizing that Whitehead did not subordinate creaturely creativity to God, argue that he *should* have. Or they at least argue that this modification must be made if Whitehead's philosophy is to be acceptable as a framework for Christian theology (Boyd 1992; Franklin 1988, 1995; Hosinski 1993). That, of course, is their privilege, just as it was Whitehead's privilege to modify the positions of some philosophers from which he had learned. Because this modification involves a rejection of one of the core doctrines of Whiteheadian process philosophy, however, the resulting position involves a substantial revision of this philosophy. If Whitehead's naturalistic theism is replaced by traditional free-will theism (which is what the modification amounts to), then many of process philosophy's main achievements are undermined, including the reconciliation of theistic religion with scientific naturalism, with evolution, and with the world's evil.

Although it is generally understood that this second option is clearly ruled out by Whitehead, the third possibility, according to which God is derivative from creativity, has often been thought to be Whitehead's actual view. The extent to which Whitehead's position is sometimes distorted in this direction is illustrated by Eric Mascall's endorsement of a statement alleging that the existence of Whitehead's God "as an actual concrete reality is totally dependent on the world; and thus, if anything, the world exists chronologically and logically prior to God" (1980, 75). Although this interpretation of Whitehead's view goes far beyond anything permitted by the relevant texts, Whitehead is himself partly to blame for less extreme distortions of his position in this direction, insofar as some of his passages can be read as implying a subordination of God to creativity. There are, for example, passages that refer to the primordial nature of God as the "primordial created fact," the "primordial creature," and a "creature of creativity" (PR 31), all of which seem to suggest that creativity created God. Whitehead even says that God is the "primordial, non-temporal accident" of creativity (PR 7), thereby seeming to make God's existence contingent.

On the basis of such passages, Laurence Wilmot has argued that Whitehead held an Arian position, so that what Whitehead called "God" is not really divine but a mere creature. The background for this conclusion is

Wilmot's perception of a similarity between Whitehead's "triad"—creativity, the primordial nature of God, and the consequent nature of God—and Plotinus's hierarchy of three "hypostases"—the One, the Divine Mind, and the World Soul (Wilmot 1979, 124–33). Focusing on the relation between the first two aspects of these triads, Wilmot says that just as Whitehead portrays creativity as an impersonal process without a character of its own, Plotinus describes the One as unknown to itself and beyond being. And just as the Whiteheadian primordial nature contains the Platonic Forms, so does the Plotinian Divine Mind. The question is how these two "hypostases" are related. In Plotinus, the second is an *emanation* from the first. Arius, however, reserved divinity for the first hypostasis ("the Father") alone, regarding the second hypostasis ("the Son") as the first of the creatures, who then served as the agent for the creation of everything else. Whitehead, Wilmot argues, holds essentially the same position as Arius. One basis for this conclusion is Whitehead's identification of creativity with "ultimate reality," which for Wilmot necessarily implies divinity (Wilmot 1979, 108–10, 122, 137–38). The other basis is provided by the Whiteheadian passages just quoted, especially the statement that God is the "creature of creativity." These statements show, Wilmot concludes (69, 86, 101, 132, 157, 172), that Whitehead hypostasized creativity so that it could serve as an agent.

As Wilmot's interpretation illustrates, Whitehead's language can certainly be misleading. The explanation for this language lies in the fact that Whitehead's first metaphysical position, which was embodied in his Lowell Lectures (which were published in revised and expanded form as *Science and the Modern World*), was somewhat Spinozistic, with "substantial activity" playing much the same role as Spinoza's one substance. Although Spinoza equated this substance with God and spoke of finite things as creatures, he meant not that the one substance created the creatures as something distinct from itself but rather that the creatures were "modes" or "accidents" of the one substance, in the sense of instantiations of it. Whitehead thought similarly of the relation between substantial activity and actual entities. When he came to affirm God, however, he did not follow Spinoza in equating God with substantial activity (PR 7) but instead thought of God as a mode, instantiation, or "accident" of the substantial activity.

When read in light of this Spinozistic background, the passages seeming to suggest a subordination of God to creativity take on a different meaning. Whitehead's references to God as a creature of creativity do not mean that God was created by creativity. This could not have been Whitehead's meaning, given his ontological principle, which says that only actual entities can exert either final or efficient causation, combined with his clear denial that creativity is an actual entity: the "protean character of the creativity,"

Whitehead says, "forbids us from conceiving it as an actual entity" (RM 90). Leaving no room for ambiguity, he says that the "creativity is not an external agency with its own ulterior purposes" (PR 222). Whitehead's references to God as an accident of creativity, furthermore, mean that God is an *instantiation* of creativity; they do not reflect the modern meaning of accident as something that might or might not have occurred. In a book that appeared the same year as Wilmot's, this issue is nicely summarized by Elizabeth Kraus:

> God too is to be construed as "a creature of the creativity" in that he shares
> with actual occasions . . . the property of being a modal individualization of
> the substantial activity. It should be noted that for Whitehead "creature" does
> not carry the connotations of existential dependence with which the me-
> dievals clothed the term. In a Scholastic context, since the act of creation is a
> production *ex nihilo sui et subjecti,* the *esse* of the creature is contingent—i.e.,
> non-necessary—and the creature is assigned a lower grade of reality than the
> creator who as a necessary being *has to be.* Whitehead does not hold to a doc-
> trine of *creatio ex nihilo;* hence, to call God a creature is not to place him be-
> low the substantial activity (but above temporal occasions) in some hierarchy
> of being. To be actual has but one meaning for Whitehead: to be an actual en-
> tity. . . . The substantial activity, lacking such individuality, *is not actual,* and
> since only actualities can function as causes, *does not cause* God, i.e., is not his
> "creator" and hence a "superior" order of being. (1979, 40)

The correct interpretation of Whitehead's position, accordingly, is the fourth one, which avoids both kinds of subordination (as well as identity). The fact that God neither created creativity nor was created by it is reflected in Whitehead's statement that contrary to the view "that the ultimate creativity of the universe is to be ascribed to God's volition," God is instead "the aboriginal instance of this creativity" (PR 225). Besides being the aboriginal instance, God is the primordial *characterization* of creativity. That is, creativity has never existed neutrally, without being shaped by God's primordial aim toward value-realization. Although creativity in itself, as an abstraction, can be said to be neutral with regard to values, therefore "beyond good and evil," it never in fact exists in such a state but always exists as primordially characterized by the primordial purpose of God. Accordingly, creativity and God mutually presuppose each other, which means, as Cobb has put it, that God and creativity are equally ultimate, so that there are *two* ultimates. There can be no subordination because, as Cobb argues,

> between reality as such and actual things there can be no ranking of superior
> and inferior. Such ranking makes sense only among actualities. Among actu-
> alities [God] is ultimate. . . . [God] is ultimate actuality, and ultimate actual-

ity is just as ultimate as ultimate reality. Although it is true that there can be no ultimate actuality without ultimate reality, it is equally true that there can be no ultimate reality without ultimate actuality. Between the two there is complete mutuality of dependence. (1988, 19)

Terminology for the Two Ultimates

Given the idea of two ultimates, the next question is how best to distinguish them terminologically. One possibility would be to call creative experience the "metaphysical ultimate" and God the "religious ultimate," but this language would be doubly prejudicial. On the one hand, it would suggest that creative experience is somehow more important metaphysically than God, the falsity of which was shown by the arguments for God in Chapter 5. On the other hand, this language would suggest that only God is of religious importance, the falsity of which is one of the main points of the present chapter. A second possibility, which I used in a prior book (Griffin and Smith 1989, 44–46), is to call creative experience the "metaphysical ultimate" and God the "axiological ultimate." This distinction has the virtue of pointing to the idea that God is the source of values, but it falsely suggests, like the first one, that God is metaphysically less ultimate than creative experience. A third possibility, suggested by Cobb in the passage above and elsewhere (1982a, 112), would be to call creativity the "ultimate reality" and God the "ultimate actuality." Given Whitehead's language and his ontological principle, this distinction avoids any suggestion of subordination, so that Cobb's statement—"God's nonidentity with ultimate reality in no way subordinates God to it, for God is the ultimate *actuality*" (1988, 18)—is fully correct. To many thinkers, however, the distinction might suggest that whereas creative experience is the ultimate reality, God is *merely* the ultimate actuality, being less ultimate than the ultimate reality. As Cobb himself notes, "For those who use 'ultimate reality' as synonymous with 'God,' what I have called God cannot truly be God" (1988, 18).[12] This usage, as we have seen, lay behind the misreading of Whitehead by Wilmot. The substantive position would probably be less likely to be misunderstood if we had a terminological distinction that did not attribute ultimate reality to creativity while denying it to God.

There is more than one way in which this could be done. One general way would be to use the term *ultimate reality* for both God and creativity—

---

[12] This understanding seems to lie behind the rejection of Cobb's position by David Tracy, who says that "if ultimate reality is to be trusted and worshipped, it (he/she) must also be God" (1990, 139).

for example, calling God the "actual ultimate reality" and creativity the "nonactual ultimate reality," calling God the "personal ultimate reality" and creativity the "impersonal ultimate reality," or calling God the "form-giving ultimate reality" and creativity the "formless ultimate reality." Another way to do it would be simply to avoid the term *ultimate reality* altogether—for example, by calling creative experience the "nonactual ultimate" and God the "actual ultimate," or by calling God the "personal ultimate" and creativity the "impersonal ultimate." For reasons that will become clear in the next section, I will adopt the distinction between "personal" and "impersonal," referring to God as the "personal ultimate" (or the "personal ultimate reality") and referring to creativity as the "impersonal ultimate" (or the "impersonal ultimate reality").

God and Being

Whatever terminology is used, the most important point is that White-headian process philosophy, which understands being or being itself in terms of creativity or creative experience, suggests that God and being itself are equally ultimate in the nature of things. This position, it should be stressed, is *not* the idea that there are two gods, as critics sometimes allege. Previous systems of thought *have* suggested various forms of this idea, especially the notion that the battle between good and evil in the world reflects a cosmic struggle between a good and an evil deity. As we have seen, however, creativity is not an actuality, not a being, not an agent, but simply the activity involved in all agential beings, so it would make no sense to think of it as a deity.

Correctly understood, Whiteheadian process philosophy presents a position that has never before been fully and explicitly articulated in the West. Extreme voluntarism has subordinated being to God, in the sense that if God had chosen not to create a world of finite beings, the notion of being itself would simply have no application. The other dominant tendency in the West, however, has been to identify God and being itself. In discussing this point in the next three paragraphs, I rely primarily on Cobb's "Being Itself and the Existence of God" (1988).

Thomas Aquinas, although he was anticipated by others, was the theologian who most thoroughly identified God with being. Presupposing Aristotle's analysis of matter and form, he saw that neither of them nor their combination could account for the very being of things. What is required, he argued, is an *act of being,* which he called being itself, *esse ipsum.* Thomas identified this act of being with God, defined as that Being whose very essence it is to exist. Contingent beings exist by virtue of their participation in being itself, which means that God is the necessary ground of their being. For Thomas, then, God is not only a concrete being, the God of the Bible, but also being itself (Cobb 1988, 7).

It is this equation that Whitehead's position rejects. One basis for White-head's different view is that he no longer needed to affirm an act of being different from the material cause of all things. Whereas Thomas followed Aristotle in regarding matter as passive, developments in modern physics have led to the idea that that which all things embody is dynamic activity, better describable as energy than as matter. Enlarging this notion to creativ-ity, Whitehead had a concept that not only filled the role played by the Thomistic act of being but also could *replace,* rather than merely supplement, the Aristotelian matter. Then, given the idea that this creativity itself—this being itself, this act of being—is simply the stuff of which all actual beings exist, it was obvious that it could not also be *a* being, so that it could not in-telligibly be called God (Cobb 1988, 10–11).

Parallel with this rejection of the identification of being itself with a su-preme being on the part of Whitehead and his followers has been an even more explicit rejection of it by Martin Heidegger and his followers. The "onto-theological" metaphysical tradition, Heidegger argued, had blurred the all-important "ontological difference" between being (*Sein*) and beings (*Seinde*)—which is exactly parallel with Whitehead's distinction between creativity and actual entities. Once this ontological difference is seen, Hei-degger insisted, the equation of being itself (*esse ipsum*) with any being, even a necessary being (*esse ipsum subsistens*), is unintelligible (Cobb 1988, 8).[13]

Some theologians have agreed with Heidegger's analysis while disagree-ing with his conclusion that being itself could not be called God. Tillich, the most influential, argued that it would be demeaning to treat God as a being, even the supreme being, because such a being would be "one being along-side of others," thereby less than being itself, which is alone truly infinite. Believing that the word *God* had to refer to that which is infinite in all re-spects, Tillich said that we should understand it to refer to being itself. Tillich's idea that God, thus understood, is the being of all beings, is intelli-gible, as is the idea, also suggested by Tillich, that God is the "power of be-ing." Not intelligible, however, is Tillich's suggestion that God, understood

---

[13] Whitehead and Heidegger evidently came to this conclusion independently. In any case, because Whitehead's metaphysics does not equate being as such with God, the tendency of Heideggerians to dismiss all metaphysics, or at least all metaphysical theism, as "ontotheology" can be seen to be an instance of overshoot.

as the pure dynamism of the world, somehow exercises a selective agency and thereby provides direction to the world. Tillich could make application of the word *God* to Heidegger's being itself somewhat plausible only by using terms suggesting that being itself exercises some kind of purposive activity. All such terms are illegitimate, however, because not only purposive activity but any kind of selective activity, in which some possibilities are chosen instead of others, can intelligibly be attributed only to concrete, actual beings.[14]

As we have seen, it was Whitehead's recognition of this point that led to his affirmation of God as a concrete actuality distinct from substantial activity or creativity. In saying that God and being itself are distinct but equally ultimate, Whitehead thereby provides a new position in Western philosophical theology. As we will see in the next section, however, it has been anticipated by some philosophical theologies in the East.

4. The Two Ultimates and Two Types of Religious Experience

The Whiteheadian way of developing the relation between God and being, especially as developed by Cobb, turns out to be directly relevant to one of the central problems for the philosophy of religion insofar as it deals with religious experience.

The Problem Arising from Conflicting Claims

For philosophers of religion and theologians who accept the genuineness of religious experience, one of the most perplexing problems has been the multiplicity of types of religious experience. For example, one problem with giving a religious interpretation of religious experiences, says Hick, is "the fact that they differ markedly from one religious tradition to another." Summarizing the sceptic's rhetorical question, he asks: "If religious experience constitutes an authentic window onto the Real, why does that reality look so different when seen through different windows?" (1989, 104). Much of Hick's position is devoted to answering this question.

This problem, under the heading of "the conflicting claims challenge" to the validity of religious experience, has also been extensively treated by Caroline Franks Davis in *The Evidential Force of Religious Experience*. The twofold

---

[14] I have discussed the illegitimacy of some of Tillich's language in a critique entitled "Being Itself and Symbolic Language" (Griffin 1973a, chap. 1).

challenge arising from "the great diversity of religious experiential claims,"
says Davis, is

> the challenge that since subjects cannot agree on a description of the alleged
> perception, their experiences must be at worst, illusory, at best, serious mis-
> perceptions, and in any case, generally unreliable; and the challenge that since
> the different descriptions tend to be correlated with the subjects' different tra-
> ditions, a reductionist explanation involving prior beliefs is more plausible
> than any explanation involving an autonomous holy power. (1989, 166)

Two Types of Religious Experience

Although there are many different issues involved in "the great diversity
of religious experiential claims," the central issue in most discussions is the
distinction between two basic kinds of reported religious experiences: the
experience of a numinous, personal being distinct from oneself, and the experience of union or identity with an impersonal, formless reality. For example, in a discussion of whether the experience of the Holy is "objective"
in the sense of being an experience of "something Holy independent of ourselves which is revealed or manifested through the experience," Ninian
Smart examines Otto's famous analysis of the "numinous" experience in *The
Idea of the Holy,* which involves an experience of something "Wholly
Other." While agreeing that Otto accurately describes one kind of religious
experience, Smart adds that Otto

> seems to be less successful in dealing with the contemplative mystic, such as
> the Buddha and Shankara. . . . Otto makes much of the separation between
> the Other and the creature. . . . But the Buddha did not—judging from the
> scriptural reports—feel himself to be confronted by an Other. . . . His reli-
> gion was not primarily one of worship. . . . It also happens that in the Upa-
> nishads and in some other phases of the Hindu tradition, there is a sense of
> the identification of the eternal Self with the ground of being, Brahman. Here
> again the subject-object distinction is washed away. It is not a matter of expe-
> riencing a Wholly Other, still less a personal Object of devotion. . . . In brief,
> there is evidence to think that Otto has only diagnosed one form of religious
> experience. (1970, 12–14)

This idea of two forms of religious experience leads Smart to speak of two
types of religion: "[T]he one sort tends to stress the gap between the human
being and the ultimate, whereas the other tends to emphasize identity"
(1992, 204). This distinction between these two kinds of religion based on

two types of religious experience, to which Smart repeatedly returns in his writings (1960, 78–81; 1996, 67–68, 95–96, 296), is also described by many other writers. In religious experience of the one kind, the experience is said to be of a personal, perfectly good, loving, Holy Being distinct from the experiencer. In the other kind, the experience is said to be of an ultimate reality, finally identical with one's own deepest reality, that is impersonal, indifferent ("beyond good and evil"), and in some Buddhist accounts, wholly "empty."

The philosophical problem, of course, is that both kinds of experience are reported, Davis points out (1989, 167), as apprehensions of "the nature of *ultimate* reality." Expressing the resulting challenge, she asks: "How can 'ultimate reality' be both a personal being and an impersonal principle, identical to our inmost self and forever 'other,' loving and utterly indifferent, good and amoral, knowable and unknowable, a plenitude and 'emptiness'?" (172–73). Although, she notes, seemingly contradictory reports of some kinds of experience can be reconciled by distinguishing between the experience itself and imported interpretations, such a solution would not be possible in this case. As Stephen Katz, whom she approvingly quotes in this regard, says:

> There is no intelligible way that anyone can legitimately argue that a "no-self" experience of "empty" calm is the same experience as the experience of intense, loving, intimate relationship between two substantial selves. (Katz 1978, 39–40)

Solutions Based on the Assumption of One Ultimate Reality

The reason why these two kinds of religious experience create a problem for most positive philosophers of religion, such as Hick and Davis, is the assumption that, in Cobb's words, "what is approached as 'ultimate reality' must be one and the same" (1987, 96). Given that assumption, there are various ways to try to solve the resulting problem.

"One rather brazen approach," as Davis calls it (1989, 172), is simply to say that logic does not apply to mystical experiences. For example, W. T. Stace, contending that mysticism is "simply nonlogical," says that the paradoxes, such as the statement that ultimate reality is both personal and impersonal, "are in fact incapable of solution" (1960, 264, 268). The problem with this "solution," as Davis says, is that "inherently contradictory experiences are poor evidence for the existence of their alleged object" (1989, 172). In other words, although Stace's solution might seem satisfactory to those who are already firmly convinced of the reality of God or the Ultimate, it does nothing to answer the charge that religious experiences, by virtue of giving rise to contradictory descriptions of that which is allegedly experienced, provide no evidence for a religious interpretation of the universe.

The most common solution, especially in the East, has been the view that the personal God, which one encounters in theistic religious experience, is derivative from the impersonal ultimate reality. In that form of Hinduism known as Advaita Vedanta, which was founded by Shankara in the eighth century, the ultimate reality is Nirguna Brahman, meaning Brahman-without-attributes (which is similar to Heidegger's being and Whitehead's creativity). Ishvara, the personal God of religious devotion, is a derivative being. Although belief in Ishvara is true at one level, it is illusory from the perspective of the highest level of truth. Those who aspire to harmony with the truly ultimate reality replace religious devotion to a personal God with the effort to realize the identity of their true essence, as Atman, with Nirguna Brahman. Greater prestige, Cobb points out, is generally accorded to those who orient themselves to Brahman in this way (1988, 18).

A similar distinction occurs in Mahayana Buddhism, as Cobb also points out:

> There, ultimate reality as such, without attributes, can be called Dharmakaya. This is identical with Sunyata or Emptiness. But there is also the Sambhogakaya, which is ultimate reality as wise and compassionate, and which can be understood by the believer as Amida, the all-wise and all-compassionate Buddha. It is Amida who is trusted and worshipped. Dharmakaya, on the other hand, is to be realized through meditational techniques. Again, on the whole, the higher status usually attaches to enlightenment as the realization of ultimate reality as such. (1988, 18)

It is this view, especially in its Advaita Vedantist form, that is presupposed in the perennial philosophy with which Huston Smith identifies. Although the personal embodiment of being itself is real, it has only a derivative reality. From the perspective of the higher truth, furthermore, it is finally illusory. Given this subordinationism, the idea of two ultimates simply does not make sense. Smith, for example, asks why process theology does not "make one of its ultimates really ultimate and productive of the other," adding that his own preference is to make the personal God derivative from the impersonal ultimate (Griffin and Smith 1989, 82). From this perspective, according to which all events are finally determined by the ultimate reality, Smith holds that there is no genuine evil in the world, thereby contending that one of our hard-core commonsense beliefs is true only from a less than ultimate perspective.

This position, as Davis points out, also provides no help with regard to the conflicting-claims challenge. The intent of this position, to be sure, is to say that both types of religious experience are real because the one type involves the experience of a numinous personal being, the other type the realization of one's identity with ultimate reality. But in effect, as Davis says, this position actually "treats all experiences other than the realization of identity with the undifferentiated Brahman as ultimately illusory" (1989, 173). The claim of theistic mystics to have experienced ultimate reality, in other words, is rejected.

Still another approach has recently been taken by Hick. At one time (1973, 144), Hick had essentially adopted the Advaita Vedantist position. Using the Kantian distinction between noumenal Reality, or the thing in itself, and the phenomenon, or the thing as it appears to us, he equated the Divine Reality in itself with Nirguna Brahman, which is beyond all our categories, while equating God as related to the creation with Saguna Brahman, the personal deity. He came to realize, however, that this position took sides with one of the two basic types of religious experience against the other. Wanting an approach that would be equally acceptable to theistic and nontheistic traditions, he has more recently distinguished *all* ideas of God from the Divine Reality, or simply "the Real," in itself. These human ideas of God are then divided into two basic types, the *personae* and the *impersonae*. Nirguna Brahman, as a divine *impersona,* is said not to correspond to the Real in itself any more than do Saguna Brahman and the God of the Bible. The Real in itself "cannot be said to be one or many, person or thing, substance or process, good or evil, purposive or non-purposive" (1989, 246). Although some purely *formal* properties, such as "being a reference of a term" and "being that than which no greater can be conceived," can be attributed to the Real (239, 246), we cannot apply *substantial* properties, such as "being good," "being powerful," and "having knowledge" (239).

This solution, however, undermines Hick's whole attempt to provide an alternative to nonrealist views of religious language, to which he devotes considerable space (1989, chaps. 11–12). The ultimate problem with the nonrealist view, Hick says, is that "it cannot credibly claim to represent the message of the great spiritual traditions" (1989, 208). What all these traditions have in common, he holds, is an "ultimate optimism" according to which all human beings will eventually reach fulfillment (206). The nature of the universe as described by nonrealist uses of religious language, however, is such that this fulfillment would be impossible. This is because for the nonrealist, "God/Brahman/the Dharmakaya are human ideas, existing only *in mente*" (206). Only if these names really refer to the Ultimate Reality of the universe, not merely to something in our minds, Hick says, would the message of the religious traditions be true.

Although Hick regards his position as superior in this respect to that of the nonrealists, it is not, because it is essentially the same. That is, there is no significant difference between saying that the word *God* refers to nothing outside our imaginations, as the nonrealists do, and saying that it refers to something about which we can know absolutely nothing, as Hick does. If that to which the word *God* refers cannot be said to be either purposive or good, belief in God provides no basis for cosmic optimism. If, as Hick says, the properties of having knowledge and being powerful do not apply to the Real in itself, then there is no basis for believing that there is an ultimate reality that knows what is going on and, even if it did, could do anything about it. And if the ultimate reality does not have the property of being good, then we have no reason for assuming that it would be interested in bringing all sentient beings to fulfillment.

This same feature of Hick's position also undermines his basic concept of salvation, which involves the transformation from ego-centeredness to Reality-centeredness. As Hick himself says, to judge whether that transformation is taking place requires criteria. But what could the criteria possibly be? Hick says that

> on the hypothesis that the major world religions constitute varying human responses to the transcendent Reality, and are thus at least to some extent *in alignment with that Reality,* the available criteria will be those that have developed within them. (1989, 300–301; emphasis added)

If we can say absolutely nothing substantive about "transcendent Reality," however, no one form of human behavior can be said to be more "in alignment with that Reality" than any other. Saints in all religious traditions, Hick rightly says, manifest "compassion/love towards other human beings or towards all life" (301). Given Hick's view that nothing can be predicated of "Ultimate Reality," however, we cannot say that "compassion/love" is "in alignment with that Reality" any more than are indifference and hate.

In view of these self-defeating implications, one might wonder why Hick has come up with this hypothesis. "The answer," he says, "is that the divine noumenon is a necessary postulate of the pluralistic religious life of humanity" (1989, 249). Hick's point is that, given the different types of reported religious experiences, some of which speak of a personal deity and some of which speak of an impersonal absolute, we would, without his postulate, have only two options: either regard all such reports as illusory or else affirm the truth of reports of one type while considering those of the other type illusory. For those who cannot accept either of these options, Hick says, his pluralistic theory becomes inevitable.

A fourth possibility, however, would be a *different type of pluralism,* based on the hypothesis that there is more than one ultimate. *If we were to assume that there are two ultimates—a personal God as well as an impersonal ultimate—then both of the two basic kinds of religious experience can be taken to be fundamentally valid.* Hick rules out this option, saying that "there cannot be a plurality of ultimates" (1989, 249). In light of the momentous nature of this claim, however, his arguments for it are remarkably weak. One of his arguments is that "what the traditions severally regard as ultimates are different and therefore cannot all be truly ultimate" (1989, 248). That argument begs the question, however, because the conclusion follows only if it is already presupposed that there is only one ultimate.

His other argument is that although there is no a priori reason to reject the hypothesis that there is more than one ultimate,

> if from a religious point of view we are trying to think, not merely of what is logically possible . . . , but of the simplest hypothesis to account for the plurality of forms of religious experience and thought, we are, I believe, led to postulate "the Real." For each of the great traditions is oriented to what it regards as the Ultimate as the sole creator or source of the universe. (Hick 1989, 248)

Surely, however, simplicity is not the only criterion for judging the relative suitability of possible hypotheses. In fact, as we saw, Whitehead warns that all simple doctrines, which regard a single causal principle as (in Hick's words) "the sole creator or source of the universe," are "shipwrecked on the rock of the problem of evil" (RM 74). The same kind of simplicity, it now seems, is equally shipwrecked on the rock of the problem of religious pluralism. In any case, although simplicity should always be a desideratum, adequacy to the facts in question, along with self-consistency, should always be given greater weight. Hick's hypothesis, as we have seen, is neither adequate nor self-consistent. We should, therefore, explore the slightly more complex idea that there are *two* ultimates, each one of which corresponds to one of the two major kinds of religious experience.

Eastern Approximations of the Idea of the Two Ultimates

Eastern thinkers over the centuries have devoted extensive thought to the distinction between a personal cosmic being, whether under the name

Sambhogakaya, Saguna Brahman, Ishvara, or something else, and that which in the West is called being itself, whether under the name Nirguna Brahman, Emptiness, the Buddha nature, or something else. Although the dominant tendency among philosophical thinkers has been to subordinate the former to the latter, there have also been some reactions against this tendency in favor of a view close to Whitehead's. Such approximations to Whitehead's views would not be purely coincidental: Whitehead himself commented that his position on the question of ultimate reality "seems to approximate more to some strains of Indian, or Chinese, thought, than to western Asiatic, or European, thought" (PR 7). In pointing to the contrast he has in mind between East and West, respectively, he says: "One side makes process ultimate; the other side makes fact ultimate" (PR 7). However, what Whitehead has in effect proposed, as Cobb has shown, is a higher reconciliation, in which "process" and "fact" are *equally* ultimate, because process as such, which is creative experience as such, both presupposes and is presupposed by its primordial factual embodiment ("the initial fact is the primordial appetition" [PR 48]). The suggestion that "some strains" of Eastern thought anticipated this higher reconciliation has been borne out in studies comparing Whitehead with Ramanuja, Aurobindo, and Shinran carried out by three Whiteheadian thinkers: Delmar Langbauer, Ernest Simmons, and John Cobb, respectively.

Most Hindu piety is theistic, being *bhakti* (devotion) to a personal deity. The central expression of this view in Indian religious literature is the Bhagavad Gita, which says that Brahman is the body of God, so that God is more inclusive (Bhagavad Gita VII.2; IX.4; XI.37). Shankara, however, said the opposite, that Nirguna Brahman (without attributes) is more inclusive, so that Saguna Brahman (*with* attributes) is derivative. Devotion to a personal God, therefore, would involve an inferior relation to ultimate reality. Some later Indian philosophers, however, have developed positions that defend the ultimacy of God, and thereby *bhakti,* against Shankara's view. The most important of these philosophers was Ramanuja, who wrote in the eleventh century, developing a position he called Visistadvaita Vedanta. Although, as Langbauer points out, the success in the West of missionaries for Shankara's position have "made Advaita Vedanta seem like *the* Hindu view," Ramanuja's Visistadvaita Vedanta is actually closer to the beliefs of most Hindus. Langbauer has shown how Ramanuja's view is similar to, albeit not identical with, Whitehead's position (1970, 200).

Ramanuja's attempt was, in Langbauer's words, "to affirm both Brahman and Ishvara as ultimate" (1970, 245). Referring to Nirguna Brahman as the universal substance, Ramanuja argued that this substance necessarily and eternally emanates attributes, the most important of which are personal attributes, such as power, knowledge, and will (147–48). Nirguna Brahman is actual, therefore, only as Saguna Brahman, as God. In abstraction from Ishvara, in other words, Nirguna Brahman is not some higher reality but merely an abstraction. Hence, Ramanuja's position is similar to Whitehead's view, according to which creativity is eternally embodied in God.

Another position rejecting the subordination of the personal God to the impersonal absolute, as Simmons has shown, was proffered in the twentieth century by Sri Aurobindo Ghose, who developed a "realistic Advaita" in opposition to the "illusionist Advaita" of Shankara (Simmons 1981, 217). In contrast with Shankara's version of Vedanta, which relegated Ishvara "to subordinate or inferior phases of the Brahman-idea," Aurobindo affirmed the position of the Gita, which "represent[s] the Ishwara [sic] . . . as higher even than the still and immutable Brahman . . . , as containing within himself the opposition of the Brahman with qualities and without qualities" (Ghose 1950, 84–85). As Simmons points out, Aurobindo did not deny the experience of Nirguna Brahman. Indeed, his first mystical experience was of "the spaceless and timeless Brahman." Rather, Aurobindo denied only that this was the sole or the highest experience (Simmons 1981, 173). Put otherwise, Aurobindo spoke of Brahman, the impersonal supercosmic existence, and Ishvara, the personal cosmic spirit, as co-equal and co-eternal, rejecting all ideas of any hierarchical ordering between them (Simmons 1981, 146–48).

Cobb has pointed out an approximation to Whitehead's position within Mahayana Buddhism. In most Mahayana schools of thought, says Cobb, Dharmakaya, the ultimate reality beyond all forms, takes on the character of the Sambhogakaya only as a concession to human weakness since most human beings are not able to realize ultimate reality as such. Sambhogakaya, with its wisdom and compassion, is not, therefore, regarded as the ultimate truth. In Shinran's True Pure Land Buddhism, however, a different view is offered. Identifying Amida Buddha with Sambhogakaya, Shinran said, in Cobb's words:

Amida is ultimate reality *for us,* because ultimate reality for us *is* wise and compassionate. . . . In Amida the *Dharmakaya* has a primordial character. This character is fully revealed in the vow of [Amida] to save all sentient beings. There is for Shinran no access to an ultimate reality that is not characterized by this primal vow. (1982a, 126)

Cobb's point, of course, is that this position is remarkably similar to Whitehead's view that although creativity is formless, being "without any character of its own," it is never experienced by us apart from its primordial characterization by God. This characterization, called the "primordial nature of

God," is an appetition for the realization of ever higher forms of value. Although creative experience *as such* is "beyond good and evil," so that it can be embodied in monsters as well as saints, creative experience *as we actually experience it* has a bias toward the good, the true, and the beautiful. This position is approximated by Shinran's position, in which emptiness is primordially characterized by the vow of Amida and thereby by wisdom and compassion.

Many Buddhist thinkers would, of course, reject this view on the grounds that, in Cobb's words, "people can realize the *Dharmakaya* as such apart from all forms" (1982a, 127). Cobb replies that this claim is "not evidently established by history or present experience," adding this explanation:

> All Buddhists expect that Buddhas will be wise and compassionate. In standard Buddhist teaching this wisdom and compassion express their full realization of ultimate reality. There is no apparent evidence of a higher state in which wisdom and compassion are left behind. Hence it is not clear how this attainment can be used to argue for the superiority of the *Dharmakaya* as such to the *Dharmakaya* as characterized by wisdom and compassion, that is, to the *Sambhogakaya* or Amida. (Cobb 1982a, 127)

From this perspective, Buddhism, like Hinduism, can be seen to have anticipated the Whiteheadian way of understanding the personal and impersonal ultimates.

It is probably wrong, furthermore, to think that True Pure Land Buddhism is the only form of Buddhism in which this anticipation occurs. In suggesting that most forms of Mahayana are ultimately nontheistic, regarding emptiness as superior to any personal embodiment of it, Cobb has probably exaggerated. That is not the view presented in the Lotus Sutra, which, as Gene Reeves points out (1994, 98), has been the most important sutra for most Buddhists in East Asia, being the fundamental document for several major schools, from T'ien T'ai to Rissho Kosei-kai. It is atheistic only in the sense that process philosophy is, says Reeves: [15]

[15] Furthermore, the appropriateness of the label *atheism* not only for certain types of Buddhism but also for Buddhism in general has been questioned by some interpreters. "Serious distortions may result," stated Evans-Pritchard, "when it is said that Buddhism and Jainism are atheistic religions" (1965, 119). Eugene Long, editor of the *International Journal for Philosophy of Religion,* defines an atheist as "one who looks to his own existence for meaning and purpose and who interprets reality as indifferent or perhaps even threatening to his efforts to achieve authentic existence." He then says: "On these grounds, at least, Buddhists do not appear to be atheists. . . . Indeed, some commentators have argued that many of the characteristics assigned to Nirvana [in early Buddhism] are very similar to those assigned to God in the Western tradition" (1986, 258). The same point about Buddhism in general is granted, furthermore, even by some authorities who at first glance appear to reject it. For example, in an anthology titled *Picturing God,* Peter Harvey begins his essay on Buddhism by saying: "In the Buddhist world-

Certainly if by "God" is meant a literally all-powerful being who is the only Creator of the universe, then the Lotus Sutra has no God. But if by "God" is meant something more like what is taught by Whitehead and Hartshorne, there can be little question but that the Sutra's "Eternal Buddha" is indeed God, or vice versa. (1994, 108)

This universal or eternal Buddha, says Reeves, is everlasting, being "the Buddha of all worlds—past, present and future," and "omnipresent, i.e., present in all places" (109). "The Lotus Sutra," furthermore, "is very insistent on personal language for talking about this universal Buddha," saying that "the Buddha is like a father whose life is incomplete and suffers so long as a son is lost" (110). Buddhism based on the Lotus Sutra, concludes Reeves, should be considered a form of panentheism (110). We can say, accordingly, that the forms of Buddhism based on the Lotus Sutra also have both a personal and an impersonal ultimate reality.[16]

Implications of the Solution Based on Two Ultimates

The two fundamentally different kinds of religious experience can thus be regarded as *equally veridical,* with the one oriented to creative experience as such (which has also been called, among other things, Nirguna Brahman, Emptiness, and Being Itself), the other to creative experience as embodied in, and therefore qualified by, the creative and responsive love of God

view, ultimate reality is generally not personalised, as a God, much less as a single God" (1994, 25). But in Harvey's discussion of the "Three body" doctrine of Mahayana Buddhism—which has far more adherents than Theravada Buddhism, with which Harvey himself identifies—he points out that "the *Dharma*-body is given a semi-personalised aspect, making it somewhat akin to the concept of God in other religions" (25).

[16] Reeves has argued that one should say that there are not simply two ultimates in Whitehead's philosophy but three, with finite actual occasions constituting the third (personal communication, November 8, 1999). As both a Unitarian Universalist and a Lotus Sutra Buddhist, Reeves makes this point in support of the ultimate importance of the world, fearing that a religion oriented around only God and/or Creativity as such might encourage a religiosity in which this world is trivialized. Given the twofold fact that much traditional religion *has* regarded the world as relatively unimportant and that Whitehead insisted that creativity is necessarily embodied in a multiplicity of finite occasions as well as in God, Reeves's point is certainly well-taken. I have not spoken of three ultimates, nevertheless, for four reasons. First, simply getting a hearing for the idea that there may be *two* ultimates is difficult enough. Second, the chapter was already sufficiently long and complex. Third, even though "the world" is ultimate in the sense that some world or other exists necessarily, our particular world—our cosmic epoch—does not exist necessarily and will not endure forever. Fourth, many of process philosophy's doctrines—such as the doctrines that all actual entities have intrinsic value, that the divine purpose is to maximize important experience in the world, and that all experiences are preserved everlastingly in the divine experience—make clear that it does not support a world-negating spirituality.

(which has also been called Saguna Brahma, Ishvara, the vow of Amida, the cosmic Christ, and simply God). We can thus avoid the two positions that Hick wishes to avoid.

On the one hand, we can avoid the exclusionary position of traditional personalistic theism, according to which those who say that ultimate reality is an impersonal, infinite reality, with which we are identical ("Atman is Brahman"), are simply wrong. They are *not* wrong, because we are each instantiations of creativity, or creative experience, which is the impersonal ultimate reality.

On the other hand, we can avoid the exclusionary view of Advaita Vedantists and many Buddhists, according to which those who say that ultimate reality is a personal, compassionate deity, with whom we can experience union but not complete identity, are simply wrong. Of course, Advaita Vedantists typically say not that theistic worshipers are simply wrong but merely that the object of their devotion has a derivative reality. Besides being condescending, however, this view rejects the claim of theistic mystics to have experienced *ultimate* reality and thereby the claim of theistic religions that ultimate reality is compassionate. This view, therefore, does not finally differ from saying that theists are simply wrong. From the perspective of the Whiteheadian hypothesis, theists are *not* wrong, because the impersonal ultimate reality is always instantiated in the everlasting, all-inclusive personal ultimate reality, whose creative and responsive love for the creatures can be experienced.

Furthermore, given the Whiteheadian hypothesis, we not only can avoid the two nonpluralistic positions, which say that either theistic or nontheistic religions are wrong. We can also avoid Hick's Kantian pluralism, according to which everyone is wrong. Hick does succeed in his effort to make all the religions equal, but only by making them equally erroneous. Whiteheadian pluralism, by contrast, allows us to see that the two basic kinds of religion, insofar as they have been describing different ultimate realities, have been equally right (at least in this respect).

If people begin thinking about the relations among the religions in terms of this Whiteheadian pluralism, the basis for the conflicting claims argument against the cognitive nature of religious experience will be removed because we will no longer assume that the reports of theistic and nontheistic religious experiences must be about the same ultimate reality. Given Whiteheadian pluralism, these reports do not cancel each other out. Rather, one type of report reflects experiences in which the existence of the personal ultimate reality has risen to consciousness, whereas the other type reflects experiences in which the existence of the impersonal ultimate reality has risen to consciousness. The fact that these two types of religious experience have evidently been reported in all cultures is a source of support, rather than embarrassment, for Whiteheadian theism.

One dimension of this explanation of the two basic types of religious experience remains to be addressed. It may be wondered why experiences of the impersonal ultimate—creative experience as such—would be *religious* experiences, given the explanation of the distinctively religious character of theistic religious experiences provided in Chapter 2. According to that explanation, which employed the category of the initial conformity of subjective form, this character is based on the conformal prehension of God, understood to be a Holy Reality, meaning that God embodies the quality of "holiness." We have "experiences of the holy" when our prehensions of the Holy One rise to the conscious portion of our experience. But why should experiences in which creative experience as such rises to consciousness also be experiences of the holy? If creative experience as such is devoid of (substantive) attributes, then it cannot be said to be holy. To be sure, as Tillich and many others have pointed out, it is of ultimate importance, because it is the "power of being," the power by virtue of which all actualities, including God, exist. But there is no reason to attribute the quality of holiness to it.

An answer can be provided by the notion that creativity never exists by itself but always exists as instantiated. We never experience creativity as such but always experience it as embodied in, and therefore characterized by, God and worldly actualities. What makes an experience of creativity as such a *religious* experience is, by hypothesis, the fact that creativity as such is always characterized by God and therefore by holiness. To say this is not to return to the view that theistic experiences are more accurate than nontheistic religious experiences. It *is* to suggest, however, that the fact that we are always prehending God is the explanation for the distinctively religious character of nontheistic religious experiences, just as this fact is the explanation for various other features of our experience—such as our experience of novel possibilities and of moral, aesthetic, and logical norms—that usually do not involve a conscious awareness of God as such.

This hypothesis, that even nontheistic religious experiences involve prehensions of God, would account for some of the paradoxical descriptions of the impersonal ultimate reality. For example, although Nirguna Brahman is by definition "without (substantive) attributes," it is also described as *sat-chit-ananda,* or existence-consciousness-bliss. And although Emptiness is said to be empty of all qualities, it is also described in terms of wisdom and compassion. The explanation suggested here is that although the description of Brahman and Nirvana as devoid of qualities reflects an accurate account of creativity as such, the addition of consciousness, wisdom, bliss, and compassion reflects the fact that the creativity as prehensively experienced is always characterized by divine attributes. The religious nature of the experience would be due to the divine attribute of holiness, which is prehended with some conformity of subjective form.

In any case, this Whiteheadian religious pluralism will also be helpful with regard to the other reasons for the importance of the topic of the relations between the religions. The basis for the mutual lack of respect among the various religions, at least insofar as this basis has been the assumption by theistic religions that nontheistic religions are simply wrong and vice versa, will be undermined. Members of the various religious traditions will thereby be encouraged not only to learn from one another but also to cooperate with one another in terms of the many values they have in common overagainst quasi-religious ideologies. They may also be inspired to work toward a "higher-order global religion" that can "embrace complementary worldviews," which has been advocated by Ninian Smart (1996, 291–94).

Another benefit of this Whiteheadian pluralism is that it actually supports the "cosmic optimism" of the full-fledged religions, to which Hick has called attention, far better than Hick's own Kantian pluralism does. Being freed from the assumption that accounts of nontheistic religious experience, which speak of an ultimate reality wholly devoid of all substantive attributes, are accounts of the one and only ultimate reality, one *can* affirm the existence of an ultimate reality that knows the world, loves it, and exercises providential power within it.[17] Accordingly, we can have an intelligible basis for faith that a loving power is leading us in the direction of wholeness — which brings us to the subject of the next chapter.

---

[17] In the Introduction, I pointed out that although Whitehead's philosophy, because of its content, can be considered a natural theology, it must, in light of its origin and basic worldview, be called a *Christian* natural theology. The present chapter, by reaffirming the existence of a personal ultimate actuality, reinforces this judgment. But it also suggests a qualification, which is that Whitehead's philosophy is Christian in a way that does not prevent it from also being appropriated by philosophers and theologians of other religious traditions. Some Buddhists, for example, have written about the helpfulness of Whitehead's conceptuality for developing Buddhist thought (Takeda 1994; Tanaka, 1977; Yakota 1994), with one of them (Tanaka) even suggesting a "Whiteheadian Buddhist Natural Theology."

[8]

Religion, Morality, and Civilization

Whitehead wrote no separate moral treatise and said, furthermore, that the moral order of the world is derivative from its aesthetic order. From this twofold fact, some critics have inferred that morality was not of central importance to him. Nothing could be further from the truth. His entire philosophy is intended to provide support for the moral life. His philosophy is a moral philosophy just as much as it is a scientific philosophy, a religious philosophy, and an aesthetic philosophy. This point has been made in the present book by including among the core doctrines of process philosophy "the provision of cosmological support for the ideals needed by contemporary civilization as one of the chief purposes of philosophy in our time." Another reason for confusion about the centrality of morality in Whitehead's philosophy has surely been the fact that his understanding of the primary task of moral philosophy in our time differs from the dominant understanding. Although this difference involves many dimensions, the primary one involves the question how to respond to the fact that the late modern worldview, which I have called naturalism$_{sam}$, portrays what Max Weber called a "disenchanted" world. (Putnam refers to this kind of naturalism, which he no longer accepts, as "disenchanted naturalism" [see Chapter 1, n. 5].)

In saying that the world is now disenchanted, Weber meant that the world as now understood *contains no objective moral norms, at least none of which we could obtain knowledge,*[1] so that the world is "ethically irrational" (1958, 122).

[1] In Weber's most well-known statement about "the disenchantment of the world," he characterizes it as the fact that "the ultimate and most sublime values have retreated from public life" (1958, 155). Weber was led by this development, which he accepted, to affirm what

This position, usually called "ethical nihilism," is sometimes taken to involve an *ontological* doctrine. In the words of Gilbert Harman: "Nihilism is the doctrine that there are no moral facts, no moral truths, and [therefore] no moral knowledge" (1977, 11). According to this view, the lack of moral knowledge is due to the fact that there are no moral truths to be known. Moral nihilism in this ontological sense is affirmed by John Mackie, who in his book on the subject—significantly titled *Ethics: Inventing Right and Wrong*—says: "There are no objective values" (1977, 15).

Moral nihilism can also be phrased in purely *epistemic* terms. The epistemic nihilist says that if there *are* moral facts, we have no way of obtaining knowledge of them. Moral nihilism in this latter sense is now widespread in intellectual circles. For example, in an encyclopedia article titled "Nihilism," Robert Olson says: "If by nihilism one means a disbelief in the possibility of justifying moral judgments in some rational way, and if philosophers reflect the intellectual climate of the times, then our age is truly nihilistic. At no period in Western history . . . have so many philosophers regarded moral statements as somehow arbitrary" (1967, 515). Nihilism in this epistemic sense follows, at least in part, from the sensationism of naturalism$_{sam}$, which would disallow any perception ("intuition") of moral norms, even if they existed.

Because this late modern worldview involves atheism and materialism as well, moral nihilism in the ontological sense is also widespread. The central meaning of Nietzsche's affirmation that "God is dead," said Heidegger with endorsement, is the denial of the existence and efficacy of a realm of supersensuous values (1977, 61).[2] Accordingly, when Mackie affirms both dimensions of moral nihilism—that moral values do not exist and that we would be unable to know them even if they did (1977, 38–39)—he is sim-

---

Habermas calls "decisionism" (1971, 64), according to which one's ultimate ends can be based only on an arbitrary decision (Turner and Factor 1984, 50, 182). Weber's own ultimate value-decision, as shown by Turner and Factor (59, 63–64, 68, 75, 91), was for German nationalism, on behalf of which he was a strong advocate of power politics.

[2] Like Weber, Heidegger affirmed decisionism. Heidegger's thought, says Hans Jonas, provides no norm to guide one's answer to the call of being—"no norm except depth, resolution, and the sheer force of being that issues the call" (1966, 247 n. 11). Jonas connects this lack to Heidegger's notorious proclamation as rector of the University of Freiburg in 1933, in which he declared: "Not doctrines and 'ideas' be the rules of your being. The Führer himself and alone is the present and future German reality and its law. Learn ever deeper to know: that from now on each and every thing demands decision, and every action, responsibility. Heil Hitler!" The relation between Heidegger's philosophy and his Nazism has been intensely discussed (Löwith 1995; Habermas 1987; Neske and Kettering 1990; Rockmore 1992; Wolin 1990, 1993; Zimmerman 1990).

ply spelling out the moral implications of the late modern worldview. Mackie is explicit about the centrality of his atheism to this conclusion, conceding that "if the requisite theological doctrine could be defended, a kind of objective ethical prescriptivity could be thus introduced" (48).

Most mainline philosophical ethicists, agreeing with Mackie that theism is false, have argued that ethics is "autonomous," meaning that it needs no cosmological support.[3] Within this mainline position, some moral philosophers have devoted at least part of their energies to the meta-ethical[4] task of providing a basis for morality, perhaps by showing that human reason itself provides a justification for the moral life (P. Taylor 1961; Gewirth 1978). Other mainline moral philosophers have ignored this meta-ethical task, instead simply trying to work out a substantive ethical theory, perhaps of a deontological or utilitarian type. Whitehead, by contrast, did not believe that morality could be autonomous. Holding that our ideals and thereby our actions are inevitably shaped by our worldviews, he believed that if a society's worldview does not support morality, the society's moral life would inevitably deteriorate. Given the nature of the late modern worldview, therefore, he considered *the overriding moral need of our time to be the development of a new morality-supporting cosmology.*

In this light, we can see the claim that he wrote no treatise on morality to be misleading. A chapter titled "Civilized Universe" begins with the statement that it seeks "the evidence for that conception of the universe which is the justification for the ideals characterizing the civilized phases of human society" (MT 105). This description can be applied to the entirety of Whitehead's philosophy, which can thereby be called a "civilizing cosmology," meaning a cosmology intended to support the ideals now needed by human civilization. The present chapter develops this side of Whiteheadian process philosophy, showing how it is intimately connected with its religious side. The first section points out how the context for Whitehead's moral philosophy is provided by the current crisis with regard to the justification for civilizational ideals. The second section discusses the various elements in Whitehead's cosmological support for a moral civilization, emphasizing in

[3] For example, although Habermas rejects Weber's decisionism, he fully accepts Weber's assumption that the universe has been irreversibly disenchanted, so that those wishing to provide a grounding for the ethical life must do so without any theistic or even metaphysical support (Habermas 1984, 1992, 1993).

[4] Whereas ethics is usually understood to include both the first-order practice of making moral judgments and the second-order task of developing a normative moral position, the term *meta-ethics* has come to be used to encompass the discussion of various third-order issues, such as the meaning of moral terms, the justification of moral principles, and motivation for living morally.

particular the extent to which this support is theistic. The third section discusses Whitehead's moral philosophy as such, stressing the intimate connection between his religious and his ethical ideas. The fourth section sketches a Whiteheadian-Hartshornean meta-ethical position.

1. The Current Crisis with Regard to Civilizational Ideals

The context for Whitehead's moral philosophy was provided by the current state of civilization, which Whitehead believed to be in crisis. I will first discuss the nature of this crisis, then what Whitehead believed to be the needed philosophical response.

The Current Crisis of Civilization

Having described the present as a time of opportunity, but with the reminder that "opportunity leads upwards or downwards," Whitehead says: "Philosophy should now perform its final service. It should seek the insight, dim though it be, to escape the wide wreckage of a race of beings sensitive to values beyond those of mere animal enjoyment" (AI 159). Writing this in 1932—and therefore prior even to the outbreak of World War II, let alone the development of atomic weapons—Whitehead already had the sense that the present trajectory of civilization could well lead to the "wide wreckage" of the human race.

The task of philosophy, in the face of this prospect, is to provide the "insight" by which this wreckage might be escaped. What Whitehead thereby means is suggested in another passage, in which he says that "[philosophy's] gifts are insight and foresight, and a sense of the worth of life, in short, that sense of importance which nerves all civilized effort" (AI 98). Observing that the "mere compulsion of tradition has lost its force," he adds that it is the task of philosophy "to re-create and reenact a vision of the world, including those elements of reverence and order without which society lapses into riot" (AI 99). To move forward, he is saying, civilization requires a sense of importance, based on a *reverence-evoking insight* into the nature of the universe.

Problems for Moral Philosophy Created by Modern Thought

"The vigour of civilized societies," Whitehead writes, "is preserved by the wide-spread sense that high aims are worth-while" (AI 288). The problem is that the view of the universe currently sanctioned by the scientific community does not support this sense. At the heart of the best features of Western civilization, in Whitehead's view, has been the "humanitarian ideal," which involves "the idea of the essential rights of human beings, arising from their sheer humanity" (AI 13). This ideal was implanted in Western civilization primarily through the combined influence of Platonism, with its doctrine of the human soul, and Christianity, which incorporated this doctrine within its theistic cosmology (AI 14–16, 26, 37). In the eighteenth and nineteenth centuries, this ideal was crucial to the abolition of slavery (AI 19–23, 26–28). "This success came only just in time," however, because several strands of thought emerged "whose combined effect was in direct opposition to the humanitarian ideal" (AI 28).

One of these strands was the denial of the human soul, whether from a materialist or a sensationist-phenomenalist basis, as represented respectively by Hobbes and Hume. With regard to the latter, Whitehead comments:

> Hume's flux of impressions and of reactions to impressions, each impression a distinct, self-sufficient existence, was very different to the Platonic soul. The status of man in the universe required re-considering. "What is man that thou are mindful of him?" The brotherhood of man at the top of creation ceased to be the well-defined foundation[5] for moral principles. There seems no very obvious reason why one flux of impressions should not be related to another flux of impressions in the relative status of master to slave. (AI 29–30)

Although Hume probably personally disliked slavery, owing to his "psychological inheritance from the Platonic religious tradition," the question is what *reason* he could give for opposing it. This question is especially pressing in the light of Hume's contention that "there is no such passion in human minds as the love of mankind, merely as such, independent of personal

---

[5] It has recently become fashionable to say that we should *not* be seeking a "foundation" for morality because to do so would be "foundationalism," which has been discredited. This argument often conflates two very different matters: the attempt to provide a foundation for moral judgments that shows how they can be both true and rationally justifiable, which can be called *foundationalism$_m$*, and foundationalism as a technical doctrine in epistemology, which can be called *foundationalism$_e$* (and which will be discussed in Chapter 10). The use of the same term, especially without differentiating subscripts, falsely suggests that the two forms of "foundationalism" are problematic for the same reason. The rejection of foundationalism$_m$, having little if anything to do with the problems involved in foundationalism$_e$, is usually based instead on the acceptance of late modernity's disenchanted universe, which provides no cosmological foundation for morality, combined with the realization that none of the attempts to provide a non-cosmological foundation has been successful. The claim that foundationalism$_m$ is bad seems, therefore, to be an example of the well-known tendency of human beings, perhaps especially philosophers, to make a virtue out of a (perceived) necessity.

qualities, of services, or of relation to ourself" (1739, Bk. III, Pt. II, Sect. I; quoted at AI 30).

The denial of the human soul, whether on phenomenalistic or materialistic grounds, is closely related to another discrepancy between modern thought and "the moral intuitions which are presupposed in the concrete affairs of life" (SMW 80), namely, the twofold intuition that we have a degree of freedom and that our behavior can be shaped by ideals consciously adopted (SMW 77–78; FR 12–16). Although the truth, Whitehead believes, is that human society always involves an interweaving of force and persuasion, or strife and harmony, the idea that *everything* is determined by efficient causation, so that ideals are impotent, implies that social relations, both within society and between societies, are based entirely upon force and strife (AI 32). The "Gospel of Force," Whitehead adds, "is incompatible with a social life" (SMW 206). Although Whitehead believes that a certain amount of force will always be necessary, he maintains that healthy societies are held together primarily by the persuasive power of shared ideals, so that force should be reduced to the absolute minimum (AI 56, 85).

The main contributor to this Gospel of Force was the Darwinian view of evolution, especially as interpreted by social Darwinists. According to this view, with its stress on natural selection (understood in terms of the "struggle for existence" and the "survival of the fit"), "the destruction of individuals was the very means by which advance was made to higher types of species" (AI 35). This doctrine supported a "gospel" quite different from that implied by Platonic Christianity: "Instead of dwelling on the brotherhood of man, we are now directed to procure the extermination of the unfit" (AI 36).[6] This evolutionary doctrine, according to which progress comes about through ruthlessness, is "a challenge to the whole humanitarian movement" (AI 36).

The extent to which this evolutionary doctrine is now assumed to be scientifically established was illustrated by the quotation from Provine in Chapter 1. Provine maintains that free will, in the sense of the freedom to make uncoerced choices among alternative courses of action, "simply does not exist." He also says that modern science implies that there are "no pur-

---

[6] Although Whitehead cites no examples of this view, he could have quoted the following passage from Nietzsche, in which Christian morality is under attack: "All 'souls' became equal before God: but this is precisely the most dangerous of all possible evaluations! If one regards individuals as equal . . . , one encourages a way of life that leads to the ruin of the species: Christianity is the counterprinciple to the principle of *selection*. . . . The species requires that the ill-constituted, weak, degenerate, perish: but it was precisely to them that Christianity turned as a conserving force. . . . What is 'virtue' and 'charity' in Christianity if not just this mutual preservation, this solidarity of weak, this hampering of selection?" (1967, 141–42).

posive principles whatsoever in nature" and that "there are no inherent moral or ethical laws." Given this disenchanted view of the universe, what should the moral philosopher do?

The Inadequacy of Non-Cosmological Solutions

The dominant approach among moral philosophers has not been to challenge this amoral cosmology but instead to try to provide a morality without cosmological support. The two examples Whitehead cites are Jeremy Bentham's utilitarian principle of "The Greatest Happiness of the Greatest Number" and Auguste Comte's "Religion of Humanity." These doctrines reflected the humanitarian ideal, which was based on "emotions [of respect and friendliness] towards men, as men." Although these emotions, says Whitehead, involve, as a matter of historical fact, "the generalization of feeling produced by the joint influence of philosophy and religion," Bentham and Comte, extending the modern revolt against metaphysics to moral and political theory, "accepted these generalized emotions as ultimate moral intuitions, clear matter of fact, requiring no justification" (AI 37). Bentham and Comte did not realize that strong emotions of respect and friendliness toward humans qua humans—as distinct from people in one's own family and tribe—have not resulted solely from self-evident moral intuitions but have depended on traditions and worldviews through which these emotions have been intentionally inculcated. These "moral intuitions" will not long seem self-evident in the absence of a worldview justifying their appropriateness.

Commenting on Bentham and Comte's failure to provide a justification of these emotions by explaining "their relationship to the rest of things," Whitehead says:

> [T]he relations of the emotions to the rest of things refused to be ignored. In the evolution of life Nature is implacable: Nature discriminates. Whence comes this universal benevolence? "The Religion of Humanity" should be replaced by a cult of a select assortment of Humanity: "The Greatest Happiness of the Greatest Number" should be replaced by "The Humane Extinction of Inferior Specimens." Hume denies that there is any "such passion . . . as the love of mankind merely as such." Modern science gives a plausible explanation why no such passion is required. It can only stand in the way of the scavenging process of evolution. If any people are subject to this passion, of course they will act on it. But no reason can be given why we should inculcate the passion in others, or why we should pervert legislation to subserve the ends of

such an unreasonable emotion. I am certainly in greater sympathy with Bentham and Comte than with this deduction from Hume and modern Zoology.
But . . . the deduction does show that Bentham and Comte were mistaken in
thinking that they had found a clear foundation for morals, religion, and leg-
islation, to the exclusion of all ultimate cosmological doctrines. (AI 38)

I have quoted this passage at length because it clearly brings out, by negative example, the connection between Whitehead's metaphysical cosmology and his moral concern. Thanks to his nonsensationist epistemology, he
agrees with those who believe that morality is partly based on moral intuitions. He does not believe, however, that these intuitions by themselves,
unsupported by cosmological beliefs, are sufficient to determine human
ideals and behavior, especially in the face of cosmological beliefs supporting
contrary principles. He also agrees with Hume that morality is based on
emotions, especially sympathy, and that such sympathy does not naturally
extend beyond a rather limited circle of human beings (AI 37). He therefore
holds that if it is to be extended further, especially to all humanity, it must
be deliberately inculcated in a society's members by that society's dominant
vision. Whitehead believes, furthermore, that this inculcation of universal
benevolence will be effective and self-perpetuating only if it seems to be a
reasonable emotion, in the sense of being appropriate in light of the ultimate
nature of things.[7] We again see the implications for moral philosophy of the
idea that religion involves the desire to be in harmony with the ultimate
power in the nature of things. If Darwinian natural selection is taken to be
that ultimate power, then the humanitarian ideal is undermined. Modern
civilization will continue—or, in some circles, resume—inculcating universal benevolence in its citizens only if the neo-Darwinian cosmology is replaced by a different cosmology, one that shows human beings who embody
universal benevolence thereby to be in harmony with the ultimate power of
the universe.[8]

Having titled this section "the inadequacy of non-cosmological solutions," which I mean to indicate Whitehead's opinion, I have discussed only
the one type of non-cosmological moral theory that he discussed, moral in-

---

[7] In relation to the contemporary discussion, this point means that a purely *local* justification, in terms of the beliefs, attitudes, and customs of some particular cultural tradition,
will not suffice. Although most traditional justifications were de facto local in this sense, the
power of the justifying reasons rested on the assumption that they reflected universal truth. Insofar as this assumption is eroded, the local justifications will not continue to be effective.

[8] The real religion of a society consists, in Clifford Geertz's language (see pp. 13–14), of
the way in which its worldview shows its ethos to be appropriate while its ethos shows its
worldview to be plausible.

tuitionism. This form of moral theory, however, has long been out of favor. Most of those who have tried to provide a non-cosmological support for a non-nihilistic position have taken different approaches, with some version of Kantianism probably being the most popular among those who have sought to defend an objective and universalistic morality. Because I consider morality inherently metaphysical and religious—holding motivation and even justification to depend finally on the desire to be in harmony with ultimate reality, with this taken, at least implicitly, to be holy—it follows that I judge all the non-cosmological solutions, including the various versions of Kantianism, to be inadequate. Here, however, I can only announce this judgment, not argue it. I can provide some support for it by pointing to commentators who argue that all actual moralities have been thought to have cosmological support[9] and by pointing to moral philosophers who have concluded that none of the modern attempts to support morality within the context of a disenchanted universe have succeeded.[10] For my own argument to this effect, however, I can only refer to other publications.[11]

[9] This claim that non-cosmological solutions are inadequate is supported not only by Geertz but also by Michael J. Perry, who says "Real moralities—the moralities that various human communities have actually lived—have always been cosmologically embedded" (1998, 16). Support is also provided by *Cosmogony and Ethical Order,* edited by Robin Lovin and Frank Reynolds (1985). Taking *cosmogony* to mean beliefs "about how things are in the world and how they came to be that way," Lovin and Reynolds suggest that an approach to ethics that follows the type of moral thinking actually employed by people worldwide cannot isolate moral propositions from cosmogonic beliefs (3–4, 18–20).

[10] Two of the best-known books to formulate this case are Mackie's *Ethics* and Bernard Williams's *Ethics and the Limits of Philosophy* (1985), which argues especially against Kantians that "there is no route to the impartial standpoint from rational deliberation alone" (70). For critiques of one of the best-known attempts to provide such a route, Alan Gewirth's *Reason and Morality* (1978), see Edward Regis (1984), especially those by Hare, Raphael, Nielsen, and Hudson. The attempts by Habermas and John Rawls have also been widely discussed. *The Divine Good* (1990) by Franklin Gamwell offers a powerful critique of the post-Kantian attempt to provide a basis for the moral life apart from a metaphysical vision of a divine telos.

[11] There will be a chapter on theism and morality in *The Divine Cry of Our Time.* In an earlier publication (Griffin 1980, 344–47), I argued that the problem with at least some non-cosmological solutions is that while claiming to be compatible with a wholly disenchanted universe, they presuppose the holiness of either the "moral point of view" (Warnock 1971) or "rationality" (Taylor 1961). In particular, I argued, these thinkers build the notion of "impartiality" into their very definitions of morality or reason, thereby ruling out as instances of morality and rationality all practices that fail to take the interests of all human beings into account. In giving the stance of impartiality this status, they are implicitly accepting the "ideal observer" theory of morality, which I discuss in the final section of this chapter. The problem is that the ideal observer is simply a secularized version of God, understood as omniscient and omnibenevolent, so that these supposedly non-cosmological accounts of morality are implicitly ascribing to impartiality the quality of holiness, for which there is no place in a wholly disenchanted universe.

The Twofold Problem with the Return to Traditional Theism

For many thinkers in the nineteenth and twentieth centuries, the solution has been to return to traditional theism. For Whitehead, this possible solution was not a live option, for both intellectual and moral reasons. His reasons for thinking traditional theism intellectually untenable have been discussed in prior chapters. In expressing his moral objection, Whitehead says of the God of traditional theism: "He stood in the same relation to the whole World as early Egyptian or Mesopotamian kings stood to their subject populations. Also the moral characters were very analogous" (AI 169). This problem with the "moral character" of the God of traditional theism was discussed in terms of the problem of evil in Chapter 6. Of course, as Whitehead says sardonically, "If we mean by [God's] goodness that He is the one self-existent, complete entity, then He is good. But such goodness must not be confused with the ordinary goodness of daily life" (RM 68). In other words, insofar as the term *good* can be applied to God only equivocally, so that its meaning when applied to God is completely different from its meaning in reference to human beings, divine "goodness" can provide no basis for human morality. This conclusion is disastrous, from Whitehead's perspective, because in an ethically purified religion the emphasis is on the "concept of the goodness of God." That is, we study God's goodness in order to be like God (RM 40). This morality is undermined if we become convinced that the divine goodness has nothing in common with what we normally mean by goodness.

Besides failing to support the moral life, traditional theism, by subordinating divine goodness to divine power, actually promotes an immoral use of human power, which now can be more dangerous than ever. Referring to the "glorification of power" in portions of the Bible, Whitehead complains: "This worship of glory arising from power is not only dangerous: it arises from a barbaric conception of God. I suppose that even the world itself could not contain the bones of those slaughtered because of men intoxicated by its attraction" (RM 54–55). By a "barbaric conception," Whitehead means one in which the "final good is conceived as one will imposing itself upon other wills" (AI 51). Given our irrepressible tendency to imitate deity as we conceive it, we will not overcome our own barbaric morality, Whitehead believes, until we overcome the remnants of barbarism in our conception of the deity of the universe.[12]

---

[12] As illustrated by social Darwinism, Marxism, and Fascism, the "deity of the universe" need not be understood as a personal being to play a religious role. The relation between cosmology and ethics in Marxism has been discussed insightfully by Anthony Giddens (1971, 18–34) and Douglas Sturm (1985).

A final problem is that traditional theism, because of its assumption of divine omnipotence, has led to exaggerated claims for moral codes, which have been taken to be incapable of improvement even though they fail to agree with our present moral intuitions: "The result is that the world is shocked, or amused, by the sight of saintly old people hindering in the name of morality the removal of obvious brutalities from a legal system. Some *Acta Sanctorum* go ill with civilization" (AI 290). The assumption that some particular moral code has been written in stone by the author of the universe has, of course, sometimes led to far more deadly results.

A New Cosmological Basis for the Ideals of Civilization

Given Whitehead's threefold belief that the ideals of civilization need cosmological support, that the late modern cosmology undermines this support, and that the traditional theistic cosmology does not provide the necessary support, what is needed, he holds, is a new cosmological basis for the ideals of civilization, one that provides, in particular, "a reconstructed justification for the doctrine of regard to man, as man" (AI 38).

2. Central Elements in Whitehead's Cosmological Support for Civilized Existence

The basic reason why Whitehead's cosmology provides support for the moral ideals of civilization, whereas the dominant modern cosmology does not, was pointed to in the final section of Chapter 1. Modern cosmology has been based almost entirely upon scientific ideas, in distinction from ideas rooted in aesthetic, ethical, and religious experience, whereas Whitehead emphasizes the need to retain "the whole of the evidence in shaping our cosmological scheme" (SMW vii). Modern thinkers, assuming the truth of a cosmology rooted only in science-based ideas, find distinctively aesthetic, ethical, and religious ideas—not surprisingly—to be cosmologically ("scientifically") unjustified. Whitehead, by contrast, says that ideas that are well grounded in aesthetic, ethical, and religious experience should be built into the cosmology from the outset. Although in previous chapters the focus has been primarily on ideas grounded in religious and aesthetic experience, ideas that are grounded in ethical experience are equally important. For example, in illustrating his point that "[p]hilosophers are [i.e., *should be*] rationalists," Whitehead quotes approvingly the following statement from moral philosopher Henry Sidgwick (1906, Appendix I): "It is the primary aim of philosophy to unify completely, bring into clear coherence, all departments of rational thought, and this aim cannot be realised by any philosophy that leaves out of its view the important body of judgments and reasonings which form the subject matter of ethics" (SMW 142). In this section, I will summarize several elements of Whitehead's metaphysical cosmology that are especially germane to his support for a moral civilization. These elements are crucial to Whitehead's "reenchantment" of the world.

Freedom

Discussing the "discrepancy between the materialistic mechanism of science and the moral intuitions which are presupposed in the concrete affairs of life" (SMW 80), Whitehead primarily has in mind the intuition that we have freedom, so that we are responsible for our decisions and actions. Whitehead prepares the way for the affirmation of human freedom, as we have seen, by attributing a mental pole to every actual entity; by construing enduring individuals as temporally ordered societies, each of which oscillates between efficient and final causation; by formulating an organizational duality between aggregational societies, which have no dominant member to give them the power of overall self-determination, and compound individuals, which do, and thereby distinguishing between the brain, as an aggregational society with billions of members, and the psyche-at-the-moment, as a single occasion of experience; by construing the "laws of nature" as the world's most well established, long-lasting habits rather than as imposed, inflexible laws; by having a hierarchy of actual occasions, the higher of which are less habit-bound; and by having a realm of eternal objects in the primordial nature of God, from which finite occasions can be confronted with alternative possibilities. Much of Whitehead's philosophy, accordingly, can be seen to support our moral intuition of freedom.

Whitehead often calls attention to the connection of his defense of freedom with his attempt to be adequate to the presuppositions of moral experience. After introducing, in a discussion of perception, the "notion of self-production arising out of some primary given phase," he adds: "I would remind you that, apart from it, there can be no moral responsibility. The potter, and not the pot, is responsible for the shape of the pot" (S 8–9). Likewise, having said that "the actual entity, in a state of process during which it is not fully definite, determines its own ultimate definiteness," Whitehead comments: "This is the whole point of moral responsibility" (PR 255). In a more detailed discussion, he says:

The subject-superject[13] is the purpose of the process originating the feelings. . . . The feelings are what they are in order that their subject may be what it is. Then transcendently, since the subject is what it is in virtue of its feelings, it is only by means of its feelings that the subject objectively conditions the creativity transcendent beyond itself. In our own relatively high grade of human existence, this doctrine of feelings and their subject is best illustrated by our notion of moral responsibility. The subject is responsible for being what it is in virtue of its feelings. It is also derivatively responsible for the consequences of its existence because they flow from its feelings. (PR 222)

In developing his metaphysical position, as this statement illustrates, Whitehead clearly had in mind its implications for moral responsibility.

Each Occasion of Experience Public as Well as Private

Also of central importance to Whitehead's cosmological grounding for the moral life is his rejection of the idea of actual entities as independent substances. Saying that the bad effects of this doctrine were fatal in the nineteenth century, given the rise of the modern industrial system, he explains:

The doctrine of minds, as independent substances, leads directly not merely to private worlds of experience, but also to private worlds of morals. The moral intuitions can be held to apply only to the strictly private world of psychological experience. Accordingly, self-respect, and the making the most of your own individual opportunities, together constituted the efficient morality of the leaders among the industrialists of that period. The western world is now suffering from the limited moral outlook of the three previous generations. (SMW 196)

That statement was written in 1925. Now, several generations later, the *whole* world is suffering, and much more extensively, from the polluting and depleting effects of this "limited moral outlook" of modern industry, which was supported by the notion of the human self as a self-enclosed, independent substance whose decisions are nobody's business but its own. In response to the fact that the public realm is now dominated by the idea of privacy in various forms—"Private Property, The Competition of Private Traders, Private Amusement"—Whitehead says: "The notion that every

---

[13] The term *subject-superject* is sometimes used by Whitehead to emphasize the self-determining nature of an actual entity—that it is "at once the subject experiencing and the superject of its experiences" (PR 29).

action is at once a private experience and a public utility had to be born
again" (AI 31).

Whitehead hoped to contribute to this moral rebirth with his doctrine
that every actual occasion, after having its moment of private subjectivity,
becomes a "superject" with objective immortality, thereby becoming an ingredient, for good or for ill, in all future occasions. The connection between
this point and moral responsibility is explicitly made in the quotation above,
in which Whitehead says that the subject is "derivatively responsible for the
consequences of its existence because they flow from its feelings."

The Objectivity of Moral Experience

Besides presupposing these ideas about human experience, the moral life
presupposes that the moral dimension of experience involves apprehensions
of truths about the nature of reality, especially the idea that some aims are
really better than others. "[O]ur moral and aesthetic judgments," Whitehead points out, "involve the ultimate notions of 'better' and 'worse'"
(ESP 80). But the dominant view, which is a deduction from naturalism$_{sam}$,
is that moral (along with aesthetic) judgments do not give us any objective
knowledge but merely express subjective feelings and preferences. In addition to Weber, Heidegger, and Mackie, cited earlier, we can quote
J. J. C. Smart, who says: "[S]ince art and morality are concerned with evoking feelings and recommending actions, not with the cognition of facts, they
would not appear to provide a counterinstance to the omnicompetence of
science as a cognitive activity" (1996, 223).

One of the main arguments for this view that there are no moral facts is
what Mackie calls "the argument from relativity," which is based on "the
well-known variation in moral codes" in different societies, periods, and
classes. "[R]adical differences between first order moral judgements," thinks
Mackie, "make it difficult to treat those judgements as apprehensions of objective truths" (1977, 36). Whitehead, by contrast, uses the fact of moral disagreement to argue *for* an element of objectivity: "The discordance over
moral codes witnesses to the fact of moral experience. You cannot quarrel
about unknown elements. The basis of every discord is some common experience, discordantly realized" (FR 86). Likewise, against the positivistic attempt to limit the cognition of facts to mere "matter-of-fact,"[14] Whitehead

---

[14] The ontological part of Mackie's "argument from queerness" seems to imply that any
entities other than mere matter-of-fact would be too queer to be plausible members of our
universe. "If there were objective values," Mackie contends, "then they would be entities
or qualities or relations of a very strange sort, utterly different from anything else in the universe"
(1977, 38). What would be queer about them, Mackie avers, is that they would be "intrinsically prescriptive," somehow having "to-be-pursuedness" or "not-to-be-doneness" built into

insists that "the impact of aesthetic, religious and moral notions is inescapable" (MT 19). This inescapability of moral notions means that they belong to our hard-core commonsense notions.[15]

The Primordial Nature of God as the Home and Source of Moral Ideals

When J. J. C. Smart endorsed "the omnicompetence of science as a cognitive activity," he expressed a widely shared conviction of late modernity. Closely related to this conviction is the modern mind's *nominalism,* to which Whitehead refers (AI 129). As we saw in Chapter 6, this doctrine, when consistently accepted, rejects the existence of a "Platonic" realm of ideal entities. In a less consistent form, it restricts this realm to purely objective, mathematical entities—which Whitehead calls "eternal objects of the objective species."[16] Because of Whitehead's acceptance of the existence of a primordial, all-pervasive actuality, he could affirm not only these mathematical entities but also "eternal objects of the subjective species," which include all possible values. His doctrine of the primordial nature of God allows him to affirm both the reality of such ideal entities and their efficacy in the world. The ideal of moral beauty, furthermore, is said to be central to the divine aims for distinctively human experience. Replacing the traditional trinity of truth, beauty, and goodness with "intellectual beauty, sensible beauty, and moral beauty," Whitehead says: "All three types of character partake in the highest ideal of satisfaction possible for actual realization, and in this sense can be termed that beauty which provides the final contentment for the Eros of the Universe" (AI 11). The ideal of moral beauty, therefore, pervades the universe as fully as do mathematical and logical notions, being prehensible wherever there are beings capable of prehending it. Whitehead's universe, far from being disenchanted, is saturated with values, including distinctively moral values.

---

them (40). Putnam, who at one time would have agreed, now rejects the contention that "an *ought-implying fact*" would be "ontologically queer" (1994, 167–68). Arguing that cognitive values are not completely different from normative values, Putnam says: "There are 'ought-implying facts' in the realm of belief fixation; and that is an excellent reason not to accept the view that there cannot be 'ought-implying facts' anywhere" (170).

[15] Mackie does not deny this claim, instead pointing out that objectivism about values has "a firm basis in . . . the meanings of moral terms" and that his own denial of this objectivism "conflicts with what is sometimes called common sense" (1977, 31, 35). The problems created by Mackie's "error theory" of common sense are at the center of a book devoted to his ethical theory, appropriately titled *Morality and Objectivity* (Honderich, ed., 1985).

[16] As we saw in note 26 of Chapter 1, mathematical objects are the only nonmaterial entities allowed in Quine's universe, and note 9 of Chapter 5 contains Hersh's statement that most mathematicians continue to believe in a remnant of Plato's Heaven "with all entities but the mathematical expelled."

The Reality of Nonsensory Perception

Besides presupposing the ontological existence of moral ideals, the cognitive interpretation of moral experience presupposes that we can directly experience such ideals. Crucial to this idea is Whitehead's nonsensationist doctrine of perception, discussed in Chapter 2 in relation to religious experience. Because God is the home of the moral ideals, our moral experience and our religious experience are closely intertwined. Whitehead says, as we have seen, that our experience of ideals "is the experience of the deity of the universe" (MT 103). It is because moral ideals are actively envisaged by the divine actuality, with appetition that they be realized in the world, that they can be causally efficacious on our experience.[17] And we can perceive (prehend) these moral ideals, even though we have not been deistically endowed with a special faculty of "moral intuition," because our perception in general is most fundamentally nonsensory, with sensory perception being merely a special case.

As we saw earlier, Whitehead rejects "moral intuitionism" in the strong sense, according to which morality can be justified in terms of moral intuitions alone, without any cosmological support. But the idea that we have direct intuitions of moral ideals is central to his position. Given the pervasiveness of the sensationist doctrine of perception, however, this idea is almost universally rejected nowadays.[18] Bernard Williams, for example, says that "the appeal to intuition as a faculty explained nothing. It seemed to say that these truths were known, but there was no way in which they were known. . . . So intuition in ethics, as a faculty, is no more" (1985, 94). As this statement shows, the idea of moral intuition has been virtually equated with the idea of a special "faculty." That equation was required, of course, by all those who defended moral intuitions while otherwise presupposing sensationism. And that equation was rightly seen to rest the case for moral intuitions upon a purely ad hoc assumption. Mackie bases much of his case against moral intuitions upon this "argument from queerness," saying that if we could be aware of objective moral values, "it would have to be by some

---

[17] The widespread belief (as discussed in note 9 of Chapter 5) that even if mathematical entities exist they could not be perceived by us—both because they are not possible objects of *sensory* perception and because they could exert no *causality*—is applied to moral norms by many philosophers, including Gilbert Harman (1977, 9–10) and Bernard Williams (1985, 94).

[18] It is important to recognize that this rejection is based on a priori considerations, not on any phenomenology of moral perception. For example, Mackie says: "'Moral sense' or 'intuition' is an initially more plausible description of what supplies many of our basic moral judgements than 'reason'" (1977, 38). A form of moral intuition has recently been defended by David Little (1993).

special faculty of moral perception of intuition, utterly different from our ordinary ways of knowing everything else" (1977, 38). In relation to Whitehead's position, however, that criticism would not apply.

The World as a Locus of Value Realization

One reason why the moral life has seemed less important than in earlier times is the late modern view that intrinsically valuable experience is not the aim of existence. For neo-Darwinism, the aim is mere "survival." For social Darwinism, the aim is victory in the military and economic competition for survival, which means power and riches.

For Whitehead, by contrast, every actuality is an occasion of experience, which as such has value for itself and for others. The idea that every actual entity enjoys value-experience is contained in the idea that each concrescence concludes with a "satisfaction." This satisfaction is discussed in terms of the aesthetic criteria of beauty: harmony and intensity. Experience that is "aesthetic" in this sense is said to be the whole point of existence: "The teleology of the Universe is directed to the production of Beauty" (AI 265). The evolution of the universe, with its increasingly complex societies supportive of higher modes of value-experience, is reflective of this divinely rooted teleology toward experiences with greater intrinsic value. "The actual world is the outcome of the aesthetic order, and the aesthetic order is derived from the immanence of God" (RM 101). Whitehead explicitly connects this idea with morality: "By reason of this character, constituting reality, the conception of morals arises. We have no right to deface the value experience which is the very essence of the universe" (MT 111). Emphasizing this point, he says: "Our enjoyment of actuality is a realization of worth, good or bad. It is a value experience. Its basic expression is—Have a care, here is something that matters!" (MT 116).

Although Whitehead used aesthetic value as the basis for *establishing* the importance of morality, some critics have assumed that he thereby *denigrated* its importance by making it derivative. As Whitehead says, however, the moral element in experience must be derivative from something more fundamental: "For otherwise there is no content for duty to operate upon. There can be no mere morality in a vacuum" (AI 11). In other words, if there were nothing deemed valuable in itself, the idea that we have moral duties—duties to do certain kinds of things, duties to refrain from doing other kinds of things—would be meaningless.[19] For example, if it were not

---

[19] Although the Kantian, deontological version of ethics is usually assumed to deny this point, what would be left of Kantian morality without the notion that other human beings are to be treated as ends in themselves, not simply as instrumental means to our own ends? Kant's

generally assumed that pain is intrinsically bad, we would have no moral duty to avoid causing needless pain. Whitehead's view that morality presupposes intrinsic value, understood in (broadly) aesthetic terms, certainly did not lead him to downplay the importance of morality. He said, for example, that "beauty, moral and aesthetic, is the aim of existence" (ESP 8).

Human Beings as Especially Persuadable by Divine Ideals

Crucial to Whitehead's defense of the ideals of civilized existence is his concern to develop a "reconstructed justification" for the doctrine of regard to humans qua humans. Although all the ideas discussed thus far are involved in this reconstructed justification, at its very heart is the idea that human life receives its distinctive worth "from the way in which unrealized ideals shape its purposes and tinge its action" (MT 27). Whitehead's development of this idea is based on the notion that the laws of nature are really its habits, which means that nature is "plastic" in the sense of being open to "the introduction of novel law" and thereby the modification of its habits (AI 41–42, 78). Humankind "is that factor *in* Nature which exhibits in its most intense form the plasticity of nature" (AI 78). Endorsing Plato's view that the creation of the world is "the victory of persuasion over force," Whitehead adds that the distinctive worth of human beings "consists in their liability to persuasion. They can persuade and can be persuaded by the disclosure of alternatives, the better and the worse" (AI 83).

Reverence for Divine Power

Having mentioned various factors that have created bonds of sympathy and thereby an inclination to base human relations on persuasion rather than force, Whitehead completes his argument by speaking of "a greater bond of sympathy," of which he says: "This bond is the growth of reverence for that power in virtue of which nature harbours ideal ends, and produces individual beings capable of conscious discrimination of such ends. This reverence is the foundation of respect for man as man" (AI 86). As this statement shows, *Whitehead's moral philosophy is finally theistic.* Respect for humans qua humans is supported not only by our direct prehension of the humanitarian ideals (which we prehend whether we "believe in God" or not) but also by explicit *reverence for a Holy Power,*[20] understood as the power that is the source

---

idea that human beings necessarily regard themselves as "self-existent ends" is, in fact, the key idea in the articulation of Kant's moral philosophy by Alan Donagan (1993, 60–65).

[20] Arguably the most serious problem in Habermas's attempt to provide a philosophical grounding for democratic ideals is that although he says "reasoning discourse" cannot speak of something Holy (the "extraordinary" or the "unconditional"), he also holds, in the words of Peter Dews (1995 10–11), "that the life of even the most democratic polity will degener-

of all ideal possibilities and also, through persuasion, creates beings who can consciously choose among these possibilities. From this point of view, therefore, those who have encouraged atheism in the name of morality have been engaged in an ultimately self-defeating enterprise.[21]

A Wholly Good Holy Reality

Agreeing with traditional theists that the moral life ultimately needs the support of a theistic meta-ethic, Whitehead differs only about the conception of God that is needed, insisting that it must be one that has itself been shaped by our best ethical intuitions (RM 32, 35). Whitehead's doctrines that God is not related to the world like a despot to slaves (AI 36), that the will and infinity of God are not to be defined at the expense of the goodness of God (RM 40, 147), that God acts by persuasion, not coercion (AI 166), that God's love is all-embracing (RM 152), that God always returns good for evil (RM 148–49)—all these doctrines are aspects of Whitehead's ethical theism, intended to support a religion that would direct "conduct towards a unified purpose commanding ethical approval" (RM 30). Given Whitehead's doctrine of God, the natural human desire to imitate the Holy Reality supports the moral life.

The Holy Reality as Enriched by Our Actions

The God of process philosophy is important to morality not only as the source of moral aims and as a Holy Reality to imitate, but also as the ultimate recipient of our experiences and of the experiences that we influence. This idea is crucial, because, as we saw in Chapter 5, Whitehead says that "'importance for the finite' involve[s] the notion of 'importance for the

---

ate into oppressive and purposeless routine unless the transcendent sources of ethical energy and moral inspiration are periodically renewed." Because of this problem, Dews suggests (10), Habermas should reconsider his assumption that religious discourse must of necessity be cognitively inadequate. For a tightly reasoned argument, formulated partly in relation to Habermas, that democratic liberalism requires a framework that is both metaphysical and religious, see Gamwell's *The Divine Good* (1990).

[21] Most of those who reject religious beliefs while having strong humanitarian convictions understandably resist the suggestion that the latter somehow depend upon the former, but an exception is provided by Jeffrie Murphy (1988, 248). Although it is for him "very difficult—perhaps impossible—to embrace religious convictions," he has concluded that "the liberal theory of rights requires a doctrine of human dignity, preciousness and sacredness that cannot be utterly detached from a belief in God or at least from a world view that would be properly called religious in some metaphysically profound sense." Saying that "the idea that fundamental moral values may require [religious] convictions . . . appears to force choices that some of us would prefer not to make," he adds that "it still might be true for all of that."

infinite'" (MT 86–87). For Whitehead, this notion is at the heart of the intuition of holiness. Describing an experience in which a "sense of the value of the details for the totality dawns upon our consciousness," Whitehead says: "This is the intuition of holiness, the intuition of the sacred, which is at the foundation of all religion" (MT 120). Just after this statement, which occurs in the context of Whitehead's attempt to provide a cosmological justification for the ideals of civilized existence, he observes: "In every advancing civilization this sense of sacredness has found vigourous expression. It tends to retire into a recessive factor in experience, as each phase of civilization enters upon its decay" (MT 120). Whitehead's doctrine that God is consequent as well as primordial is, therefore, intimately related to his concern to provide a vision of human life in the cosmos that could reinvigorate civilization.

3. Whitehead's Moral Philosophy as Such

Having discussed those elements in Whitehead's philosophy that provide cosmological support for his moral philosophy, I turn now to this moral philosophy as such. I add the phrase "as such" because Whitehead's moral philosophy, in the largest sense of the term, includes all the points in the previous sections. Indeed, as I suggested at the outset of this chapter, he evidently considered this meta–ethical cosmological reconstruction to be the primary challenge for moral philosophy today. It was certainly the challenge toward which most of his own efforts were directed. Nevertheless, he also suggested, albeit sketchily, a moral philosophy as such.

A Spirit, Not a Code

On the issue of relativism versus universalism, Whitehead takes a middle position.[22] On the one hand, he rejects the idea of a concrete moral code applicable to human beings at all times and places. "There is no one behav-

---

[22] As Putnam points out, "[M]any philosophers confuse the notion of a 'universal ethic' with the notion of a 'universal way of life'" (1994, 184). Whitehead, like Putnam, wants the former without the latter. The distinction implied by Putnam has recently been spelled out by Michael Perry, who says that a conception of human good should affirm universalism—"Human beings are alike in some respects, such that some things good for some human beings are good for every human being"—as well as pluralism: "There are many important respects in which human beings are not all alike; some things good for some human beings, including a concrete way of life, might not be good for every human being" (1998, 65). Pluralism, in other words, does not entail complete relativism.

ior system belonging to the essential character of the universe, as the uni-versal moral ideal" (MT 14). On the other hand, he maintains that the term *morality* does have a meaning because it refers to a universally valid spirit or ideal: "What is universal is the spirit which should permeate any behaviour system. . . . Thus morality does not indicate what you are to do in mytho-logical abstractions. It does concern the general ideal which should be the justification for any particular objective" (MT 14).

What is this general ideal? Given Whitehead's statements that the "teleol-ogy of the Universe is directed to the production of Beauty" and that Beauty is "the one aim which by its very nature is self-justifying" (AI 265, 266), many commentators have taken Whitehead's position to be a utilitarian ethic according to which we should seek to maximize beauty in every situation. His position is certainly heavily teleological. Instead of saying that we should always seek to maximize beauty, however, Whitehead speaks of *importance*: "Morality consists in the control of process so as to maximize importance. It is the aim at greatness of experience in the various dimensions belonging to it. . . . Whether we destroy, or whether we preserve, our action is moral if we have thereby safeguarded the importance of experience so far as it de-pends on that concrete instance in the world's history" (MT 13–15).

The next question, of course, is what Whitehead means by *importance*. This word, he says, points to an extremely general notion, not to be reduced to any one of its specific forms:

> Importance is a generic notion which has been obscured by the overwhelm-ing prominence of a few of its innumerable species. The terms *morality, logic, religion, art,* have each of them been claimed as exhausting the whole mean-ing of importance. . . . By this false limitation the activity expressing the ulti-mate aim infused into the process of nature has been trivialized into the guardianship of mores, or of rules of thought, or of mystic sentiment, or of aesthetic enjoyment. No one of these specializations exhausts the final unity of purpose in the world. The generic aim of process is the attainment of im-portance, in that species and to that extent which in that instance is possible. (MT 11–12)

On the basis of these passages, we can see that Whitehead clearly does not identify morality with the aim to maximize aesthetic enjoyment. We would come much closer to his view if we said that his ethic states that we should maximize beauty in the most general sense, so that it includes moral, intel-lectual, and spiritual beauty as well as sensible beauty and aesthetic enjoy-ment, but even this would be too narrow. The only general principle is that *in any concrete situation we should seek to maximize importance insofar as it is at-tainable by us in that situation.*

This principle has several implications. First, because we all have different backgrounds and capacities, what it is most important for one person or society to do at a given time and place is not necessarily the same thing that it is most important for others to do. Second, because there are so many things that are important, even for a given individual, there is not necessarily only one course of action in a given situation that would exemplify the general ideal of seeking to maximize importance. Third, the central objection typically raised against utilitarianism does not apply to Whitehead's principle. That is, utilitarianism is usually taken to involve the following notions: that we have equal obligations to all human beings ("each one is to count as one"); that only the future, not the past, is morally relevant; and that moral rules, such as rules against lying and breaking promises, are to be violated if so doing will fulfill the utilitarian formula (generally understood to be "maximize the happiness of the greatest number"). Against these notions, it is rightly urged that we have a greater obligation to some people (such as family members and benefactors) than to most; that the past is often morally relevant (as when one has made a promise or accepted a favor); and that certain "deontological" prohibitions, such as those against lying, stealing, cheating, killing, and promise-breaking, are objectively (even if not absolutely) valid, so that they should not be overridden for the sake of some modest increase in the total happiness of the relevant parties. Whitehead's principle, by speaking in terms of importance rather than beauty, can incorporate all these dimensions of moral importance.

Broadening Our Sympathies, Enlarging Our Interests

One commentator has classified Whitehead's moral position as a "moral interest theory" (Schilpp 1951, 572). Although this classification is not wrong, it could be misleading insofar as it could suggest that Whitehead provided a *private*-interest theory. The whole point of Whitehead's position is that the aim of religious and moral education should be to *enlarge* our interests so that they include the interests of others, ideally to the point that there would be no tension between our interests and the common good.

Whitehead's position on this issue is rooted in his doctrine that every occasion of experience has a subjective aim, which is an aim at satisfaction, or what he sometimes calls an aim at intensity. This language could indeed make it seem as if Whitehead, like some other philosophers and psychologists, had made selfishness or egoism metaphysically obligatory. That would be the case, however, only if an occasion of experience necessarily aimed solely at its own immediate satisfaction, with no interest in how its decision would affect other experiences. But Whitehead's doctrine is that the subjective aim "is at intensity of feeling (a) in the immediate subject, and (b) in the *relevant* future" (PR 27). What belongs to the "relevant future" depends upon the occasion of experience itself, because the *relevant* future is that portion of the total future that the experience anticipates influencing. An occasion of experience, in other words, does not aim solely at its own enjoyment; it also intends to influence the future. Having articulated this twofold aim, Whitehead then qualifies it, pointing out that the two aims, while distinguishable, are not fully separable: "This double aim—at the *immediate* present and the *relevant* future—is less divided than appears on the surface. For the determination of the *relevant* future, and the *anticipatory* feeling respecting provision for its grade of intensity, are elements affecting the immediate complex of feelings" (PR 27). Our immediate enjoyment, in other words, can be significantly constituted by our anticipation that the present moment will affect the future in a particular way.

Whitehead is here, of course, simply describing an obvious fact of our experience. When we put money in a savings account, buy a gift for a friend, work for a good cause, or, less admirably, act so as to bring harm to an enemy, our present *anticipation* that our action will influence future experiences contributes to the satisfaction of the present experience itself. Having made this point, Whitehead then states its relevance to our present topic: "The greater part of morality hinges on the determination of relevance in the future" (PR 27). Although he does not say, as would a strict utilitarian, that the *whole* of morality depends on this determination, he does hold that the *greater* part of morality hinges thereon. What he means is that morality primarily involves the question *how much* of the future—of the world that will in fact be affected by our present decision—we take into account in making this decision and *how* we intend this present decision to influence those future events.

If the decision is moral to the degree that it intends to maximize importance in the future, this same point can be made in terms of acting with the intention to contribute maximally to the general good. We typically seek our own satisfactions, even if by so doing we detract from, rather than contribute to, the common good. Insofar as we nevertheless feel that we *should* act otherwise, we feel the well-known tension between duty and desire. This tension, however, is not metaphysically necessitated but can in principle be transcended. Having said, "Morality of outlook is inseparably conjoined with generality of outlook," Whitehead adds: "The antithesis between the general good and the individual interest can be abolished only when the individual is such that its interest is the general good, thus exemplifying the loss of minor intensities in order to find them again with finer composition in a wider sweep of interest" (PR 15).

When one reaches this state, one is still, of course, acting in terms of one's "interest." But it would be querulous to say that one is thereby still acting in terms of one's *private* (or *selfish*) interest because that language makes sense only insofar as there is a distinction between one's own interest and the general good.

This point can also be made in terms of the notion of sympathy. As suggested by Whitehead's comment about "[g]ood people of narrow sympathies" whose "moral correctitude is . . . so like evil that the distinction is trivial" (RM 95), his view is that *true* goodness involves broad sympathies. Perfect goodness would involve an all-inclusive sympathy. Given the embodiment of universal love, one would naturally want to act so as to promote the welfare of all, just as we naturally want to act to promote our own welfare. Insofar as our sympathies are broadened, so that we truly *feel with* the feelings of others, our interests will be enlarged. I will lift up three aspects of Whitehead's philosophy aimed at encouraging movement in this direction.

One of these sources of encouragement is the doctrine of internal relations, which is aided by the doctrine that enduring individuals are really temporally ordered societies of momentary occasions of experience. According to this doctrine, we are not strictly (numerically) identical with our past or future selves, and our present relations to our own past and future experiences are not different in kind, only greatly different in degree, from our relations to the past and future experiences of other people. This means, points out Hartshorne (1962, 16–18; 1970, 191), that the religious injunction to love our neighbors *as* we love ourselves is not metaphysically impossible, whereas it would be on the traditional view, according to which I am strictly identical with my past and future experiences and strictly nonidentical with—that is, only externally related to—the past and future experiences of other people. That traditional, substantialist view of self-identity through time has been used to support psychological egoism, which says that it is impossible in principle truly to care about the welfare of others. Given the Whiteheadian view, by contrast, my past and future experiences are "others" and yet I can clearly care about them. I can feel sympathy for those experiences of a day or a month ago that suffered some great pain or disappointment, and I can make present sacrifices to try to ensure pleasant experiences for my future self, perhaps by buying health insurance. If I can truly care about the welfare of the experiences "I" will be having in another twenty or thirty years, it is absurd to deny that I can truly care about the happiness of my wife, our daughters, or our grandsons in the next few minutes, days, and months. Bringing out the religious implications of this doctrine and its importance to him, Hartshorne says: "We can love the other *as our-*

selves because even the self as future is also another. The barrier to obeying the Great Commandment is then not metaphysical or absolute, but psychological and relative. On this ground alone I would not give up the event doctrine without the most rigorous proofs of its erroneousness" (1970, 198).

Once it is admitted that we can truly care for some other people, furthermore, there is no reason to deny that we can truly care for many others or, finally, for all others—that is, for humankind as such. Whitehead refers to this state, "where the 'self' has been lost, and interest has been transferred to coordinations wider than personality," as "Peace." Calling it "the barrier against narrowness," he adds: "One of its fruits is that passion whose existence Hume denied, the love of mankind as such" (AI 285–86). In this way, simply by providing an ontology that shows it not to be impossible, Whitehead's philosophy encourages us to broaden our sympathies, thereby enlarging our interests.

A second aspect of Whitehead's philosophy designed to encourage us in this direction is his doctrine that God is doing just that:

> God is that function in the world by reason of which our purposes are directed to ends which in our own consciousness are impartial as to our own interests. He is that element in life . . . in virtue of which our purposes extend beyond values for ourselves to values for others. He is that element in virtue of which the attainment of such a value for others transforms itself into value for ourselves. (RM 151–52)

We have here not only a succinct account of the rise of moral consciousness and how the resulting tension with one's self-interest can be overcome but also Whitehead's statement that the ultimate power behind this process is the divine influence. Accordingly, insofar as we become *religiously* sensitive, becoming responsive to the divine element in our experience, we will become more *moral* in the deepest sense of the term, getting our enjoyment from our contribution to the general good. Given Whitehead's doctrine of the God-human relation, there can be, in the language of Kierkegaard, no "teleological [religious] suspension of the ethical." The divine aim for us is directed toward the production of moral beauty.

A third factor in Whitehead's encouragement of the enlargement of our interests, to the point that we will naturally want to contribute to the general good to the greatest extent open to us, is his portrayal of God, the Holy One, as so motivated: "The consciousness which is individual in us, is universal in him: the love which is partial in us is all-embracing in him" (RM 152). Therefore, truly to worship God, which involves imitating God as much as possible, means working for the good of the whole world. This is what Whitehead means by defining religion at its best as "world-loyalty," in which the human spirit has "merged its individual claim with that of the objective universe" (RM 59). This ultimate coincidence of religion and morality at their best is also expressed in the earlier discussion of morality as the aim to maximize importance, which is the "ultimate aim infused into the process of nature." To seek to maximize importance is to adopt the divine aim as one's own. Given a proper understanding of both deity and morality, therefore, the most fundamental religious drive, the *imitatio dei,* will inspire true moral goodness, the enlargement of our sympathies and interests. Religion, says Whitehead, "is directed to the end of stretching individual interest beyond its self-defeating particularity" (PR 15). Religion at its best, far from producing "people of narrow sympathies," will stretch our sympathies toward all-inclusiveness.

Responding to New Ideals

Having seen that Whitehead's moral philosophy is theistic through and through, we need to examine one more dimension of this theistic ethic for civilized existence. Included among Whitehead's ideals of civilized existence is "adventure," so that to be fully civilized is not simply to know and repeat the best that has been done and said in the past but to seek to realize new perfections (AI 273–74). This idea fits, of course, with Whitehead's idea of God, who, as the source of novelty, calls us beyond the achievements of the past. "The pure conservative," Whitehead has famously said, "is fighting against the essence of the universe" (AI 274).

In one sense, this call to realize new possibilities occurs in every moment. Whitehead also speaks, however, of a divine call to actualize radically new ideals, which occurs only occasionally. Offering "an alternative rendering of Descartes' notion of perfection," Whitehead describes it as "the notion of that power in history which implants into the form of process, belonging to each historic epoch, the character of a drive toward some ideal, to be realized within that period." For an illustration of such an ideal, Whitehead points to the "ideal of human liberty, activity, and cooperation dimly adumbrated in the American Constitution" (MT 120). Suggesting an answer to the question *when* such extraordinary ideals are implanted, Whitehead says that "as the present becomes self-destructive of its inherited modes of importance, then the deistic influence implants in the historical process new aims at other ideals" (MT 103). Insofar as Whitehead finally equates morality at its highest with devotion to the divine aims, which seek the good of the whole world, morality would involve the adventurousness entailed by responsiveness to these radically new ideals.

Given Whitehead's sense that civilization is presently in crisis, with the human race being in danger of "wide wreckage," he would surely regard our own time as one in which the divine power is seeking to implant new ideals. As for what these ideals would be, Whiteheadians could reasonably differ. There is widespread agreement, however, on some ideals. Whitehead-ians have written considerably about the need for a politics and economics for the common good,[23] for an ecological ethic,[24] and for a postpatriarchal culture.[25] I myself argue for an ideal that I take to be implied by and inclusive of those other three: the movement to a democratic world order (Griffin forthcoming a and c).

4. Panentheism and Morality

Whitehead's moral theory, as we have seen, is ultimately theistic in two senses. The idea that moral judgments are based in part on objective moral

[23] At the center of Whiteheadian political writings is the principle of internal relatedness, which means that our private good is inseparable from the common good. This notion is especially central in the publications of Douglas Sturm (1981, 1988). See also writings by Kenneth Cauthen (1987), John Cobb (1981, 1982b), Herman Daly and Cobb (1994), Franklin Gamwell (1981, 1984), Robert Hoffert (1975), Randall Morris (1991), Leslie Muray (1991), Robert Neville (1974), Widick Schroeder (1981), and William Sullivan (1986).

[24] Given the Whiteheadian-Hartshornean doctrines (1) that all individuals have intrinsic value, (2) that there are varying degrees of intrinsic value, (3) that all individuals are internally related to their environments, (4) that God is internally related to the world, feeling its joys and sufferings, and (5) that God, not being coercively omnipotent, cannot unilaterally save the world from the destructive effects of modern technological society, it is not surprising that when the ecological crisis came to public attention in the late 1960s, process thinkers were among the first to produce explicitly ecological philosophies and theologies to support an eco-logical ethic. For example, Cobb's "The Population Explosion and the Rights of the Sub-human World" appeared in 1970, and his *Is It Too Late? A Theology of Ecology,* which first appeared in 1972, was the first book on the issue by a philosopher. Also, the first dissertation written in the new field of environmental ethics was subtitled *A Whiteheadian Study* (Arm-strong 1976). For further writings, see Armstrong 1986, 1989, 1991; Birch 1993a, 1993b, 1995; Birch and Cobb 1981; Cobb 1978, 1980; Cobb and Griffin 1976, chap. 4; Ferré 1976, 1993, 1996; Gare 1995, 1996; Griffin 1972, 1994; Hartshorne 1977b; and McDaniel 1989, 1990.

[25] The Whiteheadian principle of internal relations, which is central to the political and ecological ethics of process thought, is equally central to its support for the movement to a postpatriarchal culture. See publications by Kathlyn Breazeale (1993), Rita Brock (1988), Carol Christ (1997), Sheila Davaney (1981, 1990), Susan Nelson Dunfee (1982, 1989), Nancy R. Howell (1988, 1989), Catherine Keller (1986, 1988, 1990, 1996), Lois Livezey (1988), Susan L. Nelson (1997), Ann Pederson (1993), Marjorie Suchocki (1994b), and Marilyn Thie (1978).

principles, which human beings presuppose in practice, can finally be made sense of only in theistic terms; and the justification and motivation for generalizing our natural respect and sympathy for family and friends to human beings as such depends finally on reverence for the creator who brought us forth. There has been, to put it mildly, considerable hostility to the idea that morality finally presupposes any idea of deity. Although some of this hostility is irrational, some of it has been based on, or at least supported by, reasonable objections. I suggest in this section that a Whiteheadian position can overcome those objections.[26]

The Theistic Meaning of Moral Terms

For most theists, the meaning of moral terms is understood in terms of the will of God. Whether one asks in some situation what the "good" or the "right" is or what one "ought" to do, the formal answer, whether given explicitly or only implicitly, is "what God wills." There are three great advantages to this simple answer. First, the widespread modern view that these moral terms are meaningless is avoided.[27] Second, the problem of ultimate justification is solved because the word *God* refers to that which is taken to be holy, and *the holy* is that which is intrinsically good in an ultimate, nonderivative way, so that it would be meaningless to ask whether we should do that which the Holy One prefers. And finally, the problem of motivation—surely the most difficult problem for nonreligious moralities—is solved in principle, thanks to the universal religious desire of human beings to want to be in harmony with that which they take to be holy.

This is not to say that the problem of motivation is solved *in fact,* for at least two reasons. First, to say that we have a desire to be in harmony with the Holy Reality is not to say that this desire is always or even usually stronger than other desires, which may run counter to it. Second, besides the fact that there is a distinction between the holy as *conceived* and the holy as *perceived* or *felt,* the latter generally provides much stronger motivation than the former. If the two significantly diverge, so that what we *feel* to be holy is different from what we *think* to be holy, then our "belief that God

[26] The argument of this section draws heavily on Griffin 1980.

[27] I am not hereby endorsing the semantic view that the meaning of any of these terms can be said to be strictly identical with "the will of God." Although I disagree with G. E. Moore's claim that the meaning of "good" (and by extension "right" and "ought") is analogous to the perceptual meaning of "yellow" and hence completely simple and indefinable (1965, 13–15), I do hold that the meaning of these ethical terms *involves* a perceptual element, which is based on our nonsensory prehension of moral ideals.

wills such and such" will provide little motivation. This, however, is a practical problem: it is the task of religious education, worship, prayer, and meditation to make the two holies coincide. With those provisos, we can maintain the point that theistic morality solves the problem of motivation as well as problems of meaning and justification.

The Traditional Objection to Understanding Morality Theistically

There are many reasons why philosophers may object to conceiving of morality as dependent on theism. The most obvious reason is simply that many philosophers combine atheism with a continued belief in the objectivity of moral principles. If this objectivity were really dependent on theism, they would be forced into moral nihilism or at least the relativistic conventionalism exemplified by John Mackie, Bernard Williams, and Gilbert Harman.[28] Or worse yet, they would have to reconsider theism.

Although the strong desire to show morality to be independent of a belief considered false, and perhaps even morally harmful, may lie behind the arguments against any theistic understanding of morality, such arguments *have* been given. Most of them—such as the claim that "theistic morality" is destructive of true morality by appealing to crude self-interest (the desire to attain heaven and escape hell)—can be ignored as obviously not applying to process theism. But there is one argument, which goes back to Plato's *Euthyphro,* that must be answered. This is the argument that a theistic morality either makes the good arbitrary or implicitly makes it independent of God. This dilemma is based on the premise that either the good must be good because God wills it or God must will it because it is good. If God wills the good because it is good, this means that the good is independent of God, so that we should follow it because it is good, not because God wills it. But if it is considered good merely because God wills it, then it is arbitrary, and we must still ask whether we should obey God's arbitrary commands. This second horn of the dilemma involves the notorious "is-ought" problem— namely, that an *ought*-statement usually cannot be derived from an *is*-statement. Even if the is-statement is about the will of God, it is said, one would need an independently derived ought-statement to make the transition to

---

[28] Although philosophers understandably resist describing themselves as nihilists, there is no substantive difference between nihilism as Harman describes it, according to which "there are no moral facts, no moral truths," and his own "relativism," according to which "there are no absolute facts of right or wrong, apart from one or another set of conventions" (1977, 11, 131–32).

the conclusion that we should follow it. The argument, that is, would have
to run thus:

1. It is the will of God that we do X.
2. We ought to obey the will of God.
3. Therefore, we ought to do X.

As this argument reveals, we would still need an independent argument that
we ought to obey the will of God. And, it is often added, the mere fact that
God created us or has more power than we do—perhaps even the power to
determine our everlasting destiny—provides no morally relevant reason for
obeying the will of God, if we think it wrong. In any case, whether we grasp
the first horn of the dilemma or the second, concludes the argument, the
will of God does not define what is good, or right, or what we ought to do.

The Actual Ideal Observer

The question raised to the theistic view of morality just outlined is
whether there is any way to avoid the dilemma, so that the will of God
would define that which is good or right and yet not in an arbitrary way, so
that it would follow that we ought to do that which God wills. An answer
consonant with process panentheism can be given in terms of the moral theory usually called "the ideal observer theory." According to this view, that
which is right or good in any concrete situation is that which would be pre-
ferred by an ideal observer, meaning one who is *fully informed* as to all the
relevant facts, *perfectly benevolent,* and *impartially sympathetic* to the feelings of
all parties involved. Given this view, the traditional dilemma is avoided. On
the one hand, what the right thing for one to do in a particular situation is
not some truth that exists prior to the ideal observer's response. There is no
higher standard—such as some list of timeless duties or some utilitarian formula—in terms of which the right thing could be established. On the other
hand, the preference of this ideal observer is not arbitrary, in the sense of
capricious, because this observer is fully sympathetic to the feelings of all beings involved. Its preference, therefore, could not be for actions that would
result in unnecessary pain or injustice.

There is considerable agreement among philosophical ethicists that the
ideal observer theory spells out our best intuitions as to the criterion implicit
in our notions of what is right and good (Reynolds 1970, 1972). This notion
of an ideal observer, however, corresponds exactly with process theism's no-

tion of God, which is simply the ideal observer regarded as actual. That is, in the ideal observer theory as usually understood, the ambiguous term *ideal* means not only "optimal" but also "ideal as opposed to actual." In process theism's view of God, the second meaning is rejected while the first one, referring to optimality, is retained, because God is omniscient, universally benevolent, and impartially sympathetic. Would this not mean, therefore, that there would be widespread agreement that the traditional dilemma is resolved, so that "the preferences of God" could be regarded as providing cosmological grounding for our basic ethical notions?

Although this should follow, objections will be forthcoming because when most philosophers read the word *God*, the image evoked in their minds is not the God of process theism. Calvinism's arbitrary tyrant, who predestined a majority of the human race to hell, is hardly an impartial sympathizer. According to traditional theism more generally, God is omnipotent in the sense of causing or at least permitting—while having the power to prevent—all the world's evils, and it is implausible that such a being is sympathetic to the feelings of all sentient beings. Although, as Charles Reynolds says, the ideal observer is simply a secular version of God (1970, 163), it is a secular version of a thus far *minority* view of God, so that the word *God* still evokes images that make it psychologically difficult to think of God as an ideal observer.

Being a purely psychological problem resulting from lingering connotations of the word *God*, that difficulty does not constitute a philosophical problem for process theism, given its explicit rejection of those connotations. Lying behind this psychological problem, however, is a philosophical argument that the will of God would *not* necessarily be identical with the preference of a fully informed, benevolent, impartially sympathetic perspective. It is agreed, of course, that God would be fully informed because omniscience is one of the features of our generic idea of God. But many philosophers have argued that there is no necessity that a being worthy of the name *God* would be impartial and/or sympathetic to the feelings of all sentient beings. For example, Henry David Aiken says that "there is no logical connection between the metaphysical attributes and the moral attributes. Logically, there is no reason why an almighty and omniscient being might not be a perfect stinker" (1958, 82). P. H. Nowell-Smith states: "There is nothing in the idea of an omnipotent, omniscient creator which, by itself, entails his goodness or his right to command" (1966, 97). And J. Brenton Stearns maintains that there is no necessary connection between metaphysical eminence and moral eminence (1972, 213), from which it follows that, "given any metaphysical description of God, God's goodness is logically contingent" (214). In particular, says Stearns, there is no reason why a meta-physically supreme being, having attributes such as omniscience, should not be evil (212).

Although Stearns claims that this point applies even to more adequate views of God, such as Whitehead's (219), the discussion of perception in Chapter 2, when combined with the discussion of God in Chapters 4 and 5, shows this to be false. In denying that omniscience would necessarily involve impartial sympathy, Aiken, Nowell-Smith, and Stearns are evidently think-ing of divine knowledge by analogy with sensory perception. They would not, to be sure, be making the mistake of thinking of divine knowledge as "knowledge about," as distinct from "knowledge by acquaintance," as it is generally agreed that divine knowledge would be immediate perceptual knowledge, not inferential knowledge. But they are evidently thinking of this perceptual knowledge by analogy with *sensory* (especially *visual*) percep-tion, in which sympathy with the perceived is so minimal as to seem entirely absent. According to process philosophy, however, sensory perception is so unsympathetic because it is so indirect. *Direct* perception of other actualities is physical prehension, or perception in the mode of causal efficacy, which is, in Whitehead's words, "*sympathy,* that is, feeling the feeling in another and feeling conformally *with* another" (PR 162). Our best example of this sympathetic, conformal feeling is our feeling of our own bodily members. A better term than *ideal observer* would therefore be *ideal feeler.*

Hartshorne has applied this notion to the question at hand. Reminding us that our knowledge of our bodily members is the only regular kind of knowledge we have (except memory) that is obviously sympathetic, Harts-horne emphasizes the importance of using it as the model for thinking of the God-world relation (1937, 208).[29] He points out that this kind of knowl-edge, combined with omniscience, would imply perfect sympathy: "To fully sympathize with and to fully know the feelings of others are the same rela-tionship, separable in our human case only because there the 'fully' never applies" (1941, 163). And this means, Hartshorne concludes, that God's om-niscience implies that God is *necessarily* motivated by concern for the welfare of the world because God's own welfare and that of all other sentient beings

---

[29] I inserted the word *regular* in this statement to allow for another (but irregular) type of knowledge, ignored by Hartshorne, that is typically sympathetic, namely telepathy. Telepathy often involves sympathetic feelings of another mind—the word, indeed, means "feeling at a distance." See my analogy in Chapter 2 of telepathy and religious experience understood as a conformal feeling of a Holy Reality.

necessarily coincide (162–63).[30] Contrary to Stearns, then, it is *not* true that, "given any metaphysical description of God, God's goodness is logically contingent." Given process theism's metaphysical description of God, the divine goodness, contrary to Aiken and Nowell-Smith, *is* entailed by the divine omniscience.

In light of process philosophy's interpretation of our generic idea of God, then, God would exemplify all the characteristics of the ideal observer. Accordingly, insofar as the ideal observer is seen to provide the criterion for understanding the good and the right and thereby what we ought to do, the preferences of God provide this criterion. This is a result of no small significance because it means that the "theory" assumed by ordinary theists, that the right and the good necessarily coincide with the will of God, is supported by what is arguably the best *philosophical* theory.

The Epistemic Danger and the Ideal Participant

As sound as that conclusion may be, many moral philosophers will still be reluctant to acquiesce in even this type of theistic ethical position because of what can be called the epistemic danger, which is that theism would be used not only to provide meaning and justification for our basic moral terms but also to provide a tendentious way to decide, in concrete circumstances, what ought to be done. That is, most philosophical ethicists believe that we should make this decision through rational procedures, with "rational" understood to involve learning the relevant facts, including the interests of the various parties to be affected, and deciding through impartial and cooperative reflection upon the best course of action. Theistic morality, by contrast, has often been associated with the idea that God's will with regard to most issues is already known because it has been adequately revealed in the past, perhaps in the Bible, so that we would settle ethical questions simply by appealing to this revelation. For example, after arguing that God's moral judgments are always correct, Richard Mouw says that God "has publicised his moral views," which Mouw contrasts with "our own deliberations" (1970, 65, 66). There is, accordingly, reason for ethicists to be suspicious that theistic morality would circumvent rational deliberation by claiming that the morally right course of action can be known without it.

---

[30] The following thought experiment is suggested by Hartshorne: "[S]uppose all 'others' were within the body, as its members; then, since the need of the body is for the flourishing of its own parts or members, bodily desire and altruism would be coincident" (1953, 141).

That suspicion, however, like the ones previously discussed, depends upon the traditional doctrine of omnipotence, which lies behind Mouw's assumption that we have been provided with an infallible revelation of "God's moral views." Process theists might hold that scripture contains a revelation of God's general character and purpose, but not the sort of revelation that would preclude the necessity of rational deliberations about its implications for moral issues today.

Nevertheless, process theism's conviction that the ideal observer is actual does have epistemic implications. The God of process philosophy is not merely an observer or even feeler of the world's processes but also an *active participant* in them, presenting ideal aims for all occasions. At the human level, this doctrine means that we experience God-given ideals, including moral ideals, constantly even if—compared with our experience of sensory objects—dimly. Because of this immediate experience of norms and ideals, we do not get our ideas of right and wrong solely or even originally through the process of imagining what an ideal observer would prefer. Rather, we have some immediate intuitions, not all of which can be explained by cultural conditioning, of what is right and wrong, perhaps the strongest of which involve taboos (Little 1993, 80–81). This account of immediate intuitions can explain the fact that in spite of the ideational differences among the cultures of the world, those who are attuned to recent international developments find "a remarkable kind of cross-cultural moral agreement about human rights" (Outka and Reeder 1993, 3).

The reality of moral intuitions does not, however, obviate the need for cooperative rational deliberation. Our moral intuitions are usually vague.[31] The cross-cultural element in a moral intuition is usually closely intertwined

---

[31] Peter Strawson's essay "Ethical Intuitionism" (1949) is one of the writings often credited with demolishing the doctrine named in its title. Its strongest argument—aside from the critique of the idea of a distinct moral faculty, which, as we saw earlier, process philosophy also rejects—presupposes G. E. Moore's suggestion that knowing the meaning of "good" and "right" through an intuition is something like knowing the meaning of a color through an intuition. Strawson argues that just as it would be self-contradictory to say that "I know what the word 'red' means, but I can't remember ever *seeing* red," then—if "good" and "right" are indefinable intuitive concepts—it would be self-contradictory to say that "I know what the word 'right' or the word 'good' means, but I can't remember ever *intuiting* rightness or goodness" (1949, 25). Although that argument may be valid against Moore's intuitionism, it does not apply to Whitehead's, which distinguishes systematically between the data of perception in the mode of presentational immediacy, which are occasional and often vivid, and those data of perception in the mode of causal efficacy from which our inevitable presuppositions arise, which are prehended constantly but dimly. The claim that we know what goodness means because we directly intuit it does not require, therefore, that we had some particular experience in which we had an intuition of goodness as clear and distinct as our perceptions of yellow.

with various culturally conditioned values, some of which may now be in tension with the underlying values. And the content of two intuitions, such as the rightness of truth-telling and the sacredness of human life, may sometimes suggest divergent courses of action, a fact that shows that moral intuitions should be taken to establish only prima facie, not absolute, duties. In such situations, which are *most* situations, we can decide what should be done—what is most important in that situation—only through rational deliberation, taking into account all the relevant facts as well as all the relevant moral values.

The Motivational Problem

The severest weakness of nonreligious moral theories has involved the problem of motivation. Even if philosophers have been confident of their ability to provide helpful advice to people who already live in terms of "the moral point of view," they have admitted that their theories provide no motivational basis for inducing people into this point of view (Habermas 1993, 74, 79, 146).[32] Even the theory of the ideal observer, taken as merely hypothetical, suffers from this weakness, as pointed out by Harman: "Morality gives people reasons to do things. If an ethical theory is to be adequate, it must explain why this is so. Therefore, the ideal observer theory . . . is defective in that it does not say why anyone has a reason to do what he ought morally to do . . . , because the theory does not say why anyone should care about the reactions of this imaginary person" (1977, 91). Religious theists, however, do care about *God's* reactions. Although this fact has surely been partly due to theologies that have portrayed God as holding out the promise of heaven and the threat of hell, theists who no longer share these beliefs still care about the divine "point of view." This is because, I have suggested (perhaps ad nauseam), we are inherently religious beings and thereby want to be in harmony with the Holy Reality as we understand it.[33] Theism, accordingly, provides the basis for a complete moral theory by overcoming the crucial defect in the theory of a merely hypothetical ideal observer.

32 They also may add, as does Habermas (1992, 51; 1993, 79), that religion, in spite of its superstitious beliefs and other defects, remains the most effective institution for instilling this disposition or point of view.

33. The contention of this section, that understanding the dynamics of belief in a Holy Reality is the key to answering both the is-ought problem and the question of motivation, is supported by Geertz, who in describing the source of religion's moral vitality says: "The powerfully coercive 'ought' is felt to grow out of a comprehensive factual 'is' . . . [The power of sacred symbols] comes from their presumed ability to identify fact with value at the most fundamental level" (1973, 126–27).

[9]

Religious Language and Truth

Books on philosophy of religion often have the discussion of the formal issues of religious truth, language, and knowledge at the beginning. Given the position of many authors, this practice is necessary because their understanding of these matters, at least in relation to religious issues, differs so greatly from the customary understandings that the reader needs to be informed, even forewarned. In process philosophy of religion, by contrast, there is little if any departure from customary usages. Most religious language that appears to be referential, such as "God is loving," is understood to be *really* referential. Religious beliefs are considered *cognitive*—that is, capable of being true or false—and truth is understood straightforwardly as *correspondence* between a proposition and that to which it refers. Religious knowledge is understood, like knowledge in general, as *justified true belief,* and the kind of justification needed is held to be similar to that needed for other beliefs. Given this adherence to customary understandings, the discussion of these issues can well come here at the end of the book.

This location at the end is, indeed, preferable because part of the task of these final two chapters is to show how these customary understandings can, given the substantive position of process philosophy, be defended. The defense of the correspondence definition of truth, for example, presupposes several doctrines of process philosophy, including its panexperientialism and its prehensive doctrine of perception. A statement of this defense that is brief as well as intelligible can be given only if those substantive positions have already been explained.

This defense of the notion of truth as correspondence is crucial to this book. It has been presupposed throughout that truth in general is correspondence and that religious beliefs, such as belief in God, can be true in this straightforward sense. Many philosophers have claimed, however, that the notion that religious doctrines can be true in this sense is nonsensical because this notion of truth is bankrupt in general. Others claim that although some propositions can correspond to reality, religious propositions cannot. Both positions imply that religious language cannot be referential and cognitive. This chapter, which argues against both these positions, is divided into three sections. In the first section, I discuss the notion of truth as correspondence. In the second section, I provide a Whiteheadian defense of this embattled notion. In the final section, I present a Whiteheadian view of religious language as referential and cognitive.

1. The Notion of Truth as Correspondence

It belongs to our hard-core commonsense notions, I have suggested, that to say that a proposition is true is to say that it corresponds to the reality to which it refers. For example, the statement that "the president of the United States became obviously angry before the grand jury" is true if and only if the person holding the office of presidency of the United States at the time the statement was made had gone before a grand jury, had experienced the emotion of anger, and had visibly and/or audibly expressed this emotion in front of the jury. Likewise, to say that a statement is false means that it fails to correspond to the actual facts. For example, if the president had not really been angry but had merely feigned anger, the statement would be false unless emended to say "apparently became angry."

As these examples illustrate, the idea that truth *means* correspondence is presupposed in all our discourse. Outside philosophical circles, in fact, most people would be puzzled to learn that many philosophers have said that truth must be defined in some other way, such as "works well" or "is part of a coherent set of assertions." No, most people would say, the fact that an idea works well for some purpose or that it is part of a self-consistent view might provide *evidence* for the truth of the idea, but to say that it is true *means* that it corresponds to the actual situation.

The word *true* can be used, of course, in other ways. We can speak of a true friend, of being true to oneself, and so on. The issue before us, however, is what it means to say of statements, assertions, beliefs, propositions, or declarative sentences[1]—such as "Richard Rorty rejects the idea that truth should be defined in terms of correspondence" and "a Divine Reality exists and loves us"—that they are true. It is part of our hard-core common sense, the argument here is, that to call these propositions true is to say that they correspond with the realities to which they refer.

This notion that truth means correspondence is often referred to as "the correspondence theory of truth," but this usage is misleading for two reasons. First, because this notion expresses what we all *mean* by truth and cannot help presupposing, it is misleading to speak of it as a *theory* of truth, as if it were simply one debatable view among others, which we could give up on the basis of a good argument. We should, therefore, speak simply of "truth as correspondence" when referring to this commonsense notion of truth.

A correspondence *theory* of truth, by contrast, would be an explanation and defense, in terms of some particular philosophical system, of the notion of truth as correspondence. Whitehead's philosophy provides such a theory, but other philosophical systems give more or less different explanations and defenses. Accordingly, the second reason that it is misleading to speak of "the correspondence theory of truth" is that this expression falsely implies that there is only one such theory. When speaking of attempts to explain and justify the notion of truth as correspondence, therefore, we should use the plural, speaking of "correspondence *theories* of truth." If the focus is on one particular explanation and defense, we should speak, for example, of *Whitehead's* or *the early Wittgenstein's* correspondence theory of truth.

What I am calling "the notion of truth as correspondence" is similar to what William Alston, in defending "alethic realism" (realism about truth), calls the "minimal-realist conception of truth" (1996, 32). As a first approximation of what he means, Alston says: "A statement (proposition, belief . . .) is true if and only if what the statement says to be the case actually is the case. For example, the statement that gold is malleable is true if and only if gold is malleable" (5). Alston's point, in other words, is that the gold's being malleable "is both necessary and sufficient for the truth of the statement. Nothing else is relevant to its truth value" (7). More precisely, "the truth *maker* is something that is objective vis-à-vis the truth *bearer.* It has to do with what the truth bearer is about, rather than . . . its epistemic status, its place in a system of propositions, or the confidence with which it is held" (7–8).

As Alston's final statement makes clear, the realist conception of truth is

---

[1] I say later that propositions should be regarded as the primary truth-bearers, with the other types of entities, such as sentences, being truth-bearers in a secondary, derivative sense. For the sake of simplicity, I will anticipate that later discussion by henceforth speaking only of propositions.

opposed to all *epistemic* conceptions of truth, which somehow make human knowledge essential to the very nature of truth. For example, Bradley said that truth is "that which satisfies the intellect" (1914, 223); in a phrase that rightly or wrongly has widely been taken as a definition, Peirce referred to truth as "the opinion which is fated to be ultimately agreed to by all who investigate" (1931–35, 5:268); Putnam at one time said that "truth is an *idealization* of rational acceptability," by which he meant that "we call a statement 'true' if it would be justified under [epistemically ideal] conditions" (1981, 55). These epistemic conceptions all have in common, Alston points out, the idea that "[t]he truth of a truth bearer consists not in its relation to some 'transcendent' state of affairs, but in the epistemic virtues the former displays *within* our thought, experience, and discourse. Truth value is a matter of whether, or the extent to which, a belief is *justified, warranted, rational, well grounded,* or the like" (1996, 189–90). The realist view, by contrast, says that the truth of a proposition depends entirely on its relation to the state of affairs to which it refers.

Given this explanation of what Alston means by the "minimal-realist conception of truth," it is virtually identical with what I mean by the "notion of truth as correspondence." This judgment is supported by Alston's observation that a minimal realism could be looked on as an "inchoate" or "minimalist" correspondence theory (1996, 33, 39). Indeed, the "minimalism" of his view consists precisely in the fact that he rests content with this inchoate theory rather than working out a "robust" correspondence theory as such (32). Whereas the minimal-realist conception is satisfied to say that "a true proposition is made true by a fact," a "correspondence theory sets out specifically to say what that relationship is" (33). Alston's position is substantially the same as mine on these points.

Alston also agrees that this notion of truth as correspondence is the commonsense view, saying: "[I]t seems overwhelmingly obvious that the realist conception is the one we express with 'true,' when that predicate is applied to propositions, statements, and beliefs" (188).[2] From this fact, Alston draws the conclusion that it is "proper to omit any positive argument for the position," limiting the argument "to rebutting objections to it" (85). Agreeing

---

[2] This idea is accepted by many other philosophers, such as D. J. O'Connor, who says: "The correspondence theory of truth may be regarded as a systematic development of the commonsense account of truth embodied in such dictionary definitions for 'truth' as 'conformity with fact' and the like" (1975, 17). Paul Horwich, who preceded Alston in offering a "minimalist" view of truth, refers to the "common-sense notion that truth is a kind of 'correspondence with the facts,'" adding that the traditional alternatives to correspondence theories have been problematic precisely because "they don't accommodate the 'correspondence' intuition" (1990, 1–2).

with this point, I provide a defense of the notion of truth as correspondence in the next section by rebutting objections to it. I differ from Alston, however, in holding that this notion of truth can be adequately defended only by developing a full-fledged correspondence *theory* of truth. One of the main reasons behind the recent anti-realism about truth seems to be simply the conviction that it is impossible to work out the relation of correspondence conceptually.[3] This conviction can be overcome only by actually showing otherwise. I rebut objections to the notion of truth as correspondence, accordingly, in terms of a particular correspondence *theory* of truth, that provided by Whitehead.

2. A Whiteheadian Defense of Truth as Correspondence

In the present section, I discuss various reasons given by philosophers for rejecting the notion of truth as correspondence. By showing that these reasons do not apply, at least, to Whitehead's correspondence theory of truth, I show that Whitehead's philosophy provides the basis for defending the notion of truth as correspondence against well-known criticisms. These criticisms, which are numerous, are grouped under three main headings: (1) criticisms based on confusion, (2) criticisms based on a different ontology, and (3) criticisms based on a different doctrine of perception.

(1) Criticisms Based on Confusion

Several of the reasons sometimes given for rejecting the notion of truth as correspondence involve a confusion of this notion as such with various problematic ideas that are falsely taken to be implied by it. The fact that these ideas are not necessarily implied by the notion as such can be demonstrated by showing that they are not implied by Whitehead's correspondence theory. I will explain Whitehead's theory progressively by dealing with six such confusions.

The Confusion of Verbal Statements and Propositions

Some criticisms of the notion of truth as correspondence reflect the assumption that when truth is defined as the correspondence of a proposition

---

[3] For example, Donald Davidson, having dismissed his earlier objection to realist, correspondence theories (see note 9), now rests his rejection of them solely on his conviction that they are unintelligible (1990, 302–4).

with the reality to which it refers, the word *proposition* means a *verbal statement,* a *sentence.* One criticism based on this assumption is that the idea of correspondence is nonsense: there is no intelligible way in which a sentence, being composed of a set of words, can correspond to *things, events,* or *processes.* Another criticism based on this assumption is that it is meaningless to ask whether a given statement, such as "Caesar crossed the Rubicon," is true or false: it may be understood differently by the speaker and each of several hearers—depending upon, say, whether *Caesar* is understood to refer to Julius, a puppy, or a movie star, and whether *the Rubicon* is understood to refer to a river in Italy, a local stream, or an irreversible decision.

The question of correspondence, however, directly applies not to a sentence or verbal statement but to a *proposition* in the sense of a *meaning* that may be either expressed or evoked by a sentence. The difference can be illustrated by considering the three verbal phrases "It is raining," "Es regnet," and "Il pleut." In this case, the same meaning (proposition) can be expressed by three different verbal phrases. The previous example, by contrast, showed that one and the same verbal phrase, "Caesar crossed the Rubicon," could evoke various propositions in various hearers, all of which might differ, more or less radically, from the meaning the speaker intended to express.

To call a verbal statement true, therefore, is really a shorthand way of speaking. It may be a way of saying that the proposition that a speaker *intended to express* corresponds with the facts in question. But it may also be a way of saying that the proposition that was *evoked in a hearer's mind* corresponds with reality, and that proposition may be quite different from the one intended by the speaker. The one may be true and the other false. This ambiguity does not mean, however, that the notion of truth as correspondence should be rejected. It means only that we need to be alert to the important distinction between verbal statements and propositions—a distinction so important to Whiteheadian process philosophy that in the Introduction I included it among the core doctrines.[4]

This distinction is clearly central to Whitehead's position. In listing some "prevalent habits of thought" that he rejects, Whitehead includes the "trust in language as an adequate expression of propositions" (PR xiii). Expanding on this point, he says: "It is merely credulous to accept verbal phrases as adequate statements of propositions" (PR 11). Having referred to some thinkers who "presuppose that language does enunciate well-defined propositions," Whitehead comments: "This is quite untrue. Language is thoroughly inde-

---

[4] In my statement of the tenth core doctrine, I also included the distinction between propositions as such and "propositional feelings," which will be discussed later.

terminate" (PR 12). He also speaks of "the hopeless ambiguity of language" (PR 196), pointing out that "the vagueness of verbal statements is such that the same form of words is taken to represent a whole set of allied propositions" (PR 193). But this ambiguity or indeterminateness, which has recently been emphasized by Jacques Derrida, does not render hopeless a correspondence theory of truth—because truth and falsehood are qualities of propositions, not of linguistic phrases.[5]

Once this distinction has been clearly made, it can then be said that because verbal statements can be truth-bearers in a secondary, derivative sense, the practice of referring to them as either true or false is not wholly wrong. Although truth is a relation that *directly* applies to the relation between a proposition and that to which it refers, "There is an indirect truth-relation of the sounds or of the visual marks on paper to the propositions conveyed" (AI 248). This is the case because, within any particular group of people, "There is a right and a wrong use of any particular language" (AI 249). That is, any human society, in order to communicate, must have widely shared understandings of the meanings of words and phrases, perhaps enshrined in dictionaries. Because of these shared understandings, linguistic statements have the capacity to evoke propositions in the conscious experience of readers and auditors that are identical with, or at least very similar to, the propositions the writer or speaker intended to convey. The common practice is acceptable, therefore, if we keep in mind the fact that verbal statements can be said to be true or false only in an indirect or derivative way.[6]

The Confusion of Correspondence with Identity

A second confusion is the assumption that to affirm *correspondence* between a proposition and reality is to affirm their *identity*. It is obvious, of course, that a proposition, such as "Caesar crossed the Rubicon," is not identical

---

[5] Although the view that propositions are the primary bearers of either truth or falsity is controversial, it is supported by Alston (1996, 9–17), Horwich (1990, 89–93), and Marian David (1994, 45). The main reason why many philosophers reject this view, as Alston (9, 13), Horwich (92), and David (54–55) all point out, is the nominalist rejection of "abstract entities" on the basis of the physicalist view that only material entities exist. Against this rejection, Horwich, in spite of offering a deflationary view of truth, argues that propositions "participate in an adequate account of the logical forms of belief attributions," so that "despite their peculiarities, we should not balk at propositions" (93).

[6] One of many philosophers who reject this view is Putnam, who says: "It is statements (not abstract entities called 'propositions') that are true or false" (1994, 302). One of the problems with this view can be seen by the fact that it leads Putnam to the following self-contradictory statement: "While it is true that the stars would still have existed even if language users had not evolved, it is not the case that sentences would have existed. There would have still been a world, but there would not have been any *truths*" (1992, 368).

with the actual event to which it refers. If correspondence meant identity, the notion of truth as correspondence would be absurd.

Explaining Whitehead's response to this issue requires a more complete understanding of his doctrine of propositions. Including them among the eight types of entities listed under the "categories of existence," he says that, of these eight types, "actual entities and eternal objects stand out with a certain extreme finality" (PR 22). A proposition is a *hybrid* type of entity, combining actual entities and a (more or less complex) eternal object (PR 22, 185–86). A proposition, of course, must have a logical subject and a predicate. Actual entities constitute the logical subjects of the proposition; eternal objects constitute the predicate (PR 24). "The proposition is the possibility of *that* predicate applying in that assigned way to *those* logical subjects" (PR 258). For example, if I say "my wife is hungry and thirsty," the phrase "my wife" indicates the logical subject. The proposition asserts that her present occasions of experience are physically realizing the complex eternal object indicated by the phrase "hungry and thirsty."

The assertion that a proposition combines eternal objects and actual entities would seem, if not further qualified, to imply that a proposition, like an actual entity, could exert agency. The further qualification needed is that in a proposition the actual entities constituting the logical subjects are each reduced to a bare "it," meaning that there is an abstraction from all the concrete feelings that were in fact realized by those actual entities (PR 258, 261). As a result, the proposition is merely a *possibility,* not an actuality. However, unlike an eternal object, which is a *pure* possibility, a proposition is an *impure* possibility, because it refers to some particular actual entities (PR 22, 188). With this explanation, we can now give a more formal definition. *A proposition is the possibility of a definite set of eternal objects being realized in a particular way in a particular nexus of actual entities* (PR 186, 196, 257). A proposition is, therefore, a theory about particular actual entities, which may or may not be true.

Given this explanation, we can see why correspondence does not mean identity. Explaining why the question arises, Whitehead says: "A proposition is true when the nexus does in reality exemplify the pattern which is the predicate of the proposition. Thus in the analysis of the various component factors involved the proposition, if true, seems to be identical with the nexus. For there are the same actual occasions and the same eternal objects" (AI 244). That conclusion, however, would follow only if we ignored the all-important issue of mode of togetherness: "The nexus includes the eternal object in the *mode of realization.* Whereas in the true proposition the togetherness of the nexus and the eternal object belongs to the *mode of abstract possibility.* . . . Thus a nexus and a proposition belong to different categories of being. Their identification is mere nonsense" (AI 244–45; emphasis added). The confusion involved in the charge that correspondence would mean identity, therefore, involves neglecting a distinction between categorically different modes of togetherness.

The Confusion between the Meaning and the Possession of Truth

Sometimes the notion of truth as correspondence is rejected on the grounds that those who accept it thereby claim to *possess* the truth. For example, Roman Catholics may claim to possess the ultimate truth about sexual morality because of the alleged infallibility of the pope, whereas Marxists may claim to possess the ultimate truth about the goal of history. The way to undermine these arrogant claims, some critics suppose, is to deny the very notion of truth as correspondence.

That approach, however, is triply misguided. In the first place, insofar as socially concerned individuals give up the notion of truth as correspondence, they relinquish any intellectual basis for opposing the ideologies they consider harmful. In the second place, because truth as correspondence is one of our hard-core commonsense notions, all criticisms of this notion are involved in performative self-contradiction. In the third place, the notion of truth as correspondence is a notion about the *meaning* of the relationship indicated by words such as *truth, vēritās,* and *Wahrheit.* The claim to *possess* the truth, being a claim about *knowledge,* is a categorically different kind of claim, involving the assertion that one's beliefs are both true and justified. Although the idea of truth as correspondence may be a *necessary* condition for claiming to possess the truth, it certainly is not a *sufficient* condition. The way to battle truth-claims with which one disagrees is to argue that the beliefs in question are not justified by the relevant evidence. In any case, the notion of truth as correspondence is a notion merely about what it *means* to say that a proposition is either true or false. It implies nothing about any particular truth-*claims*.

The Confusion between Meaning and Verification

A confusion that blurs the distinction just made—between the *meaning* of "truth" and its *verification*—has been involved in one of the most commonly given reasons for rejecting the notion of truth as correspondence. Part of the reason this confusion has been so widespread is that the movement known as logical positivism was based on it, arguing that the very *meaning* of a statement is its mode of verification. James, in some of his extreme formulations of the "pragmatic theory of truth," had seemed to say something similar (albeit with a much wider notion of possible modes of verification). Although logical positivism is now generally rejected, its equation of meaning with verification has lingered. With respect to the issue at hand, this equation leads many philosophers to assume that to define truth as correspondence between proposition and reality is to prescribe a method of verifying that proposition. Then, arguing that we have no direct access to "reality in itself" apart from our ideas about it, they conclude that the notion of truth as correspondence must be rejected.

Although the question of direct access to reality is important, the question what the concept "truth" *means* can be discussed independently. We can know what a proposition means, and what it means to consider it true, apart from any mode of verifying it. For example, shortly before I wrote the first draft of this chapter, the president of the United States publicly expressed contrition for some of his wrongdoing and asked forgiveness. Some people believed the contrition to be genuine; others suspected that it was feigned for political purposes. We have no way of completely verifying whether the expressed contrition reflected sincerity or political expediency (or some combination thereof). In spite of this lack of any means to verify our beliefs about the president, however, we know what they *mean*. Those who were uncertain as to whether he was genuinely contrite understand what it is about which they are in doubt, which is whether the emotion that we call "contrition" was really experienced or merely feigned.

Whitehead distinguishes clearly between truth and verification. Important to this distinction is the distinction between a proposition as such and a "propositional feeling" in which that proposition is prehended by a subject. (I have pointed to the importance of this distinction by including it in the tenth core doctrine of Whiteheadian process philosophy.) The proposition's truth or falsity depends on its relation to its *logical* subjects (the nexus of actual entities to which it refers), not its relation to any *prehending* subjects (PR 258).[7] These prehending subjects may make a judgment about the proposition's truth and may even set out to verify or falsify it. But these beliefs and operations will not affect the truth or falsity of the proposition because this truth or falsity obtained prior to the proposition's being prehended by any of us.[8] In line with this point, Whitehead affirms "a 'correspondence'

---

[7] This is another way of making Alston's point that "the truth of a truth bearer consists . . . in its relation to some 'transcendent' state of affairs, [not] in the epistemic virtues the former displays within our thought" (1996, 189).

[8] It is assumed here that the logical subject of the proposition is already fully determinate. The truth of propositions about the future, of course, can be affected by our actions, as in

theory of the truth and falsehood of propositions" (PR 191). When he discusses the attempt to *ascertain* the truth-value of particular propositions, by contrast, he speaks of "coherence" and "pragmatic tests" (PR 181, 191). To define truth as the correspondence of proposition with reality, therefore, is not to refer to some method of verification.[9]

The Confusion between Partial and Complete Truth

Still another criticism of the notion of truth as correspondence is that it rules out complementary perspectives. To say that a particular proposition corresponds to reality implies, it is charged, that it tells the *full* truth about that reality. Perhaps, however, reality is indefinitely complex, so that other perspectives on it are equally valid. For example, the claim that Western medicine works because it is based on ideas that correspond to the human body had long prevented the recognition that Chinese medicine, which is based on very different ideas, also works. We must, the argument concludes, reject the notion of truth as correspondence to overcome this arrogant narrow-mindedness.

There is no doubt that human beings have a tendency to assume that their own firmest convictions are not only "the truth" but "the whole truth." This tendency, however, is a fact about human psychology. The mere fact that a philosophy affirms the notion of truth as correspondence does not imply that it would encourage that tendency. To see if Whitehead's would, let us look again at his definition: "A proposition is true when the nexus does in reality exemplify the pattern which is the predicate of the proposition" (AI 244). To say that the nexus exemplifies that pattern of eternal objects is *not* to say that it exemplifies *only* that pattern. The possibility is left open that it may exemplify an indefinite number of other patterns. And Whitehead's position entails, in fact, that this is the case, especially with regard to nexūs involving the higher-level, more complex occasions of experience. Whitehead supports, therefore, the position suggested in the prior paragraph, ac-

---

"self-fulfilling prophecies." James's tendency to suggest a general "pragmatic" theory of truth on the basis of this characteristic of propositions about the future created much confusion, disguising the fact that James generally presupposed the notion of truth as correspondence, as Marcus Ford has shown (1982, 59–74; 1993, 117–22).

[9] Although Davidson had long rejected correspondence theories on the basis of the "usual complaint" that "it makes no sense to suggest that it is somehow possible to compare one's words or beliefs with the world," he now says: "This complaint against correspondence theories is not sound [because] it depends on assuming that some form of epistemic theory is correct" (1990, 302). Given the fact that Rorty and many others have rested their case against correspondence theories primarily on the basis of this argument, Davidson's recent acknowledgment of its circularity is of considerable importance.

cording to which the world is indefinitely complex so that an indefinite number of propositions would be true with regard to any particular set of occasions of experience. Whitehead even spells out one of the appropriate ethical conclusions: "The duty of tolerance is our finite homage," he says, "to the complexity of accomplished fact which exceeds our stretch of insight" (AI 52).

The human tendency to equate partial with complete truth is also discouraged by Whitehead's criticism of the Dogmatic Fallacy, which is "the persuasion that we are capable of producing notions which are adequately defined in respect to the complexity of relationship required for their illustration in the real world" (AI 144–45). Insisting that most of our ideas are infected with "incurable vagueness," he states: "The notions employed in every systematic topic require enlightenment from the perspective of every standpoint" (AI 145). Saying that during the Middle Ages "the theologians were the chief sinners in respect to dogmatic finality," he adds that during recent centuries "their bad preeminence in this habit passed to the men of science" (AI 145). Given Whitehead's critique of modern science's tendency to commit the fallacy of misplaced concreteness, to which he here alludes, his endorsement of the notion of truth of correspondence does not imply that "true" scientific ideas tell anything close to the *whole* truth. The aim of deflating scientistic pretensions, accordingly, does not require the drastic step of denying truth as correspondence. Indeed, the notion of truth as correspondence is *presupposed* in any criticism of a partial truth masquerading as the full truth because one is pointing out that the partial formulation does not correspond to the complexity of the actual situation. To reject truth as correspondence on the grounds that reality is far more complex than our ideas about it, therefore, is to be involved in performative self-contradiction.

The Assumption That Truth as Correspondence Implies Naive Realism

A final confusion to deal with is the assumption that any defense of the notion of truth as correspondence would have to defend naive realism. The idea of truth as correspondence does obviously presuppose some version of metaphysical realism, understood as the assumption that the actual world is real independently of our perception and conception of it. Without that assumption, it would make no sense to ask whether any particular idea about the world "corresponds" to it because "the world" would be simply, or at least in part, a product of our ideas about it.[10] *Naive* realism, however, is an

---

[10] Although Alston in his book seems to say that realism about truth does not require metaphysical realism in this sense (1996, 81), he elsewhere, in giving a more complete statement of

extreme version, which holds that the world that exists independently of us is *the world as it appears to our sensory perception.* This doctrine would mean, for example, that the red of the robin's breast, *as we see it,* exists apart from the visual perception of human beings and all other animals. It has long been accepted, however, that colors are "secondary qualities," meaning that they are produced by our sensory perception. *Red as we see it* does not exist independently of our perception.

Whitehead's correspondence theory rejects naive realism. As we saw in Chapter 2, the prominent data in sensory perception, such as colors and sounds, are data of perception in the mode of presentational immediacy, *not* of perception in the mode of causal efficacy. Whitehead fully agrees that colors as we see them are "secondary qualities" because they arise "from one of the originative modes of the percipient occasion," not from the external region onto which they are projected (PR 122).

Whitehead's theory does retain, nevertheless, a form of realism. Although the world as it is *in itself* is extremely different from the world as displayed in our sensory perception, it does exist independently of our percepts and concepts of it. To think about other actualities as they are in themselves, Whitehead's whole ontology is devoted to showing, we need to think of them in terms of categories supplied by our own *experiencing as such* (rather than in terms of categories suggested by the *data* of our *sensory* experience). We can, therefore, intelligibly affirm the existence of a real world to which our ideas may or may not correspond.

(2) Criticisms Based on a Different Ontology

The previous criticisms involved various ways in which the notion of truth as correspondence has been confused with some absurd version or supposed consequence of it. The criticisms in this and the next subsection are based less on confusion than on alternative positions. The critics point out that, assuming the truth(!) of their own positions about ontology and perception, the notion of truth as correspondence is problematic. Part of the Whiteheadian response is that, given the fact that none of us can help presupposing the notion of truth as correspondence, even in the act of criticizing it (as the parenthetical exclamation point in the previous sentence was meant to indicate), the fact that the critics' positions are incompatible with

---

his position, says: "The facts that make true [statements] true hold and are what they are independently of human cognition" (1995, 39).

the notion of truth as correspondence should be taken as an indictment of their positions, not of the notion of truth as correspondence. The other part of the Whiteheadian response is to show that, given a panentheistic, panexperientialist ontology and a prehensive doctrine of perception, we *can* make sense of truth as correspondence. I deal with three criticisms based on alternative ontologies in the present subsection, saving the criticisms based on alternative views of perception until the next.

Atheism

One ontological reason for the denial of the notion of truth as correspondence is the acceptance of atheism, which implies that there is no all-inclusive perspective, only a plurality of partial perspectives. Given this position, one could argue that the notion of truth as correspondence, which holds that our ideas are true if they correspond to the way things really are independently of our ideas about them, is nonsense because there is no way things "really" are. The manner in which process philosophy's panentheism overcomes this problem was discussed under "The Argument from Truth" in Chapter 5.

Dualism: Overt and Covert

The other main ontological doctrine that has raised a problem for the notion of truth as correspondence is dualism—whether it be the *overt* dualism of the Cartesians, according to which mind and matter are actualities of ontologically different types, or what Hartshorne calls the *implicit* or *covert* dualism of materialism (1970, 9, 27). In this latter doctrine, dualism is verbally rejected, but the "physical world" is still assumed to be composed of things that are different in kind from human experience. In any case, ontological dualism, either in the overt or the covert version, seems historically to be the original source of the rejection of the notion of truth as correspondence between an idea and the thing to which it refers. An idea, it was realized, can correspond only to another idea. Given the assumption that the material world is not (contrary to Berkeley and other idealists) simply an *idea,* and that it is not (contrary to Leibniz, Whitehead, and other panexperientialists) composed of things that can *embody* ideas, the question arises as to how our ideas about the physical world could "correspond" to it in any meaningful sense. How, for example, could the idea that the robin's breast is red correspond in any way with the physical reality? The problem arises because dualists and materialists have understood secondary qualities to be *completely different in kind* from the characteristics said to inhere in matter in itself—the so-called primary qualities, which are said to be purely *quantitative,* as when it is said that colors are "really" just wavelengths.

This problem, by itself, should not logically have led to the rejection of the notion of truth as correspondence *in general* because even if it were impossible to make sense of this notion with regard to what are sometimes called "physical object statements," the slogan that *an idea can correspond only to an idea* would still allow our ideas about other human minds or experiences to correspond to them. For example, the statement "Kant rejected the ontological argument for the existence of God" is true if, in fact, one of the ideas held by Kant was that the ontological argument is unsound. Many philosophers who purport to reject the idea of truth as correspondence show an amazing ability to ignore this point. For example, to support his argument against the idea of truth as correspondence, Richard Rorty (1979, 1982) makes numerous assertions about the views of philosophers such as James, Dewey, and Quine, which support Rorty's case only on the assumption that his assertions correspond to what James, Dewey, and Quine actually believed.

In any case, although the generalization has been illogical, the widespread rejection in philosophical circles of the notion of truth as correspondence has been due to a significant extent to the problem created by ontological dualism for so-called physical object statements. Referring explicitly to this problem, Whitehead says: "All metaphysical theories which admit a disjunction between the component elements of individual experience on the one hand, and on the other hand the component elements of the external world, must inevitably run into difficulties over the truth and falsehood of propositions" (PR 189). Spelling out the way his "philosophy of organism," with its panexperientialism, avoids these difficulties, Whitehead writes:

> There is a togetherness of the component elements in individual experience. This "togetherness" has that special peculiar meaning of "togetherness in experience." It is a togetherness of its own kind. . . . The consideration of experiential togetherness raises the final metaphysical question: whether there is any other meaning of "togetherness." The denial of any alternative meaning, that is to say, of any meaning not abstracted from the experiential meaning, is the doctrine of . . . the philosophy of organism. (PR 189)

From the perspective of this alternative, Whitehead then completes his explanation of why dualism creates difficulties for truth as correspondence: "The contrary doctrine, that there is a 'togetherness' not derivative from experiential togetherness, leads to the disjunction of the components of subjective experience from the community of the external world." This disjunction creates "an insurmountable difficulty" because there can be no cor-respondence between "togetherness in experience, and togetherness of the non-experiential sort" (PR 190).[11]

Given Whitehead's panexperientialism, by contrast, no such difficulty arises. Eternal objects can be embodied by *all* actual entities, even those con-stituting those enduring objects called "elementary particles." Although du-alism, whether overt or covert, can also allow physical particles to embody eternal objects, it can allow them to embody only the purely *quantitative* ones, which Whitehead calls "eternal objects of the objective species" (PR 291), some of which were dubbed "primary qualities" by dualists. The so-called physical world cannot, according to (overt and covert) dualists, embody eternal objects of the subjective species. This is why, given a dual-istic or materialistic ontology, none of our ideas about physical things, ex-cept perhaps purely quantitative ones, could be thought to correspond with anything really in the things themselves. Given Whitehead's panexperien-tialist ontology, by contrast, all actual entities embody eternal objects of both species, so that propositions about the inorganic world that go beyond purely quantitative description can, in principle, correspond to it.

As indicated in the discussion of naive realism, this position does not mean that molecules embody, say, colors *as we see them*. Such qualities *are* second-ary qualities, being dependent upon the perceiver. In Whitehead's position, however, such secondary qualities are *not* created (miraculously) out of purely quantitative factors. They are created out of more primitive modes of ingression of eternal objects of the subjective species. For example, *red as we see it* is a transmuted form of *red as an emotion,* which *can* be felt by low-grade occasions of experience, such as those constituting molecules (PR 315; AI 215, 245). For this reason, Whitehead points out, his version of the doctrine that qualities as we experience them in sensory perception are secondary qualities "does not have the consequences which follow in the earlier philosophies" (PR 122). Spelling out this point, he says that sensory appear-ances can be true in the sense that

> the appearance has not built itself up by the inclusion of elements that are for-eign to the reality from which it springs. The appearance will then be a gen-eralization and an adaptation of emphasis; but not an importation of qualities

___

[11] Although the "insurmountable difficulty" to which Whitehead refers in this particular statement regards the epistemological problem of making judgments, my appropriation of his phrases to refer to the metaphysical or ontological problem of correspondence does not vio-late the intent of his discussion, which he begins by saying that "all difficulties as to first prin-ciples are only camouflaged metaphysical difficulties," meaning that "the epistemological dif-ficulty is only solvable by an appeal to ontology" (PR 190).

and relations without any corresponding exemplification in the reality. This concept of truth is in fact the denial of the doctrine of Appearance which lies on the surface of Kant's *Critique of Pure Reason*. (AI 293)

Assertions employing sensory-based categories, however, are not the primary beneficiaries of the fact that Whitehead's ontology allows assertions about the inorganic world to correspond to it. The most important consequence is that analogical assertions based on our own experience—assertions involving subjective categories such as emotion (subjective form) and purpose (subjective aim)—can in principle be employed. Dualists, regarding such categories as even further removed from the real world than colors and sounds, have sometimes called them "tertiary qualities." In process philosophy's panexperientialism, however, some of these subjective qualities are the truly primary ones.

In sum, the idea that propositions about the physical, inorganic world could not possibly correspond to it, even given the Whiteheadian understanding of correspondence, follows only if one is assuming the truth of an ontology that is either implicitly or explicitly dualistic. The inadequacies of those ontologies, however, have been shown in Chapters 1 and 3. The notion of truth as correspondence, furthermore, is one of our hard-core commonsense notions, which we continue to presuppose even if we try to deny it—as these philosophers illustrate by presupposing the truth of ontological dualism, whether the explicit or the implicit variety, as the basis for rejecting truth as correspondence. We should, therefore, reject the dualistic ontologies, not try to reject the notion of truth as correspondence.

(3) Criticisms Based on a Different Doctrine of Perception

In the contemporary discussion, the rejection of the notion of truth as correspondence is usually based primarily upon the ideas (1) that there are no observation statements, or even observations, that are theory-neutral and (2) that experience includes no pre-interpretive given elements. I will argue that Whitehead's philosophy shows that the acceptance of the former idea, as normally understood, does not entail the latter idea, which is the crucial issue.

The Denial of Theory-Neutral Statements and Observations

In rejecting the definition of truth as correspondence between a theory and reality, Cornel West says that he "rejects Reality as the ultimate standard since reality-claims are theory-laden, i.e., our truth-claims are mediated by our theories" (1986, 55). The reasoning behind this statement is spelled out in an explication of the position of Rorty given by West (1985, 263–64): "[T]he theory-laden character of observations relativizes talk about the world such that realist appeals to 'the world' as a final court of appeal to determine what is true can only be viciously circular. We cannot isolate 'the world' from theories of the world, then compare these theories of the world with a theory-free world." West's statement, along with the Rortian position behind it, reflects the widespread rejection in recent philosophy of a particular form of empiricism, which claimed that our philosophical and scientific theories could be verified or falsified by checking them against observation-statements assumed to be free from contamination from the observer's theory. It is now widely recognized not only that observation-statements are inevitably affected by one's theory, most basically by the philosophical worldview implicit in one's language, but also that the observations themselves are not theory-free because our *perceptions* are inevitably influenced by our *conceptions*. For West, Rorty, and many others, that recognition suffices to discredit the notion of truth as correspondence.

There are three problems with this conclusion. The first is the fact that commentators, in the very process of rejecting the notion of truth as correspondence, presuppose it. For example, West's claim that "reality-claims are theory-laden" is itself a reality-claim, from which we should draw conclusions only if it corresponds to the reality of human reality-claims. The fact that West is discussing human reality, rather than molecular reality, makes no difference to the fact that he is presupposing the notion of truth as correspondence. His position, therefore, is self-contradictory.

The second problem with the West-Rorty conclusion is that it reflects the confusion, already discussed, of the question of the *meaning* of the word *truth* with the question how, once we have settled that prior question, we *determine* whether some particular proposition is true or false. Another way of putting this problem is that, as Donald Davidson has pointed out, the West-Rorty argument against realist conceptions of truth *presupposes,* in a circular fashion, an *epistemic* conception of truth.[12]

The third problem is indicated by the fact that Whitehead, who defends

---

[12] Davidson's criticism of this circularity was cited in note 9. Another philosopher to whom Rorty had appealed to justify his rejection of truth as correspondence was Putnam in the latter's anti-realist period, when he held an epistemic theory of truth. Putnam more recently (1994), having rejected that view of truth in favor of "common-sense realism" (v), has disassociated himself from Rorty's attempt "to show that the whole idea that our words and thoughts sometimes do and sometimes do not 'agree with' or 'correspond to' or 'represent' a reality outside themselves ought to be rejected as entirely empty" (297).

the notion of truth as correspondence, had long ago affirmed the position taken by West and Rorty on observations. "Every scientific memoir in its record of the 'facts,'" Whitehead pointed out, "is shot through and through with interpretation" (PR 15). Expressing even more fully his rejection of the kind of empiricism targeted by West and Rorty, Whitehead distinguished between the "observational order" and the "conceptual order," then noted that "the observational order is invariably interpreted in terms of the concepts supplied by the conceptual order" (AI 154–55). If Whitehead insisted on this point (long before it became fashionable), perhaps it by itself does not imply the rejection of the notion of truth as correspondence.

This rejection would require, in fact, another premise—the claim that experience includes no element that is simply "given" in the sense of being prior to, and thereby unshaped by, the linguistic, conceptual structure that clearly does shape our conscious perceptions and descriptions of the world. West makes this claim as well, endorsing the *denial* that "there is a given element—a . . . theory-neutral, noninferential element—in experience which . . . serves as the final terminating point for chains of epistemic justification" (1981, 252). Given this denial, the notion of truth as correspondence to an independently existing reality would indeed be highly problematic because, beyond the fact that there would be no way to check for correspondence with such a reality, there would not even be any basis in experience for believing in such a reality. So although the *meaning* of truth as correspondence is, as we have seen, separable from the question whether we can ever *verify* correspondence, the defense of the intelligibility of this notion of truth is not unrelated to this question.[13] Because the denial of any given element in experience is so fateful as well as currently so widespread, it requires close examination.

The Denial of Givenness to Experience

"Truth and falsehood," says Whitehead, "always require some element of sheer givenness" (PR 258). This requirement is explained in a well-known statement by Whitehead's Harvard colleague C. I. Lewis: "If there be no datum given to the mind, then knowledge must be contentless and arbitrary; there would be nothing which it must be true to" (1929, 38–39). Because philosophers use the word "datum" in its original sense, to refer to some-

---

[13] As Alston says: "Even though an account of what truth *is* is not an account of how one determines what is true, it would still be a heavy cross for the realist to bear if it should turn out that on the realist account of truth, no one could ever determine the truth value of any truth-value bearer" (1996, 87).

thing *given,* it might seem redundant for Lewis to speak of a "datum given to the mind." His point, however, is that there must be a datum given to the mind *from the world beyond the mind,* as distinct from a datum provided to some moment or aspect of the mind by its own prior functioning. In the language of H. H. Price, one needs to affirm "data *simpliciter* [in distinction from data *secundum quid*] which is not the result of any previous intellectual process" (1932, 4).

Although Lewis and Price clearly saw the kind of givenness presupposed by truth as correspondence, they tried to defend the reality of such givenness while retaining the sensationist doctrine of perception. For example, in articulating what has been called his "sensory foundationalism," Lewis said: "Our empirical knowledge rises as a structure of enormous complexity . . . all [parts] of which rest, at bottom, on direct findings of sense" (1946, 171). His defense of givenness, accordingly, had to be made in terms of the assumption that perception is most fundamentally ("at bottom") *sensory* perception. Likewise, in Price's chapter "The Given" (1932), the chief example offered is the visual perception of a tomato. Although Price does not claim that the tomato's actuality is given, he does claim givenness for various sensory data, such as redness and roundness (4–6). In the same vein, another well-known defender of givenness, Roderick Chisholm, refers to sensa such as blue, noise, hot, and bitter to illustrate the kinds of objects given in sensory perception (1977, 28, 77).

Defended in such terms, the idea of givenness has been widely, and rightly, rejected. Wilfrid Sellars, in a well-known critique of "the myth of the given" (1950), has argued cogently that sensory data are *constructed* by the perceiver, not passively received. More recently, a similar position has been supported by Michael Williams. "Evidence from the psychology of perception," says Williams, "all points to there being no such thing as a state of sensuous apprehension utterly unaffected by beliefs, desires and expectations and consequently no experience of the given as such" (1977, 45–46).

Although these critiques of givenness are fatal to the defenses offered by Lewis, Price, and Chisholm, they do not apply to Whitehead's position. As the statement by Williams most clearly illustrates, these critiques all move from the claim that *sensory* data are not given to the mind from beyond itself, with which Whitehead agrees, to the claim that there is "no experience of the given as such," which would follow only on the assumption that sensory perception is our primary mode of perception. As we saw in Chapter 2, however, the entirety of Whitehead's epistemology, with its "reformed subjectivist principle," is oriented around the rejection of this widespread assumption. Sensory perception in its fullness is a *complex* mode of perception, involving a combination of two prior modes: (1) perception in the mode of causal efficacy and (2) perception in the mode of presentational immediacy. Of these, the second—sensory perception in the Humean sense, which provides nothing but sensory data—is derivative from the first, which provides direct knowledge of other actualities.

Thanks to this distinction, Whitehead's defense of the kind of givenness required by truth as correspondence is not undermined by the awareness that the data of sensory perception are not given from without. Whitehead, in fact, insists on this latter point. As I said in my own exposition of Whitehead's position in the discussion of "Givenness and Religious Experience" in Chapter 2:

> The data of presentational immediacy arise only in a later phase (PR 172, 180): these data are "data"—that is, *given* elements—not in the sense of being given *to the occasion of experience from beyond itself* but only in the sense of being given *to perception in the mode of presentational immediacy by the prior functioning of that occasion of experience itself.*

In Price's terminology, the data of presentational immediacy are not "data *simpliciter*" but merely "data *secundum quid.*" Whitehead, nevertheless, can affirm the existence of data *simpliciter* because of his affirmation of a presensory mode of perception. While recognizing with Sellars and Williams that the data of sensory perception are self-produced, Whitehead can still, therefore, say that each act of self-production arises "out of some primary given phase" (S 8).

The data given to this phase are not only presensory but also prelinguistic and preconceptual. Nowadays the denial of givenness is often made primarily in terms of the claim that our experience of the world is shaped from beginning to end, from bottom to top, by our linguistic, conceptual categories, so that no distinction between given and interpretative elements can be made. Experience, say many philosophers, is interpretation all the way down. For example, in a statement endorsing Kant's position, Wayne Proudfoot says: "We have no access to any uninterpreted given. All the data to which we appeal are informed and categorized by antecedent judgments and interpretations" (1985, 3). That claim, however, is self-stultifying: Proudfoot is intending to tell us how experience really works, thereby presupposing that he and those on whom his account builds have some direct access to it, but his account implies that no one has such access, that we can give only interpretations of interpretations. His account, therefore, presupposes that experience includes a given, in the sense of a preconceptual element. Whitehead's analysis of experience shows how it can have such an element, in spite of the great degree to which the mind actively constructs its own perception of the world in terms of culturally conditioned concepts.

One of the crucial features of Whitehead's analysis is the idea that experience begins with physical prehensions of prior experiences (be they one's own past experiences, the experiences of one's bodily cells, the experiences of other minds, or the divine experiences), so that concepts, propositions, and consciousness arise only subsequently. As we saw in Chapter 2, the idea that experience begins with *physical* prehensions—rather than, as Hume argued, with conceptual experience—is necessary to explain many of our hard-core commonsense convictions, such as our presuppositions about causality, the external world, the past, and the functioning of our bodies in sensory perception. To be sure, this given phase is immediately followed by the rise of conceptual prehensions, propositional prehensions, and then possibly intellectual prehensions with their subjective form of consciousness. Experience is, therefore, conceptually shaped *almost* all the way down, and *conscious* experiences always involve interpretations. It is on this basis that Whitehead argued that our observations, be they sensory observations of the external world or introspective observations of our own conscious experience, are always shaped by our inherited conceptual order, so that all observation, in this sense, is theory-laden. That recognition, however, is compatible with his insistence that each moment of experience begins with a preconceptually given element, of which we *can* become more or less clearly conscious, so that, in *this* sense, our conscious observations do include theory-independent elements.

Equally crucial to Whitehead's explanation of this compatibility is his point that human experience comes in discrete *occasions* of experience, because this point shows how our experience can be influenced by given elements many times per second. Those who argue the impossibility of such elements, in light of the all-pervasiveness of our interpretative categories, seem to be presupposing the idea of the mind as an enduring entity or process in which the linguistic and other concepts and categories are simply there—lying in wait, as it were—ready to shape every percept as it enters. But if the enduring mind is really a temporal society of momentary occasions of experience, we can see how the conceptual functioning, rather than lying in wait, would be *evoked into being* in each new occasion by its prehensions of antecedent actualities.

The most important of these actualities, to be sure, would be one's own prior occasion of experience, with all *its* concepts, intellectual feelings, and other interpretations. In *this* sense, there *is* interpretation all the way down, or from the outset. This *received* interpretation, however, is part of that which is *given* to the occasion. It is not the present occasion's *own* interpretation but that of the previous occasion. This distinction explains why we are not completely at the mercy of our prior interpretations but can revise them. Because our own past experience is *given* to our present experience, rather than strictly (numerically) identical with it, we can *improve* on previous interpretations of our experience and of human experience in general—an assumption that is shared by psychotherapy, by the rise of new schools of psychology, and by attempts (such as Proudfoot's) to give better accounts of the nature of human experience.

The prior actualities given to a new occasion of experience include, of course, more than simply one's own past experience. All past occasions are given. In each moment, we receive, simultaneously with our past interpretations, raw data from God, our brains, and other things. *These data are not shaped at the entrance gate by the received interpretations but enter on an equal footing with them,* being data of fellow physical feelings. When the occasion's own interpretations of the data of all these feelings arise, therefore, the prior interpretations can be corrected in the light of some of these data. For this reason, after stating that "the observational order is invariably interpreted in terms of the concepts supplied by the conceptual order," Whitehead can also say that "novel observations modify the conceptual order" (AI 155). This modification is possible because although every conscious observation, as a whole, involves interpretations in terms of inherited concepts, every moment of experience that rises to consciousness does include preconceptual data. Thanks to these prelinguistic, preconceptual data, new observations can lead us to correct old theories. Otherwise, progress in the natural and social sciences, in the sense of replacing older theories with ones that correspond more accurately to certain aspects of the world, would be impossible, as would be progress in philosophy of religion and theology.

Whitehead's account of perception, accordingly, conceptually provides that "element of sheer givenness" that is required for truth and falsehood (PR 258). The fashionable rejection of the notion of truth as correspondence on the grounds that experience includes no such element of givenness is simply based on a different account of perception, an account that, besides creating the various problems examined in Chapter 2, is self-stultifying. Combining this conclusion with the results of the prior parts of this section, we can see that Whitehead's philosophy is able to avoid or overcome the various objections that have been raised against the notion of truth as correspondence. These objections provide, therefore, no general grounds for denying that religious doctrines can, in principle, be true in the sense of corresponding (more or less adequately) to reality.

Late modern philosophy's problems with the notion of truth as correspondence result primarily from the same source as most of its other problems: its acceptance of naturalism$_{sam}$. Each of the three aspects of this version of naturalism—its sensationism, its atheism, and its materialistic view of nature—contributes to the difficulty of formulating an intelligible correspondence theory of truth. Such a theory can be provided, however, in terms of process philosophy's naturalism$_{PPP}$. Many philosophers will consider outrageous the suggestion that to make sense of the notion of truth they cannot help presupposing, they must accept a panexperientialist ontology, a doctrine of perception based on nonsensory prehension, and a version of theism. History has proved, however, that the fact that some suggestions initially seem outrageous is no disproof of their truth—at least when what is outraged is simply culturally conditioned (soft-core) common sense. In any case, having shown that Whitehead's philosophy allows us to make sense of the notion of correspondence with regard to statements in general, we turn now to the issue of religious statements in particular.

3. Religious Language

"The central problem with religious discourse," says Lyman Lundeen at the outset of his book on the relevance of Whitehead's theory of language for religious faith, "has to do with the nature of the claims expressed. Does religious language have a cognitive significance in addition to its obvious affective appeal?" (1972, 2). For claims to have "cognitive significance" is for them to state propositions that are capable of being either true or false. Stephen Franklin, in his book on the same topic, begins by saying that he discovered in Whitehead's philosophy "a profound metaphysical vision which allowed for the possibility of God-language conveying genuine claims about what is the case" (1990, ix). I will largely rely on the fine books by Franklin and Lundeen in this section.

Although process philosophy does not consider the problems of language to be prior to ontological and epistemological problems, it does take difficulties posed by language with utmost seriousness. "The great difficulty of philosophy," says Whitehead, "is the failure of language" (MT 49). One sign of the centrality of linguistic problems in his philosophy is the fact that of the eleven habits of thought that are repudiated at the outset of *Process and Reality,* two of them involve language. One of them, the "trust in language as an adequate expression of propositions," was mentioned earlier. A second of these repudiated doctrines is the "subject-predicate form of expression" (PR xiii). The chief problem created by it is the subject-quality metaphysics, according to which the ultimate actualities are mutually independent substances with their purely private qualities. Whitehead's remedy is his doctrine that actual entities are prehensive occasions of experience, each of which arises out of internalized relations to prior actualities.

The present topic, of course, is not Whitehead's theory of language in general but its relevance for understanding religious language, especially its cognitivity and referentiality. As Franklin has pointed out, however, "Religious language is no different metaphysically from any other form of language" for Whitehead. "What is true of all language in general is also true of religious language in particular" (1990, 352, 367). Developing a process philosophy of religious language, accordingly, involves an application of Whitehead's general understanding of language to the religious domain. Unlike many other such "applications," this one does not involve an allegedly general theory that was developed without the religious domain in view. Rather, as explained in Chapter 1, Whitehead's philosophy, which includes his philosophy of language, is explicitly developed as much in light of aesthetic, ethical, and religious experience as in light of scientific and everyday sensory experience.

Although religious language is not metaphysically different from other forms of language, it is different in terms of its purposes and referents. The purpose of language in general is to elicit propositions. What is distinctive about religious language, points out Franklin, is that it "is meant to elicit propositions about such items as the coordination of values and God" (1990, 358). Lundeen, making the same point in different terms, describes the "primary characteristic of religious language [as] its expression of fundamental personal and corporate convictions about the meaning of life," along with reference to the convictions about ultimate reality "which make these attitudes appropriate" (1972, 4–7).

In philosophical reflection about theistic religion, this reference to God has been the primary source of the view that religious language is uniquely problematic. There have been three main reasons for thinking that language about God cannot be referential and cognitive, in the sense of expressing propositions that could in principle correspond to reality: (1) the idea that the purpose of religious language, including God-language, is to evoke various attitudes and emotions in people, not to communicate information; (2) the idea that God-ideas do not arise out of perceptual experience, which implies that there would be no reason to expect these ideas to correspond to anything existing independently of us; and (3) the idea that God is infinitely different from any finite thing, so that no categories developed for dealing with finite things could possibly apply to God.

Religious Language as Referential and Nonreferential, Cognitive and Noncognitive

During the past century, there has been much discussion about the non-referential, noncognitive functions of religious language. Philosophers have repeatedly pointed out that the central purpose of at least much religious language, even language in which the word *God* is used, is not to communicate information but to produce some affective or behavioral response in the reader or hearer: to evoke belief, awe, fear, gratitude, worship, praise, love, repentance, obedience, recommitment, or generosity (especially, cynics would say, when the offering plate is passed). Having realized that the central intention is not to provide information about God, some philosophers of religion, such as D. Z. Phillips (1976, 45–48, 148), have concluded that this intention is completely absent. A Whiteheadian analysis of religious language leads to a different conclusion.

Whitehead does, to be sure, emphasize the noncognitive functions of religious language because he emphasizes the noncognitive functions of language in general. In Franklin's words: "Whitehead emphasized that human language has many functions beyond that of describing what is the case. In fact, in his view, these other uses are far more foundational than that of conveying information" (1990, ix). Whitehead says, for example, that "it is a mistake to think of words as primarily the vehicle of thoughts" (PR 182). According to Whitehead's position, "the fundamental goal of language is not so much to communicate factual descriptions of the world as it is to elicit feelings of the world"—so concludes Franklin's analysis (1990, 243). "The most important aspect of language," Lundeen's analysis similarly finds, "is its capacity to elicit the deep feelings and emotions of concrete experience" (1972, 47). This fact about language in general is especially true of much religious language. Whitehead agrees, in short, with those who have stressed the nonreferential, noncognitive functions of religious language.

Speaking of "religious language," even "theistic language," in such broad generalities is, of course, problematic. The genus *religious language* has many species, and the generalizations just discussed would apply to some of them more than to others. Franklin, for example, suggests a threefold classification: language of intuition, of exemplification, and of explication. The language of explication, employed by philosophers and theologians, will usually be more oriented to communication of cognitive ideas than are the other two. Philosophers with a noncognitivist view of religious language often distinguish this philosophical-theological language of explication from the "real" religious language of seers, prophets, preachers, and ordinary believers. As Franklin's threefold classification suggests, however, there is no basis for this invidious distinction, as if the attempt to articulate the presuppositions of one's faith in a disciplined, coherent way were somehow less of a religious activity than singing hymns, preaching love of neighbor, or shouting "Praise the Lord!" Nevertheless, even given this distinction between different types of religious language, we can agree with the point that the primary purpose of most religious language is not to convey information about what is the case.

Whitehead, however, makes this point without moving to the opposite extreme of denying that religious language is intended to convey *any* such information. As we saw earlier, language serves both to *express* propositions that were in the mind of the speaker/writer and to *evoke* propositions in the mind of the hearer/reader. Language can be used to communicate because it is possible for a statement to evoke in the hearer/reader approximately the same proposition intended by the speaker/writer. Accordingly, although theistic language serves primarily to evoke emotions, attitudes, affirmations, and action, it also evokes propositions that attribute various characteristics to God. Take, for example, the exclamation "Praise God!" Propositions intended by the speaker and/or evoked in the hearer would probably include "God exists (i.e., there is a Divine Being, a Creator)" and "God is good (i.e., worthy of praise)." Besides having nonreferential functions, theistic language intends to refer, so it can be true or false. As Franklin says, "debates whether religious language is cognitive or noncognitive are quite misplaced" because religious language, like all language, "has both a cognitive and a noncognitive element" (1990, 367, 365).

Whitehead's analysis of the relations among language, propositions, and propositional feelings provides the basis for both understanding and overcoming the misplaced debates on the cognitive status of religious language. In my discussion of language thus far, I have said that language evokes propositions. Although that statement is correct, it is a shorthand way of stating the fuller truth, which is that language *indirectly* evokes propositions by *directly* evoking "propositional feelings." A propositional feeling (or prehension) is, of course, a feeling (positive prehension) that has a proposition as its datum. For example, if during a telephone conversation my German sister-in-law says, "Es regnet," her statement evokes in me a feeling of the proposition that I usually express by saying, "It is raining." This proposition has been elicited in me, but only indirectly, as the datum of the propositional feeling. The proposition is simply the meaning as such, whereas my propositional *feeling,* like every feeling, has a *subjective form* (as well as an objective datum). For example, I may feel the proposition with the subjective form of delight (if, say, her region had been having a drought) or of horror (if, say, more rain at the moment will endanger the lives of her loved ones). More simply, I may prehend it with either disbelief (if it is August and I think my sister-in-law is kidding me) or belief (if I have no reason to doubt her statement).

Because language, in Franklin's words, "elicits propositional prehensions and not just propositions" (1990, 362), it "also elicits the subjective forms with which we prehend the specified propositions." The speaker/writer can, of course, deliberately seek to elicit some particular subjective form in the hearer/reader. This attempt, indeed, is often the central goal—a fact that illustrates the point that the nonreferential, noncognitive function of language is often primary. This fact, however, must not be used to conclude that this attempt to elicit a particular subjective form of response is the real *meaning* of the statement. In a statement that nicely summarizes his position, Whitehead spoke directly to this possible confusion:

> No verbal sentence merely enunciates a proposition. It always includes some incitement for the production of an assigned psychological attitude in the prehension of the proposition indicated. It other words, it endeavours to fix the subjective form which clothes the feeling of the proposition as a datum. There may be an incitement to believe, or to doubt, or to enjoy, or to obey. This incitement is conveyed partly by the grammatical mood and tense of the verb, partly by the whole suggestion of the sentence, partly by the whole content of the book. . . . In the discussion of the nature of a proposition, a great deal of confusion has been introduced by confusing this psychological incitement with the proposition itself. (AI 312)

It has probably been in relation to religious language that the confusion to which Whitehead here refers has been greatest. For example, from the fact that the statement "God is love" is usually made with the desire to foster a loving disposition, some philosophers have concluded that the very meaning of the statement—the proposition expressed—is something like "Be loving!" or "I intend to live a loving life. Why don't you, too?" Whitehead's analysis—which clearly distinguishes between the verbal statement and the proposition, and between both of these and the propositional feeling (with its subjective form)—provides a basis for recognizing and avoiding confusion of this kind. Even if the primary purpose of a verbal statement is the evocation of some particular subjective form, a proposition, which relates some predicate to some logical subject, is always at least implied. And usually, as Franklin says, "the emphasis is on both the content of the feelings and the way that content is felt" (1990, 243–44). In saying "God forgives sinners," for example, a preacher may be equally interested in suggesting that we should be forgiving to those who have wronged us and in saying something true about God—thereby explaining why it is *appropriate* for us to forgive one another.

The Givenness of God

Even if nothing about the multiple functions of religious language counts against its referentiality and cognitivity, there are other reasons for doubt.

One of these is whether God is in any sense *given* to experience. Whitehead himself points out that "meaning" is reduced to a mystery if the logical subjects indicated by a proposition are not given to experience (PR 168). His doctrine of symbolic reference, according to which the clearer data of presentational immediacy refer to the vaguer but insistent data given in the perceptual mode of causal efficacy, "does away with any mysterious element in our experience which is merely meant, and thereby behind the veil of direct perception" (S 10). As we saw in Chapter 2, however, most modern thinkers have agreed with the judgments of Samuel Preus and Gordon Kaufman, according to which "God is not given" (Preus 1987, xv), so that, whatever the word *God* means, it does not refer "to anything we directly experience" (Kaufman 1993, 415). This assumption implies that there would be no reason to assume that God-talk even roughly corresponded to reality. But this assumption presupposes the sensationist theory of perception, which has created insoluble problems for modern epistemology.

These problems, as we have seen, can be overcome by Whitehead's prehensive doctrine of perception (suggesting that it is somewhat closer to the full truth about human perception). On the basis of this otherwise more adequate doctrine there is no reason to deny, and many reasons to affirm, that we do directly perceive a Holy Actuality. This perception, of course, is seldom if ever *given to consciousness* with the same clarity as are some sensory data. But these sensory data, as we have seen, are not really *given to experience* at all (as opposed to being created for consciousness by preconscious experiential activities). We must compare our prehension of God, accordingly, not with the data of presentational immediacy but with other prehensions of actualities in the mode of causal efficacy. And here the vagueness is comparable. We can be somewhat clearly aware of prior moments of our own experience. We are somewhat less clearly aware of our sensory organs, being, for example, much more clearly aware of a green tree than we are of the fact that we are seeing it *with the eyes*. And when we come to those bodily actualities that are most directly given to our dominant occasions of experience, namely, our brain cells, we are seldom if ever conscious of their existence, although they are contributing enormous amounts of data to our experience.

Even if human beings never became conscious of God's presence, therefore, the direct givenness of God to our occasions of experience would not be thereby negated. As we saw in Chapters 2 and 5, furthermore, we have numerous good reasons, including the arguments from religious experience, normative values, importance, and novelty, to believe that a Holy Actuality *is* directly prehended, sometimes consciously. Accordingly, we can both meaningfully and plausibly hold that language about God is attempting to formulate, however inadequately, a genuine element of our experience. As Franklin emphasizes, the materials for creating theistically religious propositions, which focus on God and the coordination of values, "are present at the initial phase of every new actual entity" (1990, 358).

Because these materials are in the *initial* phase or—to change from horizontal to vertical imagery—the *deepest* dimension of experience, religious language involves, as the title of Franklin's book suggests, "speaking from the depths." Besides allowing the speakers/writers to try to formulate their deepest intuitions about values and the Holy, such language "helps us to organize our ordinary experience so that certain implicit factors are made explicit" (1990, 358). Franklin here refers to Whitehead's well-known comparison of a religious symbol, which he calls an "expressive sign," to a tuning fork. The expressive sign, says Whitehead, "elicits the intuition which interprets it. It cannot elicit what is not there. A note on a tuning fork can elicit a response from a piano. But the piano has already in it the string tuned to the same note. In the same way the expressive sign elicits the existent intuition which would not otherwise emerge into individual distinctiveness" (RM 128). Language about God, in other words, can bring our perception of God from the depths of our experience into our conscious awareness.

God and the Categories

Whereas much traditional philosophy of religion has taken God-language to be referential, it has said, at least in effect, that such language cannot be *cognitive* because our language—or, more precisely, the propositions expressed and evoked by our language—cannot in principle correspond to the Divine Actuality. The reason for this supposed impossibility is that philosophers and theologians have often said that God does not exemplify the categories we use for speaking of finite actualities. For example, the God of classical theism is said to know and love the world, but this knowing-and-loving is then said to have no element of passivity or receptivity in it, which means that it is different in kind from the only knowing-and-loving of which we can conceive. Because of this difference, the terms *know* and *love* are said not to apply to God literally but only analogically. The so-called analogical predication, furthermore, seems indistinguishable from equivocation (Hartshorne 1964a, 119)—as was admitted by those theologians who said that we cannot know what God is, only what God is not.

In recent centuries, classical theism has been widely rejected, but this fact in itself has not necessarily increased the possibility of speaking of God intelligibly. Some of the alternative ways of conceiving of the referent of the word *God* have, if anything, made our most general categories seem even less applicable, so that the idea that language about God could in principle be true in the correspondence sense has been widely rejected.[14] As we saw in Chapter 7, for example, Tillich, following classical theism in speaking of God as "being itself," insists that God is in no sense *a* being. Thinking of "being itself" in much the same way that Whitehead thinks of "creativity as such," Tillich rightly says that no metaphysical categories, such as individuality, experience, causality, and receptivity, can apply to God (thus understood). Although Tillich sometimes fudges on this issue (Griffin 1973a, chap. 1), his position means that personal categories, such as love, purpose, and knowledge, cannot be attributed to God. The attempt to apply such terms to God analogically involves complete equivocation even more clearly than it did in classical theism.

In Whiteheadian-Hartshornean process philosophy, the situation is very different. Whitehead's doctrine that all actualities are of the same type leads to his suggestion that God should be considered the "chief exemplification" of, rather than the exception to, the general categories applying to all other actualities (PR 343). Once Whitehead's own remaining exceptionalism is overcome, by reconceiving God as a living person rather than a single actual entity (as discussed in Chapter 4), language about God can include literal elements. Hartshorne, who has dealt most extensively with this issue, has distinguished among three kinds of predicates applied to God: formal, symbolic, and analogical (1962, 133–47). In *formal* or nonmaterial predicates, God is compared with any and all finite beings, as when God is said to be perfectly absolute (in one respect) and perfectly relative (in another respect). Such terms apply literally to God. Symbolic predicates are one type of *material* predicates, a type that compares God to a particular portion of the world, as when God is called a rock, a ruler, a shepherd, or a parent. But, given a panexperientialist view of the universe, there is another type of material predicates: according to panexperientialism, material or substantive terms such as feeling, memory, and sympathy (love) are "categorial" terms, applying to all concrete individuals. These terms, applied to God, are analogical because God's feeling, memory, and love are universal in scope whereas that of the creatures is not. However, Hartshorne adds, there is also

---

[14] Alston refers to the idea that "no positive substantial concepts apply to God," which he illustrates in terms of the views of Tillich, Kaufman, and Hick, as "extreme conceptual transcendence," pointing out that it is incompatible with theistic alethic realism (1995, 51–53).

a "sense in which the analogical concepts apply literally to deity, and analogically to creatures":

> We say that human beings "know" various things, but then we have to qual-
> ify. . . . We see that the term "know" in the human case turns out to have a
> rather indefinite meaning. In the divine case, the matter is simple: . . . God
> simply knows—period. . . . In this sense, it is the theistic use only of psychi-
> cal conceptions which has literal meaning, a meaning from which all other
> meanings are derived by qualification, diminution, or negation. . . . It is the
> same with love. If this means such things as appreciating the qualities of oth-
> ers, caring about their weal and woe, wishing them well, . . . then . . . one has
> to admit that in no case of human love is it simply true that one does these
> things. . . . But God appreciates the qualities of all things—period. . . . He
> wishes all creatures well—period. (1962, 141–42)

Given a Whiteheadian-Hartshornean theistic position,[15] therefore, language
can be applied meaningfully, even literally, to God.

From the perspective of Whiteheadian-Hartshornean process philosophy,
the standard reasons for assuming that language about God cannot be referential and cognitive do not apply. The idea that religious language is cognitive, however, means only that the propositions it expresses and evokes are
in principle *capable* of being true. Determining whether some of these propositions are really true is another question, to which we now turn.

[15] With this chapter behind us, we are in position to summarize one of the most significant
features of Whiteheadian theism: its anti-nominalist affirmation of a "Platonic" realm of eternal forms. As we have seen, the modern rejection of such a realm has created numerous problems: how to make sense of the apparent objectivity of mathematics, morality, and logic, even
the law of noncontradiction; how to explain the apparent jumps in evolution; and how, without assuming (nonphysical) propositions, to account for our assumptions about truth. The
need to explain how abstract forms can exist and exert influence on our experience (and the
world more generally) was central to Whitehead's move to a new version of Platonic-biblical
theism.

Both the importance and the difficulty of this move for modern intellectuals is illustrated
by Charles Larmore's *The Morals of Modernity.* On the one hand, seeing the need to reject modern naturalism, according to which the world "consists solely of the physical and psychological phenomena that are the objects of the modern natural sciences" (1996, 89), Larmore affirms
the Platonic view that reality also involves normative values (82, 87–90, 114–17). On the
other hand, accepting the irreversibility of modern disenchantment understood as the death
of God (42–43, 55), Larmore is left with no explanation of how this normative realm can exist and exert pressure on us. Although his account of "Nietzsche's legacy" is otherwise astute,
he evidently fails to see, as Heidegger did, that the death of God *entails* the rejection of transcendent values.

Religious Knowledge
and Common Sense

"Religion is marginalized in our time," points out Adina Davidovich, "because it is thought not to be one of the central modes of our knowledge of the world" (1993, xiii). The fact that process philosophy disagrees with this late modern opinion has been implicit in the previous chapters. In the present chapter we turn explicitly to this issue, asking whether it is possible to think of some of our religious beliefs as part of our knowledge and, if so, on what basis.

Process philosophy reaffirms the traditional definition of knowledge as "justified true belief." According to this definition, there are two necessary conditions, which are jointly sufficient, for a belief to be considered knowledge. First, the belief must be true. However, the fact that a person's belief about something, such as the age of the universe, just happens to be true does not make it knowledge. The second necessary condition is that this belief is *justified,* in the sense of being well founded.[1] Some Hindu and Buddhist thinkers more than two thousand years ago, for example, said that our universe is many billions of years old. Only during the past century, however, did the scientific community develop methods for ascertaining the approximate age of the universe. Accordingly, although those early thinkers in India turned out to be correct, we should not say that they *knew* the uni-

---

[1] I include in this condition the causal element discussed in note 9 of Chapter 5, namely, that that which makes the belief true must be causally related to the belief in the appropriate way.

verse to be many billions of years old—unless their belief was based upon a direct intuition into the nature of things that has proved itself to be a reliable way of discovering truths.

As this illustration shows, we can *define* knowledge as justified true belief while disagreeing on whether particular beliefs, even if they happen to be true, are *instances* of knowledge. That fact, of course, points to the really difficult question: What counts as justification? Or, given the recognition that justification is a matter of degree, how well justified does a belief have to be for us to say that we *know* it to be true? There is no right answer to this question, partly because there is no precise way to measure the degree of justification. My own view is that the bar for claiming knowledge should be placed very high. Of things that are well justified but not beyond a reasonable doubt, we should speak of merely *probable* knowledge, as when we say: "I think I know such-and-such." With many other beliefs, including many deep convictions, we should be content to call them just that: "beliefs" or "convictions." We should claim knowledge only when the belief is justified beyond any reasonable doubt.

Given this understanding of knowledge, our question is, Can religious beliefs ever be sufficiently justified to count as knowledge? As the title of this chapter indicates, the notion of hard-core commonsense beliefs is central to process philosophy's answer to this question. The first section gives a brief overview of this answer. The second section explains how the appeal to hard-core commonsense notions avoids relativistic historicism without returning to foundationalism. The third section is devoted to showing how the appeal to hard-core commonsense beliefs is crucially different from the appeal to "basic beliefs" in the Reformed epistemology of Alvin Plantinga and Nicholas Wolterstorff.

1. Justifying Religious Beliefs

The Need for Justification

A process philosophy of religion takes it for granted that religious beliefs need to be justified. Whitehead, in fact, began his book on religion by saying that its purpose was "to consider the type of justification which is available for belief in doctrines of religion" (RM 13). To anyone who has read this far, it will come as no surprise to learn that religion, in his view, "requires a metaphysical backing" (RM 81). Whitehead agrees, as we have seen, with those who say that religion has its primary importance in generating emotional states that serve to transform character. But, he holds, "[religion's] authority is endangered by the intensity of the emotions which it generates. Such emotions are evidence of some vivid experience; but they are a very poor guarantee for its correct interpretation" (RM 81).

Already in Whitehead's time, many philosophers and theologians were saying that the only justification needed by religion is pragmatic: we call it true because it produces good fruits. Whitehead demurred. In spite of his concern to provide a metaphysical justification for science, he agreed that "science can leave its metaphysics implicit and retire behind our belief in the pragmatic value of its general description" (RM 83). But not religion: "If religion does that, it admits that its dogmas are merely pleasing ideas for the purpose of stimulating its emotions."

The reason why religious belief requires metaphysical explication is made clear by Whitehead's statement that "religion claims that its concepts, though derived primarily from special experiences, are yet of universal validity, to be applied by faith to the ordering of all experience" (RM 31). This notion, which H. Richard Niebuhr employed to explain "the meaning of revelation" in a book with that title (1941, 93), implies that although one's vision of reality may arise out of some faith experience rooted in a particular religious tradition, the truth of this vision can be supported only by showing that the ideas to which it gives rise can provide the basis for an interpretation of the universe that meets the criteria for philosophical excellence.

There are religious beliefs, of course, of various types. One of the most important divisions is between historical and (at least relatively) ahistorical beliefs, with *history* understood here to mean beliefs about events of human history. Buddhist beliefs about Gautama, Jewish beliefs about Moses, Christian beliefs about Jesus, and Islamic beliefs about Mohammed provide paradigmatic examples of historical religious beliefs. The only *strictly* ahistorical beliefs involve metaphysical doctrines, such as the doctrine that God has both an abstract essence and concrete states. Beliefs about the general features of our particular cosmos, including generalizations about human beings, are *relatively* ahistorical. Although historical beliefs are usually important for theologies of the various religious traditions (as illustrated by the importance of historical beliefs about Jesus for Christology), philosophy of religion is concerned primarily with metaphysical, cosmological, and anthropological beliefs. It focuses, in other words, on what can be called worldview beliefs (N. Smart 1995a, 33; 1995b). This focus is presupposed in the statement just made that religious concepts claim universal validity, so that the appropriate criteria for evaluating their truth are philosophical.

Criteria for Justifying Religious Beliefs

Philosophers have increasingly recognized that worldview beliefs cannot intelligibly be evaluated singly, as they were in the heyday of analytic philosophy. Rather, each such belief has its place within an overall worldview, so that its credibility hinges, in large part, on the credibility of the whole worldview to which it belongs. To ask whether some religious doctrines are justified true beliefs, accordingly, requires the evaluation of the worldview to which they belong in terms of the appropriate criteria. Although longer lists can be given (Wainwright 1988, chap. 7), these criteria are, most basically, adequacy and coherence (taken to include self-consistency). Much of this book has been devoted to showing how process philosophy fulfills these criteria better than naturalism$_{sam}$, on the one hand, and supernaturalistic theism (which usually involves mind-body dualism), on the other.

Insofar as this case has been made, the distinctive doctrines of process philosophy, which may seem implausible when judged from the perspective of another worldview, take on added plausibility. For example, the doctrine of panexperientialism has been almost universally rejected, or at least ignored as unworthy of serious attention, by modern philosophers. Hartshorne says, however, that the case for it is so strong that it is "one of the two doctrines I am most confident of" (1976, 69). Hartshorne would count this doctrine among those beliefs he *knows* to be true. Likewise, as argued in Chapters 4 and 5, insofar as process philosophy's panexperientialism and its prehensive doctrine of perception seem convincing, its panentheism becomes much more plausible than it does when evaluated from the perspective of a different ontology and epistemology. Most process philosophers of religion, however, probably would say not that they *know* it to be true but that they are deeply convinced that it is closer to the truth than other available doctrines. It is not, in other words, as well justified by the evidence as is panexperientialism. The point at hand, in any case, is that our confidence in most worldview beliefs is based upon their place within a more or less complete system of ideas, combined with the number of good reasons within that system supporting their probable truth.

If this were all that could be said, however, we would be able to judge the truth of various doctrines only by judging the coherence of the overall worldview to which they belong. We might still define the *meaning* of truth in terms of correspondence to reality rather than in terms of coherence, but this definition would have no practical import. We would never be able to say of some particular doctrine, taken in relative isolation, that it is simply false. But this implication itself seems false. Spinoza's doctrine of total determinism can be judged false apart from evaluating Spinozism as a whole. Determinism is false, we say, because it is inadequate to human experience and behavior. The point here is that we also judge a worldview in terms of the criterion of "adequacy to the facts," not only in terms of self-consistency and coherence, because we believe we have the ability, at least with some doctrines, to evaluate them singly.

The pervasive relativism of recent philosophy has been due to scepticism about this point. As discussed earlier, it has been widely argued that we never experience any data directly, prior to shaping them in terms of our conceptual systems. Given that assumption, the test of adequacy to the facts could never be applied because each worldview, by virtue of its shaping of its adherents' minds, would create its own "facts." Each philosophical system would necessarily be equally adequate to the facts because there would be no common, worldview-transcendent facts in terms of which to judge the various worldviews.

This account of adequacy to the facts, however, is itself not adequate to the facts of scientific and theological history. Previous scientific theories, such as the geocentric and the nonevolutionary views of the universe, have been replaced because scientists, *even though their perception had been shaped by those theories,* saw facts to which those theories could not do justice. Likewise, although the Darwinian account of evolution led to the expectation that the evidence would reveal a very gradualistic evolutionary process, some scientists, as mentioned in Chapter 6, have discovered that the fossil record contradicts this expectation. In a similar way, expectations created by traditional theism have been disappointed. For example, the problem of evil is a problem precisely because people see the occurrence of evils that, given their understanding of the nature of God, should not occur. Another example is provided by the history of biblical scholarship, which shows that many scholars were forced, by their perception of the facts, to give up the theory of biblical inspiration with which they began. It is not pointless, therefore, to make adequacy to the facts a criterion for determining the truth of beliefs.

The facts to which a worldview should be adequate are *all* the facts, and these facts are of various types. As argued in Chapter 1, however, the facts to which it is most important that a philosophical position be adequate are our hard-core commonsense notions. One of these notions, the notion that we experience the "external world," lies behind the examples in the previous paragraph. Other such notions include truth as correspondence to this world beyond our immediate experience, the reality of the past, causation as real influence, freedom as choice among alternative possibilities (as left open by the causation upon us), normative values (and thereby better and worse possibilities), genuine evil (involving the realization of less than optimal possibilities), and a holy reality. Insofar as we inevitably presuppose these notions in practice, no philosophical position that denies one or more of them can be deemed adequate.

To return to the criterion of coherence: one of its aspects is for the position's ontology and its epistemology to support each other. A philosophy should, at the least, avoid self-stultification, which occurs when the ontology presupposes ideas that according to the epistemology we would have no way of knowing. Better yet, the position should explain *how* we know the various ideas said to be true. Process philosophy does this with regard to its hard-core commonsense notions. We know about the external world, the past, causal efficacy, a holy reality, and normative values—and thereby genuine evil, by comparing what *is* to what *ought* to have been—because we directly prehend these realities. We know of freedom as self-determination, involving choice among alternative possibilities, both by immediately enjoying it in the moment and by remembering prior acts of self-determination. In other words, the reason why we have all these notions is neither because a supernatural deity has implanted them in our minds, as early modern thought (including Kant, evidently) assumed, nor because human beings with genes to believe these notions have won out in the evolutionary battle for survival, as late modern thought tends to assume. Rather, we presuppose all these notions in practice because we directly prehend their truth in every moment of our experience, so that they are present in the depths of our experience all the time. We can deny them with our words, but we cannot act contrary to them, and it is our action, as Hartshorne says in agreement with the pragmatists, that reveals what we really believe (1941, 79; 1991b, 634).

Deep Religious Knowledge

All the hard-core commonsense notions just mentioned, it should be noted, are of religious import. This fact is consistent with process philosophy's view that explicit religious knowledge, for the most part, consists in bringing to consciousness things that we already know at a deeper level of experience. Presupposed in this statement, of course, is the idea that there is a kind of "knowledge" that is deeper than our conscious, explicit, verbalizable knowledge. In referring to this deeper level of knowledge, Whitehead says: "[M]others can ponder many things in their hearts which their lips cannot express. These many things, which are thus known, constitute the ultimate religious evidence, beyond which there is no appeal" (RM 65). This idea lies behind Whitehead's tuning fork analogy mentioned in Chapter 9. New religious insights can evoke a positive response from us because although we ourselves had not been able to verbalize them, we already knew them at a preconscious, prelinguistic level of experience.

This idea, that the ultimate religious evidence consists in prelinguistic knowledge in the depths of our experience, is of utmost importance. Most modern thought has taken religious doctrines, especially about a Divine Reality, to be "metaphysical" ideas in the Kantian sense of the term, meaning ideas about things lying beyond all possible experience. Whitehead rejects this idea of metaphysics: "The elucidation of immediate experience is the sole justification for any thought; and the starting-point for thought is the analytic observation of components of this experience" (PR 4). This dictum applies to religious thought as much as to any other thought. Religious doctrines, therefore, are not attempts to speak about unexperienced things but, as Franklin says, attempts at "speaking from the depths" (1990).

Direct Verification

One reason that this notion is important is that it provides the basis for a direct verification of some religious ideas. We can approach this issue by seeing how Whitehead's position allows for the direct verification of commonplace ideas. According to his doctrine of symbolic reference as a *mixed* mode of perception, "meaning" involves the reference of a percept in one of the pure modes of perception, usually that of presentational immediacy, to a percept in the other pure mode, usually that of causal efficacy. For example, if a student says to me, "You gave me an B+ on my paper because you were disappointed with it," the meaning of "you" is a nexus of occasions of my experience that occurred prior to my putting the grade on the paper. I can know through direct observation, Whitehead points out, whether the student's statement is true. "[T]here is a definite determination of what is true," he says, "when the 'meaning' is sufficiently distinct and relevant, as a perceptum in its proper pure mode, to afford comparison with the precipitate of feeling derived from symbolic reference" (PR 181). What this means, in this case, is that I can clearly remember (through prehension in the mode of causal efficacy) what my state of mind was at the time, so that I can judge whether the proposition evoked by the student's statement, which affirms that my occasions of experience at the time included disappointment with the student's paper, corresponds to the actual situation. I can, perhaps, see that it is false because I had actually been pleasantly surprised by how good the paper was, having expected it to be worthy of only a C.

The point involved in this commonplace example is directly germane to religious assertions. "[T]he final opposites, joy and sorrow, good and evil, disjunction and conjunction—that is to say, the many in one—flux and permanence, greatness and triviality, freedom and necessity," Whitehead says, "are in experience with a certain ultimate directness of intuition" (PR 341). Accordingly, when a Jewish theologian speaks of our freedom in relation to good and evil, or a Buddhist speaks of flux and permanence, we can judge the truth of the statements by comparing them with our own experience. Yet another pair of opposites, "God and the World," is also present in our experience, says Whitehead, but *not* with the same directness of intuition: "God and the World introduce the note of interpretation" (PR 341).

This position has a twofold implication for statements about God. On the one hand, statements about God *are* attempts to interpret something genuinely present in our experience. On the other hand, such statements involve far more interpretation than do statements about, say, causal efficacy and freedom. The former implication is relevant in relation to the position of theologians such as Gordon Kaufman, who assume that theistic assertions are *purely* "imaginative" in the sense of not being rooted in experience at all. The latter implication is relevant in relation to philosophers of religion, such as the Reformed epistemologists discussed later, who seem to assume that one idea of God, that of traditional theism, has been rather directly *given* to human consciousness, so that little if any interpretation was involved in the origin of this idea of God.

Cross-Cultural Cooperation

Leaving aside that issue for the moment, I turn now to the implication of Whitehead's position for philosophy of religion as a cross-cultural enterprise. Philosophical theology should be understood, Hartshorne suggests, as "an effort, through cooperation, to discover what the bottom layer of our common human thought really is" (1941, 80). Although Hartshorne's statement was not explicitly presented as a program for cross-cultural philosophy of religion, it could be so taken. The doctrines of the various religions can be understood, to a significant extent, as attempts to bring to consciousness, and to develop the implications of, a few of our hard-core commonsense notions (Cobb and Griffin 1976, chap. 2). The biblical religions, for example, have lifted up our experience of God, freedom, and moral values.

Confucianism, while having considerable overlap with biblical religion, has given more attention to aesthetic values. Taoism has emphasized the idea that the divine element in our experience is a gentle, slow-working, persuasive influence. Buddhism thematizes the experience of being causally influenced—but *not* determined—by the totality of the past. And so on. The ultimate goal of philosophy of religion would be to discover, then to coordinate into a global philosophy of religion, the various deep truths to which the various religions of the world have called attention. This effort must be carried out *cooperatively,* so that the judgments made by people shaped by one tradition are checked by the judgments of those shaped by other traditions. Insofar as all agree on some doctrines, we can rightly think of them as genuine knowledge.

Historical Revelation and Vision of Reality

In discussing worldview beliefs, which are (at least relatively) ahistorical in intention, I have said that the most important facts to which they need to be adequate are our hard-core commonsense ideas, which are ahistorical in origin, being common (at the presuppositional level) to human beings in all times and places. Most worldview beliefs, however, are historical in origin, having arisen through some particular tradition, such as Judaism or Taoism, or some particular person, such as Gautama, Aristotle, Descartes, Newton, or Darwin. Conceptualizations of the world, furthermore, are explications of an underlying, preconceptual *vision of reality,* which is usually inherited from the tradition in which one is raised (Cobb 1965, 263–70; Griffin 1973a, 153–66). Those who have been brought up in a Jewish, Christian, or Islamic tradition, for example, tend to see the world as created. This is less an explicit belief, which might be doubted, than a way of seeing, which includes simply seeing the world as contingent (making it seem self-evident that, to understand it, reference to a creator is needed).

One of the realizations of recent philosophy is that all thinking begins with some such vision of reality. It used to be assumed that although theologians began by presupposing the truth of certain ideas, which they considered revealed truths, philosophers began by presupposing nothing, questioning all inherited ideas. Now it is realized that the philosopher and the theologian do not differ formally. The difference between philosophers and theologians, in this respect, is mainly that those who use the latter name are more consciously aware of the fact that they do begin with a nonrational vision (Cobb 1962, 312–18; Ferré 1967, 367–70). The vision is nonrational because we do not argue *to* it from some other point but *from* it. It is appropriately called "nonrational," rather than "irrational," because the latter term would suggest, falsely, that we could start with a wholly blank slate.

Although a vision of reality, being "second nature" for a person, may seem as self-evident as our set of hard-core commonsense beliefs, it does not have the same status. Having arisen historically, in a particular tradition, it is not universally presupposed. Once we become aware of the fact that we operate out of one vision of reality among others, therefore, we cannot rationally continue simply to presuppose its truth. Although our set of hard-core commonsense notions does not need testing, because they are universally shared and would be presupposed in any attempt to evaluate them, our vision of reality does need testing. But how is such testing possible, if our vision of reality is also presupposed in the very process of argumentation?

The first step in an answer is to see that although a vision of reality is preconceptual and usually precognitive (because prior to becoming aware of worldviews expressing different visions of reality, one is usually unaware that one has such a vision), it does have cognitive implications. Some have thought otherwise. For example, the early Paul van Buren, using R. M. Hare's term *blik* for this underlying vision of reality, said: "There is no arguing about 'bliks'" (1963, 155). However, although a vision of reality as such, being preconceptual, cannot be tested, each vision of reality can be formulated in various philosophical conceptualizations. The various Christian theologies, for example, are attempts to express the Christian—or, more generally, biblical—vision of reality. The various Buddhist philosophical systems are attempts to formulate the vision of reality expressed by Gautama and early Buddhism. The various materialistic philosophies are attempts to explicate the vision of reality underlying naturalism$_{sam}$. The truth of these and other underlying visions of reality can be *indirectly* tested by directly comparing the best philosophical conceptualizations to which they have given rise.

It is widely assumed that any such testing would be circular: those with a biblical vision of reality would see some version of Jewish, Christian, or Islamic theology as providing the most adequate conceptualization of reality; those with a Buddhist vision of reality would give the nod to some version of Buddhist philosophy; and those with a materialist vision of reality would find, on balance, some philosophical formulation of naturalism$_{sam}$ to be most adequate. This conclusion is *largely* true, mainly because the vision of reality out of which we operate will largely determine the "facts" to which we believe a philosophical system must do justice. Three factors, however, prevent that conclusion from being the whole truth. First, although a vision of reality largely colors our reading of the facts, it does not completely determine it; we are able, at times, to see disconfirming, or at least "anomalous," facts. Second, the first point is true partly because experience contains a pre-conceptual given element, as discussed in the previous chapter. Third, our hard-core commonsense notions reflect elements of experience that are given to all human beings alike, so that these notions can serve as points of agreement for all people, regardless of their different visions of reality.

Although process philosophy reflects elements from other traditions (such as the Buddhist idea of interdependent becoming), it can largely be regarded as one more attempt to explicate a biblical vision of reality. Jewish, Christian, and Muslim process theologians might regard this vision of reality as a revelation (Griffin 1973a, chap. 6). But this notion plays no role in the attempt of process philosophy to make its case. That is, there is no claim that process philosophy is true *because* it is based on revealed ideas. Rather, a philosophical system has, as Whitehead suggests, the status of a complex "working hypothesis" (AI 222). Speaking of religious doctrines in particular, he says that they stand or fall, like any other doctrines, by their success in the interpretation of life (RM 120). We judge the truth of religious doctrines, in other words, by their fruits, not their roots, with the chief philosophical fruit being the articulation of a position that can pass the twofold test of adequacy and coherence.

In summary, we can think of those religious beliefs that belong to our hard-core common sense as knowledge because such beliefs are our best-justified general beliefs. We can be confident that particular ideas belong to our set of hard-core commonsense beliefs insofar as we see that they are inevitably presupposed by all human beings, regardless of cultural-linguistic shaping. We can even think of our verbal formulations of such ideas as knowledge insofar as people from diverse religio-cultural backgrounds agree on these formulations. With regard to religious ideas that have arisen historically, they can be thought of as *probable* knowledge insofar as they are supported by a number of considerations as well as being essential elements within a worldview fulfilling the criteria of coherence and adequacy.

Now, having sketched a view of religious knowledge from the perspective of process philosophy, I will further clarify it through comparisons with two other currently popular positions, both of which, like process philosophy, reject classical foundationalism.

2. Anti-foundationalism without Relativistic Historicism

Foundationalism and Its Rejection

Epistemological foundationalism is the view (1) that a system of beliefs is distinguishable into basic and nonbasic beliefs, (2) that basic beliefs are known immediately to be true, (3) that in a rational system basic beliefs form the starting points from which all nonbasic beliefs must be derived, and (4) that the relation between basic and nonbasic beliefs is an entirely one-way relation, with basic beliefs supporting, without in any way being supported by, nonbasic beliefs. A rational system of beliefs is assumed to be like a building, in which the superstructure is supported by a solid foundation. As Reid put it, "[T]hat all knowledge got by reasoning must be built on first principles . . . is as certain as that every house must have a foundation" (1971, 558).

Foundationalism, thus understood, is now widely rejected, for a variety of reasons. For one thing, it is now generally recognized that a system of beliefs is less like a building resting on a foundation than like a web, in which the various beliefs support one another. The beliefs that were taken to be basic by classical foundationalists, such as Descartes and Reid, were in fact supported by a vast network of assumptions. Other reasons for the rejection of foundationalism will be discussed later. In any case, many thinkers have concluded that if foundationalism is untenable, we are left with no universally valid criteria for judging between truth and falsehood, especially with regard to the most fundamental assumptions underlying various systems of thought, so that we must be content with some version of historicism.

For example, Jeffrey Stout reports that he "felt driven [to historicism] by the demise of foundationalism" (1981, 12). By "historicism," he means the view that social practices can be justified not in terms of any universal criteria but only in terms of criteria accepted by some particular historical tradition (112). Historicism, he says, involves "a criticism of the philosophical tradition's quest for a perspective outside of or more fundamental than historically conditioned thought" (4). The attempt to defend this historicism, however, leads Stout into self-contradictions, as in the following statement: "We must say that by virtue of being human we are all *situated* more radically than poets and philosophers typically pretend. Descartes *seemed* to transcend his situation in part because he thought he could. Historicism says he could not *because no one can*" (66; final emphasis added). In making this universal claim, Stout is involved in the performative self-contradiction of implying that he has precisely the kind of transcendence over his particular situation that his statement says no one can have.

Universal Criteria without Foundationalism

Stout's conclusion, that we are driven to relativistic historicism by the demise of foundationalism, involves a mistake. *The mistake is to assume that if we reject foundationalism, we cannot affirm any universally valid criteria for thought.* The prevalence of this mistake is shown by the common assumption that all philosophers who affirm universal criteria are foundationalists. The contrary is shown by the fact that although Whitehead and Hartshorne affirm universal criteria, they reject the position that has come to be called foundationalism. Calling it the "fallacy of dogmatism," Whitehead rejected the idea "that metaphysical thought started from principles which were individually, clear, distinct, and certain" (FR 49). "Coherence," says Hartshorne, "is a circle, not a straight line. On the highest level of generality, nothing is essentially premise or essentially conclusion" (1991b, 684). Whitehead and Hartshorne nevertheless have a universal criterion, saying that we should reject any proposition that contradicts any of the ideas we inevitably presuppose in practice.[2] Whitehead's affirmation of this criterion was shown in Chapter 1. Hartshorne, calling it a "pragmatic principle," says that "what we have to be guided by in our decision-making, we should not pretend to reject theoretically" (1991b, 624).[3]

Although some philosophers will be tempted to call this a version of foundationalism, that would reflect confusion. Given the generally accepted definition of foundationalism just stated, hard-core commonsense notions do not function as a foundation in process philosophy (as distinct from Reid's philosophy, which has been called "common-sense foundationalism" [Helm 1983, 78]). One does not begin with them, then try to infer all other ideas from them. The philosophical enterprise is more like a journey than a building. We start wherever we happen to be.[4] The set of hard-core commonsense notions serves not as a foundation but as a compass, letting us know when we have gotten off course. That is, the use of this set of ideas is primarily negative: no proposition that contradicts any of these commonsense beliefs should be accepted. Also, our confidence in these notions is not entirely independent of other ideas in our philosophy. For example, my conscious belief in freedom is fortified by the fact that Whitehead has provided an intelligible explanation as to how it is possible.[5] Process philosophers, therefore, reject half the defining principles of foundationalism (namely, the third and fourth principles given at the outset of this section).

    [2] See note 15 of Chapter 1.
    [3] See note 13 of Chapter 1 on "pragmatic metaphysics."
    [4] As Peirce said in articulating his commonsense philosophy: "There is but one state of mind from which you can 'set out,' namely, the very state of mind in which you actually find yourself at the time you do 'set out'—a state in which you are laden with an immense mass of cognition already formed, of which you cannot divest yourself if you would" (1931–35, 5:416).
    [5] This position, which rejects the idea that the process of lending credibility always goes from basic to nonbasic beliefs, has been dubbed "up-and-back-ism" by Susan Haack (1985, 218).

Of course, one could redefine foundationalism so that it includes any position that affirms universally valid criteria—which we could call foundationalism$_{uc}$ (for "universal criteria"). But then one could not dismiss process philosophy because of its foundationalism on the grounds that "everyone knows that foundationalism is bankrupt," because in that latter phrase the reference would be to what we could call foundationalism$_{om}$ (for "original meaning"). Rather, one would have to explain why foundationalism$_{uc}$ is to be rejected.[6] And what explanation could be given for this assertion, except the claim that there are not, in fact, any notions that are universally presupposed? That would bring us back to the point made in Chapter 2, that the proper way to challenge the claimed universality of these notions is to find a society or even a single individual who is able to live without presupposing them. Until such a society or person is located, we can continue to assume their universality.

It is a further point, of course, to say that if they are in fact inevitably presupposed, we should use them as criteria for theoretical thought. Stout himself, however, implicitly provides the basis for this point. Shortly after claiming that "we do not need universal criteria of rationality" (1981, 151), he says: "I do grant without hesitation that inconsistency is often—that is, in some contexts—a mark of irrationality. If it were *always* a mark of irrationality, perhaps there would be no harm in referring to the law of noncontradiction as a criterion of rationality" (154). Although Stout tries to avoid directly contradicting himself by his qualifications ("often," "if," "perhaps"), he does accept this law as a universal criterion of rationality.[7] His apparent argument against doing so is directed only against taking it as "an absolutely overriding requirement of rationality . . . to be pursued at all costs." He concedes that it is "one virtue among the many an ideal system of beliefs would have" (155)—which is what is entailed by calling it a universal criterion of rationality. He also grants that "[c]oherence is the standard case that allows us to take reasoning seriously in the explanation of belief and behavior" (171).

Once this point is granted, it follows that if what I have called hard-core commonsense notions are indeed inevitably presupposed, they must be used as criteria for rejecting the truth of any position that contradicts any of them.

---

[6] Still another common practice is to call a philosopher's affirmation of universal criteria *quasi-foundational,* a term that seems to suggest guilt by association even while admitting that the sin of foundationalism is not actually committed.

[7] Putnam's present recognition that the law of noncontradiction must be considered a universal (a priori) criterion, which involves a reversal of his earlier position, was cited in note 11 of Chapter 1.

As I pointed out in Chapter 1, this conclusion follows from the law of non-contradiction because any thinker who verbally denied one of them would be implicitly affirming it at the same time, resulting in a performative self-contradiction. Stout's virtual admission that the law of noncontradiction is a formal ideal of rationality, then, implicitly carries with it a number of substantive criteria of rationality, once the existence of universal presuppositions of practice is recognized.

Probable Reasoning without Vacuity

This recognition is crucial to process philosophy's rejection of Stout's main claim about philosophy of religion and theology. Stout's book being cited here, *The Flight from Authority,* deals with the fate of theology after it gave up the old idea of probability, which was based on appeal to authority, for the "new probability," which is based on evidence (1981, 56–61). Claiming that theology cannot accept this new probability without becoming vacuous, Stout says that Hume made clear "the severely limited character of any religious system that embraces the new probability" (118). For further support, Stout (1981, 146) quotes with approval a statement by Alasdair MacIntyre that was occasioned by reflections upon the projects of Bultmann and Tillich: "[A]ny presentation of theism which is able to secure a hearing from a secular audience has undergone a transformation that has evacuated it entirely of its theistic content. . . . I am thus advancing not merely the weaker contention that all [the theologians'] attempts so far have failed but the stronger contention that any attempt of this kind must inevitably fail" (MacIntyre 1969, 26). It is impossible, concludes Stout, for philosophy to be "both completely secular [in approach] and completely religious [in content]" (1981, 140).

One of the main purposes of the present book is to show precisely the opposite—that a position can be fully religious substantively, including being fully theistic, while formally adhering to the standards of secular or philosophical thought. The truth in the MacIntyre-Stout claim is that if philosophers of religion and theologians accept the *substantive* assumptions currently dominant in intellectual circles, especially the materialistic view of nature and the sensationist doctrine of perception, a significantly religious position is excluded. By challenging those substantive assumptions, however, process philosophy can argue for a "completely religious" position as the most probable in light of all the evidence.

Central to this argument is the twofold claim that our various hard-core commonsense beliefs provide universally valid criteria of rationality and that process philosophy can do more justice to them than can its competitors. These commonsense beliefs are also central to the comparison of process philosophy with a position that has been much discussed in recent decades, the Reformed epistemology of Alvin Plantinga and Nicholas Wolterstorff.

3. Reformed Epistemology and the Reformed Subjectivist Principle

Central to process philosophy's epistemology, we have seen, is its "reformed subjectivist principle," according to which the datum of a subject's experience includes other actualities. Whitehead coined this phrase in response to the positions of Descartes, Locke, and Hume. In what is known as Reformed epistemology, by contrast, the term *Reformed,* which is capitalized, refers to the Reformed, or Calvinistic, version of Christian faith. Given the fact that these two uses of the word *reformed* arose out of different trajectories and in relation to different issues, one might assume that they would not have anything in common. Surprisingly, however, they do: both positions affirm the direct, immediate awareness of God. This affirmation, however, plays a very different role in the two positions, in part because they understand the content of this immediate awareness of God quite differently.

On Taking Belief in God as Basic

At the heart of the epistemology articulated by Plantinga and Wolterstorff is the rejection of "evidentialism" in relation to belief in God. They do not deny that belief in God requires grounds, but they deny that it requires evidence. Although this distinction has occasioned confusion, by "evidence" they mean *inferential* evidence. The evidentialist, says Wolterstorff, holds "that theistic conviction, to be rational, must be arrived at, or at least reinforced, by the process of inference" (1983a, 158). The claim of the Reformed epistemologists is that they and fellow believers commit no intellectual sin in taking their belief in God as a *basic* belief, one that is held "without evidence" in the sense of not being inferred from other beliefs. That is, they claim that for them belief in God is *properly* basic, meaning that they "are within their epistemic rights" in taking this belief as basic (Plantinga 1986, 9). In speaking of "belief in God," furthermore, they mean not simply belief in a divine or holy reality, which various people might define in various ways, but belief in "God as conceived in traditional Christianity, Judaism, and Islam: an almighty, all-knowing wholly good and loving person who has created the world and presently upholds it in being." The principal claim of the Reformed epistemologists is that belief in God *thus conceived* can be properly basic (Plantinga 1997, 383).

As the term *basic belief* suggests, their argument is made in terms of foundationalism. Although commentators have differed about the extent to which Plantinga and Wolterstorff still affirm a version of foundationalism, their position clearly involves a threefold rejection of *classical* foundationalism. One point rejected is the idea that the only beliefs that are properly taken as basic are those that are (1) self-evident, in the sense of tautologous, or (2) incorrigible because limited to one's immediate experience (Plantinga 1996, 330–31; 1997, 385). Plantinga sometimes describes classical foundationalism as including a third type of basic beliefs—beliefs that are "evident to the senses" (1983b, 372; 1989, 425)—which will be important for our discussion. A second feature of classical foundationalism rejected by Plantinga is the contention that belief in God cannot properly be accepted as a basic belief but must instead by inferred from other beliefs (1989, 418). He rejects, in other words, the idea that "belief in God is rationally acceptable if and only if there is adequate evidence in the form of good arguments for it" (1997, 384). A third rejected point, which brings out an implication of the second, is that one can *properly* take as basic only beliefs that are basic for all human beings (1996, 330). In a statement rejecting the second and third features of classical foundationalism, Plantinga says: "A central point at which the Reformed epistemologist differs from the classical foundationalist [is that] according to the former but not the latter, belief in God belongs in the foundations of knowledge, even if there are many people who don't believe in God at all. Reformed epistemology thus rejects the idea that knowledge is what can be proved from propositions accepted by all rational persons" (1996, 332). As this statement shows, Plantinga's aim is to be able to call his belief in God *knowledge*.

The Argument from Parity

The question, of course, is how Plantinga can argue that it is rationally justifiable for him to take God as a *properly* basic belief (and, therefore, as part of his knowledge). It is here that what I have called our hard-core commonsense beliefs come into play. Belief in God, argues Plantinga, is on an "epistemological par" with such beliefs, so that if the latter beliefs are rational, which they surely are, then belief in God is rational.

Plantinga first worked out this parity argument in terms of belief in other minds, as suggested by the title of his *God and Other Minds* (1990 [first edi-

tion 1967]). From the point of view of classical foundationalism, belief in
other minds is not a basic belief because it does not fit any of the two (or
three) criteria, being neither self-evident nor incorrigible (nor evident to the
senses). Also, continues Plantinga, belief in other minds is not supported by
"cogent arguments of the sort required" by classical foundationalism for rational nonbasic beliefs, which shows that classical foundationalism is not
true, "for a person flouts no epistemic duty in believing that there are other
minds" (xii). Having made this point, Plantinga next argues that the
strongest arguments for God and for other minds are similar (xi). That is, although the best argument for God is the teleological argument, whereas the
best argument for other minds is the analogical argument from one's own
self-knowledge, both arguments fall prey to the same objection (212, 245).
Plantinga concludes, accordingly, that "if my belief in other minds is rational, so is my belief in God. But obviously the former is rational; so, therefore, is the latter" (271).

The great advantage of this "insight," says Plantinga, is that the theist's belief in God can be seen to be reasonable even though "the theist has no very
good answer to the request that he explain his reasons for believing in the
existence of God" (1990, 268). In other words, "the believer is entirely
within his intellectual rights in believing as he does, even if he doesn't know
of any good theistic argument (deductive or inductive), even if he doesn't
believe that there is any such argument" (1986, 4).

Plantinga later extended the parity argument to include some other commonsense beliefs, especially our beliefs in an external world and the past
(1983b, 365; 1984, 26). Besides failing to meet classical foundationalism's criteria for basicality, says Plantinga, these beliefs are not supported by any
evidential arguments. But that does not matter, we realize, because these beliefs do not *need* any evidential arguments (1983b, 364−65). For example,
"hardly anyone thinks you need a good argument for the existence of the
past if you are to be rational in thinking you had breakfast this morning"
(1997, 384). Likewise, "there is nothing whatever immoral in believing in
material objects in the basic way," even though "there is no good (non-
circular) argument for the existence of material objects from propositions
that are properly basic by classical foundationalist standards" (1997, 386). By
the same token, Plantinga argues, if "after careful reflection and consideration it just seems obvious to me that there *is* such a person as God [then I]
can be perfectly justified in holding this belief in the basic way" (1997, 386).

In saying that these beliefs are without evidence, however, Plantinga does
not mean that they are *groundless*. For example, the ground for my belief that

another person is in pain is my perception of typical pain behavior on his or her part, along with other conditions, such as an absence of grounds for suspecting the behavior to be feigned. The ground for my perceptual belief that I am perceiving a real (external) tree is, to use Roderick Chisholm's language, "my being appeared treely to," along with some other circumstances, such as being generally free from hallucinations. The ground for my memory belief that I had breakfast this morning, points out Plantinga, is "a certain past-tinged experience" of having breakfast, along with other circumstances, such as not having an unreliable memory (1989, 420–21). In the same way, Plantinga argues, belief in God can be noninferential and yet not groundless. For example, observing the universe may trigger in us the belief that God created it (1989, 421–22). It is important to realize that Plantinga is not saying that this belief involves "an implicit argument—perhaps a version of the teleological argument." Indeed, the person's "belief need not be based on any other propositions at all" (1983b, 366). Rather, the person simply knows of God's existence *immediately,* just as we immediately know the existence of the past, the external world, and other minds (1996, 331–32).

At this point, the critic might reply that the argument from parity can be turned back against Plantinga. As Hume and Santayana have pointed out, the existence of other minds, the external world, and the past is not self-evident, part of my immediate consciousness, or evident to the senses, so we must, theoretically, be solipsists. That is, although Hume agreed that these natural beliefs are ineluctable, he denied that they are therefore true, because blind "Nature" may have simply constructed us so that we would believe them (Penelhum 1992, 102–3). Our "natural belief" in these things, therefore, provides no analogical basis for trusting the belief in God.

In replying to this objection, the Reformed epistemologists employ an idea articulated by Hume's anti-sceptical, Calvinistic opponent Thomas Reid. We have the dispositions to believe in the external world, other minds, and other commonsense facts, said Reid, because we were endowed with these dispositions by our creator (Wolterstorff 1983a, 150). Appealing to Calvin's notion that "God himself has implanted in all men a certain understanding of his divine majesty" so that "men one and all perceive that there is a God and that he is their Maker" (quoted in Plantinga 1983b, 365), the Reformed epistemologists enlarge Reid's notion of divinely implanted dispositions to include one that Reid himself did not include: the disposition to believe in the Divine Being itself. The Reidian approach to epistemology, says Wolterstorff, is to play down inferential reasoning in favor of "mechanisms of belief-formation" that can produce belief in God that is immediate and yet rational (1983a, 175). Stating his parity argument in these terms, Plantinga says: "Belief in the existence of God is then in the same boat as belief in truths of logic, other minds, the past, and perceptual objects; in each case God has so constructed us that in the right circumstances we acquire the belief in common" (1984, 262).

The Implausibility of the Parity Argument

Now that we have the argument from parity before us, we need to ask whether it should be accepted. Should we agree that belief in God is on par with our beliefs in the external world, other minds, and the past, so that it can equally be considered a properly basic belief? The most obvious objection is simply to deny the parity-claim. Terence Penelhum points out, for example, that theistic beliefs, unlike these other beliefs, have competitors (1992, 103). If there were really parity, there should be competition in all cases or none. In fact, adds Penelhum, Hume had, in response to an earlier argument from parity offered by Pascal, intentionally undermined the analogy between religious and commonsense beliefs, pointing out that the former, unlike the latter, are not universal, so their sources must be environmental and cultural, not natural (Penelhum 1992, 104). Stephen Wykstra, using the very term *parity* to point out a problem in Plantinga's position, argues that although inferential evidence is not needed for our commonsense beliefs, it *is* needed for belief in God because religious experience can reasonably be regarded as riddled with problems of "ostensible epistemic parity" (Wykstra 1989, 436). For an example, Wykstra quotes Flew's statement (1966, 126) that religious experience in various cultures "ostensibly authenticat[es] innumerable beliefs many of which are in contradiction with one another."

In his original argument, Plantinga had anticipated that some philosophers would hold that although we do not need to explain our belief in other minds, there are reasons for insisting on the need for evidence if belief in *God* is to be rational. Plantinga's reply was that "it is certainly hard to see what these reasons might be" (1990, 271). Penelhum and Wykstra have given one such reason. The Reformed epistemologists, however, have an answer: sin. Although unbelievers claim that there is not enough evidence for God, the real reason for their unbelief, says Wolterstorff, is a sinful desire not to acknowledge God (1981, 22). Plantinga likewise says: "Were it not for the existence of sin, we should all believe in God with the same natural and wholehearted spontaneity with which we believe in other persons, the past, and the external world. It is only because of sin in the world that some of us human beings find belief in God difficult or absurd" (1996, 334).

Arguments from sin should not necessarily be ridiculed. In the first place, our desires do influence what we notice, how we evaluate what we do notice, and thereby how we interpret the world. This point, which was emphasized by James, is enshrined in Whitehead's account of an occasion of experience, according to which the occasion's subjective aim greatly determines the subjective form with which the various data are felt. Included therein is the issue of which data will be felt with the subjective form of consciousness. In the second place, human desire is often such as to block calls reflecting the divine will, along with evidence of the divine reality, from conscious awareness. Sin, therefore, is not irrelevant to epistemology. This point has been argued with great sensitivity in Wainwright's *Reason and the Heart* (1995). The argument of the Reformed epistemologists should not be rejected out of hand, accordingly, simply because it speaks of sin.

Their particular argument is, nevertheless, problematic. One problem is that if God is the source of our dispositions to believe in other persons, the past, and the external world as well as our disposition to believe in God, it is puzzling that sin clouds only our awareness of God. Parity of a sort does exist here as well, Plantinga suggests, contending that "as a result of sin" our capacities for perception, memory, and grasping self-evident truths "sometimes malfunction" (1996, 336). If parity were even approached, however, the differences pointed out by Hume, Penelhum, and Wykstra would not obtain. If there were true parity, sinful solipsism would be as rampant as sinful atheism.

A second problem is simply that the claim involved is wholly implausible. In discussing the epistemic effects of sin, Plantinga avers that "one who does not believe in God is in an epistemically substandard position—rather like a man who does not believe that his wife exists, or thinks she is like a cleverly constructed robot which has no thoughts, feelings, or consciousness" (1983b, 366). Can we really suppose that if only the world were free of sin, the existence of God would be as obvious as that of other people? Plantinga even comes to claim that a person whose noetic structures were fully restored "would be as convinced of God's existence as of her own" (2000, 485). These comparisons provide a reductio ad absurdum of the claim for epistemic parity.

Parity and the Reformed Subjectivist Principle

Process philosophy, furthermore, can show that this prima facie lack of epistemic parity reflects a *genuine* difference. The fact that the Reformed epistemologists maintain that belief in the God of traditional theism is on an epistemic par with our hard-core commonsense beliefs reveals, from the perspective of process philosophy, that their Reformed epistemology is insufficiently reformed.

Crucial to their case for parity is the standard conviction, shared not only by Hume and Santayana but also by Reid, that there is *no apparent reason* for our commonsense beliefs in the external world, the past, and other minds. Reid said, for example, that "we are under a necessity to take [them] for granted in the common concerns of life, *without being able to give a reason for them*" (1997, 33; emphasis added). Both Hume and Reid, to be sure, gave a reason of sorts. Although both of them held that, in Reid's words (1971, 613), "we can give no other account [of these beliefs] but that they necessarily result from the constitution of our faculties," Hume attributed this constitution to (blind) Nature while Reid attributed it to a providential deity (which is why Reid assumed that our constitution could be trusted, whereas Hume did not). But these are *speculative* reasons, deemed necessary because there seemed to be no *apparent* reason for these beliefs, such as would be provided by a *direct perception* of the reality of the external world, the past, and other minds.

Herein lies the importance of the fact that Plantinga sometimes mentions that according to medieval versions of classical foundationalism, some beliefs are basic because they are "evident to the senses." This criterion is usually absent in modern versions, of course, as most modern philosophers agree with Hume that sensory perception does not vouchsafe the existence of the external things to which our sensory data seem to refer. Aside from self-evident beliefs, such as $2 + 2 = 4$, incorrigible beliefs are typically limited, as Plantinga says, to beliefs about the immediate states of one's own mind, so that properly basic beliefs based on sensory perception are limited to propositions of the type, "I am being appeared treely to" (in distinction from propositions of the type, "I see a tree"). Plantinga's argument about perceptual beliefs presupposes this purely phenomenalist analysis of the data of sensory perception. The point remains, however, that if perception *does* provide direct awareness of the existence of external actualities, then belief in the external world *should* be regarded as a properly basic belief, for two reasons: (1) it is a *universal presupposition* of all human thought and practice and (2) its truth is *evident to perception*. Plantinga's parity argument—that he is not irrational for believing in God without any generally acceptable reason because his belief in the external world is without any generally acceptable reason and yet clearly rational—would be undermined.

Process philosophy, with its reformed subjectivist principle, shows that our hard-core commonsense beliefs in the external world, the past, and other minds all *do* fit the criterion of being "evident to perception."

Perceptual Knowledge of the External World

As we have seen, Whitehead's analysis of sensory perception comes out about halfway between modern phenomenalism and the sensory realism of pre-Humean philosophy. Since Whitehead accepts the subjectivist bias introduced by Descartes, he agrees that philosophical analysis must begin with conscious human experience as such, and he also agrees with Hume that sense data as such do not necessarily tell us anything about a world external to our minds. His "reformed subjectivist principle," however, involves the rejection of a purely subjectivist, solipsistic analysis of the data of full-fledged sensory perception. By virtue of distinguishing between perception in the mode of presentational immediacy, on which Hume focused, and perception in the mode of causal efficacy, which Hume presupposed in practice but ignored in his theoretical analysis, Whitehead lifts to our awareness the fact that full-fledged sensory perception always includes the perception of the causal efficacy upon us of other *actualities*.

Whitehead's analysis enlarges the dimensions of our experience that are incorrigible. Our perception in the mixed mode of symbolic reference, which is what full-fledged sensory perception is, may be wrong, as we may attribute sense data to sources from which they did not originate. But "the two pure perceptive modes are incapable of error" (PR 168). That is, just as I cannot be wrong about my present awareness of data in the mode of presentational immediacy—such as the fact that while writing this I am, in Chisholmian language, being appeared to computerly—I also cannot be wrong about the fact that I am feeling the impress of other actualities upon my experience. This constant knowledge of the impress of "stubborn fact" may not be as clear and distinct as my awareness of changing sense data, but it always guides my responses, which is why I never, in practice, have solipsistic moments. These impressions come, most immediately, from the actualities constituting my own body, but these impressions suffice to provide knowledge of an actual world *external to my own mind*. Through the direct impressions I receive from my bodily members, furthermore, I *indirectly* receive impressions from the world external to my body, so that it is *almost* true to say, as some realists do, that in sensory perception we directly perceive things outside our bodies.

This twofold point is explained by Whitehead in terms of the "vector" character of physical prehension, by which he means that "it is referent to an external world" (PR 19). Each of our most primitive prehensions is a "vector feeling," meaning a "feeling from beyond" (PR 163). In describing the operations of an organism (an occasion of experience) as vectors, Whitehead says that they "are directed *from* antecedent organisms and *to* the immediate organism" (PR 151). More precisely, each prehension inherits "vector feeling-tone," meaning "feeling-tone with evidence of its origin" (PR 119). Contrary to Hume's contention that the data of our experience arise from "unknown causes," we are directly aware that our experience *here-now* is drawing on data from actualities *there-then*.

This doctrine of the vectorial nature of prehensions has two implications for our topic. The first implication is that in receiving data by prehending our bodily organs, we are directly aware of prehending these other actualities from there-then. The second implication is that the same vector transmission occurs when the occasions of experience constituting our bodily organs, such as our eyes, ears, and skin, prehend actualities external to the body. That is, they themselves prehend the data *as coming from antecedent actualities*. Accordingly, in directly prehending our bodily actualities, we *indirectly* prehend the actualities that *they* had prehended.

With this second implication, Whitehead accounts for the fact that I am virtually as confident of the existence of the computer before me as I am of my body—which is why I find it inadequate, even humorous, when philosophers tell me that all I *really* know is that "I am appeared to computerly." Whitehead accounts for this confidence, furthermore, in a fully naturalistic way, with no need to appeal to a supernatural deistic implant. All that is needed is the recognition that sensory perception *presupposes,* because it *includes,* a nonsensory mode of perception. Although modern philosophers, because of their sensationism, tend to think that nonsensory perception would be supernatural, this comparison of Whiteheadian with Reformed epistemology suggests that an account that is naturalistic as well as adequate to our experience can be provided only by allowing for nonsensory perception.

This allowance provides, furthermore, yet another way to explain our hard-core commonsense conviction as to the reality of the world beyond our bodies. I discussed in Chapter 2 Whitehead's endorsement of telepathy, which is the direct feeling of another mind. Although we tend to use the word *telepathy* only when such prehensions rise to consciousness, we are, according to Whitehead's principles, unconsciously having telepathic experiences of other minds all the time. "The fundamental principle," says Whitehead, "is that whatever merges into actuality, implants its aspects in every individual event" (SMW 150). This principle means that our experience is always being colored by what we could call "background telepathy." Whitehead refers to evidence of this background telepathy in speaking of our "instinctive apprehension of a tone of feeling in ordinary social intercourse" (PR 308). Our direct perception of actualities beyond our own bodies would not be limited to other minds, however, because they are not different in kind from any other actualities. Accordingly, although we tend to speak of "clairvoyance" only when we have a *conscious* perception of some physical object or situation, we would in reality be having background clairvoyance of things such as trees and computers all the time. If so, this dim but constant dimension of our perception would help explain our incurable realism about such things.

From the perspective of Whitehead's epistemology, in sum, we know the existence of the external world because it is evident to perception (prehension) in a threefold way: through our direct perception of our own bodies, through our indirect perception via our sensory perceptions of the world external to our bodies, and through our direct, nonsensory prehension of that external world.

Perceptual Knowledge of the Past

Our perceptual knowledge of the past, having been extensively treated in Chapter 2, needs little discussion here. The reason why we do not "need a good argument for the existence of the past" is not, as Plantinga suggests, because God implanted in us a past-believing disposition but because we directly prehend the pastness of prior occasions of experience—as Plantinga in effect admits in speaking of a memory as a "past-tinged experience" (1989, 120–21). The existence of the past, like that of the external world, is a hard-core commonsense belief because it is evident to perception.

Perceptual Knowledge of Other Minds

We come now to our knowledge of other minds, which provided the original basis for Plantinga's parity argument. The Whiteheadian account of this knowledge is more complex than its account of our knowledge of the past and even of that of the external world. In the first place, it is surely true that our belief in other minds is to a considerable extent analogical. On the basis of our immediate awareness of our own conscious experience, combined with our perception of other people behaving in roughly the same ways that we do, we infer—so spontaneously that it does not even seem like inference—that they have experiences like unto our own. If this were the only basis we had for believing in other minds, then there would be some basis for claiming parity with belief in God, insofar as belief in God is based on inferring from the world's "behavior" that it is directed by a cosmic mind. This basis would not, however, be very strong. Even though process philosophers use the mind-body relation analogically for thinking of the God-world relation, we do not pretend that the world's behavior suggests a cosmic mind with anything approaching the same clarity as the behavior of fellow human beings suggests that they have minds. That is, even if we grant Plantinga's point that the analogical argument for other minds is not coercive, because it is subject to the same kind of objection as the teleological argument for God, it could still be true, as most philosophers believe, that the analogical argument for other minds is *far closer to coercive* than is the teleological argument for a divine mind.

Inference from the bodily behavior of others by itself, furthermore, would not seem to account for the firmness of our conviction as to—indeed, our *knowledge* of—the existence of other minds. Much of the truth is surely indicated by those who point out that, given the fact that we acquire our language and most of our conceptual ability from our parents and other people, the existence of other minds is *presupposed* by the very ability to raise the question. By the time we are able to make the analogical inference, it merely supplies a reinforcement of, rather than the original basis for, our knowledge of the reality of other minds. The idea that belief in other minds and belief in God are in the same epistemic boat, therefore, is undermined because we have no similar interaction with God.

To be sure, assuming the truth of theism as understood by either process or Reformed philosophers, we *are* interacting with God even more constantly than we are with human beings. Through the divine influence, furthermore, we acquire many of our presuppositions, such as those involving logical truths and normative values. The analogy with influence from other people, however, is too remote to provide anything approaching epistemic parity because the fact that we acquire truths and values from God—assuming it to be a fact—is not *obvious* in the way that it is obvious that we acquire our language from our parents and other people. Reformed epistemologists might claim that it *is* equally obvious in communities in which children are taught from the earliest age to understand themselves in relation to God. That claim, however, would be disconfirmed by the fact that although children raised in such communities sometimes later become atheists, they never come to doubt the existence of the people from whom they learned to speak.

Although that point would suffice to undermine the claim for parity, there is a third factor that further helps explain our unquestioning acceptance of the reality of other minds, a factor that unites this hard-core commonsense belief with our beliefs in the external world and the past. This third factor, already mentioned, is an immediate prehension of other minds occurring at the subliminal level all the time. Plantinga's original parity argument in *God and Other Minds,* by contrast, included an explicit denial of the possibility of a direct perception of other minds:

> [W]hile a person can observe another's behavior and circumstances, he cannot perceive another's mental states. "The thoughts and passions of the mind are invisible," says Thomas Reid. "Intangible, odorless, and inaudible," we might add; and they cannot be tasted either. Hence we cannot come to know that another is in pain in the way in which we can learn that he has red hair; unlike his hair, his pain cannot be perceived. (1990, 188)

This analysis forms the basis for Plantinga's contention that although "no one has direct access to the mental states of another," we "can know the mental states of another" (1990, 204). By thereby suggesting that we have a properly basic belief that is not based on perception (as well as not being self-evident or simply a truth about our own state of mind), Plantinga has prepared the way for his argument that belief in the God of traditional theism, being in the same epistemic boat, can also be properly basic.

However, Plantinga's claim that we cannot directly perceive the mental states of others, such as their pains, is contradicted by a massive amount of empirical evidence (Broughton 1991; Edge et al. 1986; Griffin 1997a). This evidence suggests that the existence of other minds belongs to our hard-core commonsense notions partly for the same reason as do our beliefs about the past and the external world.

Plantinga's only acknowledgment of this possibility is his comment that "Baron von Hügel suggested that we know the mind of another (on at least some occasions) directly, in the same way we know our own minds." But Plantinga quickly dismisses this possibility by interpreting it in such a way that it is obviously false. Von Hügel, opines Plantinga, "apparently believed that just as a man has 'direct access' to his own mind, so he may on some occasions have direct access to someone else's. It is not easy to understand the suggestion, but presumably it comes to supposing that some propositions ascribing mental states to others are incorrigible for me—and this seems to be just false" (1990, 190–91). Direct access, however, need not mean incorrigibility. For example, I have direct access to my own past experiences, but sometimes I misremember, perhaps thinking I had actually written a letter that I had only planned to write. Parapsychologists who accept the reality of telepathy, understood as the direct nonsensory perception of another mind, certainly do not equate it with incorrigibility. The same is true of telepaths themselves. In some experiments, for example, subjects are given the opportunity to make "confidence calls," in which they indicate that they are especially confident of being correct. Subjects typically make confidence calls only rarely. And although such guesses usually have a higher percentage of "hits" than other guesses, even some of them are wrong (Edge et al. 1986, 156, 171).

In any case, given the evidence that we directly prehend other minds, combined with the twofold fact that the existence of other minds is presupposed by our very ability to ask the question and that the argument from analogy is very strong, the original basis for Plantinga's parity argument is undermined because *we have very good, universally valid reasons for believing in other minds.* When this point is combined with the prehensive explanations of our beliefs in the past and the external world, the whole argument is undermined.

Plantinga is right that there are basic beliefs that do not fit the criteria of classical foundationalism. But if, on the basis of the recognition of the reality of nonsensory perception, the criterion of "evident to the senses" is enlarged to "evident to perception," we can include our hard-core common-sense beliefs in the external world, the past, and other minds in our list of basic beliefs. Once we recognize that this is the way to handle the problem to which Plantinga has called attention, we can see why his claim of epistemic parity is prima facie so implausible. The truth of the belief in the God of traditional theism, unlike the truth of these hard-core commonsense beliefs, is *not* evident to perception and (therefore) not universally presupposed in practice. The recognition that these three commonsense beliefs should be considered properly basic, therefore, provides no justification for claiming that one can legitimately take belief in the God of traditional theism as properly basic.

In speaking of some beliefs as properly basic, I am assuming that the notion of basic beliefs can be separated from foundationalism. In calling a belief *basic,* I am referring to how we know it (namely, immediately, without inferring it from other beliefs), not to the idea that it should come first in developing a rational system of thought. The position I am suggesting is that our hard-core commonsense beliefs should be included among the beliefs that are properly basic for all thinkers, that this is so because we inevitably presuppose them, that *this* is so because their truth is always evident to our primal mode of perception, and that the set of basic beliefs should be used as a compass, to warn us when our intellectual journey is going off course, not as a foundation stone from which all nonbasic beliefs must be derived.

Parity Reconceived

From the perspective of Whitehead's reformed subjectivist principle, we have seen that the principal claim of Reformed epistemology, that God as construed by traditional theism can be properly basic, should be rejected. This conclusion does not mean, however, that Reformed epistemology contains no element of truth but only that it has exaggerated the truth it has seen, which is that our knowledge of God is not entirely inferential. Given Whitehead's reformed subjectivist principle combined with his theism, it follows that we are directly prehending God all the time. *God* here, of course, refers to God as construed by process philosophy and theology, not as construed by Reformed epistemology.

These two construals are not as different as might be assumed from the fact that "Reformed" refers to Calvinism because Plantinga and Wolterstorff have partly modified Calvin's own doctrine of God in the direction of process theology. With regard to divine action in the world, the notion of complete divine determinism of all events in the world has been rejected to allow for freedom, at least for that of human beings (Plantinga 1974). With regard to the world's influence on God, the traditional views of divine eternity and impassibility have been rejected (Wolterstorff 1988). The two construals still differ, however, on the question of divine power, as the Reformed thinkers retain the traditional doctrine, according to which God *could* totally determine events within the world. This difference is correlated with the different ways in which the two schools think of God as immediately given to human experience.

In light of the fact that process philosophy regards God as directly prehended, one might assume that it would regard belief in God to be on an epistemic par with our hard-core commonsense beliefs—indeed, to be one of them. That is partly true. As argued in Chapters 2 and 5, because we directly prehend God, we all have an awareness, at some level, of the existence of *a Holy Reality.* We are also aware of a *principle of rightness,* through which we know that there are better and worse actions and outcomes. And we have a sense of *ultimate importance,* that somehow what we do matters in the long run. These three beliefs can be said to belong to our hard-core commonsense beliefs, even if less obviously than is the case with the other examples we have been discussing.

Although from the perspective of a theist, especially a process theist, these three beliefs add up to a basic belief in God, it is not universally obvious that this is the case. As pointed out by Penelhum, a person can have experiences of God without *knowing* that they are experiences of God (1992, 117). To explicate our immediate experience in terms of "God and the World," Whitehead has noted, is to introduce a greater element of interpretation than when we speak of many other opposites, such as "the many and the one" (which implies the external world) and "freedom and necessity" (which implies both causation and self-determination) (PR 341). We cannot say, accordingly, that "belief in God" is a properly basic belief. We *can* claim this status for belief in a Holy Reality, along with the beliefs in a principle of rightness and ultimate importance, but not for any highly ramified doctrine of God, be it that of Reformed or of process philosophers. For any such doctrine to be rationally held, at least after one knows of the existence of competing doctrines, arguments in terms of self-consistency and adequacy to the relevant evidence are required.

Immediacy and Evidence

The position suggested in the previous paragraph is in line with those of Wykstra and Penelhum, who have given two of the most cogent critiques of Reformed epistemology. Wykstra, arguing for a "sensible evidentialism," points out that for Plantinga evidentialism about God presupposes classical foundationalism, which assumes that we have no noninferential access to God. Plantinga assumes that by rejecting classical foundationalism he has overcome the primary basis for evidentialism about God. Wykstra argues, however, that there is a better rationale for this evidentialism. This rationale presupposes a distinction between two kinds of inferential evidence: derivational and discriminational. In rejecting the need for inferential evidence, Plantinga has in mind the derivational type, which is used to derive "truths to which our basic faculties give no access" (Wykstra 1989, 434). To employ derivational inferential evidence for God would be to deny one of the essential points of theism, which is that we do have a capacity for being aware of God's presence and character (a *Sensus Divinitatis*). But there are also some truths for which, although we do have direct access to them, we need inferential evidence "because our basic faculties give us, as it were, conflicting signals about their truth." The result is, in Wykstra's phrase quoted earlier, "ostensible epistemic parity." In such situations, an appeal to evidence is needed to "resolve the ostensible parity by functioning as a discriminating feature" (434). In relation to religious experience, Wykstra suggests, one's direct access to the divine reality would provide the *force* for belief, while the inferential evidence would discriminate "a *direction* for one's believing" (435–36). Penelhum argues, similarly, that although one can be rational in *adopting* the beliefs of one's tradition as basic beliefs, one cannot be rational in *maintaining* these beliefs without supporting evidence after becoming aware of the competing truth-claims made by other religious traditions and by nonreligious interpretations of the universe. Accordingly, Penelhum says, because the world exhibits "multiple religious ambiguity," one needs to engage in natural theology to "disambiguate our world" (1992, 111–12).

The recommendations of Wykstra and Penelhum support the position of the present book: religion has been so pervasive of human culture because all people share, at the depths of their experience, an awareness of the existence of a Holy Reality.[8] This universal religious experience even includes elements suggesting that this Holy Reality is a personal being. These elements are not sufficiently unambiguous, however, to make belief in a personal deity universal. Furthermore, pervasive nonreligious interpretations of reality can lead people even to deny that they have any awareness of a Holy Reality. So although our immediate experience of the Divine Holiness provides the basic reason for believing in God, this reason must be supplemented by a cumulative case for the existence God, and our inherited concepts of the nature of God must be evaluated for their self-consistency and their adequacy in the face of all the relevant evidence, such as the evil and evolutionary nature of our world as well as its order and beauty.

Ambiguity and Revelation

One relevant part of the evidence is precisely the "multiple religious ambiguity," with the resulting "ostensible epistemic parity," to which Wykstra and Penelhum call attention. Would traditional theism lead us to expect such ambiguity? Wykstra points to this problem in commenting that Reformed theists may think that although the discriminational evidentialism he has proposed does not contradict theism, it is not very harmonious with it: "If theism is true, and God himself has given humans a *Sensus Divinitatis,*" says Wykstra, "is it not odd that our experiential religious beliefs should need so much evidential refining?" (1989, 437). Yes, it is odd. If God were omnipotent in the traditional sense as well as perfectly loving, we would ex-

---

[8] Contrary to the view that Wykstra shares with Plantinga and Wolterstorff, however, Whitehead's explanation of this awareness requires no implanted *Sensus Divinitatis,* in fact no special religious sense of any sort (RM 120), because of his recognition of a nonsensory mode of perception. Whiteheadian process philosophy, accordingly, need not violate domain uniformitarianism in order to defend the reality of genuine religious experience.

pect—especially if, as Calvinists usually hold, there will be divinely imparted retribution for those who do not believe and live properly—that God would make the divine existence, nature, and will unambiguously clear, and equally so to all peoples.[9] The solution suggested by Wykstra to this problem is to appeal to sin, suggesting that "our fallenness depraves (as Calvin put it) not just part but the totality of our nature: it corrupts even our spiritualities, distorting . . . our dispositions to form experiential beliefs about God" (1989, 437).

Although that solution to the problem avoids any outright contradiction—at least if we do not probe further to ask why God, being omnipotent as well as loving, has allowed human history to be dominated by this fallenness—it is not the only possible answer. Process philosophy suggests that we can avoid the problem, as well as the more general problem of evil of which it is a part, by revising our doctrine of divine power. That is, given the nonoverridable capacity of human beings to be shaped intellectually by the tradition in which they stand, to exercise intellectual self-determination, and to shape the thinking of future human beings, God simply cannot provide the kind of unambiguous revelation presupposed in the statement of the problem.

Plantinga has, as mentioned above, modified the Calvinistic idea of divine power so as to allow for genuine human freedom, which he rightly sees not to be compatible with complete divine determination of human belief and action. As we saw in Chapter 1, however, he has retained the belief that God has the power to override human freedom at any time. Because of this belief, Plantinga can hold that God has used this power to provide a revelation in the Christian scriptures that is qualitatively clearer about the divine nature and purposes than any other revelation. This conviction, as we saw in Chapter 7, lies behind his religious exclusivism. It also lies behind his defense of the claim that belief in the God of traditional theism can be properly basic, which involves his conception of the very nature of philosophy of religion.

Basic Beliefs, Revelation, and Defensive Rationality

The purpose of philosophical reflection about religion, according to Reformed epistemologists, is not to seek the truth but to defend the beliefs of their religious community—or, more precisely, to defend the right of

[9] As we saw in Chapter 7, several religious philosophers, from Matthew Tindal to Huston Smith, have argued for this conclusion.

members of their community, including themselves, to retain their beliefs even after becoming aware of the existence of competing beliefs. With regard to the existence of the God of traditional theism, their concern, unlike that of Swinburne, is not to show that this existence is more probable than not but simply to argue that they are within their "intellectual rights" in taking it as basic for them—that they are not thereby committing any "epistemic sin." However, as George Mavrodes points out, those who want their beliefs to be rational in this sense have a very "minimal ambition," rather like those who merely want their actions to be legal. Just as we usually desire more for our actions, such as that they also be moral and useful, we also generally desire more for our beliefs, namely, that "those beliefs should be true, should correspond somehow with reality" (1983, 208).

The fact that the Reformed epistemologists understand philosophy of religion as a defensive rather than a truth-seeking enterprise, however, does not mean that they are indifferent to the question of truth. Their approach, rather, reflects the conviction that they already had the truth about God before engaging in philosophical reflection. It is here, of course, that their belief in the Christian revelation plays a decisive role. As suggested by the title of Wolterstorff's book *Reason within the Bounds of Religion* (1976), they hold that the Christian philosopher should simply take for granted the truth of ideas that seem to be clearly enunciated in the Bible. For example, although he generally agrees with Reid's position, Wolterstorff criticizes "Reid's Enlightenment insistence that revelation must be tested by reason," asking rhetorically: "Does this not fundamentally subordinate revelation to reason? What then is left of the authority of Scripture? But is it not fundamental to the identity and the direction of the Christian community that Scripture function as canon within it—that it be accepted as authoritative?" (1983b, 67).

With regard to the idea of God in particular, the position of the Reformed epistemologists means, says Plantinga, that they are entirely within their rights "in *starting with* belief in God, in accepting it as basic, and in taking it as a premise for arguing to other conclusions" (1983b, 371). In stating this, furthermore, Plantinga is not simply saying that it is his role, as a Christian philosopher, to take this belief for granted, without worrying about whether it is really true. Rather, he claims, Christians *know* that God exists (1996, 331–32). That is what it means to say that belief in God is properly basic for them.

The fact that philosophy's task in relation to these basic beliefs is purely defensive, to be sure, does not mean that philosophy has no role to play at all. The mere fact that he may be initially justified in accepting belief in God as basic, Plantinga acknowledges, does not mean that he can *remain* justified, without doing anything, if some apparently good argument or evidence arises that suggests the falsity of his belief (1983b, 381). In this situation, he can remain justified only if he can "defeat the defeater," that is, show that the argument or evidence does not prove the falsity of his belief in God.

The philosophical task in this situation, however, remains primarily defensive. For example, in response to the problem of evil, Plantinga has provided a free-will defense (1974), which argues that, assuming that God has granted genuine freedom to rational creatures, there is no inconsistency in believing in the existence of an all-powerful, all-good God while recognizing the occurrence of genuine evils. The point of calling it a "defense" rather than a "theodicy" is that it *need not be plausible.* "Clearly it need be neither true, nor probable, nor plausible, nor believed by most theists, nor anything else of that sort," says Plantinga. "The fact that a particular proffered [explanation] is implausible," he contends, "is utterly beside the point" (1981, 26–27). The explanation needs to be only barely possible. Indeed, Plantinga says, to defeat the prima facie defeater posed by the problem of evil, he does not even have to give a possible reason for the existence of evil. He can simply say: "If God is good and powerful as the theist believes, then he will indeed have a good reason for permitting evil; but why suppose the theist must be in a position to figure out what it is?[10] . . . [If] the best the atheologian can do by way of an antitheistic argument from evil is to point out that theists do not have an explanation for evil: then theism has nothing to fear from him" (1981, 28). If this is all that theistic philosophers must do to defend the rationality of their beliefs, then the ambition involved in wanting their beliefs to be considered "rational" is extremely minimal indeed. Reformed epistemology operates, says Wolterstorff, in terms of the assumption that beliefs "are innocent until proved guilty" (1983a, 163). Although there is something to be said for this "credulity principle," Reformed epistemologists employ it in such a way as to make the guilt of any of their basic beliefs virtually impossible to prove.

An even more disturbing implication of the program of Reformed epistemology, however, is that its approach, if generally adopted, would promote what Penelhum has called "a Balkanized world."

[10] Given Plantinga's belief in a God who is good as well as omnipotent, the critic could wonder why this God had not clearly revealed the reason for allowing so much evil, especially in light of Plantinga's belief that this God has revealed other details of the divine plan in such exquisite detail.

Basic Beliefs and Balkanization

Claiming that there are no universally valid necessary and sufficient conditions for proper basicality, Plantinga holds that each community has the right to form its criteria in terms of its own examples of beliefs that it takes to be properly basic. The likely result, he says, is that different communities will come up with different examples and therefore different criteria:

> [T]here is no reason to assume, in advance, that everyone will agree on the examples. The Christian will of course suppose that belief in God is entirely proper and rational; if he doesn't accept this belief on the basis of other propositions, he will conclude that it is basic for him and quite properly so. Followers of Bertrand Russell and Madelyn Murray O'Hare may disagree; but how is that relevant? Must my criteria, or those of the Christian community, conform to their examples? Surely not. The Christian community is responsible to *its* set of examples, not to theirs. (1989, 425)

If we generalize this principle, the implication is that each religious and ideological community is to decide upon its own criteria for basicality in terms of the beliefs that *it* takes to be properly basic. Given the assumption that there are no universally valid criteria of proper basicality, each community would simply ignore criticisms from any other community, be it the scientific, the philosophical, or some other religious community. Plantinga explicitly says this about the Christian community in an article called "Advice to Christian Philosophers," in which he is seeking to bolster "Christian self-confidence" (1984, 269). If the Christian's "pre-philosophical opinions"—the term used here for basic beliefs—"are widely rejected as naive, or pre-scientific, or primitive," says Plantinga, "that is nothing whatever against them" (1984, 268). Given the number of communities in the world, this principle would seem to mean that virtually any belief could be taken to be properly basic by some community or other. Plantinga, being aware of this objection, formulates it thus:

> [I]f belief in God is properly basic, why can't *just any* belief be properly basic? Couldn't we say the same for any bizarre aberration we can think of? . . . What about the belief that the Great Pumpkin returns every Halloween? Could I properly take *that* as basic? . . . If we say that belief in God is properly basic, won't we be committed to holding that just anything, or nearly anything, can properly be taken as basic, thus throwing wide the gates to irrationalism and superstition? (1989, 423)

Although that certainly would seem to be the implication of Plantinga's position, he claims otherwise, saying that his rejecting the traditional criterion of proper basicality without proposing a substitute "does not mean that he is committed to supposing just anything is properly basic" (1989, 424). With regard to his denial that belief in the Great Pumpkin is properly basic, a relevant difference is said to exist between it and belief in God: there is a natural tendency to believe in God, which was itself implanted by God, but "the same cannot be said for the Great Pumpkin." Far from having to take belief in the Great Pumpkin as properly basic, Plantinga "may take belief in the Great Pumpkin as a paradigm of irrational basic belief" (1989, 425–26).

This answer, however, completely misses the point. The point of the objection is not that Plantinga's Christians would have to accept just any belief as properly basic but that they would "be committed to holding that just anything, or nearly anything, can properly be taken as basic"—that is, *by other communities*. Because Plantinga's Christian community insists that it rightly has its own criterion of proper basicality, so that it has the right to take any belief it pleases as properly basic and hold to it regardless of disagreement from other communities, it would have to grant the same right to all other communities, including the right to maintain the innocence of their beliefs in the same defensive spirit employed by Plantinga.

Plantinga trivializes the implication of this point by using belief in the Great Pumpkin as an example. It is not a good example precisely because, as Plantinga says, there is no community with a natural tendency to believe in the Great Pumpkin. The concern becomes much less laughable, however, if we use real-life examples, such as the natural tendency for each religious tradition to believe that it is superior to all others—a tendency exemplified not only in the Christian exclusivism embodied in Plantinga but also in Judaism, Islam, Confucianism, Buddhism, and virtually every other tradition. Each such tradition has its basic beliefs, which it, according to Plantinga's principles, would be justified in taking to be *properly* basic. Some Jews, for example, take it as a properly basic belief that God gave them a particular piece of the Earth, so that regardless of the fact that other people have been living there for many centuries, it rightfully belongs to Jews. This belief became so dangerous in the twentieth century, of course, because Nazism had *its* basic beliefs, which it took to be proper. Much of the political history of the twentieth century involved the rise and spread of Communism, with quite different basic beliefs, which its true believers took to be properly basic. The clash between Islam and the modern West is becoming so dangerous partly because these two traditions have very different basic beliefs, with each taking its own as properly basic and those of the other side as false, perhaps demonic.

In citing these examples, to be sure, I am pointing out that the world already is, and long has been, politically and religiously Balkanized, in the sense of being divided into hostile, mutually uncomprehending units with different fundamental beliefs and values. Intellectual representatives of various traditions, however, have made considerable progress in recent centuries in overcoming the mutual incomprehension and even forging shared beliefs and values. If the stance of Reformed epistemology were adopted by Christians generally, Christian leadership in this enterprise would be undercut. With regard to the debate about the existence of God, Plantinga says that "the Christian community ought *not* to think of itself as engaged in this common effort to determine the probability or philosophical plausibility of belief in God" (1984, 261). Given what Plantinga has said about the irrelevance of other people's opinions regarding any beliefs that Christians of his type take as properly basic, we can see that he would be against thinking of the Christian community as engaged in *any* common effort to find a basis for agreement on fundamental religious beliefs and values.

The intellectual leaders of the various other religious and ideological communities would be encouraged, by analogy, to adopt a similar attitude, thereby giving up all efforts to reach interreligious and intercultural agreement. Plantinga perhaps thinks that it is uniquely appropriate for Christians to take their basic beliefs as virtually unquestionable starting points because these beliefs are *true,* being based on genuine divine revelation. But true believers in other traditions are equally convinced of the truth of *their* basic beliefs, which are often considered revealed. Plantinga's advice to Christian philosophers would, if generalized, lead to the development of Buddhist epistemology, Hindu epistemology, Jewish epistemology, Islamic epistemology, Marxist epistemology, Nazi epistemology, and so on. The Balkanized units would, in fact, be even smaller. For example, within Christianity, besides traditional Roman Catholic epistemology, which would take the infallibility of the pope as properly basic, there would be Lutheran epistemology, Southern Baptist epistemology, and so on. Within Buddhism, there would be Zen epistemology, Pure Land epistemology, Nichiren epistemology, and so on. Many of these denominations, furthermore, would likely—as the adjective "traditional" before "Roman Catholic" suggests—be divided into epistemological subcommunities.

Again, this is the state of affairs that to a great extent we have de facto had. The aim of the liberal tradition, however, has been to forge a common basis for conversation among all peoples. This aim has thus far been carried out very imperfectly, largely because of the adoption of substantive Enlighten-ment assumptions, especially the sensationist theory of perception—along with, of course, typical human blindness and arrogance. Even so, it has had some success. Progress has been made, furthermore, in overcoming the ar-rogance and problematic assumptions, so that the degree of success needed if human civilization is to survive may yet be achieved. But Plantinga's post-liberal approach to basic beliefs, if widely adopted, would put an end to this effort. The de facto religious–cultural–ideological Balkanization of the world would be accepted as ideal, or at least inevitable.

Penelhum has pointed out this dangerous implication of Reformed epis-temology. Mere "parity between commonsense beliefs and religious ones," says Penelhum, "is not enough for religion" because it leads to "a Balkanized world" (1992, 111). While sharing Penelhum's concern, process philoso-phers would partly disagree with his analysis. From our perspective, the problem with Plantinga's program is not that parity between commonsense beliefs and belief in God is not enough but that there is no real parity. The hard-core commonsense beliefs are ahistorical, in the sense of being com-mon to people in all times and places. Belief in a Holy Reality, I have sug-gested, is one of these beliefs. Belief in the God of traditional theism, by contrast, is a highly particularized way of understanding this Holy Reality, which arose historically in one particular tradition and is not universally pre-supposed, even among adherents of the biblically rooted religious traditions. The peculiarity of Reformed epistemology is its attempt to justify treating this historically particular belief as if it were in the same class as, or at least on a epistemic par with, ahistorical universal beliefs, so that it, like them, can be considered properly basic.

The rationale for this attempt is the idea, shared with Stout and many other contemporary philosophers, that rationality is radically situational, or contextual. That claim is certainly correct at one level, in that what it is ra-tional for people raised in one religious community to believe may be radi-cally different from what it is rational for persons raised in different com-munities to believe, at least before they have been exposed to one another's beliefs. What Reformed epistemologists mean by speaking of situated ra-tionality, however, is that when the people of the different communities be-come exposed to one another's beliefs, there are no universally valid criteria of rationality, at least of a substantive nature, in terms of which to evaluate their respective inherited beliefs. The problem with this claim is shown in Wolterstorff's attempt to illustrate it. Having said (correctly) that some be-liefs that would be rational for persons in a tribal society would not be ra-tional for intellectuals in the modern West, Wolterstorff makes the further claim that we cannot "ask in abstract, nonspecific fashion whether it is rational to believe that God exists, . . . that there is an external world, . . . that there are other persons" (1983a, 155). The problem with this argument is that people in tribal societies and the modern West all *do* believe in other persons and the external world. It is only the belief in God, as understood by Wolterstorff, that is not universal. What his illustration really shows is that his belief in God, if it is to be considered rational, has to be justified in terms other than those that justify the rationality of belief in persons and the external world.

The difference between the Reformed position and that of process philosophy can be brought out more precisely in terms of the discussion, in the first section above, of a "vision of reality." That discussion supported the idea that rationality is (largely) situated by pointing out that we all inevitably philosophize in terms of some such preconceptual vision, which we usually have inherited from the tradition in which we stand. From this perspective, Plantinga is entirely correct to say that philosophy "is in large part a clarification, systematization, articulation, relating, and deepening of pre-philosophical opinions." And he is right, furthermore, to add that this fact is largely inevitable because "we come to philosophy with pre-philosophical opinions; we can do no other" (1984, 268).

There are, however, two crucial differences between Plantinga's position and the one I have suggested. In the first place, in speaking of the "pre-philosophical opinions" with which the thinker begins, Plantinga means not merely a *preconceptual* vision of reality but a very particular, highly ramified concept of God. The difference is manifested in the fact that Plantinga says that "we must strive to be Christian philosophers" (1984, 271). One does not, by contrast, need to "strive" to see things in terms of one's vision of reality; that is simply how one does see things. The second difference involves the fact that process philosophers clearly distinguish one's vision of reality from one's set of basic (hard-core commonsense) beliefs because the former, unlike the latter, is not universally shared but merely one vision among others. As such, it cannot, after one becomes aware of other visions, be taken as properly basic. In Reformed epistemology, however, no such distinction in kind is made. The whole approach, in fact, is to try to convince us that historically particular beliefs, such as traditional theism, can be treated as if they were in the same class as universal beliefs, such as our beliefs in the past, the external world, and other minds.

Reformed epistemology is based on a realistic recognition. Plantinga and Wolterstorff, unlike Swinburne, realize that the existence of the God of traditional theism cannot be shown, in any sort of objective way, to be more probable than not. Their epistemology is designed to allow themselves and fellow traditional theists, in spite of this fact, to regard themselves as rational. Plantinga expresses this motive explicitly, saying that his epistemology enables him to answer the claim that theistic belief is "irrational or unreasonable or intellectually second- or third-rate because there is insufficient evidence for it" (1990, xi). From the perspective of process philosophy, the better approach would be to reformulate theism so that it *can* be shown to be, among other things, more probable than not.

That, of course, has been a central purpose running throughout this book. The panexperientialist ontology, besides providing a better basis for science and philosophy than does either dualism or materialism, shows how variable divine influence can be a normal part of the world's causal processes. The prehensive doctrine of perception, besides overcoming numerous problems bequeathed to modern science and philosophy by sensationism, shows how genuine religious experience can occur without any violation of normal perceptual processes. This ontology and this epistemology, as we saw in Chapter 5, provide the basis for a strong cumulative case for the existence of a Divine Power as the best explanation of many features of the world in general and human experience in particular. The naturalism of process panentheism, with its rejection of creation ex nihilo and thereby the possibility of supernatural interruptions of the world's normal causal processes, overcomes the main arguments *against* the existence of a Divine Power, such as the problem of evil, the evolutionary nature of our universe, and the existence of many religions. A central feature of this naturalistic theism, its distinction between God and creative experience, explains in particular the existence of both theistic and nontheistic religious experience. When all these elements are combined, the existence of a Divine Reality of the sort portrayed by process theism can be seen to be overwhelmingly more probable than the alternatives presented by atheism and supernaturalism.

To summarize my argument with regard to religious knowledge: I have suggested that we can rightfully claim to have knowledge of those religiously important ideas that belong to our hard-core common sense, especially insofar as we have an ontology that shows how they can be true and an epistemology that shows how we can have immediate knowledge of this truth. We can, accordingly, claim knowledge of such things as the reality of freedom, normative values, genuine evil, a Holy Power, and ultimate meaning. We can be said to know the falsity, therefore, of a wholly disenchanted worldview.

With regard to the distinctive ideas of process philosophy that do not belong to our set of hard-core commonsense ideas, I would venture to say that in spite of the fact that majority opinion is thus far overwhelmingly on the other side, one can claim to know that the truth involves some form of non-sensationist doctrine of perception and some form of panexperientialist ontology (without thereby making the wholly improbable claim that White-headian process philosophy has provided the permanently best way to formulate these doctrines). To put the point negatively, we have sufficient warrant to say that we know sensationism, dualism, and materialism all to be false. With regard to process panentheism as an explication of our hard-core commonsense knowledge of a Holy Power, normative values, and ultimate meaning, I would say the following. Having placed the bar very high for us-ing the term *knowledge,* we certainly should not claim knowledge for any highly ramified doctrine, such as that of process theism. Even with regard to the truth of *some sort* of naturalistic theism—which I indicated in the previ-ous paragraph by speaking of "the existence of a Divine Reality of the sort portrayed by process theism," I speak not of knowledge but only of "over-whelming probability," and this in comparison with atheism and supernat-uralism. Or, to put the issue of theism in context, I would say that some form of naturalism$_{ppp}$ is overwhelmingly more probable than either some form of supernaturalistic dualism or some form of naturalism$_{sam}$.

With regard to life after death, my position is somewhat parallel. I cer-tainly do not think we have a sufficient basis for speaking of knowledge of any particular form of life after death. I would not even say that we can know (for sure) that our present existence is followed by *some* form, or forms, of continued conscious existence beyond bodily death. I do think, however, as I argued in Chapter 6 and more fully in *Parapsychology, Philosophy, and Spir-ituality* (1997a), that a quite strong cumulative case can be made for the re-ality of such an existence, especially when the various types of empirical evi-dence are examined from the perspective of a worldview, such as that of process philosophy, that allows this evidence to be taken seriously. From such a perspective, we can think of the belief in some form of life after death as considerably more probable than its denial. With these final reflections about ultimate matters, I conclude this presentation of a process philosophy of religion.

References

Abraham, William. 1985. *An Introduction to the Philosophy of Religion.* Englewood Cliffs, N.J.: Prentice-Hall.

Adler, Julius, and Wing-Wai Tse. 1974. "Decision-Making in Bacteria." *Science* 184: 1292–94.

Aiken, Henry David. 1958. "God and Evil: A Study of Some Relations between Faith and Morals." *Ethics* 68, no. 2 (January): 77–97.

Alston, William P. 1995. "Realism and the Christian Faith." *International Journal for Philosophy of Religion* 38, nos. 1–3 (December): 37–60.

———. 1996. *A Realist Conception of Truth.* Ithaca: Cornell University Press.

Anselm, Saint. 1903. *Proslogium; Monologium; An Appendix in Behalf of the Fool by Gaunilon; and Cur Deus Homo.* Translated by S. N. Deane. LaSalle, Ill.: Open Court.

Apel, Karl-Otto. 1987. "The Problem of Philosophical Foundations in Light of a Transcendental Pragmatics of Language." In *After Philosophy: End or Transformation?* edited by Kenneth Baynes, James Bohman, and Thomas McCarthy, 250–90. Cambridge: MIT Press.

Aquinas, St. Thomas. 1952. *Summa Theologica.* Translated by Fathers of the English Dominican Province as revised by Daniel J. Sullivan. A volume in *Great Books of the Western World,* edited by Robert M. Hutchins. Chicago: W. Benton.

Armstrong, Susan. 1976. "The Rights of Nonhuman Beings: A Whiteheadian Study." Ph.D. dissertation, Bryn Mawr College, Bryn Mawr, Pa.

———. 1986. "Whitehead's Metaphysical System as a Foundation for Environmental Ethics." *Environmental Ethics* 8, no. 3 (fall): 241–59 (under the name Armstrong-Buck).

———. 1989. "Nonhuman Experience: A Whiteheadian Analysis." *Process Studies* 18, no. 1 (spring): 1–18 (under the name Armstrong-Buck).

———. 1991. "What Process Philosophy Can Contribute to the Land Ethic and Deep Ecology." *Trumpeter* 8, no. 1 (winter): 29–34 (under the name Armstrong-Buck).

Augustine, Saint. 1948a. *Enchiridion.* Translated by J. F. Shaw. In *Basic Writings of St. Augustine,* 2 vols., edited by Whitney J. Oates. New York: Random House.

———. 1948b. *Grace and Free Will*. Translated by P. Holmes. In *Basic Writings of St. Augustine*, 2 vols., edited by Whitney J. Oates. New York: Random House.

———. 1953. *The Nature of the Good*. Translated by John H. S. Burleigh. In *Augustine: Earlier Writings*, vol. 6 of Library of Christian Classics. Philadelphia: Westminster Press.

Ayer, A. J. 1952. *Language, Truth, and Logic*. New York: Dover.

Bartley, William Warren. 1984. *Retreat from Commitment*. LaSalle, Ill.: Open Court.

Barbour, Ian G. 1990. *Religion in an Age of Science*. San Francisco: Harper & Row.

———. 1995. "Ways of Relating Science and Theology." In *Physics, Philosophy, and Theology: A Common Quest for Understanding*, 2d ed., edited by Robert John Russell, William R. Stoeger, and George V. Coyne, 21–45. Vatican City State: Vatican Observatory.

Baumer, Franklin. 1960. *Religion and the Rise of Scepticism*. New York: Harcourt, Brace.

Becker, Carl. 1932. *The Heavenly City of the Eighteenth-Century Philosophers*. New Haven: Yale University Press.

Behe, Michael J. 1996. *Darwin's Black Box: The Biochemical Challenge to Evolution*. New York: Free Press.

Benacerraf, Paul. 1983. "Mathematical Truth." In *Philosophy of Mathematics*, 2d ed., edited by Paul Benacerraf and Hilary Putnam, 403–20. Cambridge: Cambridge University Press.

Bertocci, Peter. 1972. "Hartshorne on Personal Identity: A Personalistic Critique." *Process Studies* 2, no. 3 (fall): 216–21.

Birch, Charles. 1993a [1976]. *Confronting the Future*. Rev. ed. New York: Penguin Books.

———. 1993b. *Regarding Compassion for Humanity and Nature*. Kensington, Australia: New South Wales University Press; St. Louis: Chalice Press.

———. 1995. *Feelings*. Sydney: University of New South Wales Press.

Birch, Charles, and John B. Cobb, Jr. 1981. *The Liberation of Life: From the Cell to the Community*. Cambridge: Cambridge University Press.

Bohm, David, and B. J. Hiley. 1993. *The Undivided Universe: An Ontological Interpretation of Quantum Theory*. London: Routledge.

Bowler, Peter J. 1983. *The Eclipse of Darwinism: Anti-Darwinian Evolution Theories in the Decades around 1900*. Baltimore: Johns Hopkins University Press.

Boyd, Gregory A. 1992. *Trinity and Process: A Critical Evaluation and Reconstruction of Hartshorne's Di-Polar Theism towards a Trinitarian Metaphysics*. New York: Peter Lang.

Bradley, F. H. 1893. *Appearance and Reality: A Metaphysical Essay*. Oxford: Clarendon Press.

———. 1914. *Essays on Truth and Reality*. Oxford: Clarendon Press.

Braun, Herbert. 1965. "The Problem of New Testament Theology." In *The Bultmann School of Biblical Interpretation: New Directions?* edited by Robert Funk, 169–83. New York: Harper & Row.

Breazeale, Kathlyn A. 1993. "Don't Blame It on the Seeds: Toward a Feminist Process Understanding of Anthropology, Sin, and Sexuality." *Process Studies* 22, no. 2 (summer): 71–83.

Broad, C. D. 1969. *Religion, Philosophy, and Psychical Research: Selected Essays*. New York: Humanities Press.

Brock, Rita. 1988. *Journeys by Heart: A Christology of Erotic Power*. New York: Crossroad.

Broughton, Richard S. 1991. *Parapsychology: The Controversial Science*. New York: Ballantine Books.

Brown, Delwin. 1997. "Academic Theology and Religious Studies." *Bulletin of the Council of Societies for the Study of Religion* 26, no. 3 (September): 64–66.

Bultmann, Rudolf. 1958. *Jesus Christ and Mythology*. New York: Charles Scribner's Sons.

Byrne, Peter. 1989. *Natural Religion and the Nature of Religion: The Legacy of Deism*. London: Routledge.

Calvin, John. 1960. *Institutes of the Christian Religion*. Edited by John T. McNeill. Translated by Ford Lewis Battles. Philadelphia: Westminster Press.

Campbell, Keith. 1984. *Body and Mind*. 2d ed. Notre Dame: University of Notre Dame Press.

Čapek, Milič. 1991. *The New Aspects of Time: Its Continuity and Novelties: Selected Papers in the Philosophy of Science*. Edited by Robert S. Cohen. Boston: Kluwer Academic.

Cauthen, Kenneth. 1987. *The Passion for Equality*. Totowa, N.J.: Rowman & Littlefield.

Chihara, C. 1982. "A Gödelian Thesis Regarding Mathematical Objects: Do They Exist? And Can We Perceive Them?" *Philosophical Review* 91:211–17.

Chisholm, Roderick. 1977. *Theory of Knowledge,* 2d ed. Englewood Cliffs, N.J.: Prentice-Hall.

Christ, Carol P. 1997. *Rebirth of the Goddess: Finding Meaning in Feminist Spirituality*. New York: Addison Wesley.

Christian, William A. 1959. *An Interpretation of Whitehead's Metaphysics*. New Haven: Yale University Press.

——. 1964. "The Concept of God as a Derivative Notion." In *Process and Divinity: The Hartshorne Festschrift,* edited by William L. Reese and Eugene Freeman, 181–204. LaSalle, Ill.: Open Court.

Cobb, John B., Jr. 1962. *Living Options in Protestant Theology*. Philadelphia: Westminster Press.

——. 1965. *A Christian Natural Theology: Based on the Thought of Alfred North Whitehead*. Philadelphia: Westminster Press.

——. 1967. *The Structure of Christian Existence*. Philadelphia: Westminster Press (reprinted with a new preface, Lanham, Md.: University Press of America, 1990).

——. 1969. *God and the World*. Philadelphia: Westminster Press.

——. 1970. "The Population Explosion and the Rights of the Subhuman World." *IDOC-International: North American Edition* (September 12): 40–62 (abridged version in *Dimensions of the Environmental Crisis,* edited by John A. Day, F. F. Fost, and P. Rose, 19–32 [New York: John Wiley, 1971]).

——. 1971. "The 'Whitehead without God' Debate: The Critique." *Process Studies* 1, no. 2 (summer): 91–100.

——. 1972a. *Is It Too Late? A Theology of Ecology*. Beverly Hills, Calif.: Bruce (rev. ed., Denton, Tex.: Environmental Ethics Books, 1995).

——. 1972b. "Regional Inclusion and the Extensive Continuum." *Process Studies* 2, no. 4 (winter): 277–95.

——. 1975. *Christ in a Pluralistic Age*. Philadelphia: Westminster Press.

——. 1978. "Beyond Anthropocentrism in Ethics and Religion." In *On the Fifth Day,* edited by Richard Knowles Morris and Michael W. Fox, 137–53. Washington, D.C.: Acropolis Books.

——. 1980. "Process Theology and Environmental Issues." *Journal of Religion* 60, no. 4 (October): 440–58.

———. 1981. "The Political Implications of Whitehead's Philosophy." In *Process Philosophy and Social Thought,* edited by John B. Cobb, Jr., and W. Widick Schroeder, 11–28. Chicago: Center for the Scientific Study of Religion.

———. 1982a. *Beyond Dialogue: Toward a Mutual Transformation of Christianity and Buddhism.* Philadelphia: Fortress Press.

———. 1982b. *Process Theology as Political Theology.* Philadelphia: Westminster Press.

———. 1984. "Overcoming Reductionism." In *Existence and Actuality: Conversations with Charles Hartshorne,* edited by John B. Cobb, Jr., and Franklin I. Gamwell, 149–64. Chicago: University of Chicago Press.

———. 1987a. "Toward a Christocentric Catholic Theology." In *Toward a Universal Theology of Religion,* edited by Leonard Swidler, 86–100. Maryknoll, N.Y.: Orbis Books.

———. 1987b. "The Resurrection of the Soul." *Harvard Theological Review* 80, no. 2: 213–27.

———. 1988. "Being Itself and the Existence of God." In *The Existence of God,* edited by John R. Jacobson and Robert Lloyd Mitchell, 5–19. Lewiston, N.Y.: Edwin Mellen.

Cobb, John B., Jr., and Franklin I. Gamwell, eds. 1984. *Existence and Actuality: Conversations with Charles Hartshorne.* Chicago: University of Chicago Press.

Cobb, John B., Jr., and David Ray Griffin. 1976. *Process Theology: An Introductory Exposition.* Philadelphia: Westminster Press.

———, eds. 1977. *Mind in Nature: Essays on the Interface of Science and Philosophy.* Washington, D.C.: University Press of America.

Cobb, John B., Jr., and Christopher Ives, eds. 1990. *The Emptying God: A Buddhist-Jewish-Christian Conversation.* Maryknoll, N.Y.: Orbis Books.

Cole, K. C. 1988. "Missing Pieces of the Cosmic Puzzle." *Los Angeles Times,* June 15, A1, A16.

Cronin, Helena. 1991. *The Ant and the Peacock: Altruism and Sexual Selection from Darwin to Today.* Cambridge: Press Syndicates of University of Cambridge.

Cupitt, Donald. 1981. *Taking Leave of God.* New York: Crossroad.

Daly, Herman E., and John B. Cobb, Jr. 1994. *For the Common Good: Redirecting the Economy toward Community, the Environment, and a Sustainable Future.* 2d ed. Boston: Beacon Press.

Daly, Mary. 1973. *Beyond God the Father.* Boston: Beacon Press.

Dancy, Jonathan, ed. 1988. *Perceptual Knowledge.* Oxford: Oxford University Press.

Darwin, Charles. 1868. *The Variation of Animals and Plants under Domestication.* 2 vols. New York: Orange Judd.

———. 1958 [1872]. *The Origin of Species.* 6th ed. New York: Mentor Books.

———. 1964. *The Origin of the Species.* Facsimile of the first edition. Cambridge: Harvard University Press.

Davaney, Sheila Greeve. 1990. "God, Power, and the Struggle for Liberation: A Feminist Contribution." In *Charles Hartshorne's Concept of God,* edited by Santiago Sia, 57–75. Dordrecht: Kluwer Academic.

———, ed. 1981. *Feminism and Process Thought.* New York: Edwin Mellen.

David, Marian. 1994. *Correspondence and Disquotation: An Essay on the Nature of Truth.* Oxford: Oxford University Press.

Davidovich, Adina. 1993. *Religion as a Province of Meaning: The Kantian Foundations of Modern Theology.* Minneapolis: Augsburg Fortress.

Davidson, Donald. 1990. "The Structure and Content of Truth." *Journal of Philosophy* 87, no. 6 (June): 279–328.

Davis, Caroline Franks. 1989. *The Evidential Force of Religious Experience.* Oxford: Clarendon Press.

Dawkins, Richard. 1987. *The Blind Watchmaker: Why the Evidence of Evolution Reveals a Universe without Design.* New York: Norton.

———. 1989. *The Selfish Gene.* 2d ed. Oxford: Oxford University Press.

Dean, Thomas. 1995. "Introduction: Cross-Cultural Philosophy of Religion." In *Religious Pluralism and Truth: Essays on Cross-Cultural Philosophy of Religion,* edited by Thomas Dean, 1–5. Albany: State University of New York Press.

Denton, Michael. 1991. *Evolution: A Theory in Crisis.* London: Burnett Books.

Dewey, John. 1934. *A Common Faith.* New Haven: Yale University.

Dews, Peter. 1995. *The Limits of Disenchantment: Essays on Contemporary European Culture.* London: Verso.

Donagan, Alan. 1993. "Common Morality and Kant's Enlightenment Project." In *Prospects for a Common Morality,* edited by Gene Outka and John P. Reeder, Jr. Princeton: Princeton University Press.

Drees, Willem. 1996. *Religion, Science, and Naturalism.* Cambridge: Cambridge University Press.

Dummett, Michael. 1978. *Truth and Other Enigmas.* Cambridge: Harvard University Press.

Dunfee, Susan Nelson. 1982. "The Sin of Hiding: A Feminist Critique of Reinhold Niebuhr's Account of the Sin of Pride." *Soundings* 65, no. 3 (fall): 316–27.

———. 1989. *Beyond Servanthood: Christianity and the Liberation of Women.* Lanham, Md.: University Press of America. (See also Susan L. Nelson.)

Durkheim, Emile. 1963 [1912]. *The Elementary Forms of the Religious Life.* Translated by Joseph Ward Swain. New York: Free Press.

Easlea, Brian. 1980. *Witch Hunting, Magic, and the New Philosophy: An Introduction to Debates of the Scientific Revolution, 1450–1750.* Atlantic Highlands, N.J.: Humanities Press.

Ebeling, Gerhard. 1967. *God and Word.* Philadelphia: Fortress Press.

Edge, Hoyt L., Robert L. Morris, John Palmer, and Joseph H. Rush. 1986. *Foundations of Parapsychology: Exploring the Boundaries of Human Capability.* Boston: Routledge & Kegan Paul.

Edwards, Rem. 1975. "The Human Self: An Actual Entity or a Society?" *Process Studies* 5, no. 3 (fall): 195–203.

Einstein, Albert. 1931. "Maxwell's Influence on the Development of the Conception of Physical Reality." In *James Clerk Maxwell: A Commemorative Volume,* by J. J. Thomson et al., 66–73. Cambridge: Cambridge University Press.

Eldredge, Niles. 1995. *Reinventing Darwin: The Great Debate at the High Table of Evolutionary Theory.* New York: John Wiley & Sons.

Eldredge, Niles, and Stephen Jay Gould. 1972. "Punctuated Equilibria: An Alternative to Phyletic Gradualism." In *Models of Paleobiology,* edited by T. J. M. Schopf, 82–115. San Francisco: Freeman, Cooper & Co.

Eliade, Mircea. 1978. *History of Religious Ideas.* 2 vols. Translated by W. R. Trask. Chicago: University of Chicago Press.

Ely, Stephen Lee. 1983 [1942]. "The Religious Availability of Whitehead's God: A Critical Analysis." In *Explorations in Whitehead's Philosophy,* edited by Lewis S. Ford and

George L. Kline, 170–211. New York: Fordham University Press. (Ely's critique was originally published as a little book by the University of Wisconsin Press.)

Erickson, Millard J. 1985. *Christian Theology.* Grand Rapids, Mich.: Baker Book House.

Evans-Pritchard, E. E. 1965. *Theories of Primitive Religion.* Oxford: Clarendon Press.

Ferré, Frederick. 1967. *Basic Modern Philosophy of Religion.* New York: Charles Scribner's Sons.

———. 1976. *Shaping the Future: Resources for the Post-Modern World.* New York: Harper & Row.

———. 1993. *Hellfire and Lightning Rods: Liberating Science, Technology, and Religion.* Maryknoll, N.Y.: Orbis Books.

———. 1996. *Being and Value: Toward a Constructive Postmodern Metaphysics.* Albany: State University of New York Press.

Fetz, Reto Luzius. 1991. "In Critique of Whitehead." Translated by James W. Felt. *Process Studies* 20, no. 1 (spring): 1–9.

Field, Hartry. 1980. *Science without Numbers.* Princeton: Princeton University Press.

Flew, Antony. 1966. *God and Philosophy.* New York: Dell.

Florschütz, Gottlieb. 1993–96. "Swedenborg's Hidden Influence on Kant: Swedenborg and Occult Phenomena in the View of Kant and Schopenhauer." Translated by Kurt Nemitz and J. Durban Odhner. Serialized in seven issues of *New Philosophy: The Journal of the Swedenborg Scientific Association* 96–99 [January–June 1993 to January–June 1996]).

Ford, Lewis S. 1984. *The Emergence of Whitehead's Metaphysics.* Albany: State University of New York Press.

———, ed. 1973. *Two Process Philosophers: Hartshorne's Encounter with Whitehead.* Tallahassee, Fla.: American Academy of Religion.

Ford, Marcus Peter. 1982. *William James's Philosophy: A New Perspective.* Amherst: University of Massachusetts Press.

———. 1993. "William James." In *Founders of Constructive Postmodern Philosophy,* by David Ray Griffin et al., 89–132.

———. 1998. "James's Psychical Research and Its Philosophical Implications." *Transactions of the Charles S. Peirce Society* 34, no. 3 (summer): 605–26.

Forrest, Peter. 1996. *God without the Supernatural: A Defense of Scientific Theism.* Ithaca: Cornell University Press.

Franklin, Stephen T. 1988. Review of *Process Theology,* edited by Ronald Nash. *Process Studies* 17, no. 2 (summer): 131–35.

———. 1990. *Speaking from the Depths: Alfred North Whitehead's Hermeneutical Metaphysics of Propositions, Experience, Symbolism, Language, and Religion.* Grand Rapids, Mich.: Eerdmans.

———. 1995. "God and Creativity: A Revisionist Proposal within a Whiteheadian Context." Unpublished paper (available at the Center for Process Studies, 1325 N. College, Claremont, Calif. 91711).

Gamwell, Franklin I. 1981. "Happiness and the Public World." In *Process Philosophy and Social Thought,* edited by John B. Cobb, Jr., and W. Widick Schroeder, 38–54. Chicago: Center for the Scientific Study of Religion.

———. 1984. *Beyond Preference: Liberal Theories of Independent Associations.* Chicago: University of Chicago Press.

——. 1990. *The Divine Good*. San Francisco: Harper Collins.

Gare, Arran E. 1995. *Postmodernism and the Environmental Crisis*. London: Routledge.

——. 1996. *Nihilism, Inc.: Environmental Destruction and the Metaphysics of Sustainability*. Sydney: Eco-Logical Press.

Geertz, Clifford. 1968. *Islam Observed: Religious Development in Morocco and Indonesia*. New Haven: Yale University Press.

——. 1973. *Interpretation of Cultures: Selected Essays*. New York: Basic Books.

Gewirth, Alan. 1978. *Reason and Morality*. Chicago: University of Chicago Press.

Ghose, Sri Aurobindo. 1950. *Essays on the Gita*. New York: Sri Aurobindo Library.

Giddens, Anthony. 1971. *Capitalism and Modern Social Theory*. Cambridge: Cambridge University Press.

Gillespie, Neal C. 1979. *Charles Darwin and the Problem of Creation*. Chicago: University of Chicago Press.

Gödel, Kurt. 1990. "What Is Cantor's Continuum Problem? Supplement to the Second [1964] Edition." In *Collected Works*, vol. 2, edited by Solomon Feferman et al., 266– 69. New York: Oxford University Press.

Goldbeter, A., and D. E. Koshland, Jr. 1982. "Simple Molecular Model for Sensing and Adaptation Based on Receptor Modification with Application to Bacterial Chemotaxis." *Journal of Molecular Biology* 161:395–416.

Gould, Stephen Jay. 1977. *Ever since Darwin*. New York: W. W. Norton.

Greene, John C. 1981. *Science, Ideology, and World View: Essays in the History of Evolutionary Ideas*. Berkeley and Los Angeles: University of California Press.

Griffin, David Ray. 1967. "Schubert Ogden's Christology and the Possibilities of Process Philosophy." *Christian Scholar* 50 (fall): 290–303 (reprinted in *Process Philosophy and Christian Thought*, edited by Delwin Brown, Ralph E. James, Jr., and Gene Reeves, 347–61 [Indianapolis: Bobbs-Merrill, 1971]).

——. 1972. "Whitehead's Contributions to a Theology of Nature." *Bucknell Review* 20 (winter): 3–24.

——. 1973a. *A Process Christology*. Philadelphia: Westminster Press (reprinted with a new preface, Lanham, Md.: University Press of America, 1990).

——. 1973b. "Gordon Kaufman's Theology: Some Questions." *Journal of the American Academy of Religion* 41, no. 4 (December): 554–72.

——. 1976. *God, Power, and Evil: A Process Theodicy*. Philadelphia: Westminster Press (reprinted with a new preface, Lanham, Md.: University Press of America, 1991).

——. 1977. "The Subjectivist Principle and Its Reformed and Unreformed Versions." *Process Studies* 7, no. 1 (spring): 27–36.

——. 1980. "The Holy, Necessary Goodness, and Morality." *Journal of Religious Ethics* 8, no. 2 (fall 1980): 330–48.

——. 1981. "Creation out of Chaos and the Problem of Evil." In *Encountering Evil: Live Options in Theodicy*, edited by Stephen T. Davis, 101–17. Atlanta: John Knox.

——. 1982. "Rupert Sheldrake's *A New Science of Life*." *Process Studies* 12, no. 1 (spring): 38–40.

——. 1983. "Relativism, Divine Causation, and Biblical Theology." In *God's Activity in the World: The Contemporary Problem* (AAR Studies in Religion, no. 31), edited by Owen C. Thomas, 117–36. Chico, Calif.: Scholars Press.

——. 1986a. "Critique of Lewis S. Ford, *The Emergence of Whitehead's Metaphysics*." *Process Studies* 15, no. 3 (fall): 194–207.

———. 1986b. "Introduction: Physics and the Ultimate Significance of Time." In *Physics and the Ultimate Significance of Time: Bohm, Prigogine, and Process Philosophy*, edited by David Ray Griffin, 1–48. Albany: State University of New York Press.

———. 1988. "On Ian Barbour's *Issues in Science and Religion:* A Review Essay." *Zygon* 23, no. 1 (March): 57–81.

———. 1989a. *Archetypal Process: Self and Divine in Whitehead, Jung, and Hillman.* Evanston, Ill.: Northwestern University Press.

———. 1989b. Review of Marjorie Suchocki's *The End of Evil. Process Studies* 18, no. 1 (spring): 57–62.

———. 1989c. *God and Religion in the Postmodern World.* Albany: State University of New York Press.

———. 1991. *Evil Revisited: Responses and Reconsiderations.* Albany: State University of New York Press.

———. 1992a. "Hartshorne, God, and Relativity Physics." *Process Studies* 21, no. 2 (summer): 85–112.

———. 1992b. "Griffin Response to Peters" (to Ted Peters's review of *The Reenchantment of Science* and *Spirituality and Society*). *Zygon* 27, no. 3 (September): 343–44.

———. 1993. "Parapsychology and Philosophy: A Whiteheadian Postmodern Perspective." *Journal of the American Society for Psychical Research* 87, no. 3 (July): 217–88.

———. 1994. "Whitehead's Deeply Ecological Worldview." In *Worldviews and Ecology: Religion, Philosophy, and the Environment,* edited by Mary Evelyn Tucker and John Grim, 190–206. Maryknoll, N.Y.: Orbis Books.

———. 1996. "Modern and Postmodern Liberal Theology: A Response to Alvin Reines." In *Jewish Theology and Process Thought,* edited by David Ray Griffin and Sandra Lubarsky, 289–308. Albany: State University of New York Press.

———. 1997a. *Parapsychology, Philosophy, and Spirituality: A Postmodern Exploration.* Albany: State University of New York Press.

———. 1997b. "A Richer or a Poorer Naturalism? A Critique of Willem Drees's *Religion, Science, and Naturalism.*" *Zygon* 32, no. 4 (December): 593–614.

———. 1998a. *Unsnarling the World-Knot: Consciousness, Freedom, and the Mind-Body Problem.* Berkeley and Los Angeles: University of California Press.

———. 1998b. "Christian Faith and Scientific Naturalism: An Appreciative Critique of Phillip Johnson's Proposal." *Christian Scholar's Review* 28, no. 2 (winter 1998): 308–28.

———. 2000a. *Religion and Scientific Naturalism: Overcoming the Conflicts.* Albany: State University of New York Press.

———. 2000b. "Religious Experience, Naturalism, and the Social Scientific Study of Religion." *Journal of the American Academy of Religion* 68, no. 1 (March): 99–125.

———. Forthcoming a. *Beyond Anarchy and Plutocracy: The Need for Global Democracy.*

———. Forthcoming b. "Creation Out of Nothing, Creation Out of Chaos, and the Problem of Evil." In *Encountering Evil,* 2d ed., edited by Stephen T. Davis. Atlanta: Westminster/John Knox.

———. Forthcoming c. *The Divine Cry of Our Time.*

———. Forthcoming d. "Pantemporalism and Panexperientialism." In *The Textures of Time,* edited by Paul A. Harris.

Griffin, David Ray, William A. Beardslee, and Joe Holland. 1989. *Varieties of Postmodern Theology.* Albany: State University of New York Press.

Griffin, David Ray, John B. Cobb, Jr., Marcus P. Ford, Pete A. Y. Gunter, and Peter Ochs. 1993. *Founders of Constructive Postmodern Philosophy: Peirce, James, Bergson, Whitehead, and Hartshorne.* Albany: State University of New York Press.

Griffin, David Ray, and Huston Smith. 1989. *Primordial Truth and Postmodern Theology.* Albany: State University of New York Press.

Griffin, Donald R. 1992. *Animal Minds.* Chicago: University of Chicago Press.

Gruber, Howard. 1981. *Darwin on Man: A Psychological Study of Scientific Creativity.* 2d ed. Chicago: University of Chicago Press.

Gustafson, James M. 1981. *Ethics from a Theocentric Perspective.* Vol. 1. Chicago: University of Chicago Press.

Gutting, Gary. 1982. *Religious Belief and Religious Scepticism.* Notre Dame: University of Notre Dame Press.

Haack, Susan. 1985. "C. I. Lewis." In *American Philosophy,* edited by Marcus G. Singer, 215–38. Cambridge: Cambridge University Press.

Habermas, Jürgen. 1971. "Value-Freedom and Objectivity." In *Max Weber and Sociology Today,* edited by Otto Stammer, 59–66. New York: Harper & Row.

——. 1982. "A Reply to My Critics." In *Habermas: Critical Debates,* edited by John B. Thompson and David Held, 219–83. Cambridge: MIT Press.

——. 1984. *The Theory of Communicative Action.* Vol. 1. Translated by Thomas McCarthy. London: Heinemann.

——. 1987. *The Philosophical Discourse of Modernity.* Translated by Frederick G. Lawrence. Cambridge: MIT Press.

——. 1992. *Postmetaphysical Thinking: Philosophical Essays.* Translated by William Mark Hohengarten. Cambridge: MIT Press.

——. 1993. *Justification and Application: Remarks on Discourse Ethics.* Translated by Ciaran Cronin. Cambridge: Polity Press.

——. 1997. "Kant's Idea of Perpetual Peace, with the Benefit of Two Hundred Years' Hindsight." In *Perpetual Peace: Essays on Kant's Cosmopolitan Ideal,* edited by James Bohman and Matthias Lutz-Bachmann, 113–53. Cambridge: MIT Press.

Hahn, Lewis Edwin, and Paul Arthur Schilpp, eds. 1986. *The Philosophy of W. V. Quine.* Library of Living Philosophers, vol. 18. LaSalle, Ill.: Open Court.

Hameroff, Stuart R. 1994. "Quantum Coherence in Microtubules: A Neural Basis for Emergent Consciousness?" *Journal of Consciousness Studies* 1, no. 1: 91–118.

Harman, Gilbert. 1977. *The Nature of Morality: An Introduction to Ethics.* New York: Oxford University Press.

Hartshorne, Charles. 1937. *Beyond Humanism: Essays in the New Philosophy of Nature.* New York: Willett, Clark, & Co.

——. 1941. *Man's Vision of God and the Logic of Theism.* New York: Harper & Row.

——. 1945. "Omnipotence." In *An Encyclopedia of Religion,* edited by Vergilius Ferm, 545. New York: Philosophical Library.

——. 1951 [1941]. "Whitehead's Idea of God." In *The Philosophy of Alfred North Whitehead,* 2d ed., edited by Paul Arthur Schilpp, 513–59. Library of Living Philosophers, vol. 3. New York: Tudor.

——. 1953. *Reality as Social Process: Studies in Metaphysics and Religion.* Glencoe: Free Press; Boston: Beacon Press.

——. 1960. "The Buddhist-Whiteheadian View of the Self and the Religious Traditions." In *Proceedings of the Ninth International Congress for the History of Religions*, 298–302. Tokyo: Maruzen.

———. 1961a. "Whitehead and Contemporary Philosophy." In *The Relevance of Whitehead: Philosophical Essays in Commemoration of the Centenary of the Birth of Alfred North Whitehead*, edited by Ivor Leclerc, 21–43. New York: Humanities Press.

———. 1961b. "Whitehead, the Anglo-American Philosopher-Scientist." *Proceedings of the American Catholic Philosophical Association*, 163–71. Washington, D.C.: Catholic University of America.

———. 1962. *The Logic of Perfection and Other Essays in Neoclassical Metaphysics*. LaSalle, Ill.: Open Court.

———. 1963. "Whitehead's Novel Intuition." In *Alfred North Whitehead: Essays on His Philosophy*, edited by George L. Kline, 18–26. Englewood Cliffs, N.J.: Prentice-Hall.

———. 1964a [1948]. *The Divine Relativity: A Social Conception of God*. 2d ed. New Haven: Yale University Press.

———. 1964b. "Interrogation of Charles Hartshorne." In *Philosophical Interrogations*, edited by Sydney Rome and Beatrice Rome, 321–54. New York: Holt, Rinehart & Winston.

———. 1965. *Anselm's Discovery*. LaSalle, Ill.: Open Court.

———. 1967. *A Natural Theology for Our Time*. LaSalle, Ill.: Open Court.

———. 1968. "Preface to the Bison Book Edition." *Beyond Humanism*. Lincoln: University of Nebraska Press.

———. 1970. *Creative Synthesis and Philosophic Method*. LaSalle, Ill.: Open Court; London: SCM Press.

———. 1972 [1936]. "The Compound Individual." In *Whitehead's Philosophy: Selected Essays, 1935–1970*, by Charles Hartshorne, 41–46. Lincoln: University of Nebraska Press (originally published in *Philosophical Essays for Alfred North Whitehead*, edited by Otis T. Lee [New York: Longmans, Green]).

———. 1976. "Why Psychicalism? Comments on Keeling's and Shepherd's Criticisms." *Process Studies* 6, no. 1 (spring): 67–72.

———. 1977a. "Physics and Psychics: The Place of Mind in Nature." In *Mind in Nature: Essays on the Interface of Science and Philosophy*, edited by John B. Cobb, Jr., and David Ray Griffin, 89–96. Washington, D.C.: University Press of America.

———. 1977b. "Cobb's Theology of Ecology." In *John Cobb's Theology in Process*, edited by David Ray Griffin and Thomas J. J. Altizer, 112–15. Philadelphia: Westminster Press.

———. 1979. "Whitehead's Revolutionary Concept of Prehension." *International Philosophical Quarterly* 19, no. 3 (September): 253–63 (reprinted in Hartshorne's *Creativity in American Philosophy* [Albany: State University of New York Press, 1984]).

———. 1984. *Omnipotence and Other Theological Mistakes*. Albany: State University of New York Press.

———. 1987. *Wisdom as Moderation: A Philosophy of the Middle Way*. Albany: State University of New York.

———. 1989. "General Remarks." In *Hartshorne, Process Philosophy, and Theology*, edited by Robert Kane and Stephen H. Phillips, 181–96. Albany: State University of New York Press.

———. 1990. *The Darkness and the Light: A Philosopher Reflects upon His Fortunate Career and Those Who Made It Possible*. Albany: State University of New York Press.

———. 1991a. "Some Causes of My Intellectual Growth." In *The Philosophy of Charles*

Hartshorne, edited by Lewis Edwin Hahn, 3–45. Library of Living Philosophers, vol. 20. LaSalle, Ill.: Open Court.

——. 1991b. "A Reply to My Critics." In *The Philosophy of Charles Hartshorne,* edited by Lewis Edwin Hahn, 569–731. Library of Living Philosophers, vol. 20. LaSalle, Ill.: Open Court.

——. 1994. Letter (January 4) to David Griffin (available at the Center for Process Studies, 1325 N. College, Claremont, Calif. 91711).

——. 1997. *The Zero Fallacy and Other Essays in Neoclassical Philosophy.* Edited by Mohammed Valady. Peru, Ill.: Open Court.

Hartshorne, Charles, and William L. Reese, eds. 1953. *Philosophers Speak of God.* Chicago: University of Chicago Press.

Harvey, Peter. 1994. "Buddhism." In *Picturing God,* edited by Jean Holm with John Bowker, 9–40. London: Pinter.

Hasker, William. 1994. "A Philosophical Perspective." In *The Openness of God,* by Clark H. Pinnock et al., 126–54.

——. 1995. "*Darwin on Trial* Revisited: A Review Essay." *Christian Scholar's Review* 24, no. 4 (May): 479–88.

Heidegger, Martin. 1977. *The Question Concerning Technology: Heidegger's Critique of the Modern Age.* Translated by William Lovett. New York: Harper & Row.

Hellman, G. 1989. *Mathematics without Numbers.* Oxford: Oxford University Press.

Helm, Paul. 1983. "Thomas Reid, Common Sense, and Calvinism." In *Rationality in the Calvinian Tradition,* edited by Hendrik Hart, Johan van der Hoeven, and Nicholas Wolterstorff, 71–89. Lanham, Md.: University Press of America.

Henderson, L. J. 1913. *The Fitness of the Environment: An Inquiry into the Biological Significance of the Properties of Matter.* New York: Macmillan.

Hersh, Reuben. 1997. *What Is Mathematics, Really?* New York: Oxford University Press.

Heschel, Abraham Joshua. 1962. *The Prophets.* New York: Harper & Row.

Hick, John. 1966. *Evil and the God of Love.* San Francisco: Harper & Row.

——. 1973. *God and the Universe of Faiths.* London: Macmillan; New York: St. Martin's Press.

——. 1985. *Problems of Religious Pluralism.* New York: St. Martin's Press.

——. 1989. *An Interpretation of Religion: Human Responses to the Transcendent.* London: Macmillan.

——. Forthcoming. "An Irenaean Theodicy." In *Encountering Evil,* 2d ed., edited by Stephen T. Davis. Atlanta: Westminster/John Knox.

Hintikka, Jaakko. 1962. "Cogito, Ergo Sum: Inference or Performance." *Philosophical Review* 71:3–32.

Hocking, William E. 1963. "Whitehead as I Knew Him." In *Alfred North Whitehead: Essays on His Philosophy,* edited by George L. Kline, 7–17. Englewood Cliffs, N.J.: Prentice-Hall.

Hoffert, Robert W. 1975. "A Political Vision for the Organic Model." *Process Studies* 5, no. 3 (fall): 175–86.

Honderich, Ted, ed. 1985. *Morality and Objectivity: A Tribute to J. L. Mackie.* London: Routledge & Kegan Paul.

Horwich, Paul. 1990. *Truth.* Oxford: Basil Blackwell.

Hosinski, Thomas E. 1987. "The 'Kingdom of Heaven' and the Development of Whitehead's Idea of God." *Process Studies* 16, no. 3 (fall): 203–15.

———. 1993. *Stubborn Fact and Creative Advance: An Introduction to the Metaphysics of Alfred North Whitehead.* Lanham, Md.: Rowman & Littlefield.

Howell, Nancy R. 1988. "The Promise of a Feminist Theory of Relations." *Process Studies* 17, no. 2 (summer): 78–87.

———. 1989. "Radical Relatedness and Feminist Separatism." *Process Studies* 18, no. 2 (summer): 118–26.

Hoy, David Couzens. 1994. "Conflicting Conceptions of Critique: Foucault versus Habermas." In *Critical Theory,* by David Couzens Hoy and Thomas McCarthy, 144–71. Cambridge, Mass.: Basil Blackwell.

Hubbeling, H. G. 1987. *Principles of the Philosophy of Religion.* Assen, Netherlands: Van Gorcum.

Hume, David. 1739. *A Treatise of Human Nature.* Vols. 1 and 2 of *The Philosophical Works of David Hume,* 4 vols. Boston: Little, Brown; Edinburgh: Adam & Charles Black, 1854.

———. 1902. *An Enquiry Concerning Human Understanding.* 2d ed. Edited by L. A. Selby-Bigge (bound together with Hume's *Enquiry Concerning Morals*). Oxford: Clarendon Press.

Huxley, Aldous. 1945. *The Perennial Philosophy.* New York: Harper & Brothers.

Huxley, Thomas H. 1893. *Method and Results.* London: Macmillan.

———. 1989. "Evolution and Ethics." In *Thomas Huxley's Evolution and Ethics: With New Essays on Its Victorian and Sociobiological Context,* by James Paradis and George C. Williams, 57–116. Princeton: Princeton University Press.

James, William. 1902. *Varieties of Religious Experience.* New York: Longmans, Green, & Co. (reprinted in Penguin Classics by Penguin Books [New York], 1985).

———. 1956. *The Will to Believe.* New York: Dover.

———. 1960. *William James on Psychical Research.* Edited by Gardner Murphy and Robert O. Ballou. New York: Viking Press.

———. 1971. *Essays in Radical Empiricism* and *A Pluralistic Universe.* Edited by Ralph Barton Perry. Introduction by Richard J. Bernstein. New York: E. P. Dutton.

———. 1975. *The Meaning of Truth.* Cambridge: Harvard University Press (reprint of 1907 edition).

———. 1986. *Essays in Psychical Research.* Edited by Robert McDermott. Cambridge: Harvard University Press.

Jay, Martin. 1993. "The Debate over Performative Contradiction: Habermas versus the Poststructuralists." In *Force Fields: Between Intellectual History and Cultural Critique,* by Martin Jay, 25–37. New York: Routledge.

Johnson, A. H. 1969. "Whitehead as Teacher and Philosopher." *Philosophy and Phenomenological Research* 29:351–76.

Johnson, Gregory R. 1999a. "A Commentary on Kant's Dreams of a Spirit-Seer." Ph.D. dissertation, Catholic University of America, Washington, D.C.

———. 1999b. Review of *Swedenborg's Hidden Influence on Kant: Swedenborg and Occult Phenomena in the View of Kant and Schopenhauer,* by Gottlieb Florschütz. *Journal of Scientific Exploration* 13, no. 3: 545–49.

Johnson, Phillip E. 1993a. *Darwin on Trial.* 2d ed. Downers Grove, Ill.: InterVarsity Press.

———. 1993b. *Reason in the Balance: The Case against Naturalism in Science, Law, and Education.* Downers Grove, Ill.: InterVarsity Press.

Jonas, Hans. 1966. *The Phenomenon of Life: Toward a Philosophical Biology*. New York: Harper & Row.

———. 1988. *Materie, Geist und Schöpfung*. Frankfurt: Suhrkamp.

Kane, Robert, and Stephen Phillips, eds. 1989. *Hartshorne, Process Philosophy, and Theology*. Albany: State University of New York Press.

Kant, Immanuel. 1952. *The Critique of Pure Reason*. In *Great Books of the Western World*, ed. Robert Maynard Hutchins, vol. 42, *Kant*. Chicago: Encyclopedia Britannica.

———. 1960. *Religion within the Limits of Reason Alone*. Translated by Theodore M. Greene and Hoyt H. Hudson. New York: Harper & Row.

Katz, Stephen. 1978. "Language, Epistemology, and Mysticism." In *Mysticism and Philosophical Analysis*, edited by Stephen Katz, 22–74. New York: Oxford University Press.

Kaufman, Gordon D. 1993. *In Face of Mystery: A Constructive Theology*. Cambridge: Harvard University Press.

Keller, Catherine. 1986. *From a Broken Web: Separation, Sexism, and Self*. Boston: Beacon Press.

———. 1988. "Toward a Postpatriarchal Postmodernity." In *Spirituality and Society: Postmodern Visions*, edited by David Ray Griffin, 63–80. Albany: State University of New York Press.

———. 1990. "Warriors, Women, and the Nuclear Complex: Toward a Postnuclear Postmodernity." In *Sacred Interconnections: Postmodern Spirituality, Political Economy, and Art*, edited by David Ray Griffin, 63–82. Albany: State University of New York Press.

———. 1996. *Apocalypse Now and Then: A Feminist Guide to the End of the World*. Boston: Beacon Press.

Keller, Evelyn Fox. 1983. *A Feeling for the Organism: The Life and Work of Barbara McClintock*. New York: W. H. Freeman.

Kim, Jaegwon. 1993. *Supervenience and Mind: Selected Philosophical Essays*. Cambridge: Cambridge University Press.

Kirkpatrick, Frank G. 1973. "Subjective Becoming: An Unwarranted Abstraction?" *Process Studies* 3, no. 1 (spring): 15–26.

Koyré, Alexandre. 1968. *From the Closed World to the Infinite Universe*. Baltimore: Johns Hopkins University Press.

Kraus, Elizabeth. 1979. *The Metaphysics of Experience*. New York: Fordham University Press.

Küng, Hans. 1980. *Does God Exist? An Answer for Today*. Translated by Edward Quinn. New York: Doubleday.

Lamont, Corliss. 1965. *The Illusion of Immortality*. 4th ed. New York: Frederick Ungar.

Langbauer, Delmar. 1970. "Santana Dharma and Modern Philosophy: A Study of Indian and Whiteheadian Thought." Ph.D. dissertation, Claremont Graduate School, Claremont, Calif.

Larmore, Charles E. *The Morals of Modernity*. New York: Cambridge University Press, 1996.

Leclerc, Ivor. 1958. *Whitehead's Metaphysics: An Introductory Exposition*. London: George Allen & Unwin.

———. 1972. *The Nature of Physical Existence*. London: George Allen & Unwin.

———. 1977. "Some Main Philosophical Issues Involved in Contemporary Scientific

Thought." In *Mind in Nature: Essays on the Interface of Science and Philosophy,* edited by John B. Cobb, Jr., and David Ray Griffin, 101–8. Washington, D.C.: University Press of America.

———. 1990. "Whitehead and the Dichotomy of Rationalism and Empiricism." In *Whitehead's Metaphysics of Creativity,* edited by Friedrich Rapp and Reiner Wiehl, 1–20. Albany: State University of New York Press.

Levenson, Jon D. 1988: *Creation and the Persistence of Evil: The Jewish Drama of Divine Omnipotence.* San Francisco: Harper & Row.

Lewis, C. I. 1929. *Mind and the World Order.* New York: Charles Scribner's Sons.

———. 1946. *An Analysis of Knowledge and Valuation.* LaSalle, Ill.: Open Court.

Lewis, C. S. 1965. *The Problem of Pain.* New York: Macmillan.

Lewontin, Richard. 1997. "Billions and Billions of Demons" (review of *The Demon-Haunted World: Science as a Candle in the Dark,* by Carl Sagan). *New York Review of Books,* January 9, 28–32.

Little, David. 1993. "The Nature and Basis of Human Rights." In *Prospects for a Common Morality,* edited by Gene Outka and John P. Reeder, Jr., 73–92. Princeton: Princeton University Press.

Livezey, Lois Gehr. 1988. "Women, Power, and Politics: Feminist Theology in Process Perspective." *Process Studies* 17, no. 2 (summer): 67–77.

Livingston, James C. 1998. *Anatomy of the Sacred: An Introduction to Religion.* 3d ed. Upper Saddle River, N.J.: Prentice Hall.

Long, Eugene Thomas. 1986. "An Approach to Religious Pluralism." In *Being and Truth: Essays in Honour of John Macquarrie,* edited by Alistair Kee and Eugene Thomas Long, 247–63. London: SCM Press.

Lovin, Robin W., and Frank E. Reynolds, eds. 1985. *Cosmogony and Ethical Order: New Studies in Comparative Ethics.* Chicago: University of Chicago Press.

Lowe, Victor. 1985. *Alfred North Whitehead: The Man and His Work.* Vol. 1. Baltimore: Johns Hopkins University Press.

Löwith, Karl. 1995. *Martin Heidegger and European Nihilism.* Edited by Richard Wolin. Translated by Gary Steiner. New York: Columbia University Press.

Lubarsky, Sandra, and David Ray Griffin, eds. 1996. *Jewish Theology and Process Thought.* Albany: State University of New York Press.

Lundeen, Lyman T. 1972. *Risk and Rhetoric in Religion: Whitehead's Theory of Language and the Discourse of Faith.* Philadelphia: Fortress Press.

Luther, Martin. 1957. *On the Bondage of the Will.* Translated by J. I. Packer and O. R. Johnston. Grand Rapids, Mich.: Fleming H. Revell.

MacIntyre, Alasdair. 1969. "The Fate of Theism." In *The Religious Significance of Atheism,* by Alasdair MacIntyre and Paul Ricoeur, 3–29. New York: Columbia University Press.

Mackie, John. 1976. *Problems from Locke.* Oxford: Oxford University Press.

———. 1977. *Ethics: Inventing Right and Wrong.* New York: Penguin.

———. 1982. *The Miracle of Theism: Arguments for and against the Existence of God.* Oxford: Clarendon Press.

Maddy, Penelope. 1990. *Realism in Mathematics.* Oxford: Clarendon Press.

Madell, Geoffrey. 1988. *Mind and Materialism.* Edinburgh: Edinburgh University Press.

Mascall, Eric L. 1949. *Existence and Analogy.* London: Longmans, Green.

——. 1980. *Whatever Happened to the Human Mind? Essays in Christian Orthodoxy*. London: SPCK.

Mavrodes, George I. 1983. "Jerusalem and Athens Revisited." In *Faith and Rationality: Reason and Belief in God*, edited by Alvin Plantinga and Nicholas Wolterstorff, 192–218. Notre Dame: University of Notre Dame Press.

May, Gerhard. 1994. *Creatio ex Nihilo: The Doctrine of "Creation out of Nothing" in Early Christian Thought*. Translated by A. S. Worrall. Edinburgh: T. & T. Clark.

Mayr, Ernst. 1970. *Populations, Species, and Evolution*. Cambridge: Harvard University Press.

McCarthy, Thomas. 1993. *Ideals and Illusions: On Reconstruction and Deconstruction in Contemporary Critical Theory*. Cambridge: MIT Press.

McDaniel, Jay B. 1989. *Of God and Pelicans: A Theology for the Reverence of Life*. Louisville: Westminster/John Knox.

——. 1990. *Earth, Sky, Gods, and Mortals: Developing an Ecological Spirituality*. Mystic, Conn.: Twenty-Third Publications.

McGinn, Colin. 1982. *The Character of Mind*. Oxford: Oxford University Press.

——. 1991. *The Problem of Consciousness: Essays toward a Resolution*. Oxford: Basil Blackwell.

McHenry, Leemon. 1992. *Whitehead and Bradley: A Comparative Analysis*. Albany: State University of New York Press.

——. 1997. "Quine and Whitehead: Ontology and Methodology." *Process Studies* 26, nos. 1–2 (spring–summer): 2–12.

McMullin, Ernan. 1991. "Plantinga's Defense of Special Creation." *Christian Scholar's Review* 21, no. 1: 55–79.

——. 1995. "Natural Science and Belief in a Creator: Historical Notes." In *Physics, Philosophy, and Theology: A Common Quest for Understanding*, 2d ed., edited by Robert John Russell, William R. Stoeger, and George V. Coyne, 49–79. Vatican City State: Vatican Observatory.

McTaggart, J. M. E. 1906. *Some Dogmas of Religion*. London: Edward Arnold.

Min, Anselm. 1997. "Dialectical Pluralism and Solidarity of Others: Towards a New Paradigm." *Journal of the American Academy of Religion* 65, no. 3 (fall): 587–604.

Mitchell, Basil. 1981 [1973]. *The Justification of Religious Belief*. Oxford: Oxford University Press.

Montefiore, Hugh. 1985. *The Probability of God*. London: SCM Press.

Moore, G. E. 1965. *Principia Ethica*. Cambridge: Cambridge University Press.

Moreland, J. P. 1988. "An Enduring Self: The Achilles' Heel of Process Philosophy." *Process Studies* 17, no. 3 (fall): 193–99.

Morris, Randall C. 1991. *Process Philosophy and Political Ideology*. Albany: State University of New York Press.

Moschovakis, Y. N. 1980. *Descriptive Set Theory*. Amsterdam: North Holland.

Mouw, Richard. 1970. "The Status of God's Moral Judgments." *Canadian Journal of Theology* 16: 61–66.

Muray, Leslie A. 1991. "Human Rights in a Process-Relational Perspective." In *Human Rights: Christians, Marxists, and Others in Dialogue*, edited by Leonard Swidler, 101–16. New York: Paragon House.

Murphy, Jeffrie G. 1988. "Afterword: Constitutionalism, Moral Skepticism, and Religious Belief." In *Constitutionalism: The Philosophical Dimension,* edited by Alan S. Rosenbaum, 239–49. New York: Greenwood.

Nagel, Thomas. 1986. *The View from Nowhere.* New York: Oxford University Press.

Nash, J. Madeleine. 1995. "When Life Exploded." *Time,* December 4, 66–77.

Nelson, Susan L. 1997. *Healing the Broken Heart: Sin, Alienation, and the Gift of Grace.* St. Louis: Chalice. (See also Susan Nelson Dunfee.)

Neske, Gunter, and Emil Kettering, eds. 1990. *Martin Heidegger and National Socialism: Questions and Answers.* New York: Paragon House.

Neville, Robert C. 1974. *The Cosmology of Freedom.* New Haven: Yale University Press.

———. 1993. "Religious Studies and Theological Studies." *Journal of the American Academy of Religion* 61, no. 2 (summer): 185–200.

Newell, Norman D. 1959. "The Nature of the Fossil Record." *Proceedings of the American Philosophical Society* 103, no. 2: 264–85.

Niebuhr, H. Richard. 1941. *The Meaning of Revelation.* New York: Macmillan.

Nielsen, Kai. 1982. *An Introduction to the Philosophy of Religion.* New York: St. Martin's Press.

———. 1985. *Philosophy and Atheism: In Defense of Atheism.* Buffalo, N.Y.: Prometheus Books.

———. 1989a. *God, Scepticism, and Modernity.* Ottawa: University of Ottawa Press.

———. 1989b. "God and the Soul: A Response to Paul Badham." In *Death and Afterlife,* edited by Stephen Davis, 53–64. London: Macmillan.

Nietzsche, Friedrich. 1967. *The Will to Power.* Edited by Walter Kaufmann. Translated by Walter Kaufmann and R. J. Hollingdale. New York: Random House.

Nitecki, Matthew H., ed. 1988. *Evolutionary Progress.* Chicago: University of Chicago Press.

Nobo, Jorge. 1989. "God as Essentially Immutable, Imperishable, and Objectifiable: A Response to Ford." In *Hartshorne, Process Philosophy, and Theology,* edited by Robert Kane and Stephen H. Phillips, 175–80. Albany: State University of New York Press.

Nowell-Smith, P. H. 1966. "Morality: Religious and Secular." In *Christian Ethics and Contemporary Philosophy,* edited by Ian T. Ramsey, 95–112. London: SCM Press.

O'Connor, D. J. 1975. *The Correspondence Theory of Truth.* London: Hutchinson University Library.

Olson, Robert G. 1967. "Nihilism." In *Encyclopedia of Philosophy,* edited by Paul Edwards, 5:514–17. New York: Macmillan.

Oomen, Palmyre M. F. 1998. "The Prehensibility of God's Consequent Nature." *Process Studies* 27, nos. 1–2 (spring–summer): 108–33.

Otto, Rudolf. 1907. *Naturalism and Religion.* London: Williams & Norgate; New York: G. P. Putnam's.

———. 1931. "Darwinism and Religion." In *Religious Essays: A Supplement to "The Idea of the Holy,"* by Rudolf Otto, 121–39. Translated by Brian Lunn. Oxford: Oxford University Press; London: Humphrey Milford.

———. 1958 [1917]. *The Idea of the Holy.* Translated by John H. Harvey. New York: Oxford University Press.

Outka, Gene, and John P. Reeder, Jr., eds. 1993. Introduction to *Prospects for a Common Morality,* 3–28. Princeton: Princeton University Press.

Pailin, David. 1989. *God and the Processes of Reality: Foundations of a Credible Theism.* London: Routledge.

Pannenberg, Wolfhart. 1968. *Jesus— God and Man*. Translated by Lewis L. Wilkins and Duane A. Priebe. Philadelphia: Westminster Press.

Pascal, Blaise. 1965 [1670]. *Pensées: Thoughts on Religion and Other Subjects*. Translated by William F. Trotter. Edited by H. S. Thayer and Elisabeth B. Thayer. New York: Washington Square Press.

Pederson, Ann. 1993. "Forensic Justification: A Process Feminist Critique and Construction." *Process Studies* 22, no. 2 (summer): 84–92.

Peirce, Charles Sanders. 1931–35. *Collected Papers of Charles Sanders Peirce*. 6 vols. Edited by Charles Hartshorne and Paul Weiss. Cambridge: Harvard University Press.

Penelhum, Terence. 1992. "Parity Is Not Enough." In *Faith, Reason, and Skepticism*, edited by Marcus Hester, 98–120. Philadelphia: Temple University Press.

Penrose, Roger. 1994. Interview (with Jane Clark). *Journal of Consciousness Studies* 1, no. 1: 17–24.

Perry, Michael J. 1998. *The Idea of Human Rights: Four Inquiries*. New York: Oxford University Press.

Perry, Ralph Barton. 1935. *The Thought and Character of William James*. 2 vols. Boston: Little, Brown.

Phillips, D. Z. 1970. *Faith and Philosophical Inquiry*. London: Routledge.

——. 1976. *Religion without Explanation*. Oxford: Basil Blackwell.

——. 1986. *Belief, Change, and Form of Life*. London: Macmillan.

Pinnock, Clark H., and John B. Cobb, Jr., eds. 2000. *Searching for an Adequate God: A Dialogue between Process and Free Will Theists*. Grand Rapids, Mich.: Eerdmans.

Pinnock, Clark H., Richard Rice, John Sanders, William Hasker, and David Basinger. 1994. *The Openness of God: A Biblical Challenge to the Traditional Understanding of God*. Downers Grove, Ill.: InterVarsity Press.

Plantinga, Alvin. 1974. *God, Freedom, and Evil*. New York: Harper & Row.

——. 1979. "Is Belief in God Rational?" In *Rationality and Religious Belief*, edited by Cornelius F. Delaney, 7–27. South Bend, Ind.: University of Notre Dame Press.

——. 1981. "Reply to the Basingers on Divine Omnipotence." *Process Studies* 11, no. 1 (spring): 25–29.

——. 1983a. "Reason and Belief in God." In *Faith and Rationality: Reason and Belief in God*, edited by Alvin Plantinga and Nicholas Wolterstorff, 16–93. Notre Dame: University of Notre Dame Press.

——. 1983b. "The Reformed Objection to Natural Theology." In *Rationality in the Calvinian Tradition*, edited by Hendrik Hart, Johan van der Hoeven, and Nicholas Wolterstorff, 363–83. Lanham, Md.: University Press of America.

——. 1984. "Advice to Christian Philosophers." *Faith and Philosophy* 1, no. 3 (July): 253–71.

——. 1986. "On Taking Belief in God as Basic." In *Religious Experience and Religious Belief: Essays in the Epistemology of Religion*, edited by Joseph Runzo and Craig K. Ihara, 1–17. Lanham, Md.: University Press of America.

——. 1989. "Is Belief in God Properly Basic?" In *Philosophy of Religion: Selected Readings*, 2d ed., edited by William L. Rowe and William J. Wainwright, 417–26. Fort Worth: Harcourt Brace.

——. 1990 [1967]. *God and Other Minds*. 2d ed. Ithaca: Cornell University Press.

——. 1991a. "When Faith and Reason Clash: Evolution and the Bible." *Christian Scholar's Review* 21, no. 1: 8–32.

———. 1991b. "Evolution, Neutrality, and Antecedent Probability: A Reply to McMullin and Van Till." *Christian Scholar's Review* 21, no. 1: 80–109.

———. 1995. "Pluralism: A Defense of Religious Exclusivism." In *The Rationality of Belief and the Plurality of Faith,* edited by T. D. Senor, 191–215. Ithaca: Cornell University Press.

———. 1996. "On Reformed Epistemology." In *Philosophy of Religion: Selected Readings,* edited by Michael Peterson, William Hasker, Bruce Reichenbach, and David Basinger, 330–36. New York: Oxford University Press (reprinted from *Reformed Journal,* January 1982).

———. 1997. "Reformed Epistemology." In *A Companion to Philosophy of Religion,* edited by Philip L. Quinn and Charles Taliaferro, 383–89. Cambridge, Mass.: Basil Blackwell.

———. 2000. *Warranted Christian Belief.* New York: Oxford University Press.

Pols, Edward. 1967. *Whitehead's Metaphysics: A Critical Examination of Process and Reality.* Carbondale: Southern Illinois University Press.

———. 1975. *Meditation on a Prisoner: Towards Understanding Action and Mind.* Carbondale: Southern Illinois University Press.

———. 1982. *The Acts of Our Being: A Reflection on Agency and Responsibility.* Amherst: University of Massachusetts Press.

Popper, Karl R. 1963. "What Is Dialectic?" In *Conjectures and Refutations: The Growth of Scientific Knowledge,* by Karl Popper, 312–25. London: Routledge & Kegan Paul.

Popper, Karl R., and John C. Eccles. 1977. *The Self and Its Brain: An Argument for Interactionism.* Heidelberg: Springer.

Pratt, James Bissett. 1939. *Naturalism.* New Haven: Yale University Press.

Preus, J. Samuel. 1987. *Explaining Religion: Criticism and Theory from Bodin to Freud.* New Haven: Yale University Press.

Price, H. H. 1932. *Perception.* London: Methuen.

Price, Richard. 1969. "A Review of the Principal Questions in Morals." In *British Moralists, 1650–1800,* edited by D. D. Raphael, 2:130–98. Oxford: Clarendon Press.

Proudfoot, Wayne. 1985. *Religious Experience.* Berkeley and Los Angeles: University of California Press.

Provine, William. 1988. "Progress in Evolution and Meaning in Life." In *Evolutionary Progress,* edited by Matthew H. Nitecki, 49–74. Chicago: University of Chicago Press.

Puccetti, Roland. 1964. "The Concept of God." *Philosophical Quarterly* 14 (July): 237–45.

Putnam, Hilary. 1979. *Mathematics, Matter, and Method.* Cambridge: Cambridge University Press.

———. 1981. *Reason, Truth, and History.* Cambridge: Cambridge University Press.

———. 1983. *Realism and Reason.* New York: Cambridge University Press.

———. 1992. "Replies." *Philosophical Topics* 20, no. 1 (spring): 347–408.

———. 1994. *Words and Life.* Edited by James Conant. Cambridge: Harvard University Press.

Quine, Willard Van. 1941. "Whitehead and the Rise of Modern Logic." In *The Philosophy of Alfred North Whitehead,* edited by Paul A. Schilpp, 125–63. Library of Living Philosophers, vol. 3. New York: Tudor.

———. 1953. *From a Logical Point of View.* Cambridge: Harvard University Press.

——. 1969. *Ontological Relativity and Other Essays*. New York: Columbia University Press.

——. 1981. *Theories and Things*. Cambridge: Harvard University Press.

——. 1990. *The Pursuit of Truth*. Cambridge: Harvard University Press.

——. 1995. *From Stimulus to Science*. Cambridge: Harvard University Press.

——. 1997. "Response to Leemon McHenry." *Process Studies* 26, nos. 1–2 (spring–summer): 13–14.

Rauschenbusch, Walter. 1917. *A Theology for the Social Gospel*. New York: Macmillan.

Reeves, Gene. 1994. "The Lotus Sutra and Process Thought." *Process Studies* 23, no. 2 (summer): 98–118.

Regis, Edward, ed. 1984. *Gewirth's Ethical Rationalism*. Chicago: University of Chicago Press.

Reichenbach, Hans. 1938. *Experience and Prediction*. Chicago: University of Chicago Press.

Reid, Thomas. 1971. *Essays on the Intellectual Powers of Man*. New York: Garland (facsimile of 1785 edition).

——. 1997 [1764]. *An Inquiry into the Human Mind on the Principles of Common Sense*. A Critical Edition. Edited by Derek R. Brookes. University Park: Pennsylvania State University Press.

Rennie, Bryan S. 1999. "The View of the Invisible World: Ninian Smart's Analysis of the Dimensions of Religion and of Religious Experience." *Bulletin of the Council of Societies for the Study of Religion* 28, no. 3 (September): 63–69.

Rensch, Bernard. 1977. "Arguments for Panpsychistic Identism." In *Mind in Nature: Essays on the Interface of Science and Philosophy*, edited by John B. Cobb, Jr., and David Ray Griffin, 70–78. Washington, D.C.: University Press of America.

Reynolds, Charles. 1970. "A Proposal for Understanding the Place of Reason in Christian Ethics." *Journal of Religion* 50, no. 2 (April): 155–68.

——. 1972. "Elements of a Decision Procedure for Christian Social Ethics." *Harvard Theological Review* 65: 509–30.

Rhine, J. B. 1953. *New World of the Mind*. New York: William Sloane.

Riley, Gregory. 1995. *Resurrection Reconsidered: Thomas and John in Controversy*. Minneapolis: Fortress Press.

Robinson, William S. 1988. *Brains and People: An Essay on Mentality and Its Causal Conditions*. Philadelphia: Temple University Press.

Rockmore, Tom. 1992. *On Heidegger's Nazism and Philosophy*. Berkeley and Los Angeles: University of California Press.

Rorty, Richard. 1979. *Philosophy and the Mirror of Nature*. Princeton: Princeton University Press.

——. 1982. *Consequences of Pragmatism*. Minneapolis: University of Minnesota Press.

Russell, Bertrand. 1957. *Why I Am Not a Christian and Other Essays on Religion and Related Subjects*. Edited by Paul Edwards. New York: Simon & Schuster.

Santayana, George. 1955. *Scepticism and Animal Faith*. New York: Dover.

Sartre, Jean-Paul. 1956. *Being and Nothingness*. Translated by Hazel Barnes. New York: Philosophical Library.

Schilpp, Paul Arthur. 1951 [1941]. "Whitehead's Moral Philosophy." In *The Philosophy of Alfred North Whitehead*, 2d ed., edited by Paul Arthur Schilpp, 561–618. Library of Living Philosophers, vol. 3. New York: Tudor.

Schleiermacher, Friedrich. 1928. *The Christian Faith*. Translated by H. R. Mackintosh and J. S. Stewart (from the 2d, rev. ed. of *Der Christliche Glaube* [1830]). Edinburgh: T. & T. Clark.

Schroeder, W. Widick. 1981. "Structure and Context in Process Political Theory: A Constructive Formulation." In *Process Philosophy and Social Thought*, edited by John B. Cobb, Jr., and W. Widick Schroeder, 63–80. Chicago: Center for the Scientific Study of Religion.

Schuon, Frithjof. 1975. *The Transcendent Unity of Religions*. New York: Harper & Row.

Seager, William. 1991. *Metaphysics of Consciousness*. New York: Routledge.

———. 1995. "Consciousness, Information, and Panpsychism." *Journal of Consciousness Studies* 2, no. 3: 272–88.

Searle, John R. 1984. *Minds, Brains, and Science: The 1984 Reith Lectures*. London: British Broadcasting Corporation.

———. 1992. *The Rediscovery of the Mind*. Cambridge: MIT Press.

Segal, Robert A. 1989. *Religion and the Social Sciences: Essays on the Confrontation*. Atlanta: Scholars Press.

———. 1992. *Explaining and Interpreting Religion: Essays on the Issue*. New York: Peter Lang.

Sellars, Wilfrid. 1950. "Empiricism and the Philosophy of Mind." In *Foundations of Science and the Concepts of Psychology and Psychoanalysis*, edited by Herbert Feigl and Michael Scriven, 253–329. Minneapolis: University of Minnesota Press (reprinted in Sellars, *Science, Perception, and Reality* [New York: Humanities Press, 1963]).

Setzer, J. Shoneberg. 1970. "Parapsychology: Religion's Basic Science." *Religion in Life* 39: 595–607.

Sharma, Arvind. 1997. "On the Distinction between Religious Studies and Theological Studies." *Bulletin of the Council of Societies for the Study of Religion* 26, no. 3 (September): 50–51.

Sherburne, Donald W. 1967. "Whitehead without God." *Christian Schoolman* 50: 251–72 (reprinted in *Process Philosophy and Christian Faith*, edited by Delwin Brown, Ralph E. James, and Gene Reeves [Indianapolis: Bobbs-Merrill, 1971]).

———. 1971. "The 'Whitehead without God' Debate: The Rejoinder." *Process Studies* 1, no. 2: 101–13.

———. 1986. "Decentering Whitehead." *Process Studies* 15, no. 2 (summer): 83–94.

Sidgwick, Henry. 1906. *Henry Sidgwick: A Memoir*. London: Macmillan.

Simmons, Ernest Lee, Jr. 1981. "Process Pluralism and Integral Nondualism: A Comparative Study of the Nature of the Divine in the Thought of Alfred North Whitehead and Sri Aurobindo Ghose." Ph.D. dissertation, Claremont Graduate School, Claremont, Calif.

Smart, J. J. C. 1996. "Religion and Science." In *Philosophy of Religion: A Global Approach*, edited by Stephen H. Phillips, 217–24. Fort Worth: Harcourt Brace (reprinted from *Encyclopedia of Philosophy*, edited by Paul Edwards [New York: Macmillan Press, 1967], vol. 7).

Smart, Ninian. 1960. *World Religions: A Dialogue*. Baltimore: Penguin Books.

———. 1970. *The Philosophy of Religion*. New York: Random House.

———. 1983. *Worldviews: Crosscultural Explorations of Human Beliefs*. New York: Scribner's.

———. 1992. "Soft Natural Theology." In *Prospects for Natural Theology*, edited by Eugene Thomas Long, 198–206. Washington, D.C.: Catholic University of America Press.

———. 1995a. *Worldviews: Crosscultural Exploration of Human Beliefs.* 2d ed. Englewood Cliffs, N.J.: Prentice Hall.

———. 1995b. "The Philosophy of Worldviews, or the Philosophy of Religion Transformed." In *Religious Pluralism and Truth: Essays on the Cross-Cultural Philosophy of Religion,* edited by Thomas Dean, 17–31. Albany: State University of New York Press.

———. 1996. *Dimensions of the Sacred: An Anatomy of the World's Beliefs.* Berkeley and Los Angeles: University of California Press.

———. 1997. "Religious Studies and Theology." *Bulletin of the Council of Societies for the Study of Religion* 26, no. 3 (September): 66–68.

Smith, Huston. 1977. *Forgotten Truth: The Primordial Tradition.* New York: Harper & Row.

———. 1988. "Philosophy, Theology, and the Primordial Claim." *Cross Currents* 38, no. 3 (fall): 276–88.

Smith, John E. 1961. "Ultimate Concern and the Really Ultimate." In *Religious Experience and Truth,* edited by Sydney Hook, 65–69. New York: New York University Press.

Spencer, Herbert. 1908. *The Life and Letters of Herbert Spencer.* Edited by David Duncan. London: Methuen.

Stace, W. T. 1960. *Mysticism and Philosophy.* London: Macmillan.

Stanley, Steven M. 1981. *The New Evolutionary Timetable.* New York: Basic Books.

Stearns, J. Brenton. 1972. "The Naturalistic Fallacy and the Question of the Existence of God." *Religious Studies* 8, no. 3 (September): 207–20.

Stout, Jeffrey. 1981. *The Flight from Authority: Religion, Morality, and the Quest for Autonomy.* Notre Dame: University of Notre Dame Press.

Strawson, Galen. 1994. *Mental Reality.* Cambridge: MIT Press.

Strawson, Peter. 1949. "Ethical Intuitionism." *Philosophy* 24, no. 88 (January): 23–33.

———. 1988. "Perception and Its Objects." In *Perceptual Knowledge,* edited by Jonathan Dancy, 92–112. Oxford: Oxford University Press.

Sturm, Douglas. 1981. "Process Thought and Political Theory: Implications of a Principle of Internal Relations." In *Process Philosophy and Social Thought,* edited by John B. Cobb, Jr., and W. Widick Schroeder, 81–102. Chicago: Center for the Scientific Study of Religion.

———. 1985. "Cosmogony and Ethics in the Marxian Tradition: Premise and Destiny of Nature and History." In *Cosmogony and Ethical Order: New Studies in Comparative Ethics,* edited by Robin W. Lovin and Frank E. Reynolds, 353–80. Chicago: University of Chicago Press.

———. 1988. *Community and Alienation: Essays on Process Thought and Public Life.* Notre Dame: University of Notre Dame Press.

Suchocki, Marjorie Hewitt. 1975. "The Metaphysical Ground of the Whiteheadian God." *Process Studies* 5, no. 4 (winter): 237–46.

———. 1988. *The End of Evil: Process Eschatology in Historical Context.* Albany: State University of New York Press.

———. 1989. "Evil, Eschatology, and God: Response to David Griffin." *Process Studies* 18, no. 1 (spring): 63–69.

———. 1991. "Original Sin Revisited." *Process Studies* 20, no. 4 (winter): 233–43.

———. 1994a. *The Fall to Violence: Original Sin in Relational Theology.* New York: Continuum.

———. 1994b. "God, Sexism, and Transformation." In *Reconstructing Christian Theology*, edited by Rebecca Chopp and Mark L. Taylor, 25–48. Minneapolis: Fortress Press.

Sullivan, William M. 1986. *Reconstructing Public Philosophy*. Berkeley and Los Angeles: University of California Press.

Swinburne, Richard. 1977. *The Coherence of Theism*. Oxford: Oxford University Press.

———. 1979. *The Existence of God*. New York: Oxford University Press.

———. 1986. *The Evolution of the Soul*. Oxford: Clarendon Press.

———. 1996. *Is There a God?* Oxford: Oxford University Press.

Takeda, Ryusei. 1994. "Mahayana Buddhism and Whitehead's Philosophy." *Process Studies* 23, no. 2 (summer): 72–86.

Tanaka, Takao. 1977. "From a Buddhist Point of View." In *John Cobb's Theology in Process*, edited by David Ray Griffin and Thomas J. J. Altizer, 99–111. Philadelphia: Westminster Press.

Taylor, Charles. 1987. "Overcoming Epistemology." In *After Philosophy: End or Transformation?* edited by Kenneth Baynes, James Bohman, and Thomas McCarthy, 464–88. Cambridge: MIT Press.

Taylor, Gordon Rattray. 1983. *The Great Evolution Mystery*. London: Secker & Warburg.

Taylor, Paul. 1961. *Normative Discourse*. Westport, Conn.: Greenwood.

Tennant, Frederick. 1930. *Philosophical Theology*. Vol. 2. Cambridge: Cambridge University Press.

Thie, Marilyn. 1978. "Feminist Concerns and Whitehead's Theory of Perception." *Process Studies* 8, no. 3 (fall): 186–91.

Tillich, Paul. 1951. *Systematic Theology*. Vol. 1. Chicago: University of Chicago Press.

Tindal, Matthew. 1730. *Christianity as Old as Creation*. London: Thomas Astley.

Tracy, David. 1990. "Kenosis, Sunyata, and Trinity: A Dialogue with Masao Abe." In *The Emptying God: A Buddhist-Jewish-Christian Conversation*, edited by John B. Cobb, Jr., and Christopher Ives, 135–54. Maryknoll, N.Y.: Orbis Books.

Trigg, Roger. 1997. "Theological Realism and Antirealism." In *A Companion to Philosophy of Religion*, edited by Philip L. Quinn and Charles Taliaferro, 213–20. Cambridge, Mass.: Basil Blackwell.

Turner, Stephen P. L., and Regis A. Factor. 1984. *Max Weber and the Dispute over Reason and Value: A Study in Philosophy, Ethics, and Politics*. London: Routledge & Kegan Paul.

Tylor, Edward B. 1871. *Primitive Culture: Researches into the Development of Mythology, Philosophy, Religion, Language, Art, and Customs*. 2 vols. London: J. Murray.

Van Buren, Paul. 1963. *The Secular Meaning of the Gospel: Based on an Analysis of Its Language*. New York: Macmillan.

Van Till, Howard J. 1991. "When Faith and Reason Cooperate." *Christian Scholar's Review* 21, no. 1: 33–45.

Viney, Donald Wayne. 1985. *Charles Hartshorne and the Existence of God*. Albany: State University of New York Press.

Wainwright, William J. 1988. *Philosophy of Religion*. Belmont, Calif.: Wadsworth.

———. 1995. *Reason and the Heart: A Prolegomenon to a Critique of Passional Reason*. Ithaca: Cornell University Press.

———. 1997. "Christianity." In *A Companion to Philosophy of Religion*, edited by Philip L. Quinn and Charles Taliaferro, 56–63. Cambridge, Mass.: Basil Blackwell.

———. 1998. "Worldviews, Criteria, and Epistemic Circularity." In *Philosophy of Religion:*

Selected Readings, 3d ed., edited by William L. Rowe and William J. Wainwright, 337–53. Fort Worth: Harcourt Brace.

Warnock, G. J. 1971. *The Object of Morality.* London: Methuen.

Weber, Max. 1958. *From Max Weber.* Edited by H. H. Gerth and C. Wright Mills. New York: Oxford University Press.

Weinberg, Steven. 1994. *Dreams of a Final Theory: The Scientist's Search for the Ultimate Laws of Nature.* 2d ed. New York: Vintage Books.

Wesson, Robert. 1991. *Beyond Natural Selection.* Cambridge: MIT Press.

West, Cornel. 1981. "Nietzsche's Prefiguration of Post-Modern Literature." *Boundary 2: A Journal of Post-Modern Literature* 9–10 (spring–fall): 241–70.

———. 1985. "Afterword: The Politics of American Neo-Pragmatism." In *Post-Analytic Philosophy,* edited by John Rajchman and Cornel West, 259–75. New York: Columbia University Press.

———. 1986. "Dispensing with Metaphysics in Religious Thought." *Religion and Intellectual Life* 3, no. 3 (spring): 53–56.

Whitehead, Alfred North. 1922. *The Principle of Relativity.* Cambridge: Cambridge University Press (R).

———. 1929. *The Aims of Education and Other Essays.* New York: Macmillan (AE)

———. 1947. *Essays in Science and Philosophy.* New York: Philosophical Library (ESP).

———. 1959 [1927]. *Symbolism: Its Meaning and Effect.* New York: Capricorn (S).

———. 1960 [1926]. *Religion in the Making.* Cleveland: World (RM). (The pagination of this volume is slightly different from that of the original [1926] edition, which was reprinted, with an introduction by Judith A. Jones, by Fordham University Press in 1996.)

———. 1967a [1933]. *Adventures of Ideas.* New York: Free Press (AI).

———. 1967b [1925]. *Science and the Modern World.* New York: Free Press (SMW).

———. 1968a [1929]. *The Function of Reason.* Boston: Beacon Press (FR).

———. 1968b [1938]. *Modes of Thought.* New York: Free Press (MT).

———. 1978 [1929]. *Process and Reality,* corrected edition. Edited by David Ray Griffin and Donald W. Sherburne. New York: Free Press (PR).

Widgery, Alban G. 1954. *What is Religion?* London: Allen and Unwin.

Wieman, Henry Nelson. 1946. *The Source of Human Good.* Chicago: University of Chicago Press.

Williams, Bernard. 1985. *Ethics and the Limits of Philosophy.* Cambridge: Harvard University Press.

Williams, Daniel Day. 1949. *God's Grace and Man's Hope.* New York: Harper & Brothers.

Williams, Michael. 1977. *Groundless Belief: An Essay on the Possibility of Epistemology.* Oxford: Basil Blackwell.

Wilmot, Laurence. 1979. *Whitehead and God: Prolegomena to Theological Reconstruction.* Waterloo, Ont.: Wilfrid Laurier University Press.

Wilson, Edward O. 1998. *Consilience: The Unity of Knowledge.* New York: Alfred A. Knopf.

Wolin, Richard. 1990. *The Politics of Being: The Political Thought of Martin Heidegger.* New York: Columbia University Press.

———, ed. 1993. *The Heidegger Controversy: A Critical Reader.* Cambridge: MIT Press.

Wolterstorff, Nicholas. 1976. *Reason within the Bounds of Religion.* Grand Rapids, Mich.:

Eerdmans.

———. 1981. "Is Reason Enough?" *Reformed Journal* 31, no. 4 (April): 20–24.

———. 1983a. "Can Belief in God Be Rational if It Has No Foundations?" In *Faith and Rationality: Reason and Belief in God,* edited by Alvin Plantinga and Nicholas Wolterstorff, 135–86. Notre Dame: University of Notre Dame Press.

———. 1983b. "Thomas Reid on Rationality." In *Rationality in the Calvinian Tradition,* edited by Hendrik Hart, Johan van der Hoeven, and Nicholas Wolterstorff, 43–69. Lanham, Md.: University Press of America.

———. 1988. "Suffering Love." In *Philosophy and the Christian Faith,* edited by T. V. Morris, 196–237. Notre Dame: University of Notre Dame Press.

———. 1997. "The Reformed Tradition." In *A Companion to Philosophy of Religion,* edited by Philip L. Quinn and Charles Taliaferro, 165–70. Cambridge, Mass.: Basil Blackwell.

Woozley, A. D. 1941. Introduction to *Essays on the Intellectual Powers of Man,* by Thomas Reid, edited and abridged by A. D. Woozley, vii–xl. London: Macmillan.

Wykstra, Stephen J. 1989. "Toward a Sensible Evidentialism: On the Notion of 'Needing Evidence.'" In *Philosophy of Religion: Selected Readings,* 2d ed., edited by William L. Rowe and William J. Wainwright, 426–37. Fort Worth: Harcourt Brace.

Yakota, John S. 1994. "A Call to Compassion: Process Thought and the Conceptualization of Amida Buddha." *Process Studies* 23, no. 2 (summer): 87–97.

Zimmerman, Michael E. 1990. *Heidegger's Confrontation with Modernity: Technology, Politics, and Art.* Bloomington: Indiana University Press.

Index

Cornell Studies in the Philosophy of Religion
A Series Edited by William P. Alston